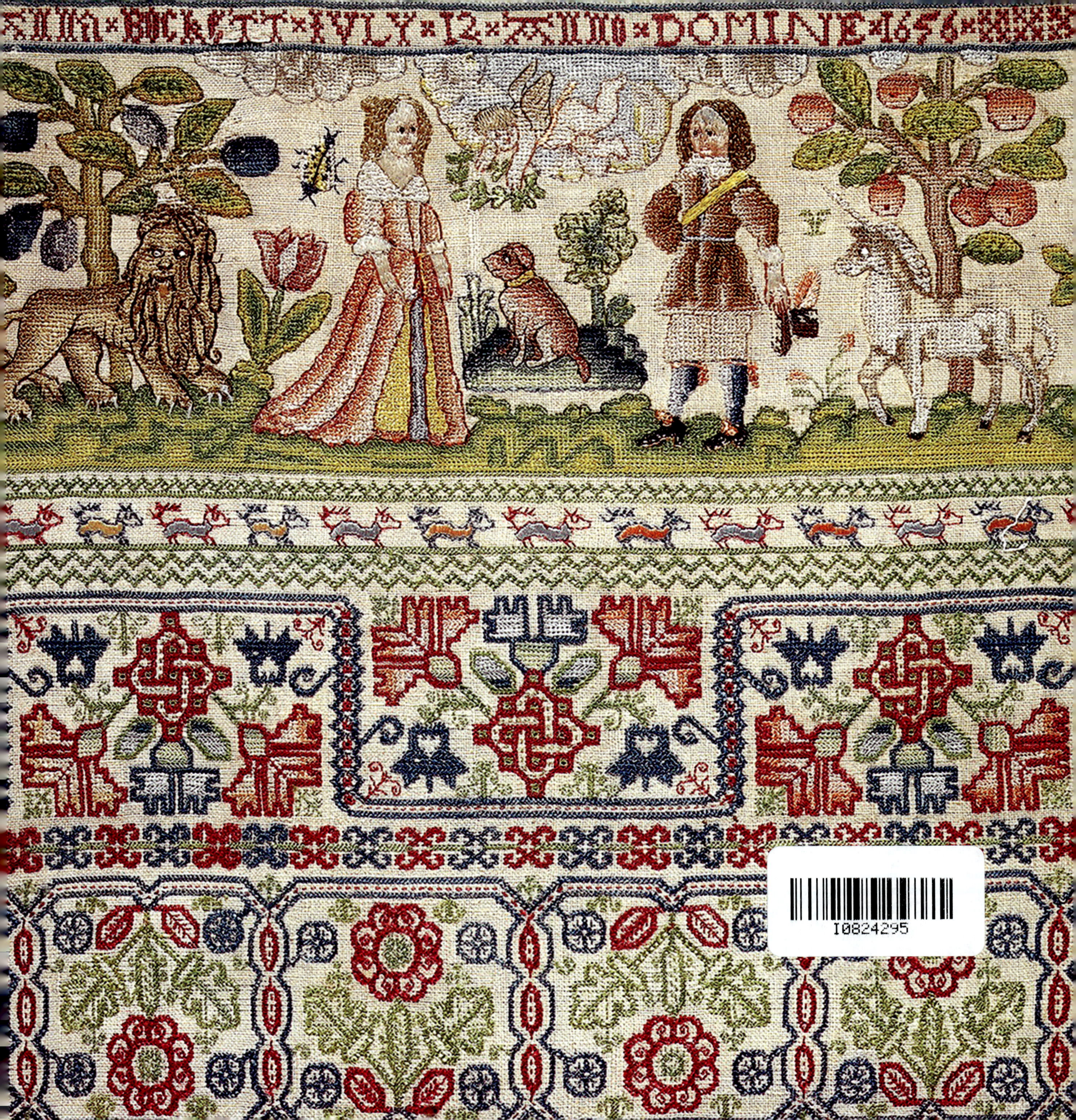
I0824295

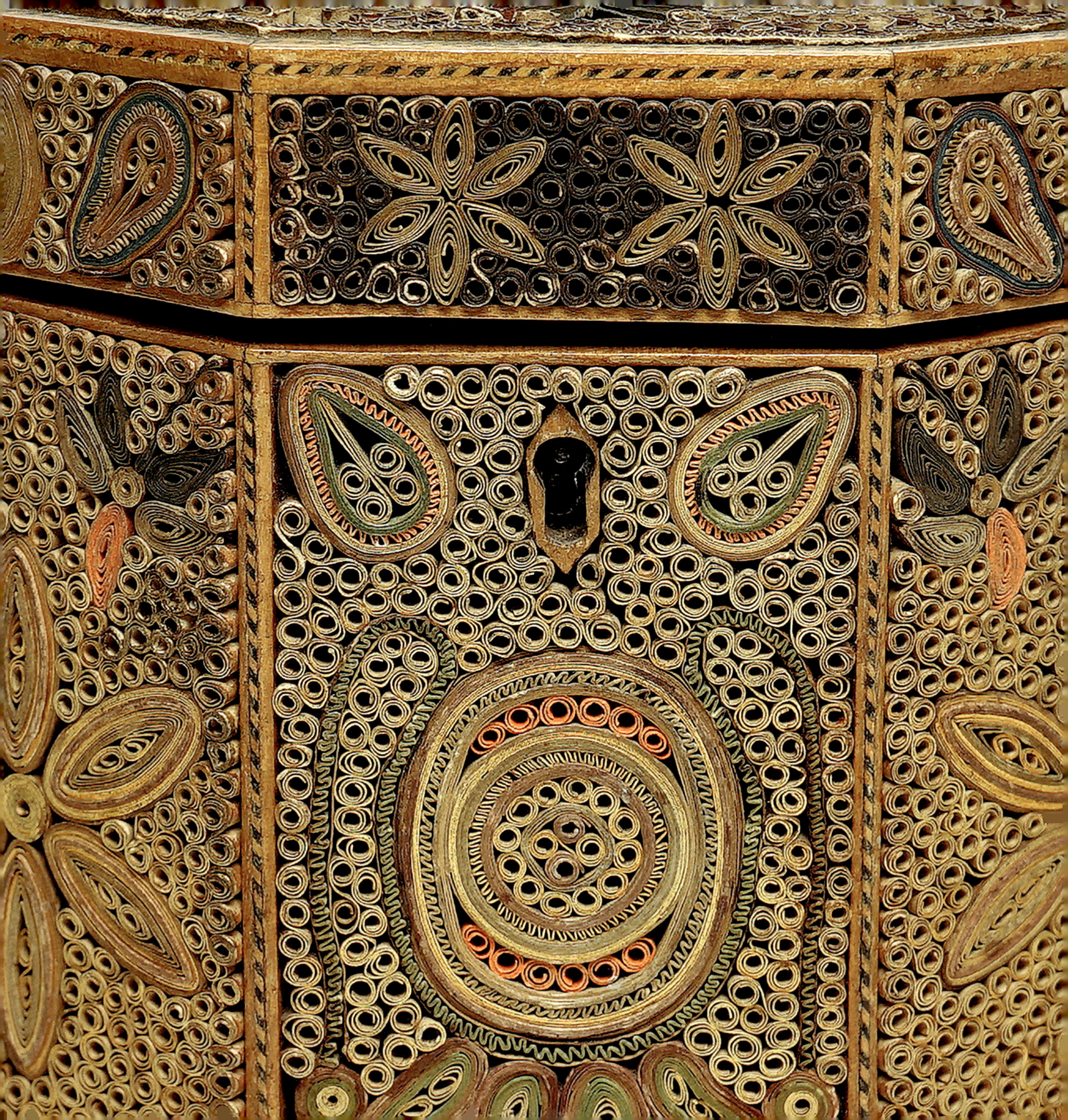

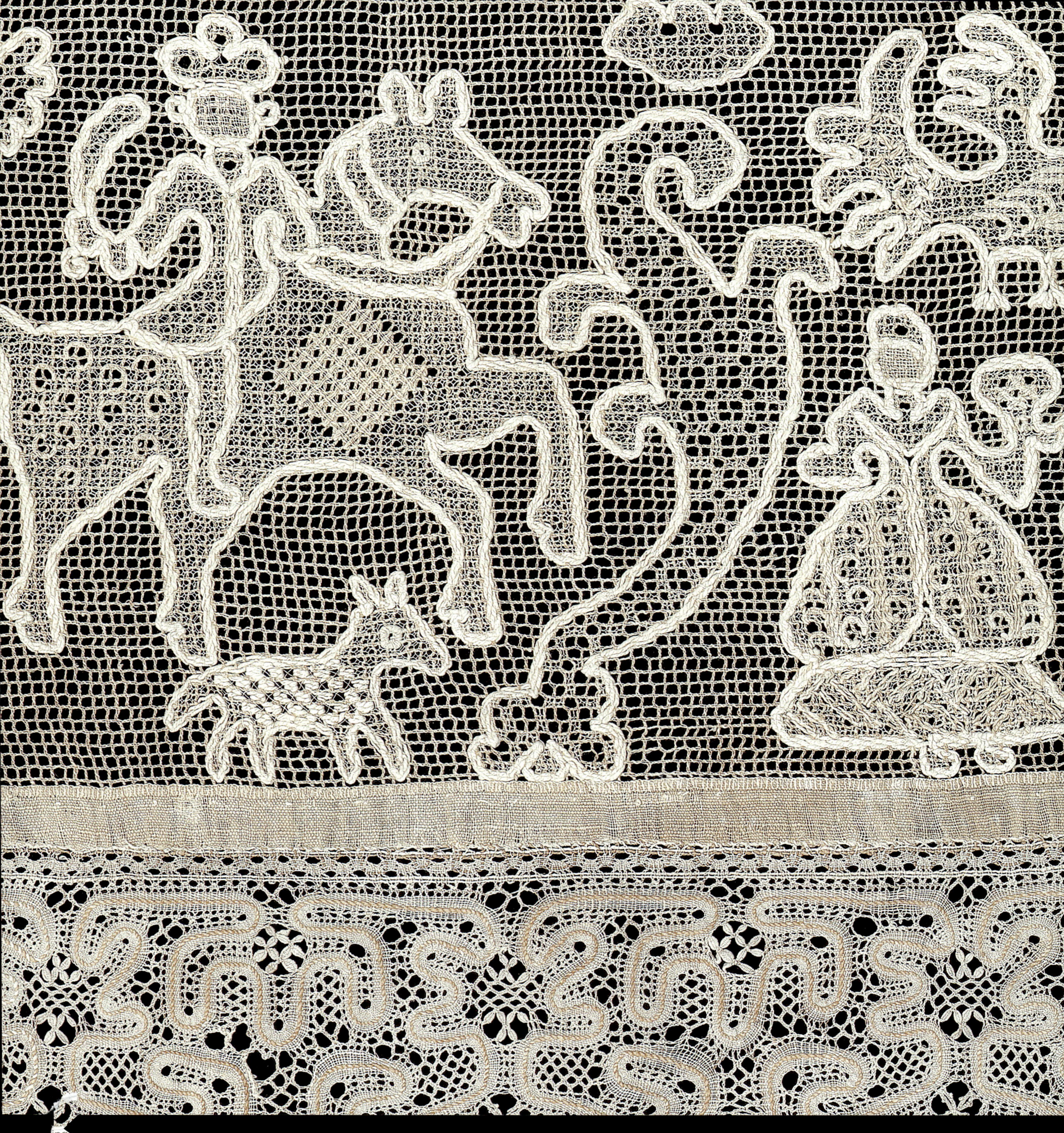

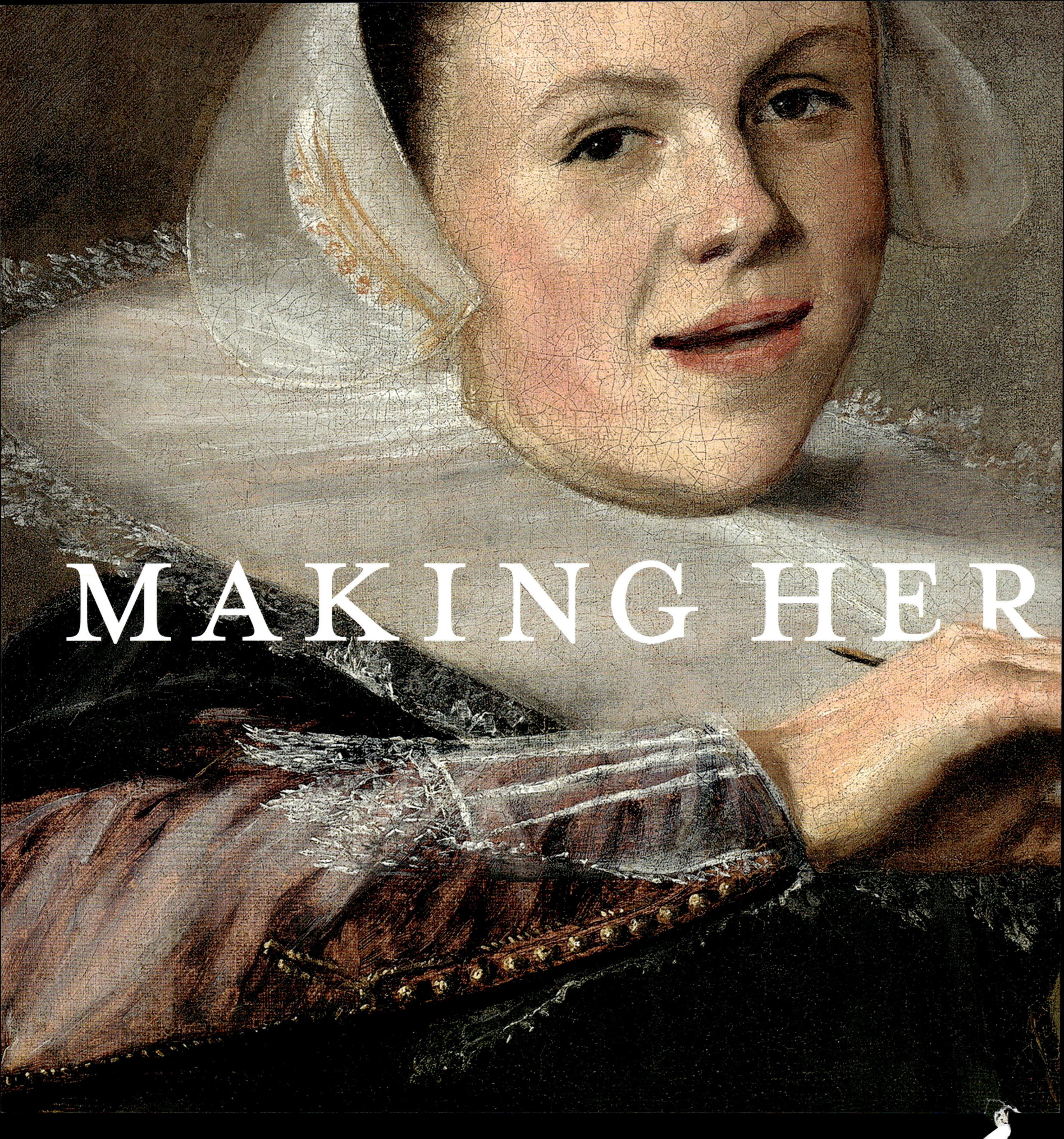
MAKING HER

EDITED BY Andaleeb Badiee Banta and Alexa Greist, with Theresa Kutasz Christensen

MARK

A HISTORY *of* WOMEN ARTISTS *in* EUROPE, 1400–1800

AGO

BALTIMORE MUSEUM OF ART

Goose Lane Editions

Contents

6 DIRECTORS' FOREWORD
Stephan Jost and Dr. Asma Naeem

9 EDITORS' FOREWORD
Andaleeb Badiee Banta, Alexa Greist, and Theresa Kutasz Christensen

14
Not Seen, Not Heard
In Search of the Unexceptional Woman Artist
Andaleeb Badiee Banta

30
Prints and Needles
Women Makers and European Textile Pattern Books, 1500–1800
Alexa Greist

42
Designing Women
Drawings by Women Artists in Early Modern Italy
Babette Bohn

58
Multiple Challenges, or the Challenge of Multiples
Early Modern Women as Creators of Prints
Madeleine C. Viljoen

76
Unravelling the Threads
Women Working with Silk in Italy, France, and England, 1500–1800
Yassana Croizat-Glazer

92
Women in Workshops
Brittany Luberda

106
Women and the Art of Science
Virginia Treanor

122
Art and Politics
Women Artists and the Rulers of the Revolutionary World
Paris A. Spies-Gans

138
Women of the World
European Women Makers in a Global Context
Andaleeb Badiee Banta and Theresa Kutasz Christensen

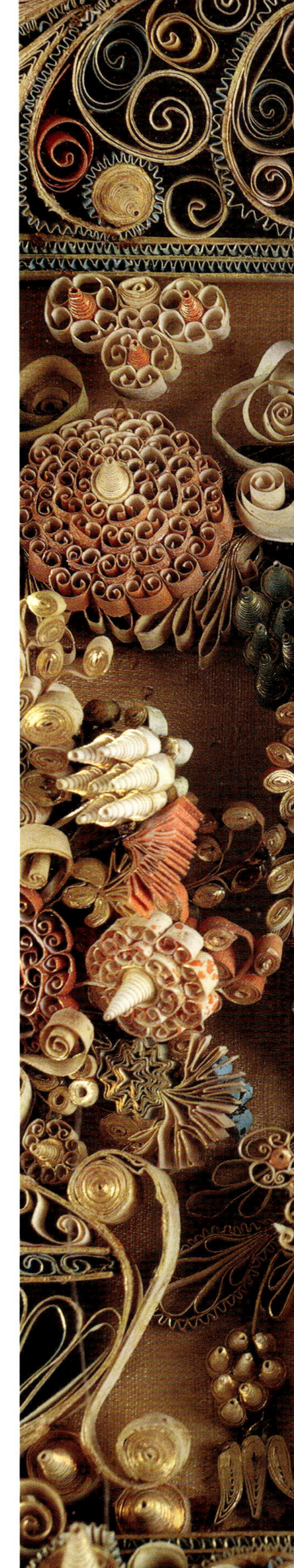

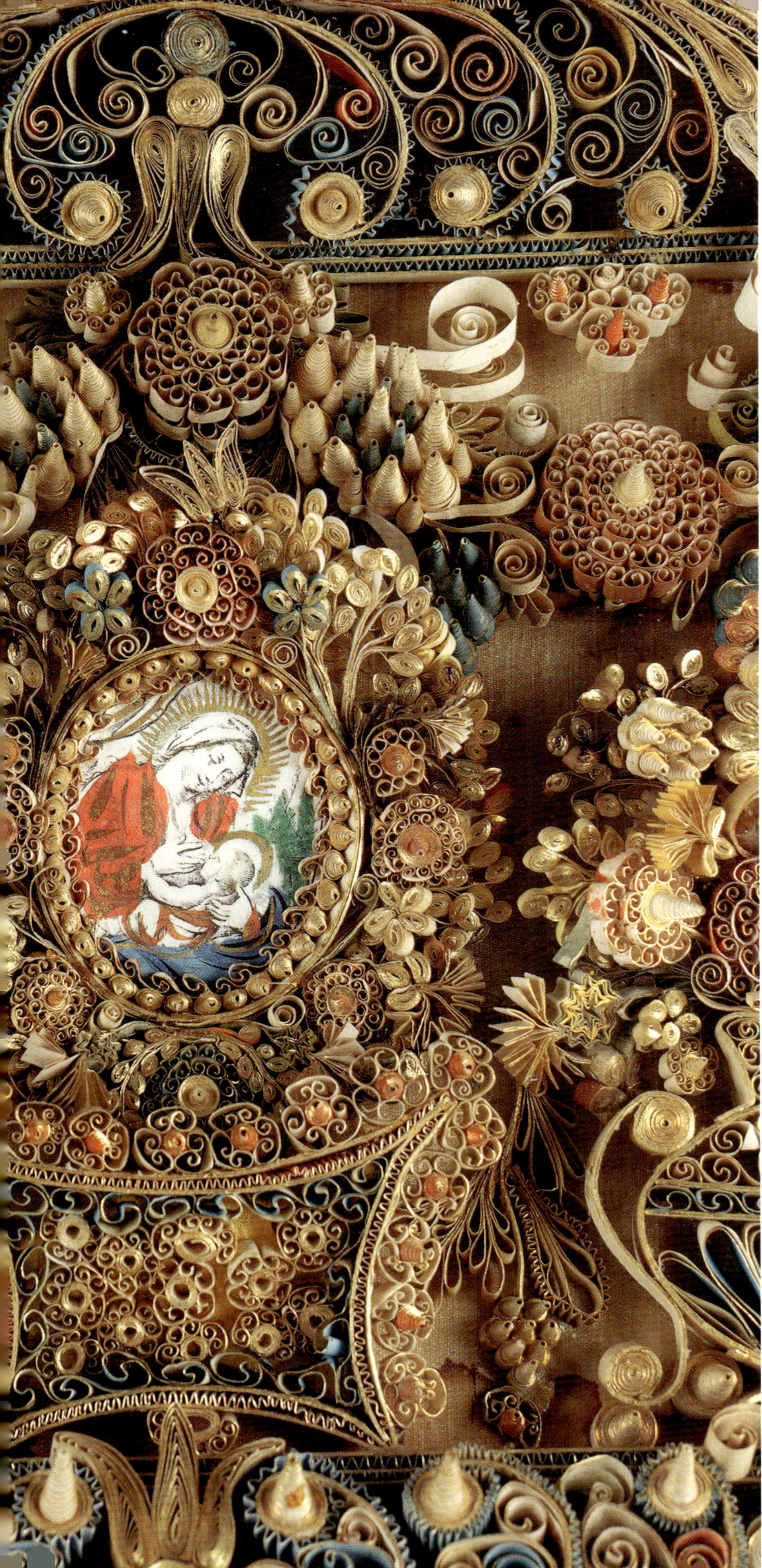

159

Works Exhibited

160 Book Arts and Publishing
164 Ceramics
172 Cloister Work
176 Drawings, Pastels, and Watercolours
186 Furniture
190 Lace
194 Manuscript Illumination
197 Painting: History
202 Painting: Miniatures
205 Painting: Portraiture
210 Painting: Still Life
215 Painting: Women at Work
218 Prints
225 Scientific and Natural Illustration
234 Sculpture
239 Silver and Enamel
244 Tapestry, Woven Fabrics, and Embroidery

256 Index of Women Makers Illustrated
259 Contributors
261 Credits

Detail (cat. no. 31) • Unknown European maker, *Quillwork (paper filigree) picture with Madonna and Child*, 18th century. Rolled paper, gilding, paint, wood, and glass, 27.3 × 35.6 × 5.4 cm. Peabody Essex Museum, acquired before 1919, 109453. Image courtesy of the Peabody Essex Museum.

Directors' Foreword

Even though women comprise half of the world's population, works by women artists make up significantly less than 50 percent of art holdings in most museum collections. If one looks for women working before 1800, galleries are even more sparsely populated. And yet, women makers had been present and active throughout Europe well before they were granted official entrance into the Salons and academies of art in the nineteenth century. To follow the advice offered in Chimamanda Ngozi Adichie's *We Should All Be Feminists*, we need to do better. Pursuing goals of equity and social justice has prompted both the Art Gallery of Ontario and the Baltimore Museum of Art to make significant changes to our exhibition programs and collecting strategies in order to address this and other groups' lack of representation. Co-presented by the BMA and the AGO, *Making Her Mark: A History of Women Artists in Europe, 1400–1800* endeavours to correct the record and prompt questions about which artists and artworks are featured within our walls, and why others historically have not received this prominence. This wide-ranging and ambitious investigation of women's diverse contributions to the history of European art makes clear that there is still plenty of work to be done to bring women's stories and creations of the past to the fore.

Curated by Andaleeb Badiee Banta, Senior Curator and Department Head, Prints, Drawings & Photographs at the Baltimore Museum of Art, and Alexa Greist, Curator & R. Fraser Elliott Chair, Prints & Drawings at the Art Gallery of Ontario, with research support from Theresa Kutasz Christensen, this exhibition seeks to make visible historical women who produced across media, within lauded high-art categories—including painting, drawing, printmaking, sculpture, and the decorative arts—as well as those typically cast as material culture, such as embroidery, paper-cutting and rolling, and lacemaking. These makers worked in a variety of spaces and contexts: as the heads of workshops and businesses making tapestries, furniture, ceramics, silver, and printing books, but also as anonymized labourers in factory spaces, at home, and from within the walls of cloisters. Some of these women's names are recorded within their compositions, in archives, or in advertisements for the goods they oversaw or made, but many more are not captured in the historical record. Acknowledging the varied essential roles that women played in producing art enriches and complicates our understanding of the shifting circumstances for historical women artists. It also challenges our assumptions about which formats qualify as serious artistic expression. Additionally, by highlighting collaborative approaches to art-making, which were more the norm than previously acknowledged, *Making Her Mark* pushes back against the historical idolatry of individual (male) genius.

The AGO extends heartfelt thanks to the Volunteers of the AGO for their lead support and to Robert & Cecily Bradshaw, Philip R.L. Somerville, and the Women's Art Initiative for their generous support. The Baltimore Museum of Art gratefully acknowledges generous support for this project by the National Endowment for the Humanities, Laura Freedlander, PNC Foundation, The Gladys Krieble Delmas Foundation, Dutch Culture USA program by the Consulate General of the Netherlands in New York, Samuel H. Kress Foundation, and Sheela Murthy/MurthyNAYAK Foundation.

We are deeply grateful to numerous institutions and collectors for participating in this expansive exploration of women makers by lending objects and providing research and staff time to help us learn more about them. In Canada, Gardiner Museum; Montreal Museum of Fine Arts; Pôle culturel du Monastère des Ursulines; Royal Ontario Museum; and The Thomson Collection at the Art Gallery of Ontario. In Italy, Museo Correr and Ca' Rezzonico, Fondazione Musei Civici di Venezia; and Museo della Specola, Università di Bologna. In Portugal, The Gaudium Magnum Collection and Museu Nacional de Arte Antiga, and, in Sweden, Nationalmuseum, Stockholm. In the United Kingdom, Arnold Wiggins & Sons; Fitzwilliam Museum, University of Cambridge; Katrin Bellinger Collection; Victoria and Albert Museum; Walker Art Gallery, National Museums Liverpool; and The Wallace Collection. In the United States, Allen Memorial Art Museum, Oberlin College; Art Institute of Chicago; Clay H. Barr and the Barr Foundation; Michele Beiny Harkins; Babette Bohn; Cathedral of St. John the

Divine; Chrysler Museum of Art; Cincinnati Art Museum; Clark Art Institute; The Cleveland Museum of Art; Collection of the Embassy of Portugal, Washington, DC; The Colonial Williamsburg Foundation; Cooper Hewitt, Smithsonian Design Museum; Cummer Museum of Art & Gardens; David M. Rubenstein Rare Book & Manuscript Library, Duke University; Davis Museum at Wellesley College; Detroit Institute of Arts; Dominican Sisters of San Rafael; Dumbarton Oaks Research Library and Collection; Frances Lehman Loeb Art Center, Vassar College; Sophie Guiny and Charles Bushman; Hillwood Estate, Museum & Gardens; The Hispanic Society of America; Houghton Library, Harvard University; Institute of the History of Medicine, Johns Hopkins University; The Jewish Museum; The John & Mable Ringling Museum of Art; Linda H. Kaufman; Kislak Center for Special Collections, Rare Books and Manuscripts, University of Pennsylvania Libraries; Lewis Walpole Library, Yale University; Los Angeles County Museum of Art; The Metropolitan Museum of Art; Milwaukee Art Museum; Minneapolis Institute of Art; The Morgan Library & Museum; Museum of Fine Arts, Boston; National Gallery of Art, Washington; National Museum of American History, Smithsonian Institution; National Museum of Women in the Arts; The New York Public Library; North Carolina Museum of Art; Oak Spring Garden Foundation; Old Barracks Museum; Peabody Essex Museum; Philadelphia Museum of Art; Museum of Art, Rhode Island School of Design; Saint Louis Art Museum; San Diego Museum of Art; Sheridan Libraries, Johns Hopkins University; Smith College Museum of Art; Toledo Museum of Art; Lisa Unger Baskin; The Walters Art Museum; and Yale Center for British Art.

The AGO and BMA commend our co-curators for their vision in bringing such an important show to life. The staff at both museums have been instrumental in the success of this endeavour and we are grateful for their passionate efforts on this project. The AGO thanks Julian Cox, Deputy Director & Chief Curator; Jessica Bright, Chief, Exhibitions, Collections & Conservation; Laura Comerford, Director of Exhibitions; the Production team of Malene Hjørngaard and Evelyn Quinn; Exhibition Designer Theodora Doulamis; Graphic Designer Evelina Petrauskas; Project Manager Melissa Ramage; Curatorial Coordinator Wendy Hebditch; Interpretive Planner Nadia Abraham; and Registrar, Exhibitions Joel Herman. This comprehensive and visually stunning publication would not have been possible without the intuition of our extraordinarily talented designer, Lara Minja of Lime Design, as well as the management and dedication of Publication Coordinator Kathryn Yuen, alongside Editor, Publications & Exhibitions Nives Hajdin-Rorabeck, and Jim Shedden, Curator, Special Projects & Director, Publishing. The BMA is grateful to Interim Chief Curator Kevin Tervala; Exhibition Research Assistant Theresa Kutasz Christensen; Associate Director of Exhibitions Kirsten MacKenzie; Registrar and Department Head Caitlin Perry-Vogelhut; Interpretive Planner Verónica Betancourt; Exhibition Designer David Zimmerman; and Graphic Designers Kristine Ferg and Olivia Tucker. In addition, we are profoundly thankful to the various authors of the illuminating contributions to this catalogue: Babette Bohn, Yassana Croizat-Glazer, Elena Naomi Kanagy-Loux, Joanna Karlgaard, Brittany Luberda, Catherine Powell-Warren, Isabella Rosner, Paris A. Spies-Gans, Virginia Treanor, Annelies Verellen, Madeleine C. Viljoen, and Lara Yeager-Crasselt.

This exhibition is by no means a definitive representation of women's creative output in Europe between 1400 to 1800, but we hope that it acts as the seed for future explorations of artists or objects that have yet to formally receive the attention they deserve.

Stephan Jost
Michael and Sonja Koerner Director, and CEO, Art Gallery of Ontario

Dr. Asma Naeem
Dorothy Wagner Wallis Director, Baltimore Museum of Art

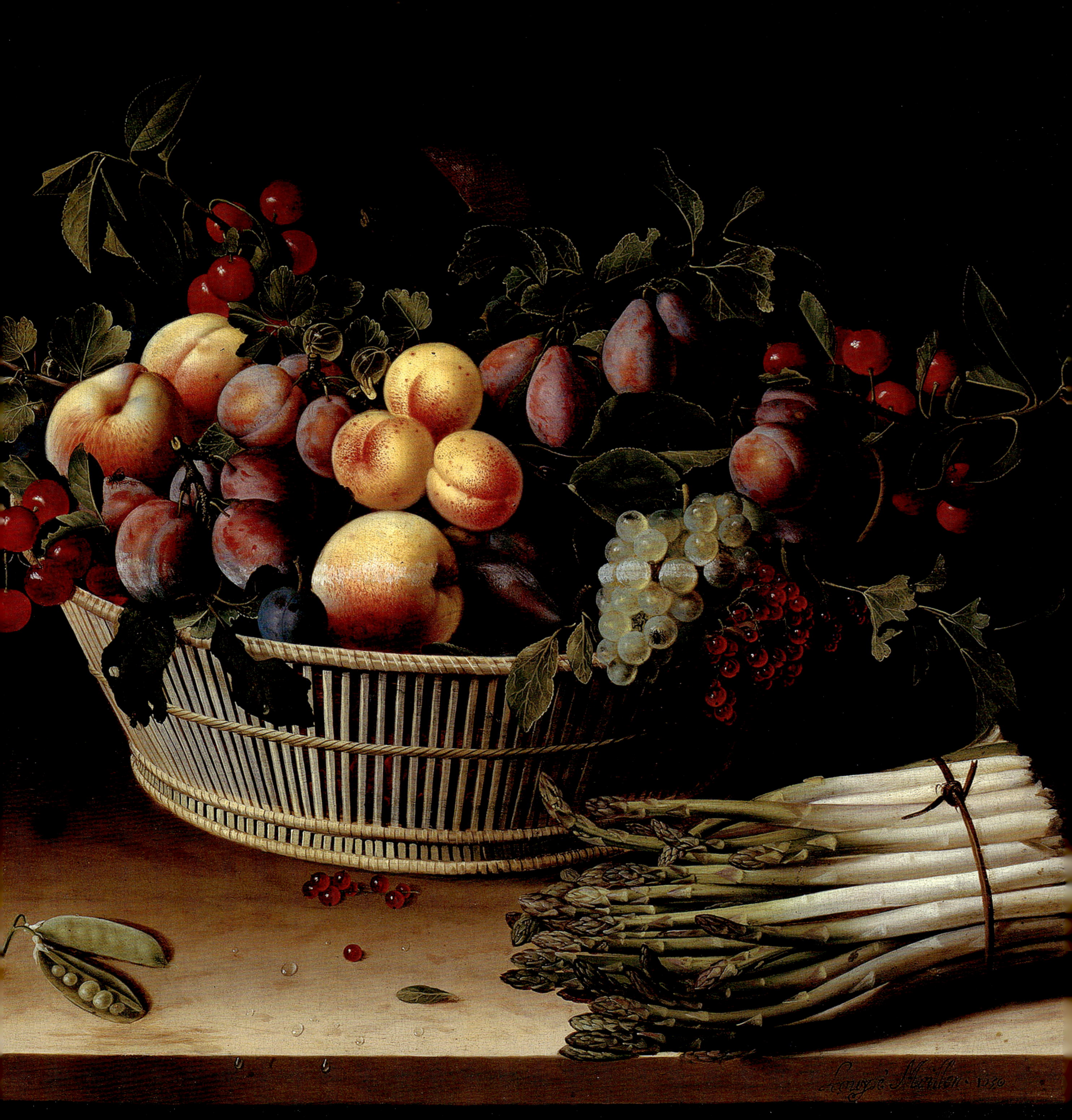

Editors' Foreword

The topic of historical women artists has garnered a fair amount of attention in museums lately, encouraging a shift in institutional policies to address the paucity of women makers in their collections. As museums try to rectify this long-standing oversight, pre-modern European women artists' works are achieving greater status within the art market and the public imagination. Organizing an exhibition devoted to women makers during this moment has been exciting and gratifying, to be sure, but also makes clear how our collective perspective continues to be shaped by biases toward narratives of exceptional and solitary genius.

In our efforts to counter this prevailing approach, we found ourselves—as many have—returning to a foundational exhibition of women artists of the past: Anne Sutherland Harris's and Linda Nochlin's *Women Artists, 1550–1950*, first installed in 1976 at the Los Angeles County Museum of Art. Their laudable and historic efforts resulted in increased scholarly interest in women artists and makers from the Middle Ages to the present, establishing a robust tradition in which this exhibition takes part. The curators' broad sweep of geography and chronology inspired our scope, as did their general intention to bring greater awareness to women's artistic accomplishments.

Yet, despite the important findings this exhibition offered, its approach to understanding women's contributions to, and status within, the artistic culture of early modern Europe still subscribed largely to the male-established criterion of singular brilliance with a paintbrush. Even in the face of significant development of gender and women's art historical studies in the nearly fifty years since then, women artists continued to be categorized as rare and comparatively less talented against this standard.

Making Her Mark: A History of Women Artists in Europe, 1400–1800 challenges this characterization and shifts focus onto the wide variety of objects made by women. With the aim of presenting a more accurate and diverse range of women's creative accomplishments, we established several underlying parameters. Foremost was the decision to expand upon the typical painting-centric focus and include various channels of visual creativity that reflect women's collaborative, silent, or adjacent roles in that production. A purposefully broad geographic scope helps elucidate the variety of women's socioeconomic situations and how they played out in differing religious and societal contexts. Diversified market forces in the Netherlands and German city-states offered different opportunities than those available to women living in essentially still feudal territories within Italy and the Iberian Peninsula. Similarly, a wide chronological span allows for the tracking of societal changes over time, such as the lessening of social and professional restrictions imposed on women as well as the impact of major political events or intellectual developments. Traditional art historical methodologies—such as sorting out attributions or identifying makers' relationships to prevailing stylistic movements—are less of a concern as they have long been used to exclusionary effect and discount the different priorities and circumstances that dictated creative production.

We do not deny male artists' involvement or attempt to present a fantastical world in which women makers operated independently from their circumstances, thereby risking what Griselda Pollock calls the "ghettoisation" of feminist art history. We have also endeavoured to curb the impulse to impose current feminist and gender ideologies that would have been largely incomprehensible to women of the past. Instead, we hope to focus the spotlight on the polyphonic contributions of women makers—exceptional and unexceptional alike—active during the four centuries between the origins of the Western canon and the modern era. While the absence of documentary evidence for the lion's share of creative women makes it difficult to treat each individual or society with the same degree of detail, we do hope that calling attention to the prevalence of silent labour or the many facets of artistic production will encourage consideration of unnamed women's participation.

As many have noted since Nochlin's provocation to go in search of the "great" women artist, the true reach of women's work has long been hidden in private collections and in museum storerooms, frequently obscured by the attribution of their work to male artists. Closely related is the inherent delicateness of the objects many women made. Women's works for the domestic sphere—such as shell work, embroidery, paper rolling, wax, and hair work—are particularly limited by their fragility, which drastically impacts access to extant examples in good repair. While literature produced by women resides tucked away in archives and libraries, the material goods made by even the most accomplished women makers were often utilitarian, meaning that they frequently deteriorated due to daily use or fell out of fashion over time. Some of these works have suffered from later appraisals by scholars and curators who determined that objects based on mass-produced patterns or kits were not the result of an authentic creative process. In addition to containing light-sensitive materials, like textiles or paper, these works are often intermedial, existing between museum-collecting departments and therefore less likely to receive sustained attention from curators. Certain media are so fragile and difficult to lend that a number of important works—including those by Anna Morandi Manzolini (1714–1774), Caterina de Julianis (1670–1743), Mary Delaney (1700–1788), and the enclosed garden altarpieces of the women of the Flemish Beguine convents—cannot be properly represented here.

By no means does this exhibition or catalogue offer an exhaustive representation of women makers in Europe in the centuries selected. Even as we committed to the final checklist, new works surfaced. Readers may note greater representation of work from later centuries; this is not intended to favour those periods or imply that women across Europe necessarily played greater roles overall in the production of art in those periods. Instead, this imbalance is a reflection of better archival support for the documented professionalization of women in the arts as well as greater numbers of extant examples stable enough to travel or be put on display.

Although there are episodes of global reach woven throughout, the focus remains on Western Europe in a conscious effort to subvert the dominant narrative of male-centred standards for the Western canon and to prevent an unwieldy checklist. This restriction, however, hampered our ability to thoroughly engage with the question of women makers of non-European origin, or the exchange between European women artists and those trained in non-Western traditions. Further, the topic of artistic output by historical gender non-conforming individuals was not something we could address properly with the works we were able to include. We do not intend to negate their existence or erase their contributions, as surely they were part of these artistic communities. Rather, the state of scholarship has not yet led us to specific artistic examples that could concretely illuminate their identities. Equally frustrating was the inability to include objects representing named women makers of colour. While women of colour doubtlessly engaged in the broader production of works of art during this period, thus far it appears to have remained in the same silent or undocumented capacity that applies to the majority of women during this period. We hope to be proven wrong in these last statements, and that future discoveries will lead to many more inclusive and expanded explorations into women makers of the past.

Major essays in this catalogue address a broad range of media, with the goal of offering a variety of perspectives on women's far-ranging and ubiquitous involvement with all manner of artistic materials and sites of creative production during the centuries covered in this exhibition. Following these broader investigations are concise object-focused essays, organized by media, that take the place of traditional catalogue entries for the works presented in the exhibition. This format is intended to undermine the traditional monographic approach, one that has long favoured male artists. Further, abandoning the focus on individual identities allows for an integrated discussion of the objects with unknown makers, and builds a picture of how women worked in medium-specific contexts. To find a work from the exhibition, consult the medium-specific chapters starting on page 159; to find an artist, consult the index of women makers with works illustrated in the catalogue, located at the end of the volume.

As with any major project, this undertaking was the result of a collaborative effort. The team dynamic that undergirded its research, organization, and execution felt wholly appropriate to a project that aims to decentre the traditional concept of the individual male artist working in isolation. We are grateful to the dozens of colleagues, scholars, and friends who have contributed generously and with great enthusiasm.

It has been deeply satisfying to see the power of cooperation bring to light the historical reality of women making their mark collaboratively throughout the centuries. Locating and learning about the objects made by women in collections across North America and Europe required the expertise, patience, and goodwill of our colleagues at the lending institutions and collections. Our deep appreciation goes to Kira d'Alburquerque, Ellenor Alcorn, Silvija Banić, Peter Bell, Arnaud Bessière, Rachel Bradshaw, Laurie Brewer, Michael Brown, Charlotte Brumpton, Catherine Burce, Joaquim Caetano, Fiona Campbell, Bonnie Campbell Lilienfeld, Danielle Carrabino, Sarah Cartwright, Kelsey Champagne, Sarah Chasse, Tara Chicirda, Elizabeth Cleland, Caitlin Condell, David Conradsen, Tara Contractor, Genevieve Cortinovis, Alberto Craievich, Caroline Danforth, Lloyd DeWitt, Judith Dolkart, Jack Doran, Martina Droth, Marlene Edelheit, Tara Emsley, Anne-Marie Eze, Paola Focardi, Jerry Forehand, Aprile Gallant, Gabriel Goldstein, Michael Gregory, Courtney Harris, Earle Havens, Kate Heller, Rena Hoisington, Olivia Horsfall, Jan Howard, Heather Hughes, Nick Humphrey, Lyle Humphrey, Lisa Hurst, Neal Hurst, Kim Ivey, Yuriko Jackall, Jennifer Jarvis, Eva-Lena Karlsson, Simon Kelly, Holly Keris, Sarah Kirk, Cory Korkow, Angelika Kuettner, Nicole LaBouff, Abigail Lang, Leah Lehmbeck, Alexandra Libby, Karla Livingston, Mary-Kay Lombino, Rebecca Long, Paula Lopes, Judith Mann, Louis Marchesano, John Marciari, Katharine Martin, Rachel McGarry, Carie McGinnis, Leela Meinertas, Sandra Mendonça Pires, Sequoia Miller, Sarah Mirseyedi, Bo K. Mompho, Kathleen Morris, Mary Morton, Cristina Nisi, Maureen O'Brien, Nadine Orenstein, Tanya Paul, Chloe Pelletier, Emily J. Peters, Laurel Peterson, Mei Mei Rado, Mark Ramirez, Abigail Rapoport, Sarah Reidell, Kelly Reynolds, Paula Richter, Cynthia Roman, Kim Schenck, Robert Schindler, Michael Seminara, Anita Sganzerla, Natalie Shores, Daniel Slater, Joaneath Spicer, Nick Stagliano, Moyna Stanton, Lucille Stiger, Anatole Tchikine, Karine Tsoumis, Rachel Tu, Jessica Urick, Tricia Walker, Henrietta Ward, Betsy Wieseman, Aaron Wile, Tony Willis, Diane Wright, and Wilfried Zeisler.

In addition to our knowledgeable and generous contributing authors, we wish to thank Zara Anishanslin, Sheila Barker, Catherine Hall-van den Elsen, Suzanne Karr Schmidt, Lia Markey, Denise Murrell, Jill Pederson, Lindsey Schneider, Katlijne Van der Stighelen, and Courtney Wilder for their generous subject-matter expertise. For their assistance with the indemnity application, a huge thank-you goes to Sandra Hindman and David Rueger.

Just as women makers worked alongside their family members in households humble to grand, we could not have accomplished this project without the support of our families. Andaleeb wishes to acknowledge the unflagging and loving support provided by her husband, James, and son, Jasper, throughout the long hours invested in this project. Further heartfelt thanks also go to her friends-like-family who offered advice and encouragement to see this endeavour through. Alexa wishes to thank her husband, Seth, for his assistance in providing the mental space to do the travel and work required for this exhibition. Her daughter, Livia, who accompanied her on loan trips in Italy, deserves an award for her museum tolerance, while Jonathan keeps it all just wild enough. A special thank-you to her parents for hosting us in Madison and for a lifetime of love and support. Theresa would like to express her immense gratitude to her husband, Owen, for his enthusiastic support of her passion for this project and she would additionally like to recognize his contributions in 3D modelling for the exhibition. She extends heartfelt thanks to her friends and family for their encouragement, curiosity, love, and patience.

Andaleeb Badiee Banta
Senior Curator and Department Head, Prints, Drawings & Photographs, Baltimore Museum of Art

Alexa Greist
Curator and R. Fraser Elliott Chair, Prints & Drawings, Art Gallery of Ontario

Theresa Kutasz Christensen
Exhibition Research Assistant, Prints, Drawings & Photographs, Baltimore Museum of Art

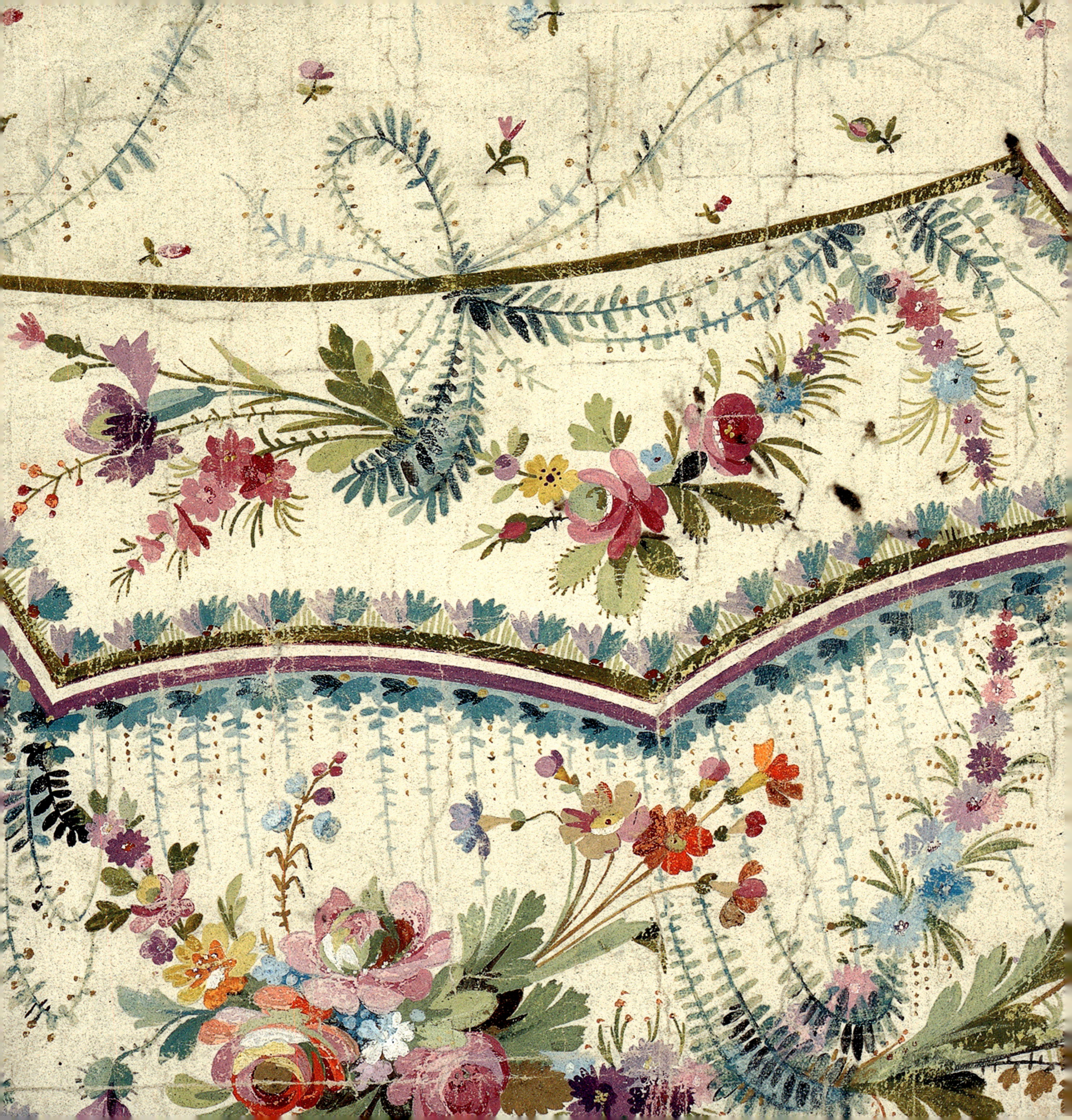

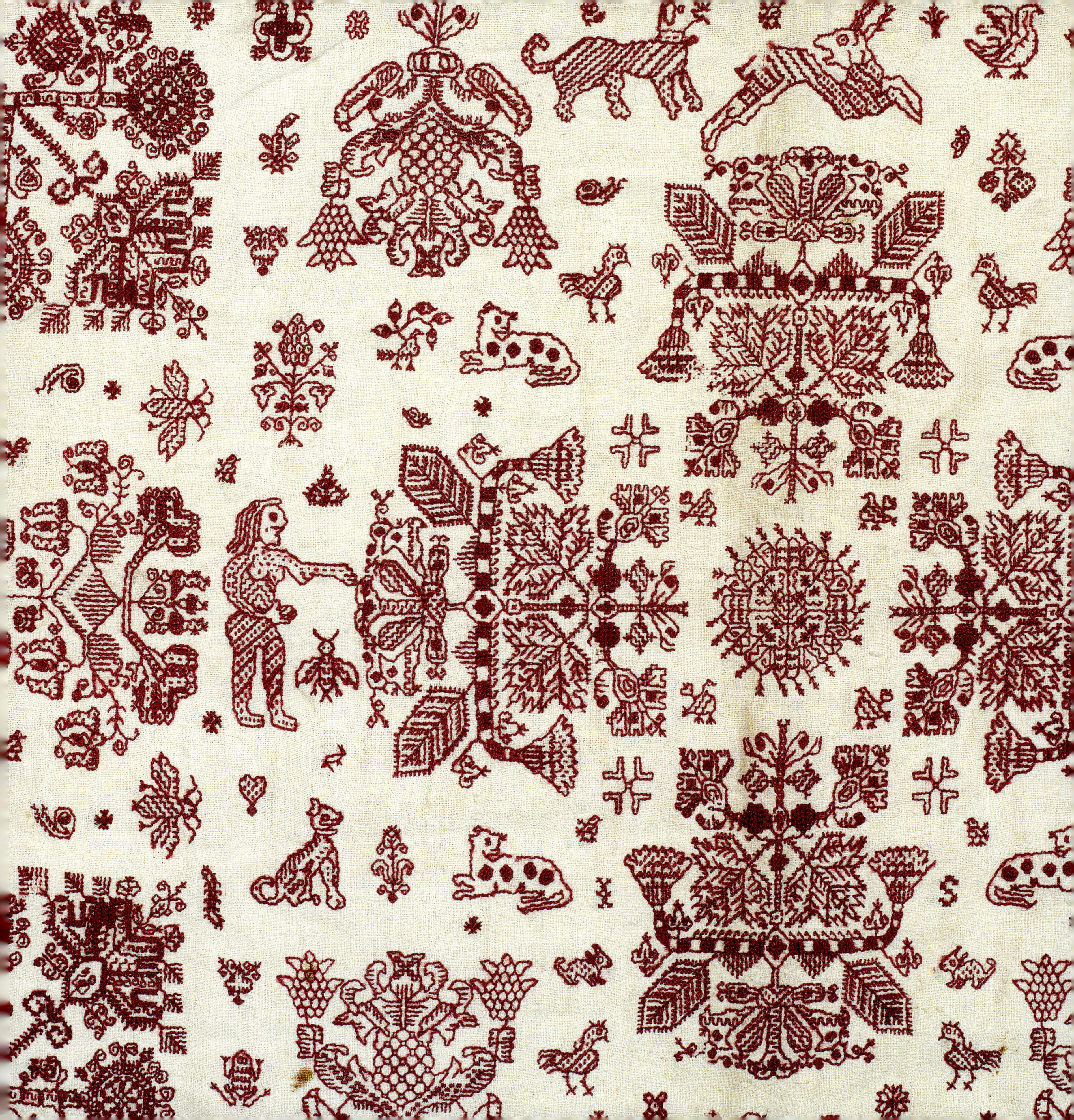

NOT SEEN, NOT HEARD

In Search of the Unexceptional Woman Artist

Andaleeb Badiee Banta

"The notion of the 'exceptional' woman artist may be one of the most insidious means of undermining the likelihood of women's entering the creative arts."

—NANETTE SALOMON, "The Art Historical Canon: Sins of Omission"[1]

Fortune favours the bold. This adage, based on an ancient Latin proverb, has resonated over the centuries because it supports an appealing belief: that history is shaped by noteworthy or extraordinary actions taken by brave souls who forged new paths to work against established norms. Historical sources and contemporary narratives have asserted that it was unusual to be a professional woman artist during the early modern period in Europe—here defined as the fifteenth through the eighteenth centuries—precisely because many societal expectations and practices prevented women from pursuing such an "un-ladylike" path. Those whose names appear in the annals of Western European art history—including Sofonisba Anguissola, Artemisia Gentileschi, Luisa Roldán, Maria Sibylla Merian, Rosalba Carriera, and Elisabeth Louise Vigée-LeBrun—were indeed women who lived extraordinary lives, earning favour at royal courts, travelling great distances, supporting their families, and navigating the restrictions that excluded them from traditional paths of artistic education and professionalism. In many ways, these women found a way to play by rules that were decidedly established *by* men *for* men, and for this reason they are worthy of celebrated status and should be regarded as exceptional.

Their stories, however, are not reflective of the majority of women who were involved—professionally or otherwise—in the production of visual art during this period. In fact, most of these largely anonymous or less-documented lives and experiences of women makers were decidedly unexceptional by contemporary critical standards, even if their contributions resulted in extraordinary objects that embody sophisticated and compelling aspects of creativity. In considering each object as a locus for the intersection of various circumstantial factors related to its production, context, materials, and audience, we are able to expand our understanding of women's contributions to sourcing materials as well as to their administrative and supervisory capacity that was essential to the business of making art. In this light, the finished product integrally mirrors the diverse experiences of the many unexceptional women involved in the numerous procedural steps of its creation.

Exceptionality evokes notions of genius, celebrity, innovation, and quality—all concepts that were constructed for and by a privileged class of men as ideological cornerstones of the Western artistic canon. The myth of exceptionalism was required of figures included in historical compendia about artists; the perceived "unnatural" status of the few women artists who achieved professional reputations earned them entry into the category of exceptionalism.[2] That women's names do not appear in equal measure in the laudatory artistic biographies of both the past and the present is an indicator of pervasive biases that continue to shape our understanding of the history of Western art, both in terms of an artist's gender and the type of work created, which tend to be linked. Even the term "artist" implies that certain extrinsic standards—historically defined by men—determine whether a woman who creates, fabricates, or labours toward an aesthetic product can be considered worthy of this professional classification. These documentary lacunae around unexceptional women artists and makers not only tell us about the limitations imposed on these women of the past but are indicative of the prejudices still embedded in the discipline of art history itself. Examination of historical women's creative output through this lens, particularly as it applies to museum collections, speaks volumes about the types of artistic production considered worthy of inclusion, and the marginalization of women's artistic contributions to the visual culture of the early modern period.

How does one locate and discuss the woman maker who was never meant to be included in the history of European art? What place does the unexceptional woman maker occupy in a narrative that insists on distinction and recognition? Even the parameters by which historians operate depend on basic data—such as a name, birth and death dates, or a body of work—that are often absent when considering the role of creative women of the past. This is especially true for women and girls who were enslaved or coerced to work without remuneration, but it applies also to many women working on the lower rungs of the manufacturing process, and to those producing objects for domestic use or for sale to support a household. Their history is not lost, as some presentations of women artists have claimed; rather, it is more likely that their history was not recorded in the first place. One must peer through the critical and methodological framework staunchly established by patriarchal art historical traditions to find the unsung, the anonymous, the silent makers who often have few or no written records or encomia to represent them. This approach often requires stepping outside the sanctioned category of "artist"—historically wrapped up with ideas of individual (invariably male) "genius"—to expand notions of creative responsibility that include women who contributed to the production of art in less romantic, more logistical or collaborative ways.[3] To include women in the visual history of humanity, we must look beyond the exalted categories and narratives imposed in the past that still shape our vision today, and abandon our preoccupation with exceptional individuals and heroic deeds. In the face of a persistent bias in art museums toward the "fine" arts authored by named (mostly male) individual artists, orchestrating an exhibition devoted to women makers of the past requires a unique approach: one that de-centres existing expectations about how women participated in artistic culture of the fifteenth through eighteenth centuries and that questions assumptions about what kind of works should be included.

This essay is far from the first to call out the inherent sexism of art history as a formalized discipline. As generations of feminist scholars have made clear, this exclusion of women artists can be attributed to the early records of art history and has been perpetuated over the centuries through the establishment and maintenance of the patriarchic canon, the privileged bastion of quality and excellence. Well-founded criticism and significant recuperative scholarly investigations of the past half century have reclaimed the work and voices of many historical women artists, reassessed the art historical discipline, and identified the various ways that chauvinism and sexism have prevented women from participating on the same playing field.[4] More recently, the feminist

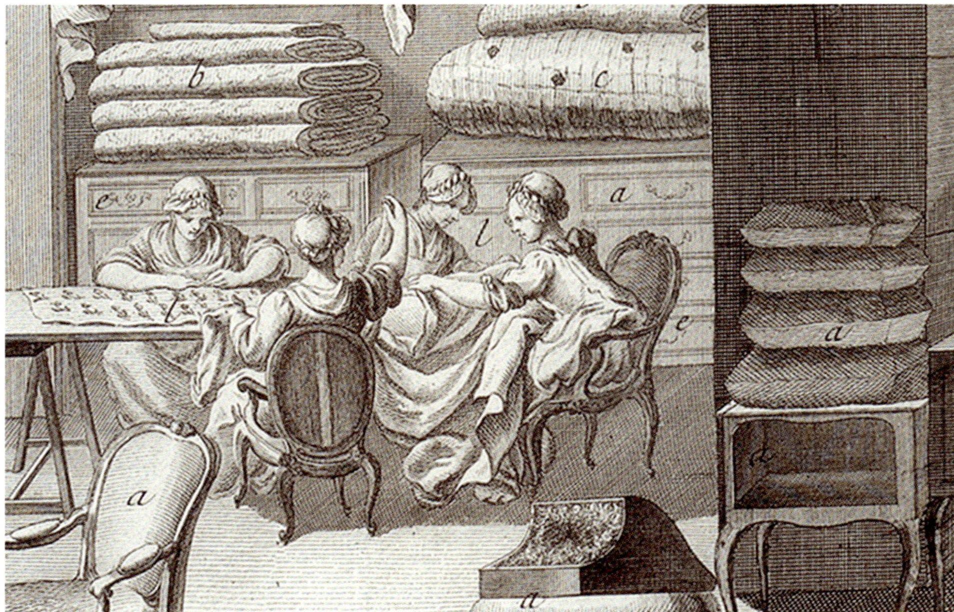

Fig. 1 • Detail: Denis Diderot and Jean le Rond d'Alembert, *Upholstery [Tapissier, interieur d'une boutique et différens ouvrages]*, plate 1 in *Encyclopédie, ou Dictionnaire raisonné des sciences, des arts et des métiers*, vol. 9, Paris, 1751–1772. Printed book on paper, illustrated with engravings, 43.8 × 29.5 cm. Victoria and Albert Museum, London, museum no. NAL.38041008210395. Image © Victoria and Albert Museum, London.

movement within and beyond academia has worked to identify its own ideological blind spots in terms of essentialism, intersectionality, and agency.[5] While academic scholarship has made notable strides in calling out the historical and continuing forces that erase women from history—contributing to the foundation of entire fields of study and activism—the application of these lessons learned have made far less progress in the symbiotic world of museums and the art market, particularly in the arena of pre-modern art. This circumstance has everything to do with the long-standing and intrinsic connection of museums and the market to the history of connoisseurship, collecting, and the canon-supporting privilege of exceptionality (in the guise of such subjective terms as "quality" and "importance"). In turn, this dynamic illustrates and perpetuates the inextricable link between identity, oppression, and economics that had defined and motivated Western society for centuries.

The presence of women as makers remains largely anomalous or anonymized in the halls displaying pre-modern art of European and North American museums, reflecting these institutions' reliance on masculinist ontological and commercial systems. Unsurprisingly, the postmodernist dismantling of the notion of individual heroic genius narratives has not found fertile ground in art museums' presentations of historical European art. Significantly, over the past decade, interdisciplinary developments centring materiality within art historical discourse also have not been applied uniformly in museums. In the rarified setting of an art museum, these approaches are reserved for objects that have been relegated to the historically feminized categories of the decorative arts, textiles, craft, or, even more problematically, non-Western cultures' artistic production.[6]

The last two decades have seen a pronounced uptick in the presentation of pre-modern women artists as the subject of museum exhibitions and high-profile acquisitions. But many of these laudable endeavours to prove the worth of historical women artists subscribe to the same criteria and parameters that originate with the hegemonic structure of individual exceptionalism and its legacy. Works by women makers remain resolutely in the minority and treated as entirely exceptional, either in their isolation as the single example (or one of a handful) by a named woman in a museum's collection, or in the ardent efforts of curators to argue for their inclusion in the first place. Market forces are clearly part of the equation, as the monetary and canonical value of works by women artists are determined by the fame of the makers, which is in turn supported or abandoned by museums' willingness to acquire and display their works. As a result, unexceptional women makers—those that lack recognition endorsed by the canon or those that work in media outside of painting—generally do not appear in museum galleries or are relegated to lower-profile auction sales.

At the core of this quandary is the disregard for works that diverge from the established dominance of paintings and monumental sculpture as the de facto representational categories of the fine arts. Works rendered in smaller formats, from ephemeral or more fragile materials—what Sheila ffolliott terms the "anomalous media"[7]—or those that employ aesthetic standards that diverge from the expectations of the approved stylistic trajectories that make up the Western canon have been relegated to a lower status in the hierarchy of the arts, occupying the division of "craft" or "decorative arts."[8] By the logic of exceptionality, inexpensive common materials—such as cloth, thread, wax, and clay—tend not to promote the celebration of an object or its maker, a measure of the ingrained biases against materials to which most women had access. Further, many of these types of objects do not comply with unwritten but enforced rules of what is put on display in a museum gallery. "Wall power" should be added to the list of terms that have doomed the majority of early modern women makers and their creations to secondary or tertiary status. Elaborately constructed small-scale devotional objects or painstakingly embroidered and beaded boxes and baskets have a hard time visually competing with the monumental dynamism of large-scale paintings, gilded furniture, and objets d'art. Instead, many of the types of objects that unexceptional women makers created reward close, contemplative looking at a pace hardly afforded works of art anymore.[9]

Women makers were active in nearly every means of artistic production of the early modern period. Beyond the time-honoured trifecta of the "major" arts of painting, monumental sculpture, and architecture lies a broader, richer landscape in terms of makers' social status, methods of working, and variety of materials. This pronouncement comes as no surprise to historians of craft, fibre arts, and material culture, but for those who have isolated their study to the "fine" arts, it broadens the search for women artists considerably. The unexceptional woman maker operated at almost all social levels, whether as a manager of a workshop or manufactory, as a procurer of raw materials used in artistic fabrication by others, or as an amateur creating at home with her peers. While most of these makers lack the celebrity status of the familiar exceptional artistic heroines, their contributions are impressive—less for their groundbreaking bravura than for their reflection of the diversity of voices and hands operating outside canonical mainstream aesthetics and art theory.

Anomalous or Anonymous

The myth of exceptionalism in the history of Western European art arguably originates with the artist-biographer Giorgio Vasari. Although the practice of recording the names of remarkable practitioners dates back to classical antiquity, Vasari is recognized as the progenitor of art historical biography as an independent genre. His biographical compendium *Le vite de' più eccellenti pittori, scultori e architettori* [*The Lives of the Most Excellent Painters, Sculptors, and Architects*], first published in 1550 and then again in a revised and expanded edition in 1568, established a foundational methodological framework that promoted creative genius independent of manual craft. Through the identification of significant (male Florentine) artists who illustrated a proposed trajectory of artistic development based on its approximation of antique Greco-Roman ideals, Vasari formulated a heroic, individualistic narrative of Renaissance art history that served as a model for the next four centuries of scholars, connoisseurs, and art theorists.[10] Vasari's anthology reflects socially inculcated priorities and norms of his time, including chauvinism related to language, geography, class, and gender.[11] Further, Vasari's biographies are known to be filled with fictions and fabrications that support these biases, making it impossible to regard his narratives as wholly factual accounts, which they may never have been intended to be in the first place.[12] Nevertheless, *The Lives* remains the most fulsome resource for information about artists of Renaissance Italy and, most importantly, it functioned as the basis for the subsequent development of art history as a discipline, affecting how artists have been discussed well into the modern age. Whatever Vasari's intentions may have been, *The Lives* codified exclusionary exceptionalism, a hierarchy of the arts, the primacy of life drawing, and heroism or celebrity as the fundamental components of the history of art, asserting its inherent biases against craft, anonymous and collective labour, and domestic production—categories that were perceived then and continue to be associated with women makers.

Vasari's prioritization of fame as a measure of success necessitated that the artists he promoted were, by nature, extraordinary, placing exceptionalism at the core of his methodology. He necessarily included a few biographies of women working in the arts, if only because it would have been inaccurate to ignore them entirely. Despite their inclusion, this publication resulted in establishing art historical methodologies that categorized women artists as anomalous or anonymous. In the 1550 edition of *The Lives*, Vasari included the biography of only one woman artist, the Bolognese sculptor Properzia de' Rossi (c. 1490/91–c. 1530),[13] while the second edition appended brief, independent biographies of three additional women artists to de' Rossi's biography: Sister Plautilla Nelli (1523–1588),[14] Lucrezia Quistelli dalla Mirandola (1541–1594),[15] and Sofonisba Anguissola (c. 1535–1625).[16]

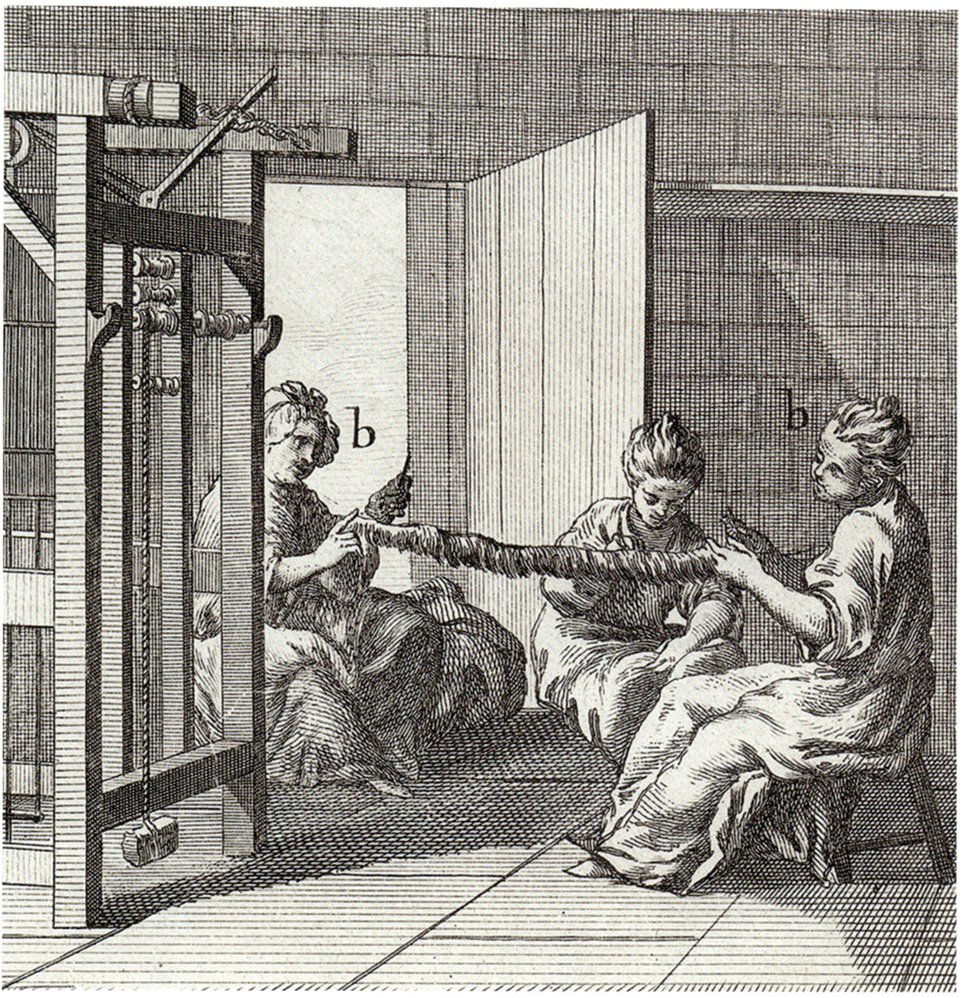

Fig. 2 • Detail: Denis Diderot and Jean le Rond d'Alembert, *Making trimmings* [*Passementerie, mètier à franges*], plate 15 in *Encyclopédie, ou Dictionnaire raisonné des sciences, des arts et des métiers*, vol. 11, Paris, 1751–1772. Printed book on paper, illustrated with engravings, 42.7 × 28 cm. Victoria and Albert Museum, London, museum no. NAL.38041800774804. Image © Victoria and Albert Museum, London.

Others can be found only in passing mention within other male artists' entries, without any elaborated or critical discussion of their work.[17] It is likely that the four women for whom Vasari did write standalone, albeit short, biographical entries were selected as much for their exceptionality as for their talent.[18]

Subsequent regional artistic biographers, within Italy and beyond, also emulated this format with little variation, perpetuating the standards of exceptionalism and fame in an effort to bring such reputations to their own cities and hometown artists. These biographic compendia remain today the best resources, in some cases the only, for information about women's accomplishments in the centuries following Vasari's *The Lives*, and shed light on regional differences in women artists' access to paths to professionalism. Some seventeenth- and eighteenth-century authors showed greater awareness of women artists, such as Carlo Cesare Malvasia and his fellow Bolognese authors, whose biographies of women artists contributed support for higher numbers of professional women artists thriving there than elsewhere in Italy.[19] Arnold Houbraken's unprecedented presentation of twenty-five women artists in his *De groote schouburgh der Nederlantsche konstschilders en schilderessen* (1718–1721) likely reflects Netherlandish women's greater flexibility to operate outside restrictive guild systems.[20] Despite these standout examples, however, the majority of art biography during the early modern period remained faithful to Vasari's legacy.

Writing at a moment when professional artists were keen to distinguish their creative production as intellectually separate from the manual output of craft guilds, Vasari constructed a cult of personality around his chosen heroes, gifting them with impossibly perfect, near-superhuman qualities that elevated the status of the art they practised.[21] As such, this emphasis on individual artists' personal characteristics was tied to moral judgements about their behaviour. In the case of women artists, these judgements were inextricably wrapped up with contemporary ideas about what women could and should be. Therefore, "feminine" virtues like chastity and faithfulness were highly prized, as were beauty and musical talent.[22] Vasari's commentary on these women's exceptional qualities occasionally included reference to their diligence, intellect, and popularity with patrons, but their status would never be considered on par with that of their male counterparts because of women's perceived biological and base nature.[23] With their inclusion, however, Vasari was faced with the dilemma of reconciling the discrepancy between the qualities he promoted in his artistic heroes that were historically categorized as male attributes (active, ambitious, intellectual, divine) with those traditionally associated with women (passive, circumspect, feebleminded, biological).[24] Women had to have remarkable qualities in order to warrant examination of their careers, but as Nanette Salomon asserts, "what can and has been done for men cannot simply and unproblematically be done for women."[25] The type of details that appeared in a male artist's biography to convey the heroic and appealing qualities of his artistic genius conversely functioned within a woman's profile to promote her as an oddity or anomalous. In an age that idolized the marvellous and fantastic, the "unusual" nature of a female artist functioned as justification for including women in Vasari's characterization of the pervasive flowering of creativity that defined the Renaissance.[26]

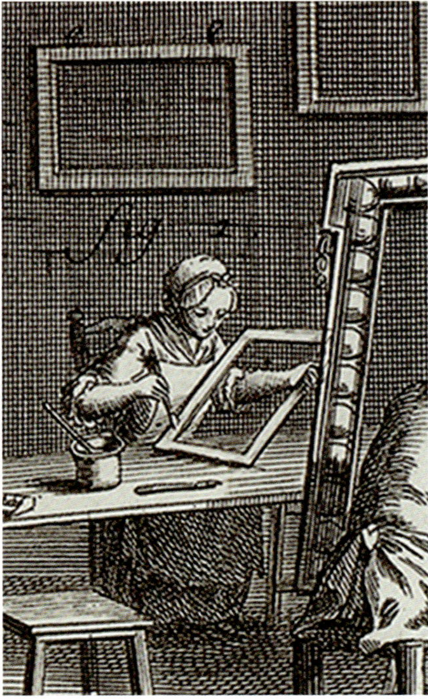

Fig. 3 • Detail: Denis Diderot and Jean le Rond d'Alembert, *Gilding [Doreur, sur bois]*, plate 4 in *Encyclopédie, ou Dictionnaire raisonné des sciences, des arts et des métiers*, vol. 3, Paris, 1751–1772. Printed book on paper, illustrated with engravings, 43.8 × 29.5 cm. Victoria and Albert Museum, London, museum no. NAL.38041800786170. Image © Victoria and Albert Museum, London.

Even the very format of *The Lives* as a compendium of biographies required focus on famous individuals as the subjects of the entries, an organizing principle that ultimately disqualified many women makers from the start.[27] Vasari constructed his entries as lionizing vehicles for his artistic heroes, with Michelangelo and Raphael at the forefront, disregarding the important role that collaborative or silent labour played in any large-scale artistic undertaking. This approach excluded consideration of female practitioners in convents, family workshops, larger manufactories, and domestic settings.[28] The family workshop was the typical model for artistic production by men and women during the late medieval and early Renaissance periods, and countless women contributed to the commercial success of such family enterprises well through the eighteenth century. By disassociating the famous women artists he chose to profile from any artisanal workshop origins, Vasari dismissed other women's collaborative creative output as domestic work more closely tied to the labour required to run and support a household or convent rather than an expression of talent or aesthetic achievement. To be fair, his intent was to document the "most excellent" professional Italian artists' lives, not to provide an account of artistry in every format. But the restrictions and assumptions inherent in the publication informed subsequent centuries' standards by which any artistic practitioner was to be judged, establishing an androcentric and hierarchical reading of the creative landscape for Western art.

Vasari's ideological devotion in *The Lives* to the fundamental role of drawing as the basis for the "major" arts of painting, sculpture, and architecture also contributed to standards of exceptionalism that had an enduring misogynist effect. His championing of draughtsmanship—particularly of the nude male body—as the core skill required to master the other arts not only was decidedly biased toward the stylistic developments occurring in Florentine art during his lifetime but it also effected the exclusion of the majority of women artists. Women's access to study from live male nude models—the assumed gold standard for artistic educational practice—was severely restricted in the sixteenth century, as it would have been deemed a threat to the chaste honour of an unmarried woman, and wholly inappropriate for any woman of society. Historical subjects, the most respected of the pictorial genres, required a command of the depiction of the human body based upon carefully drawn observation. Drawing was also a fundamental activity within the academy, the beginnings of which were taking shape during Vasari's time. By the late seventeenth century, the academy became the educational and social nexus for artistic creativity, camaraderie, and networking.[29] This general lack of official access to an essential component of formal artistic education and socialization affected the types of subjects women could portray as well as the scale and format of their work, a hindrance that affected the types of official commissions for which they could compete well into the eighteenth century.[30]

With the establishment of art history as a legitimate field of historical inquiry in the eighteenth century—significantly, the same period in which art museums began to take shape as formalized public cultural institutions—the Vasarian prejudices and qualifying standards were applied to the formation of the field and its physical manifestation in museum galleries. The increasing differentiation between works that should be treated as fine art as opposed to those that reflect human industry and craft—later categorized as material culture or anthropological artifacts—was determined largely along the same classically centred lines that had informed Vasari's history of chosen heroic artistic (male) individuals. By the late eighteenth century, a named woman rarely appeared in written histories or on the walls of museums, unless she qualified as exceptional.[31]

Fig. 4 • Detail: Denis Diderot and Jean le Rond d'Alembert, *Paper making workshop [Papetterie, etendage]*, plate 12 in *Encyclopédie, ou Dictionnaire raisonné des sciences, des arts et des métiers*, vol. 5, Paris, 1751–1772. Printed book on paper, illustrated with engravings, 43.8 × 29.5 cm. Victoria and Albert Museum, London, museum no. NAL.38041800786188. Image © Victoria and Albert Museum, London.

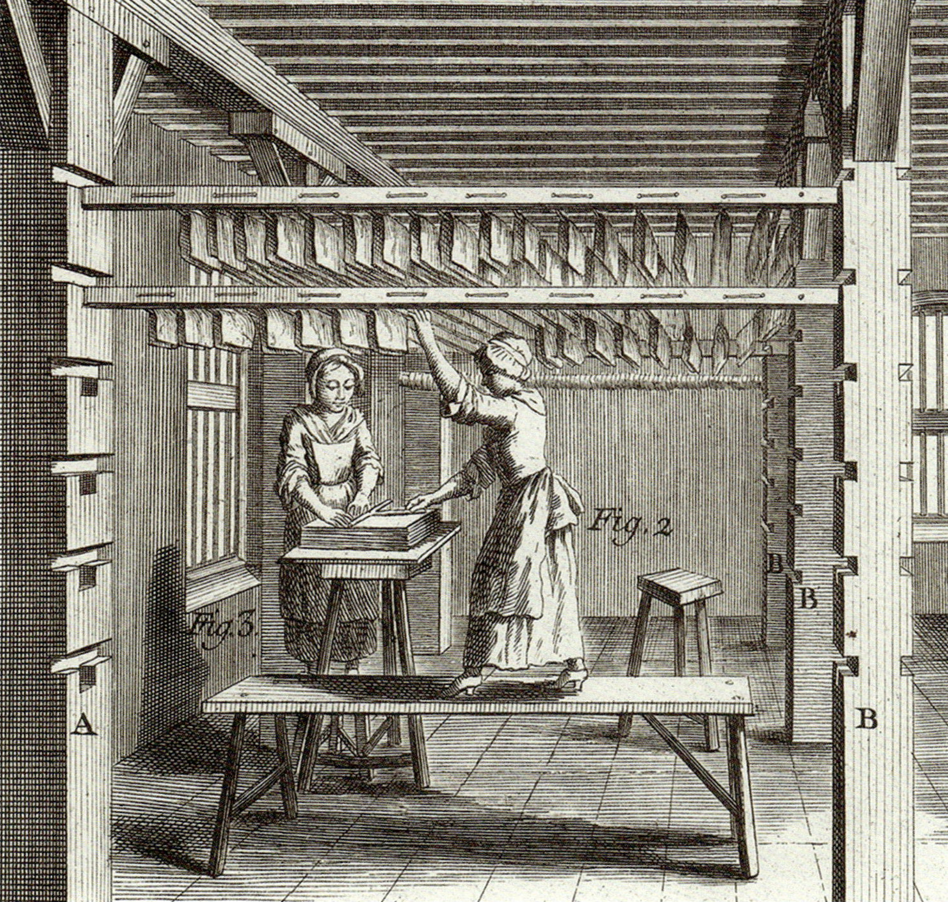

What's in a Name?

The modern scholarly manifestations of Vasari's legacy are the monographic study and its close cousin the catalogue raisonné, both of which developed over the course of the eighteenth and nineteenth centuries. In these essential formats for the study of a single artist's contribution, Vasari's laudatory superlatives and compelling anecdotes were supplanted with more procedural standards in determining an individual's biography, historical circumstances, and body of work.[32] Yet, as with Vasari's biographies, the baseline requirement for a monographic study is the identity of an individual artist—a name. Its reliance on biographical knowledge about an artist excluded anyone for whom this information no longer survived or was never recorded in the first place. For the majority of women makers, their birth, marriage, or death dates are the most we have to work with, and the absence of signatures on works—let alone those that were later obscured or erased—makes it very difficult to recover their oeuvre.[33] To be sure, monographic studies have contributed enormously to the recuperation of many early modern women's artistic careers and they remain vital resources, but it is important to note the role this genre has played in the discourse around fame and historical recognition.[34]

Aside from relying on documented biographical information, the monographic study also promoted the concept of single-person authorship, an idea that attained mythic proportions by the nineteenth century, when it combined with the Romantic notion of the lone genius of the artist, which also had its basis in Vasari's promotional biographies. Although this characterization of an artist functioning entirely independently—toiling to give form to his inner (inspired, often misunderstood) genius—is now recognized as an outdated trope, it nevertheless lives on in the form of the monographic study's promotion of named individualized creativity and exclusion of unnamed or polyphonic contributions. This distaste for anonymity remains at the core of historical analysis of post-medieval Western art, and continues to be a

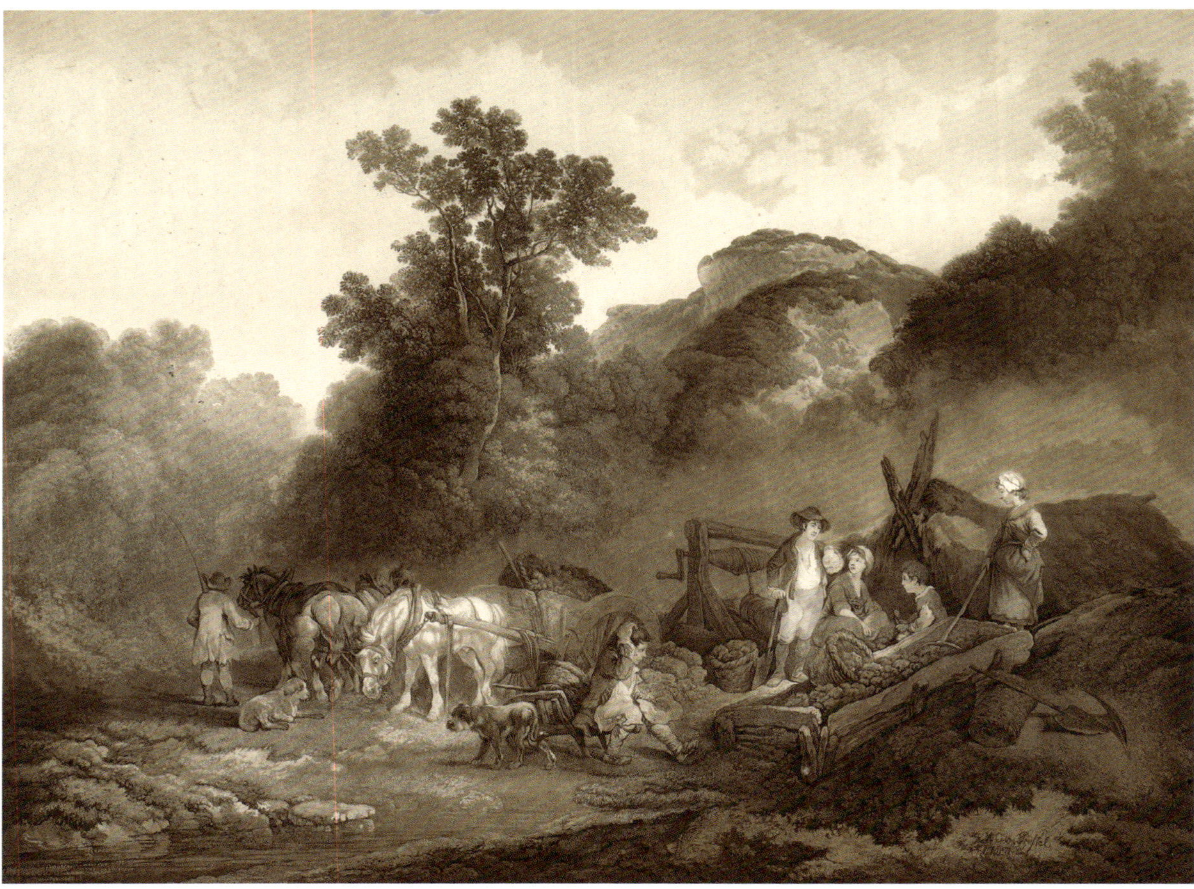

Fig. 5 • Maria Catharina Prestel, after Philippe Jacques de Loutherbourg, *A View of the Black-Lead Mine, in Cumberland*, 1788. Aquatint and etching, sheet: 54.8 × 68.5 cm; image: 46.5 × 64 cm. Baltimore Museum of Art: Garrett Collection, 1984.81.2394. Photo: Mitro Hood.

driving force in scholarship as well as in methods of organization and display practised in museums.[35] This enduring anxiety around anonymity in museums is evident in the persistent popularity of the monographic exhibition, the prominence given to an artist's name (if one is known) on object labels,[36] and the general perception that anonymity of an object is a problem that can be resolved with enough sustained research.[37]

In an even more pronounced way, the catalogue raisonné has played a crucial and decidedly mercantile role in the cultivation of exceptionality around the work of a particular artist. At the heart of its methodology are the intertwined concepts of quality and connoisseurship, used by the earliest eighteenth-century authors—themselves art dealers—as authoritative validation of a specific individual's contributions and, by extension, market value.[38] Connoisseurship—the act of determining whether a work is by a particular author—requires the acceptance of quality as the qualifying standard for that determination. Maintaining a decisive catalogue of an artist's work creates a paradigm of exclusion that directly affects the perception of rarity and quality essential to establishing an artist's market value, which eventually becomes synonymous with historical resonance. The combined anxieties around anonymity and quality have contributed consistently to women's exclusion from the canon, as much of their work has been compared unfavourably with what men made, ignoring the contributing external factors in its creation or whether it was intended for audiences outside of market environments.[39] These omissions doom the works to be disregarded by collectors, museum curators, scholars, and ultimately the public.

It seems more than coincidental that critical focus on the exceptional, named maker formalized during the nineteenth century, by which time women artists had largely disappeared from art historical scholarship.[40] By the twentieth century, even those women who had met the standards of exceptionality during the early modern period were systematically erased from modern surveys and did not receive monographic treatment, leaving those women mentioned by Vasari and biographical writers of earlier centuries to seem even more anomalous.[41] It is worth pointing out that this active erasure coincided with the first wave of feminist advocacy movements occurring in Europe and the United States during the nineteenth century in reaction to the widespread acceptance of Victorian standards for feminine domesticity.[42] Around the same time, the artistic and literary archetype of the femme fatale—a pernicious threat to men and patriarchal society, arguably another type of exceptional woman—achieved new heights of popularity, primarily in the overtly masculinist and misogynist movement of Symbolist art and literature in Europe at the end of the nineteenth century.[43] Julia Dabbs has also noted that the early-twentieth-century edition of Vasari's *The Lives*, translated by Gaston du Vere between 1912 and 1915, used particularly strong sexist language in the biographies for the women artists, amplifying Vasari's statements through a gendered bias specific to that moment of shifting paradigms.[44] As women began to assert their human rights in Western society, misogynist standard bearers were doubling down in their assessment of women's art historical (un)worthiness.

As part of the seismic shift in the critical landscape of the 1970s and '80s, second-wave feminist philosophies and political movements prompted investigations into the exclusion of early modern women from the art historical canon. From a museological perspective, the 1976 exhibition *Women Artists: 1550–1950*, curated by Ann Sutherland Harris and Linda Nochlin at the Los Angeles County Museum of Art, functioned as a watershed endeavour in bringing together works by women artists practising before the nineteenth century, many of whom were unknown to specialists, much less to most American museum visitors.[45] Although not the first exhibition devoted to women makers of the past, this exhibition, in its parameters and exclusions, established the model for addressing the absence of women artists in a museum setting. In the first sentence of the exhibition's preface, the authors state:

> Our intention … is to make more widely known the achievement of some fine artists whose neglect can in part be attributed to their sex[,] and to learn more about why and how women artists first emerged as rare exceptions in the sixteenth century and gradually became more numerous until they were a largely accepted part of the cultural scene.[46]

The authors' reference to women artists' status of exceptionalism during the Renaissance indicates the pervasiveness of this myth, which, to their credit, Harris undermines by recounting the long history of women's diverse contributions in European art in the lead essay. Significantly, the exhibition's structure did not follow a monographic format, allowing for a more collective consideration of women artists and providing a larger stage on which to highlight recuperated heroines. But the catalogue did rely heavily on the Vasarian tradition of individual biographies of named makers as a means of acquainting the reader with presumably unknown historical figures. Perhaps the most limiting factor was their restriction to paintings, rationalized as a means of maintaining focus and continuity, while revealing a bias against other formats and media and perpetuating painting's historical status as the benchmark of women artists' accomplishment and exceptionality.[47] The enduring strength of Harris and Nochlin's legacy is reflected in formidable efforts over the past four decades to recentre women artists in exhibitions devoted to the pre-modern period within Europe. Some exhibitions have maintained the broader geographical and chronological aspects of the 1976 exhibition, and others have focused on specific regions or time periods, but the monographic exhibition remains the predominant format, celebrating individual genius in the fields of the "major" arts.[48] Even those with a more generalized or inclusive approach still focus overwhelmingly on paintings by women artists, perpetuating the patriarchal standards historically used to regard their works, and with only passing reference to media and formats outside of the "fine" arts. The desire to elevate the lesser-known woman artist to the same heroic, named status as her male counterparts remains the norm.

Materiality Matters

In 1981, Rozsika Parker and Griselda Pollock issued a compelling argument in favour of the unexceptional woman artist in *Old Mistresses: Women, Art and Ideology* that has yet to be widely reflected in museum and exhibition practices in North America and Europe.[49] Rather than augment the patriarchal canon, as Harris and Nochlin had done, Parker and Pollock aimed to subvert it entirely, disrupting the hierarchy of the arts established in the structurally sexist origins of the discipline.[50] While Parker and Pollock did not specifically identify exceptionalism as part of the problem, they do home in on the shifting historical status of craft as an indicator of women artists' critical fortune. By the early Renaissance, needlework and other media associated with women and the domestic arts were demoted in status, while drawing, painting, and sculpture were elevated with a masculine association as the "major" arts. With this downgrading of the "feminine" arts came the associated de-intellectualizing of craft and its assignment to the private, domestic sphere rather than the public, professional realm. According to this rationale, in order for a woman maker to be recognized as an artist, she had to distance herself from craft production and its association with the lower class. This meant she had to make a name for herself according to standards established by male-determined authority, such as those framed by Vasari, and pursue the high-profile arts of painting or sculpture. Norma Broude and Mary Garrard, in their introduction to *Reclaiming Female Agency*, reference the discourse between "high art" and "crafts" central to feminist literature of the 1970s and '80s as a battle already won.[51] Judging from the current landscape of museum galleries and exhibitions, paintings continue to reign.

Taking as a point of departure Parker and Pollock's call for re-interpolating craft and domestic production into the consideration of women artists, this exhibition aims to include a wide variety of women's contributions to art-making. As a result, many of the objects are small,[52] made from ephemeral or fragile materials (watercolour, textile, pastel), and often have no assigned named maker. Encountering such so-called anonymous objects in conjunction with the "familiar" large-scale paintings and sculpture functions against the entrenched myth of exceptionality, purposefully creating a disjuncture of scale and materials that diverges from the current aesthetically driven practices of museum display. Doing so also places works in context with each other in order to provide the visitor with a sense of the diverse nature of display and use practised during the early modern period. At the centre of this exhibition's rationale is a focus on the multivalency of objects and the women who made them. Stepping away from the exceptional genius model allows for interjections from the arena of material culture and opens the door to a consideration of several categories of unexceptional women makers.

Women in convents (cloistered or not) have long been recognized as active creative producers throughout the medieval and early modern periods, both in the domain of religious art and as cultivators of material goods meant to support their community, such as lace production by girl orphans taken in and trained by the priory.[53] Widows also play significant roles in the history of artistic production. Generally excluded from legal claims to a deceased husband's workshop or business, the widow did the work of administratively continuing the manufacture of goods under her spouse's name, thus often being overlooked in historical documentation or referred to merely as the widow of the recognized male artisan. These entrepreneurial widows also shared a class with women who established their renown as business managers alongside their husbands or

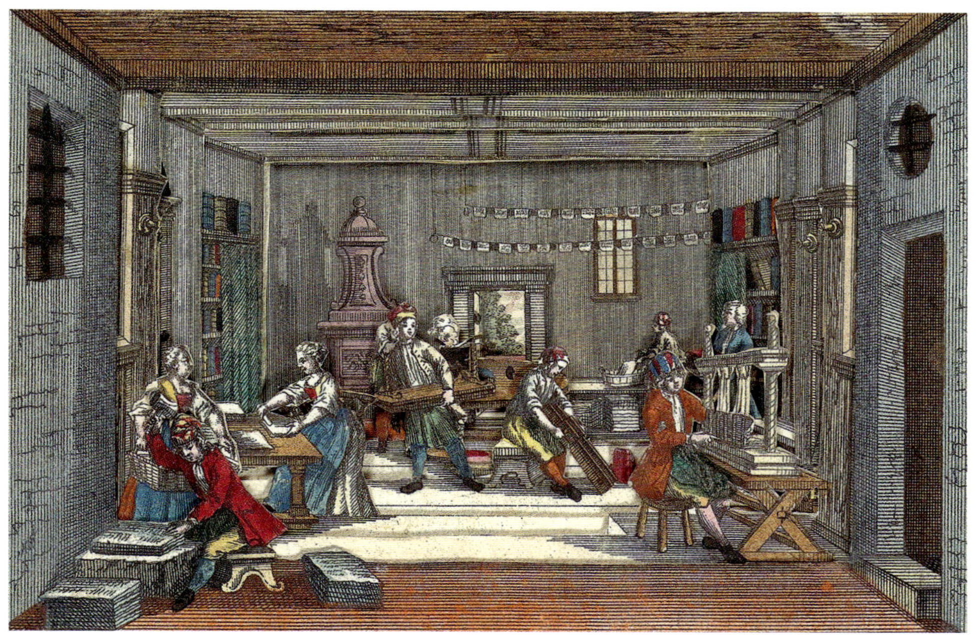

Fig. 6 • Martin Engelbrecht, *Perspective of a bookbindery* [*Perspectivische vorstellung einer buchbinderei*], Augsburg, c. 1750. Hand-coloured engraving, 9.2 × 14.4 cm. Special Collections, The Sheridan Libraries, Johns Hopkins University, inv. no. 9887111. Photo: Digitization Services Unit, Johns Hopkins University.

male children. In some cases, such women became known in their own right as significant forces in their particular area of artistic production. At the other end of the mercantile spectrum is the category of the amateur women makers who produced artistic objects for their own amusement and enjoyment, or for a small group of friends and acquaintances. The decidedly uncommercial nature of their production contributed to their near-complete exclusion from any consideration of their place in art history.[54] Their private engagement with the arts—usually in a self-taught capacity and often labelled as *retardataire* (out of style) or provincial—had nothing to do with Vasarian standards of celebrity, adherence to an approved degree of innovation, or subscription to accepted stylistic developments. In the cases, however, of women amateurs who were educated and of higher classes, they were often keenly aware of the latest developments in arts and culture, and collaborated with leading tastemakers in their creative output.[55] Deeply connected to the prevailing developments in areas beyond the aesthetic are the women who we would today recognize as scientific practitioners. Active in the fields of anatomy, childbirth, and natural sciences such as zoology, entomology, botany, and astronomy, these women often provided visual form to their own discoveries, marking major milestones in the early history of science. They in turn relied frequently on other women to procure the base materials and anecdotal experiences used in their creative work.

Acknowledging the silent labour of these women further raises the question of class and how it intersects with women makers at vastly differing levels of society. Not surprisingly, we have almost no specified documentation for the countless women and girls who were engaged in manual labour in domestic or professional workshop or manufactory settings, making it more difficult to grasp the details of their experience. Much of what is known about women's involvement in craft trades follows the family workshop model, since women largely were excluded from guilds through most of the early modern period.[56] As such, daughters and wives were employed in the family workshop, an entity that blurred commercial and private domestic space. As part of the family labour force, their contributions to craft production would be unpaid and unrecorded, except in the rarest of situations. If they were paid for their work at all—orphans or enslaved labourers certainly were not—workers of lower classes were often engaged in the so-called "terrible trades," menial and physically demanding work that was essential to the production of luxury goods and manufactured production that increasingly occurred outside of the home by the eighteenth century.

Several contemporary illustrations provide confirmation of women's largely unacknowledged roles in the gruelling trades of artistic production, albeit through idealized imagery. Throughout the *Encyclopédie, ou Dictionnaire raisonné des sciences, des arts et des métiers* (figs. 1–4), women are shown working in workshop, manufactory, or commercial shop settings, from textile fabrication (figs. 1 & 2) to furniture production (fig. 3) to printing and publication (figs. 4 & 6).[57] Indeed, if women did not contribute directly to the construction or embellishment of these objects, they often worked in shops as the salesperson or evaluated the quality and worth of proposed wares for trade or resale. Women were also involved in the sourcing of materials: women and girls were tasked with shredding linen and cotton rags to create the fibrous slurry that would be transformed into laid paper used for drawings and in printing presses. Maria Catharina Prestel's print of *A View of the Black-Lead Mine, in Cumberland* (fig. 5) provides visual evidence that women were tasked with the arduous work of mining and hauling graphite, which would have been used for both artistic and industrial lubrication purposes. Whether these women should be classified as artists in the Vasarian sense is debatable, but to exclude them entirely from the story of art and its production only contributes to historical inaccuracy. These women may not fit into the construct of a "creative genius" solely responsible for the heroic moments in the history of art, but their labour directly contributed to the realization of the objects that make up the history of aesthetic accomplishment.

This exhibition attempts to quiet the volume of the hegemonic voice of the male-oriented art world of past and present that demands attention only for the exceptional. In order to give the silent makers and labourers their due, it focuses as much as possible on presenting only women's creations on their own terms. One might point out that this separation is not historically accurate, but to assert that a gathering of women's contributions to early modern European visual culture should reflect the same standards that undergird the patriarchal canon is beside the point. In this collection of evidence highlighting women's involvement in artistic production, we aim to distinguish the material and aesthetic resonance of what they made from the misogynist standards that have dictated what should be considered art. To do so requires a loosening of parameters, a thematic rather than categorical exploration, and the employment of a philosophy of inclusiveness and generosity rather than of stricture and hierarchy. This approach understandably rankles against centuries of tradition that have foregrounded the pursuit of quality as a defining characteristic of art. But to foreground quality at the expense of inclusivity risks perpetuating biases and prejudices—consciously or not—determined by those who had other priorities; namely, to preserve the privileges for a finite group of an elect few, promoting the same chauvinist standards that contributed to the establishment of the notion of quality. This is not a rejection of the concepts of beauty, skill, or accomplishment; rather, we present a range of objects so that they may resonate with audiences through differing modes of emotional, intellectual, spiritual, and aesthetic pleasure. The collective effect—varied in touch, technique, scale, and material—reflects the human spirit on multiple levels, as memorable and affecting art always has. In this case, however, we invite the unexceptional maker to have her say as well.

Notes

1 In Donald Preziosi, ed., *The Art of Art History: A Critical Anthology* (Oxford: Oxford University Press, 1998), 347–48.

2 Mary Garrard, "Review of *The Women Artists of Bologna*," *Woman's Art Journal* 1 (1980–81): 63; Julia K. Dabbs, *Life Stories of Women Artists, 1550–1800: An Anthology* (Farnham, UK: Ashgate, 2009), 17, 47.

3 Carolyn Korsmeyer, *Gender and Aesthetics: An Introduction* (New York: Routledge, 2004), 6. See also Paris A. Spies-Gans, "Why Do We Think There Have Been No Great Women Artists? Revisiting Linda Nochlin and the Archive," *Art Bulletin* 104, no. 4 (2022): 83–86.

4 Feminist art historical literature and its application to the period of interest here is significant in size and scope. Since Linda Nochlin's landmark essay "Why Have There Been No Great Women Artists?" was published in 1971 (*ARTNews* 69, no. 9 [January 1971]: 22–39), feminist art history established its own field of inquiry and ideology, transforming the discipline. For a review of recent research in gender studies, see Jane Couchman, Allyson M. Poska, and Katherine McIver, eds., *The Ashgate Research Companion to Women and Gender in Early Modern Europe*, rev. ed. (New York: Routledge, 2021). Milestone publications in the twenty years following Nochlin's essay include Ann Sutherland Harris and Linda Nochlin, *Women Artists: 1550–1950* (Los Angeles: Los Angeles County Museum of Art, 1976); Germaine Greer, *The Obstacle Race: The Fortunes of Women Painters and Their Work* (New York: Farrar Straus and Giroux, 1979); Rozsika Parker and Griselda Pollock, *Old Mistresses: Women, Art and Ideology*, rev. ed. (1981; London: Bloomsbury, 2021); Norma Broude and Mary D. Garrard, eds., *Feminism and Art History: Questioning the Litany* (New York: Harper and Row, 1982); Wendy Slatkin, *Women Artists in History from Antiquity to the 20th Century*, rev. ed. (Englewood Cliffs, NJ: Prentice Hall, 1990); Whitney Chadwick, *Women, Art, and Society* (New York: Thames and Hudson, 1990); and Mary Garrard and

Norma Broude, eds., *The Expanding Discourse: Feminism and Art History* (New York: HarperCollins, 1992).

5 See Griselda Pollock, *Differencing the Canon: Feminist Desire and the Writing of Art's Histories* (New York: Routledge, 1999); Norma Broude and Mary D. Garrard, eds., *Reclaiming Female Agency: Feminist Art History after Postmodernism* (Berkeley: University of California Press, 2005); Maura Reilly and Linda Nochlin, eds., *Global Feminisms: New Directions in Contemporary Art* (London: Merrell Publishers, 2007); and Jenna Ashton, ed., *Anonymous Was a Woman: A Museums and Feminism Reader* (Edinburgh: MuseumsEtc, 2020).

6 Sara Pennell, "'For a crack or flaw despis'd': Thinking about Ceramic Durability and the 'Everyday' in Late Seventeenth- and Early Eighteenth-Century England," in *Everyday Objects: Medieval and Early Modern Material Culture and Its Meanings*, ed. Tara Hamling and Catherine Richardson (Farnham, UK: Ashgate, 2010), 27–40; Michael Yonan, "Toward a Fusion of Art History and Material Culture Studies," *West 86th: A Journal of Decorative Arts, Design History, and Material Culture* 18, no. 2 (Fall–Winter 2011): 232–48; and Ann-Sophie Lehmann, "The Matter of the Medium: Some Tools for an Art Theoretical Interpretation of Materials," in *The Matter of Art: Materials, Technologies, Meanings, 1200–1700*, ed. C. Anderson, A. Dunlop, and P.H. Smith (Manchester: Manchester University Press, 2015), 21–41.

7 Sheila ffolliott, "'Più che famose': Some Thoughts on Women Artists in Early Modern Europe," in *Women Artists in Early Modern Italy: Careers, Fame, and Collectors*, ed. Sheila Barker (London: Harvey Miller, 2016), 20.

8 In the study of art of the Middle Ages, there is less hesitancy to assign such media to the realm of "great art" even when individual names cannot be linked to them. This does not preclude the field of medieval art from its own oversight in assuming that most artists were men and that women were the exception to the rule. See Therese Martin, "Exceptions and Assumptions: Women in Medieval Art History," in *Reassessing the Roles of Women as "Makers" of Medieval Art and Architecture*, vol. 7 of *Visualising the Middle Ages*, ed. Therese Martin (Leiden: Brill, 2012), 1–33, and Leslie Ross, *Artists of the Middle Ages* (Westport, CT: Greenwood Press, 2003), 3–10.

9 Studies conducted at the Metropolitan Museum of Art and the Art Institute of Chicago determined that visitors spent an average of twenty-seven to twenty-eight seconds looking at individual works of art. See Lisa F. Smith, Jeffrey K. Smith, and Pablo P.L. Tinio, "Time Spent Viewing Art and Reading Labels," *Psychology of Aesthetics, Creativity and the Arts* 11, no. 1 (2017): 77–85.

10 For various interpretations of Vasari and his text, see Anne B. Barriault, Andrew T. Ladis, Norman E. Land, and Jeryldene M. Woods, eds., *Reading Vasari* (Athens, GA: Philip Wilson and Georgia Museum of Art, 2005), and Patricia Lee Rubin, *Giorgio Vasari: Art and History* (New Haven, CT: Yale University Press, 1995).

11 Significant research and analysis have been invested in feminist readings of Vasari's *Lives of the Artists*; see especially Fredrika H. Jacobs, *Defining the Renaissance "Virtuosa": Women Artists and the Language of Art History and Criticism* (Cambridge: Cambridge University Press, 1997); Nanette Salomon, "The Art Historical Canon," in Preziosi, *The Art of Art History*; Katherine McIver, "Vasari's Women," in Barriault et al., *Reading Vasari*, 179–88; and Dabbs, *Life Stories*, 45–49.

12 Paul Barolsky, "Fear of Fiction: The Fun of Reading Vasari," in Barriault et al., *Reading Vasari*, 31–37.

13 Frederika Jacobs, "The Construction of a Life: Madonna Properzia De' Rossi *"Scultrice* Bolognese," *Word and Image* 9 (April–June 1993): 122–32.

14 Jonathan Nelson, ed., *Plautilla Nelli (1523–1588): The Painter-Prioress of Renaissance Florence* (Florence: Syracuse University in Florence, 2008); Jonathan K. Nelson, ed., *Suor Plautilla Nelli (1523–1588): The First Woman Painter of Florence* (Fiesole, Italy: Cadmo, 2000).

15 Sheila Barker, "Lucrezia Quistelli (1541–94): A Woman Artist in Vasari's Florence," in Barker, *Women Artists*, 47–80.

16 Michael W. Cole, *Sofonisba's Lesson: A Renaissance Artist and Her Work* (Princeton, NJ: Princeton University Press, 2019); Leticia Ruiz Gómez, ed., A *Tale of Two Women Painters: Sofonisba Anguissola and Lavinia Fontana* (Madrid: Museo Nacional del Prado: 2019).

17 Dabbs, *Life Stories*, 46. Other Italian women artists appearing in male artists' entries are the Anguissola sisters (Minerva, Lucia, Europa, and Anna), Irene di Spilembergo, Barbara Longhi, and Diana Mantuana. Flemish miniaturists include Susanna Horenbout, Clara Keysere, Anna Segher, Levina Teerlinc, and Catherina van Hemessen.

18 Viewing each of these women as a typology in the same way that many of the male protagonists in *The Lives* have been interpreted, their biographical details may have been meant to be understood as instructional examples of the different ways in which women managed to pursue professional status during the Renaissance. See McIver, "Vasari's Women," 179–88.

19 Babette Bohn, *Women Artists, Their Patrons, and Their Publics in Early Modern Bologna* (University Park, PA: Penn State University Press, 2021), chap. 1.

20 Hendrik J. Horn, *The Golden Age Revisited: Arnold Houbraken's Great Theatre of Netherlandish Painters and Paintresses* (Doornspijk, Netherlands: Davaco, 2000).

21 See Patricia Rubin, "What Men Saw: Vasari's Life of Leonardo da Vinci and the Image of the Renaissance Artist," *Art History* 13, no. 1 (March 1990): 34–46.

22 Dabbs, *Life Stories*, 18.

23 Jacobs, *Defining the Renaissance "Virtuosa,"* 4.

24 A larger list of gender-associated dialectic terminology and their antique origins can be found in Jacobs, *Defining the Renaissance "Virtuosa,"* 12–13.

25 Salomon, "The Art Historical Canon," 351. Significantly, none of the four women Vasari treated with individual biographies were trained by their artist fathers or brothers, a typical educational route for women artists of this time. This detail may have contributed to their exceptional stature, but it also could have been an indicator of Vasari's desire to maintain the separation of the fine arts from that of craft or commercialism.

26 Garrard, "Review of *The Women Artists of Bologna*," 63; Jacobs, *Defining the Renaissance "Virtuosa,"* 15; Dabbs, *Life Stories*, 47. For more on the concept of the marvel, see Joy Kenseth, ed., *Age of the Marvelous* (Dartmouth, NH: Hood Museum of Art, 1991).

27 Part of this omission was also because *The Lives* was intended to serve as a historical source as much as it was to be received as literature. To depart from the individualized format would have deprived it of its intrigue and narrative appeal. See Andrew Ladis, *Victims and Villains in Vasari's Lives* (Chapel Hill: University of North Carolina Press, 2008).

28 An exception was Plautilla Nelli, who was a member and later prioress of the Dominican convent at Santa Caterina da Siena at Piazza San Marco in Florence. But Vasari makes no mention of other women artists working in that same convent, or that Nelli had any engagement with them, as a teacher or otherwise. See Catherine Turrill, "Compagnie and Discepole: The Presence of Other Women Artists at Santa Caterina da Siena," in Nelson, *Suor Plautilla Nelli*, 90–97.

29 Academies and other mechanisms for artistic learning were in development during the sixteenth and seventeenth centuries; their characteristics did not become uniform or standardized until the subsequent century. For more on the evolution of early art academies, see Anton W.A. Boschloo, Elwin J. Hendrikse, Gert Jan van der Sman, and Laetitia C. Smit, eds., *Academies of Art: Between Renaissance and Romanticism, Leids Kunsthistorisch Jaarboek* 5/6 (The Hague: SDU Uitgeverij, 1989); Carl Goldstein, *Teaching Art: Academies and Schools from Vasari to Albers* (Cambridge: Cambridge University Press, 1988); and Thomas E. Crow, *Painters and Public Life in Eighteenth Century Paris* (New Haven, CT: Yale University Press, 1985).

30 Harris, "Introduction," *Women Artists*, 40–44. By the eighteenth century, increased access by women painters active in London and Paris to more formalized training through private or academy resources—and eventually being allowed to show in the official Salon—contributed to a broader acceptance of women pursuing professional artistic status. See Paris A. Spies-Gans, *A Revolution on Canvas: The Rise of Women Artists in London and Paris, 1760–1830* (London: Paul Mellon Centre for Studies in British Art in association with Yale University Press, 2022), chap. 2.

31 Further, direct sources stated or written by women artists of the early modern period about the nature of their profession are scant. Wendy Slatkin, *The Voices of Women Artists* (Englewood Cliffs, NJ: Prentice Hall, 1993), brings together a selection of autobiographical texts (letters, journals, memoirs) by professional women artists. For the period before 1800, only three artists are included: Artemisia Gentileschi, Rosalba Carriera, and Elisabeth Louise Vigée-LeBrun. This paucity may be because of many intervening centuries and the vicissitudes of archival survival that have silenced countless voices of the past, male and female alike. But this does not account for the relative void of sources from women artists compared with the plethora of letters, journals, treatises, polemics, anecdotes, biographies, and so on, penned by men—many of whom were artists—that have contributed to the establishment and development of the critical art historical canon.

32 G. Guercio, *Art as Existence: The Artist's Monograph and Its Project* (Cambridge: Cambridge University Press, 2004), 34–46.

33 Even when there is biographic documentation of a woman's artistic career, as in the case of Irene di Spilimbergo or Marietta Tintoretto, the absence of securely attributed works stalls attempts to learn more about their creative production. See Jacobs, *Defining the Renaissance "Virtuosa,"* 1–2.

34 By contrast, see Guercio, *Art as Existence*, 263–65, for a discussion of the relationship between the shared aims of the monograph and feminism to "capture identities in the making." See also Ross, *Artists of the Middle Ages*, 3–10.

35 In Heinrich Wöfflin's first edition of *Principles of Art History* (1915), his quest for identifying universal formal and stylistic qualities in art led him to call for an "art history without names," but the negative critical response caused him to dispense with the phrase in subsequent editions. See Arnold Hauser, *The Philosophy of Art History*, rev. ed. (1958; repr., Evanston, IL: Northwestern University Press, 1985;), 120–25.

36 Current reconsideration of how to refer to works that have no named maker associated with them lately has been a topic of urgency in museum circles. Phrases such as "name once known" are beginning to appear on museum labels but, disturbingly, are still relegated primarily to the display of works from non-Eurocentric traditions.

37 Alison Wright, "Life in the 'Anonymous' Box," in *Nameless: Anonymous Drawings of 15th & 16th Century Italy from the British Museum, The Courtauld Gallery and National Galleries of Scotland*, ed. Alison Wright (Findhorn, Scotland: Moray Art Centre, 2010), 4–5: "Dismissal of the nameless effectively denies works without attribution a place both in scholarship and in public view ... nameless is not only assumed unworthy of exhibition but prejudged to be unpopular."

38 Antoinette Friedenthal, "Defining the Oeuvre: Shaping the Catalogue Raisonné," in *The Challenge of the Object: 33rd Congress of the International Committee of the History of Art*, ed. G. Ulrich Grossmann and Petra Krutisch (Nuremberg: Verlag des Germanischen Nationalmuseums, 2013), 723–27. Significantly, the earliest catalogues raisonnés treated prints, rather than paintings, as they were more readily available to be consulted and acquired.

39 In her assessment of the 2001–2002 exhibition "Orazio and Artemisia Gentileschi: Father and Daughter Painters in Baroque Italy," held at the Metropolitan Museum of Art and the Saint Louis Art Museum, Nanette Salomon outlines the detrimental effect of establishing a comparative model when considering women artists in relation to the male counterparts in their lives. See N. Salomon, "Judging Artemisia: A Baroque Woman in Modern Art History," in *The Artemisia Files: Artemisia Gentileschi for Feminists and Other Thinking People*, ed. Mieke Bal (Chicago: University of Chicago Press, 2005): 33–61.

40 See Mary Sherriff, "Pour l'histoire des femmes artistes: Historiographie, politique, et théorie," *Perspective* 1 (2017): 91–112.

41 The legacy of this unquestioned exclusion of women artists–addressed critically by Linda Nochlin in her 1971 essay "Why Have There Been No Great Women Artists?"—continued unabated well into the late twentieth century. In a 1978 interview with H.W. Janson, the architect of the foundational and widely distributed textbook *History of Art*, the author stated that the primary criterion of an artist's "importance" was justification to not include any woman maker among the over three thousand objects represented. See Eleanor Dickinson, "Sexist Texts Boycotted," *Women Artists News* 5, no. 4 (September–October 1979): 12.

42 This context is further explored in Eve Straussman-Pflanzer, "Why Have There Been No Exhibitions of Early Italian Women Artists in Hartford or Detroit?" in *By Her Hand: Artemisia Gentileschi and Women Artists in Italy, 1500–1800*, ed. Eve Straussman-Pflanzer and Oliver Tostmann (New Haven, CT: Yale University Press in association with Detroit Institute of Arts, 2021), 17–30.

43 For the decisively male gendering of Symbolist art, see Norma Broude, "The Gendering of Impressionism," in Broude and Garrard, *Reclaiming Female Agency*, 221–24.

44 Dabbs, *Life Stories*, 48–49.

45 An exhibition at the Walters Art Gallery (as it was then known) in Baltimore titled "Old Mistresses: Women Artists of the Past" was held in 1972, but the absence of a substantial accompanying publication meant that the Los Angeles County Museum of Art exhibition would become the more prominent historiographic point of reference. See Straussman-Pflanzer, "Why Have There Been No Exhibitions?," 23.

46 Harris, "Introduction," *Women Artists*, 11.

47 Harris, "Introduction," *Women Artists*, 17: "The history of women as embroiderers, however significant in its own right, is only relevant as background to the later emergence of women as painters."

48 For example, see the appendix of Italian women artists' exhibition history since 1972 included in Straussman-Pflanzer, "Why Have There Been No Exhibitions?" 27.

49 Parker and Pollock, *Old Mistresses*.

50 Lawrence Alloway, in his review of "Old Mistresses: Women, Art and Ideology," *Woman's Art Journal* 3 (Fall 1982/Winter 1983): 60, claims: "Parker and Pollock require a total dismantling of art history." Griselda Pollock states in the preface to the 2013 reissued edition of *Old Mistresses*, "We need to challenge the entire apparatus and its underlying ideological function that distorts all of our understandings of who we are and who we can be" (p. xxxviii).

51 Broude and Garrard, *Reclaiming Female Agency*, 3.

52 The issue of size and scale of objects women made is explored further in Oliver Tostmann, "The Advantages of Painting Small: Italian Women and the Matter of Scale," in Straussman-Pflanzer and Tostmann, *By Her Hand*, 31–41.

53 See Sheila Barker, ed., "Artiste nel chiostro: produzione artistica nei monasteri femminili in età moderna," *Memorie Domenicane* 46.

54 Noël Riley, *The Accomplished Lady: A History of Genteel Pursuits, c. 1660–1860* (Wetherby, UK: Oblong Creative, 2017).

55 For further discussion of "amateur" as a category, see Kim Sloan, *A Noble Art: Amateur Artists and Drawings Masters, ca. 1600–1800* (London: British Museum Press, 2000), and Spies-Gans, "Why Do We Think There Have Been No Great Women Artists?," 82–83.

56 Clare Crowston, "Women, Gender, and Guilds in Early Modern Europe: An Overview of Recent Research," *International Review of Social History* 53, supplement 16: *The Return of the Guilds* (2008): 19–44.

57 Denis Diderot, "Encyclopedia," The Encyclopedia of Diderot & d'Alembert Collaborative Translation Project, trans. Philip Stewart (Ann Arbor: Michigan Publishing, University of Michigan Library, 2002), hdl.handle.net/2027/spo.did2222.0000.004 (accessed October 4, 2022), originally published as "Encyclopédie," *Encyclopédie, ou Dictionnaire raisonné des sciences, des arts et des métiers*, 5:635–648A (Paris, 1755). Illustrations from the *Encyclopédie* organized by object and trade can be found in a helpful interactive resource provided by the Victoria and Albert Museum in London: vam.ac.uk/europetrades/#/.

Detail (fig.6, opposite) • Martin Engelbrecht, *Perspective of a bookbindery* [*Perspectivische vorstellung einer buchbinderei*], Augsburg, c. 1750. Hand-coloured engraving, 9.2 × 14.4 cm. Special Collections, The Sheridan Libraries, Johns Hopkins University, inv. no. 9887111. Photo: Digitization Services Unit, Johns Hopkins University.

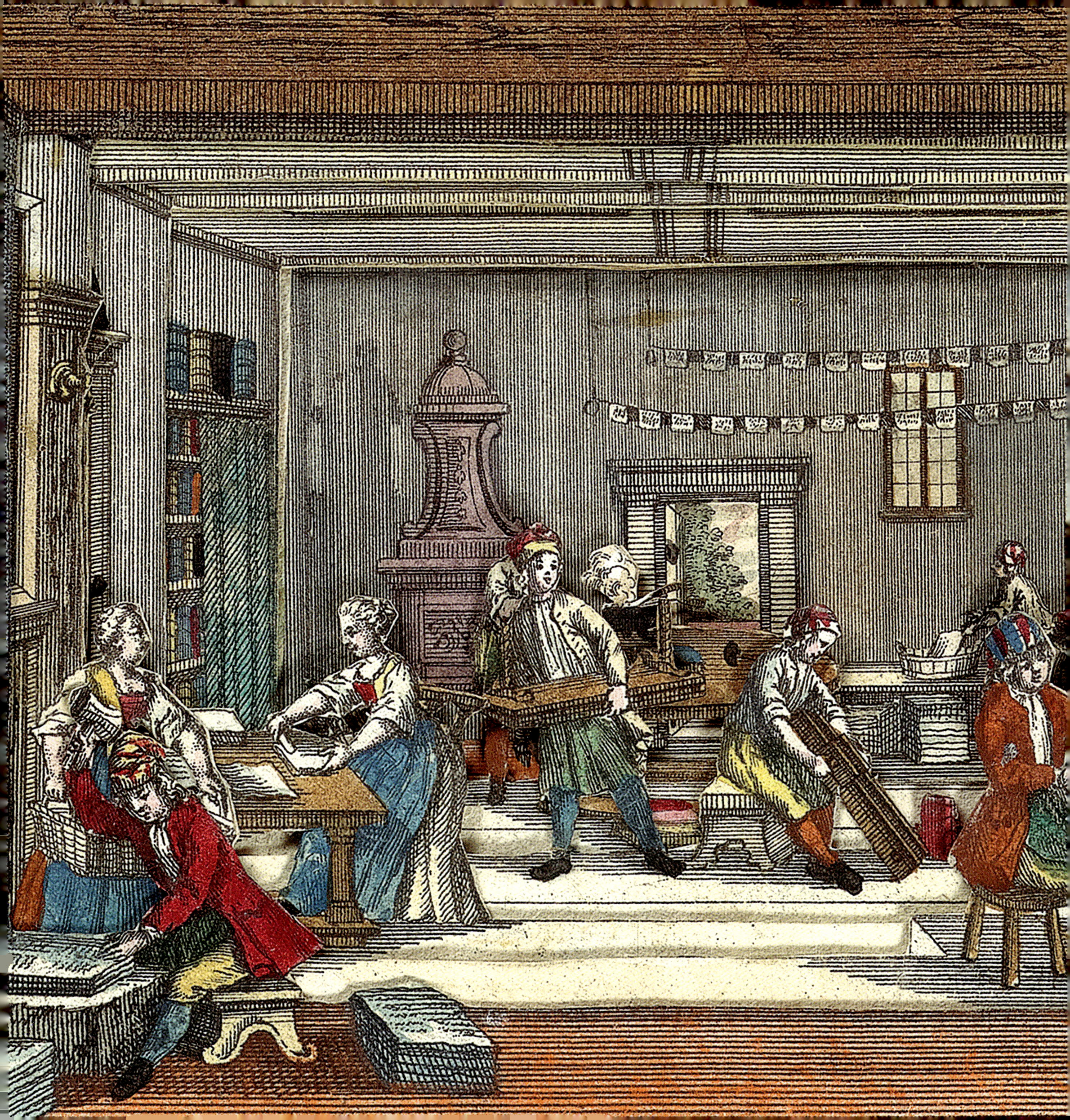

PRINTS AND NEEDLES

Women Makers and European Textile Pattern Books, 1500–1800

Alexa Greist

The sixteenth century saw the creation of many genres of printed books in Europe. Among these novel texts were instructional manuals intended to educate the user in basic skills such as writing, reading, and arithmetic, as well as more specialized texts such as those on drawing, fencing, embroidery, and lacemaking. The latter two categories of books were most often intended for use by women but not for beginners who had never picked up a needle. Rather, they existed for those with advanced skills who needed patterns to create numerous embellished textiles their family would use, or who sought income through the sale of such textiles. Beginning in the sixteenth century north of the Alps, genres of instructional books with images and occasional text evolved from earlier pattern prints that circulated throughout Europe as individual sheets. This essay explores the prevalence of printed instructional or pattern books—primarily lacemaking and embroidery patterns—frequently used by women, with a focus on the surviving pattern books designed by women.[1]

Although lace in Europe was made almost exclusively by women, embroidery has a bifurcated history. Historically, early modern embroidery has been divided between professional work (by men) and amateur work (by women), but what did it mean to be an amateur in the sixteenth and seventeenth centuries? Until the late seventeenth century, the word "amateur" signified someone who loved the arts and practised them for pleasure rather than profit. "Amateur" did not refer to a distinction between professional and nonprofessional status or mean that the work created was of a lesser quality, rendering it unprofessional.[2] Without access to training within guilds and workshops, women could not gain professional status; even if they were born into families where they were taught to participate in the activities of a workshop, their work was often uncredited, and any status they received was by virtue of a male relative's membership. Much as women working in embroidery were considered amateur by later scholars, pattern prints for textiles were likewise dismissed as amateur and less worthy of study than those for metalwork or sculpture.[3] Women's use of patterns, either as named or anonymous makers (in the case of lace), was seen as copying by amateurs rather than as highly skilled interpretations made by professionals. As this exhibition aims to make clear, these definitions are not useful for defining what is worthy of study, display in a museum, or consideration in the history of art.

Important societal shifts in Italy in the fifteenth and sixteenth centuries led to changes in the role of women in society, with women increasingly excluded from professional activities outside of the domestic space. Artisan guilds, which were controlled by men, followed suit and prevented women from attaining leadership roles or equal membership.[4] Fourteenth-century tax rolls show women in guilds, but by the next century, women's membership in these organizations all but disappeared.[5] Women in the lowest social positions would have felt these changes more acutely than those in the upper and middle classes, who were more often able to limit their work to the home.[6] As discourses on sexual difference gained prominence among European theologians, doctors, and writers, women were further restricted to only a few specific roles and activities within the home. While this societal shift limited women's access to professional artisan craft industries, it also required them to have more specialist knowledge within the home, including how to use plants to treat ailments. In order to access the relevant knowledge in herbals, women required basic literacy and numeracy skills, which could be learned by studying printed manuals.[7]

With women largely excluded from professional training and production, pattern books and other sources for inspiration in design took on a great importance in their creative lives. Women used pattern books to make embroidery and lace, as well as to create calligraphy and to decorate objects throughout the home and as gifts for friends. A brief overview of how women across social classes gained these necessary skills in reading, writing, and arithmetic will inform the discussion of the format and use of textile pattern books that follows.

Basic Skills and Printed Books

Most children were taught in the household, often by their mother, until the age when boys were sent to grammar school (girls remained at home). Children learned many basic skills much as they do today—through imitation and play, and by watching adults around them complete tasks. For young women, these models would have been their mothers, nurses, or other older women living in the household who had a supervisory role. The most critical responsibility for adult women would have been the spiritual education of their charges and preparing young women for running a household. Girls were often encouraged to pursue domestic tasks in order to remain productively occupied and out of trouble.[8] Women's education was elevated by expanding definitions of what household management entailed. Middle- and upper-class women were increasingly expected to gain fluency in topics such as the previously mentioned plant cultivation and the use, basic accounting, production, and embellishment of domestic furnishings that included textiles. Upper-class families were not the only members of society who made it a priority for their daughters to possess skills in needlework, a status that denoted their worthiness as a lady of the house. According to surviving dowry records, women marrying into the craftsman classes brought objects that denoted the skills they brought to the union, including needle holders, pin cushions, and looms.[9] Unlike their upper-class counterparts, whose attention was focused on embellishments such as monogramming clothing or decorating table linens, these women contributed to the household in a more practical manner. They made and mended garments and textiles, and in some cases sold their work to supplement their husband's income. Regardless of class, the tools of embroidery and weaving—and any pattern or instructional books—possessed by a woman were symbols of her virtue, reflecting activities that were appropriate for her gender at the time while also allowing for a display of skill.[10]

Most women's basic education was limited to the home in the early modern era, as was their artistic training, if they received any. Most women did not learn to draw as male artists did, in a workshop, as an apprentice in a guild, or later in an academy; the majority were also only permitted to copy two-dimensional works, including prints displaying patterns for other art forms. These patterns were shared and passed down between makers in workshops or in family circles well before printers created compendia of examples. Johann Andreas Graff's drawing of his and Maria Sibylla Merian's older stepsister, Sara Marrel, embroidering in a workshop space (an easel leans on a wall behind her) affirms the presence of women creators in a space often considered male (fig. 1). The repeated reuse of designs was not seen as limiting creativity but rather as a continuation of timeless traditions of decoration,[11] as printed patterns were used by goldsmiths, armourers, and leatherworkers for centuries. Painters used prints as models for educating draughtsmen, and as sources for new work, borrowing compositions or figures for paintings, ceramics, and other prints. The audience for printed patterns would also have included print collectors; therefore, there was a large market ready to support new printed books of patterns.[12] The first textile pattern books were utilized by both men and women, without a specific audience courted in the title or introduction. This is unsurprising, as all manner of patterns had been used by both genders and redrawn from other media—including goldsmith patterns to be adapted into embroidery—long before media-specific pattern books came to market.

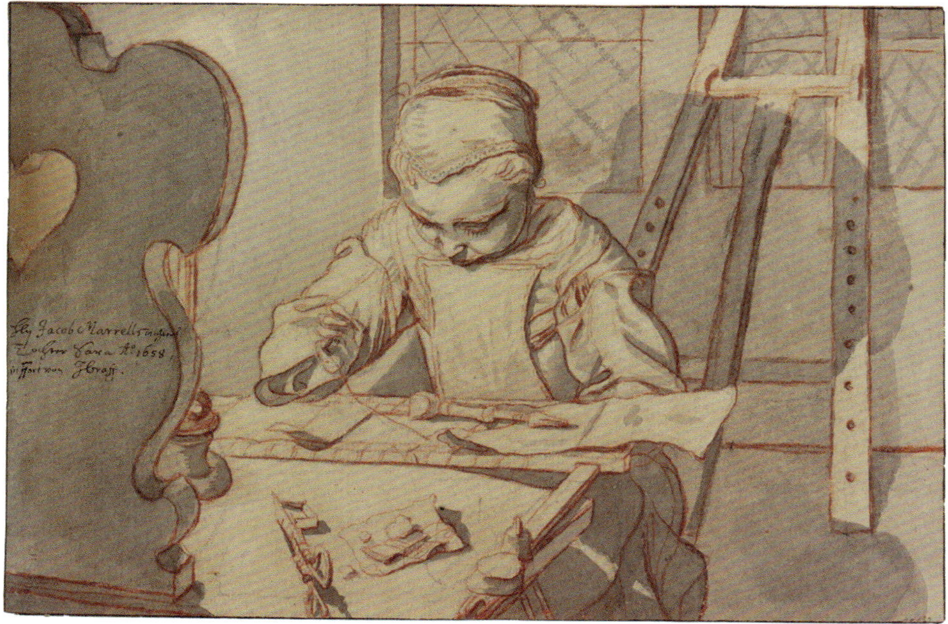

Fig. 1 (above) • Johann Andreas Graff, *Sara Marrel, seated at a table and engaged in embroidery*, 1658. Red chalk, wash, pencil, and charcoal on paper, 18.7 × 29 cm. Städel Museum, Frankfurt am Main, Acquired in 1867, inv. no. 5744.

Printed Patterns for Textiles

The rise of the printed textile pattern book came at a moment in Europe when women's roles in society were changing, and middle- to upper-class women were increasingly excluded from activities outside the domestic sphere.[13] Embroidery came to be seen as the proper hands-on task for women, in addition to their managing the household linen and other textiles; keeping them in presentable shape was a key duty of the *donna di casa*.[14] From making their own embroidered textiles to overseeing the everyday sewing and weaving in their households, women were involved at every level of maintaining fabric. By the fifteenth century, the idea that spinning and weaving was suited only to women of lower classes was common throughout Italy. Although this division was not absolute, most upper-class women did not partake in weaving aside from supervising servants' activities within the home.[15] As upper-class women were also experiencing an increase in basic literacy, they were the ideal audience for the nascent genre of printed textile pattern books.[16] For middle- and upper-class women, these skills were practised within the home either as a leisure activity to increase its decoration or as a means of supplementing income, but only through indirect sale using an agent.[17]

Just as women educated the girls in their care in elementary math and reading, they shared their knowledge of sewing, embroidery, and lacemaking with their charges. Images often show girls of various ages at work on textiles side by side, giving visual form to the reality of women passing knowledge down through the generations. Not only did pattern books provide examples for artistic production, but many examples include prints that suggest the settings in which women created embroidery or lace. One example is found in the frontispiece to Nicolò Zoppino's book of embroidery patterns titled *Convivio delle Belle Donne* [*Banquet of Goodly Women*] (fig. 2).[18] Here, four seated women are embroidering, and at the right, a younger woman looks at the work held by a more senior figure. One of the women even holds an infant in her arms, a reminder of the reality of constant interruptions faced by working women in a domestic

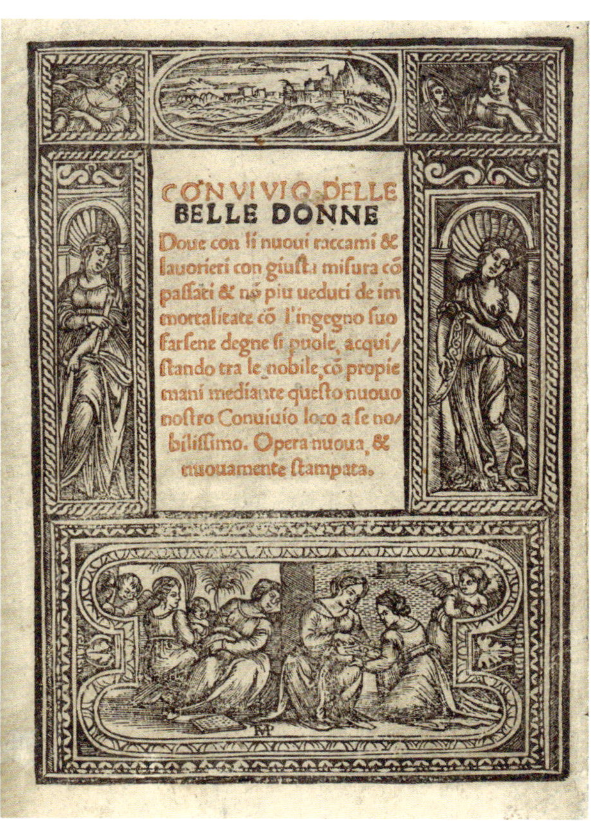

CONVIVIO DELLE
BELLE DONNE
Doue con li nuoui raccami &
lauorieri con giuſti miſura cõ
paſſati & nõ piu ueduti de im
mortalitate cõ l'ingegno ſuo
farſene degne ſi puole, acqui/
ſtando tra le nobile cõ propie
mani mediante queſto nuouo
noſtro Conuiuio loco a ſe no/
biliſſimo. Opera nuoua, &
nuouamente ſtampata.

Fig. 2 (right) • Matteo da Treviso, title page from *Convivio delle Belle Donne* [*Banquet of Goodly Women*], Venice, 1532. Woodcut, 20 × 14 cm. The Metropolitan Museum of Art, New York, Rogers Fund, 1922, inv. no. 22.66.6(1-43).

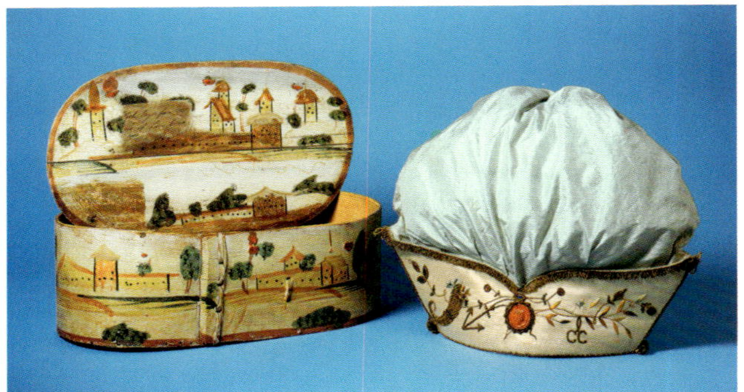

Fig. 3 • Bridgettine nuns of Syon House, Lisbon, Portugal, *Work bag and box*, c. 1787. Silk and gold embroidery, sequins, paste stones, wax seals, and painted wood; bag: 40.6 × 39.4 × 12.1 cm; box and lid: 13.3 × 39.7 × 21.9 cm. Los Angeles County Museum of Art, Gift of Mr. and Mrs. Michael Laykin, inv. no. M.81.94a-c.

setting. The younger woman may be showing her work for criticism or advice from the more experienced women.

Such an image, although idealized, reflects the way that women transferred knowledge about activities in the home. Instruction in the most basic skills of sewing and embroidery stitches would come first, but the use and sharing of patterns likely followed soon after, as evidenced by the prevalence of girls as young as nine who embroidered their names and ages onto their embroidered samplers. The ubiquitous need to have basic proficiency in sewing and needlework is supported by surviving Bolognese inventories of women's *trousseaux* (personal belongings a woman brought into her new household upon marriage), in both the lower and upper classes, which—in addition to embroidered textiles either purchased or made themselves—include materials such as sewing baskets, threads, thimbles, and sewing cushions (fig. 3; cat. no. 26).[19] Women could take part in glorifying the family name both by keeping heirloom textiles in peak condition and through the decoration and personalization of all manner of fabric. Textiles were visible throughout the home: tapestry, embroidered fabrics used as seat cushions (fig. 4; cat. no. 246), bed curtains (fig. 5; cat. no. 245), or as part of clothing. For example, the embroidered designs by an anonymous maker, likely a woman, on an English man's nightcap (fig. 6; cat. no. 229) are similar to florals found in pattern books from the Continent. Because patterns were copied in varying degrees by the compilers of pattern books, it can be difficult to identify exactly which book might be connected to a surviving embroidered textile. In addition, women had agency to adapt patterns,

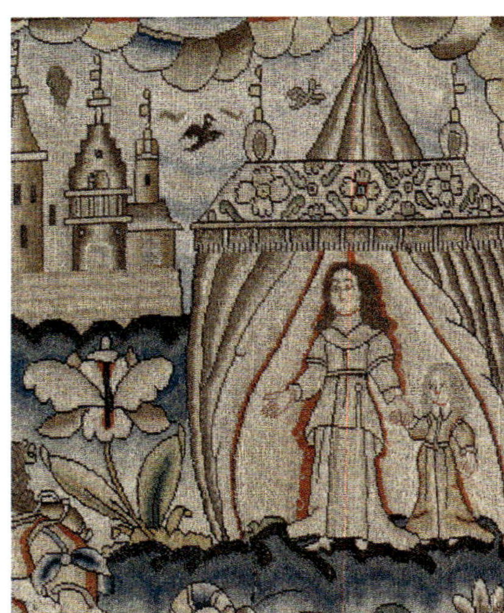

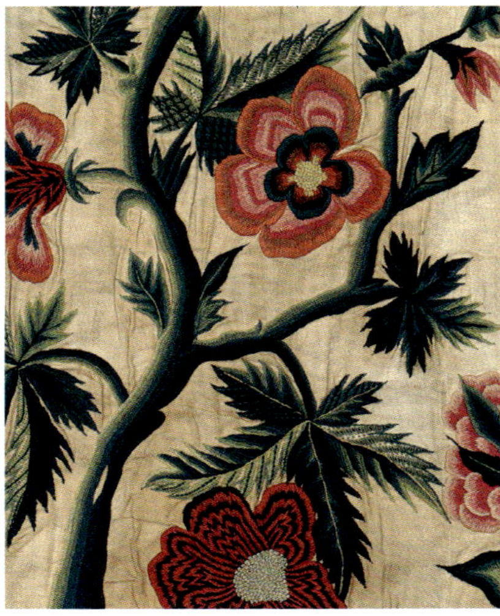

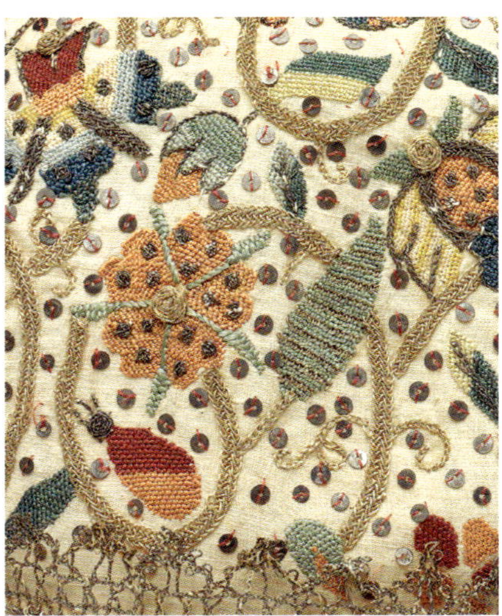

Fig. 4 (below, left) • *Detail:* Unknown British embroiderer, *Abraham Banishing Hagar and Ishmael*, c. 1650. Linen canvas ground, silk embroidery threads, silk backing, and metallic bobbin lace, 43.8 × 51.4 cm. Baltimore Museum of Art: Purchase with exchange funds from Gift of Mrs. A. Taylor Bragonier; Gift of Mrs. H.P. Bray; Gift of Mrs. Charles Collier; Gift of Mrs. Symington Dorsey; Gift of Mrs. J. Edward Duker; Gift of Maria Lovell Eaton and Mrs. Charles R. Weld, from the Estate of Mary M. Eaton; Gift of Mr. and Mrs. Manuel L. Hendler; Gift of Mrs. Gerald W. Johnson; Gift of Mrs. F.A. Korff; Gift of Ruth Young Lachman; Gift of Eleanor B. Leitch; Gift of Sara B. Lipscomb; Gift of Cornelius Ruxton Love, Jr.; Gift of Henry A. Ludwig; Gift of Fanny Lyon; Gift of Mrs. Florence Milliken; Gift of Mrs. Frank Primrose; Gift of Mrs. Jesse Rider; Gift of Mrs. Ralph K. Robertson; Gift of Mrs. C. Rogulih; Gift of Mrs. Dudley Shoemaker; and Gift of Louisa Gilmore Riach Wade, 1998.528. Photo: Mitro Hood.

Fig. 5 (below, middle) • *Detail:* M.K. Herbert, *Crewelwork bed curtain*, 1692. Linen (warp) and cotton (weft) ground; wool, silk, and cotton embroidery threads, 246.4 × 111.8 cm. Baltimore Museum of Art: Gift of Judge Irwin Untermyer, New York, 1956.151a. Photo: Mitro Hood.

Fig. 6 (below, right) • *Detail:* Unknown British embroiderer, *Man's nightcap*, c. 1580. Linen plain weave embroidered with silk, metallic thread, and metal sequins, and trimmed with metallic-thread lace, height: 25.4 cm. Lent by Museum of Art, Rhode Island School of Design, Providence, Helen M. Danforth Acquisition Fund, inv. no. 1987.042. Image courtesy of the RISD Museum, Providence, RI.

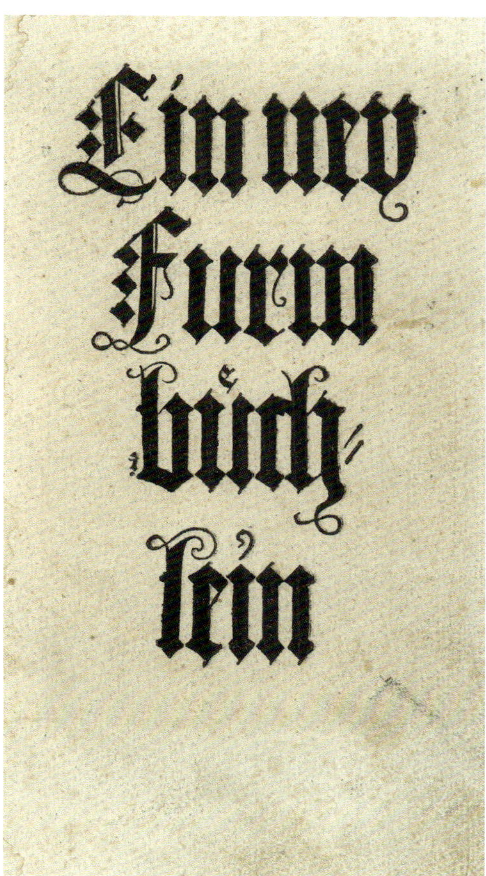

Fig. 7 • *Ein ney Furmbüchlein* [*A New Booklet of Forms*], Augsburg, c. 1525–1529. Woodcut, 20 × 15.5 cm. The Metropolitan Museum of Art, New York, Rogers Fund, 1918, inv. no. 18.66.1(1-33).

Openings illustrated (left to right):

Fig. 7a • title page

Fig. 7b • example of an interior woodcut image

whether through resizing (using a grid), combining patterns, or choosing specific imagery to hold hidden messages, such as symbols of love or loyalty.[20]

Surviving textile pattern books produced in Europe are extremely rare, considering the number of titles recorded.[21] Most of the pattern books that were printed were quite literally used up, and extant examples often have pages missing. Patterns could be transferred through various means, including tracing, but the cutting-out of entire patterns was a common practice. Another method of transfer was pouncing, where the design is pricked with a needle, outlining the form to be copied, and the design is repeatedly patted with a soot-filled container, leaving dots on the fabric where the pin holes are located. The earliest printed pattern books for textiles were produced in northern Europe, appearing in 1523 in Augsburg. One such publication by Johann Schönsperger the Younger (fig. 7) featured patterns to be used in embroidery and needlework lace (as opposed to bobbin or pillow lace).[22] This book, illustrated with woodcuts, included decorative friezes and pages of grids likely intended for the user to create their own designs next to printed ones.[23] Although this feature would seem useful, it was rarely repeated in future examples. As was often the case with the earliest examples of a genre of printed books, characteristics of the first titles did not necessarily determine the standard form that the genre would take.[24] The types of patterns reflected the uses to which they would be put: rectangular areas of repeating forms for embroidered borders, all-over patterns that could be repeated to fill a larger area, alphabets for names or inscriptions, or even narrative scenes of either lace (figs. 8a & 8c) or embroidery (figs. 8b & 8d).

Patterns could be shown in two manners: either a white design on black or a black design on white,

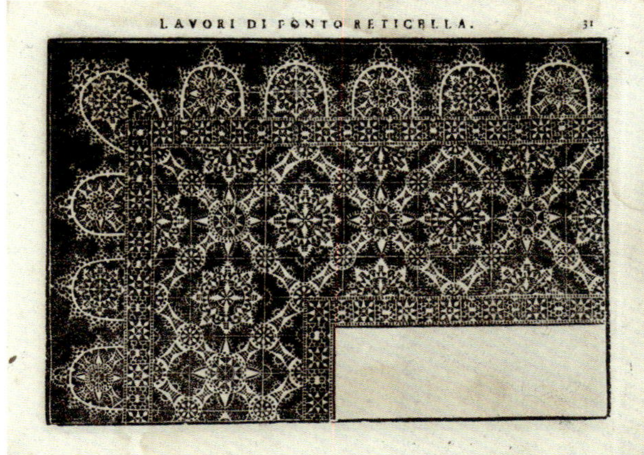

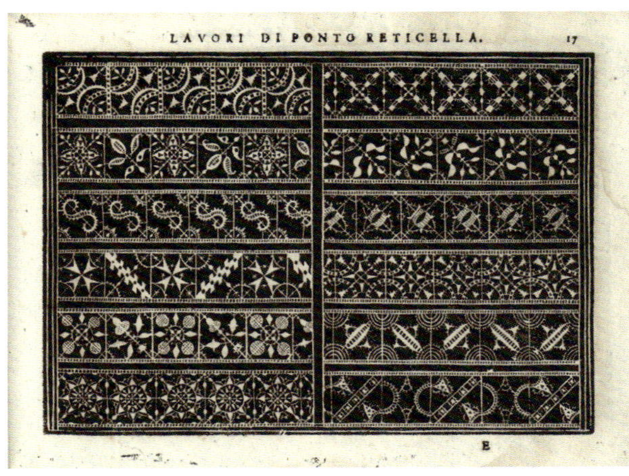

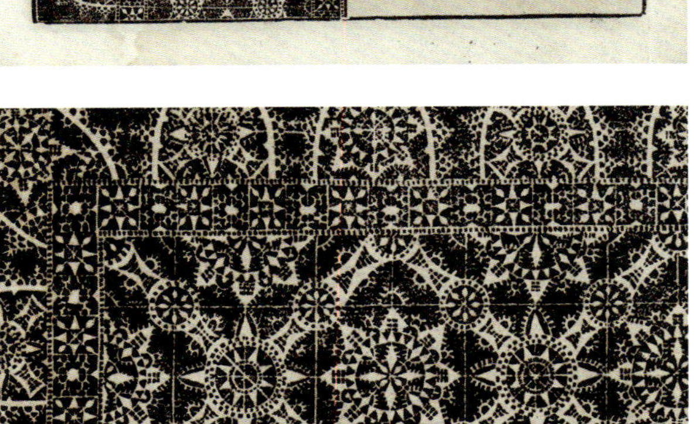

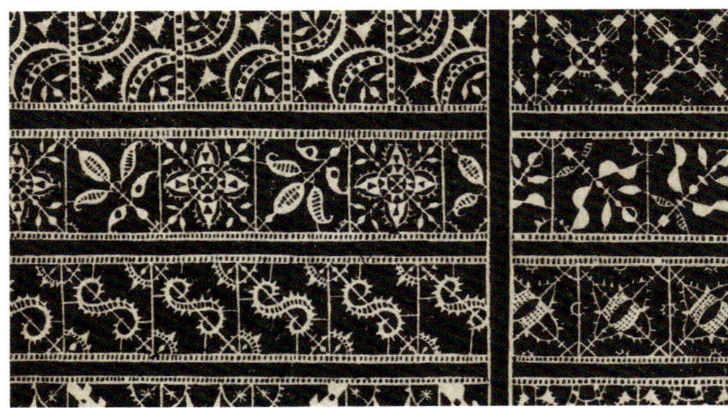

Fig. 8 • Elisabetta (or Isabella) Catanea Parasole, *Teatro delle Nobili et Virtuose Donne* [*Theater of Noble and Virtuous Women*], 1616. Woodcut engraving, 19 × 26.5 cm. The Metropolitan Museum of Art, New York, Rogers Fund, 1919, inv. no. 19.51(1-46).

Openings illustrated (left to right, above then below):

Fig. 8a • plate 31

Fig. 8b • plate 17

Fig. 8c • detail of lace pattern, plate 31

Fig. 8d • detail of embroidery pattern, plate 17

almost always on a grid. Sometimes a design was shown in both formats and the user was encouraged in the introductory text to try both approaches to the pattern. The technical challenge of how to depict a pattern within a grid on a woodblock was significant but worth pursuing for the publisher, as it aided in the transfer of designs to fabrics that have a natural grid formation because of the warp and weft of the threads. The style of lace called "cutwork" features prominent open spaces, and to show a white pattern on a grid meant that the woodblock cutter had to cut away all the wood around the fine lines of the regular grid. Some of the first examples of woodcut pattern books to depict this type of lace were included in Federico de Vinciolo's *Les Singuliers et Nouveaux Portraicts pour les ouvrages de lingerie* (fig. 9). First printed in Paris in 1587 and dedicated to Catherine de' Medici, the work was a collaboration between Vinciolo and the publisher, Jean Le Clerc, who also likely cut some of the blocks and designed some of the patterns. The decision of Vinciolo and/or Le Clerc to show the white lace on a black background created a striking, more accurate approximation of how the finished product would look against a dark fabric, with the added benefit of allowing grids to be cut into the block more easily.

As the popularity of printed textile pattern books spread, publishers in Germany, Italy, France, and the Netherlands began to sell similar products. Many of these new titles borrowed from extant books, pulling together various styles into one source. This amalgamation of popular styles and patterns was often advertised as a selling point rather than hidden from the buyer. Novelty was not necessarily the motivating factor in textile patterns, as variety was of equal or greater importance. The large number of pattern book titles published throughout Europe within a decade of Schönsperger the Younger's genre-establishing 1523 volume is evidence of the demand for the printed patterns. No fewer than 150 titles were known to the first thorough bibliographer of textile

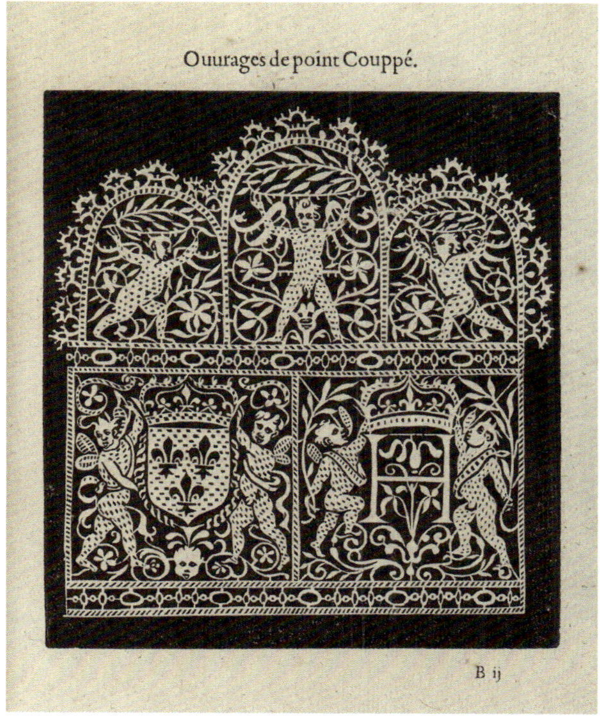

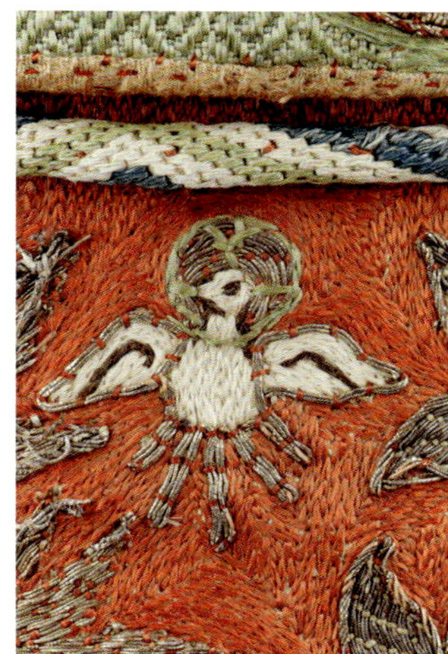

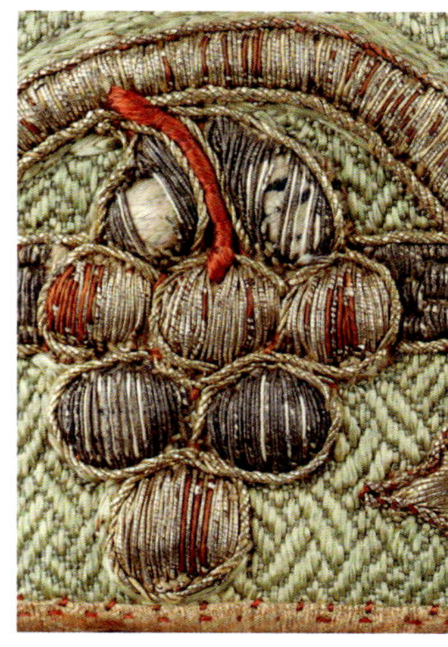

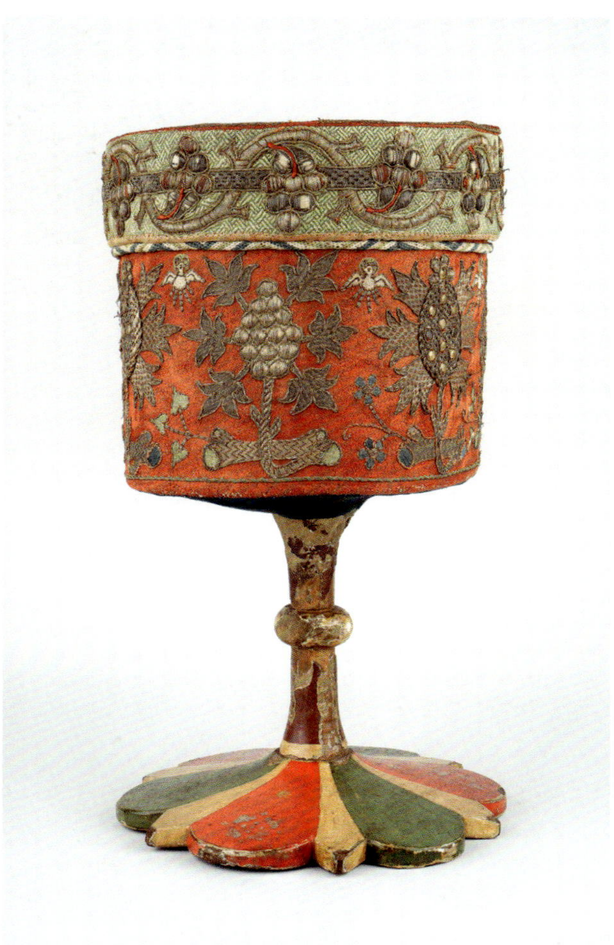

Fig. 9 (left) • Unknown makers with Federico de Vinciolo, *Les Singuliers et Nouveaux Portraicts pour les ouvrages de lingerie*, Paris, 1588. Woodcut, 20.5 × 16 cm. The Metropolitan Museum of Art, New York, Rogers Fund, 1918, inv. no. 18.68(1-93).

Fig. 10 (right, and details middle above and middle below) • Bridgettine nuns of Vadstena Abbey, *Embroidered reliquary*, 1350–1500. Wood, metal thread, and silk, 35 × 21 cm. Historiska museet, Stockholm, inv. no. 96362_HST. Photo: Myrin, Ola, Historiska museet/SHM.

pattern books, Arthur Lotz, with many more likely lost over the centuries.[25] Considering the large potential market made possible through increasing literacy for middle- and upper-class women, a very small number of printed textile pattern books survive to the present day, as most were destroyed through active use of the patterns held within.

Activities of Virtue

Young girls' time was carefully controlled and structured around their education under the primary direction of the women in their lives. What grown women should do with their leisure time inside the home was the subject of treatises, primarily by male writers, on the education and behaviour of women.[26] The trope of the virtuous woman at work on textiles goes back at least as far as Homer's eighth-century BCE *Odyssey* description of Odysseus's wife, Penelope, who holds an army of suitors at bay by promising to remarry once she finishes weaving a funeral shroud for her father-in-law. She weaves during the day and unravels her work in secret at night to remain faithful to her husband. Central to the events surrounding the mythical foundation of the Roman Republic in 508 BCE is the figure of Lucrezia, a woman whose rape by an Etruscan king, and her subsequent suicide, is the catalyst for the collapse of the monarchy. Her virtue is shown through two acts: the one most often discussed is her suicide even though she knows she is innocent of adultery, but she is also praised as a paragon of virtue known to work at her wool while the other women of her rank drink wine and socialize.

Another woman considered central to ideal womanhood in Catholic Europe was the Virgin Mary. Needlework as a pastime of the Virgin Mary became unofficial doctrine in the Middle Ages and was embraced by convents and secular women as an appropriate activity for any Christian woman regardless of status or role in society (fig. 10).[27] With increasing frequency throughout the sixteenth century, the introductory writings in textile pattern books for lacemaking and embroidery cited their utility as tools for virtuous women. The titles of several Italian lace pattern books immediately make clear their intended purpose, including *Il spechio di pensieri delle belle et virtudiose donne* [*The Mirror of the Thoughts of Beautiful and Virtuous Women*], *Teatro delle Nobili et Virtuose Donne* [*Theater of Noble and Virtuous Women*] (fig. 11; cat. no. 70), and *Corona delle Nobili et Virtuose Donne* [*Crown of Noble and Virtuous Women*]. The word "virtuose," in addition to referring to the appropriateness of behaviour, can also function as a play on "virtuosity."[28] Some authors of pattern books went so far as to suggest that users of the texts might learn enough to distinguish themselves in the art of embroidery or even "paint with the needle" and compete with poets and painters alike.[29]

Women and the Production of Model Books

Published by Christoph Froschauer in Zurich in 1561, *Nüw Modelbuch* features the first known woman involved in the production of images for model books; however, her name remains unknown, as she signed only the initials "M.K." Despite this veil of anonymity, the introductory text makes clear that the designer was a woman who taught bobbin lace to girls in Zurich.[30] The first woman whose name is signed to her designs in a textile pattern book is the Italian maker Elisabetta (or Isabella) Catanea Parasole (c. 1570–c. 1620; fig. 11a; cat. no. 70). It would seem to make sense for women, as the intended audience of the genre, to be the authors of these pattern books—yet Parasole was the only sixteenth-century Italian woman currently known to have signed her name to her work.[31] This scarcity of signed published patterns by women is not unique to Italy; examples are uncommon in other European countries as well. This raises the question of why

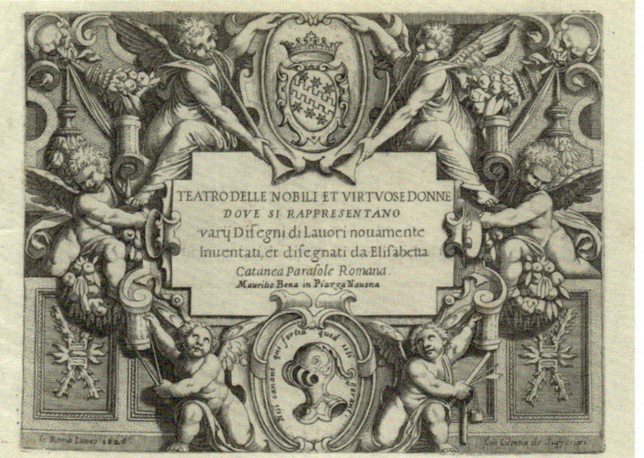

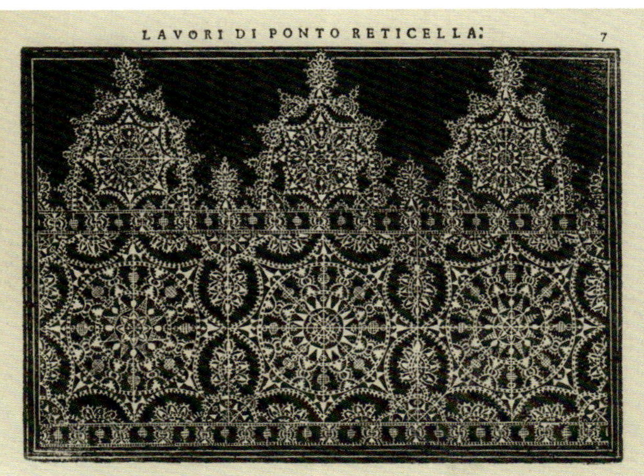

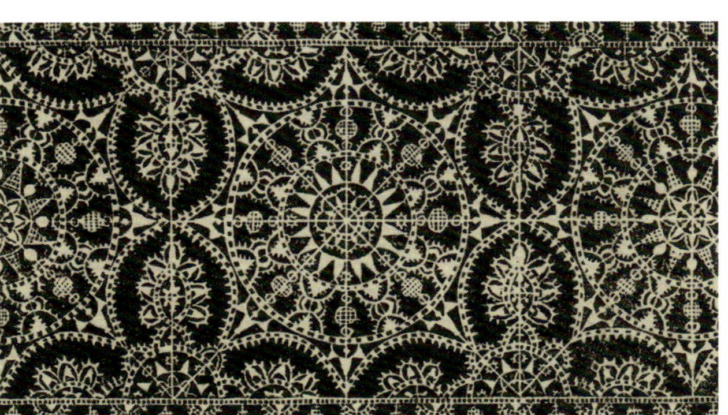

Fig. 11 · Elisabetta (or Isabella) Catanea Parasole, *Teatro delle Nobili et Virtuose Donne* [*Theater of Noble and Virtuous Women*], Rome, 1620. Printed bound volume of engravings, 22 × 28 cm. Harvard University, Houghton Library, Gift of Philip Hofer, TYP 625.20.674.

Openings illustrated (above to below):

Fig. 11a · frontispiece

Fig. 11b · plate 7

Fig. 11c · detail of plate 7

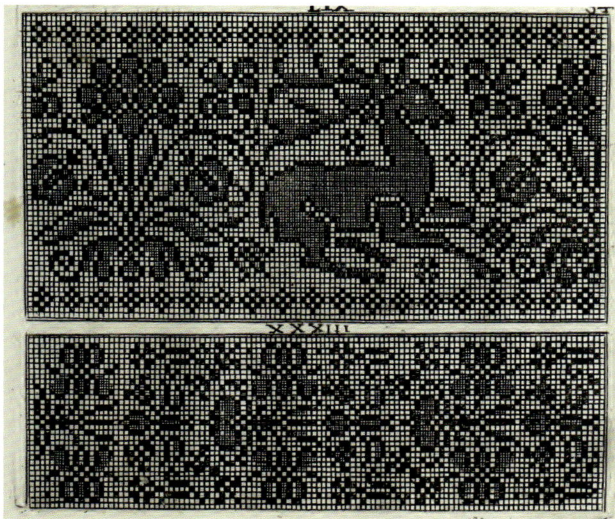

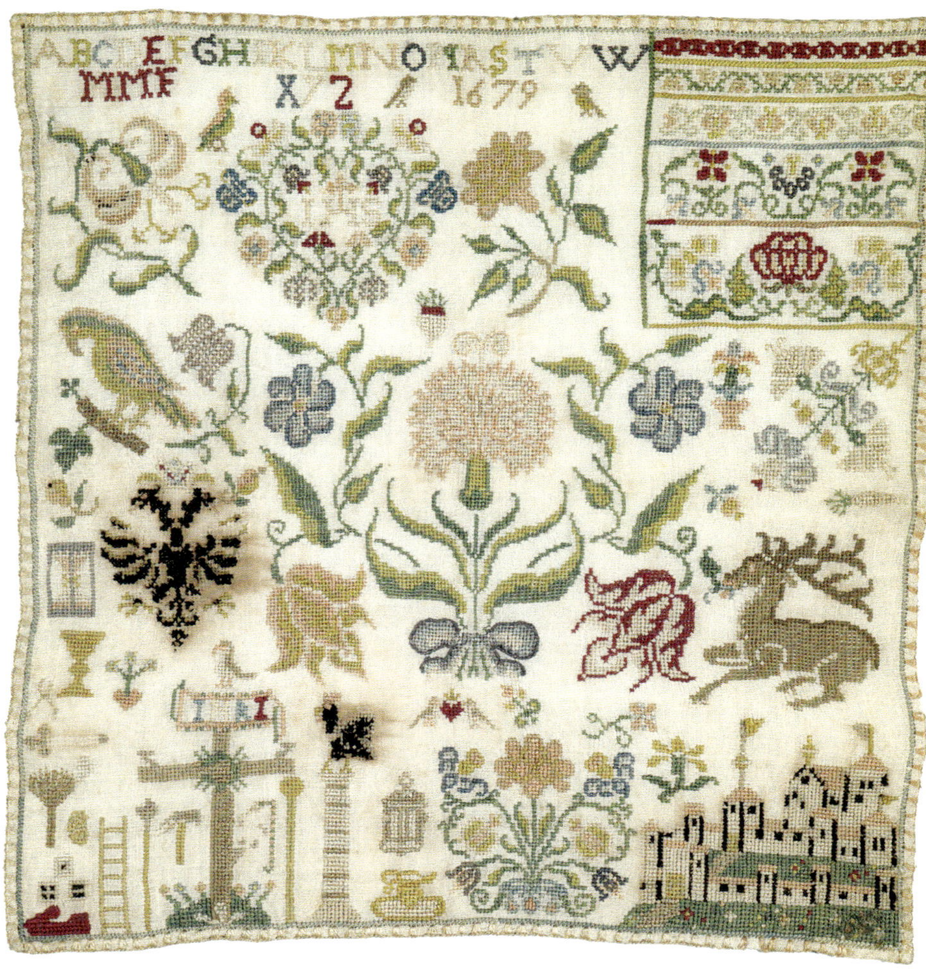

Fig. 12 (left) • Rosina Helena Fürst, plate 34 in *Dass Neüe Model Buch Andererthei*l, 1666. Bound volume of engravings, 18 × 20 cm. Sterling and Francine Clark Art Institute Library, Mary Ann Beinecke Decorative Art Collection, call no. NK9205 F8 1666-1689.

Fig. 13 (right) • Unknown German embroiderer, *Embroidery sampler with motifs from Rosina Helena Fürst's model book*, 1679. Linen, silk embroidery, cross stitch, double running stitch, stem stitch, buttonhole stitch, and picot stitch, 30.5 × 30.5 cm. Germanisches Nationalmuseum, Nürnberg, inv. no. Gew2647. Photo: M. Runge.

women's names would be as rare in the history of printed textile design as they are in most printed materials. Evelyn Lincoln has suggested that Parasole signed her lace pattern books because they were a genre where her female identity helped sell the work.[32] Although they might have brought a valuable female perspective to these works that were designed in large part for use by other women, the paucity of extant examples of lace and embroidery patterns produced by women is more likely a reflection of women's general lack of access to training as professional printmakers than it is of their direct exclusion from the particular medium of pattern book production. Parasole's contributions to the pattern book genre were facilitated by her training in embroidery and then marriage into a family where her sister-in-law was trained as a woodblock carver. Through her own education and familial connection to both woodblock carving and book publishing, she was perfectly positioned to create a pattern book.[33]

Although Parasole was the first woman to use her full name to sign textile patterns, there were at least two other women openly involved in the genre during the seventeenth century. In Nuremberg, Rosina Helena Fürst (1642–1709), the daughter of art dealer and printer Paul Fürst, engraved four model books for embroidery: *Das Neüe Model Buch Erster Theil* (1660), *Dass Neüe Model Buch Andererthei*l (1666), *Des Neuen Model-Buchs Dritter Theil* (1676), and *Neues Model-Buch, Vierten Theil* (1689).[34] Fürst states clearly in the introductory texts of the second, third, and fourth books that the patterns in the books are her own and

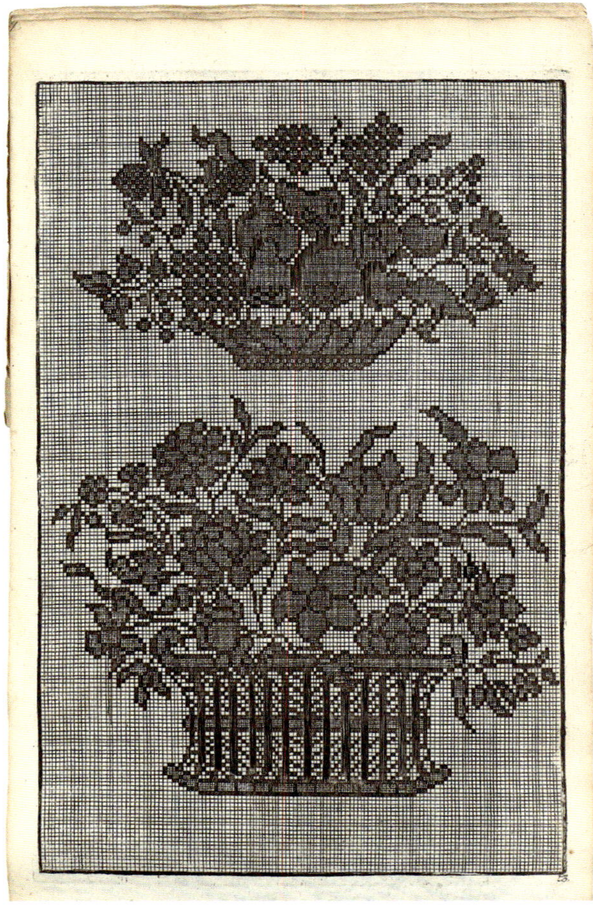

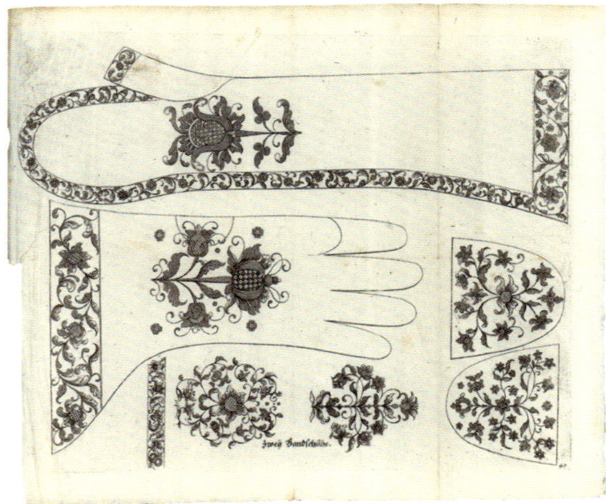

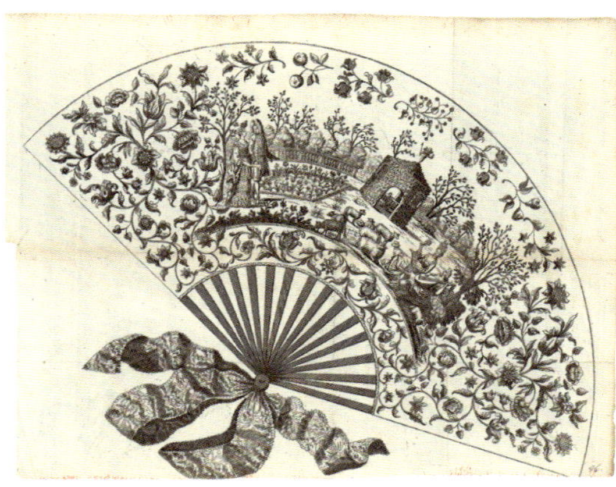

Fig. 14 • Margaretha Helm, *Kunst- und Fleiss-übende Nadel-Ergötzungen... [The Art and Diligence of Practicing Needle Delights]*, c. 1720–1746. Bound volume of engravings. Royal Ontario Museum, Toronto, Canada, inv. no. RB TT 771 H45 1700z. Photos: courtesy of the Royal Ontario Museum, © ROM.

Openings illustrated (from top left, clockwise):

Fig. 14a • *Design for an embroidery* (band 1, plate 13). Book: 21.5 × 34 × 2.8 cm; page: 20.7 × 32.5 cm.

Fig. 14b • *Design for gloves* (band 1, plate 47). Book: 21.5 × 34 × 2.8 cm; foldout page: 34.6 × 42.3 cm.

Fig. 14c • *Design for a fan* (band 2, plate 46). Book: 21.2 × 34 × 3 cm; foldout page: 38 × 52 cm.

are intended to provide the user with a variety of flowers, geometric patterns, animal motifs (fig. 12), religious motifs, armorial examples, and letters and numbers from which to embroider (fig. 13).

Living in Nuremberg around the same time as Fürst, Margaretha Helm (1659–1742) engraved more than 150 plates of patterns for embroidery that feature a wider variety of examples than Fürst's or Parasole's books. Printed in Nuremberg in three volumes by Johann Christoph Weigel between 1720 and 1742,[35] Helm's extant plates are rare in terms of the variety of objects included. In addition to sheets of floral bands (fig. 14a; cat. no. 227) or abstract motifs, letters, and numbers, there are patterns to decorate gloves (fig. 14b; cat. no. 227), stomachers, and hats of different sizes, as well as shoes and even fans (fig. 14c; cat. no. 227). Helm's designs are a combination of reused patterns from previous books; the novelty lies in the variety.[36] The survival of Helm's patterns suggests that older designs and novel styles could be adapted for specific articles of clothing and could have spread easily throughout Europe.

As women found themselves barred from textile guilds, embroidery and lacemaking took on increased importance in their lives. Whether demonstrating proficiency through samplers, decorating garments for their families, or creating highly finished altar frontals within a convent workshop, women consistently shared knowledge and patterns. This was a crucial process that became linked to the sixteenth-century publishing boom and, thanks to the influence of these largely unnamed women, has continued to the present day.

Detail (fig. 8, opposite) • Elisabetta (or Isabella) Catanea Parasole, *Teatro delle Nobili et Virtuose Donne [Theater of Noble and Virtuous Women]*, 1616. Woodcut engraving, 19 × 26.5 cm. The Metropolitan Museum of Art, New York, Rogers Fund, 1919, inv. no. 19.51(1-46). Opening illustrated: plate 17.

Notes

1 For more on the topic of lacemaking, see Emma Cormack and Michele Majer, eds., *Threads of Power: Lace from the Textilmuseum St. Gallen* (New Haven, CT: Yale University Press, 2023).
2 Kim Sloan, *A Noble Art: Amateur Artists and Drawing Masters, c. 1600–1800* (London: British Museum Press, 2000), 7.
3 Moira Thunder, "Deserving Attention: Margaretha Helm's Designs for Embroidery in the Eighteenth Century," *Journal of Design History* 23, no. 4 (2010): 409.
4 Rozsika Parker, *The Subversive Stitch: Embroidery and the Making of the Feminine* (London: Bloomsbury, 2020; reprint), 60–61.
5 Parker, *The Subversive Stitch*, 60–61. Only 4 percent of the names mentioned in the register of craftspeople and artists working in eighteenth-century Nuremberg were women. German textile pattern designer Margaretha Helm (1659–1742) was alive and working during this time, yet she is not mentioned as one of them. See Thunder, "Deserving Attention," 421.
6 Marta Ajmar-Wollheim, "Housework," in *At Home in Renaissance Italy*, ed. Marta Ajmar-Wollheim and Flora Dennis; summary catalogue ed. Elizabeth Miller (London: V&A; New York: Harry N. Abrams, 2006), 152–53.
7 Ajmar-Wollheim, "Housework," 153.
8 For examples of treatises on the education of women, see Michele Nicole Robinson, "The Material Culture of Female Youth in Bologna, 1550–1600," in *The Youth of Early Modern Women*, ed. Elizabeth S. Cohen and Margaret Reeves (Amsterdam: Amsterdam University Press, 2018), 244.
9 See Joyce de Vries, "Setting up House: Artisan Women's Trousseaux in Seventeenth-Century Bologna," in *Challenging Women's Agency and Activism in Early Modernity*, ed. Merry E. Wiesner-Hanks (Amsterdam: Amsterdam University Press, 2016), 65–84.
10 Robinson, "The Material Culture of Female Youth in Bologna," 248.
11 Femke Speelberg, "Fashion & Virtue: Textile Patterns and the Print Revolution, 1520–1620," *Metropolitan Museum of Art Bulletin* 73, no. 2 (Fall 2015): 25–26.
12 Evelyn Lincoln, "Models for Science and Craft: Isabella Parasole's Botanical and Lace Illustrations," *Visual Resources* 17, no. 1 (2001): 10–11.
13 Speelberg, "Fashion & Virtue," 19.
14 Ajmar-Wollheim, "Housework," 155.
15 Men wove cloth outside of the home as members of guilds, including as those dealing with the import and production of wool, silk, and linen.
16 Ajmar-Wollheim, "Housework," 157.
17 Ajmar-Wollheim, "Housework," 160.
18 Robinson, "The Material Culture of Female Youth in Bologna," 247.
19 Robinson, "The Material Culture of Female Youth in Bologna," 248.
20 Parker, *The Subversive Stitch*, 76.
21 David Brafman and Lisa Cambier, "Needlework Pattern Books: Early Printed 'Lace-Books' from the Research Institute's Collection," Getty Research Foundation Museum, July 19, 2012, blogs.getty.edu/iris/treasures-from-the-vault-needlework-pattern-books/, accessed September 6, 2022.
22 For an understanding of these terms and additional context, please see Elena Naomi Kanagy-Loux's text "Lace" on pages 190–93 of this volume as well as Isabella Rosner and Theresa Kutasz Christensen's text "Tapestry, Woven Fabrics, and Embroidery" on pages 244–55 of this volume.
23 Speelberg calls this "perhaps the first iteration of prefabricated point (graph) paper." She points out that the Met's collection has a book purely of graph paper, suggesting that the two became separate products. Speelberg, "Fashion & Virtue," 20.
24 For examples, see printed drawing books such as Fialetti's *Il Vero Modo* [...], which contained text providing step-by-step directions only in its earliest known form. Alexa Greist, "A Rediscovered Text for a Drawing Book by Odoardo Fialetti," *Burlington Magazine* 156, no. 1330 (2014): 12–18.
25 Arthur Lotz, *Bibliographie der Modelbücher: Beschreibendes Verzeichnis der Stick- und Spitzenmusterbücher des 16. und 17; Jahrhunderts* (Leipzig, 1933).
26 For a consideration of the way that sexual difference pushed women further into the domestic sphere, see Rozsika Parker, "The Domestication of Embroidery," in Parker, *The Subversive Stitch*, 60–81.
27 Speelberg, "Fashion & Virtue," 41.
28 Speelberg, "Fashion & Virtue," 75.
29 Speelberg refers specifically to the introduction in Matteo Pagono's *Giardineto novo di punti tagliati et gropposi per exercitio & ornamento delle donne* (Venice 1554); "Fashion & Virtue," 43. But the virtuous behaviour of women was not to be found in competition with men. Ideas about creation, procreative power, and creativity were firmly rooted in male terms of virility. Frederika H. Jacobs, "Woman's Capacity to Create: The Unusual Case of Sofonisba Anguissola," *Renaissance Quarterly* 47, no. 1 (1994): 74–101.
30 Speelberg, "Fashion & Virtue," 39.
31 Lincoln, "Models for Science and Craft," 19.
32 Lincoln, "Models for Science and Craft," 30–31.
33 Evelyn Lincoln, "Artemisia Gentileschi, Geronima and Isabella Parasole and Lavinia Fontana (*By Her Hand: Artemisia Gentileschi and Women Artists in Italy, 1500–1800*)," *Print Quarterly* 40, no. 1 (March 2023): 62.
34 She and her sister Magdalena, a flower painter, both spent time in Maria Sibylla Merian's school, where she taught drawing and painting to the daughters of wealthy Nuremberg families, a group Merian referred to as her *jungfrauen companie* (group of maidens). See Kay Etheridge, *The Flowering of Ecology: Maria Sibylla Merian's Caterpillar Book* (Leiden: Brill, 2021), 58.
35 For arguments dating the publication to 1742, see Thunder, "Deserving Attention," 423–24, where she notes that Helm's husband is mentioned as "choirmaster," which he became in 1742. Although Helm likely made the plates before this date, it is also possible the book was published posthumously.
36 Thunder, "Deserving Attention," 420.

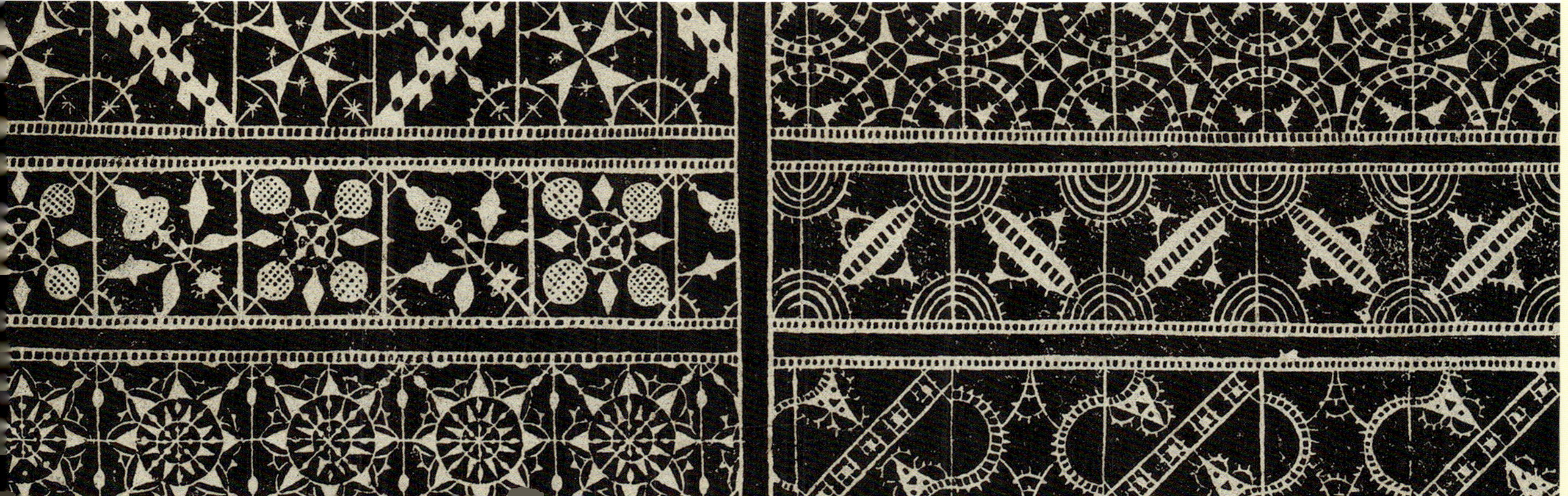

DESIGNING WOMEN

Drawings by Women Artists in Early Modern Italy

Babette Bohn

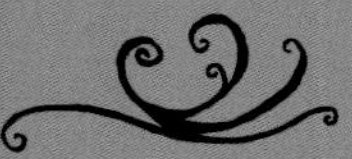

Although most women artists from early modern Italy are no longer known in extant works, this meagre survival rate applies even more dramatically to their drawings. Of the roughly 250 women artists whose names are recorded from the sixteenth and seventeenth centuries in Italy, only about 6 percent can be credited even when including drawings of uncertain attribution, and fewer still have significant existing oeuvres on paper that broadly reveal their preparatory procedures and creative ingenuity. Of course, this paucity of currently identifiable works does not mean that most Italian women did not draw. As was widespread practice in early modern Italy, artists created drawings both for educational purposes and as preparatory studies for their paintings, prints, and sculptures. But the situation does suggest that drawings by women artists were infrequently valued by early collectors and were rarely preserved as a result, impeding a full understanding of their artistic production today. The few women artists who were explicitly celebrated for their drawings—and whose drawings were avidly collected—constitute exceptions, and their achievements are illuminating to consider.

Given the growing interest in women artists during the past five decades, there is every reason to hope that more of their drawings will come to light. This essay introduces the subject, explaining and interpreting the parameters of our current knowledge. Following a brief consideration of the earliest extant drawings by Italian women and their treatment by early writers, I discuss the extant drawings and pertinent evidence for women artists, particularly in four major Italian cities during the sixteenth through eighteenth centuries, in addition to a few important figures who worked in multiple locations.

Early Drawings by Women

The earliest Italian woman to be credited with drawings by an early writer is Properzia de' Rossi (c. 1490/91–c. 1530), a Bolognese sculptor and the sole woman to receive a biography in the first edition of Giorgio Vasari's *The Lives*, in 1550. Vasari reported that he had obtained some drawings by the artist after Raphael that were "molto buoni" (very good).[1] Notwithstanding Vasari's praise, it is telling that these were not original designs but copies after another artist, a harbinger of limited appreciation for women's capacity for invention that persisted for centuries. Early modern women were rarely appreciated for their originality,[2] a prejudice that was exacerbated by the scarcity of known drawings testifying to their capacity for invention. Such claims (at least by implication) for limited invention were frequently directed to other women, too, such as Plautilla Nelli and Teresa Muratori, whose contributions will be subsequently explored in more detail. Another difficulty with Vasari's description is his failure to specify any subjects of de' Rossi's drawings, and no other early writers supplied this information either. In the absence of such specifics, it is not surprising that only two drawings—both based on early inscriptions—are ascribed to de' Rossi today, though her authorship seems questionable in both cases. One of the two drawings,[3] *Studies of a Lion and Dog* (fig. 1), is unimpressive in quality and not connected to any of the artist's identifiable sculptures, and no other autograph drawings provide a basis of comparison. So, by which criteria should this attribution be accepted? The argument rests on its inscription at upper right: "di Properzia dei Rossi, scultrice Bolognese nel 1530," an attribution that is repeated on the verso as "76/disegno

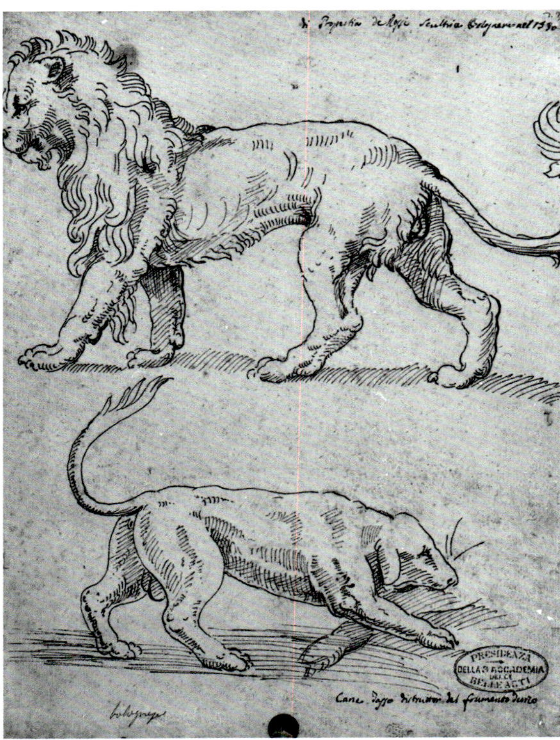

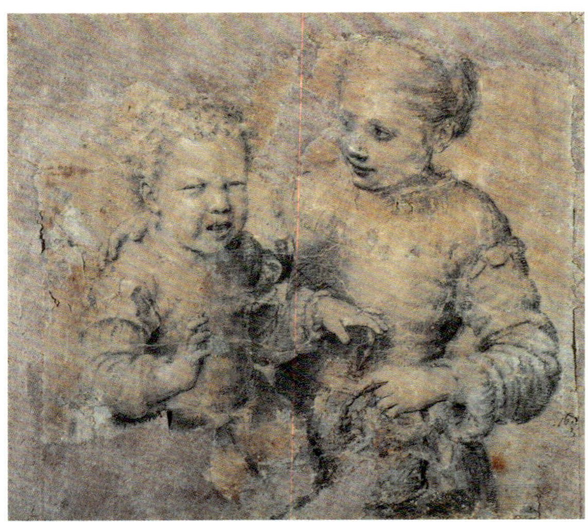

Fig. 1 (above) • Attributed to Properzia de' Rossi, *Studies of a Lion and Dog* [*Leone e cane o tasso*], 1530. Pen and brown ink on paper, 27 × 21.5 cm. Gallerie Accademia, Venice, inv. no. 719. © G.A.VE Gallerie dell'Accademia di Venezia, Archivio fotografico "su concessione del Ministero della Cultura."

Fig. 2 (below) • Sofonisba Anguissola, *Boy Bitten by a Crayfish*, c. 1554. Black chalk and charcoal heightened with white; reinforced in ink by a later hand on faded blue paper, 32.2 × 37.5 cm. Museo di Capodimonte, Naples, inv. no. 1039.

della Rossi/52." Although it is tempting to accept traditional attributions to rare artists such as de' Rossi, viability must be weighed against other evidence, a consideration that I will subsequently revisit. In this case, with no additional supporting evidence, the attribution seems questionable.

In the second edition of his *Lives*, published in 1568, Vasari added brief discussions of several other women to de' Rossi's biography, including Sofonisba Anguissola (c. 1535–1625), whose drawings he also mentioned. Here as well, Vasari begins with the implication of limited invention, remarking that Anguissola made excellent copies of works by others. His consideration of one drawing, however, includes unusual praise. He notes that a drawing of a girl laughing at a boy who is weeping because he has just been bitten by a crayfish is both graceful and true to nature ("non si puo veder cosa più graziosa nè simile al vero").[4] Vasari's discussion of this drawing (fig. 2), still extant but in poor condition,[5] is one of the earliest written accounts of a specific drawing by an Italian woman. His praise remained unequalled by any other account of a woman's drawings for a century. For Vasari, Anguissola's achievement was validated by the appreciation of her work by several sophisticated connoisseurs who each owned the drawing in succession: Michelangelo, Michelangelo's friend Tommaso Cavalieri, and Duke Cosimo de' Medici. The naturalism of the sketch marked Anguissola as a rarity: a *pittrice* (woman painter) who created figures that appeared truly alive. Another early commentary on the work, expressed in a letter written by Cavalieri in 1562, praised its invention—another critical component of artistic ability that, like naturalism, was rarely credited to women.[6]

It is telling, however, that only three drawings have been generally accepted as Anguissola's work,[7] and none has been conclusively connected with her paintings. Thus, although we have precious, if limited, proof of her naturalistic skills on paper, we lack material evidence to elucidate her preparatory procedures as a painter. The best candidate for a preliminary study for a painting is a self-portrait

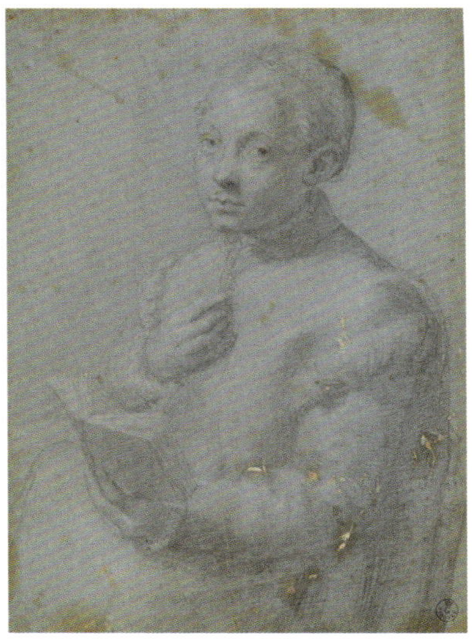

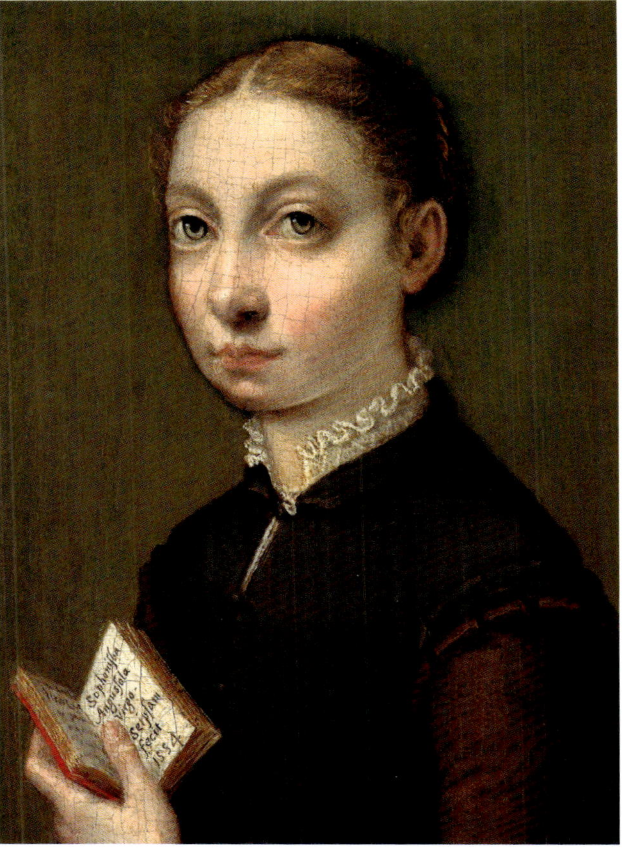

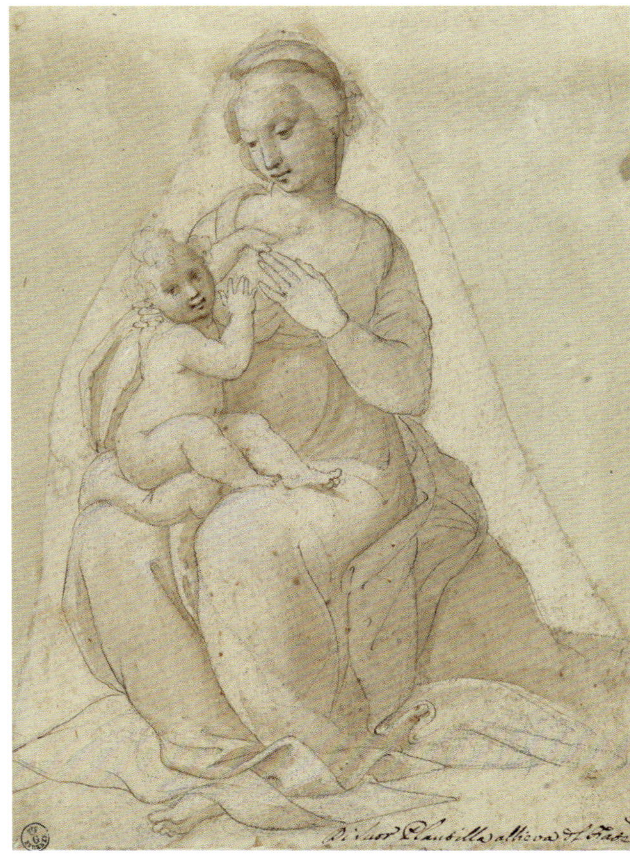

Fig. 3 (left) • Sofonisba Anguissola, *Self-Portrait (Young woman with a book)*, c. 1554. Black chalk heightened with white on blue paper, 35.1 × 26.5 cm. The Uffizi Galleries, Florence, inv. no. 13248 F. Photo: Gabinetto Fotografico delle Gallerie degli Uffizi.

Fig. 4 (middle) • Sofonisba Anguissola, *Self-Portrait (with a Book)*, 1554. Oil on wood panel, 19.5 × 14.5 cm. Kunsthistorisches Museum, Vienna, Gemäldegalerie (Picture Gallery), inv. no. GG 285. Photo: © KHM-Museumsverband.

Fig. 5 (right) • Plautilla Nelli, *Madonna and Child Nursing*, 16th century. Pen, brown ink, and brown wash, highlighted with white lead, over black chalk, 24 × 19.2 cm. The Uffizi Galleries, Florence, inv. no. 249 S. Photo: Gabinetto Fotografico delle Gallerie degli Uffizi.

drawing (fig. 3) that features Anguissola holding a book, as she also does in her 1554 painting *Self-Portrait (with a Book)* (fig. 4).[8] The drawing is more naturalistic than the painting, as one might expect if the drawing was made from life and the painting from the drawing. The painting eliminates the prominent right hand in the drawing, perhaps because Anguissola felt that it distracted from the coherent presentation of the figure. This type of revision was typical for many artists who rehearsed their ideas in preliminary drawings, but we have no further evidence of Anguissola's design procedures.

Drawings by Women Artists in Florence, Rome, and Beyond

Two fundamental issues for Anguissola and de' Rossi—the reluctance of early male biographers to credit women with powers of invention, as well as a shortage of extant preliminary studies for finished works—recur frequently for later women artists. This is certainly the case with two Florentine women, Plautilla Nelli (1523–1588) and Agnese Dolci (1659–1686), whose drawings are still known today. Nelli, another artist whom Vasari appended to his biography of Properzia de' Rossi in 1568, enjoyed a very different artistic inception. Nelli was a nun in the convent of Santa Caterina da Siena in Florence and the maker of a dozen drawings, now in the Uffizi, that were catalogued convincingly by Marzia Faietti.[9] None of these sheets appears to be a preparatory study for one of her paintings, and some copy works by other artists. Vasari disparagingly considered such copies her best efforts, hence belittling her capacity for invention. Nelli exemplifies the woman artist who, deprived of access to conventional artistic training, was a talented autodidact. She evidently learned largely from copying the drawings of Fra Bartolommeo that were available to her in the convent, as seen in *Madonna and Child Nursing* (fig. 5), which closely replicates another sheet by Fra Bartolommeo.[10] With only a dozen candidates

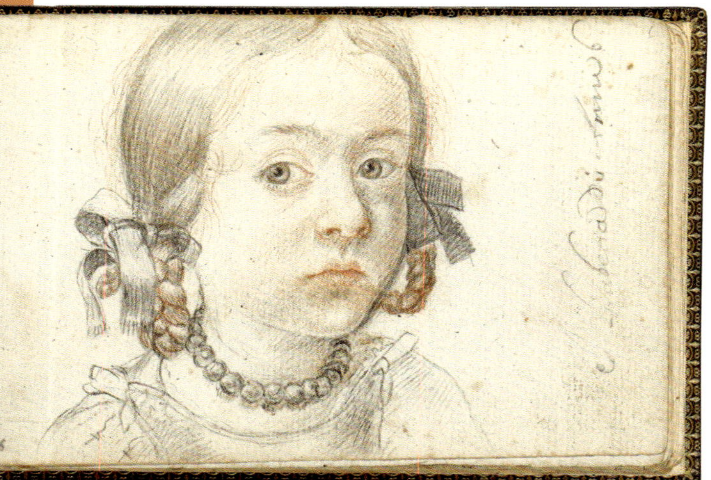

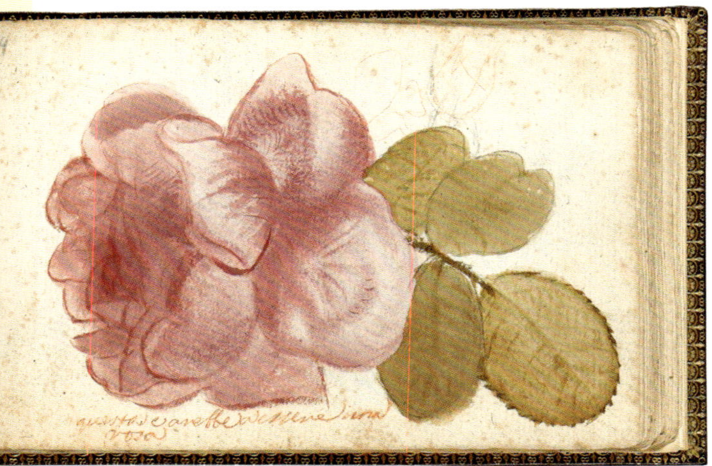

Fig. 6 • Agnese Dolci and Carlo Dolci, *Sketchbook*, 1667–1670. Red and green wash, and traces of red chalk and black chalk on paper; sheets: 9.3 × 14.8 cm; closed volume: 11.2 × 16.7 × 2.9 cm. The Syndics of the Fitzwilliam Museum, University of Cambridge, inv. no. 904*3. Images © The Fitzwilliam Museum, Cambridge.

Openings illustrated (above then below):

Fig. 6a • *Head and shoulders of Elisabetta Dolci* (folio 6r)

Fig. 6b • *Rose with a leaf* (folio 25r)

for Nelli's authorship and none securely connected to her paintings, we lack an authoritative understanding of her skills and interests as a female creator of drawings (*disegnatrice*).

Nelli's Florentine successor, Agnese Dolci, was one of seven daughters born to the painter Carlo Dolci. Her little-known artistic career was overshadowed by her famous father, and the central problem for understanding her drawings is to separate her work from his in the absence of any clarifying insights from early writers. This challenge is pivotal in assessing a small sketchbook in the Fitzwilliam Museum that includes the only known drawings (and almost the only extant work in any medium, with the exception of a single attributed painting) by Agnese Dolci. The fifty-one-page sketchbook carries an inscription by Agnese that appears to date the book to 1667–70, when she was still quite young. Although this inscription suggests Agnese's authorship, scholar David Scrase contested this uniform attribution, ascribing many of the included drawings to her father. Scrase's view was disputed by Lisa Goldenberg Stoppato, who argued for re-ascribing the three portraits of Agnese's sisters, Elisabetta (fig. 6a), Agata, and Caterina, to Agnese, based on stylistic discrepancies between these works and another portrait drawing by Carlo.[11] Scrase's principal argument seems to be that the better drawings, such as the portraits of his other three daughters, are more likely Carlo's work than that of Agnese, and in a few cases (including the portrait of Caterina), Carlo's authorship is confirmed by a signature. Stoppato engages more specifically with the style of the individual drawings but does not address the presence of Carlo's signature on Caterina's portrait, which she assigns to Agnese. Most of the drawings in the sketchbook, however, are not signed. For those sheets, simply assuming that the better works are by Carlo rather than Agnese seems insufficient. Some drawings reproduce prints by Jacques Callot, further complicating a determination of authorship.

Some pages of the sketchbook feature unusual watercolour depictions of fruit or flowers, such as the charming illustration of a rose (fig. 6b; cat. no. 44). Such still-life subjects were often treated by women artists, but without further corroborative information about Agnese, a clear understanding of her drawings remains elusive. Nevertheless, it seems logical that the daughter of an artist who drew frequently would also have adopted this practice. The absence of information about Agnese Dolci's drawings is particularly ironic, since her sketchbook may be the only known volume of drawings from the period that was demonstrably assembled by an Italian woman artist herself, confirming that drawings had particular value for the artist. Three other books of drawings by Italian women—two by Giovanna Garzoni (1600–1670) and one by Lavinia Fontana (1552–1614)—were probably bound together only later, most likely by a collector.

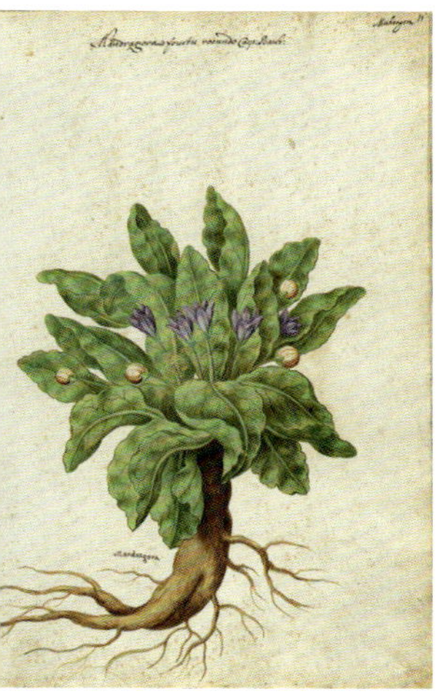

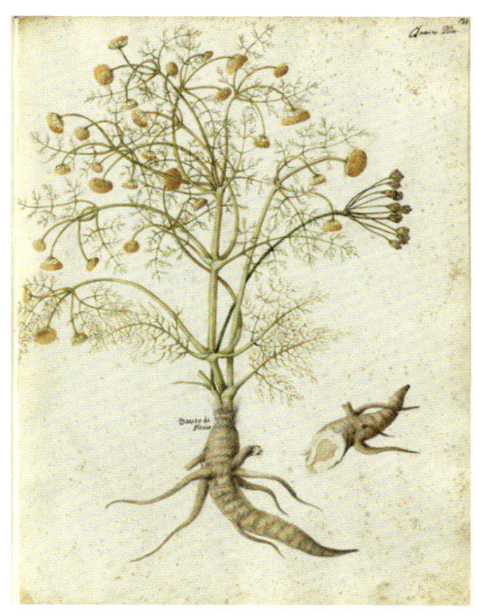

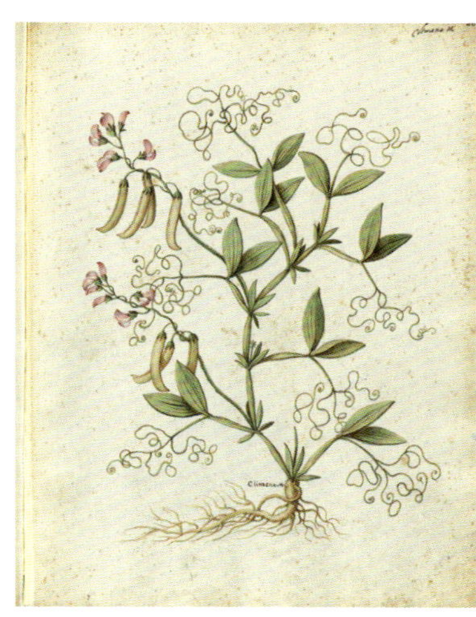

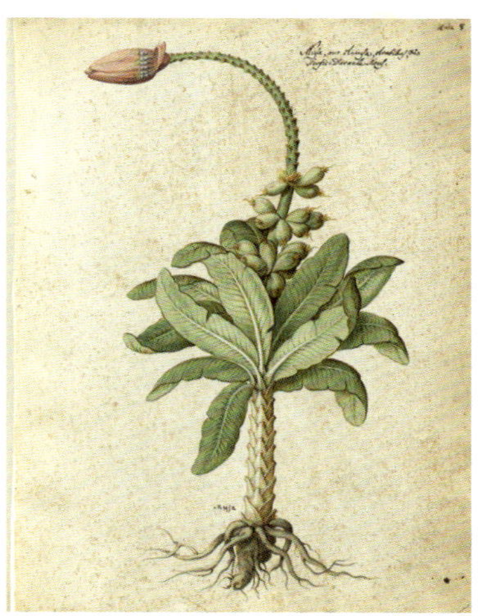

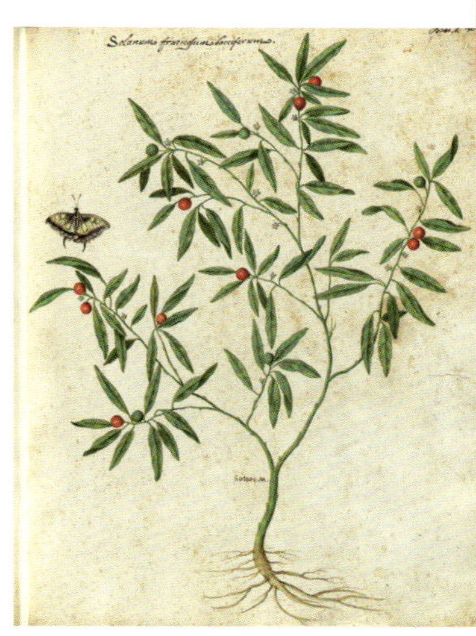

Fig. 7 • Giovanna Garzoni, *Piante varie*, c. 1630–1632. Watercolour on paper, 49.5 × 38 cm. Dumbarton Oaks Research Library and Collection, Trustees for Harvard University, Washington, D.C., inv. no. G-3-3.

Openings illustrated (left to right):

Fig. 7a • *Mandragora* (folio 11)

Fig. 7b • *Ferula communis* (folio 29)

Fig. 7c • *Lathrys clymenum* (folio 46)

Fig. 7d • *Musa* (folio 8)

Fig. 7e • *Solaro* [*Butterfly with fruit and flower*] (folio 38)

Garzoni, a painter and calligrapher from the Marches region of Italy who worked in Florence, Rome, Venice, and elsewhere, is more decisively associated with still life. In contrast to Agnese Dolci, Garzoni enjoyed considerable success and is still known in many existing works. Although we have no preparatory drawings by Garzoni, a sketchbook that the artist bequeathed to the Accademia di San Luca in Rome includes a sheet of sketches in pen and ink after Albrecht Dürer, confirming the artist's adherence to the traditional practice of making drawings after the works of other artists.[12] More typical of her production, however, is a bound book of finished botanical watercolour studies at Dumbarton Oaks in Washington, DC, that constitutes an extraordinary artifact in the history of women's production on paper. In its present form, the book is something of a palimpsest; it consists of fifty of the original seventy-one botanical drawings in watercolour (a few of arguable authorship), each page inscribed with the vernacular name of the plant in the artist's distinctive, calligraphic script. Almost half of the sheets are also inscribed with Latin names and references in an eighteenth-century hand, and all are stitched together in what is likely a twentieth-century binding. Sheila Barker and Anatole Tchikine assert that the original function, patronage, and provenance of these watercolours are unclear. The most convincing hypothesis suggests that the collection was commissioned by a Roman apothecary and naturalist, probably in the early 1630s in Rome, to provide botanists with useful models to facilitate the identification of plants, whether herbal, poisonous, or exotic.[13] Although the illustrations frequently derive from printed herbals, Garzoni's introduction of colour, sensitivity to detail, calligraphic skills, and even her occasional scientific errors impart a strongly individual character to the collection.

Such watercolours as the impressive *Mandragora* (fig. 7a; cat. no. 156) demonstrate the artist's detailed and colourful approach. Like many studies in the book, this illustration combines both the stages of flowering (evidenced here in the purple blooms) and fructification, thereby providing full visual information and embellishing the beauty and complexity of the image. Garzoni's synthesis of artistic and scientific purposes is further confirmed by the judicious placement of the images on each page, a goal that is particularly striking in the numerous details of the flowering *Ferula communis* (fig. 7b; cat. no. 156). This example also shows the cut of the roots, one of many details based solely on her own direct observation that is not strictly pertinent to its botanical identification. One of the most striking instances of what we might consider artistic licence in an interpretation of botanical materiality is her marvellous watercolour rendering of the *Lathrys clymenum* (fig. 7c; cat. no. 156). This image fills the sheet with a graceful composition that owes a good deal to the calligraphic ornamentality of its meandering stems—an illustrated feature that has no actual parallel in the plant itself. And yet Garzoni simplifies the colouring of the flowers for this edible plant: in nature, they are red and purple, but Garzoni employs only a pinkish red. She signed three of the fifty sheets, including the exotic *Musa* (fig. 7d; cat. no. 156), the name—"G Garzoni," with the two Gs interlocking—cleverly inscribed within the banana flower at the summit of the gracefully arching plant. Another image (fig. 7e; cat. no. 156) juxtaposes a handsome butterfly adjacent to a fruit- and flower-bearing Solaro plant. In short, the album is filled with individual differences and details that may confound scholars seeking a clear consensus on questions of attribution and function. They also suggest an intriguing originality of invention, though perhaps Garzoni's prolific creativity inevitably undermined full fidelity to scientific accuracy in her watercolours. She likely made preliminary sketches on separate sheets of paper for these finished, coloured botanical illustrations, but no such working drawings have been recovered to date.

Artemisia Gentileschi (1593–after 1654) is another seventeenth-century woman painter who, like Garzoni, worked in Rome, Florence, Venice, and Naples. Gentileschi is rarely discussed in considerations of women's drawings, but a few sketches have been attributed to her, with arguable plausibility. A Roman artist by birth, Artemisia, like her father, Orazio, is not generally credited with working procedures that necessarily employed the intermediary step of preliminary drawings. As with most early followers of Caravaggio, both Artemisia and Orazio are often assumed to have painted from a live model. However, this theory is not entirely warranted, as she herself mentions her drawings both early and late in her career. The earliest reference appears in the documentation of Agostino Tassi's trial for raping Artemisia in 1612, and the second in a letter of 1649 to the collector Don Antonio Ruffo.[14] Even so, the four drawings that have been ascribed to Artemisia are stylistically dissimilar; none is conclusively connected to paintings and none has early inscriptions confirming the attribution to the artist, with one unverifiable exception.[15] Moreover, since three of the four are in private collections, significant challenges remain in confirming her authorship and ascertaining her graphic style and use of drawings. Although some of these attributions may prove to be correct, it seems prudent to suspend judgement until further evidence emerges. At this time, no drawings known to this writer can be conclusively credited to any women working in Rome before the eighteenth century.

Drawings by Women Artists in Bologna

This scarcity of identifiable drawings by women artists in Rome—and, to a lesser extent, in Florence—offers a striking contrast to the situation in Bologna, where surviving drawings are still ascribed to at least six women artists from the sixteenth through eighteenth centuries. Although these artists represent a small minority of the sixty-eight women artists whose names were recorded in early modern Bologna, they constitute a significantly larger group of *disegnatrici* than are known from any other Italian city. Moreover, in one case—that of Elisabetta Sirani (1638–1665)—we have a successful painter who was also famous explicitly for her drawings. This unusual situation facilitates some meaningful insights into women's drawings during the period.

Aside from the two questionable attributions to the Bolognese sculptor Properzia de' Rossi previously noted, the earliest Bolognese woman to whom drawings can be attributed today is the aforementioned Lavinia Fontana. The daughter of a painter, Fontana was both a portraitist and a history painter, and today about thirty-five drawings are convincingly credited to her—far more than to any other woman artist of the sixteenth century. Nonetheless, Fontana was not celebrated for her drawings during her lifetime. In fact, despite a thriving artistic biography industry in early

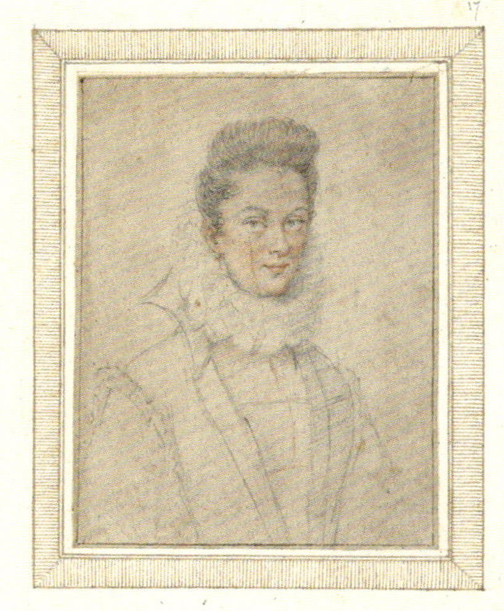

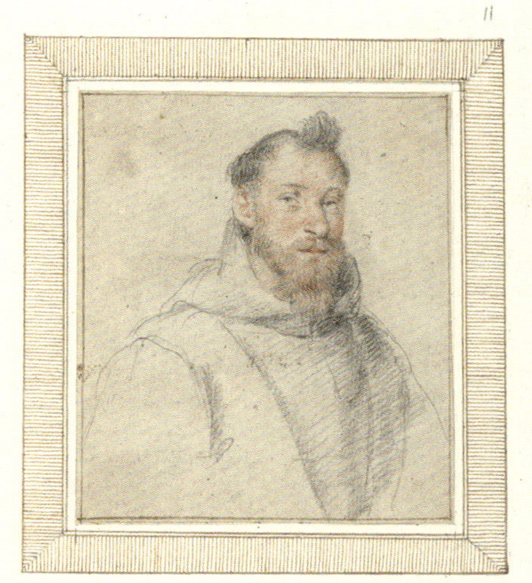

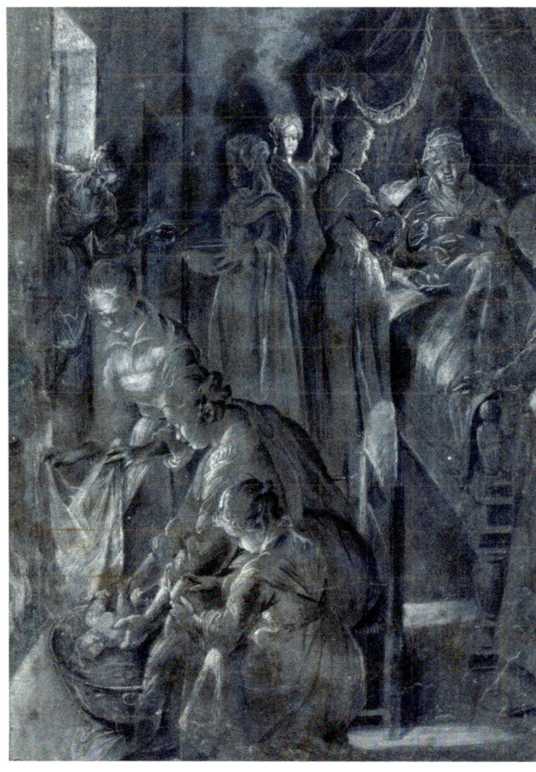

Fig. 8 (left and middle) • Lavinia Fontana, *Album of Portrait Studies*, c. 1593. Red chalk and black chalk, ruled border in pen and brown ink, simulated frame in pen and brown ink. The Morgan Library & Museum, New York, Purchased by Pierpont Morgan (1837–1913) in 1909, inv. no. IV, 158. Photos: The Morgan Library & Museum, New York.

Openings illustrated:

Fig. 8a • *Portrait of a Young Noblewoman*, 13 × 10.2 cm (158q, folio 17)

Fig. 8b • *Portrait of a Friar*, 10.1 × 9 cm (158k, folio 11)

Fig. 9 (right) • Lavinia Fontana, *Study for The Birth of the Virgin*, c. 1590. Blue wash heightened with white and squared in red chalk, 35.2 × 25 cm. Musée du Louvre, Paris, Département des Arts graphiques (Department of Graphic Arts), INV 21111. Photo: © Musée du Louvre, Dist. RMN-Grand Palais / Marc Jeanneteau / Art Resource, NY.

modern Bologna, no local writers even mentioned her drawings, nor did any of her non-Bolognese biographers. For Count Carlo Cesare Malvasia in 1678, this inattention to Fontana's drawings may be explained by a perceived lack of technical originality, in contrast to his admiration for Elisabetta Sirani's innovative wash technique.[16] Moreover, Fontana's drawings were not widely collected; only one known Bolognese inventory—that of Marchese Alessandro Facchinetti in 1685[17]—includes a drawing ascribed to her. Even so, a collection of nineteen drawings credited to the artist and pasted into an album during the early eighteenth century, now in New York's Morgan Library & Museum, suggests that some early collectors did appreciate Fontana's work on paper.[18] The entire collection consists of small portrait drawings in red and black chalk; some were preparatory for known pictures like *Portrait of a Young Noblewoman* (fig. 8a), while others were more likely created as independent exercises in observation.[19] The *Portrait of a Friar* (fig. 8b), with the man's unruly tuft of hair sticking straight up, seems too charmingly unidealized to have been the basis for a painting, but its unadorned naturalism confirms an inception in life drawing. In short, Fontana used preparatory drawings to design her detailed paintings, but she also drew from life without such an ulterior motive. Almost all of the artist's drawings known today are small portrait studies in chalk, like these examples. Only two compositional studies can currently be connected to any of Fontana's narrative paintings, including her *Study for The Birth of the Virgin* (fig. 9),[20] suggesting that most such drawings have been lost or misattributed. Thirty-five is a small number for an artist's total drawn oeuvre, but it far outstrips the quantity of drawings currently credited to most women in early modern Italy.

Fontana's successor and another successful painter, Elisabetta Sirani was the first Italian woman to be explicitly famous for her drawings, which were celebrated by many of her earlier biographers and popularly collected throughout Bologna, resulting in a sizable extant oeuvre of some 150 sheets. Malvasia's enthusiastic admiration for Sirani's wash drawings, expressed in a lengthy biography in 1678, marks her as an exceptional talent, with gifts that were rarely credited to women:

> ...when some commission for a painting came, she [Elisabetta Sirani] quickly took the chalk, and placing the sketch down swiftly in two marks on white paper (this was the great master's only method of drawing,

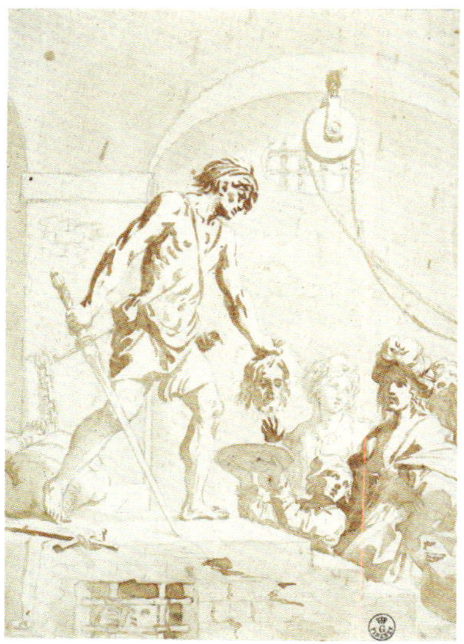

Fig. 10 • Elisabetta Sirani, *Beheading of Saint John the Baptist*, 1657. Brush and brown wash over black chalk, 19.6 × 14.9 cm. The Uffizi Galleries, Florence, inv. no. 6300 F. Photo: Gabinetto Fotografico delle Gallerie degli Uffizi.

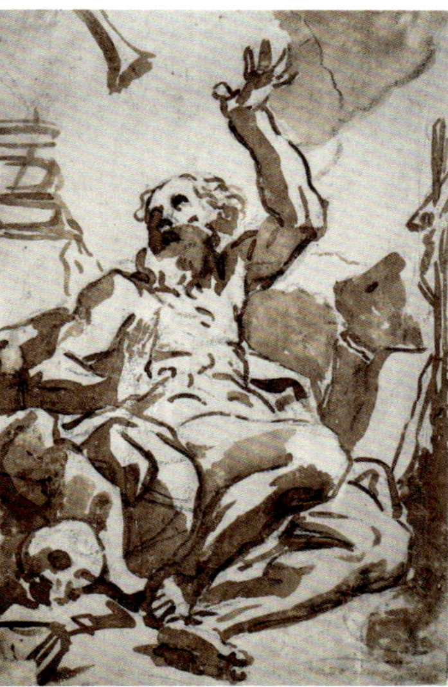

Fig. 11 • Elisabetta Sirani, *Study of Saint Jerome*, 1661. Black chalk, brush, and wash on paper, 30 × 20.5 cm. Pinacoteca Nazionale di Bologna, Department of Prints and Drawings (Gabinetto Disegni e Stampe), inv. no. 1736. Photo: Marco Baldassari, su concessione del Ministero della Cultura – Pinacoteca Nazionale di Bologna.

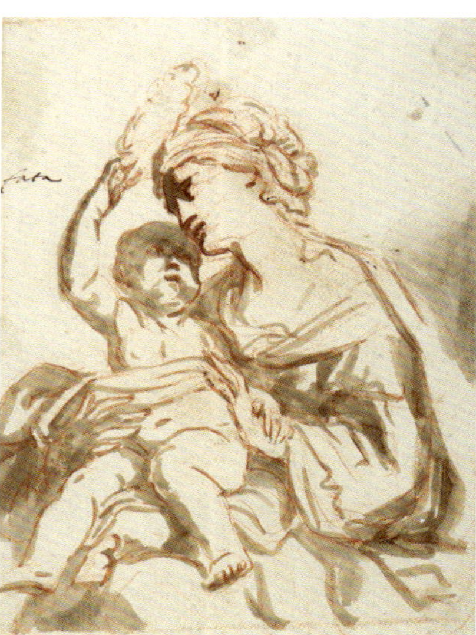

Fig. 12 • Elisabetta Sirani, *The Virgin Crowned by the Christ Child with Roses*, 1663. Red chalk and grey wash on paper, 21 × 16.5 cm. National Museums Liverpool, Walker Art Gallery, Purchased from the Trustees of the Weld Heirlooms Settlement with the assistance of the National Heritage Memorial Fund, Art Fund, Sir Denis Mahon and British Nuclear Fuels, in 1995, inv. no. WAG 1995.76.

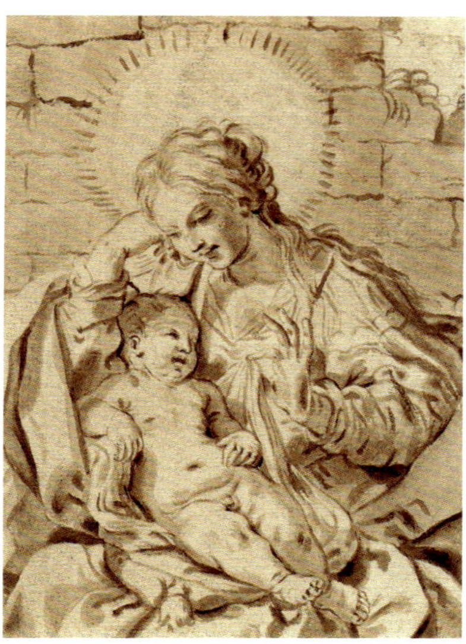

Fig. 13 • Elisabetta Sirani, *Madonna and Child*, c. 1664. Brush drawing in brown wash, over red chalk, on light brown prepared paper, 18.5 × 14.7 cm. British Museum, Donated by: Count Antoine Seilern, inv. no. 1946,0713.1413. Image: © The Trustees of the British Museum.

> which was practiced by few, not even by her father…), dipped a small brush in ink wash; from this quickly appeared a spirited invention that seemed to be without drawn or shaded strokes, and heightened together all at once.[21]

Malvasia's praise for Sirani's dazzling, virtuoso wash technique encompasses his appreciation for speed, technical facility, and original invention, also implying the allegedly exceptional character of such accomplishments for women. This unusual situation facilitates some meaningful insights into women's draughtsmanship during this period. Even in Bologna, where women artists were more appreciated than in most Italian cities, women's drawings are rarely identified in early inventories—unless they were created by Sirani. Her drawings are identified in at least fourteen Bolognese inventories of the seventeenth and eighteenth centuries, making her not only the most frequently collected *disegnatrice* in Bologna but also one of the most popular draughtsperson, male or female, of the entire Bolognese school.[22]

Beginning with Malvasia, Sirani was particularly revered for her virtuoso wash drawings. The early *Beheading of Saint John the Baptist* (fig. 10) confirms that Sirani had already developed her technique of rapid, fluid modelling in wash over minimal preliminary sketches in chalk by 1657, when she was only nineteen.[23] Three later examples, all studies for paintings, are the dynamic *Study of Saint Jerome* (fig. 11), *The Virgin Crowned by the Christ Child with Roses* (fig. 12; cat. no. 43; for a painting of 1663, see cat. no. 85), and the highly finished *Madonna and Child* (fig. 13). Although Sirani was more celebrated for her wash technique than for her drawings in other media, a number of red chalk drawings have come to light, revealing her exceptional skills in this medium as well. Her *Portrait of Annibale Ranuzzi* (fig. 14) demonstrates her lively and effective command of chalk in this independent portrayal of an important patron,[24] and her *Sibyl (study)* at Windsor (fig. 15), for a painting of 1660 (fig. 17), illustrates how such studies were used to prepare even her smaller paintings.[25] A rare early self-portrait drawing in three chalks (fig. 16; cat. no. 35)

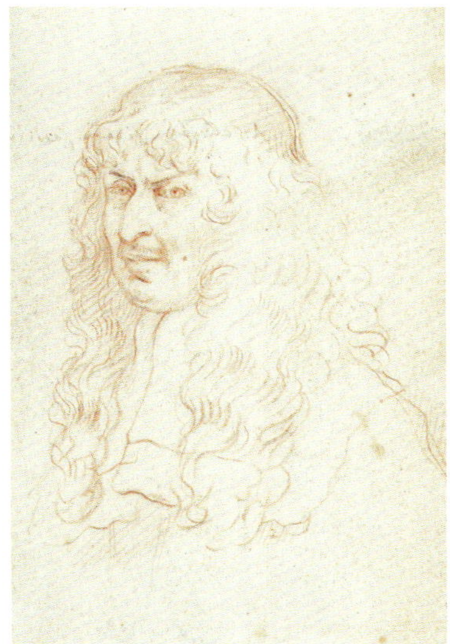

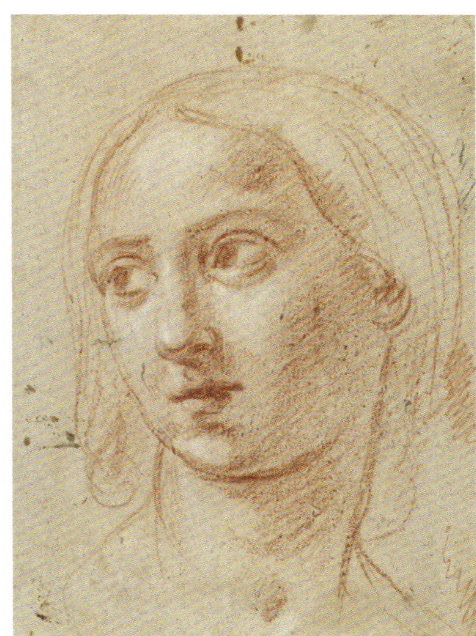

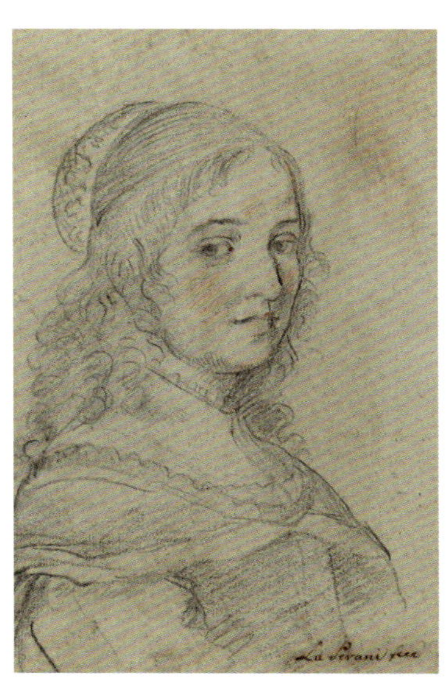

Fig. 14 (left) • Elisabetta Sirani, *Portrait of Annibale Ranuzzi*, c. 1664. Red chalk on paper, 25.7 × 16.9 cm. The Uffizi Galleries, Florence, inv. no. 15568 F. Photo: Gabinetto Fotografico delle Gallerie degli Uffizi.

Fig. 15 (middle) • Elisabetta Sirani, *Sibyl (study)*, c. 1660. Red chalk on paper, 25.8 × 19.3 cm. Royal Collection Trust, RCIN 905371. Image: Royal Collection Trust / © His Majesty King Charles III 2023.

Fig. 16 (right) • Elisabetta Sirani, *Self-Portrait*, c. 1658. Black chalk, red chalk, and white chalk on paper, 22.9 × 15.4 cm. Purchased with the Diane A. Nixon, class of 1957, Fund, and the gift of the Almathea Charitable Foundation, Smith College Museum of Art, Northampton, Massachusetts, inv. no. SC 2020.7.1.

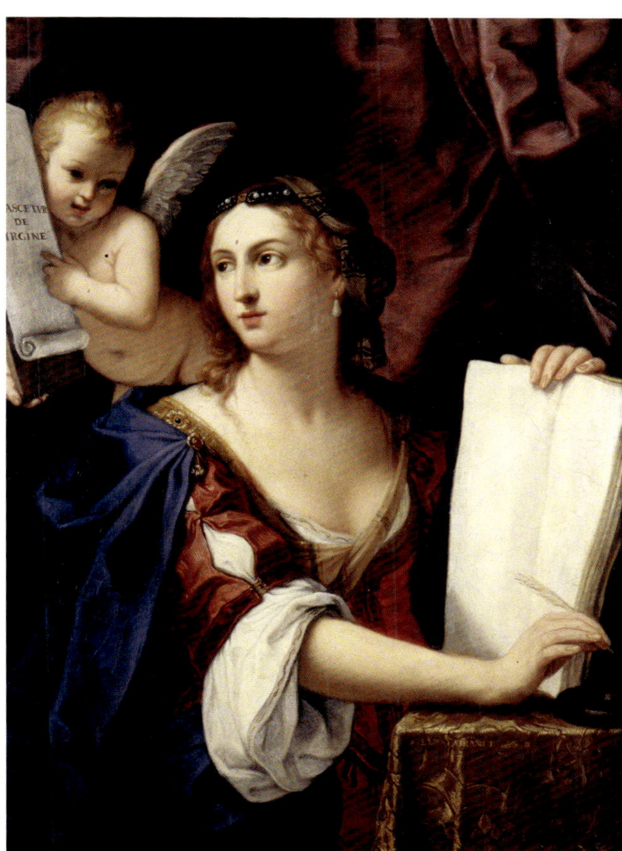

Fig. 17 • Elisabetta Sirani, *Sibyl*, 1660. Oil on canvas, 110 × 86 cm. Pinacoteca Nazionale di Bologna, inv. no. 6940. Photo: Marco Baldassari, su concessione del Ministero della Cultura – Pinacoteca Nazionale di Bologna.

showcases the diversity of Sirani's drawing media and documents her debt to her great predecessor Guido Reni, who popularized such *trois crayons* heads in Bologna.

Despite Sirani's success with drawings, few examples by her successors in Bologna are still known. Although some sheets have been convincingly ascribed to her sister Barbara Sirani (1641–1692), several attributions to Elisabetta's assistant Ginevra Cantofoli (1618–1672) are less plausible.[26] Four drawings by the prolific woodcutter Veronica Fontana (1651–1688) are still known (fig. 18), all likely studies for prints.[27] Prints almost inevitably required preliminary drawings in their creation, but to my knowledge, no earlier Italian female printmakers are still known in identifiable drawings—and only one later Bolognese woman painter, Teresa Muratori (1661–1708), can still be convincingly credited with drawings, both related to her paintings. The *Study for the Annunciation* (fig. 19), for her altarpiece in SS. Trinità, Bologna, is the only extant drawing connected to one of her many public religious pictures.[28] It employs red chalk, perhaps suggesting that Sirani's work in this medium influenced her successors. Given the limited information about drawings by Bolognese women artists after Sirani from early writers and the absence of any drawings by them in early inventories, however, the challenges for future identifications remain daunting.

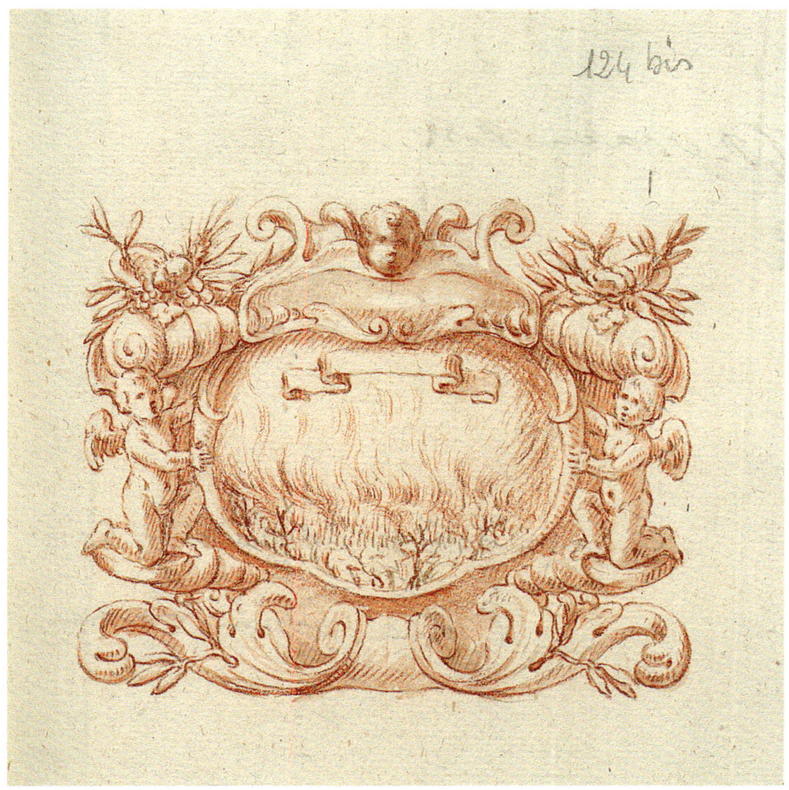

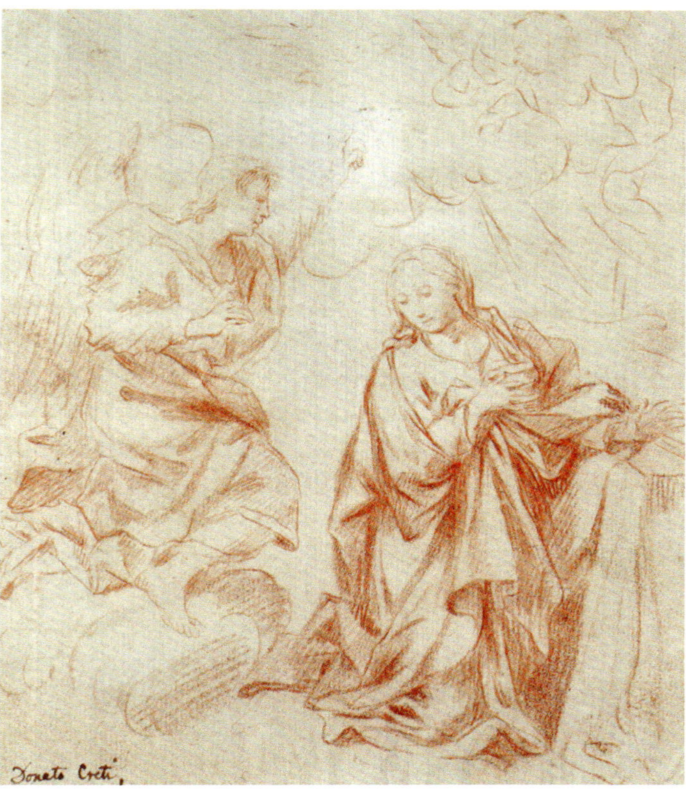

Fig. 18 (left) • Veronica Fontana, *Study for the Title Page (featuring Emblem of the Accademia dei Gelati) of Lorenzo Legati's "Museo Cospiano,"* before 1677. Red chalk with pen and brown ink and brown wash, 15.5 × 15.5 cm. The Archiginnasio Public Library, Bologna (Biblioteca Comunale dell'Archiginnasio, Bologna), inv. no. B.129, 124 bis.

Fig. 19 (right) • Teresa Muratori, *Study for the Annunciation*, undated. Red chalk on paper, 20 × 18 cm. Pinacoteca Nazionale di Bologna, inv. no. 32516.

Drawings by Women Artists in Venice: Marietta Robusti, Giulia Lama, and Rosalba Carriera

Although fewer women artists in Venice can be credited with surviving drawings compared with their contemporaries in Bologna, Venetian *disegnatrici* did in fact play a central role in the history of Italian women's drawings. In Venice, as in Florence and Bologna, a few drawings are plausibly ascribed to one sixteenth-century painter, Marietta Robusti (c. 1554/60–c. 1590). Two eighteenth-century Venetian women, Rosalba Carriera (1673–1757) and Giulia Lama (1681–1747), were pioneers in two distinct developments: the creation of pastel portraits and the drawing of nude models from life.

Marietta Robusti, the daughter of Jacopo Robusti, il Tintoretto, is the earliest Venetian woman to whom drawings are attributed today. Although early biographers such as Raffaele Borghini and Carlo Ridolfi discussed Marietta, none mentions her drawings. A half-dozen drawings were ascribed to her by the Tietzes in their studies of Venetian drawings,[29] and two of these attributions are corroborated by early inscriptions. One inscribed drawing is a copy after the antique, a bust of Vitellius that was reproduced in several drawings from the Tintoretto workshop. The sheet is inscribed: "Questa testa si è di ma[no] de madona Marietta" (fig. 20).[30] Catherine Whistler notes that deliberate signatures are not common on Venetian drawings but suggests that this may be one of the exceptions.[31] This drawing, like several previously discussed examples by other women, is a copy after another artwork and hence does not elucidate the artist's creative capabilities. That limitation does not apply, however, to a study of *A Bishop Saint Baptizing Plague Victims* (fig. 21), a compositional drawing in a Tintorettesque style that is inscribed on the verso with "Ma.tta Tintoretta."[32] Although the drawing cannot currently be connected to a painting, this design for a dozen figures was likely a preparatory study for a narrative painting. Given the paucity of paintings conclusively ascribed to Marietta Robusti, however, the chances of connecting the drawing to an autographed picture seem unpromising. As with those of Agnese Dolci, Marietta Robusti's accomplishments have been eclipsed by those of her more famous father, complicating the identifications of both her paintings and her drawings (and the criteria for attributions, as for Agnese Dolci, are limited). For the Tietzes, the basis for ascribing *A Bishop Saint Baptizing Plague Victims* was the inscription, the Tintorettesque style, and the lower quality, which they believed suggested Marietta. Without more information from early writers, the challenges of establishing her oeuvre are daunting. The early inscriptions on two Tintorettesque drawings, however, provide precious early clues to her authorship, making these two drawings arguably the most convincing of any attributions to the artist today.

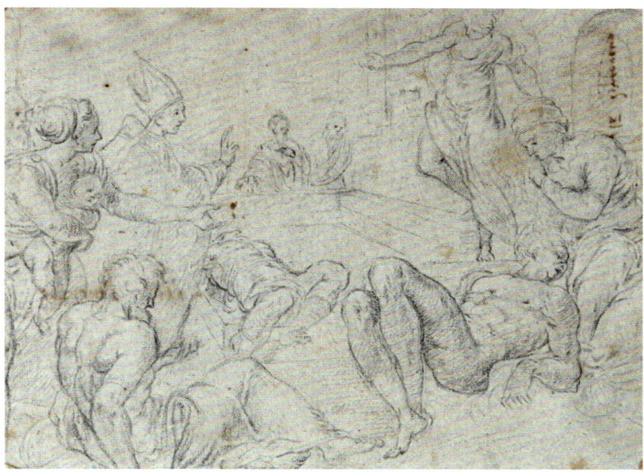

Fig. 21 • Marietta Robusti, known as Tintoretta, *A Bishop Saint Baptizing Plague Victims*, 16th century. Black chalk on blue paper, 19.5 × 27 cm. Museo Civico Ala Ponzone, Cremona, Archivio Fotografico Musei Civici Cremona, inv. no. B04.

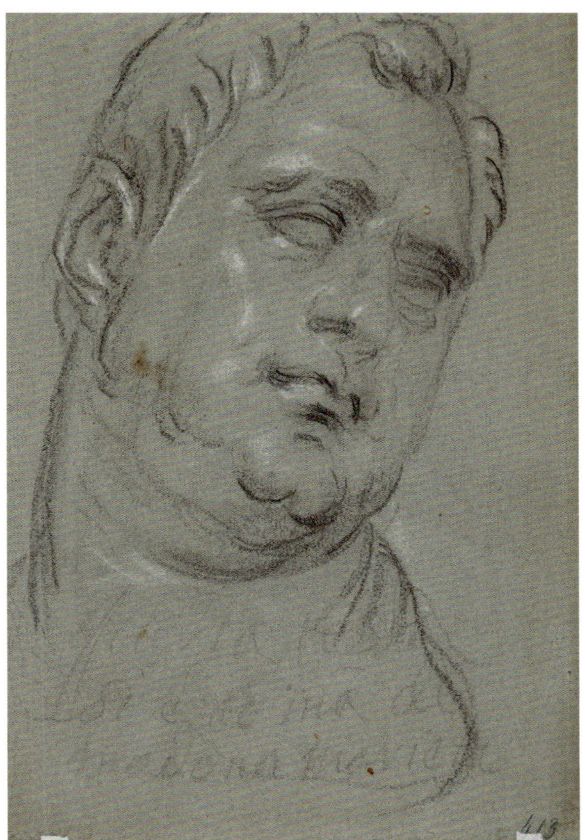

Fig. 20 • Marietta Robusti, known as Tintoretta, *Bust of Vitellius*, undated. Black chalk and white chalk on blue paper, 39 × 28 cm. Private collection. Photo © Christie's Images / Bridgeman Images.

Although twenty-nine women artists from seventeenth-century Venice are still recorded by name thanks to early Venetian writers, none can be securely credited with any drawings today, even though life drawing flourished in Venice during this period.[33] However, works on paper by two women artists from the eighteenth century are still known. Giulia Lama, a painter in Giovanni Battista Piazzetta's circle, must have been one of the most successful female artists of her day, as she produced impressive pictures for Venetian churches and also wrote poetry. Unfortunately, however, she attracted little attention from eighteenth-century Venetian writers on art, although one contemporary literary critic, Antonio Maria Zanetti, published her poetry and praised her as erudite in philosophy and valorous in painting.[34] Zanetti noted five of Lama's public paintings, only one of which is still traceable.[35] Recently, Cleo Malca Nisse discovered that another painting by the artist carries her signature.[36] Early writers entirely ignored Lama's drawings, even though such impressive works as her *Crucifixion* altarpiece for San Vitale, Venice, were clearly dependent upon drawing from life for their naturalistic, dramatically illuminated, and volumetric figures. The reconstruction of Lama's oeuvre, both drawn and painted, is otherwise based entirely on modern attributions. Rodolfo Pallucchini and Ugo Ruggeri began ascribing drawings to Lama in the 1960s and '70s, predicated partially on the connections of some sketches to Lama's few identifiable paintings.[37] To the best of my knowledge, none of these attributions is confirmed by a signature or early inscription, with one exception: a female nude in the British Museum that is not connected to a known painting.[38]

Despite this problematic situation, Ruggeri and Pallucchini ascribed almost two hundred drawings to Lama. Only a few are linked to paintings, and the large corpus of drawings seems to be the work of more than one hand. Although these attributions still await thorough study, if Lama was indeed responsible for the extraordinary series of twelve finished life studies now housed at Ca' Rezzonico in Venice,[39] she ranks as a brilliant and pivotal figure in the history of women's art. The group includes spectacular life studies of both female and male nudes (fig. 22; cat. nos. 40, 45–49), all breathtakingly naturalistic in recording anatomical details and the convincing play of light and shadow to model forms three-dimensionally. The highly finished character of these nudes suggests that they were made as collectible, finished works of art in their own right, a hypothesis that is reinforced by the similar size and finish of all twelve sheets in this collection. All of these drawings feature complex twists and turns of the torso, head, and appendages that emphasize muscular calves, buttocks, and backs. Although Lavinia Fontana created one study of a female nude that may have been drawn from life (fig. 23) and is the earliest known drawing of a female nude by a woman artist,[40] Lama's studies would be the first attributable drawings by an Italian woman artist to portray male nude models from life. Her authorship of these sheets challenges the long-standing and widespread assumption that women were not permitted to draw the male nude until well into the nineteenth century—though it has been documented recently that French women artists had already begun to draw from nude male models during the late eighteenth century. If she engaged in this practice, presumably in private studios rather than

Fig. 22 (left) • Giulia Lama, *Sketch of a man seen from behind, reclining*, first half of 18th century. Red chalk and white chalk on paper, 43 × 57 cm. Fondazione Musei Civici di Venezia, Gabinetto dei disegni e delle stampe, Ca' Rezzonico, Inv. Cl. III n. 6993.

Fig. 23 (right) • Lavinia Fontana, *Nude Andromeda*, c. 1613. Red chalk and black chalk on paper, dimensions unknown. Formerly Sotheby's, London, July 10, 2002, Lot 123, present location unknown.

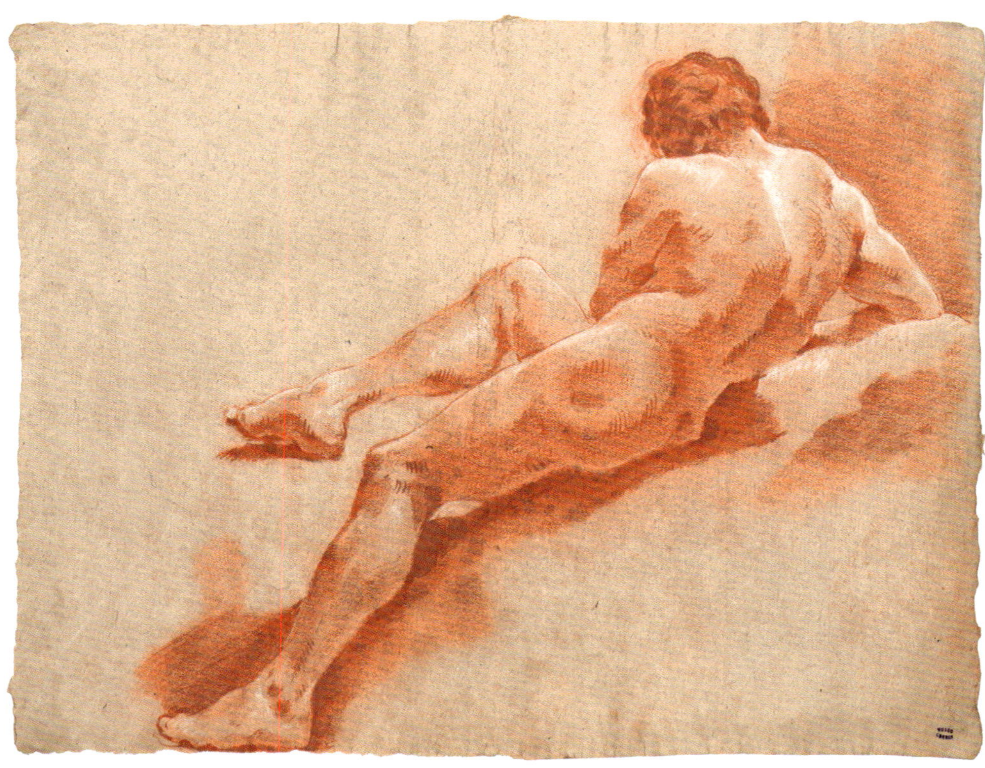

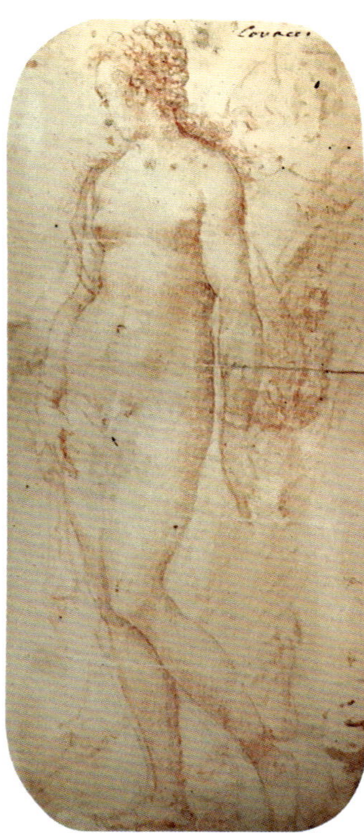

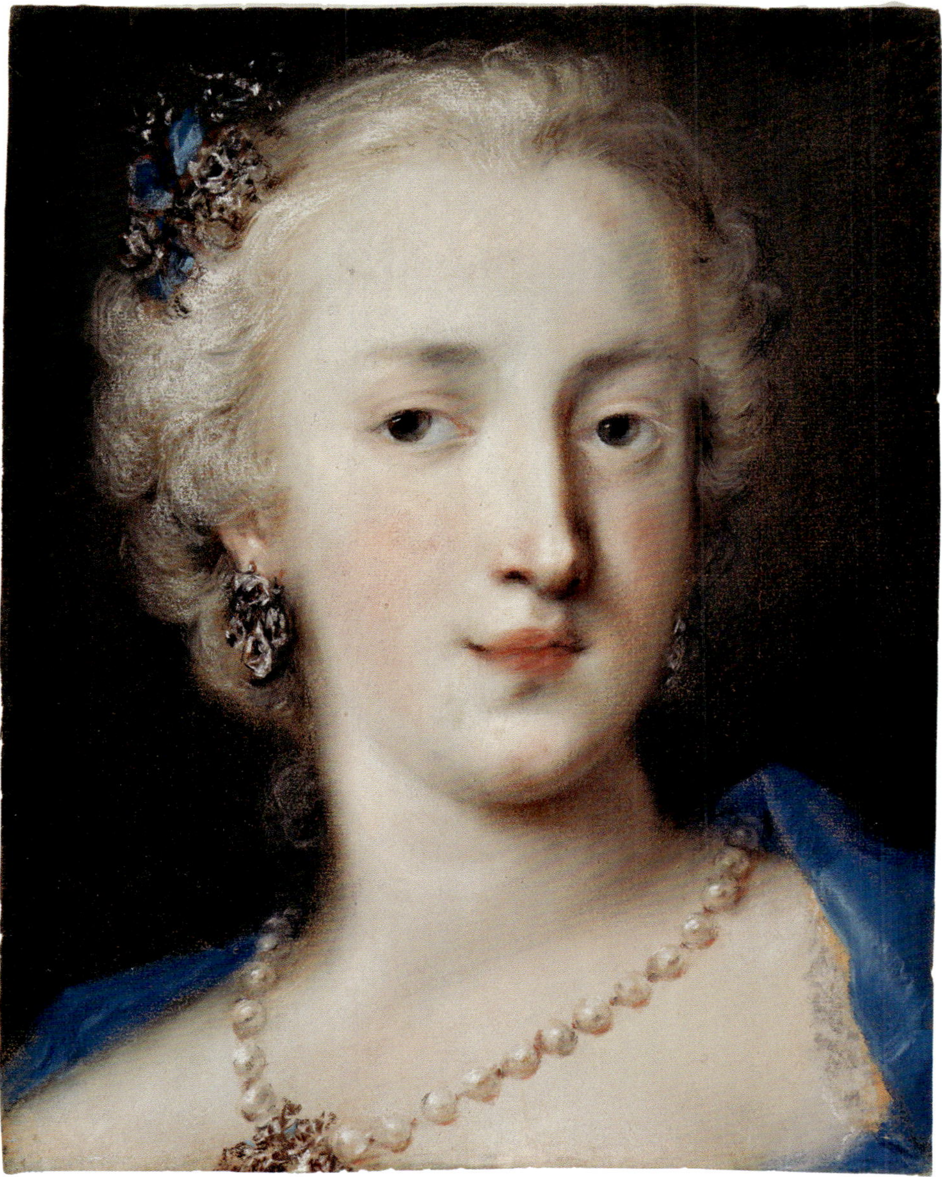

Fig. 24 • Rosalba Carriera, *Portrait of a Woman*, c. 1720s. Pastel on blue paper, 31 × 25 cm. Art Gallery of Ontario, Purchased as a gift from Mrs. Walter Gordon, 1995, 94/308. Photo: AGO.

in a public forum,[41] did other women artists likewise participate in this supposedly male-exclusive practice? Might their drawings be currently misattributed to male contemporaries? Such questions exemplify the many gaps in our current knowledge about women's drawings and drawing practices during the period. But whatever remains for us to learn, we are long overdue in examining and appreciating the accomplishments of this talented *disegnatrice* whose remarkable achievements were overlooked for centuries.

If Lama's accomplishments on paper have been overlooked for centuries and underappreciated, the same cannot be said for her compatriot Rosalba Carriera, whose brilliant contributions to pastel portraiture were celebrated during her lifetime and have been ever since.[42] These finished pastels (fig. 24; cat. no. 36) are more equivalent to paintings than to drawings, so I will discuss them only briefly. But it is important to the history of women's art on paper that Carriera was arguably the most famous European woman artist of the eighteenth century—an international celebrity whose works were widely sought after across Europe. She was admitted to three artists' academies, in Rome, Paris, and Bologna; in the latter case, she was the first female member,[43] establishing a precedent for the admission of numerous other women. Carriera's successes played a critical role in expanding the possibilities for women in the male-dominated artistic professions.

The few women who are still known in identifiable drawings, and the small number of sheets ascribed to most of them, pose significant challenges to understanding women's artistic practices in early modern Italy. Modern scholars have struggled with a lack of reliable information, sometimes offering unwarranted assumptions, such as presuming that women's drawings were less competently executed or that these artists worked only in certain genres or media. In addition, women's drawings were frequently misattributed to their male collaborators.

Given early biographers' usual inattention to women's drawings, their disinclination to credit women with skills in original invention, and the pervasive lack of interest in collecting most women's drawings, we have scant basis today for understanding women artists' accomplishments on paper. The principal exceptions to this pattern—by Lavinia Fontana, Giovanna Garzoni, Elisabetta Sirani, Rosalba Carriera, and Giulia Lama—suggest that other women also created drawings that we no longer recognize. Until we can recover more of women's accomplishments on paper, the issue will remain one of the most significant obstacles to appreciating the extraordinary accomplishments of early modern women artists in Italy.

Notes

1 Giorgio Vasari, *Le vite de' più eccellenti pittori, scultori e architetti*, vol. 4, pt. 1, ed. Paola Barocchi and Rosanna Bettarini (Florence: SPES, 1966), 403.

2 On the gendering of artistic invention, see Fredrika H. Jacobs, *Defining the Renaissance "Virtuosa": Women Artists and the Language of Art History and Criticism* (Cambridge: Cambridge University Press, 1997), 3–4, 37–40.

3 Mario Di Giampaolo, *Disegni emiliani: Galleria dell'Accademia di Venezia* (Milan: Electa, 1993), 39, cat. no. 17. A second drawing with a traditional attribution to de' Rossi is at Christ Church Oxford, as noted by Thalmann; she illustrates the *Design for a Sculptural Ornament*, in pen and brown ink (inventory number and measurements not given). To my eye, this drawing is of higher quality than the Accademia example but appears to be by a somewhat later hand than de' Rossi's. Jacqueline Thalmann, "Bolognese Women Artists at Christ Church Oxford: Drawings by Elisabetta Sirani and Properzia de' Rossi," *Art Herstory*, March 9, 2021, artherstory.net/bolognese-women-artists-at-christ-church-oxford/.

4 Vasari, *Le vite de' più eccellenti pittori, scultori e architetti*, 405.

5 Michael W. Cole, *Sofonisba's Lesson: A Renaissance Artist and Her Work* (Princeton, NJ: Princeton University Press, 2019), 179–80, cat. no. 28.

6 Cavalieri to Duke Cosimo I de' Medici, January 20, 1562, cited in Ilya Sandra Perlingieri, "Sofonisba Anguissola's Early Sketches," in *Woman's Art Journal* 9, no. 2 (1988–89): 12.

7 Cole, *Sofonisba's Lesson*, 159, 171, 179–80, cat. nos. 6, 20, 28.

8 Cole, *Sofonisba's Lesson*, 172–73, cat. no. 21.

9 Marzia Faietti, "'In the Shadow of the Friar': The Uffizi Drawings Attributed to Plautilla Nelli," Appendix I, in *Plautilla Nelli, 1523–1588: The Painter-Prioress of Renaissance Florence*, ed. Jonathan K. Nelson (Florence: Syracuse University in Florence, 2008), 99–117.

10 On Nelli's training, see Andrea Muzzi, "The Artistic Training and Savonarolan Ideas of Plautilla Nelli," in Nelson, *Plautilla Nelli*, 28–44.

11 David Scrase, *Italian Drawings at the Fitzwilliam Museum, Cambridge: Together with Spanish Drawings* (Cambridge: Cambridge University Press, 2011), 220–35, cat. no. 195; Lisa Goldenberg Stoppato, "Ritratto di una figlia di Carlo Dolci," in *Carlo Dolci, 1616–1687*, ed. Sandro Bellesi and Anna Bisceglia (Florence: Sillabe, 2015): 332–35, cat. no. 74.

12 Sheila Barker, ed., *"The Immensity of the Universe" in the Art of Giovanna Garzoni*, exh. cat. (Florence: Gallerie degli Uffizi, 2020), 132–33, cat. no. 7.

13 Sheila Barker and Anatole Tchikine, "Art in the Service of Botany: Giovanna Garzoni's *Piante varie* at Dumbarton Oaks," in Barker, *"The Immensity of the Universe,"* 36–45.

14 As noted by Francesca Baldassari, "Autoritratto," in *Artemisia Gentileschi e il suo tempo*, ed. Francesca Baldassari, exh. cat. (Rome: Palazzo Braschi, 2016), 128–29.

15 Three are in private collections: the head of a woman in black chalk on blue paper, inscribed "Domenichino" (unconvincingly termed a self-portrait of Gentileschi by Baldassari) in Baldassari, *Artemisia Gentileschi*, 128–29; a study of hands and an arm in red and white chalk on blue paper (as a preparatory study for Gentileschi's early *Lute Player* at the Wadsworth Atheneum Museum of Art in Hartford, Connecticut, in Sheila Barker, *Artemisia Gentileschi* [London: Lund Humphries; Los Angeles, Getty, 2022], 47); and the head of a youth in red chalk (sold by Sotheby's London, February 27, 1964, lot 73, present location unknown). According to the auction catalogue, the latter is inscribed on the verso in red chalk with "A. Gentileschi," but the work is currently untraceable; it is known today only in a black-and-white photograph of the recto. See the fascinating discussion of this sheet by Cristiana Romalli, "Due ritratti alla sangiugna: nuove proposte per i Gentileschi," in *Gli amici per Nicola Spinosa*, ed. Francesca Baldassari and Maria Confalone (Rome: Ugo Bozzi Editore, 2019), 43–46. Both the first and second drawings are apparently attributed to the artist based on their alleged connections to specific paintings, but neither connection is convincing. The fourth drawing attributed to Gentileschi is the *Head of a Woman* in red chalk in the Eskenazi Museum of Art, Indiana University, inv. no. 2019.186. I am grateful to Sheila Barker for her guidance on the vexed issue of Gentileschi's drawings.

16 See Babette Bohn, *Women Artists, Their Patrons, and Their Publics in Early Modern Bologna* (University Park, PA: Penn State University Press, 2021), 175–81.

17 Archivio di Stato di Bologna, fondo notarile, notaio Magnani, Giuseppe, Marchese Alessandro Facchinetti, May 19, 1685; Raffaella Morselli, *Collezioni e quadrerie nella Bologna del Seicento: Inventari, 1640–1707*, ed. Anna Cera Sones (Los Angeles: J. Paul Getty Trust, 1998), 221–27; Bohn, *Women Artists*, 239.

18 On the Morgan's album and its nineteen drawings ascribed to Fontana, see themorgan.org/search/site/Lavinia%20Fontana. Cardinal Leopoldo de' Medici also collected Fontana's drawings. In his list of Medici's drawings, Baldinucci noted ten by Fontana in 1673, adding another in 1675 ("Listra," in Anna Forlani Tempesti and Anna Maria Petrioli Tofani, *I grandi dsegni italiani degli Uffizi di Firenze* [Milan: Silvana, 1972], 79); Miriam Fileti Mazza, *Rapporti con il mercato Emiliano*, vol. 2, pt. 1, of *Archivio del collezionismo mediceo: Il Cardinal Leopoldo* (Milan: Ricciardi, 1993), 547–48. See Bohn, *Women Artists*, 175–78.

19 See Bohn, *Women Artists*, 176–77.

20 Fontana's *Birth of the Virgin* (SS. Trinità, Bologna, signed, c. 1590) was prepared in the Louvre drawing; Bohn, *Women Artists*, figs. 98–99.

21 Carlo Cesare Malvasia, *Felsina pittrice: Vite de' pittori bolognesi* (Bologna: Erede di Domenico Barbieri, 1678), 2:478–79; Carlo Cesare Malvasia, *Felsina pittrice: Vite de' pittori bolognesi*, ed. Giovanni Pietro Zanotti and Vicente Victoria (Bologna: Tipografia Guidi all'Ancora, 1841), 2:402, author's translation.

22 See Babette Bohn, "'Infinità di disegni': Le raccolte di disegni a Bologna tra Seicento e Settecento," in *Il Guercino: Atti del Convegno internazionale di studi in onore di Sir Denis Mahon*, ed. Daniele Benati (Milan: Fondazione di Piacenza e Vigevano, 2019), 145–54.

23 Bohn, *Women Artists*, 185–86.

24 Uffizi, inv. no. 15568 F., red chalk heightened with white, 132 × 109 mm. The work is inscribed by the artist on the verso with "L'Ill. Sig.re Co. Annibale Ranuzzi" and "Elisabetta Sirani fato di me"; Bohn, *Women Artists*, 191–93.

25 Otto Kurz, *Bolognese Drawings of the XVII & XVIII Centuries in the Collection of Her Majesty the Queen at Windsor Castle* (London: Phaidon, 1955), cat. no. 763 (as anonymous Bolognese), for a painting in the Pinacoteca Nazionale, Bologna, that is signed and dated 1660; Bohn, *Women Artists*, 191–92.

26 On Barbara Sirani's drawings, see Bohn, *Women Artists*, 201–02. For drawings previously accepted as Cantofoli's, see Babette Bohn, "Elisabetta Sirani and Drawing Practices in Early Modern Bologna," in *Master Drawings* 32 (2004): 228–29.

27 Oretti included four of her drawings, all probably preparatory studies for her prints, in his *Notizie de' professori del dissegno*. See Marcello Oretti, *Notizie de' professori del dissegno cioè de' pittori scultori ed architetti bolognesi e de' forestieri di sua scuola raccolta da Marcello Oretti bolognese*, n.d. (eighteenth century) (MS, Archiginnasio, Bologna), B.129:124 bis–125 bis; Bohn, *Women Artists*, 201–22. The example illustrated here, *Study for the Title Page of Lorenzo Legati's Museo Cospiano* (before 1677), is in red chalk, pen and brown ink, brown wash.

28 "Donato Creti" is inscribed in brown ink at lower left.

29 Hans Tietze and Erica Tietze-Conrat, *The Drawings of the Venetian Painters in the 15th and 16th Centuries* (1944; repr. New York: Hacker Art Books, 1979), 293; Erica Tietze-Conrat, "Marietta, fille du Tintoret, peintre de portraits," *Gazette des Beaux-Arts* 12 (1934): 258–61.

30 Christie's attributed another sketch in the same media on the recto, a portrait of Giuliano de' Medici after Michelangelo, simply to Tintoretto's workshop (black and white chalk on blue paper, 390 × 280 mm; sold by Christie's, online auction, March 23, 2021, lot 10, and now in a private collection); see also Tietze and Tietze-Conrat, *Drawings of the Venetian Painters*, 293.

31 Catherine Whistler, *Venice and Drawing, 1500–1800: Theory, Practice and Collecting* (New Haven, CT: Yale University Press, 2016), 181.

32 Tietze-Conrat, "Marietta, fille du Tintoret"; Tietze and Tietze-Conrat, *Drawings of the Venetian Painters*, 293, cat. no. 1760, in black chalk on blue paper, 195 × 270 mm; Museo Civico, Cremona, inv. no. 4. As Savage notes, Jacopo Tintoretto painted a picture of this subject (Museo Civico, Vicenza, c. 1550), but the two compositions are distinctly different. Alicia Jeane Savage, "Marietta Robusti, la Tintoretta: A Critical Discussion of a Venetian *Pittrice*" (MA thesis, Texas Christian University, 2018), 43–44.

33 Whistler observes that the drawings of most seventeenth-century Venetian artists have been underappreciated (*Venice and Drawing, 1500–1800*, xxx–xxxii).

34 Luisa Bergalli, *Componimenti poetici delle più illustri rimatrici d'ogni secolo, fino all'anno 1575* (Venice: Antonio Mora, 1726), 2:226–33, 283.

35 Antonio Maria Zanetti, *Descrizione di tutte le pubbliche pitture della città di Venezia e isole circonvicine: osia rinnovazione delle Riche Minere di Marco Boschini* (Venice: Presso Pietro Bassaglia, 1733), 76, 171, 189, 224, 258, 381.

36 As she revealed in a wonderful paper at the Renaissance Society of America conference in 2022.

37 See especially Ugo Ruggeri, "Giulia Lama disegnatrice," in *Critica d'Arte* 14, no. 87 (1967): 49–59; Rodolfo Pallucchini, "Per la conoscenza di Giulia Lama," in *Arte veneta* 24 (1970): 161–72; Ugo Ruggeri, *Dipinti e Disegni di Giulia Lama* (Bergamo: Monumenta Bergomensia, 1973); and, more recently, Daniele D'Anza and Alberto Craievich, *Giulia Lama Nudi* (Mirano/Venice: Editrice Eidos, 2018).

38 British Museum, inv. no. 1946,0713.99, in black chalk on blue paper, 205 × 189 mm, inscribed on a label attached to the mount: "Originalle di Giulia Lama / Scolara di piacetta." A.E. Popham, *Catalogue of Drawings in the Collection Formed by Sir Thomas Phillipps, Bart., F.R.S., now in the possession of his grandson, T. FitzRoy Phillipps Fenwick of Thirlestaine House, Cheltenham* (London, 1935), 147, cat. no. 1.

39 All but one of these were first published by Ruggeri, *Dipinti e Disegni di Giulia Lama*, in 1973. Pignatti explains the provenance of these sheets: all came from an album of thirty-one similarly sized, large life studies by several hands that were acquired by the Comune di Venezia in 1935. Terisio Pignatti, *Disegni antichi del Museo Correr di Venezia, IV: Guercino-Longhi* (Venice: Neri Pozza Editore, 1987), 44–51.

40 *Study of a Nude Andromeda*, current location unknown, in red chalk, Sotheby's London, July 10, 2022, lot 123, as "attributed to Lavinia Fontana;" c. 1613; Bohn, *Women Artists*, fig. 100.

41 Whistler argues that the practice of life drawing was far more prevalent in Venice than scholars have realized, beginning in the Cinquecento; she also discusses the many private "academies" that flourished there. Catherine Whistler, "Life Drawing in Venice from Titian to Tiepolo," in *Master Drawings* 42, no. 4 (2004): 370–96, 380–88; Whistler, *Venice and Drawing, 1500–1800*, 45–61.

42 On recent publications about Rosalba, see Neil Jeffares, "Pastels in the Pandemic," *Burlington Magazine* 164 (2022): 780–87.

43 Michelangelo L. Giumanini, "Catalogo degli accademici d'onore nell'Accademia Clementina (1710–1803)," in *Accademia Clementina: Atti e memorie* 38–39 (1998–99): 215.

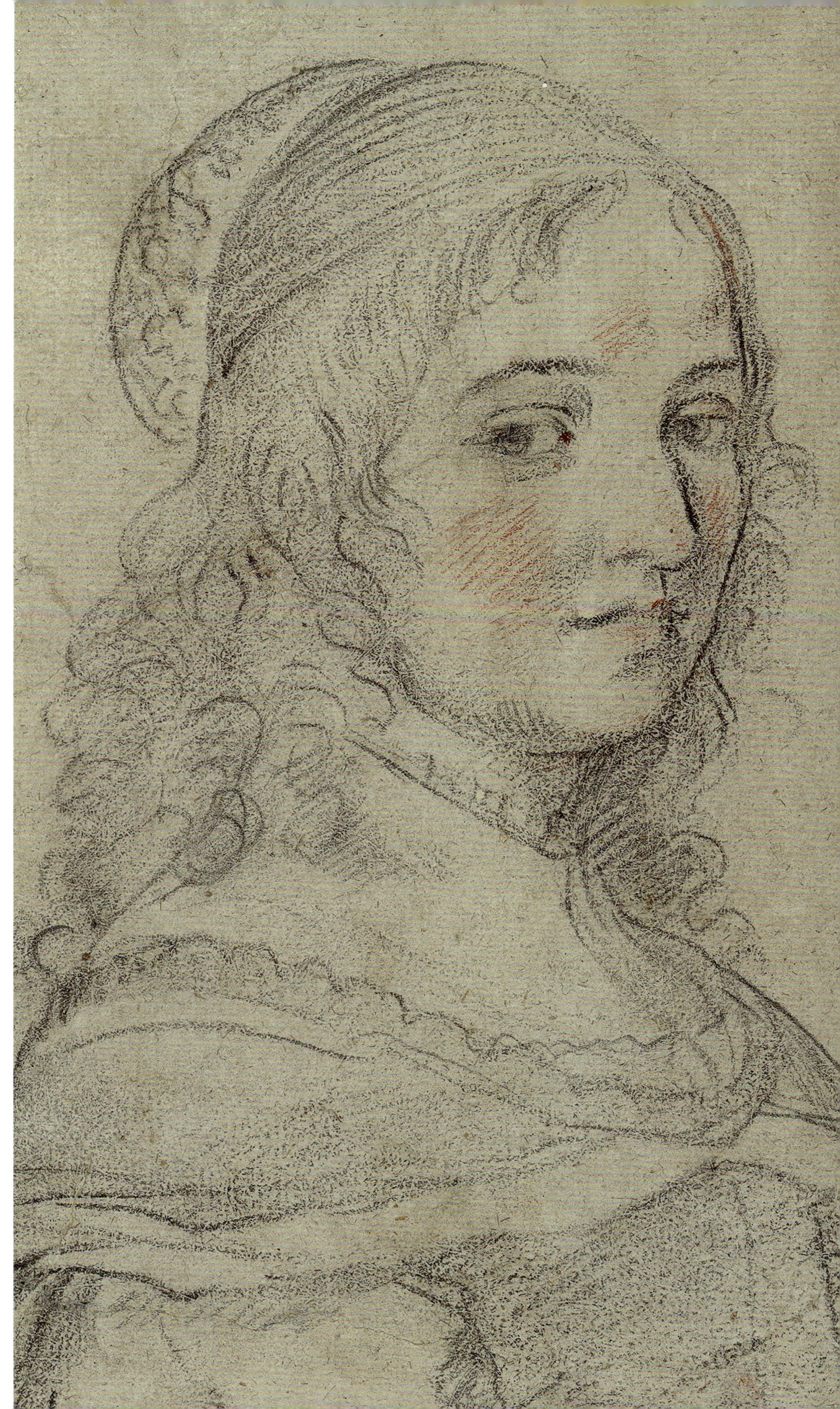

Detail (cat. no. 35; fig. 16) • Elisabetta Sirani, *Self-Portrait*, c. 1658. Black chalk, red chalk, and white chalk on paper, 22.9 × 15.4 cm. Purchased with the Diane A. Nixon, class of 1957, Fund, and the gift of the Almathea Charitable Foundation, Smith College Museum of Art, Northampton, Massachusetts, inv. no. SC 2020.7.1.

MULTIPLE CHALLENGES, OR THE CHALLENGE OF MULTIPLES

Early Modern Women as Creators of Prints

Madeleine C. Viljoen

Rowdy, grimy, and demanding, printmaking was not an enterprise in which early modern women engaged—at least, that is what an iconic image of a late-sixteenth-century engraving workshop by Giovanni Stradano would have us believe (fig. 1).[1] The image depicts a group of twelve men and three boys squeezed into a claustrophobically crowded workspace, absorbed in a series of independent but interconnected tasks. Young apprentices learn to draw, and men of varying ages incise, heat, ink, and imprint copper printing plates before finally hanging up the finished pages to dry.[2] Pictured in the *Nova Reperta*, a well-known publication dedicated to Renaissance inventions and discoveries, the print presents the act of engraving as an all-male preserve.[3] Thanks to widely shared conventions about how prints were inscribed, the identities of the individuals involved in their creation are well established—knowledge we owe in large part to the development of large *intaglio* workshops in mid-sixteenth-century Europe.[4] Print production had by this time instituted protocols that relied on collaboration to augment output

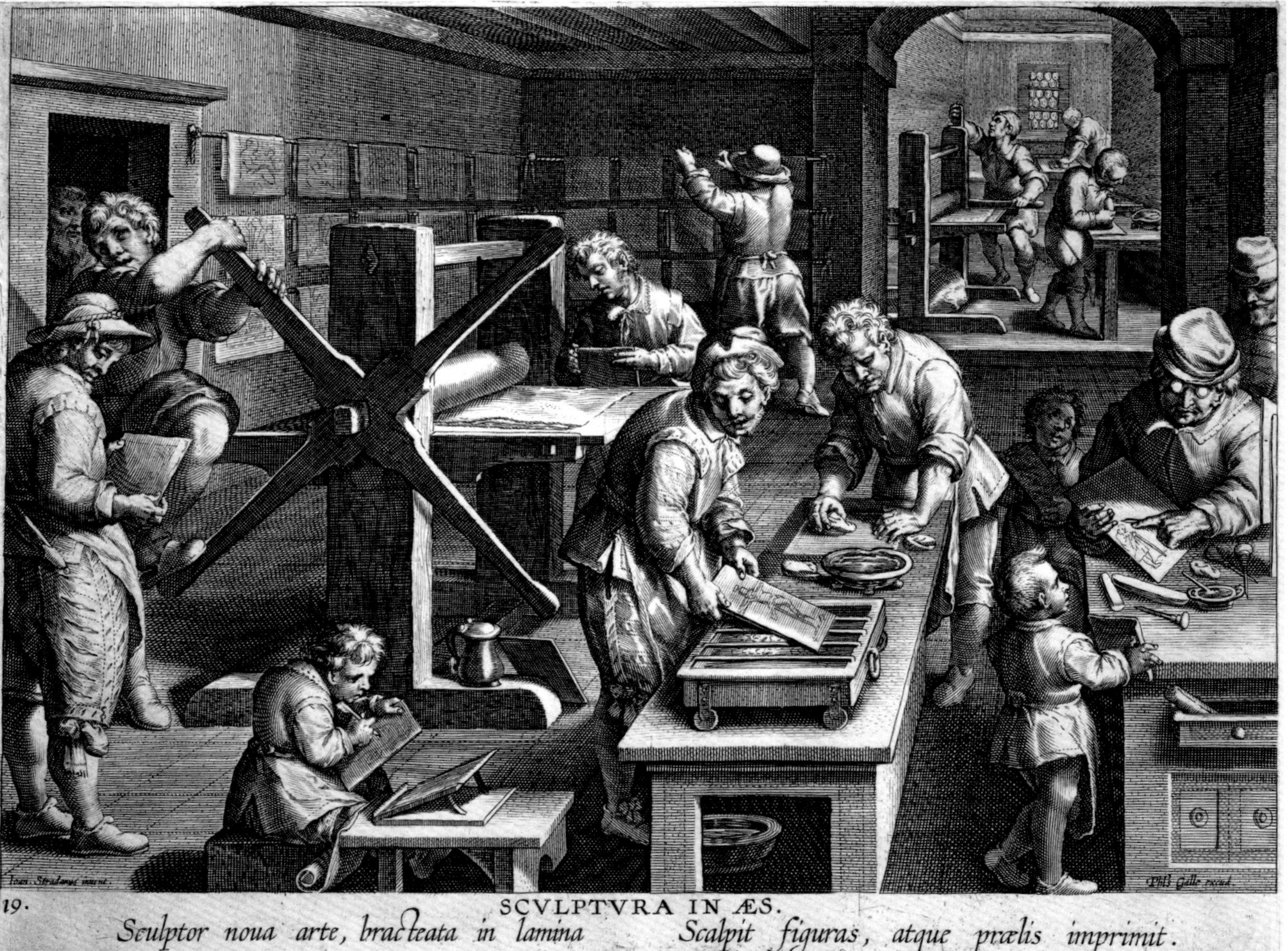

Fig. 1 • After Jan van der Straet (Giovanni Stradano, called Stradanus), *The Workshop of an Engraver* [*Sculptura in Aes*], plate 19, from the series *Nova Reperta*, c. 1600. Engraving, 20.2 × 27.1 cm. The Metropolitan Museum of Art, New York, Harris Brisbane Dick Fund, 1953, inv. no. 53.600.1823.

and financial reward, objectives that were largely accomplished by employing the talents of a variety of individuals—each performing a unique task and requiring appropriate credit. These generally included an inventor or designer, a printmaker, and a publisher, roles that are reflected in a range of Latin verbs, including *invenit* (invented), *disegnavit* (drew), and *pinxit* (painted); *fecit* (made), *sculpsit* (engraved, etched, or incised) or *caelavit* (incised); and *excudit* (published).[5] Commonly included along the bottom of the print, the terms—in conjunction with the name of the artist—offer clear proof that women in fact played an important role in the creation of early modern prints, even as their traditional duties and place within the private or domestic realm often put them at odds with fully committing themselves to the profession. In broad strokes, this essay aims to describe both the opportunities and the considerable challenges that early modern women faced when they chose to pick up the burin or etching needle and work in a medium of multiples.[6]

Family Business

The function of the print inscription was not merely to identify the print's creators, printers, and publishers. Active in her father's small family workshop, Diana Mantuana (c. 1547–1612)—the first woman known to sign her own engravings—was sensitive to the role the print inscription could play in crafting her identity and marketing her skills to prospective patrons and buyers.[7] Both entrepreneurial and remarkably self-possessed, she signed her prints "Diana Mantovana," "Diana Mantuana Civis Volaterana," or simply "Diana."[8] Just as often, though, she framed her work in relation to two central figures: her father, Giovanni Scultori, the person who enlisted her in the practice of making prints, and her husband, the architect Francesco da Volterra, both of whose careers she aimed to promote by circulating prints after their designs. These include, among others, an image of the *Descent from the Cross,* a work she signed "Giovanni Battista Mantovano engraver and inventor. His daughter Diana engraved (this)," and an engraving of an Ionic volute with egg and dart moulding, to which she added the following inscription: "This volute from an ancient capital of a Numidian stone column of a composite order, in St. Peter's in the Vatican, was drawn by Francesco da Volterra and Baptista Petra Santa for the common use of students of this art. Diana Mantuana, wife of the same Francesco [da Volterra], engraved [it] in Rome. 1576."[9] Employing the Latin terms *filia* (daughter) and *uxor* (wife) to describe her relationship to the prints' inventors, she signals the twin circumstances under which many if not most early modern female printmakers executed their work. Commonly recruited by their fathers to make prints, women regularly reproduced compositions or lent a hand to enterprises that belonged to men, a process that privileged the heroic male act of invention and invariably relegated their work to the lesser status of copy. By the same token, the act of signing their own prints gave female printmakers unprecedented visibility, reflecting their roles as active participants in early modern print culture.[10]

Mundane economic considerations are in many ways at the heart of early modern women's employment in the production of prints. If the daughters of established printmakers and publishers showed any aptitude for art, they were taught to use the burin or etching needle, affording them a chance to contribute, usually alongside male siblings, to the family business of making prints. The Dutch publisher and scion of a dynasty of engravers, Crispin de Passe, for example, had several children, four of whom became professional printmakers, including one girl, Magdalena van de Passe (1600–1638).[11] Just fourteen years old when she signed two prints from *The Seven Wonders of the World* series (figs. 2 & 3), van de Passe exemplified the tender age at which girls could be drafted to support the family's bottom line.[12] As in the case of Mantuana, van de Passe regularly made prints after her father's designs, as well as after the prolific painter Maarten de Vos, to whom she was distantly related, suggesting the role that printmaking

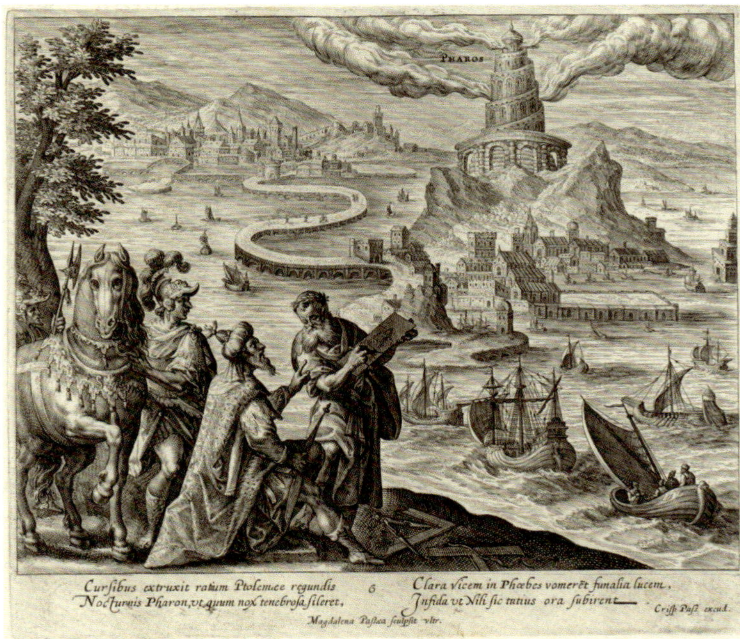

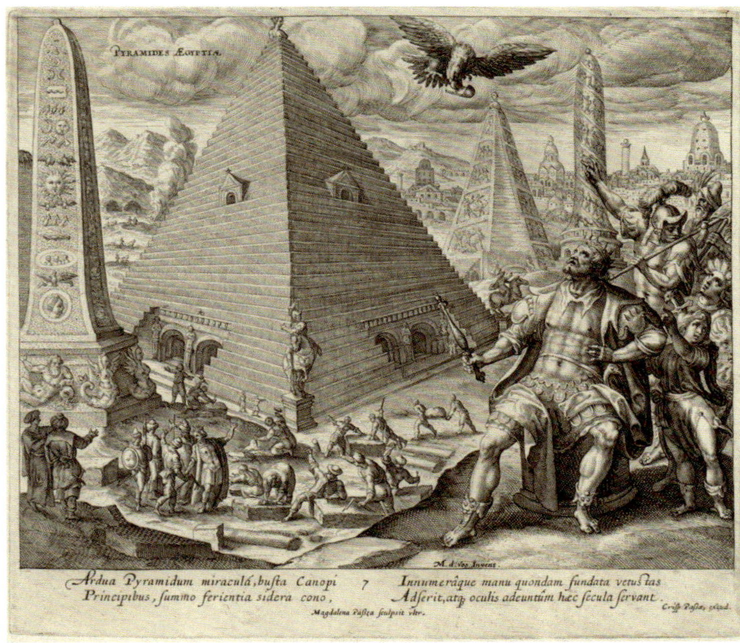

Fig. 2 (left) · Magdalena van de Passe, after Maarten de Vos, *The Lighthouse of Alexandria*, from the series *The Seven Wonders of the World*, 1614. Engraving, sheet: 24.1 × 28.6 cm; plate: 21.7 × 25.5 cm; image: 19.1 × 25 cm. Baltimore Museum of Art: Garrett Collection, 1946.112.4036. Photo: Mitro Hood.

Fig. 3 (right) · Magdalena van de Passe, after Maarten de Vos, *The Pyramids of Egypt*, from the series *The Seven Wonders of the World*, 1614. Engraving, sheet: 24.3 × 28.5 cm; plate: 21.2 × 25 cm; image: 18.7 × 24.3 cm. Baltimore Museum of Art: Garrett Collection, 1946.112.4037. Photo: Mitro Hood.

played in supporting the fiscal concerns of larger familial artistic networks.[13] By focusing on landscape subjects, including reproductions of works by Paul Bril, Roelandt Savery, and Adam Willaerts, she developed her own creative niche, actively setting herself apart within the parameters of the van de Passe workshop.[14] Upon marrying at age thirty-three or thirty-four, she ceased making prints altogether—her new role in her husband's household appearing to have precluded her continued participation in the home of her father. Given the care she gave to crafting works that could identify her, the abruptness with which her activities as an engraver came to an end is startling—pointing to the possibility that, for many early modern women, the task of making prints had to be treated more as a part-time occupation than as a lifetime calling.

The career of another seventeenth-century artist, Susanne Maria von Sandrart (1658–1716), follows a similar trajectory, suggesting that van de Passe's reasons for leaving the profession were not an anomaly and that for many early modern women, printmaking, while lucrative, was secondary to other socially dictated, gender-normative roles.[15] The daughter of Jacob von Sandrart, Susanne Maria began making prints at an early age but stopped in 1683 when she married her first husband, artist Johann Paul Auer.[16] When he died in 1687, just four years later, she once again returned to printmaking, creating some of her best-known prints at this time, including her impressive set of prints after Jean le Pautre's *Vases à la moderne* (fig. 4). A book that von Sandrart compiled later in life for her second husband contains the following statement, shedding light on the circumstances for her momentous career choices:

> I, Susanna Maria, daughter of deceased Jacob von Sandrart, having been taught by my blessed mother in my tender youth about household and other work, I also was struck with a desire to draw and in my free time, I made the etchings in this book. When my father saw that I had a natural inclination for this art, he arranged other works and gave me copper to etch, eventually also ones he could use in his print business. This work was interrupted when in 1683 I was married to my now deceased husband Johann Paul Auer. After his death soon after the marriage, I was allowed to assist my father and brother and to feed myself without becoming a burden, making the

prints by own hand in this book, and most of them during my widowhood, until divine providence and upon the advice of my parents I was married again in 1695 to Wolfgang Moritz Endter, also a widow, on account of whose large household I had to cease this work entirely.[17]

Susanne Maria's disarmingly frank account reflects how women's activities responded to their status not merely as daughters and wives but also—when their husbands died—as widows. More specifically, it presents a picture of the monetary considerations that shaped when and why women would make prints; it also helps explain why less is known about the careers of female printmakers than about their male counterparts. For von Sandrart, while engraving was a means to contribute to the economy of her father before she married, it also provided her financial independence after she became widowed. As in the case of van de Passe, matrimony brought von Sandrart's activities as a printmaker to a grinding halt, resulting in a smaller print oeuvre and diminished opportunities for achieving the sorts of renown with which the careers of men were regularly crowned.

Both of these artists' circumstances notwithstanding, not all women were compelled to give up printmaking when they wed. After marrying her father's pupil Johann Ulrich Kraus, Johanna Sibylla Küsel (c. 1650–1717) played a critical part in making prints under the auspices of the publishing business that Kraus took over from her father, Augsburg printmaker Melchior Küsel, shortly after his death.[18] Her output includes the impressive folio-size republication of Sébastien Le Clerc's 1655 prints after Charles Le Brun's *Tapisseries du Roy: ou sont representez les quatre elemens et les quatre saisons* [*Tapestries of the four elements and four seasons*] (fig. 5; cat. no. 220). As representations of the newly established royal textile manufacture, the prints reproduce Le Clerc's etchings; now rendered in reverse, however, the images have the added virtue of appearing in the correct orientation. In the preface to the volume, Kraus foregrounds both Küsel's talents and her marital and filial status, stating: "In which my dearest wife Johanna Sibylla Kraus, Mister Melchior Küsel's widely famed daughter in art and engraving, whose beautiful artistic talent (to her credit not to mention fame) can mostly be seen in Augsburg, has applied her subtle hand."[19] In this instance, her value as a printmaker within her husband's new enterprise appears not only to have outweighed a wife's customary obligations to the domestic realm but even to have been a ploy to market the volume and

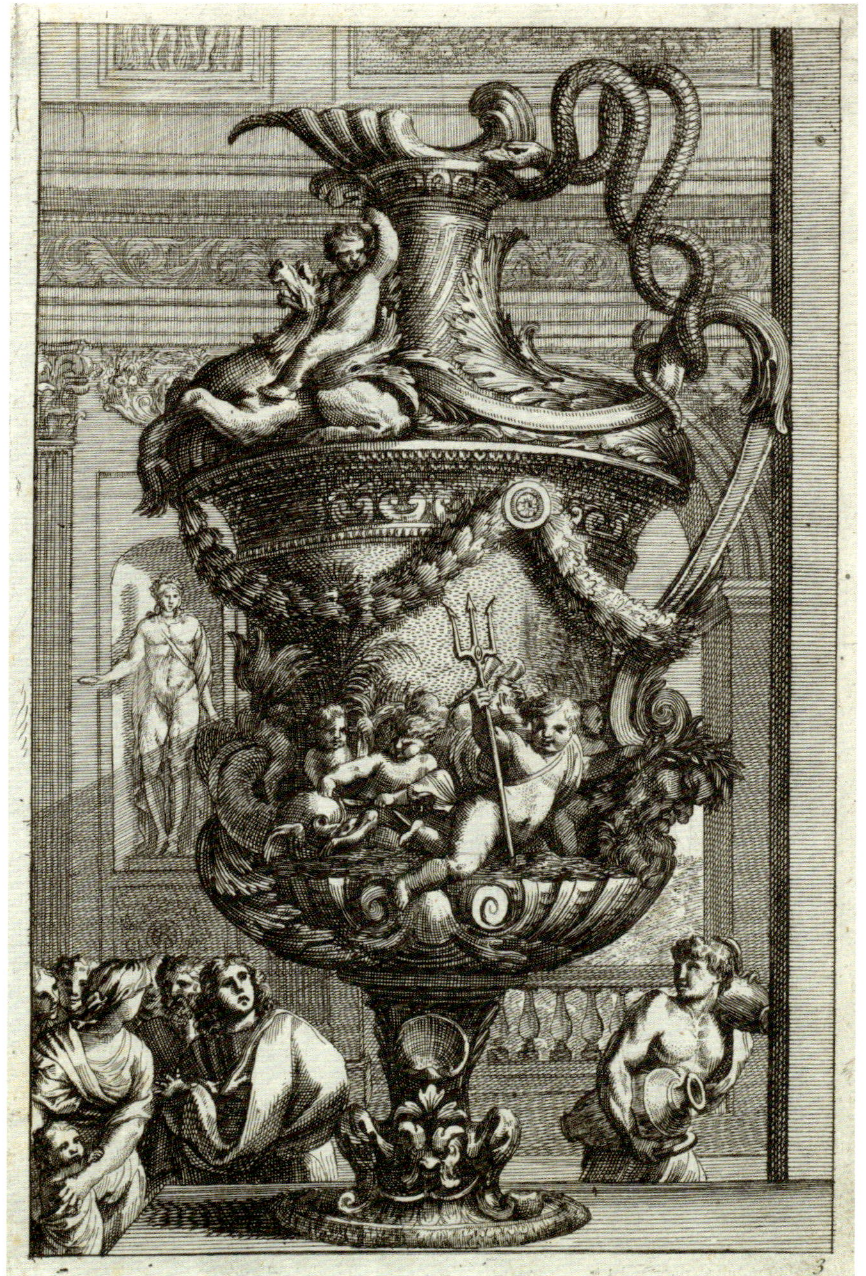

Fig. 4 • Susanne Maria von Sandrart, after Jean Le Pautre, *Large Vase with a Putto Holding a Triton*, from the series *Vases à la moderne*, c. 1678. Engraving and etching, sheet: 32 × 29.5 cm; plate: 22.6 × 15.2 cm. Baltimore Museum of Art: Purchased as a gift in Honour of Leonard and Barbara Scherlis' Fiftieth Wedding Anniversary, 2002.563.3. Photo: Mitro Hood.

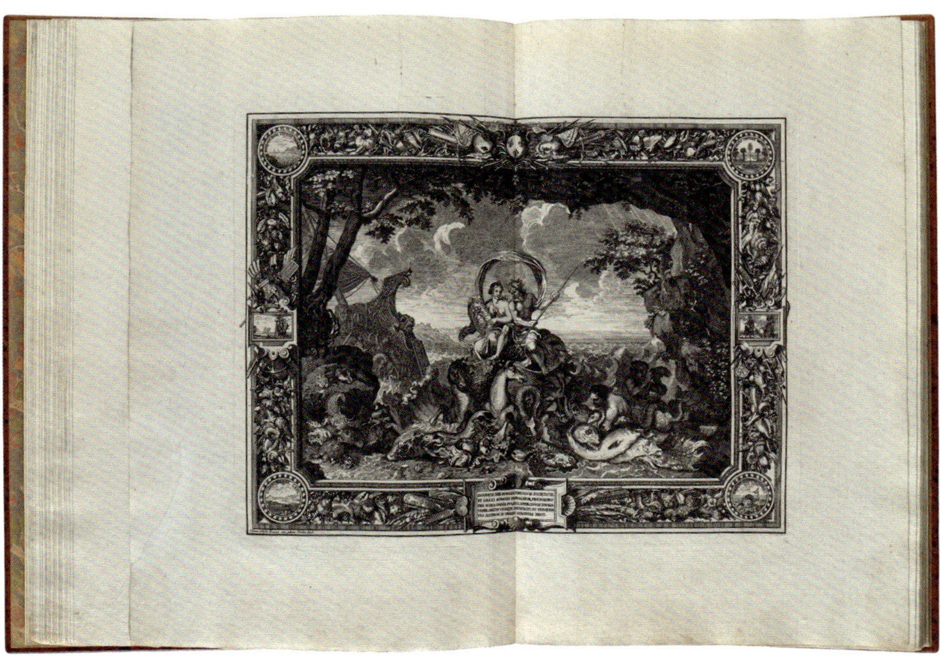

Fig. 5 · Johanna Sibylla Küsel and Johann Ulrich Kraus, after Sébastien Le Clerc the elder, *Tapisseries du Roy : ou sont representez les quatre elemens et les quatre saisons : avec les devises qui les accompagnent et leur explication* [*Tapestries of the four elements and four seasons*], 1687. Bound volume of engravings, book (closed): 38.5 × 28.5 × 2.6 cm; book (open, spread): 37.5 × 47 cm; image: 24.9 × 32.8 cm. Art Gallery of Ontario, E.P. Taylor Library & Archives, Purchase funds generously donated by Janet E. Dewan in honour of Randall Speller and by the Janet E. Hutchison Foundation (2018), R.B.F. 746.3944 L49 K86. Photo: Craig Boyko, AGO.

Opening illustrated:

The Element of Water

buoy sales. By engaging his wife in the workshop that he had taken over from her father, and by promoting her extraordinary gifts as an engraver, Kraus could reasonably expect to consolidate and capitalize upon his father-in-law's prior success—a plan that required it to be known that Johanna Sibylla Kraus was Melchior Küsel's offspring. The Küsel name was synonymous with prestige: like her father, Johanna Sibylla descended from an illustrious line of printmakers.[20]

Nuns may seem a category apart, but upon taking their vows, they accepted Christ as their celestial spouse and were expected to contribute their labour toward supporting their religious communities, thus mirroring aspects of how wives were expected to participate in the finances of their husband's households.[21] As early as the fifteenth century, holy sisters in Belgium, Germany, and Italy were making prints—largely woodcuts and metal-cut prints designed for pilgrims or visitors.[22] Among the best known of the later generation of printmaker-nuns was Suor Isabella Piccini (1644–1734; figs. 6 & 7; cat. no. 5). Born in Venice as Elisabetta Piccini, she was instructed in the art of making prints by her father, the etcher and engraver Giacomo Piccini. In 1666, she entered the Franciscan order, joining the Convent of Santa Croce in Venice, where she changed her name from Elisabetta to Isabella. As a nun, she continued her activities as a printmaker, prominently signing her works "Suor Isabella da Santa Croce," leaving no doubt as to where and by whom her prints were made. She gave the proceeds of her work, around two hundred ducats, to her convent.[23] Similarly, Suor Marietta (active 1478) from the Convent of San Jacopo di Ripoli, who was fluent in Latin, worked for pay as a typesetter and is among the first women known to have been directly involved in the creation of printed books in Florence (fig. 8; cat. no. 1).[24] For this task, she received wages that went to support her religious community. Noteworthy, in both instances, is the role of women in issuing works that were not exclusively devotional—suggesting that the business of making prints trumped sensitivities around the secularity of their pursuits.

Paths to Independence

Marriages between printmakers were not just common but even—by combining skill sets within the family—desirable.[25] They include, among others, Louise Magdelaine (1686–1767) and Marie-Anne Horthemels (1682–1727), sisters who married the well-known printmakers Charles Nicolas Cochin the Elder and Nicolas-Henri Tardieu respectively. Louise Magdelaine actively cultivated the career of her son, printmaker Charles Nicolas Cochin the Younger, pointing to the role female printmakers could play in ensuring the art they shared with their husbands was handed down to the next generation and that the family line of business was continued.[26] Where some women printmakers, like Küsel, chose to sign their work with their married names, Marie-Anne signed her works exclusively with her maiden name, and Louise Magdelaine did so most of the time, only on rare occasions signing her works "Magd. Horthemels Sponsa C. Cochin" or "Magdelaine Cochin." Similarly, Catherine Cousinet (born 1726), who married the reproductive printmaker Louis Simon Lempereur, consistently signed her works with her maiden name. The choice, which signals a surprising

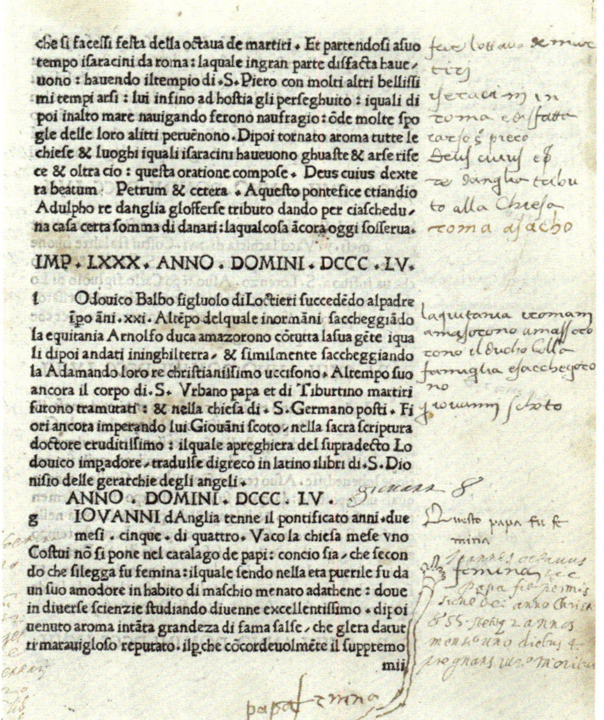
che ſi faceſſi feſta della octaua de martiri. Et partendoſi aſuo tempo iſaracini da roma: laquale ingran parte diſſacta haueuono: hauendo iltempio di. S. Piero con molti altri belliſſimi tempi arſi: lui infino ad hoſtia gli perſeghuito: iquali dipoi inalto mare nauigando ferono naufragio: ōde molte ſpogle delle loro alitti peruēnono. Dipoi tornato aroma tutte le chieſe & luoghi iquali iſaracini haueuono ghuaſte & arſe riſece & oltra cio: queſta oratione compoſe. Deus cuius dextera beatum Petrum & cetera. Aqueſto pontefice etiandio Adulpho re danglia glofferſe tributo dando per ciaſchedu-na caſa certa ſomma di danari: laqualcoſa ācora oggi ſoſſerua.

IMP. LXXX. ANNO. DOMINI. DCCC. LV.

1 Odouico Balbo figluolo di Lottieri ſuccedēdo alpadre īpo āni. xxi. Altēpo delquale inormāni ſaccheggiādo la equitania Arnolfo duca amazorono cōtutta laſua gēte iquali dipoi andati ininghilterra, & ſimilmente ſaccheggiando la Adamando loro re chriſtianiſſimo uccisono. Altempo ſuo ancora il corpo di. S. Vrbano papa et di Tiburtino martiri furono tramutati: & nella chieſa di. S. Germano poſti. Fiori ancora imperando lui Giouāni ſcoto, nella ſacra ſcriptura doctore eruditiſſimo: ilquale apreghiera del ſupradecto Lodouico impadore, tradulſe digreco in latino ilibri di. S. Dioniſio delle gerarchie degli angeli.

ANNO. DOMINI. DCCC. LV.

g IOVANNI dAnglia tenne il pontificato anni. due meſi. cinque. di quattro. Vaco la chieſa meſe vno Coſtui nō ſi pone nel catalago de papi: concio ſia, che ſecondo che ſilegga fu femina: ilquale ſendo nella eta puerile fu da un ſuo amodore in habito di maſchio menato adathene: doue in diuerſe ſcienzie ſtudiando diuenne excellentiſſimo. dipoi uenuto aroma intāta grandeza di fama ſalſe, che glera datutti marauigloſo reputato. ilpche cōcordeuolmēte il ſuppremo mii

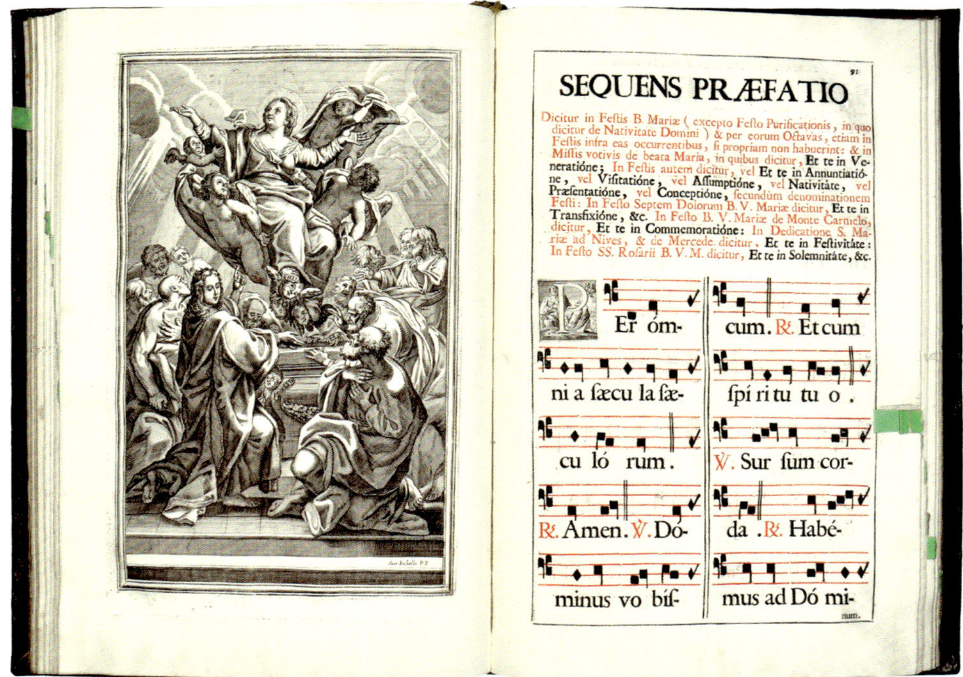
SEQUENS PRÆFATIO 91

Dicitur in Feſtis B. Mariæ (excepto Feſto Purificationis, in quo dicitur de Nativitate Domini) & per eorum Octavas, etiam in Feſtis infra eas occurrentibus, ſi propriam non habuerint: & in Miſſis votivis de beata Maria, in quibus dicitur, Et te in Veneratióne; In Feſtis autem dicitur, vel Et te in Annuntiatióne, vel Viſitatióne, vel Aſſumptióne, vel Nativitáte, vel Præſentatióne, vel Conceptióne, ſecundùm denominationem Feſti: In Feſto Septem Dolorum B. V. Mariæ dicitur, Et te in Transfixióne, &c. In Feſto B. V. Mariæ de Monte Carmelo, dicitur, Et te in Commemoratióne: In Dedicatione S. Mariæ ad Nives, & de Mercede dicitur, Et te in Feſtivitáte: In Feſto SS. Roſarii B. V. M. dicitur, Et te in Solemnitáte, &c.

PEr óm- ni a ſæcu la ſæ- cu ló rum. ℟. Amen. ℣. Dó- minus vo biſ- cum. ℟. Et cum ſpí ri tu tu o. ℣. Sur ſum cor- da. ℟. Habé- mus ad Dó mi- num.

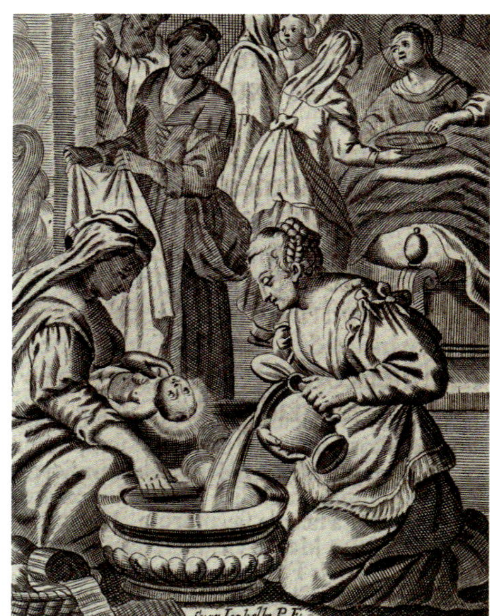

Fig. 6 (above, right) · Elisabetta (Isabella) Piccini, *Assumption of the Virgin* in *Canon Missae ad usum episcoporum, ac praelatorium solemniter vel private celebrantium*, 1735. Printed volume, 43 × 29 × 3 cm. Bridwell Library Special Collections, Southern Methodist University, BRB1254 Oversize.

Fig. 7 (below, right) · Detail: Elisabetta (Isabella) Piccini, *Nativity of the Virgin Mary* in *Officium B. Mariae Virginis: S. Pii C. Pontificis max. jussu editum, et ab. Urbano VIII...* [*Engraved illustrations for the Offices of the Virgin Mary*], Venice, 1727. Bound volume of engravings, page: 20 × 10 cm. Harvard University, Houghton Library, Gift of Philip Hofer, TYP 725.27.262.

Fig. 8 (left) · Detail: Nuns of the Convent of San Jacopo di Ripoli (printer & publisher), Pseudo-Petrarch's *Incominciano Le uite de pontefici et imperadori Romani* [*The Early Stories of the Popes and Roman Emperors*], vol. 2, Florence, 1478. Printed handset type text, 28.4 × 21.7 × 2.5 cm. Lisa Unger Baskin Collection, David M. Rubenstein Rare Book & Manuscript Library, Duke University, BX953 .V584 1478 8vo c.2.

level of autonomy, was also practical: by using their maiden names, women avoided having their work mixed up with that of their printmaker husbands.

The hazards of setting up shop with a spouse and the attendant confusion around the identities of the artists involved are illustrated by the career of Maria Catharina Prestel (1747–1794).[27] A gifted artist, she led a strikingly independent and even liberated life, even as important aspects of it were overshadowed by her husband, painter and printmaker Johann Gottlieb Prestel. Born to a well-to-do merchant family in Nuremberg, Prestel learned to draw at the age of thirteen. In 1769, she began formal instruction in drawing and painting with Johann Gottlieb, and three years later they were married.[28] Together they set up a printmaking practice in Nuremberg, aiming to create a market for high-quality etchings and aquatints after well-known paintings and drawings. Particularly celebrated are the prints they produced of the so-called "Praunsche Kabinett," a famed collection of drawings owned by Paulus Praun.[29] Signed with the Latinate version of Johann Gottlieb's name, "J. T. Prestel sc." [Joseph Theophilus Prestel *sculpsit*], an image from the famous suite *Truth Subduing Envy* (fig. 9; cat. no. 149), after a drawing by Jacopo (or Giacomo) Ligozzi, presents itself as the work of Prestel's husband, yet has been recognized as the work of her own hand.[30] A technical tour de force, the print is executed using two plates, one printed in chocolate brown and a second in ochre, then enhanced with powdered gold

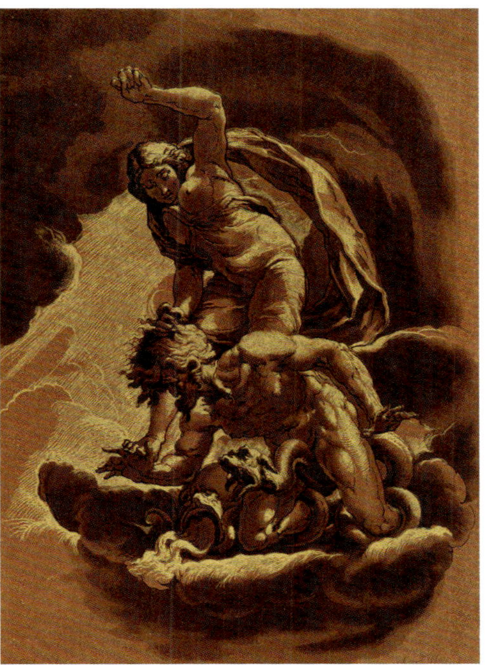

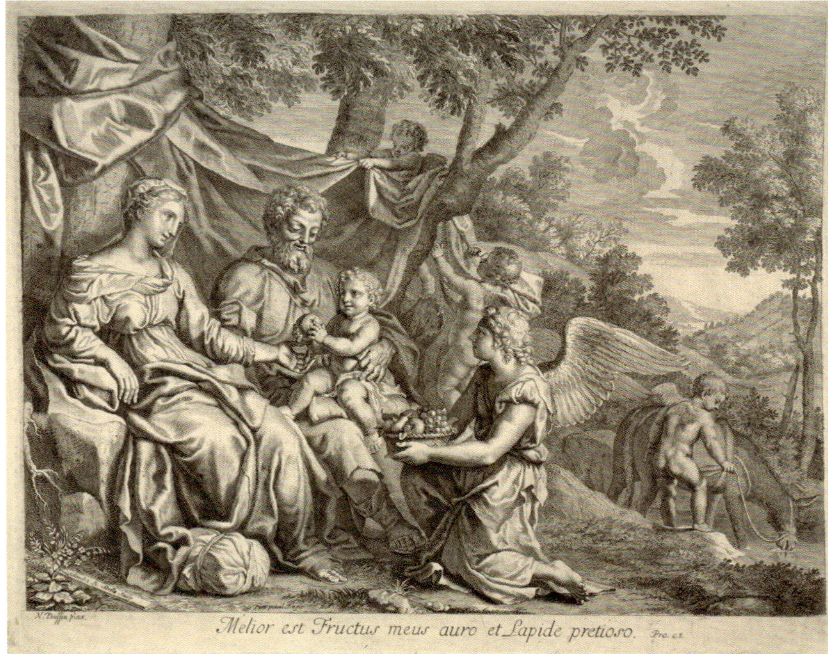

Fig. 9 (left) · Maria Catharina Prestel, after Jacopo Ligozzi, *Truth Subduing Envy*, 1781. Colour etching and aquatint, sheet (trimmed within platemark): 30.7 × 22.8 cm. Baltimore Museum of Art: Garrett Collection, 1984.81.3742. Photo: Mitro Hood.

Fig. 10 (right) · Claudine Bouzonnet Stella, after Jacques Stella, *The Holy Family in a Landscape with a Kneeling Angel Offering a Basket of Fruit*, undated. Engraving, sheet: 35.9 × 44.9 cm; plate: 34.4 × 43.4 cm; image: 31.9 × 42.9 cm. Baltimore Museum of Art: Garrett Collection, 1946.112.13750. Photo: Mitro Hood.

leaf, possibly in emulation of contemporary French prints that were trendy during this period.[31] Neither the business nor the marriage was a success, however, forcing the pair to first move to Frankfurt and then to declare bankruptcy. In 1785, Prestel finally took the highly unusual step of leaving her husband.[32] Ambitious and capable, she set out on her own a year later, establishing herself as a printmaker in London, but this time without Johann Gottlieb at her side (or to misleadingly claim that works she created were made by him). Calling herself "Mary Catherine" but still using the Prestel name, she worked primarily for the publisher John Boydell, achieving a level of success that allowed her to provide for herself and four children.[33]

If women could lend their skills to support printing enterprises directed by men, it should come as no surprise that under certain conditions they could also take over the management of an engraving or book publishing shop. Drafted into the profession of making prints, Claudine Bouzonnet Stella (1636–1697) and her sisters, Antoinette (1641–1676) and Françoise (1638–1691), moved from Lyon to Paris to reside with their uncle, the artist Jacques Stella, at the Louvre, a royal building that then housed the apartments and studios of the great artists of the day. Jacques, who was named painter to the king, had conceived the idea of establishing a family print workshop to reproduce prints after his paintings, and for this he required a team of able assistants. The girls' father, Étienne Bouzonnet, a goldsmith by profession, likely introduced them to the art of engraving, while Jacques tutored them in etching.[34] Claudine, the most talented of the trio, was not only an accomplished printmaker—praised for her ability to capture the cerebral brand of classicism associated with Nicolas Poussin, a close friend of her uncle—but also a painter.[35] Among the prints she created is a striking portrait of her uncle, titled *Jacques Stella Eques et Pictor Regius* [*Jacques Stella Knight and Painter to the King*], exemplifying the role prints played in projecting Stella's social and artistic standing. After he died in 1657, Claudine was granted exclusive rights by the king to publish prints after Stella's designs, giving her command of the family printmaking workshop (fig. 10). Her sizable will provides ample evidence of the considerable wealth she accumulated during her lifetime; included in the extensive inventory of her possessions are high-value items, including jewellery, paintings, and money.[36]

Widowhood, we have seen, could leave early modern women in straitened circumstances. When von Sandrart's husband died, von Sandrart chose to return to her former work within her father's shop in

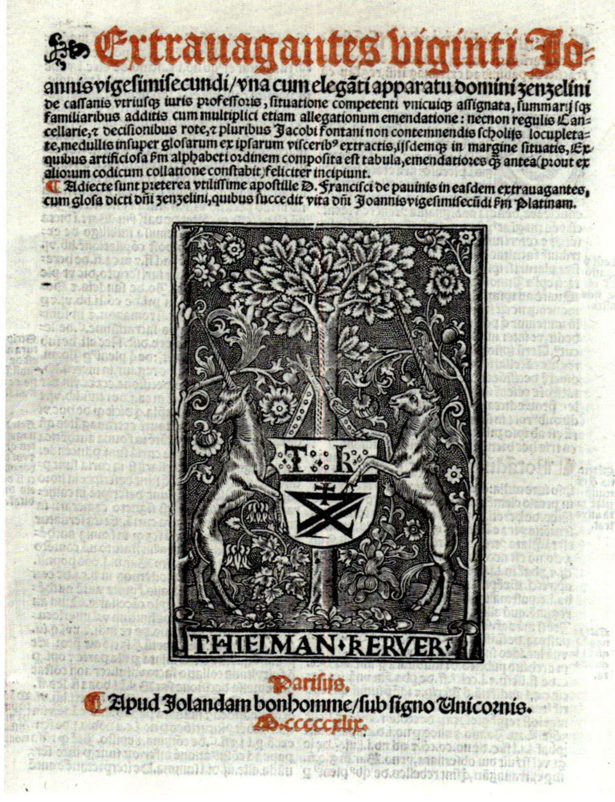

Extrauagantes viginti Joannis vigesimisecundi/vna cum elegāti apparatu domini zenzelini de cassanis vtriusqꝫ iuris professoris, situatione competenti vnicuiqꝫ assignata, summarijs qꝫ familiaribus additis cum multiplici etiam allegationum emendatione: necnon regulis Cancellarie, ⁊ decisionibus rote, ⁊ pluribus Jacobi fontani non contemnendis scholijs locupletate, medullis insuper glosarum ex ipsarum viscerib⁹ extractis, ijsdemqꝫ in margine situatis, Ex quibus artificiosa ſm alphabeti ordinem composita est tabula, emendatiores ꝙ antea (prout ex aliorum codicum collatione constabit) feliciter incipiunt.

¶ Adiecte sunt preterea vtilissime apostille D. Francisci de pauinis in easdem extrauagantes, cum glosa dicti dñi zenzelini, quibus succedit vita dñi Joannis vigesimisecūdi ſm Platinam.

THIELMAN·KERVER·

Parisijs.

¶ Apud Jolandam bonhomme/sub signo Unicornis.

M.ccccc.xlix.

Fig. 11 • Detail: Yolande Bonhomme (publisher), Pope John XII's *Extravagantes viginti Joannis Vigesimisecundi una cum elega[n]ti apparatu Domini Zenzelini de Cassanis utriusq[ue] juris professoris...*, Paris, 1549. Bound volume of woodcut text and illustrations, 23.4 × 17 cm. Collection of Lisa Unger Baskin. Photo: Stephen Petegorsky.

order to make ends meet. A similar story could be told of the widows of established print shops, who assumed the running of their deceased husband's practice, allowing them to continue to make a comfortable living. Volcxken Diericx (active 1570–1600), wife of Hieronymus Cock, took over her husband's flourishing business Aux Quatre Vents in Antwerp after he died in 1570, focusing largely on maintaining and marketing the press's existing plate stock.[37] Prints published after Cock's death, from 1570 to 1600, bear the name of the press without reference to him, suggesting the level of independence Volcxken had by this time achieved. Similarly, Yolande Bonhomme (c. 1490–1557), daughter of Pasquier Bonhomme, a printer and one of four appointed booksellers at the University of Paris, likely assumed various responsibilities associated with printing in her father's shop before she married.[38] After the death of her husband, Thielmann Carver, she took control of his prosperous shop at the "Sign of the Unicorn" on rue St. Jacques in Paris. Building on the imprint's reputation for publishing religious works (fig. 11; cat. no. 2), especially illustrated Books of Hours, Bonhomme excelled at producing volumes for the devout, and in 1526 she became the first documented woman to print an edition of the Bible.

Gendered Norms and "Manly" Pursuits

While many of the early modern female printmakers discussed here focused on the reproduction of works invented by men and/or supported male-led enterprises, there are also significant examples of women who produced original compositions and established themselves independently. One case is the well-known Bolognese artist Elisabetta Sirani (1638–1665). It is commonly understood that the invention of etching, a medium that was considerably less technically challenging than engraving, freed painters to make their own prints instead of having to hire professional printmakers to produce works after their designs.[39] Many artists were eager to try their hand at the medium not least for the opportunity to take responsibility for circulating their own ideas rather than relying on a professional engraver to do so on their behalf. Trained by her father, Sirani was the most prolific female painter and draughtswoman of early modern Italy.[40] She created fifteen etchings, some inspired by the work of her father, Giovanni Andrea, including *Holy Family with John the Baptist and Elizabeth* (fig. 12) and *Rest on the Flight into Egypt*—pointing to the way that even independent artists like herself remained in thrall to their patriarchs and teachers—while others, like *The Virgin Mary* (fig. 13), were based on her own drawings. When, by 1654, Giovanni Andrea Sirani became incapacitated by debilitating gout, Elisabetta assumed the running of the workshop, becoming at this point the family's primary breadwinner. In this new capacity, etching played a critical role in enabling her to attract fresh markets for her art. Executed in 1657 when she was just nineteen years old, the *Virgin of Sorrows Seated among Angels Holding the Implements of the Passion*

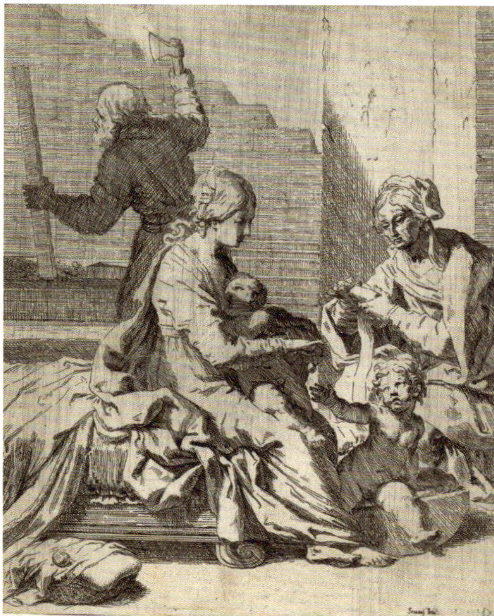

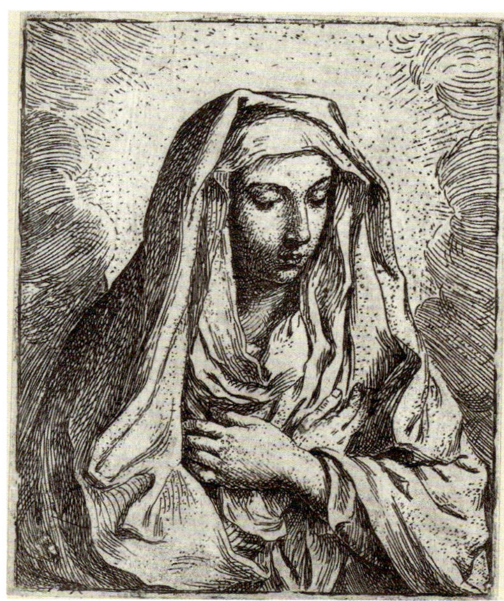

Fig. 12 (left) · Elisabetta Sirani, *Holy Family with John the Baptist and Elizabeth*, 1648–1665. Etching, 26.1 × 21.5 cm. Rijksmuseum, Amsterdam, inv. no. RP-P-OB-37.391.

Fig. 13 (right) · Elisabetta Sirani, *The Virgin Mary*, 1648–1665. Etching, 12.8 × 10.8 cm. Rijksmuseum, Amsterdam, inv. no. RP-P-OB-38.752.

was produced the same year she received her first large public commission. The print is dedicated to Ettore Ghislieri, a minister of the Order of San Filippo Neri, who was also an important collector and the founder of an art academy in 1647. Sirani's dedication of the etching to Ghislieri points to her business acumen, as she hoped to secure his patronage at a pivotal moment in her career.

Celebrated in her own day as a *virtuosa*—not least for the "virile" manner in which she wielded her paintbrush—Sirani exemplifies the acclaim extraordinary women could achieve by excelling in fields in which men had staked their preeminence.[41] As the manliness attributed to her painting style suggests, Sirani was accorded the prestige only by calling her femininity into question. Aspects of her story are echoed in accounts of other early modern women printmakers. When Giorgio Vasari wrote his foundational history of the great painters, sculptors, and architects of his day, for example, he devoted a small section in his second edition of 1568 to the history of print. In it, he singles out the work of three female printmakers, including Properzia de' Rossi (c. 1490/91–c. 1530), the unnamed wife of engraver Marcantonio Raimondi, of Bologna, and Diana Mantuana.[42] About Mantuana's work (fig. 14; cat. no. 135), he stated that "she engraved so well that it is a marvelous thing, and I, having seen her—a most charming and gracious girl—remain stupefied by her works, which are most beautiful."[43] Among just three other female printmakers of whom he was aware, she was a rarity, indeed an oddity, whose work Vasari deemed worthy of special recognition

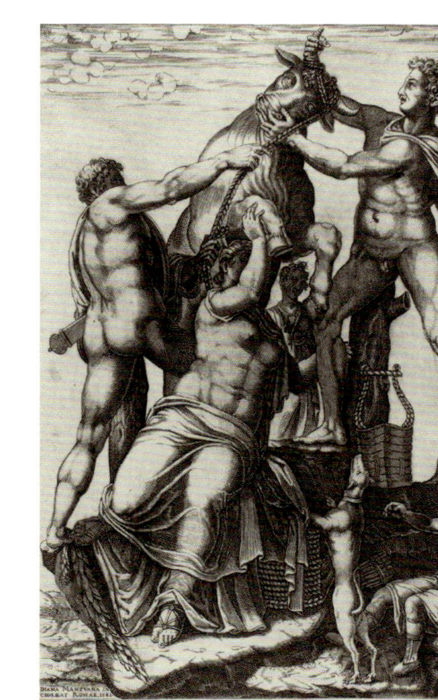

Fig. 14 · Detail: Diana Mantuana, *Amphion and Zethus Tying Dirce to a Wild Bull (The Farnese Bull)*, 1581. Engraving with plate tone, plate: 39.5 × 27.2 cm; sheet: 46.1 × 34.2 cm. Philadelphia Museum of Art: The Muriel and Philip Berman Gift, acquired from the John S. Phillips bequest of 1876 to the Pennsylvania Academy of the Fine Arts, with funds contributed by Muriel and Philip Berman, gifts (by exchange) of Lisa Norris Elkins, Bryant W. Langston, Samuel S. White 3rd and Vera White, with additional funds contributed by John Howard McFadden, Jr., Thomas Skelton Harrison, and the Philip H. and A.S.W. Rosenbach Foundation, 1985, inv. no. 1985-52-32541.

and even adulation for embodying the sorts of values contemporaries might attribute to the contents of a wondrous cabinet of curiosities.[44]

Perhaps no other figure better epitomizes the "manly" skills women could master and parlay into international fame than the seventeenth-century Dutch polymath Anna Maria van Schurman (1607–1678). A precocious scholar and prodigious intellect—who would eventually be admitted as the first female student to the university in Utrecht—van Schurman not only published her writings on an array of subjects but was widely celebrated for her incisive mind and gift for mastering difficult and obscure languages. Although not a professional artist, she made art on the side of her scholarly pursuits. Van Schurman's output—including works that ranged from paper-cutting to glass etching, painting, and even wax modelling—was never intended for the market but seems to have been motivated in part as evidence of her boundless virtuosity. Thanks to her father, Frederick van Schurman, she, too, experienced the benefits of tutorship in the art of engraving. Anna Maria was taught how to make prints by Magdalena van de Passe, with the expectation, no doubt, that her mastery of the medium would add to her burgeoning fame. It also allowed her to exchange prints she made with her learned friends, a practice that was well established among men. Frederick's choice to have his daughter learn the art from another woman points to his understanding of the part van de Passe could play as a role model, and his recognition more generally of the leading and exceptional part women could take in activities that were customarily thought to be the province of men.[45]

Noteworthy is van Schurman's focus on portraiture and especially self-portraiture for her work in prints (fig. 15; cat. no. 140). Examples of the first female self-portrait etchings, van Schurman's images of herself are preceded only by works like the woodcuts that Geronima Cagnaccia Parasole (c. 1569–1622) executed for *Teatro delle Nobili et Virtuose Donne* (cat. no. 70), a work designed by her sister-in-law Elisabetta (or Isabella) Catanea Parasole (c. 1570–c. 1620), and the print-inspired drawings by Esther Inglis (c. 1569–1624; cat. no. 76) for *Le Livre de l'Ecclesiaste*, whose title pages feature diminutive vignettes of their creators.[46] Unlike van Schurman's full-page etchings, however, Parasole's and Inglis's self-representations are not only miniature but also explicitly addressed to women, thus side-stepping the problem of making themselves explicit subjects of the male gaze.[47] Aged just twenty-six, van Schurman shows herself bust-length and barricaded behind a cartouche resembling an enormous imaginary paper scroll. She wears her hair unbound and is clothed in a brocaded dress with a lace neckline that covers her décolleté and fastens primly under the chin. The writing on the frame in front of her reads: "Neither my

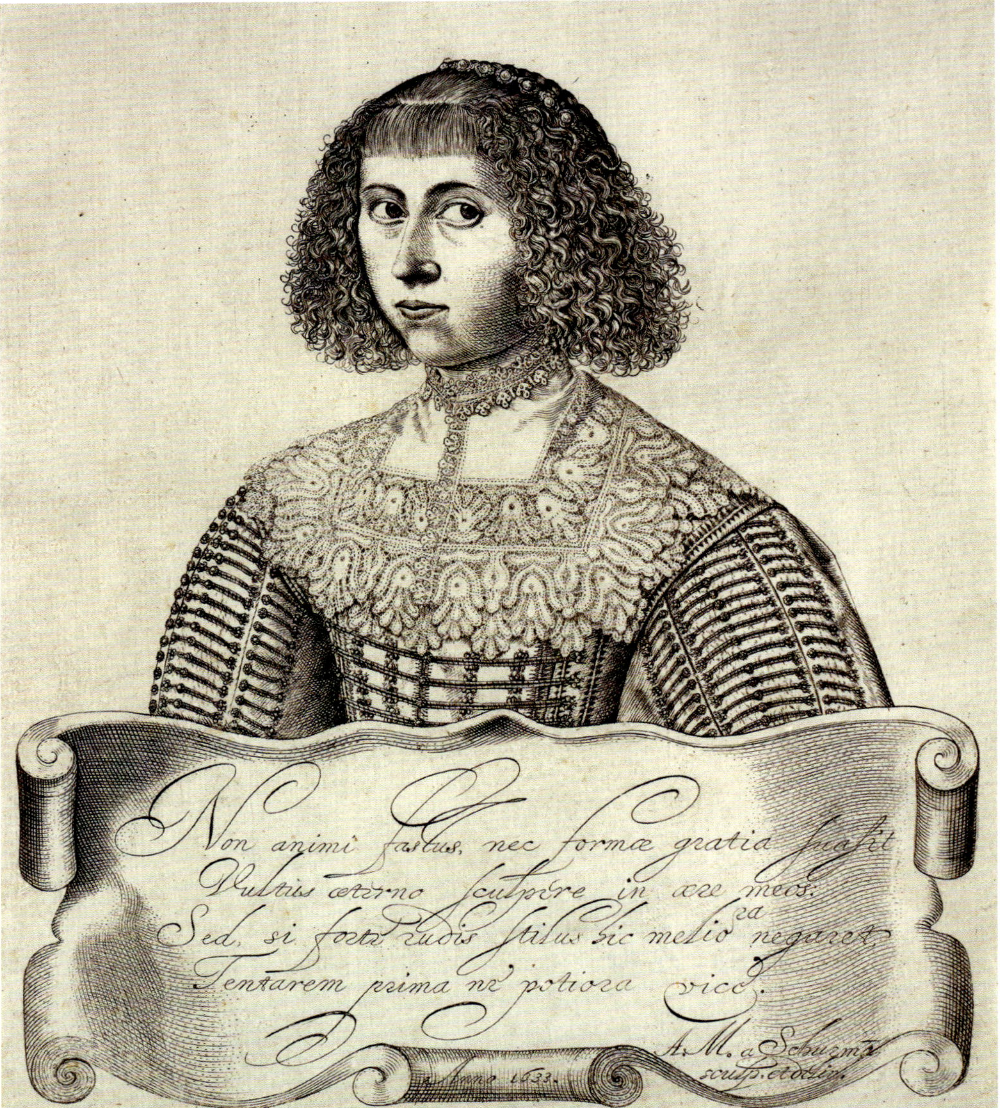

Fig. 15 · Anna Maria van Schurman, *Self-Portrait*, 1633. Engraving, 16.6 × 15 cm. Lent by Museum of Art, Rhode Island School of Design, Providence, Jesse Metcalf Fund, inv. no. 2002.30. Image courtesy of the RISD Museum, Providence, RI.

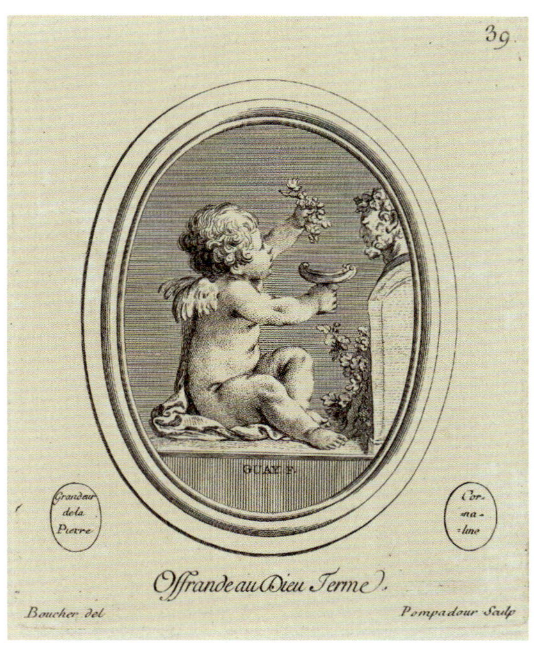

Fig. 16 • Jeanne Antoinette Poisson, called Madame de Pompadour, after François Boucher, after Jacques Guay, *Offrande au Dieu Terme*, from the series *Suite d'Estampes Gravées Par Madame La Marquise De Pompadour d'Après les Pierres gravées de Guay Graveur du Roy*, 1755. Etching and engraving, sheet: 25.5 × 20 cm; plate: 13 × 10.9 cm. Baltimore Museum of Art: The George A. Lucas Collection, purchased with funds from the State of Maryland, Laurence and Stella Bendann Fund, and contributions from individuals, foundations, and corporations throughout the Baltimore community, 1996.48.13394. Photo: Mitro Hood.

mind's arrogance, nor my physical beauty/ Has urged me to engrave my portrait in ever-lasting bronze./ It was, rather, the impulse to not work on more powerful subjects on my first attempt,/ If perhaps this crude stylus (my novice as an artist) were forbidding better ones."[48] Unwilling to describe herself in overly complimentary terms, the inscription reflects van Schurman's denial of her claims either to beauty or skill, a statement that might lead one to conclude that she held her work in little regard. Shortly after etching it, however, she gave it to the leading Dutch intellectual Constantijn Huygens, likely in an effort to get him to focus on her scholarship. The gesture hints not only that the sentiments she inscribed on the etching were designed to project an image of modest femininity but also that she understood the self-portrait print as an artifact that was designed to be shared and that could assist in situating her in the public eye, as it had done so successfully for men before her.

If her intention in giving the print to Huygens was to capture his attention, the ploy was a resounding success. In the weeks that followed, Huygens addressed a flurry of excited and erotically charged verse to van Schurman, including the following:

> Anna, I will confess, you could appeal to me more
> in a drawing
> And your charm, which had not yet been etched in
> copper, could be more pleasing to me
> But etched you appeal to me even more. A girl,
> whose face shines
> And is made up colorfully, is, it is said, a loose woman.
> Instead a girl who only loves virtue and knows no lover
> Who rather takes pleasure in—may I say it—not
> thinking much of her appearance
> A girl who if she was kind to a few men and would marry
> Binding her unique talent to a man with exceptional
> talents
> A girl who wants to be seen spiritually and regards
> suffering as an excess burden
> Must such a girl shine with unction and carelessly
> wear the finery of powder
> Etched must she be, and by her own etching needle.[49]

Using the etching as a point of departure to contemplate its subject and creator, Huygens states that van Schurman could appeal to him in a drawing but that she is even more desirable to him in print. His reasoning is that, just as the etching lacks colour, he favours virginal women, the application of cosmetic pigments and unguents being the hallmark of a sex worker. By praising the work's "chaste" monochromaticity and the plainness of its subject, he seems intent on redeeming the etching and with it the work's creator, discharging both from the imputation of licentiousness—a gesture that merely reminds of the medium's reputation for promiscuity. Women's engagement with the printing *matrix* (an archaic Latin term that meant "womb") may indicate women's suitability for the profession, but in reality the peripatetic, sociable life of prints—works that were liberally shared, passed around, and even transported on the body—meant that the medium could compromise their female makers, particularly if they used it to shine a light directly on themselves.[50]

Alleviated from the pressures of making prints to sustain a living, aristocrats and noblewomen like the Marquise Jeanne Antoinette Poisson (1721–1764), and Sophia Fredericka Caroline Louise, Princess of Saxe-Coburg-Saalfeld (1778–1835), likewise made a handful of prints. Modest in size and scope, works like

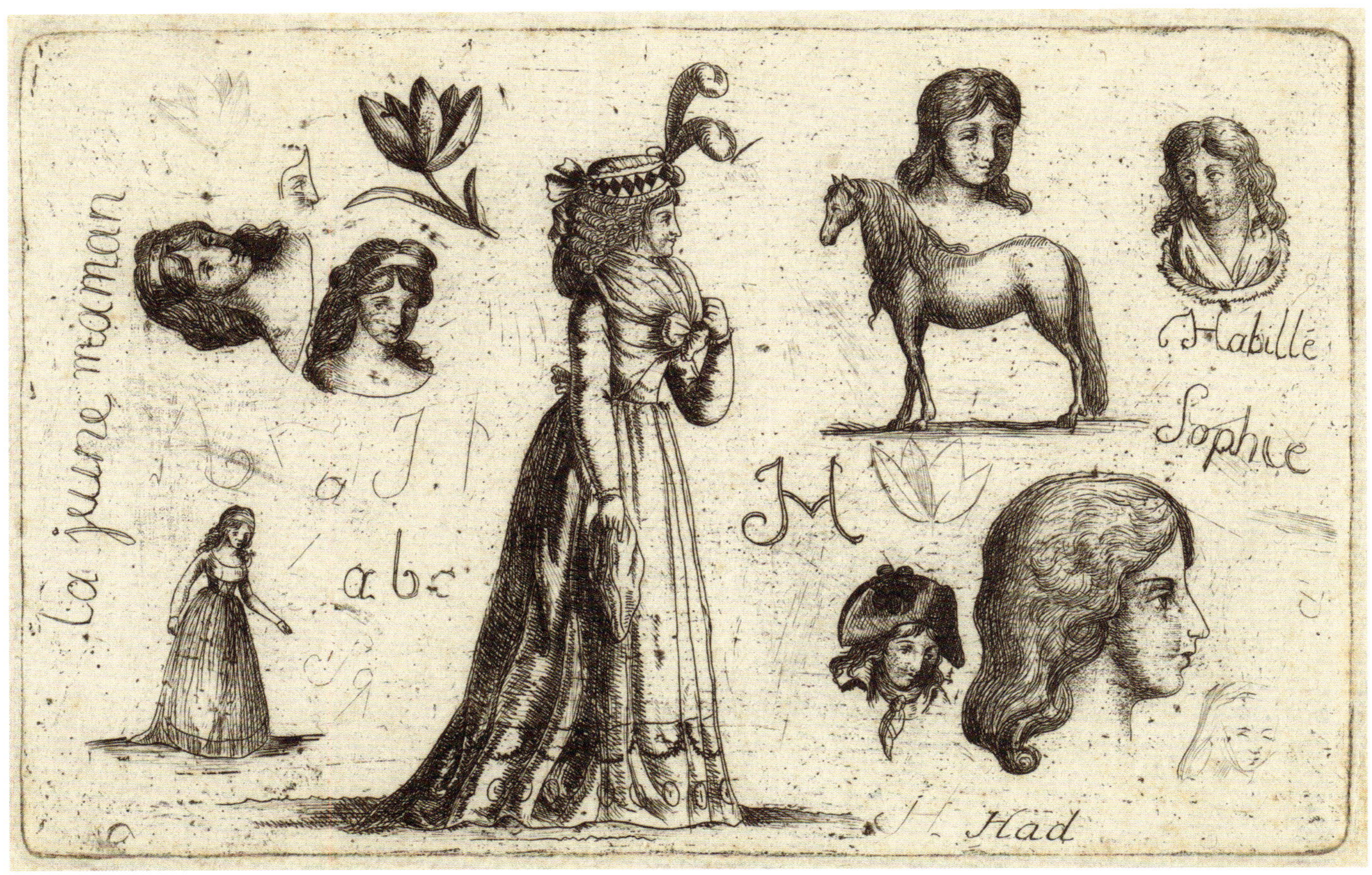

Fig. 17 · Sophia Fredericka Caroline Louise, Princess of Saxe-Coburg-Saalfeld, *A sheet of sketches and studies: two figures, eight heads, a horse, two flowers. Words and letters are scribbled on the plate, among them la jeune maman, Habille, and Sophie.*, c. 1795. Etching, 10 × 16 cm. The New York Public Library, The Miriam and Ira D. Wallach Division of Art, Prints and Photographs: Print Collection, Grolier 444, Object number 113950.

these were intended for a small circle of friends and family and never for mass circulation. The Marquise, better known as Madame de Pompadour, was the official chief mistress of King Louis XV from 1745 to her death in 1764. An intelligent and refined woman who counted Voltaire among her close friends, she received instruction in art from the fashionable court painter François Boucher and produced around eighty etchings (fig. 16).[51] Her example led many other women of her class to try their own hand at making prints. Among the compositions she produced are a handful of prints after Boucher, including one showing a seated child blowing bubbles, a common *vanitas*, or "vanity," subject and a comment on the fleeting nature of earthly delights but also, given its focus on childhood, an appropriate topic for a woman. Aunt of Queen Victoria, Princess Sophia of Saxe-Coburg-Saalfeld likewise created a series of charming but inexpert etchings at the age of seventeen. Reading like a sort of printed sampler, one of the etchings shows the fledgling artist struggling to write in reverse but managing to compose her name, the beginning of the alphabet, the words "*la jeune maman*" (the young mother), and a monogram (fig. 17). These scribbles appear next to a constellation of compositions showing a full-length figure of a young woman as well as several heads of young men and fashionable women. Ideas of love and courtship, and possibly even childbearing, seem central to its design.

The moneyed, intellectual, and leisure classes, who described themselves as "amateurs," similarly turned their hand to printmaking, with little thought of pecuniary compensation. Seventeenth-century Dutch prints were among those most avidly imitated, especially the etchings of Rembrandt as seen in the work of the amateur Marguerite Le Comte (c. 1720–c. 1786). Pointing to the role that internationally renowned inventors continued to play in the work of female printmakers, Le Comte reproduced Rembrandt's *Obelisk,* reflecting the compulsion among amateurs to

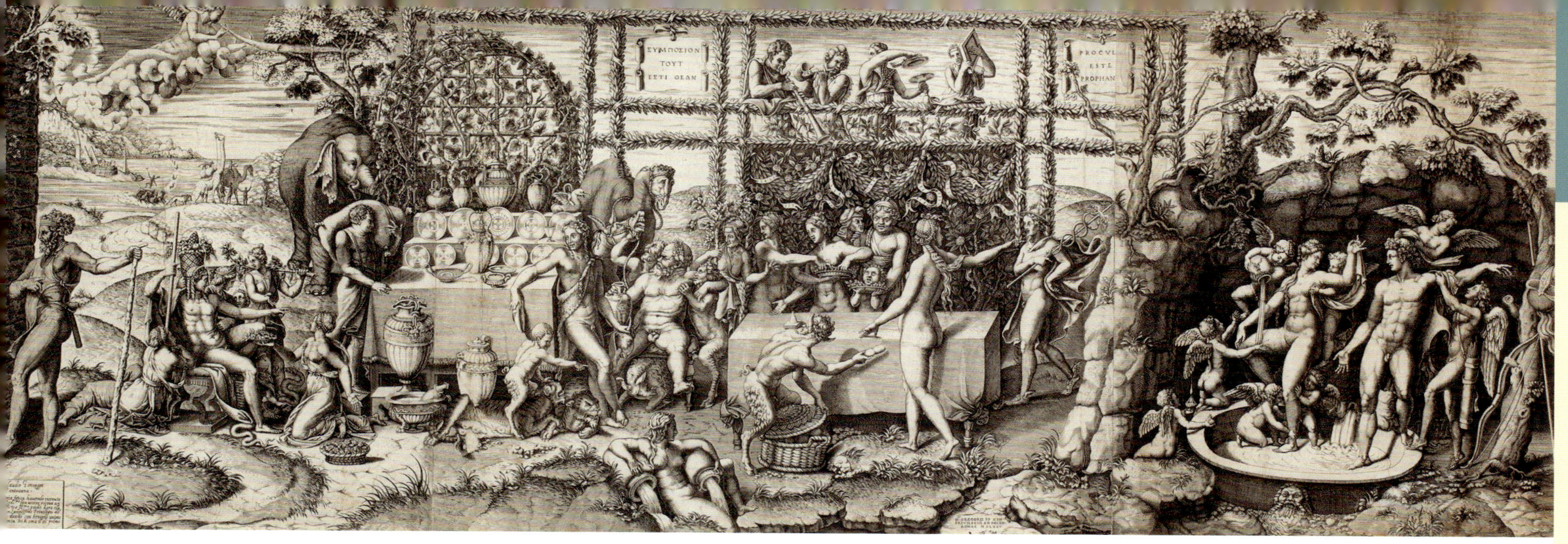

Fig. 18 • Diana Mantuana, *Preparations for the Wedding Banquet of Cupid and Psyche*, 1575. Engraving, plate and sheet: 37.6 × 112.1 cm. Milwaukee Art Museum, Gift of the DASS Fund, inv. no. M2013.34. Photo: John R. Glembin.

produce so-called "Rymbranesques"—that is, to give particular attention to the Dutch master's style of etching, work that clearly showed signs of the labour or facture involved in its production.[52]

Not without its drawbacks, women's focus on reproducing the work of acclaimed artists also brought unprecedented opportunities to treat both large, ambitious subjects and topics not normally deemed appropriate for their sex. Diana Mantuana's *Preparations for the Wedding Banquet of Cupid and Psyche* of 1575 (fig. 18) is a case in point: the large three-print composition replicates a fresco by Giulio Romano in the Palazzo Te. Known for his salacious subject matter—not least his role in the completion of an infamous series of pornographic prints—Romano was averse neither to treating the nude nor to frank representations of sexual intercourse.[53] By taking on the role of reproducing his work, Mantuana participated vicariously in similar sorts of subject matter. Her access to the material was facilitated by her father, who, under Romano's direction, helped decorate the Palazzo Te and who gave her drawings from which to work. Even as the long horizontal print represents many features of Romano's famous fresco, it excludes perhaps the most graphic of them: Cupid and Psyche naked, lounging languidly, limbs intertwined, on a fantastic Roman-style chaise longue. The subject was treated as an independent theme by Giorgio Ghisi, a protégé of Mantuana's father, however, suggesting that some of Romano's most explicit subject matter could simply not be handled by a woman.[54] Even as Mantuana tamed the most overtly sexual elements of Romano's treatment, her print is noteworthy for including several full-frontal nudes, including those of Venus and Mars bathing in a pool. Her pride in the subject is palpable in her dedication to Cardinal Claudio Gonzaga, suggesting that women's exclusion from the study of the unclothed body was not universal.[55] The idea is underscored by contemporary praise of the piece by Francesco Peranda, secretary to two Roman cardinals, which described her engraving as "*cosa stupenda*" (a stupendous thing). The study of the nude, a topic generally preserved for men, may be the most controversial "male" subject to which women's printmaking activities gave them access, but it was by no means the only one. Thanks to their engagement in large print shops, women were involved in tasks related to science and exploration, areas of expertise that were often framed as male endeavours. Violante Vanni (1732–1775/76) and the Horthemels sisters, for example, were instrumental in making maps, while Marie Briot (active seventeenth century), Rosina Helena Fürst (1642–1709), Marie-Geneviève-Charlotte Darlus Thiroux d'Arconville (1720–1805), and the Lister sisters, Anna (1671–1700) and Susanna (c. 1670–1738), worked on subjects related to the study of anatomy, flora, and fauna.

Solitary Needlework

Der Reisser.

Ich bin ein Reisser frü vnd spet/
Ich entwürff auff ein Linden Bret/
Bildnuß von Menschen oder Thier/
Auch gewechß mancherley monier/
Geschrifft/auch groß Versal buchstaben/
Historj / vnd was man wil haben/
Künstlich/daß nit ist außzusprechen/
Auch kan ich diß in Kupffer stechen.
Der

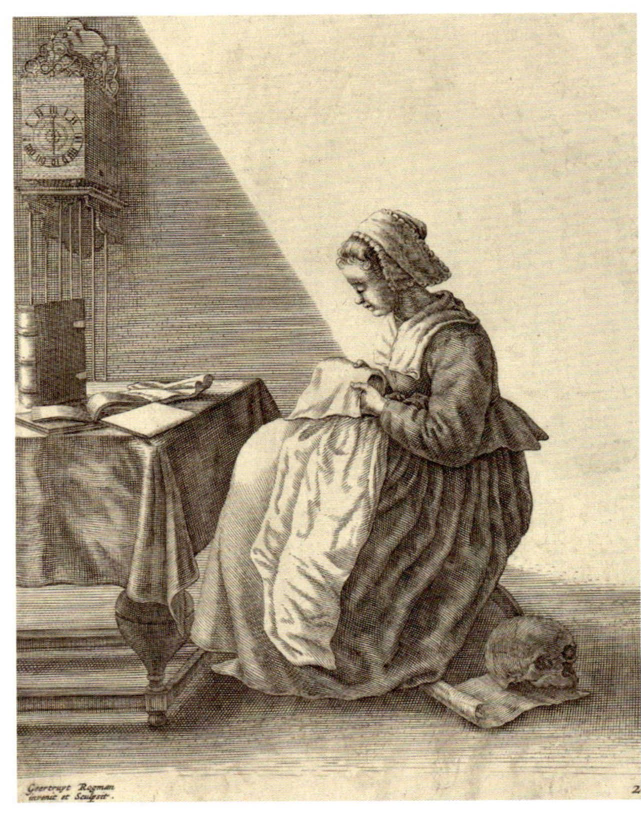

Fig. 19 (left) • Jost Amman, *The Reisser* [*Der Reißer*] from *Eigentliche Beschreibung aller Stände auf Erden*, 1568. Woodcut, 7.9 x 6.1 cm. Image courtesy of Europeana.edu.

Fig. 20 (right) • Geertruydt Roghman, *Young Girl Sewing*, from the series *Domestic Occupations*, 1640–1647. Engraving, sheet: 22 × 18.3 cm; plate: 20.6 × 16.8 cm. Baltimore Museum of Art: Garrett Collection, 1946.112.4350. Photo: Mitro Hood.

In light of extant documentation relating to women's wide-ranging involvement with early modern print production, it is appropriate to return to Stradano's engraving and to reconsider its representation of an all-male engraving shop. While the image has the virtue of showing the full cycle of print production, it is neither the most accurate portrayal of how plates were incised nor of the individuals involved in their production. Women, we have seen, were critical members of large workshops, contributing their efforts to incising plates and setting type, and occasionally even to managing their own shops. To better appreciate some of the skills they brought to bear on the art of making prints, it may be more helpful to consider another close contemporary illustration. Created a few years before Stradano, yet markedly different, Jost Amman's woodcut of the *Reisser* (fig. 19) focuses on the person responsible for incising the copper matrix.[56] Seated at a table with elaborately ornate carved legs on which a vase of flowers rests, Amman's figure is not inside a busy studio but alone and very possibly in the comforts of his own home—an idea that is supported by the fluffy pillow or folded mattress visible just behind his right shoulder. There was no practical necessity for plates to be cut inside the workshop; Stradano himself seems to hint at this by locating the engraver and his apprentices working at tables that are entirely separate from those at which the matrices are being inked, wiped, and then imprinted. Often described as lonesome work that demanded intense focus and a meticulous attention to detail, printmaking, as the series of domestic scenes by Geertruydt Roghman (1625–1657) suggests, was consistent with aspects of women's traditional duties within the home.[57] Comparable with Amman's lone Reisser, Roghman features solitary figures (with the exception of children by their side) absorbed in painstaking tasks like sewing and ruffing (fig. 20; cat. nos. 141–143).

In as much as Roghman is intent on telling us about women's aptitude for certain kinds of work, the set also draws attention to the artist's distinctive gifts as a printmaker. Where Roghman's women ply their needles through cloth, the artist applies hers to copper, an analogy that suggests an implicit understanding of printmaking as an activity at which women could excel.[58] Rosina Helena Fürst makes a similar point in the introduction to her book of textile patterns, noting: "Others by contrast are gentler and more adroit and have finer manual dexterity, including those who are responsible for the arts of sewing, silk embroidery, gold weaving and others. The praiseworthy female sex is most capable of this sort of work."[59] Men worked with pens and women with needles, it has been said, referring to the gendered idea—common since at least the Renaissance—that men expressed their unique talents by authoring texts and women by producing embroidery and other forms of textiles.[60] Fürst may be referring specifically to how women's handiness with the sewing needle allowed them to stand out in the textile arts, but, as her prints show, she used a very similar tool to etch the designs for this volume, pointing to the commensurability of the two tasks.[61] Capable of working alone, accomplished with small, pointed instruments, and endowed with fine-motor skills, Roghman and Fürst would agree, women made terrific printmakers.

Notes

1 For more on the dirt, noise, and rowdyism of the early modern engraving shop, see Robert Darnton, "Work and Culture in an Eighteenth-Century Printing Shop," *Quarterly Journal of the Library of Congress* 39, no. 1 (1982): 34–47; Madeleine C. Viljoen, "Diligent Labor in Stradanus's Engraving Shop," in *Renaissance Invention: Stradanus's "Nova Reperta,"* ed. Lia Markey (Evanston, IL: Northwestern University Press, 2020), 63–64; and Madeleine C. Viljoen, "Mysterious Noises: Orphic Strings, Rough Music and the Sounds of Early Modern Ornament Prints," in *Quid est Secretum? Visual Representation of Secrets in Early Modern Europe, 1500–1700* (Leiden: Brill, 2020), 332–34.

2 For a detailed discussion of the various members of the shop and their associated roles, see Ad Stijnman, "Stradanus's Printshop," *Print Quarterly* 27 (2010): 11–29.

3 For more on Stradano's set of illustrations featuring teams of mostly male workers engaged in industry with a range of state-of-the-art technology, see Lia Markey, *Renaissance Invention: Stradanus's "Nova Reperta."*

4 See, for example, Timothy Riggs and Larry Silver, eds., *Graven Images: The Rise of Professional Printmaking in Antwerp and Haarlem, 1540–1640* (Chicago: Mary and Leigh Block Gallery; Evanston, IL: Northwestern University, 1993); Ad Stijnman, *Engraving and Etching, 1400–2000: A History of the Development of Manual Intaglio Printmaking Processes* (London: Archetype Publications; Houten: Hes & De Graaf, 2012), 76–81; David Landau and Peter Parshall, *The Renaissance Print* (New Haven, CT: Yale University Press, 1996), 120–46; Rebecca Zorach and Elizabeth Rodini, *Paper Museums: The Reproductive Print in Europe* (Chicago: Smart Museum of Art and University of Chicago, 2005), 1–29; and Michael Bury, *The Print in Italy, 1550–1620*, exh. cat. (London: British Museum, 2001), 10–11.

5 For more on this topic, see, among others, Stijnman, *Engraving and Etching, 1400–2000*, 413–18; Rosemary Simmons, *Dictionary of Printmaking Terms* (London: A&C Black, 2002); Evelyn Lincoln, *The Invention of the Italian Renaissance Printmaker* (New Haven, CT: Yale University Press, 2000), 6–8; and Bury, *The Print in Italy, 1550–1620*, 68–80.

6 For an earlier account of women's print production, see Judith K. Brodsky, "Some Notes on Women Printmakers," *Art Journal* 35, no. 4 (1976): 374–77.

7 Evelyn Lincoln, "Making a Good Impression: Diana Mantuana's Printmaking Career," *Renaissance Quarterly* 50 (1997): 1102–03. The Getty Union List of Artist Names lists the name variously as Diana Sculptor, Diana Scultor, Diana Scultore, Diana Scultori, Mantovana, Diana Mantuana, Mantovana Sculptor, Mantovana Scultor, Mantovana Scultore, Mantovana Scultori, Diana Mantovana, Diane de Mantoue, Diane La Mantuana Ghisi, Diana Ghisi, Diane Ghisi, and Diana Ghisi Scultori. This volume uses the preferred spelling of "Diana Mantuana."

8 Lincoln, "Making a Good Impression," 1103.

9 Diana Mantuana's work with her husband is explored in Lincoln, *The Invention of the Italian Renaissance Printmaker*, 111–46.

10 Lia Markey, "The Female Printmaker and the Culture of the Reproductive Print Workshop," in *Paper Museums: The Reproductive Print in Europe, 1500–1800* (Chicago: University of Chicago Press, 2005), 51–75. Elizabeth Alice Honig notes that most Dutch women were motivated by their fathers to make art, in "The Art of Being 'Artistic': Dutch Women's Creative Practices in the 17th Century," *Woman's Art Journal* 22, no. 2 (2002): 32.

11 Ilja M. Veldman, *Crispijn de Passe and His Progeny* (Rotterdam: Sound and Vision, 2001), 199–201.

12 Veldman, *Crispijn de Passe and His Progeny*, 200.

13 Crispijn de Passe the Elder married a niece of Maarten de Vos's wife. Veldman, *Crispijn de Passe and His Progeny*, 20–21.

14 Markey, "The Female Printmaker," 58.

15 The Getty Union List of Artist Names lists her variously as Susanne Maria Sandrart, Susanne Maria von Sandrart, Susanne Maria Auer (married name), Susanne Maria Alt (version of her married name), and Susanne Maria Endter (during second marriage). Sabina Lessmann refers to her as Susanna Maria von Sandrart. This volume uses the preferred spelling of "Susanne Maria von Sandrart."

16 Sabina Lessmann, "Susanna Maria von Sandrart: Women Artists in 17th-Century Nürnberg," *Woman's Art Journal* 14, no. 1 (1993): 10–14.

17 Sabina Lessmann, *Susanna Maria von Sandrart (1658–1716): Arbeitsbedingungen einer Nürnberger Graphikerin im Jahrhundert* (Hildesheim: G. Olms, 1991), 242.

18 Eckhard Leuschner, ed., *Johann Ulrich Kraus*, pt. 1, The New Hollstein German Engravings, Etchings and Woodcuts, 1400–1700, comp. Jörg Diefenbacher (Ouderkerk aan den Ijssel: Sound and Vision, 2018), xxvii.

19 The statement appears in the unpaginated preface to *Tapisseries du Roy, ou sont representez les quatre elemens et les quatre saisons : avec les devises qui les accompagnent & leur explication*. The translation is my own.

20 Leuschner, *Johann Ulrich Kraus*, pt. 1, xxvii: "After Theodor de Bry had died, his son and successor, Johan Theodor de Bry took over the workshop. It then passed to the latter's former assistant Matthäus Merian the Elder through his marriage to de Bry's daughter Maria Magdalena de Bry. Melchior Küsel completed his apprenticeship under Merian and married his daughter, also named Maria Magdalena, in 1649. With [Johann Ulrich] Kraus's marriage, history repeated itself for a third time in a row, in that a former apprentice or assistant again married the master's daughter. The transition to the next generation thus always involved a name change, rendering the workshop's long-standing tradition less recognizable at first glance."

21 About the San Giovannino Convent in Florence in the early years of the seventeenth century, Silvia Evangelisti notes: "The convent appropriated profits from individual work. Nuns were required to be productive, as work would keep them away from immoral thoughts and conversations. They could engage in embroidering and knitting, and prepare herbal remedies, jams, cakes and biscuits. However, no commissions could be received independently for their superiors, nor could nuns keep their earnings for themselves; instead each earnings were to be handed straight to the sister-bursar or the abbess." See Silvia Evangelisti, "Monastic Poverty and Material Culture in Early Modern Convents," *Historical Journal* 47, no. 1 (March 2004): 5.

22 Ann Roberts, "Convents," in *Dictionary of Women Artists*, vol. 1 (London: Fitzroy Dearborn, 1997), 23.

23 Antony Griffiths, *The Print Before Photography: An Introduction to European Printmaking* (London: British Museum, 2016), 522n27.

24 Deborah Parker, "Women in the Book Trade in Italy, 1475–1620," *Renaissance Quarterly* 49, no. 3 (1996): 511.

25 Delia Gaze, ed., *Dictionary of Women Artists*, vol. 1 (London: Fitzroy Dearborn, 1997), 62–63.

26 Elizabeth Poulson, "Louise-Magdeleine Horthemels: Reproductive Engraver," *Woman's Art Journal* 6, no. 2 (1985): 20–23.

27 The Getty Union List of Artist Names records the artist's name variously as Katharina Prestel, Maria Katharina Prestel, Marie Catherine Prestel, Maria Catharina Prestel, M.C. Prestel, Maria Catherine Prestel, Maria Katharine Prestel, Mrs. Prestal, Maria Katharina Holl, Katharina

Hoell, Maria Catherine Höll, and more. This volume uses the preferred spelling of "Maria Catharina Prestel."

28 Joseph Kiermeier-Debre and Fritz Franz Vogel, *Kunst kommt von Prestel: Das Künstlerehepaar Johann Gottlieb und Maria Katharina Prestel* (Cologne: Böhlau, 2008), 13.

29 Rena Hoisington, *Aquatint from Its Origins to Goya* (Washington, DC: National Gallery of Art; Princeton, NJ: Princeton University Press, 2021), 129.

30 Claudia Schwaighofer, "Eine tüchtige, ihrem Gatten helfende Frau," in *Blickwechsel: Frankfurter Frauenzimmer um 1800*, ed. Ursula Kern (Frankfurt: Kramer, 2007), 31–39, and Fondation Custodia, 64: "Maria Katharina Prestel (d'après Giacomo Ligozzi)," www.fondationcustodia.fr/64-Maria-Katharina-Prestel-d-apres-Giacomo-Ligozzi, accessed June 9, 2023: "The signature of Johann Theophilus, visible on several copies including ours, as well as the double cataloging of the print by GKNagler, attest to the difficulty in separating the prints of Maria Katharina from those of Johan Theophilus. Nevertheless, the author of the recent catalogue raisonné of the work of Maria Katharina Prestel returned to her many prints which are signed with the name of Johann Theophilus in the three collections in which they collaborated; and it is to her that we owe our engraving."

31 Hoisington, *Aquatint from Its Origins to Goya*, 143.

32 Walter Prestel claims the couple separated but were never formally divorced, in "Johann Gottlieb Prestel | Maria Katharina Prestel, 1739–1808: Daten zu Leben und Werk," in Kiermeier-Debre and Vogel, *Kunst kommt von Prestel*, 16.

33 "At the time, the self-sufficient London life that the Prestel women created was truly exceptional, and few female printmakers, or women artists for that matter, found such independence." See Markey, "The Female Printmaker," 61.

34 Anthony Blunt, "Jacques Stella, the De Masso Family and Falsifications of Poussin," *Burlington Magazine* 116 (December 1974), 744–49.

35 Sue Welsh Reed notes that Claudine's works after Poussin were based on paintings her brother inherited from Jacques's estate. See Sue Welsh Reed, *French Prints from the Age of the Musketeers* (Boston: Museum of Fine Arts, 1988), 260.

36 J.J. Guiffrey, "Testament et Inventaire des Biens: tableaux, dessins, planche de cuivre, bijoux etc. de Claudine Bouzonnet Stella," *Nouvelles archives de l'art français* (1877), 1–109.

37 Elizabeth Wyckoff, "Hieronymus Cock and the Invention of the Print Market in Antwerp," *Beyond Bosch: The Afterlife of a Renaissance Master in Print* (Saint Louis, MO: Saint Louis Art Museum, 2015), 42.

38 Beatrice Hibbard Beech, "Yolande Bonhomme: A Renaissance Printer," *Medieval People* 6, no. 2 (1985): 80–81.

39 See, among others, Michael W. Cole and Madeleine C. Viljoen, *The Early Modern Painter-Etcher* (University Park, PA: Penn State University Press, 2006), and Catherine Jenkins, Nadine Orenstein, and Freyda Spira, eds., *The Renaissance of Etching* (New York: The Met, 2019).

40 Adelina Modesti, *Elisabetta Sirani "Virtuosa": Women's Cultural Production in Early Modern Bologna* (Belgium: Brepols, 2014); Babette Bohn, *Women Artists, Their Patrons, and Their Publics in Early Modern Bologna* (University Park, PA: Pennsylvania State University Press, 2021); Patricia Rocco, *The Devout Hand: Women, Virtue, and Visual Culture in Early Modern Italy* (Montreal: McGill-Queen's University Press, 2017); and Adelina Modesti, *"A Casa con I Sirani*: A Successful Family Business and Household in Early Modern Bologna," in *The Early Modern Domestic Interior, 1400–1700: Objects, Spaces, Domesticities*, ed. Erin Campbell, Stephanie Miller, and Elizabeth Carroll Consavari (Farnham, UK: Ashgate, 2013), 47–66.

41 The seventeenth-century biographer Carlo Cesare Malvasia describes Elisabetta's style as manly [*virile*]. See Frederika H. Jacobs, *Defining the Renaissance Virtuosa: Women Artists and the Language of Art History and Criticism* (Cambridge: Cambridge University Press, 1997), 26.

42 Lincoln, "Making a Good Impression," 1116.

43 Giorgio Vasari, *Le Vite Le Vite de' Piv Eccellenti Pittori Scultori et Architettori* [...] (1568): "Intaglia anch'ella tanto bene, che è cosa maravigliosa, et io che ho veduto lei, che è molto gentile e graziosa fanciulla, e l'opere sue che sono bellissime, ne sono restato stupefatto."

44 For more examples of female makers detailed within Vasari's volume, see Babette Bohn's discussion in "Designing Women: Drawings by Women Artists in Early Modern Italy" on pages 42–57 of this volume.

45 Anna Maria van Schurman is thus among the earliest artists to be formally trained by another woman. Markey, "The Female Printmaker," 60.

46 For more on the identities of Isabella (Elisabetta) and Geronima Parasole, see Evelyn Lincoln, "Artemisia Gentileschi, Geronima and Isabella Parasole and Lavinia Fontana (*By Her Hand: Artemisia Gentileschi and Women Artists in Italy, 1500–1800*)," *Print Quarterly* 40, no. 1 (2023): 62: "Baglione had stated that Isabella Parasole was the wife of Leonardo and therefore was the woodblock engraver who worked with him on various commissions. In fact, Leonardo Parasole's wife, who collaborated with him, was Geronima (or Gerolama) Parasole. She has her own interesting body of work, and is, in this author's opinion the most likely engraver of Isabella Parasole's lace designs. Isabella was trained in lace and embroidery—but probably not in woodblock carving."

47 Parasole's volume is addressed to female lacemakers and Inglis's to Princess de Rohan.

48 The translation of the original Dutch inscription is taken from Martha Moffitt Peacock, "Mirrors of Skill and Renown: Women and Self-Fashioning in Early-Modern Dutch Art," *Mediaevistik* 28 (2015): 329.

49 The translation is my own from the Dutch rendered in Katlijne Van der Stighelen and Jeanine de Landtsheer, "Een suer-soete Maeghd voor Constantijn Huygens: Anna Maria van Schurman," *De Zeventiende Eeuw: Cultuur in de Nederlanden* 25 no. 2 (2009): 149–202. The text provides translations into Dutch from the original Latin poems.

50 For more on the challenges of female self-presentation in print, see Madeleine C. Viljoen, "Show-Offs: Women's Self-Portrait Prints, c. 1700," in *Female Printmakers, Printsellers and Print Publishers in the Eighteenth Century: The Imprint of Women*, c. 1700–1830, ed. Cristina S. Martinez and Cynthia E. Roman (Cambridge: Cambridge University Press, 2023).

51 Elise Goodman, *The Portraits of Madame de Pompadour: Celebrating a Femme Savante* (Berkeley: University of California Press, 2000), 128–31.

52 Perrin Stein, "Echoes of Rembrandt and Castiglione: Etching as Appropriation," in *Artists and Amateurs: Etching in 18th-Century France* (New York: The Metropolitan Museum of Art, 2014), 158–60.

53 For more about Romano's penchant for erotic subject matter, see Bette Talvacchia, *Taking Positions: On the Erotic in Renaissance Culture* (Princeton, NJ: Princeton University Press, 1999).

54 Lincoln, "Making a Good Impression," 1127.

55 "To the most illustrious Lord Claudio Gonzaga. Diana Mantuana. It is fitting that this labor of mine, having come to life under the rule of your most excellent house, receives new life under your lordship's name, because now it enters the world favored by you with the most ample privilege of the sanctity of Our Lord." Lincoln, "Making a Good Impression," 1126.

56 See the figure of the "Reisser" in Theodore Rabb, trans., *A Sixteenth-Century Book of Trades: Das Ständebuch* (Palo Alto: Society for the Promotion of Science and Scholarship, 2009).

57 Griffiths offers the following description: "The engraver had to sit at his window carefully cutting lines into the same rectangle of copper for months on end, sometimes for years … it was lonely work in a secluded room and not all could cope with it." In *The Print Before Photography*, 234.

58 Martha Moffitt Peacock, "Geertruydt Roghman and the Female Perspective in 17th-Century Dutch Genre Imagery," *Woman's Art Journal* 14, no. 2 (1993–94): 3–10.

59 Rosina Helena Fürst, *Neues Modelbuch von Unterschiedlicher Art der Blumen und anderer genehten Mödel nach itziger Manier allen Liebhaberinnen dieser Kunst zumbesten vorgestellt* (Nuremberg: Paulus Fürsten, 1689), preface. The translation is my own.

60 Margaret W. Ferguson, "Renaissance Concepts of the 'Woman Writer,'" in *Women and Literature in Britain, 1500–1700*, ed. Helen Wilcox (Cambridge: Cambridge University Press, 1996), 153, and Kathryn R. King, "Of Needles and Pens and Women's Work," *Tulsa Studies in Women's Literature* 14, no. 1 (1995): 77–93.

61 Stacey Shimizu, "The Pattern of Perfect Womanhood: Feminine Virtue, Pattern Books and the Fiction of the Clothworking Woman," in *Women's Education in Early Modern Europe*, ed. Barbara J. Whitehead (New York: Garland, 1999), 76.

Detail (cat. no. 149; fig. 9, opposite) · Maria Catharina Prestel, after Jacopo Ligozzi, *Truth Subduing Envy*, 1781. Colour etching and aquatint, sheet (trimmed within platemark): 30.7 × 22.8 cm. Baltimore Museum of Art: Garrett Collection, 1984.81.3742. Photo: Mitro Hood.

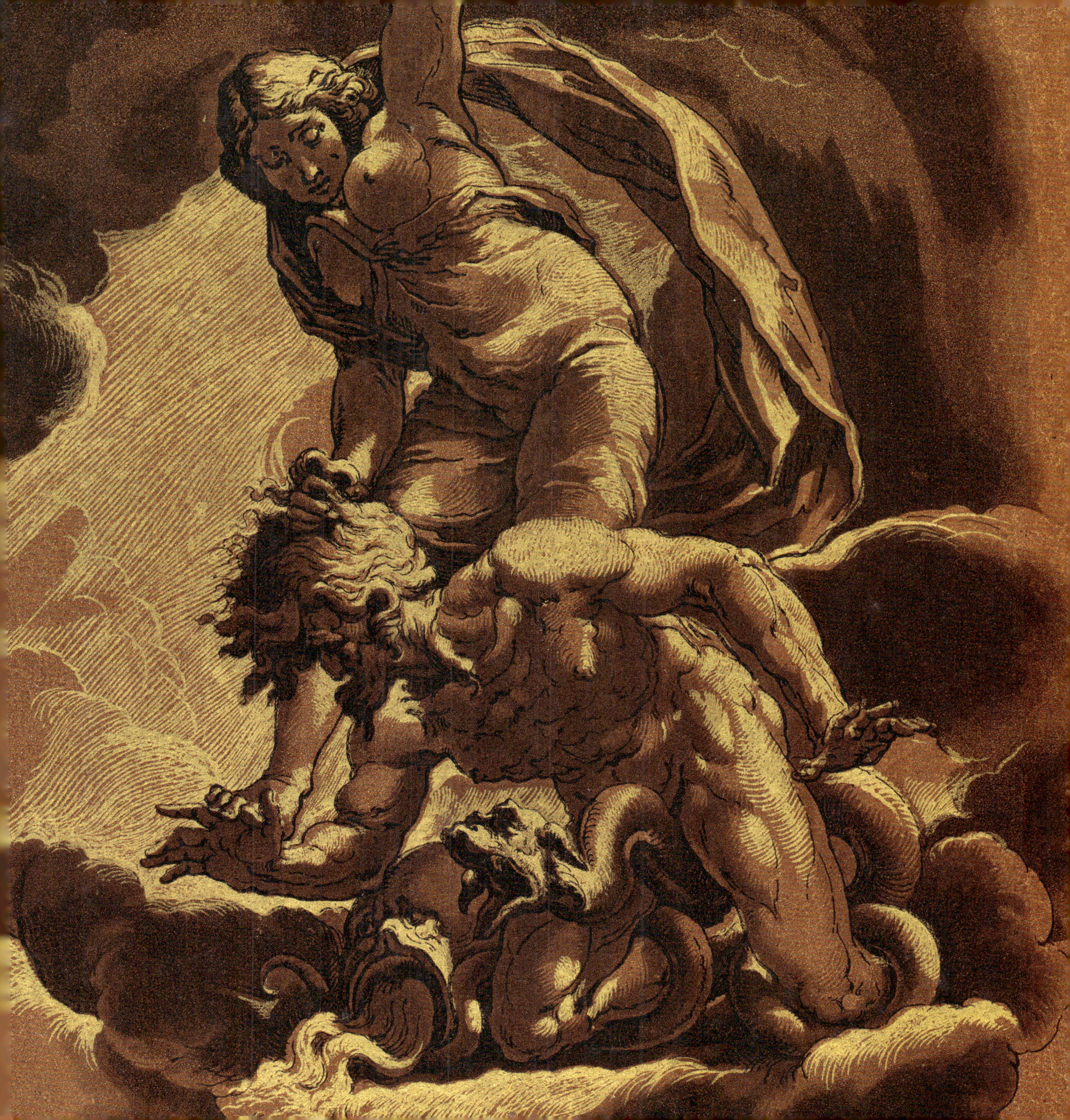

UNRAVELLING THE THREADS

Women Working with Silk in Italy, France, and England, 1500–1800

Yassana Croizat-Glazer

Nothing invites a lingering look quite like silk; strong yet delicate, it has long been treasured for its versatility and capacity to hold a dazzling array of colours. While it may be easy to find beauty in a satin jacket or length of brocaded velvet that has retained its texture and vibrancy across centuries, the details of their past lives may not reveal themselves so easily. And yet, embedded in every silk thread we see—whether in a painting, skirt panel, or embroidered sampler—is a multifaceted, at times startling, history in which women played diverse and essential roles.

The purpose of this essay is not to provide an exhaustive survey of women's contributions to the success of silk in Europe during the period covered by this exhibition. Such an undertaking would require tomes. Rather, my goal is to highlight a range of technical, creative, and mercantile achievements by women who worked with silk, whether for financial or personal gain, primarily in Italy, France, and England—areas where the material held special economic significance. The aim is also to consider how women were perceived, and perceived themselves, in relation to their silk work, as well as some of the ways their activities increased their agency. Although these women's identities remain largely unknown, the records we possess enable us to retrieve from oblivion certain aspects of their lives, and so help restore their hard-earned place in our cultural consciousness.

Picturing Women at Work

By the sixteenth century in Italy, the manufacturing and trading of silk had a well-established history in many areas, including Florence, Lucca, Genoa, Venice, and Milan. Initially, raw silk was imported from Eastern lands such as Syria and Persia, but the practice of raising silkworms (sericulture)—introduced to Sicily and Calabria by Arab and Byzantine populations by the eleventh century—gradually took root in other regions.[1] From cocoon to woven cloth, obtaining and processing silk involved numerous stages, and women of different ages and backgrounds played key roles throughout most of them.[2] We know this thanks to documentary evidence and, more rarely, contemporary imagery; most notable is the *Vermis Sericus*, a series of detailed engravings designed by the Flemish artist Jan van der Straet, known as Stradanus, during his employ at the Medici ducal court in Florence (figs. 1 & 2).[3]

As spring bloomed, women fed silkworms their favourite food, mulberry leaves, over a period of six weeks until they spun their cocoons, which were then immersed in hot water to loosen their natural glue (sericin). The ends of filaments from multiple cocoons were combined to form a single thread that was passed around a reel to form a skein of silk, a task performed throughout the Italian countryside by female specialized workers. The next step, "throwing," involved plying multiple strands together to create yarn and was often conducted in urban centres with skeins sent from the countryside. Afterward, the silk was washed and dyed, the latter a guarded process done mainly by men. While men were heavily involved in weaving, particularly of costly figured textiles, warping was done mainly by women, who also made gold- and silver-wrapped silk thread.[4]

Women from the highest social echelons were engaged in the silk industry as well, notably by promoting sericulture within their territories. Such was the case of Duchess Bianca of Monferrato living in Piedmont, who, around 1490, obtained mulberry leaves for her own silkworms and hired personnel to raise and process them.[5] Silk, resplendent and resilient, satisfied the elite's taste for luxury, scientific edification, and economic expansion. Originating in Neolithic China, sericulture remained a source of awe in early modern Italy, prompting a rise in texts

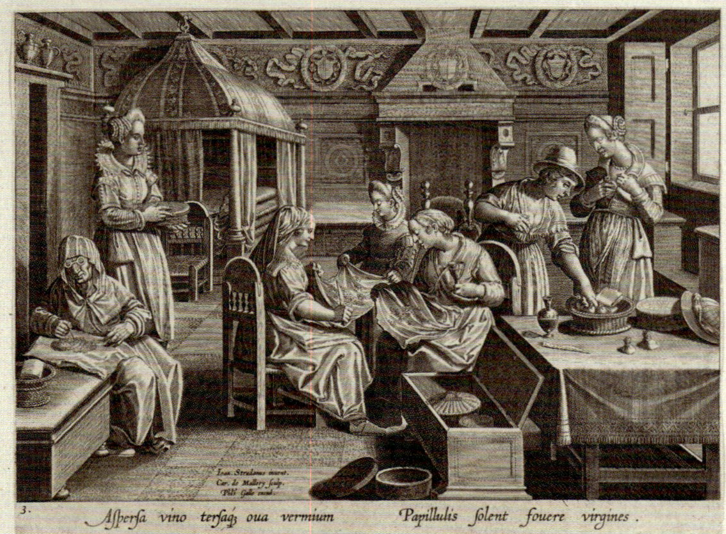

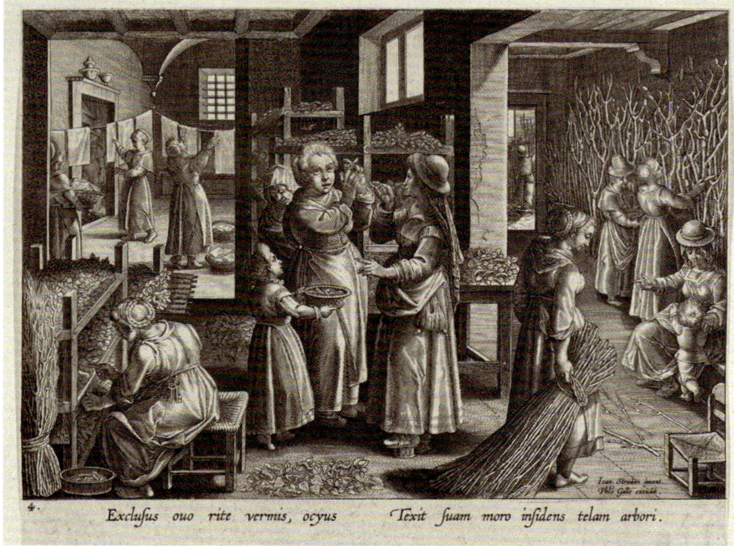

that praised silk and often singled out women as particularly knowledgeable on the subject.[6] Among the most notable of these reflections was that written by Magino Gabrielli, who wished to share his technique for ensuring not one but two yearly crops of cocoons yielding exceptional silk.[7] Gabrielli dedicated his dialogue to Pope Sixtus V and was invited to supervise a colony of silk workers operating at a court administered at the Villa Montalto by Camilla Peretti, the pope's sister.[8]

Woodcuts illustrating Gabrielli's text depict luxurious settings inhabited by women stylishly attired in the very material they were generating—a universe designed to appeal to a courtly audience. One image shows the proper way to incubate silkworm eggs, a subject accorded much importance in Gabrielli's texts and others like it. Related practices may be observed in plate 3 of the *Vemis Sericus* (fig. 1), where women of different ages place wine-soaked fertilized eggs into handkerchiefs. Two young women then insert these bundles into their décolletages, using their body heat to help the eggs reach maturity. Gabrielli specifies that silkworm eggs should be matured against the bosom of "young women, healthy and clean, of good disposition, and better a bit plump than otherwise, and better if they are virgins, or young girls in their first flower, because they have natural heat and are the most sincere."[9] Furthermore, he asserts that women menstruating, or otherwise "infirmed," should not perform this task. Interestingly, many of these criteria coincide with those listed by contemporary physicians describing ideal wet nurses.[10] Virginal yet maternal, these "surrogate mothers" paralleled the Virgin Mary, and from their breasts symbolically "flowed" a great good for their communities in the form of silk.[11] Such notions helped ensure the continued dominance of women in the early phases of silk production.

This method of incubation is also referenced in a drawing (fig. 3a) by the Milanese artist Giuseppe Arcimboldo, part of a group of thirteen sketches on silk production that he made in 1587 for the painted decorations of a palace in Prague.[12] Responding to the Rudolfine court's fascination with nature and technology, Arcimboldo strove for accuracy in many ways, particularly in his representation of a silkworm and cocoon, and of women reeling silk (the artist would likely have had occasion to observe practices tied to sericulture in his native Milan) (fig. 3b). Yet Arcimboldo's graceful workers wear vaguely classicizing dresses, recalling his costume studies for mythological characters and endowing the sketches with a performative dimension, a touch of fantasy that speaks of their fundamental aesthetic function rather than a need to share unglamorous truths about this

Fig. 1 (left) • Karel van Mallery, after Jan van der Straet (Giovanni Stradano, called Stradanus), *The Incubation of the Silkworm Eggs*, plate 3 from the series *The Introduction of the Silkworm* [*Vermis Sericus*], c. 1595. Engraving, 20 × 27 cm. The Metropolitan Museum of Art, New York, The Elisha Whittelsey Collection, The Elisha Whittelsey Fund, 1949, inv. no. 49.95.869(2).

Fig. 2 (right) • Karel van Mallery, after Jan van der Straet (Giovanni Stradano, called Stradanus), *The Silkworm Eggs Spread Out on Shelves*, plate 4 from the series *The Introduction of the Silkworm* [*Vermis Sericus*], c. 1595. Engraving, 20 × 26.8 cm. The Metropolitan Museum of Art, New York, The Elisha Whittelsey Collection, The Elisha Whittelsey Fund, 1949, inv. no. 49.95.869(4).

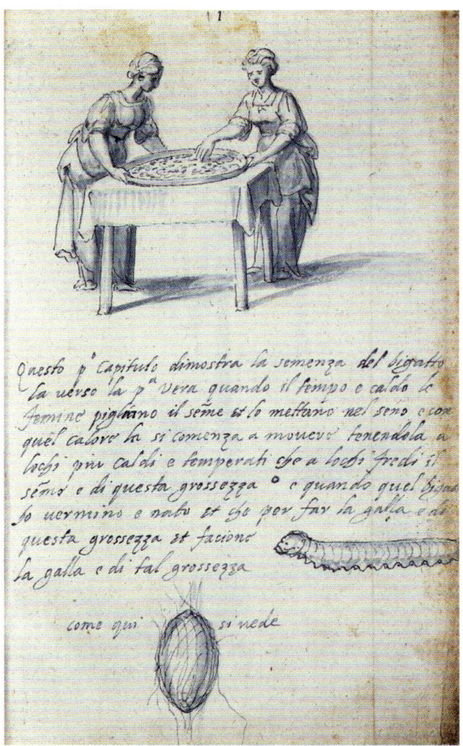

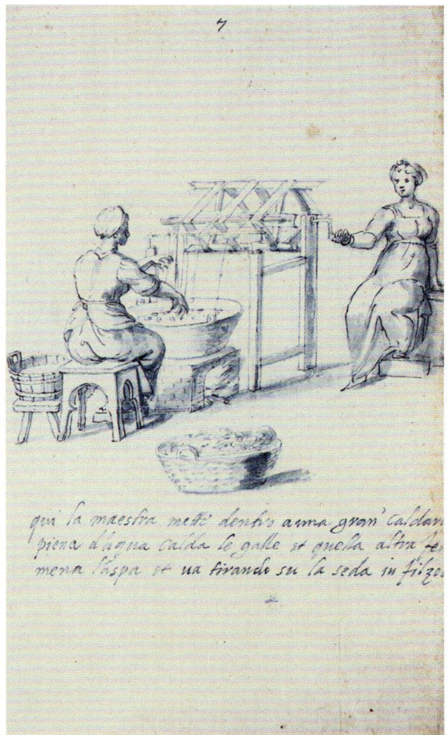

Fig. 3 • Giuseppe Arcimboldo, *Treatise on Silk Culture and Manufacture*, c. 1586. Pen and blue ink and brush with blue wash, each: 30.8 × 19 cm. Museum of Fine Arts, Boston, William A. Sargent Fund, inv. no. 50.6.15. Photographs © 2023 Museum of Fine Arts, Boston.

Openings illustrated (left to right):

Fig. 3a • *Preparing the Eggs of Silkworms* (plate 1)

Fig. 3b • *Reeling off the Raw Silk from the Cocoons* (plate 7)

form of labour. Among these were low wages, which sometimes compelled workers to steal silk to then attempt to sell to complicit weavers and craftsmen. In Genoa, thieving was so rampant that, in 1527, the government allowed the Silk Guild to establish a special "women's jail" solely for winders.[13] Italy was not alone in being affected by this issue. In eighteenth-century Lyon—by then a shining star of a French silk industry largely supported by women's work—there thrived a complex underground economy based on materials stolen by underpaid female workers.[14]

Economic reforms introduced by Jean-Baptiste Colbert, controller-general of finances under King Louis XIV, paved the way for Lyon's success, in particular by leading to the reorganization of its silk industry, which included formalizing the "Grande Fabrique" that regulated production and restricted entry into the trade.[15] The jobs performed by women, both legally and illegally, were varied, from basic tasks like sweeping to specialized work commanding higher wages, like that of the *liseuses* (readers), who read the patterns and called out the colours, thread by thread.[16] Women were technically excluded from weaving, the most prestigious occupation, although in reality female relatives often worked at the loom, both at home and in outside workshops, provided they could demonstrate their relationship to a master weaver.[17]

Given women's significant contributions to the industry, it is interesting to examine their representation in Denis Diderot and Jean le Rond d'Alembert's *Encyclopédie* (1751–1772). Featuring seventy-four thousand articles on various subjects by 140 authors and supplemented by three thousand plates, this mammoth undertaking reflects the Enlightenment's quest to advance and disseminate knowledge. As a key source of France's wealth and innovation, silk is given significant attention, both in a thirty-eight-page article on the subject and in many others dealing with related topics, from silk stockings to upholstery.[18] Female workers are mentioned, though not with a frequency or specificity indicative of their numbers and output.[19] Their presence is more readily felt in the illustration plates.[20]

Some images in the *Encyclopédie, ou Dictionnaire raisonné des sciences, des arts et des métiers* feature only women (fig. 4), such as embroideresses working on waistcoat patterns. Decorative touches like the paintings on the wall suggest they are in a domestic

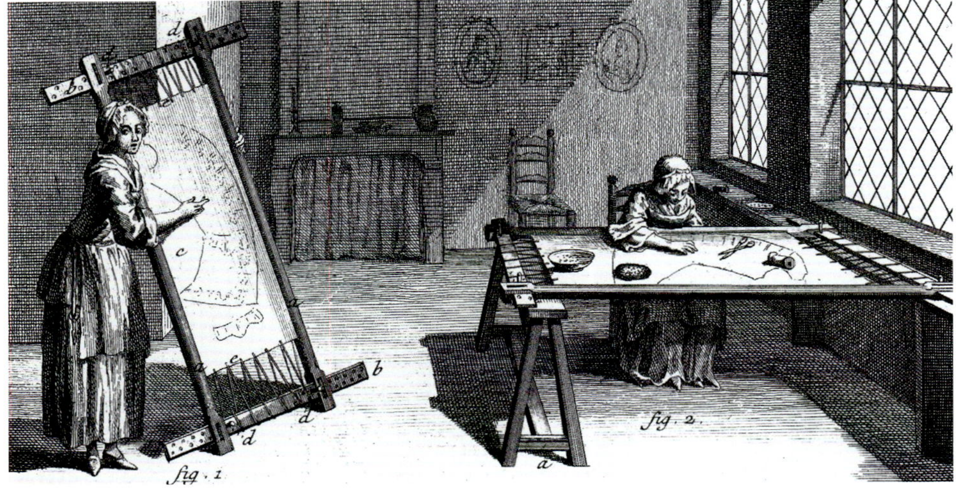

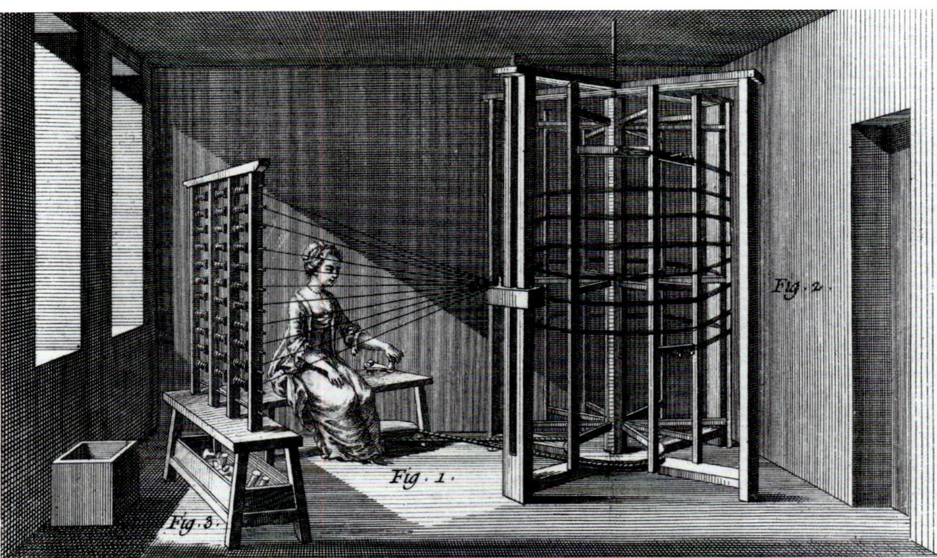

Fig. 4 (above) · *Detail:* Denis Diderot and Jean le Rond d'Alembert, *Embroidery* [*Brodeur*], plate 1 in *Encyclopédie, ou Dictionnaire raisonné des sciences, des arts et des métiers*, vol. 2, Paris, 1751–1772. Printed book on paper, illustrated with engravings, 43.8 × 29.5 cm. Private collection. Photo: © Patrice Cartier. All rights reserved 2023 / Bridgeman Images.

Fig. 5 (below) · *Detail:* Denis Diderot and Jean le Rond d'Alembert, *Warping with a Circular Frame* [*Soierie*], plate 23 in *Encyclopédie, ou Dictionnaire raisonné des sciences, des arts et des métiers*, vol. 11, Paris, 1751–1772. Printed book on paper, illustrated with engravings, 43.8 × 29.5 cm. Private collection. Photo: Bridgeman Images.

setting, possibly belonging to the establishment of a male relative.[21] Most unusual is the figure who looks at the viewer while touching the pattern in her frame, an exceptional moment in the *Encyclopédie* in which a female worker invites us to acknowledge her work.[22] As in many other plates, particular attention is given to the windows, indicating that the workers have enough light to perform their duties, while also hinting at the notion of work as an illuminating activity that enhances progress. The corresponding article indicates that embroidery on heavy fabric is exclusively the purview of men, while linen is worked on by women, who are excluded from the guild.[23] Interestingly, as Geraldine Sheridan has noted, this statement is contradicted by a plate from a contemporary treatise on embroidery, which shows women embroidering church vestments alongside men.[24]

Other images in the *Encyclopédie* present women in nondescript workshops using equipment to create various silk fabrics and related products. That women are often shown operating machines reflects their expertise and dexterity as well as the reality of the time, as inventors increasingly took into consideration the fact that their products were destined to be manipulated and calibrated by women.[25] An *ourdisseuse* (warper) (fig. 5) turns a crank to operate a circular warping frame, which draws together different threads from bobbins, interlaces them, and winds them onto the cage.[26] The woman focuses on the thread to ensure there are no breaks. Her seated position and use of an axle were considered progress, and while her activity would have been monotonous, it would not have been gruelling like that of drawgirls, who could spend up to eighteen hours a day pulling cords for large looms.[27]

Just as the *Encyclopédie*'s quest to provide accurate, usable information reveals itself in its articles and plates, so too does its desire to promote a dignified vision of labour devoid of unpalatable realities, which included disease, exhaustion, and, in the case of reelers, severely damaged skin as a result of plunging cocoons in near boiling water.[28] Above all, the value of labour, craftsmanship, and technological progress needed to come across both through the word and image for the *Encyclopédie* to achieve what Roland Barthes described as "a kind of golden legend of the artisanal class."[29] For this to be possible, its work environments needed to be rational spaces where application, neatness, and contentment ruled.

Stitching, Cutting, Transforming

The long and successful reign of Queen Elizabeth I from 1558 until her death in 1603 brought with it the stability and prosperity necessary to allow needlework to flourish among different strata of English society. While guild membership remained limited to men, women were still active in workshops and performed a wide range of activities involving needlework. The availability of luminous, coloured silk threads made it possible to achieve many effects, and by the late sixteenth century, milliners selling richly decorated accessories were long established in London.[30] These included purses, gloves, and waistcoats, as well as nightcaps, such as the ornate sixteenth-century head covering (fig. 6; cat. no. 229) that features a scrolling vine pattern enhanced with light-reflecting metallic thread and spangles. Such decoration is typical of the period's more luxurious embroidered nightcaps, worn by men around the house while entertaining informally.[31] Print books, especially herbals, were an important source of inspiration for the natural motifs that became a hallmark of English needlework.[32]

By the seventeenth century, needlework had become an integral part of a girl's education, serving as proof that she had acquired the skills necessary to establish her own household.[33] Embroidered objects, the most decorative of which would have been displayed in the home, were often signed and dated, thus amplifying their personal dimension. Stitched between 1668 and 1673, six pieces by Martha Edlin (1660–1725)—including samplers, pin cushions, an elaborate casket, and a jewellery box intricately beaded

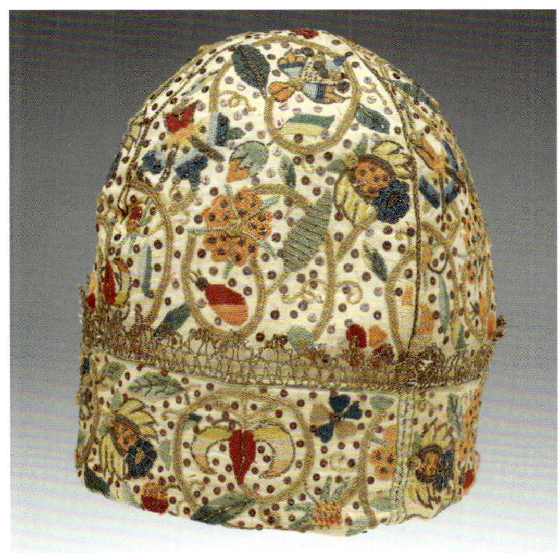

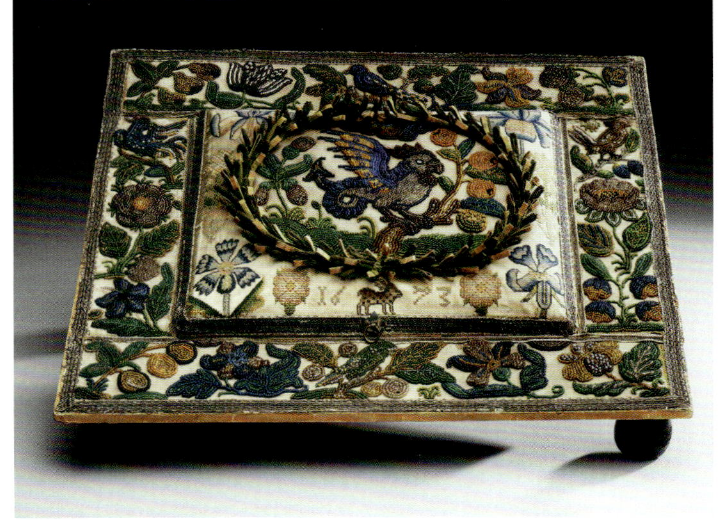

Fig. 6 (left) • Unknown British embroiderer, *Man's nightcap*, c. 1580. Linen plain weave embroidered with silk, metallic thread, and metal sequins, and trimmed with metallic-thread lace, height: 25.4 cm. Lent by Museum of Art, Rhode Island School of Design, Providence, Helen M. Danforth Acquisition Fund, inv. no. 1987.042. Image courtesy of the RISD Museum, Providence, RI.

Fig. 7 (right) • Martha Edlin, *Jewellery case*, 1673. Wood, covered with embroidered silk satin with coloured silks, metal purl and glass beads, padded, lined with silk and paper, parchment, and silver braid, 31.8 × 36.8 × 8.9 cm. Victoria and Albert Museum, London. Bequeathed by Sir Frederick Richmond, Bt, inv. no. T.41-1954. Image © Victoria and Albert Museum, London.

with a dazzling cockatrice, which she completed at age thirteen (fig. 7)—represent the largest group of works by a single hand to have survived from seventeenth-century England. Around age eight, girls typically commenced with samplers, which allowed them to track their progress as they practised different stitches and patterns. Likely produced under the guidance of an instructor, Anna Bockett's band sampler includes her name, the date (1656), and a courting scene, set in a lush garden evocative of Eden and featuring a couple separated by Cupid and a dog, symbols of love and fidelity respectively (fig. 8; cat. no. 228).[34] Beyond demonstrating her skill, Bockett (active seventeenth century) was perhaps pondering her own future marriage when adding this vignette, suggesting how such objects could also function as repositories for personal reflections.

A young woman often concluded her education by embroidering a casket, used to store jewellery, sewing equipment, and other items. Such objects could feature a lock and secret compartments, offering women their own portable, private sphere—one embellished by their hands over long stretches of time, and so possessing a distinctly personal dimension. Professional draughtspersons typically furnished designs for caskets, which were sometimes made from kits with panels on which the scenes to be embroidered were already drawn.[35] Biblical stories, especially of exemplary female heroines such as Judith and Esther, were popular subjects.

A cabinet (fig. 9; cat. no. 218) illustrates an Old Testament story rarely seen in needlework from the period—that of Ruth, known for her loyalty, hard work, and ability to take initiative.[36] The work is executed in complex queen stitch, a style rarely employed for figural elements. Other distinctive features include a costly mirrored receptacle on the casket's interior as well as a coat of arms around the lock, identified by Isabella Rosner as that of the Perwich family, whose most famous member, Susanna Perwich (1636–1661), was praised for her embroidery skills by her brother-in-law,

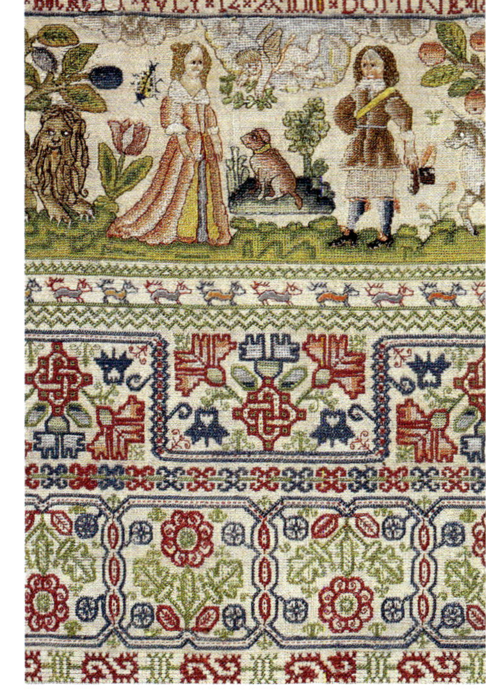

Fig. 8 (above) · *Detail:* Anna Bockett, *Sampler*, 1656. Linen worked with silk thread; long-and-short, split, stem, back, tent, cross, and satin stitches, 70.8 × 26.4 cm. Lent by The Metropolitan Museum of Art, New York, Gift of Irwin Untermyer, 1964, inv. no. 64.101.1327.

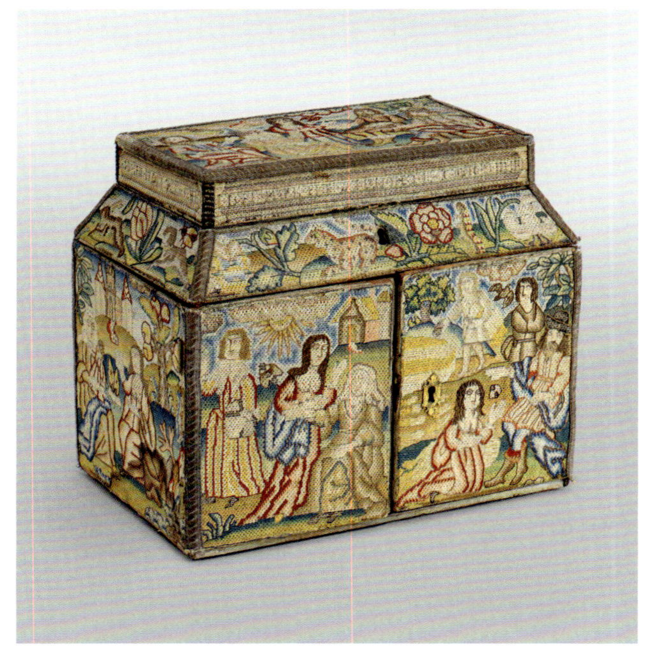

Fig. 9 (below, left) · Susanna Perwich, *Embroidered cabinet*, 1645–1655. Linen plain weave and silk satin with silk embroidery, metallic braid, silk plain weave, and mirrored glass with metal and wood, 26 × 30.8 × 20 cm. Los Angeles County Museum of Art, Gift of Mr. and Mrs. John A. McCone, inv. no. M.79.39.3a-g. Digital Image © 2023 Museum Associates / LACMA / Licensed by Art Resource, NY.

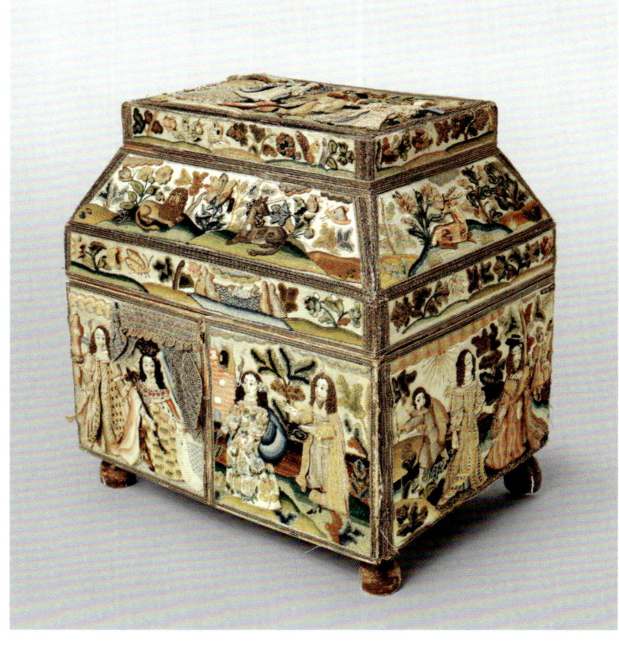

Fig. 10 (below, right) · Rebecca Stonier Plaisted, *Casket depicting scenes from the Old Testament*, 1668. Silk, warp-float faced satin weave; embroidered with silk floss, silk yarns, and silk-wrapped metal purl in brick, bullion, Ceylon, chain, knot, lattice filling, overcast, running, satin, Smyrna cross, tent, and a variety of buttonhole stitches; laid work, couching, and padded couching; French and Turkey knots; applied areas of linen, plain weave; seed pearls, coral beads, and mica; and silk, plain weave with ground weft fringe; edged with gilt-metal-strip-wrapped silk and gilt-metal strip, plain weave; silver hardware; wooden frame; lined with marbled paper; silk, plain weave; and silk, plain weave with supplementary pile warps forming cut solid velvet, 39 × 38.3 × 29 cm. Art Institute of Chicago, Purchased with funds provided by Mrs. Chauncey B. Borland and Mrs. Edwin A. Seipp, inv. no. 1959.337.

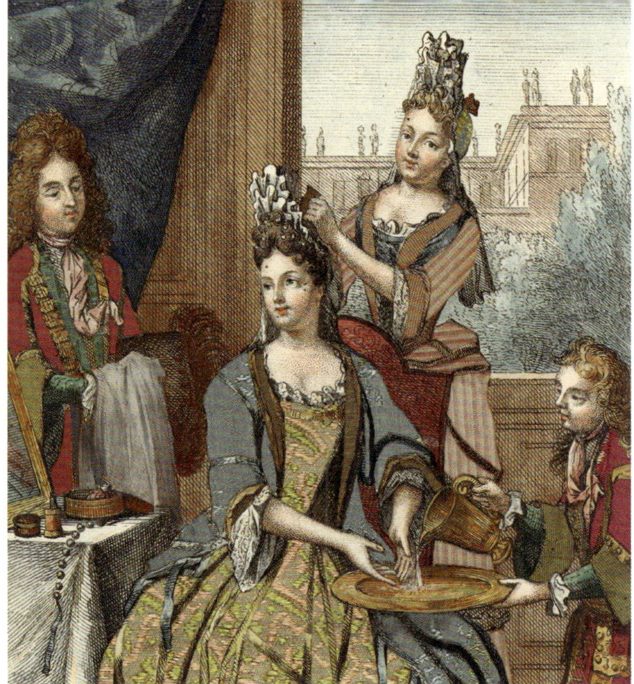

Fig. 11 (above) • Detail: Embroidered or "dressed" interventions by an unknown European maker, on an engraving by Robert Bonnart, *A Woman of Quality at Her Toilette* [*Dame de qualité à sa toilette*], originally printed c. 1690–1710, altered c. 1750. Hand-coloured engraving, faced on reverse with fabrics, 26.2 × 18.9 cm. The Morgan Library & Museum, New York, inv. no. 2002.31. Photo: The Morgan Library & Museum, New York.

John Batchiler, in *The Virgins Pattern*, his 1661 printed eulogy in her honour. Pointing to the casket's high degree of craftsmanship, its unusual features, and the object's very survival, Rosner has proposed Susanna, a celebrated musician and composer, as the author of its embroidery. It is tempting to see in its imagery, as Rosner does, further evidence of Perwich's authorship, including a musical connection through Ruth, the great-grandmother of legendary harpist King David.[37]

Ruth may have appealed because of her boldness and determination, qualities that possibly resonated with the unconventional Perwich, who chose not to marry. In fact, many of the biblical heroines stitched by women during this period travel, take action—even risks—and wield power in certain ways.[38] Among them is the Queen of Sheba, a wealthy, independent ruler who visits King Solomon in Jerusalem and tests his wisdom through her questions. She is typically presented delivering gifts to the king as a reward for his correct answers, as on the front of the casket embroidered by Rebecca Stonier Plaisted (active c. 1668; fig. 10).[39] Although domestic embroidery was intended as a stationary activity that kept women homebound, the subjects they chose could allow them to retrace the transformative journeys of others, and also to suggest their own views on authority.[40]

While our knowledge of seventeenth-century English embroidery is relatively rich, the same cannot be said of another art form that appears to have enjoyed great favour on the Continent. The fad for "dressing" prints—a process of cutting out elements of costume and decor and replacing them with brocaded silks and other fabrics[41]—was part of a larger craze in France for cut-paper work, which seems to have hit its zenith around 1727 as a source of gallant interaction between women and men.[42] Many extant examples combine late-seventeenth-century prints of fashionable individuals with fabric datable to the second quarter of the eighteenth century or later. This discrepancy may reveal that the prints were part of a witty game allowing participants to demonstrate their knowledge of quickly changing styles, and through this, their social belonging.[43] An example of this trend may be found on an engraving by Robert Bonnart (fig. 11; cat. no. 219), where attendants assist an elegant young woman in the performance of her toilet. Her pose reveals the sumptuous details of her floral damask

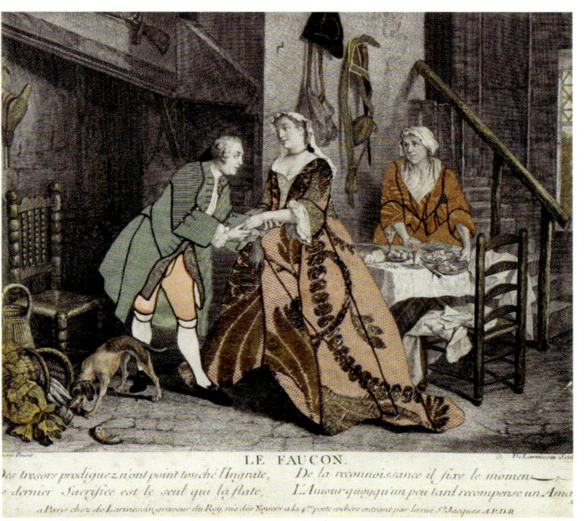

Fig. 12 (above, right) • Embroidered or "dressed" interventions by Sabine Louise d'Hervart, known as Lady Winn, on a print by Nicolas Larmessin IV, after Nicolas Lancret, *Le Faucon*, 1761–1765. Print, aquatint enriched with coloured silks, fabrics, and embroidery, 31.8 × 35.6 cm. Nostell Priory, National Trust. © National Trust / Robert Thrift.

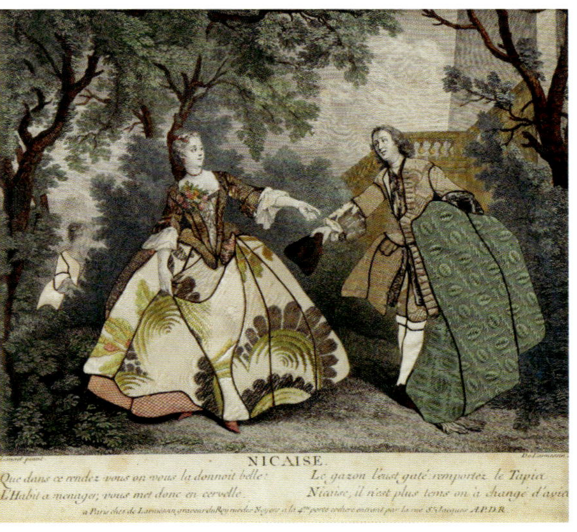

Fig. 13 (below, right) • Embroidered or "dressed" interventions by Sabine Louise d'Hervart, known as Lady Winn, on a print by Nicolas Larmessin IV, after Nicolas Lancret, *Nicaise*, 1761–1765. Print, aquatint enriched with coloured silks, fabrics, and embroidery, 31.8 × 35.6 cm. Nostell Priory, National Trust. © National Trust / Robert Thrift.

gown and blue silk morning coat, which, like the composition's many other sartorial elements, are made of real fabric inserted in the place of the original engraved paper.

In addition to embellishing the home, dressed prints may have also filled more intimate functions. For example, a gentleman, having just fetched a blanket of green silk for his rendezvous, is chided for taking too long by his married companion, now fretful about their tryst. This amorous scene illustrates one of Jean de la Fontaine's popular fables that was translated into a series of prints known as the *Suite Larmessin* (fig. 12), with their dressing ascribed to Sabine Louise d'Hervart, Lady Winn (1734–1798).[44] Sometime between their wedding in 1761 and 1765, Sir Rowland Winn gifted the engravings to his Swiss wife, who inscribed the reverse of each one.[45] With their French captions and what were deemed playful, amorous subjects, the prints would likely have appealed to Lady Winn's Francophile roots. Dressing the engraving would have taken time (and filled it), the objects serving as a link to her often-absent husband as well as to her heritage.[46] It would also have allowed her to demonstrate her skills to her new entourage, from precise cutting to meticulous embroidery, as well as her flair for composition and fashion. Many of the fabrics, such as the pink brocaded silk with silver thread in *Nicaise*, appear in different guises within several of the prints (fig. 13). These may be remnants of Winn's own garments, some possibly brought from home, and so add another layer of meaning to the engravings—one tied to memory and the need for women, often uprooted from their place of origin for marriage, to maintain tangible connections to their homes and past selves.[47]

Visions in Silk

Throughout continental Europe and England, women entertained complex relationships to fashion, as time and again sociopolitical constraints affected their agency in matters of dress. And yet, in the period under consideration here, women were deeply involved in the fabrication of garments and accessories, acting as entrepreneurial trendsetters and making use of changing styles to expand their influence and wealth.

France's persecution of Protestantism under King Louis XIV would go on to have important consequences for England's silk industry.[48] Fleeing northern France, Huguenots established themselves in the Spitalfields district of London's East End, bringing with them a set of skills and trade secrets.[49] Although herself not a Huguenot, it is there that Anna Maria Garthwaite (1688–1763) took up residence with her widowed sister in the late 1720s.[50] Garthwaite set about developing a thriving business from her house, producing designs for brocaded silks, damasks, and other fabrics for local master weavers and mercers, who then translated them into garments for men and women. Her designs, often containing annotations that reveal her technical expertise and working practices, survive in large numbers, as do many fabrics woven from them.

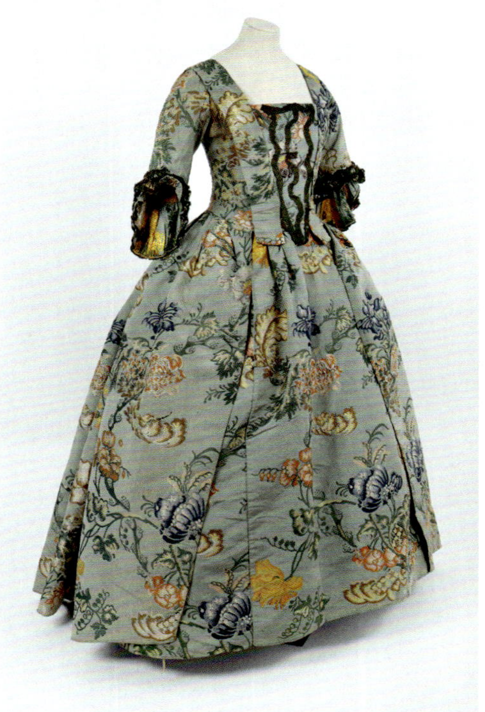

Fig. 14 (below, left) • Textile designed by Anna Maria Garthwaite, clothing designed by Jean Revel, *Blue floral silk dress*, c. 1736–1739, remodelled c. 1760s. Tabby ground brocaded with coloured silks, bust: 79 cm; waist: 67.5 cm; sleeve length: 38 cm; nape to hem: 127 cm; across back: 32 cm; pattern repeat: 65 × 60 cm (selvedge to selvedge); footprint: 100 × 90 × 144 cm. Fashion Museum Bath, inv. no. BATMC III.09.1. Photo: © Fashion Museum Bath / Bridgeman Images.

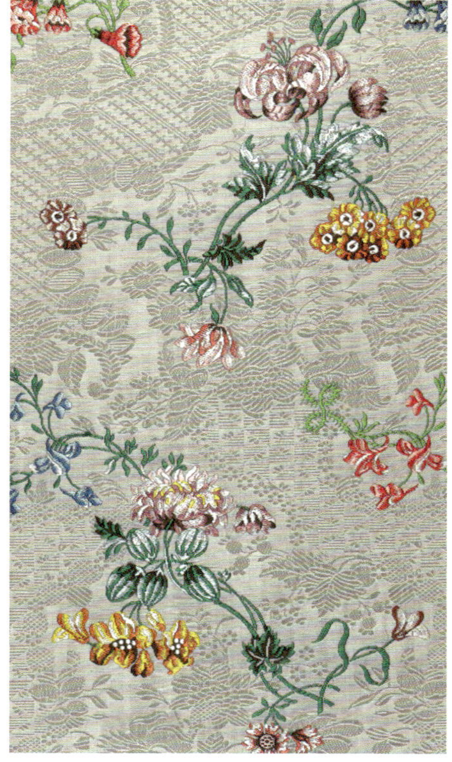

Fig. 15 (below, right) • *Detail:* Anna Maria Garthwaite, *Length of brocaded silk tobine*, 1749. Silk, 88.3 × 49.5 cm. Baltimore Museum of Art: Angelica Yonge Pearre Fund, 1999.156. Photo: Mitro Hood.

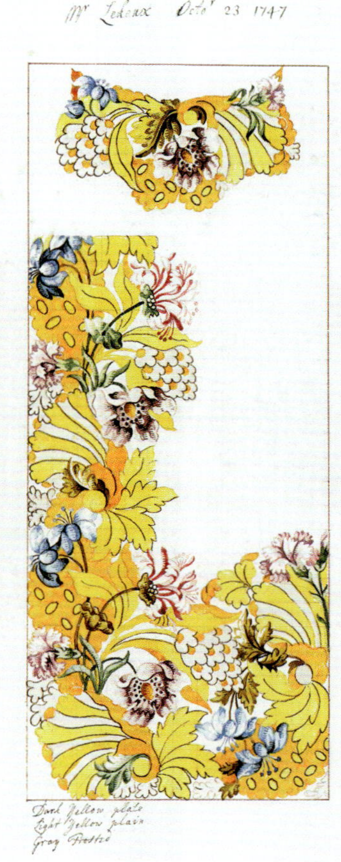

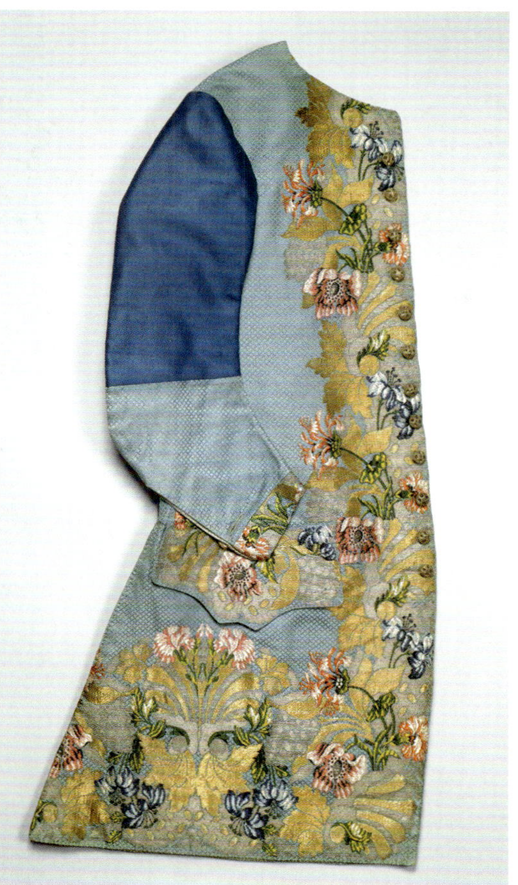

Fig. 16 (above, left) • Anna Maria Garthwaite, *Design for a woven silk*, 1747. Watercolour on paper, 48.6 × 30.2 cm. Victoria and Albert Museum, London, inv. no. 5985:13. Image © Victoria and Albert Museum, London.

Fig. 17 (above, right) • Anna Maria Garthwaite and Peter Lekeux, *Waistcoat*, 1747. Silk, wool, and metallic. The Metropolitan Museum of Art, New York, Purchase, Irene Lewisohn Bequest, 1966, inv. no. C.I.66.14.2.

Fig. 18 (below, right) • Detail: Anna Maria Garthwaite, *Dress fabric*, 1742. Silk, brocaded with silver thread, 125.2 × 55.2 cm. Victoria and Albert Museum, London, Given by F.A. Rawlence, inv. no. T.81-1938. Image © Victoria and Albert Museum, London.

This material evidence offers crucial insight into Garthwaite's remarkable career, as well as into changing tastes in English silk patterns. By the 1730s, her designs grew significantly larger, the grounds nearly covered with lush blooms and showing off to full effect the *point rentré* method of three-dimensional shading as perfected by the Lyon designer Jean Revel (fig. 14).[51] Garthwaite's distinctly English interpretation of the exuberant Rococo style fully emerged by the 1740s, characterized by lighter silks with naturalistic renditions of sprays of flowers scattered on open grounds (fig. 15; cat. no. 234).[52] The rich floral repertoire found in Garthwaite's oeuvre, in addition to her approaches to articulating the natural world, speak of her interaction with naturalists and her access to hothouses.[53]

Among our most illuminating records of Garthwaite's career are a watercolour design (fig. 16) and a waistcoat woven from it (fig. 17).[54] The former specifies the colours of the metal threads to be used ("dark yellow plate," "light yellow plain," and "gray frosted"), the name of the person who commissioned the work ("Mr. Lekeux"), and the date of sale ("October 23, 1747"). A comparison of both objects reveals the degree to which Garthwaite's design was faithfully translated, and how she anticipated the elegant pattern that her gently bending blooms and scintillating foliage would create as it filled the edges of a gentleman's waistcoat. One of England's wealthiest master weavers, Captain Peter Lekeux purchased several designs for luxurious fabrics from Garthwaite, including one that same year for a blue silk tabby brocaded with silver thread to be used for women's gowns (fig. 18).[55]

While Garthwaite spent her career in Spitalfields, her designs travelled, allowing her talent and entrepreneurial spirit to circulate well beyond her geographic confines.[56] In the American colonies, where English fashion exercised a strong hold, Garthwaite's flowered silk patterns were in demand, as revealed by family inventories and other extant evidence. Among these records is a portrait of

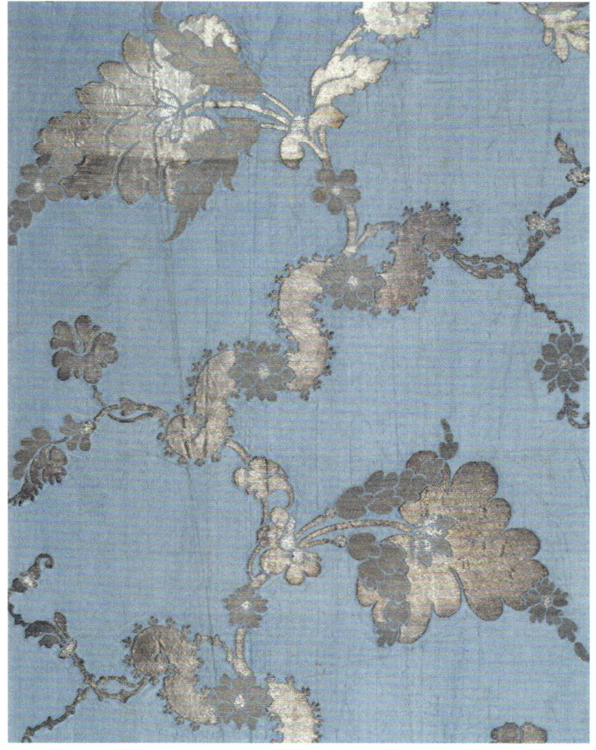

Anne Shippen Willing (fig. 19), wife of a wealthy merchant and two-time mayor of Philadelphia, who chose to have her likeness painted in a damask gown featuring a 1742 design by Garthwaite that was woven by Spitalfields master weaver Simon Julins.[57] A similar design attributed to Garthwaite adorns dress panels now at Colonial Williamsburg, which, according to family tradition, belonged to Martha Dandridge Curtis, future wife of George Washington.[58] Women in the colonies were connected to Garthwaite not only as consumers of her designs but also, in some instances, as producers of silk, which was sent back to Spitalfields to be fashioned into cloth. In the mid-1700s, Eliza Lucas Pinckney and her daughter Harriott established sericulture in their South Carolina plantation, relegating the physically taxing labour of caring for the worms and reeling the silk to enslaved individuals—mostly women and children—whose stories have yet to be fully told.[59]

As of yet, no clear equivalent to Garthwaite has made herself known to us in France, England's great rival in matters of silk during the eighteenth century. In Lyon, men either worked as designers on a freelance basis or were attached to a merchant-manufacturer, within whose headquarters they produced sketches and technical drawings that were then sent to weavers' workshops.[60] Save for a few individuals—namely designer, master weaver, and inventor Philippe de Lasalle—relatively little is known about Lyon's *dessinateurs*, who worked mostly anonymously.

Precious information about the profession emerges in a manual from 1765 by Antoine-Nicolas Joubert de L'Hiberderie.[61] Himself a Lyonnais designer, Joubert decries the "ridiculous custom" of allowing only men to pursue draughtsmanship, when women seem so well disposed to it. To those who might object to young ladies drawing silk designs for manufactories on the grounds that it is simply not done, the author replies: "So what! Shall we never shake a prejudice that deprives us of Subjects that enrich our State and honor our Homeland?"[62] To conclude, Joubert remarks:

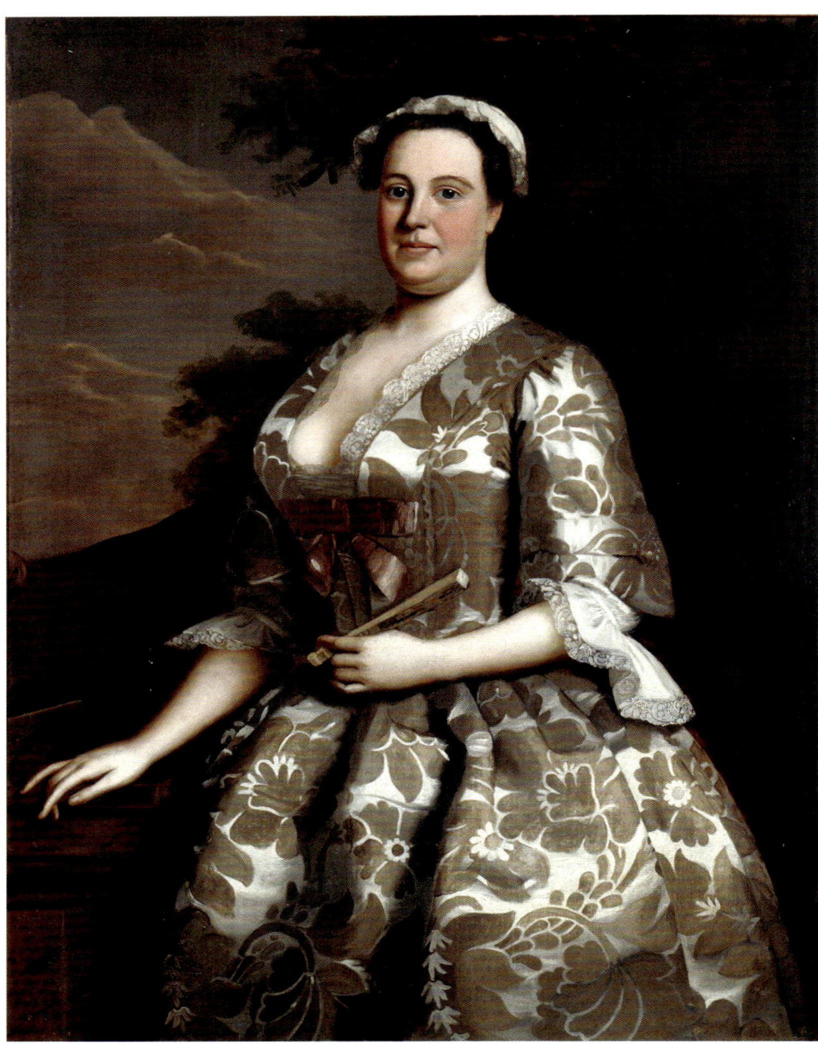

Fig. 19 • Robert Feke, *Anne Shippen Willing (Mrs. Charles Willing)*, 1746. Oil on canvas, 127 × 101.6 cm. Courtesy of Winterthur Museum, Garden & Library, Museum purchase with funds provided by Alfred E. Bissell in memory of Henry Francis du Pont, inv. no. 1969.0134A.

> I therefore say that a father who is the head of his Manufactory, could have drawing taught to his daughter, and when she will be able to run the Fabrique, she could train other students of her sex. In this way, in each house, we could occupy quantities of young ladies disgraced by Nature, or who have incommodities that prevent them from marrying, and who often become a burden to their parents.[63]

Ending on a sadly misogynistic note, Joubert's defence is firm that young women were excluded from the profession of silk designer. And yet, given the ample evidence that women routinely undertook activities technically forbidden to them, such as weaving, it is possible that Joubert's scenario of fathers employing their daughters for this purpose was not

Fig. 20 (right) • Mademoiselle Montalent, *Design for Gilet*, c. 1785. Brush and opaque watercolour on paper, 31.9 × 24.3 cm. Cooper Hewitt, Smithsonian Design Museum, Smithsonian Institution, Gift of Eleanor and Sarah Hewitt, inv. no. 1920-36-84.

Fig. 21 (below, left) • Marie Victoire Lemoine, *Portrait of a Youth in an Embroidered Vest*, 1785. Oil on canvas, 65.1 × 54.6 cm. Purchased with funds from the Cummer Council, Cummer Museum of Art & Gardens, Jacksonville, Florida, inv. no. AP.1994.3.1. Image: Douglas J. Eng Photography.

Fig. 22 (below, right) • Unknown maker, *Man's waistcoat*, 1780s–1790s. Ivory silk taffeta with multicoloured silk embroidery in satin stitch, natural linen plain weave, and natural wool flannel, centre-back length: 45.7 cm; waist: 83.8 cm. Philadelphia Museum of Art: Gift of Mrs. N. Dubois Miller, 1943, inv. no. 1943-17-6.

outside reality. In *L'Art du brodeur* (1770), Charles Germain de Saint-Aubin, also a designer, asserts that "drawing is the basis and foundation of embroidery," but speaks only of men in this capacity.[64] Preserved at the Metropolitan Museum of Art, a scrapbook of designs for embroidered waistcoats and other items from the Fabrique de St. Ruf is annotated with pattern numbers and names, some of which are prefaced with "Mad" ("Madame") or "Mlle" ("Miss").[65] Coloured drawings corresponding to these designs are now at the Cooper Hewitt (fig. 20; cat. nos. 236–238), though they contain only the pattern numbers. Several inscriptions in the Met's scrapbook identify not only the author of the design but also the embroiderer, such as pattern #1778 for a waistcoat pocket drawn by Mademoiselle Montalent (active c. 1785), which was then submitted to a woman whose name is indecipherable.[66] Little is known about St. Ruf, which may have operated in Lyon; further research will hopefully yield additional information about the women employed there and their practices.[67] The designs reflect the period's taste for bird motifs, as well as for festoons and delicate sprigs of wildflowers. Floral elements of this kind appear in the trim and buttons of

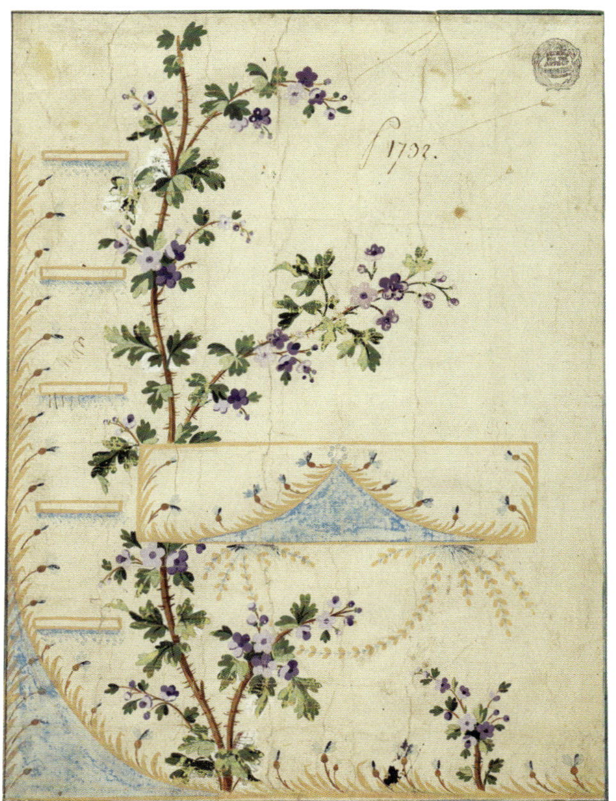

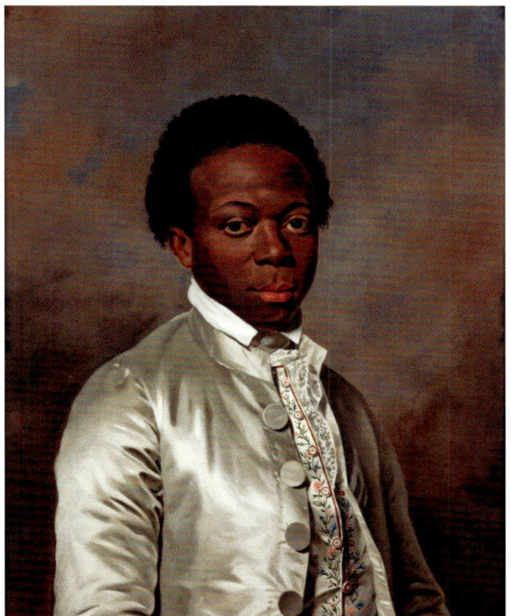

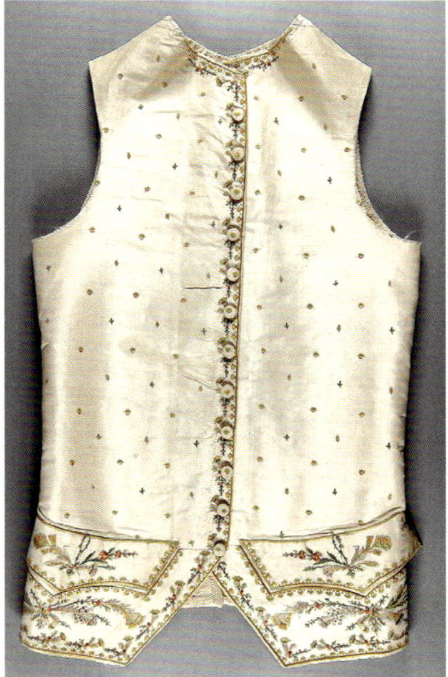

the embroidered waistcoat worn by the young man in a portrait by Marie Victoire Lemoine (1754–1820; fig. 21; cat. no. 106), painted in 1785, and therefore contemporary with the St. Ruf designs (fig. 22).[68]

Women also left their creative imprint on eighteenth-century silk fashions in other ways. By 1675, *couturières* (seamstresses) had established their own guild, where they could make certain clothing for women and children. In addition to sewing garments, women were instrumental in shaping taste and creating demand. This is particularly evident in the activities of the *marchandes de modes* (fashion merchants) who achieved independent status as a corporation in 1776.[69] Like a painter expertly combining the colours of her palette, the fashion merchants drew on a staggering selection of sartorial goods, including silk flowers, ribbons, and lace, to compose new looks. One contemporary commentator estimated that, through their astute combinations, Parisian fashion merchants increased the value of the individual elements they worked with by one hundredfold.[70] By constantly introducing new styles, these women helped fuel consumption. The most famous of these entrepreneurs, Marie-Jean "Rose" Bertin (1747–1813), who was among other things a dressmaker and milliner, worked for the French court under Queen Marie Antoinette during the late eighteenth century.[71]

While Marie Antoinette delighted in Bertin's creations, the queen's detractors saw in them evidence of her love of excess. Bertin excelled at formal court dress, with panniers (large hoops), and swaths of taffeta, moiré, and other silks embellished with embroidery and gemstones (fig. 23). On one occasion, Bertin even sent a lock of Marie Antoinette's hair to the Gobelins manufactory to have a new shade of silk made after it.[72] As criticism mounted and Marie Antoinette retreated into her own private world, Bertin encouraged her to adopt a new style that took the form of a loose gown, likely inspired by the cotton dresses worn by free women of colour in the French colonies and appropriated by colonialists' wives who found the climate too hot for silk.[73] Divorced from its original context, the style could be invested with echoes of Greco-Roman aesthetics and praised for its simplicity, bringing it in line with Enlightenment values. The gown proved controversial, not only because it was judged by many as too informal for a queen but also because the dress was made chiefly of foreign muslin, and through its popularity, threatened France's lucrative silk industry.[74]

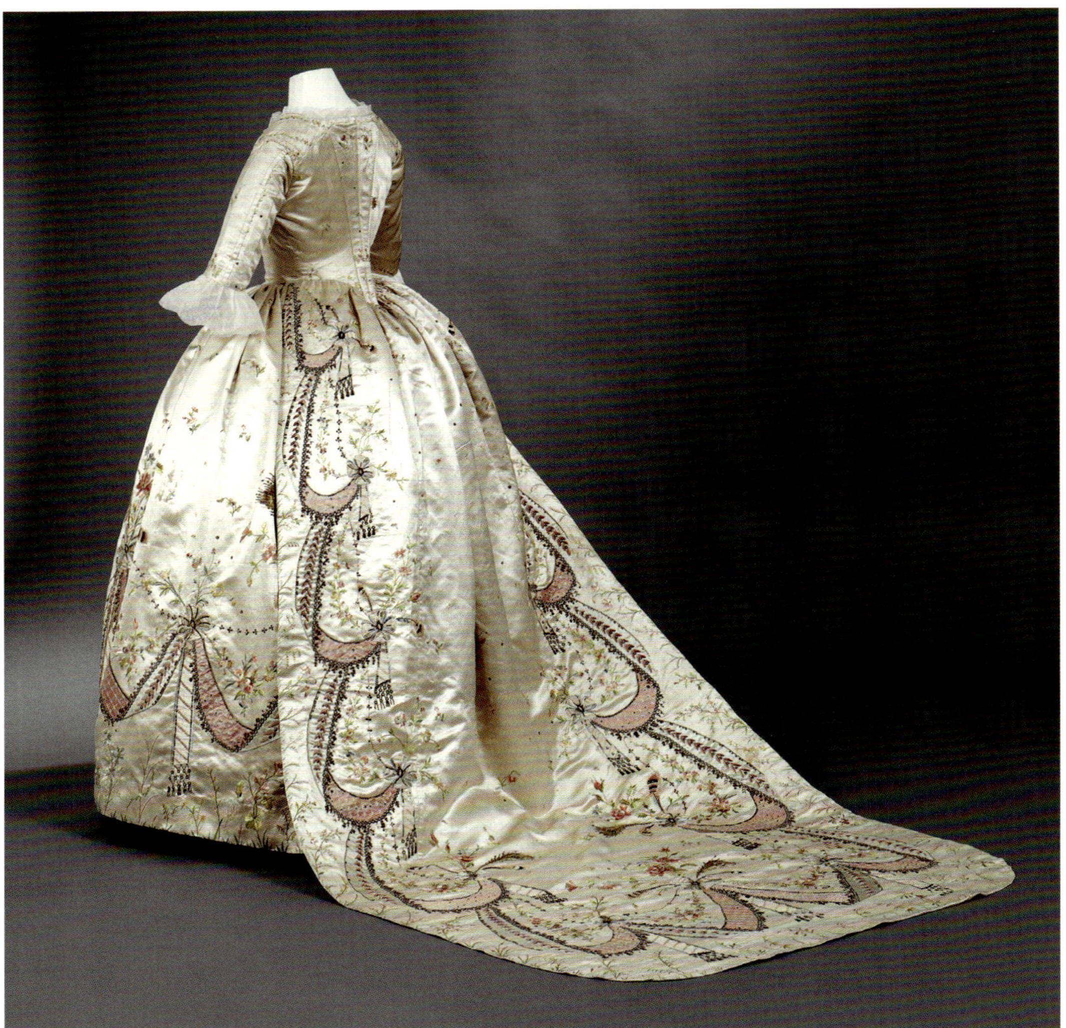

Fig. 23 • Attributed to Marie-Jean "Rose" Bertin, *Court dress* [*Robe en fourreau or robe à l'anglaise or grand habit*], 1780s, altered in 1870s. Embroidered satin with ribbon appliqués, sequins, faceted glass stones mounted on silver facings, and silver filé; fitted, boned bodice. Royal Ontario Museum, Toronto, Canada, inv. no. 925.18.3.A-B. Photo: courtesy of the Royal Ontario Museum, © ROM.

~

By contextualizing some of the material records that have come down to us from early modern Europe, this essay seeks to highlight the intersection of silk, power, and women as makers and consumers of this precious and symbolically charged material. At the root of much of this discussion is the issue of visibility—of silk workers, often compelled to operate in the shadows; of well-to-do women working their needles at home; and of designers creating anonymously or circulating their wares widely. While the works of many women, both known and unidentified, have been brought to light, there are still many threads left to be unravelled and histories to be told.

Notes

1 Luca Molà points out that the spread of sericulture in Italy followed the spread of the mulberry tree, of which a highly adaptable variety producing white fruit first appeared in Florence in 1434, then spread to the rest of Tuscany. Luca Molà, "A Luxury Industry: The Production of Italian Silks, 1400–1600," in *Europe's Rich Fabric: The Consumption, Commercialisation, and Production of Luxury Textiles in Italy, the Low Countries and Neighbouring Territories (Fourteenth–Sixteenth Centuries)*, ed. Bart Lambert and Katherine Anne Wilson (Abingdon, UK: 2016), 212.

2 Silk work in the Italian countryside provided work for nearly all segments of the female population, including nuns, noble women, and the elderly, and governments particularly targeted women workers. See Luca Molà, *The Silk Industry of Renaissance Venice* (Baltimore: Johns Hopkins University Press, 2000), 35.

3 The subject of silk is also addressed in plate 8 from another series of prints after Stradanus, the *Nova Reperta* (c. 1600), which shows in the foreground the Byzantine emperor Justinian receiving silkworm eggs from China, while in the background women are portrayed preparing raw silk. See Luca Molà, "On *Ser, Sive, Sericus Vermis, Saccarum, Oleum Olivarum*, and Intellectual Property," in *Renaissance Invention: Stradanus's* "Nova Reperta," ed. Lia Markey (Evanston, IL: Northwestern University Press, 2020), 166.

4 For example, in 1592, Giovan Stefano Cerruti, a goldbeater from Milan, offered to give a job to a thousand women the first year his business was active in Rome, eventually employing up to four thousand women. Molà, *The Silk Industry*, 35. On the different processes of silk production, see Molà, "A Luxury Industry," 213–21, and Edoardo Demo, "New Products and Technological Innovation in the Silk Industry of Vicenza in the Fifteenth and Sixteenth Centuries," in *Innovation and Creativity in Late Medieval and Early Modern European Cities*, ed. Karel Davids and Bert De Munck (London: Routledge, 2019), 81–94, esp. 83–87.

5 Molà, *The Silk Industry*, 217.

6 Among the most celebrated of these is Marcus Hieronymus Vida's Virgilian poem *The Silkworm* (1527), which he dedicated to Isabella d' Este, Marchoness of Mantua. About twenty texts about silk from the sixteenth century, mainly didactic poems, including Corsucccio di Sascorbaro's *Il vermicelli della seta* (Rimini, 1581), have been identified. See Marcus Hieronymus Vida, *The Silkworm: A Poem; In Two Books* trans. Reverend Samuel Pullein (Farmington Hills, MI: Kessinger, 2018), and Claudio Zanier, "La fabrication de la soie: un domaine reservé au femmes," *Travail, genre et sociétés* 18, no. 2 (2007): 113.

7 *Dialoghi di m. Magino Gabrielli Hebreo, sopra l'utile sue inventioni circa la seta: Ne' quali anche si dimostrano in vaghe figure historiati tutti gli' essercitij, & instrumenti, che nell'arte della seta si ricercano* (Rome, 1588). Lincoln provides a thorough analysis of Magino's dialogue, particularly in relation to his Jewish identity, noting the privileges he was able to obtain from the Pope because of his expertise on sericulture. Evelyn Lincoln, "The Jew and the Worms: Portraits and Patronage in a Sixteenth-Century How-to Manual," *Word & Image* 19 (2003): 86–99. See also Molà, "On *Ser, Sive, Sericus Vermis*," 166–67, for more on this Venetian inventor's fascinating career.

8 Among other privileges, Pope Sixtus guaranteed Magino and his heirs a percentage of any profits relating to his invention acquired by individuals in the Papal States. As for Magino, he promised a portion of his earnings to Camilla Peretti, which highlights her position as a silk entrepreneur. See Lincoln, "The Jew and the Worms," 92–93.

9 See Lincoln, "The Jew and the Worms," 95. For example, as Zanier, "La fabrication de la soie," 122, observes, Levanzio da Guidicciolo uses similar language in his *Avvertimenti* [...], 1564.

10 See, for example, the definition advanced by the French royal physician Ambroise Paré, who asserts among other things that the ideal wet nurse should be of good disposition, neither too fat nor thin, not menstruating nor sexually active. See Ambroise Paré, *Deux livres de chirurgie, de la génération de l'homme, & manière d'extraire les enfans hors du ventre de la mère,*[...] (Paris, 1573), 108–17. Zanier, "La fabrication de la soie," 122, notes that a silk worker is referred to as a "wet nurse of silkworms" in Giacomo Lubrano's *Scintille poetiche* (Naples, 1690). Fear of menstruation was likely tied to the concern that it might cause sterility in the worms.

11 It is even tempting to see a link between the young virgin who tends the worm born on her breast and the young virgin who tames the unicorn, the latter allegories of the Virgin Mary and Christ. Religion was certainly tied to the practice of women incubating and caring for silkworms. As Zanier "La fabrication de la soie," 118, observes, several contemporary authors encouraged women to give a percentage of the money they earned from their silk work to the Church to help ensure their continued success. Composed in medieval Spain by King Alfonso X el Sabio (r. 1252–1284), "Cantiga 18" of the *Cantigas de Santa Maria* tells the story of a woman whose sick silkworms were cured by the Virgin Mary, for whom she was supposed to make a silk wimple, directly underscoring Mary's role as protector of the silkworms and the women who cared for them. For a translation, see John E. Keller, "The Miracle of Divinely Motivated Silkworms: *Cantiga 18* of the *Cantigas de Santa Maria*, *Hispanófia*, no. 82 (1984): 3–4.

12 The project, planned for Baron Hoffman, a nobleman of Styrian origins, never came to fruition. Thomas DaCosta Kaufmann, "'Ancients and Moderns' in Prague: Arcimboldo's Drawings for Silk Manufacture," *Leids Kunsthistorisch Jaarboek* 2 (1983): 195. The author has analyzed the letter written by Arcimboldo to his prospective patron, now preserved with the sketches, observing that the subject of sericulture was novel in Bohemia and would have allowed Arcimboldo to demonstrate his artistic inventiveness.

13 Molà, "A Luxury Industry," 218. Winders, who were responsible for winding and doubling silk to make it more resistant, were unspecialized workers, especially wives and daughters with a male relative working in the silk industry.

14 For an extensive discussion of this phenomenon, see Daryl M. Hafter, "Women in the Underground Business of Eighteenth-Century Lyon," *Enterprise & Society* 2, no. 1 (2001): 11–40.

15 Hafter notes that, in some cases, Colbert's efforts to strengthen and prioritize the guild system had a direct positive effect on women workers, such as, for instance, with the establishment of guilds of *couturières* (women dressmakers) in Paris and Rouen. Daryl Hafter, *Women at Work in Preindustrial France* (University Park, PA: Penn State University Press, 2007), 32.

16 The job of *liseuse* was very important, as it consisted of transposing the patterns to be woven from point paper into simples, composed of several chords and designed to lift a group of warp threads when triggered by the drawgirl. Similar to graph paper, point paper was essential to translating the drawing produced by the designer into a form that allowed it to be used on the loom. See Lesley Ellis Miller, "Between Engraving and Silk Manufacture in Late Eighteenth-Century Lyons: Marie-Anne Brenier and Other Point Papermakers," *Studies in the Decorative Arts* 3, no. 2 (Spring–Summer 1996): 52–76.

17 Merchants increasingly feared weavers gaining an edge by using the labour of women who were basically operating as independent artisans being paid wages for their work outside the home. This resulted in a 1744 ordinance revoking the rights of wives and daughters to work outside the family workshop. See Daryl Hafter, "Women Who Wove in the Eighteenth-Century Silk Industry of Lyon," in *European Women and Preindustrial Craft*, ed. Daryl M. Hafter (Bloomington: Indiana University Press, 1995), 42–64, esp. 48–54. There were other exceptions as well, such as the girls abandoned to the Charité, a local Lyon hospital, who received training to work as weavers. Jean-François Budin, "Les ouvrières de la soie à Lyon au XVIIIe siècle," in *Le travail dans la revolution industrielle: Actes du 127e Congrès national des sociétés historiques et scientifiques, "Le travail et les hommes," Nancy, 2002* (Paris: Éditions du CTHS, 2006), 118–19.

18 "Soie," in *Encyclopédie, ou Dictionnaire raisonné des sciences, des arts et des métiers*, ed. Denis Diderot and Jean d'Alembert (Paris, 1751–72), 15:268–306, enccre.academie-sciences.fr/encyclopedie/. The author of the article is unknown. Related articles include, among many others, those on the making of artificial flowers, braids (*passementeries*), ribbons, lace, and goldbeating.

19 Cayez estimates that women accounted for 69 percent of all silk workers. Pierre Cayez, *Métiers, jacquards et hauts fourneaux: aux origines de l'industrie lyonnaise* (Lyon, 1978), 44.

20 Plates featuring work scenes are typically combined with sections illustrating corresponding tools or manufactured goods.

21 Sheridan observes that the women could also be "illegal workers operating from their family home, or a shared room as outworkers, selling their services to master tradesmen who commonly contravened their own

trade regulations." Geraldine Sheridan, *Louder Than Words: Ways of Seeing Women Workers in Eighteenth-Century France* (Lubbock: Texas Tech University Press, 2009), 105.

22 The corresponding caption describes in detail how to properly prepare a frame for this kind of embroidery, which explains in part why the figure appears to present it to the viewer.

23 "Brodeur," in *Encyclopédie, ou Dictionnaire raisonné des sciences, des arts et des métiers*, ed. Denis Diderot and Jean d'Alembert (Paris, 1751–72), 2:434, enccre.academie-sciences.fr/encyclopedie/.

24 Sheridan, *Louder Than Words*, 107–8. See Charles Germain de Saint-Aubin, *L'Art du Brodeur* (Paris: 1770), plate 2.

25 Women were therefore often selected to demonstrate the functioning of new textile machines. See Daryl Hafter, "French Industrial Growth in Women's Hands," in *Women and Work in Eighteenth-Century France*, ed. Daryl M. Hafter and Nina Kushner (Baton Rouge: Louisiana State University Press, 2015), 190.

26 The process of milling thread in this manner helped give silk its distinctive softness and sheen. Interestingly, in the *Encyclopédie*'s article "*Ourdir*" (Warping), work connected to silk is described as male. As Sheridan recognizes in *Louder Than Words* (164), this plate closely relates to plate 15 of Paulet's *L'Art du fabriquant d'étoffes de soie: Première et seconde sections* (2nd series), now at Houghton Library, Harvard (A 10.10.1015 F [v. 16]).

27 Hafter, *Women at Work*, 127. On the difficult working conditions of drawgirls, see Sheridan, *Louder Than Words*, 143–45. For more on the nature of their activity, see Miller, "Point Papermakers in Lyons," 55.

28 Reelers were prone to losing sensation in their hands. The threat of injury or death was high, particularly among women working in the most physically demanding, less prestigious jobs. Humid workshop conditions were conducive to tuberculosis, long hours led to exhaustion, and sexual predation was a grave concern. On working conditions for women workers of the silk industry, see Sheridan, *Louder Than Words*, 143–44, and Budin, "Les ouvrières de la soie," 120–22.

29 Roland Barthes, Introduction, *Recueil de planches sur les Sciences, les arts libéraux et les arts méchnaniques avec leur explication*, facsimile edition of *Encyclopédie, ou Dictionnaire raisonné des sciences, des arts et des métiers*, ed. Denis Diderot and Jean d'Alembert ([1751–72] Parma: F.M. Ricci, 1970), 2:38. Roland Barthes, "Les Planches de l'Encyclopédie," in *Le Degré zéro de l'écriture suivi de Nouveaux essais critiques* (Paris: Seuil, 1972), 92.

30 Already throughout the fourteenth and fifteenth centuries, silk trimmings and other items related to haberdashery were fabricated by a nearly exclusively female workforce. See Molà, *The Silk Industry*, 46.

31 Comparable motifs, such as the roses and strawberries, may be found in similar nightcaps from the period in several museums, such as the Metropolitan Museum of Art (64.101.1241) and the Victoria and Albert Museum (2016-1899). See also the example that belonged to Sir Thomas Cave illustrated in Joy Jarrett, Stephen Jarrett, and Rebecca Scott, "*Wrought with the Needle*": *Art Treasures of English Domestic Embroidery, Elizabeth I-George II / Witney Antiques* (Witney, UK: Witney Antiques, 2010).

32 For more on the topic of print books, see Alexa Greist's essay "Prints and Needles: Women Makers and European Textile Pattern Books, 1500–1800" on pages 30–41 of this volume.

33 For a thorough study of this, see Kathleen Staples, "Embroidered Furnishings: Questions of Production and Usage," in *English Embroidery from the Metropolitan Museum of Art, 1580–1700: 'Twixt Art and Nature*," ed. Andrew Morrall and Melinda Watt (New Haven, CT: Yale University Press, 2008), 23–29.

34 Andrew Morrall and Melinda Watt, eds., *English Embroidery from the Metropolitan Museum of Art, 1580–1700: 'Twixt Art and Nature"* (New Haven, CT: Yale University Press, 2008), cat. no. 19, 148–49. Band samplers are thus named because the embroidery is organized in neat rows. Girls were to be instructed by their mothers. Staples, "Embroidered Furnishings," 32, posits that the rise of challenging raised-work technique in embroidery by girls during this period may be because of their training by professional embroiderers formerly in the service of courtly patrons who made the transition to working in schools and other private settings.

35 Professionals were likely also involved in the final assembly of the caskets. For more on the collaborative nature of caskets embroidered in a domestic context by young women, see Staples, "Embroidered Furnishings," 29–32, and Isabella Rosner, "'A Cunning Skill Did Lurk': Susanna Perwich and the Mysteries of a Seventeenth-Century Needlework Cabinet," *Textile History* 49, no. 2 (November 2018): 156–59.

36 Told in the book of Ruth, the story of Ruth is depicted on the cabinet's six exterior panels. Having lost her husband in Moab, Ruth refused to abandon her mother-in-law, Naomi, and heed her call to remarry. Instead, she and Naomi went to Bethlehem, where Ruth humbly asked for permission to take on the gruelling work of gleaning barley in the fields. Later in the narrative, Ruth visits Boaz in the field at night and sleeps at his feet. Impressed by her many qualities, Boaz ultimately marries Ruth, and Naomi becomes nurse to their son, Obed. See Rosner, "'A Cunning Skill Did Lurk,'" 146–50.

37 A further musical allusion may be found on the underside of the cabinet's lid in the form of an allegorical figure representing Hearing, who plays the lute. Rosner, "'A Cunning Skill Did Lurk,'" 154.

38 For an in-depth discussion of the portrayal of biblical heroines in this context, see Ruth Geuter, "Embroidered Biblical Narratives and Their Social Context," in Morrall and Watt, *English Embroidery*, 57–77. As the author observes (59), the bold, even violent actions taken by figures such as Judith were tempered through representations of them engaging in quiet domestic work, including embroidery.

39 The casket is said to have been embroidered over a twenty-year period by Rebecca Stonier Plaisted (see "A Stuart Needlework Casket," *Art Institute of Chicago Quarterly* 53/54 (1960): 25–27, jstor.org/stable/4120544). The addition of seed pearls and coral beads adds a further note of luxury to the scene represented, as well as to the object itself.

40 See Rosner, "'A Cunning Skill Did Lurk,'" 160, and also Geuter's discussion of embroidery and monarchy, 68–73. Regarding the embroidery of the story of King David and Bathsheba during the reign of Charles I (1600–1649), the author observes (71): "Depending on the sympathies of the embroiderer she might have chosen to depict Charles in the part of royal villain or identified him with David the anointed kind, a man with passions and weaknesses."

41 More research is required on this intriguing practice in continental Europe and England, which was both a domestic activity and a professional one. Writing of France, Pullins observes that although textual sources described them as an elite activity, dressed prints "were likely also produced with more or less professional involvement. This would have been part of the post-printing modification made in the workshop.... As with the colouring of prints, there is very little documentation of how this was done." David Pullins, "The State of the Fashion Plate, c. 1727: Historicizing Fashion between Dressed Prints and Dezailler's *Recueils*," in *Prints in Translation, 1450–1750: Image, Materiality, Space*, ed. Suzanne Karr Schmidt and Edward H. Wouk (London: Routledge, 2017), no. 29, 154. For more on dressed prints, see Pullins, "State of the Fashion Plate"; Alice Dolan, "An Adorned Print: Print Culture, Female Leisure and the Dissemination of Fashion in France and England, around 1660–1779," *V&A Online Journal*, no. 3 (Spring 2011), vam.ac.uk/content/journals/research-journal/issue-03/an-adorned-print-print-culture,-female-leisure-and-the-dissemination-of-fashion-in-france-and-england,-c.-1660-1779/; Serena Dyer, *Material Lives: Women Makers and Consumer Culture in the 18th Century* (London: Bloomsbury, 2021), 131–59; and Maria Pia Pettinau Vescina, "Gioco e artificio," in *Seta: Potere e glamour; Ttessuti e abiti dal Rinascimento a XX secolo*, ed. Roberta Orsi Landini (Silvana, Italy: Silvana Editoriale, 2006), 114–17. The present discussion addresses only secular prints, but the practice also extended to religious ones, where the fabric would have served to enhance the reader's devotional experience. For more on religious dressed prints, see Suzanne Kathleen Karr Schmidt, *Altered and Adorned: Using Renaissance Prints in Daily Life* (Chicago and New Haven, CT: Art Institute of Chicago and Yale University Press, 2011), 67–69, 104–5.

42 See Pullins, "State of the Fashion Plate," 139–44. Cut-paper work (*découpure* in French) included cutting up prints from different sources and affixing them to objects and furniture, such as fans and screens.

43 Pullins, "State of the Fashion Plate," 140–41. On the notion of the dressed print as "game," see also Pettinau Vescina, "Gioco e artificio."

44 Sabine Winn was born to a prosperous family in Vervey (her father was the governor and a baron). Her relationship to Sir Rowland Winn (her second husband) is well documented thanks to the many letters they exchanged. The pair acquired Nostell and the baronetcy in 1765. Both shared a love of culture, and Rowland frequently solicited his wife's opinion on what paintings and furnishings to purchase. A portrait of the couple by Hugh Douglas Hamilton (Nostell Priory) shows them surrounded by art amid a decorative scheme devised by

Robert Adam. For more on Sabine Winn's life, see Dyer, *Material Lives*, 123–31.

45 The inscriptions on the back of each of the sixteen prints read "Mister Roland Winn gave me the painting Sabine Winn born d'Herwart" (Monsieur Roland Winn ma donné le tableau Sabine Winn née d' Herwart), suggesting Winn's pleasure at receiving this gift from her husband. According to Dyer, *Material Lives*, 151, there are no identifiably English examples of dressed prints prior to those made by Winn.

46 Winn was frequently alone, as her husband regularly travelled to London and elsewhere.

47 Dyer, *Material Lives*, 152.

48 The king's revocation of the Edict of Nantes (1684), which protected religious freedom in France, helped spur the exodus.

49 For an in-depth discussion, see Natalie Rothstein, "Huguenots in the English Silk Industry in the Eighteenth Century," in *Huguenots in Britain and Their French Background, 1550–1800*, ed. Irene Scouloudi (Basingstoke, UK: Macmillan, 1987) 125–40.

50 On Garthwaite's life, see Zara Anishanslin, *Portrait of a Woman in Silk: Hidden Histories of the British Atlantic World* (New Haven, CT: Yale University Press, 2016), 25–41.

51 The small size of the gown illustrated suggests it was made for a child. Natalie Rothstein, *Silk Designs of the Eighteenth Century: In the Collection of the Victoria and Albert Museum, London, with a Complete Catalogue* (London: Thames and Hudson, 1990), 286, counts this piece among damasks woven from designs by Garthwaite. The Bath design exists also in the form of a brocaded silk with ivory ground that was turned into a man's coat and waistcoat for a costume ball in the late 1800s, though it may have previously been a banyan (a loose dressing gown), itself made from an earlier dress (T. 740-1974, V&A Museum).

52 The flowers represented included lilies of the valley, daisies, and heartsease. On the evolution of Garthwaite's designs, see Rothstein, *Silk Designs*, 40–52.

53 Anishanslin, *Portrait of a Woman*, 50–57.

54 See Rothstein, *Silk Designs*, cat. nos. 238–239, 230.

55 The corresponding design (5981.20), dated September 20, 1742, is in the V&A Museum. See Rothstein, *Silk Designs*, cat. no. 154, 180. Lekeux's origins are discussed by Rothstein, "Huguenots," 127–32.

56 See Anishanslin, *Portrait of a Woman*, for a fascinating account of the meanings surrounding the circulation of Garthwaite's designs.

57 On Garthwaite's damask in connection to the portrait, see Anishanslin, *Portrait of a Woman*, 5–11; on Simon Julins's life and career, see Anishanslin, *Portrait of a Woman*, 107–23. The author posits (183), that Willing was either heavily pregnant or nursing in 1743–1744, and so her husband may have been the one to acquire the damask in London during a trip according to her wishes.

58 The four damask panels (1975-342,1) are now badly faded but still reveal a large-scale pattern of scrolling floral elements similar to those seen in the Willing portrait.

59 Anishanslin, *Portrait of a Woman*, 310. Eliza Lucas Pinckney (1722–1793) is best known for developing indigo as a cash crop in South Carolina. For more on her involvement in sericulture there and on her exploitation of enslaved workers to produce silk to be woven in Spitalfields, see Anishanslin, *Portrait of a Woman*, 102–3, 158–60. On the attempts made to promote sericulture in South Carolina and the treatment of enslaved labourers in that context, see Ben Marsh, *Unravelled Dreams: Silk and the Atlantic World, 1500–1840* (Cambridge: Cambridge University Press 2020), 238–311.

60 See Marie Bouzard, *La Soierie lyonnaise: du XVIIIe au XIX siècle dans les collections du musée des Tissus Lyon* (Lyon: Éditions Lyonnaises d'Art et d'Histoire, 1997), 8–10; Lesley Ellis Miller, *Selling Silks: A Merchant's Sample Book, 1764* (London: Victoria and Albert Museum, 2014), 34. According to Bouzard (9), fifty-nine "*dessinateurs*" are recorded in Lyon in 1759, and over eighty in 1790. To keep abreast of current fashions, they regularly travelled to Paris, and by 1751 a project was in place to establish a school (the foundation of the École des Beaux-Arts) to formally train draughtsmen. By the end of the century, it included a "flower class" intended to enhance skill in drawing the natural motifs favoured for silks in that period.

61 On Joubert and his manual, see Lesley Ellis Miller, "Representing Silk Design: Nicolas Joubert de l'Hiberderie and *Le Dessinateur pour les étoffes d'or, d'argent et de de soie* (Paris, 1765)," *Journal of Design History* 17, no. 1 (2004): 29–53.

62 Antoine-Nicolas Joubert de L'Hiberderie, *Le Dessinateur, pour les fabriques d'étoffes d'or, d'argent et de soie, avec la traduction de six tables raisonnées tirées de "l'Abecedario pittorico," imprimé à Naples en 1733* (Paris: Sébastien Jorry, 1765), xxix. "Eh quoi! Ne voudra-t-on jamais secouer un prejugé qui nous prive de Sujets qui enrichiroient l'Etat, & honoreroient la Patrie?" As for concerns about allowing the sexes to mingle in a workshop, Joubert reminds us that such a practice is nothing new.

63 Joubert de L'Hiberderie, *Le Dessinateur*, xxx. "Je dis donc qu' un père à la tête de la Manufacture, pourroit faire apprendre à dessiner à sa fille, & lorsqu'elle seroit en état de régir la fabrique, elle pourroit former d'autres éléves de son sexe. Ainsi dans chaque maison on occuperait quantité de Demoisellles disgraciées de la Nature, ou qui ont des incommodités qui les empêchent de se marier, & qui souvent deviennent à charge à leurs parens par défaut de fortune."

64 Saint-Aubin, *L'Art du Brodeur*, 4. "Le Dessin est la base & le fondement de la Broderie."

65 Folio 4r bears the annotation "Mad autelme" alongside drawings for men's lapels (patterns #1901 and #1902). The scrapbook (49.50.206), which also contains designs for buttonholes, fields, and dress borders, was discussed by Wunder in a 1956 article. S.E. Wunder, "Some Observations on Textile Designs at the Cooper Union Museum," *Chronicle of the Museum for the Arts of Decoration of the Cooper Union* 2, no. 8 (June 1956): 245–49.

66 Folio 49r: "1778 Drawing of Miss Montalan submitted to Mlle (?)" (1778 Dessin de Mlle Montalan remis a Mlle [?]). In some instances, payments appear to be indicated as well, as on folio 48r.

67 Wunder, "Some Observations," 247, suggested that all the women might be designers and noted that all the embroiderers were women. If this were the case, it raises the question of why only a few are given titles that identify their gender while others are not.

68 The following is inscribed on folio 50v: "1789 Montalent Drawing for waistcoats with bow and branche of feathers given to (?) Duclos on 30 November 1785" (Dessin de gilets a noeud Montalent et branche de plumes donné a [?] Duclos le 30 novembre 1785).

69 Daniel Roche's *La Culture des apparences* remains an essential study on the professions of tailors, dressmakers, linen-drapers, and fashion merchants in Paris. Daniel Roche, *La Culture des apparences: une histoire du vêtement, XVIIe-XVIIIe siècle* (Paris: Fayard, 1989), 279–312.

70 Clare Haru Crowston, *Credit, Fashion, Sex: Economies of Regard in Old Regime France* (Durham, NC: Duke University Press, 2013), 151.

71 For more on Bertin's life, see Michelle Sapori, *Rose Bertin: ministre des modes de Marie Antoinette* (Paris: Institut français de la mode, 2003).

72 Caroline Weber, *Queen of Fashion: What Marie Antoinette Wore to the Revolution* (New York: Macmillan, 2006), 159.

73 Weber, *Queen of Fashion*, 150. The dress was also known as the *gaulle*.

74 Weber, *Queen of Fashion*, 156–57. Silk manufacturers were said to have fought back by circulating a rumour about a young woman who burned to death after her muslin dress caught on fire.

WOMEN IN WORKSHOPS

Brittany Luberda

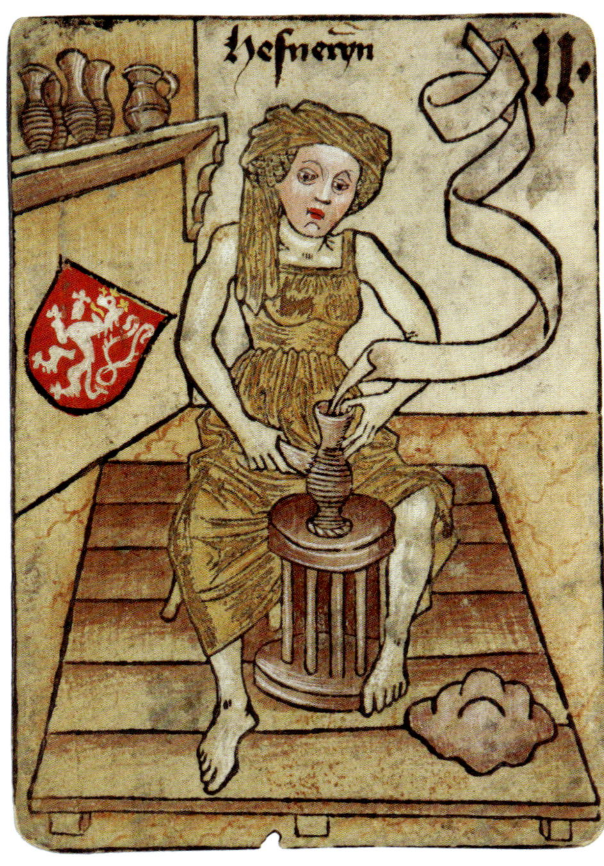

Fig. 1 • Unknown maker, *Playing Card, Bohemia, Potter (two), from the so-called Hofamterspiel*, c. 1455. Woodcut, watercolour and opaque watercolour, gold and silver leaf, and Indian ink on paper, 13.9 × 9.9 cm. Kunsthistorisches Museum, Vienna, Kunstkammer, inv. no. KK 5105. Photo: © KHM-Museumsverband.

A playing card attributed to a Viennese maker from around 1455 shows a woman ceramicist with her hair wrapped and sleeves rolled up as she trims a vessel on a kick wheel (fig. 1).[1] In the deck of cards, this industrious craftswoman, with her dirty brown dress and muscular arms, is assigned the low value of two. As a craftswoman, she starkly contrasts cards of vibrant, silk-clad women who are variously illustrated playing musical instruments, lounging in gardens, or seated on a throne as the queen of hearts. Yet her image as a working woman in a ceramic workshop confirms the everyday acceptance of female professional potters in fifteenth-century Austria.[2] Her image also proves the presence of women artists despite the absence of known works by named female potters during this period. Sourcing examples like this industrious ceramicist, this essay unites visual and archival evidence to survey women's roles in workshops that produced ceramics, silver, glass, textiles, and furniture in Europe between 1400 and 1800.

This cross-chronological, multimedia introduction to women's craftsmanship is a new narrative within existing art historical publications and exhibitions.[3] In 1981, Alice Irma Prather-Moses published *The International Dictionary of the Women Workers in the Decorative Arts*, a reference list of names and biographies of named women associated with the production of objects and furniture.[4] This record bearing hundreds of names of women makers from the Renaissance to the twentieth century touches on the breadth of female leaders in textiles, ceramics, silver, and other media across time but without citation, images, or context. Critical engagement with makers has often been the purview of socioeconomic study, highlighting women's agency in markets but minimizing a celebration of skills and artistry.[5] Scholarship on women and the decorative arts is also dominated by histories of patronage rather than artistic agency, reinforcing the misconception that female consumers lead the story of women and craftsmanship in early modern Europe.[6] In fact, women of all social and economic levels were found in commercial workshops in early modern Europe, in positions ranging from owner to artisan to the professional preparing materials. This essay engages with a plethora of media and myths of autonomous creative practice. The results reveal the integrated, multigenerational, and expert roles played by unnamed and named craftswomen in communal production across centuries and artistic mediums.

Within this context, a workshop is defined as a place of production with multiple participants of varying degrees of skill, and its purpose is commercial trade. The workshops discussed here range from the cottage industry, such as family-run shops in rural areas, to specialized departments within large, urban factories. Excluding a handful of aristocratic female designers and artists, the craftswomen presented worked for financial gain. Girls' schools and orphanages, where the purpose of production is education or household decoration, are not extensively explored in this survey. Equally, domestic collectives of women makers—such as the ladies-in-waiting who embroidered in the court of Mary Stuart, queen of Scotland (r. 1542–1567); the shell, paper filigree, and scrapbooking circles of Georgian aristocrats like Mary Delany (1700–1788); or the sisters Sophia Jane Maria Bonnell (c. 1748–1841) and Mary Anne Harvey Bonnell (1763–1853; cat. no. 66)—are beyond the bounds of this discussion.[7] Examining the context of women in workshops adds to these previously explored histories of women's education and courtly artistic production by evaluating gender through the dual lens of self-determination and industry.

In terms of methodology, identifying the presence of women in workshops can require a gymnastic approach to interpreting archives and images. In ideal cases, a work is marked, or the maker, designer, or owner is recorded in a factory inventory or city directory. But when a signature, mark, or written record is absent, we can turn to a re-examination of prints, paintings, and archival materials through a feminist lens to provide proof of female skill and presence. Written sources, such as workshop archives or guild inventories, are often limited to male names, unless the woman is the widow of a maker. Reconstructing female artist biographies and object histories then prompts a reading of a craftswoman's education, cultural norms, and movements between the lines of her relatives and partnerships. Data banks in digital art history and museum catalogues, which consciously enter the names of wives and husbands, generate a more complete picture of gender and artistry. Similarly, images of women makers in paintings and prints are invaluable period accounts of workshop history and inclusivity beyond textual sources.

Drawing on these research methods, this essay surveys women makers of objects from three perspectives: first and most expansively, by presenting highlights from the lives of women workshop owners in Europe between 1400 and 1800, as the number and consistent presence of these female leaders in the industry affirm women's legacy in workshop industries; second, by identifying how women within workshops assumed positions of authority to distinguish themselves and their skills; and finally, by acknowledging that communal production encompassed hundreds of thousands of known and unknown makers with specialized artistry in early modern Europe. Between 1400 and 1800, many of these household workshops and small-scale industries developed into holistic manufactories modelled on village communities, with women as integral entities. As maker histories are shared, it quickly becomes evident that it is impossible to encompass all forms of women's contributions to three-dimensional works. Rather, the women workshop owners and makers presented here address a diversity of materials and a range of time periods that show the pervasiveness of women's engagement with decorative arts, craft, and design histories. This variety of roles gives a sense of the far-reaching contributions of women to workshop production.

Women-Run Workshops

In 1446, Philip the Good, Duke of Burgundy, purchased tapestries from the workshop of Jehanne de Pottequin (active mid-fifteenth century), also known as the Veuve Baubrée (widow of Jean Baubrée).[8] The tapestries featured fields of flowers and scenes of children going to school. While the works are lost today, the purchase shows that de Pottequin's tapestries were of the highest quality and made in Tournai, one of the most prestigious centres of Renaissance tapestry production in Europe. De Pottequin is one of numerous women who owned or founded both small and massive workshops from the fifteenth through eighteenth centuries. Although not always the case, her story is an example of how women's knowledge of workshop production and business was revealed because of a husband's death. The transfer of ownership from a deceased husband to the wife has been found in examples of tin-glazed earthenware,

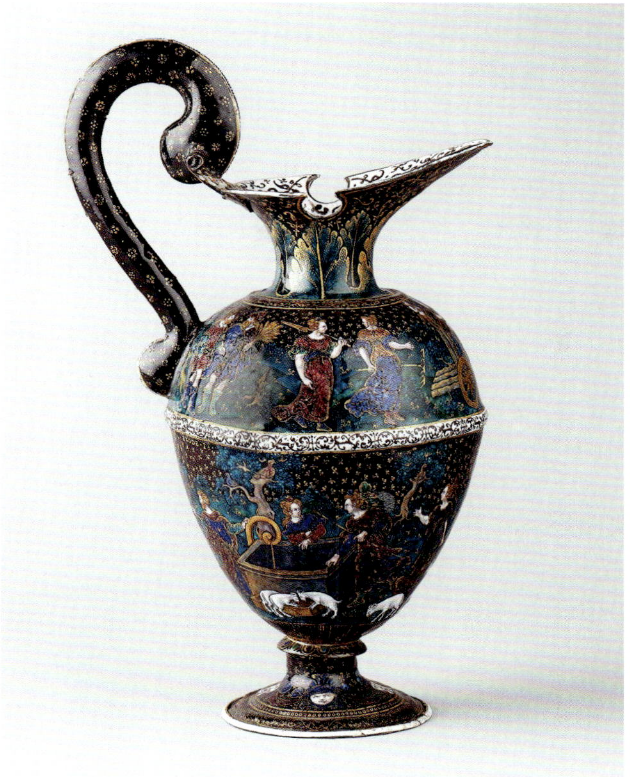

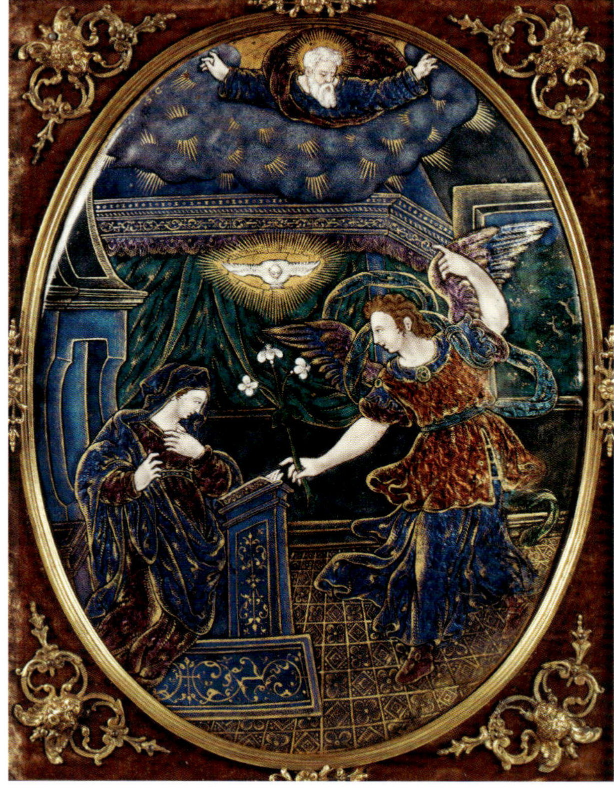

Fig. 2 (left) • Suzanne de Court, *Triumph of Ceres*, probably late 16th–early 17th century. Painted enamel, partly gilt and partly silvered, on copper, 28.7 × 17.8 × 12.1 cm. The Metropolitan Museum of Art, New York, Robert Lehman Collection, 1975, inv. no. 1975.1.1234.

Fig. 3 (right) • Suzanne de Court, *Oval plaque with the Annunciation*, c. 1600. Painted enamel and gilding on copper, 18.8 × 13 cm. The Walters Art Museum, Baltimore, Maryland, inv. no. 44.191.

printmaking, cabinetmaking, tapestry weaving, and, most notably, silver, where widow marks are registered with the local assay office. Whether through an inheritance or the founding of studios, female workshop owners created and sometimes signed artworks made either personally or by the apprentices and journeymen employed in their establishments, just as male owners did.

Suzanne de Court (active 1575–1625) produced vivid works in enamel (fig. 2)—glass and metal foil melted on a copper base—in Limoges, France. De Court often signed her works with either "svzanne covrt" or her initials, "S.C." Her biography is unconfirmed, but it is likely she was a member of the de Court family of enamellers. Perhaps she married a de Court who died and then continued the practice as a widow, or broke from her family workshops to found her own business. De Court's range of subjects includes both sacred and profane themes, and some of her works even marry the religious and secular by depicting scenes from the Bible and classical mythology.[9] The scale of enamelling was limited by the durability of hammered copperplates and lent itself to smaller, handheld objects, such as devotional plaques featuring annunciation scenes (fig. 3; cat. no. 203). Although she was the only French female enamellist to sign her works in the sixteenth century, de Court was not the first female specialist to create objects with molten glass.

Between 1400 and 1800, glassmaking proliferated across Europe, with concentrations on the island of Murano in Italy, and in the Netherlands, the Black Forest in Germany, the Czech Republic, and England. The names of Italian women in the glass trade appear in archival documents as designers, makers, and enamellers. From at least the 1200s, the Barovier workshop in Venice was one of the most prominent and innovative in Renaissance Europe, and known for introducing a new type of crystal in the fifteenth century. Elena de Lando (active mid-fifteenth century) is one of two recorded female glass painters who worked on commission on Murano before 1517.

Between 1443 and 1445, the Barovier workshop paid Lando for "work made on glass by her," possibly through the technique of enamelling on glass that had reappeared in the mid-fifteenth century.[10] From the Barovier family dynasty, Maria (or Marietta) Barovier (c. 1431–1496) operated an independent workshop specializing in millefiori—glass canes with multiple colours called "rosettes"—which remain some of the most recognizable forms in Murano glass to the present day.[11] Barovier also worked with new opaque watercolour and forms and, for her experimentation, was granted permission to build a custom kiln for a unique unblown-glass technology.[12] In the following century, Ermonia Vivarini (1490–1569) designed one of the most striking forms of the Italian Renaissance: a blown-glass ship complete with mast and rigs, sailing on a thin foot as if it floats atop a table. Vivarini was granted the exclusive privilege to produce her design by the Venetian city magistrates in 1521.[13] While these three women chart the excellence of women's technical and aesthetic achievements at the centre of European glassmaking,[14] women glassmakers also competed in the industry beyond Murano's fabled furnaces. In Antwerp, Sarah Vincx (died 1647) ran a successful workshop after her husband died in 1595. The Beilby family in Newcastle upon Tyne, England, specialized in enamelled heraldry on glass in the latter half of the eighteenth century (cat. nos. 210 & 211). In addition, Sarah Worrall Grazebrook (1722–1799) ran Audnam Flint Glasshouse, an enormous industrial factory, in the late eighteenth century.[15]

The decoration of glass offered women opportunities for financial gain and to express themselves artistically. By the seventeenth century, particularly in the Netherlands, women would become identified with two types of glass decoration: diamond-point and stipple-point engraving. Diamond-point engraving was a technique of drawing linear words or images using a diamond attached to the edge of a pen. Employed on ancient Roman glass, this technique was revived in the fifteenth century, its later use resulting in images of insects, florals, strapwork, and script completed by the accomplished poets and artists Maria Tesselschade Roemers Visscher (1594–1649) and Anna Roemers Visscher (1584–1651),[16] considered some of the first and finest engravers on glass in the Netherlands.[17] Engraving on glass was something women could complete in their home studios; one such example is a green wine glass engraved in diamond point attributed to Maria Visscher with the inscription "Sic Soleo Amicos" (meaning "Thus am I accustomed to treat friends") and decorated with a dragonfly, whose colloquial name in Dutch is *glazenmaker* (glassmaker) (fig. 4).

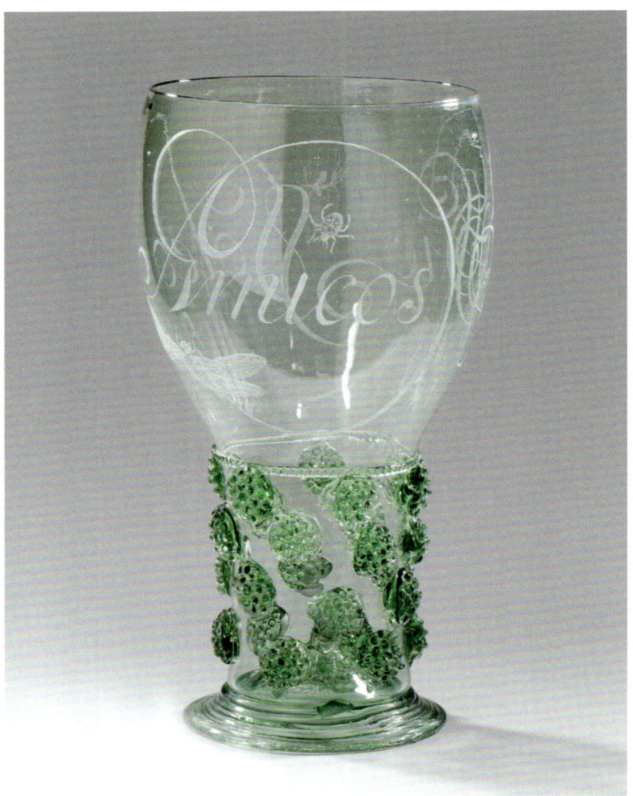

Fig. 4 · Attributed to Maria Tesselschade Roemers Visscher, *Roemer*, c. 1625–c. 1650. Glass, 23 × 13 × 10 cm. Rijksmuseum, Amsterdam, A.J. Enschedé Bequest, Haarlem, 1896, inv. no. BK-NM-10754-50.

A similar narrative for workshop ownership and independent decorators applied to ceramics. From the 1400s to the 1600s, tin-glazed earthenware—regionally known as maiolica, delftware, or faience—was the primary European ceramic body used for food and storage. These thick-bodied vessels were made from local clays in regional workshops. Centres of production emerged in central Italy, where maiolica was produced in household studios and ownership could be transferred to widows. For example, upon the death in 1538 of Nicola da Urbino, one of the most talented maiolica painters in Urbino, his wife inherited

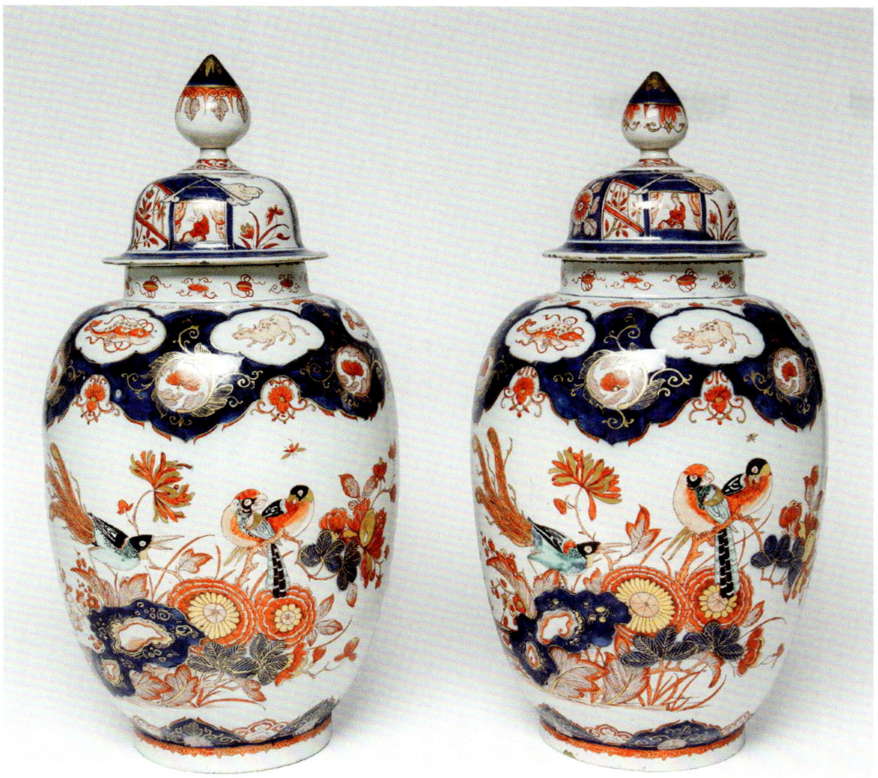

Fig. 5 • Johanna van der Heul, workshop owner of the Greek A Factory, *Pair of jars with lids*, 1701–1722. Tin-glazed earthenware with polychrome and gilt decoration, each: 46.5 × 24.1 cm. Philadelphia Museum of Art: Gift of Mrs. Henry W. Breyer, Sr., 1966, inv. no. 1966-22-1ab, 2ab.

the studio and proceeded to rent it, suggesting ownership but not necessarily her continued production of ceramics.[18] Other widows are known to have assumed ownership of tin-glazed earthenware workshops in the Netherlands, Italy, and France, and performed a more significant role in the creation of objects.[19] In the Netherlands, the city of Delft was a small metropolis of family workshops where women and girls were integrated into the industry. Some of the best-known factories, like the Greek A Factory, were led by women at multiple stages of centuries-long production. Johanna van der Heul (active early eighteenth century), the Greek A Factory's second female owner (from 1703 to 1722), was recognized as an excellent potter as well as manager (fig. 5), and she did so well that she was able to employ four specialist painters in gold in addition to decorators in underglazes.[20] From 1733 to 1757, a respected delftware factory owner and the same factory's third female head, Cornelia van Willigen, maintained an inventory of nearly ten thousand ceramics and corresponded with clients across continental Europe. In Marseilles, the Veuve Perrin workshop produced an enormous amount of tin-glazed earthenware, called "faience" in France, in the same styles as the porcelain factories (cat. no. 9). Pierette Candelot, known as the Veuve Perrin (1709–1794; owner after 1748), benefitted from the port city's location and easy access to a global market, as tin-glazed earthenware was easier to produce and reached a wider market than porcelain. For this reason, female manufactory owners had more success with tin-glazed ceramics than with porcelain, which required significant investment and often aristocratic patronage.

Beyond the opportunities of workshop ownership, women ceramic decorators worked across continental Europe and England. In late-eighteenth-century London, husbands and wives, such as John and Mary Shaw, worked on independent orders for painting on ceramics in their home studio. Women ceramic decorators in urban areas had greater possibilities for recognition and independent prosperity than those in the larger rural factories.[21] In Germany, sisters Anna Elizabeth Auffenwerth Wald (born 1696) and Sabina Auffenwerth Hosennestel (1706–1782) ran decorating studios where they painted on either blanks or seconds—products with minor defects—from the Meissen porcelain manufactory. Barring signed works, each woman's decoration is indistinguishable from one another, but their expressive brushwork and elaborate painted bandwork is distinctive within German decorated porcelains of the period (fig. 6; cat. no. 10). In a tea and coffee service now distributed between the Smithsonian Institution (fig. 7; cat. no. 12) and the Museum of Fine Arts, Boston (fig. 8; cat. no. 11) collections, the decorative scenes portray Asian figures brewing tea or smoking pipes, which self-reflexively references tea drinking on objects for tea consumption.[22] Entrepreneurial and erudite, these women porcelain painters worked in business partnerships with factories as well as independently from studios.

The most extensive study of women in workshops, particularly as workshop owners, is found in the field of silver. A coloured print of a woman silversmith by Martin Engelbrecht from the 1730s captures

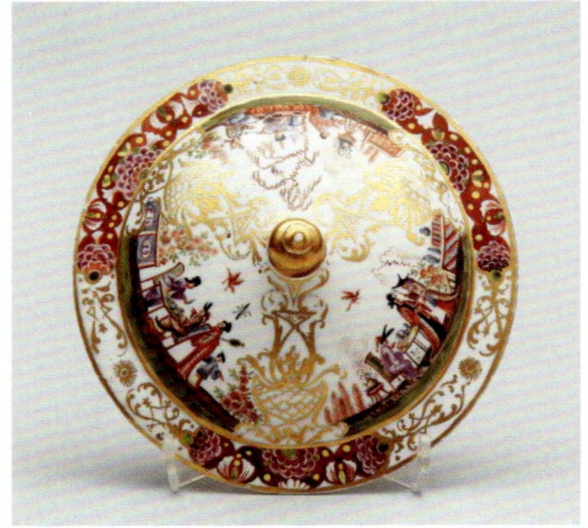

Fig. 6 • Probably Anna Elizabeth Auffenwerth Wald, and possibly Sabina Auffenwerth Hosennestel, decorators at Meissen Porcelain Factory, view of tureen lid from *Tureen and stand*, c. 1725. Hard-paste porcelain with overglaze enamels and gilding, 17.8 × 22.9 × 22.9 cm. Gardiner Museum, Toronto, Canada, Gift of George and Helen Gardiner, inv. no. G83.1.0717.1-.3.

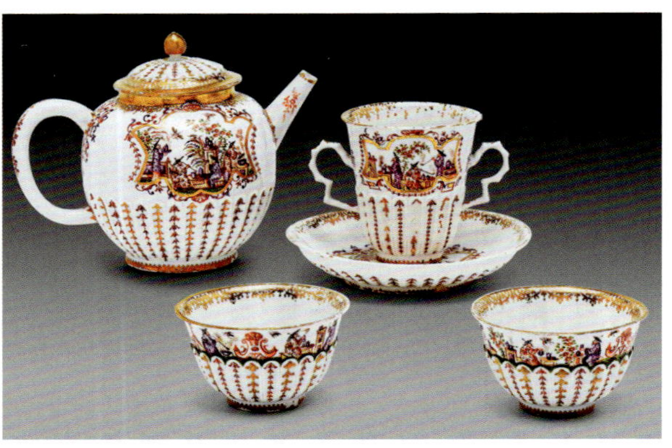

Fig. 7 • Probably Anna Elizabeth Auffenwerth Wald, and possibly Sabina Auffenwerth Hosennestel, decorators at Meissen Porcelain Factory. *Partial tea service*, 1730. Hard-paste porcelain with polychrome and gold, tea bowl: 4.5 × 7.6 cm; chocolate cup: 8 cm; saucer: 31.1 cm; teapot: 12.7 × 16.8 cm. National Museum of American History, Smithsonian Institution, inv. no. 1987.0896. 34 A,B; 36 a,b; 37 a,b. Photo: Division of Home and Community Life, National Museum of American History, Smithsonian Institution.

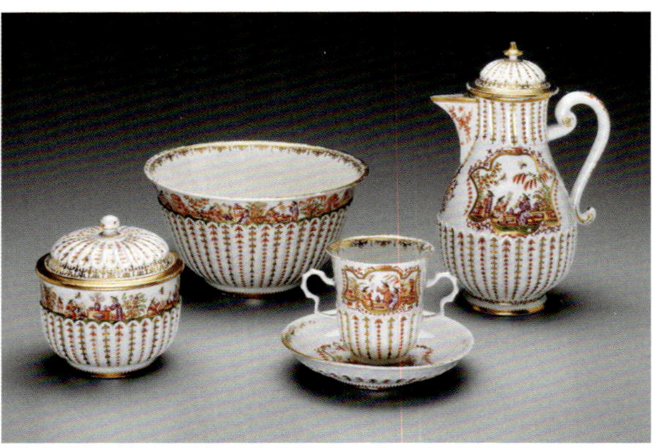

Fig. 8 • Probably Anna Elizabeth Auffenwerth Wald, and possibly Sabina Auffenwerth Hosennestel, decorators at Meissen Porcelain Factory. *Partial coffee service*, c. 1723, decorated c. 1725–1730. Hard-paste porcelain with coloured enamel and gilded decoration, coffee pot: 19.6 × 13.6 × 10.6 cm; cup: 7.8 × 10.7 × 7.3 cm; saucer: 2.7 × 13.2 cm; covered sugar bowl: 10.4 × 10.2 cm; waste bowl: 9.1 × 17.9 cm. Museum of Fine Arts, Boston, Bequest of Forsyth Wickes—The Forsyth Wickes Collection, inv. no. 65.2076a-b, 65.2077a-b, 65.2079a-b, 65.2080. Photograph © 2023 Museum of Fine Arts, Boston.

the dual roles of a woman smith as purveyor and artist, as she both presents silver goods and carries silversmithing tools (fig. 9). English assay marks registered by independent female silversmiths date to the 1690s, but the mid- to late eighteenth century represents the apex of female-led production, able to be studied thanks to excellent record-keeping by guilds that allowed widows to register marks. The most prolific workshop was run by Hester Bateman (1708–1794), who first registered a mark in 1761. Bateman inherited her husband's workshop where her two sons, among others, were apprenticed. She proceeded to lead the workshop for the next thirty years, registering nine marks with the central assay agency in London. At the helm, Bateman transformed this workshop into an urban industrial enterprise by capitalizing on innovations in sheet metal and homing in on the middle-class market (fig. 10; cat. nos. 213 & 215).[23] Debate persists about whether Bateman held the tools at any stage of the process, but based on her responsibilities and adroit business decisions, her knowledge of silversmithing is evident. Artisanal expertise seems even more likely for Elizabeth Godfrey (c. 1720–1758; fig. 11; cat. no. 208), Bateman's contemporary, who registered marks after the death of her first and second husbands. The trade card for Godfrey—in which she has identified herself as "E. Godfrey, Goldsmith, Silversmith, and Jeweler"—presents a vast array of silver for dining and display surrounded by an exuberant Rococo framework (fig. 12). The somewhat repetitious use of "goldsmith" and "silversmith" is purposeful; by

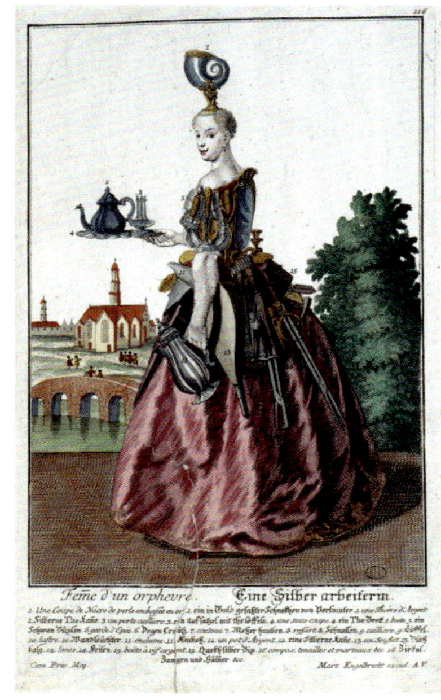

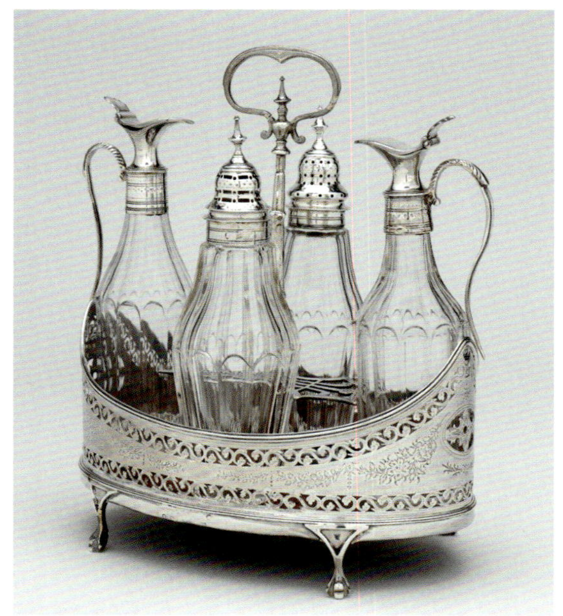

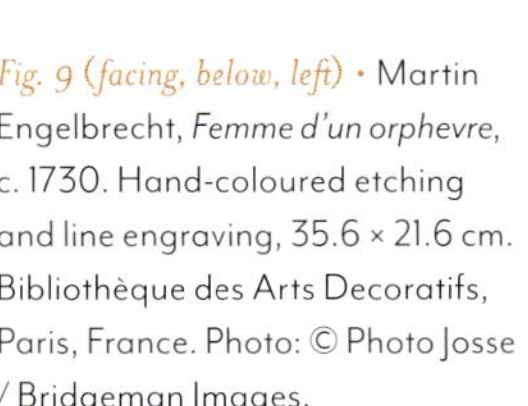

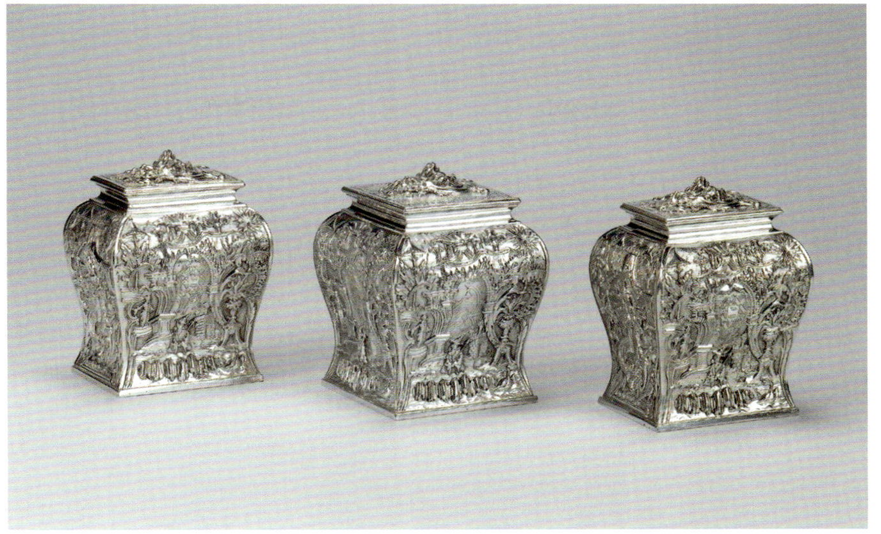

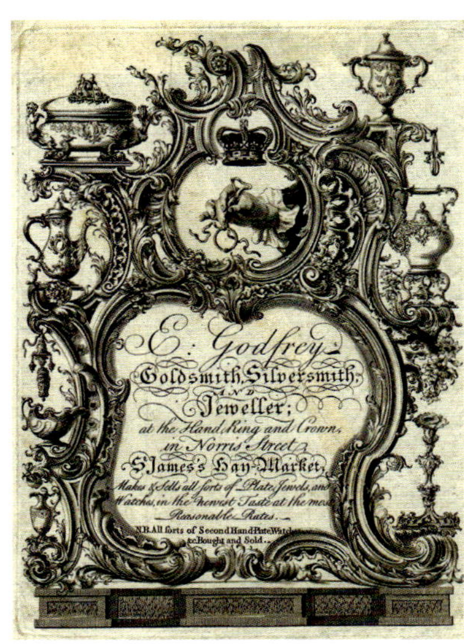

Fig. 9 (facing, below, left) • Martin Engelbrecht, *Femme d'un orphevre*, c. 1730. Hand-coloured etching and line engraving, 35.6 × 21.6 cm. Bibliothèque des Arts Decoratifs, Paris, France. Photo: © Photo Josse / Bridgeman Images.

Fig. 10 (facing, below, right) • Hester Bateman, *Cruet stand*, 1784–1790. Silver and mahogany, 22.5 × 20.3 × 12.7 cm. Baltimore Museum of Art: Gift of Elizabeth F. Cheney, Oak Park, Illinois, 1981.103.1-.5. Photo: Mitro Hood.

Fig. 11 (above, left) • Elizabeth Godfrey, *Tea canister set*, 1754–1755. Silver, largest canister: 14 × 10.2 × 10.2 cm; two smaller canisters: 13.3 × 10.2 × 7.6 cm. Saint Louis Art Museum, Funds given by Lewis and Amanda Smith; and gift of John M. Harney in memory of Florence M. Warfield and Charlotte W. Harney, funds given by Joseph Pulitzer in memory of his wife, Elinor Wickham Pulitzer, and funds given in honour of Joseph Pulitzer II, by exchange, inv. no. 4:2010.1a,b-.3a,b.

Fig. 12 (above, right) • Unknown maker, *Trade card of Elizabeth Godfrey, Goldsmith, Silversmith, and Jeweller; at the Hand, Ring and Crown, in Norris Street, St. James's, Haymarket, London*, 1740s–1760s. Etching and engraving, 19.3 × 14.2 cm. British Museum, Bequeathed by: Sir Ambrose Heal, 1960, inv. no. Heal,67.167. Image: © The Trustees of the British Museum.

the mid-eighteenth century, the term "goldsmith" implied a retailer, whereas the term "silversmith" referred to a manufacturer or artisan.[24] This card details Godfrey's wide range of talents, from the creation of works to their retail. Notably, Bateman's and Godfrey's creations are exceptional in form and scale. Most female silversmiths during the early modern period, either in France or England, were producing undecorated useful wares, such as spoons or thimbles.

The furniture trade offered a less accessible, though equally prestigious, professional field for women in early modern Europe.[25] The first woman furniture maker to appear in the English royal accounts after 1660 was Elizabeth Price (active from 1685). Price took over the post of "royal joyner" in 1685 after the death of her husband, a position later taken over by Catherine Naish (active second half of eighteenth century), who held it for thirteen years, beginning in 1759.[26] Beyond court, outside the steps of St. Paul's Cathedral in London, the thriving furniture-making industry of seventeenth- and eighteenth-century England was dominated by male workshop owners, with exceptions like Grace Coxed (active 1700–1735).[27] First listed under the surname of her first husband, joiner John Mayo, Grace inherited the business and relocated it to new premises in 1704, where it is identified as "Grace Mayo &c." in tax records.[28] For three years, the business was then identified as "Grace Mayo and partner," before her name was replaced by that of John Coxed, presumably an apprentice in the workshop, whom Grace married in 1708. When John died, Grace's name returned to the business record by 1719, at which point she founded The White Swan with Thomas Woster. This prolific workshop hosted apprentices and supplied veneered furniture for both metropolitan and rural clients. Her furniture is noted for its use of imported Brazilian rosewood as well as burr veneers, as seen on the labelled bureau (cat. no. 63) in the collection of The Colonial Williamsburg Foundation, Virginia.[29]

Women-owned furniture workshops also completed commissions for courts across Europe. Françoise-Marguerite Vandercruse (1731–1775) led a celebrated French furniture workshop under the name Veuve Oeben (Widow Oeben) from 1763 to 1767 in Paris.[30] Born into a furniture dynasty, Vandercruse lived in the Louvre, the Gobelins, and then the Arsenal manufacturing district in Paris, side by side with other cabinetmakers for the king. In Italy, Lucia Barbarossa Landucci (c. 1728–died after 1782) collaborated with her first husband, Giuseppe Corsini, on commissions for the Corsini Palace on Via della Lungara and for the Palazzo Borghese.[31] With her second husband, Antonio Landucci, Lucia provided a significant amount of furniture for the renovations

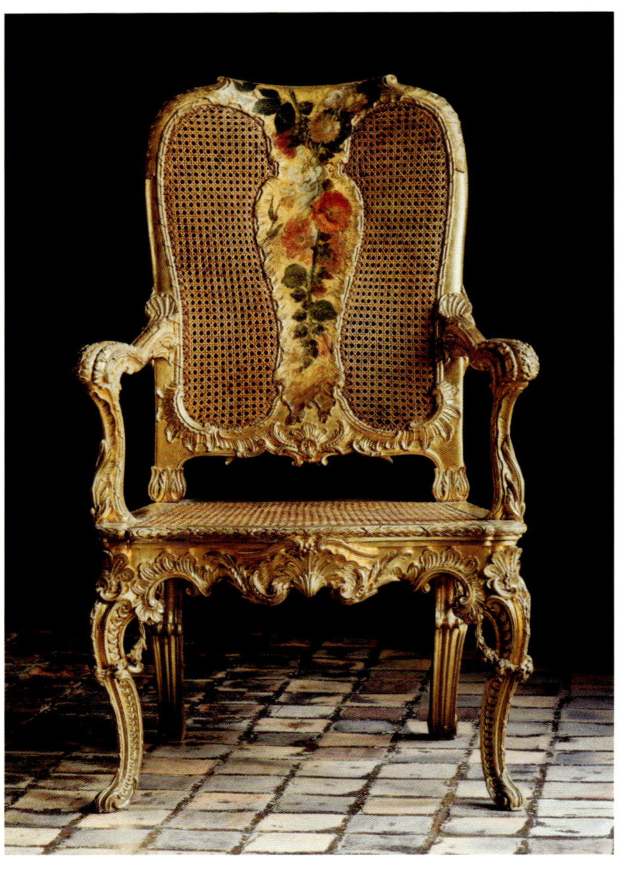

Fig. 13 • Attributed to Antonio Landucci and Lucia Barbarossa Landucci, *Armchair* from *Set of seven armchairs*, c. 1773. Gilded and painted walnut, 108 × 67.5 × 50 cm. Isabella Stewart Gardner Museum, Boston, inv. no. F26e9.1-7.

Fig. 14 (facing, above) • Marie-Henriette Gravant, workshop director at Manufacture Nationale de Sèvres, *Individual flowers*, c. 1748. Soft- and hard-paste porcelain, sizes vary, approx. life-size; smallest flower: 1.9 × 1.9 × 1.3 cm; largest flower: 5.7 × 5.7 × 3.2 cm. Courtesy of Michele Beiny Harkins. Photo: Richard Goodbody.

of the Palazzo Borghese between 1773 and 1782, including twenty tables, thirty-seven chairs, two sofas, two corner cabinets, and two tables for the audience room alone (fig. 13).[32] This furniture represents some of the most ornate examples of *trompe l'oeil* giltwood carving in existence. When Antonio died, presumably in 1782, the receipts were sent to Lucia, who continued to run the workshop and fulfill orders for the refurbishment of the Palazzo Borghese.

The grandest of all female-owned workshop productions are tapestries, the most expensive possessions of early modern Europeans. In one of the workshops owned by Cardinal Barberini, three female master weavers served as heads of the *arazzeria delle donne* (women's tapestry workshop) from 1648 to 1683: Caterina della Riviera (active as head of manufacture 1648–1653), Maria Maddalena della Riviera (1611–1676), and Anna Zampieri (active 1678–at least 1679). All three women were appointed because of their mastery in weaving and produced tapestries reflecting a wide range of subjects, from religious cycles (cat. no. 221) to a history of Pope Urban VIII to ancient Roman mythology, such as *Apollo and Attendants Flaying Marsyas* (cat. no. 222). Aristocratic funding also supported a women-led and -employed workshop founded by Queen Ulrika Eleonora of Sweden.[33] The tapestry manufacture was located in her palace at Karlberg and was active from around 1688 to 1695 under the direction of Anna Maria Schmilau (active late seventeenth century) and Katarina von Hacken (active late seventeenth century). This studio, unlike others discussed, utilized the labour of orphaned girls as weavers. A set of four tapestries in the Swedish Royal collection in Stockholm created by this workshop depicts the story of Meleager and Atalanta from Ovid's *Metamorphosis*—based on cartoons made for Louis XIV by Charles Le Brun, but known to the manufactory through tapestries woven by Jan II Leyniers in Brussels and brought to Sweden with the dowry of Queen Eleanora.[34] In the eighteenth century, while not as grand as the Baroque productions of the Barberini workshops, the tapestries produced under Katharine Ghuys Werniers (active 1738–1778) in Lille are exemplars of the painterly weaves popular in that period. Werniers inherited her husband's workshop after his death and for forty years maintained the enormous enterprise consisting of twenty looms.[35]

Leading Women within Workshops

Named women craftspeople appear in the specialty departments of workshops and factories as influential figures in production history. These women specialists and department heads function between the workshop or factory owner and its employees, both male and female. For example, at the Karlberg tapestry manufactory in Sweden, three Finnish noblewomen, Maria Helena, Emerenzia, and Anna Elisabet Klingbyl (active late seventeenth century), were paid instructors,

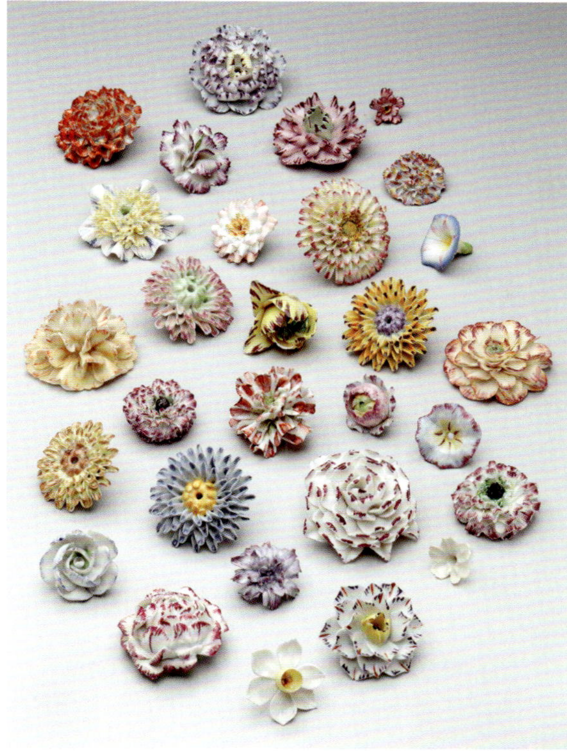

working between the directors and the labourers in vital roles. These women in leadership roles within entrepreneurial structures led innovative change in style and technology.

Ceramic factories are a clear case study. As porcelain production expanded in the eighteenth century, regional factories sought to distinguish themselves through patterns and glaze. The three-dimensional, lifelike florals from the Vincennes porcelain manufactory in France awed contemporaries across Europe (fig. 14; cat. nos. 16 & 17). The director of the floral workshop, Marie-Henriette Gravant (active mid-1700s), was considered "a vital part of the enterprise" from the earliest years of the Vincennes factory—the 1740s—where Gravant and her husband led production lines.[36] Gravant's workshop grew with the young factory, and by 1749 she employed forty-five women who would craft botanically accurate florals to embellish luxury objects bound for European courts.[37] The Gravants' knowledge of porcelain exceeded that of the factory investors and, in 1745, they extorted the company owners by withholding clay and glaze formulas for ransom. The investors eventually conceded to a small sum because Madame Gravant was indispensable to the factory's prospective success. She continued to lead the floral workshop when the factory moved to Sèvres as the royal porcelain manufactory of Louis XV.

Gravant was far from the only woman in the porcelain industry to master specialized knowledge of her craft. In 1789, scientist Charlotte Hampton (active after 1789) was named head of the gilding department at Flight in Worcester, after introducing mercury gilding on porcelain. It is unclear if Hampton studied metalwork to generate her formula; before her

Below (left to right)

Fig. 15 • Elizabeth Upton Templetown, designer at Wedgwood, known as Lady Templetown, *Vase*, 1790–1800. Earthenware, height: 36.8 cm. Victoria and Albert Museum, London, Bequeathed by Herbert Allen, inv. no. C.799-1935. Image © Victoria and Albert Museum, London.

Fig. 16 • *Detail*: Diana Beauclerk, designer at Wedgwood, *Jug*, c. 1800–1810. Red stoneware with applied black basalt reliefs and glazed interior, 23.5 × 17.8 cm. Victoria and Albert Museum, London, inv. no. 3480-1855. Image © Victoria and Albert Museum, London.

Fig. 17 • Diana Beauclerk, designer at Wedgwood, *Plaque*, c. 1789–1800. White Jasperware with black dip and applied white bas relief, 14.6 × 10.5 cm. Victoria and Albert Museum, London, inv. no. 3506-1855. Image © Victoria and Albert Museum, London.

Fig. 18 • Francesco Bartolozzi, after Diana Beauclerk, *Children at play*, 1791. Etching and stipple on paper, 20.4 × 16.1 cm. British Museum, Bequeathed by: Clayton Mordaunt Cracherode, 1799, inv. no. S,6.26. Image: © The Trustees of the British Museum.

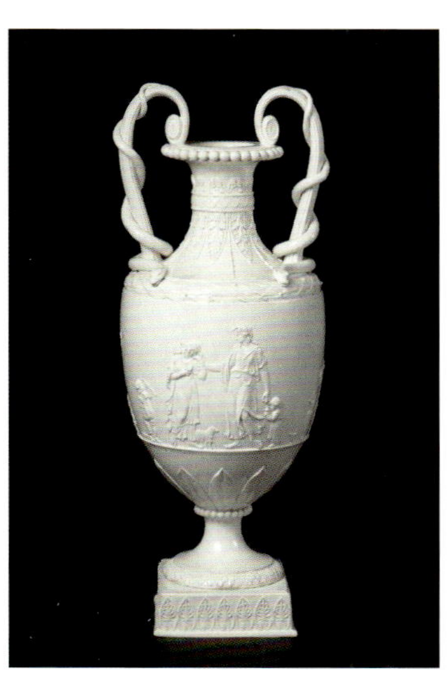

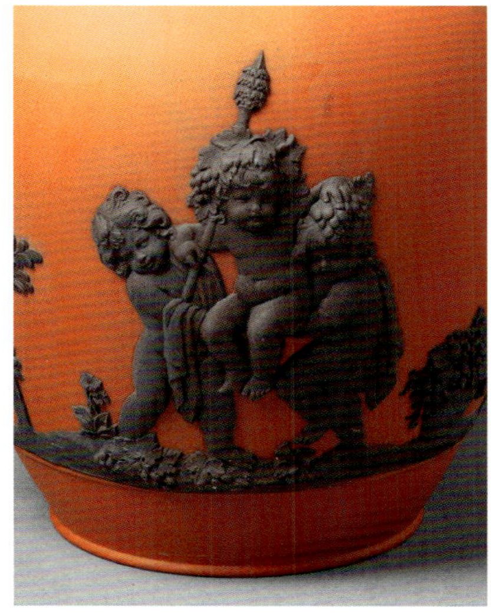

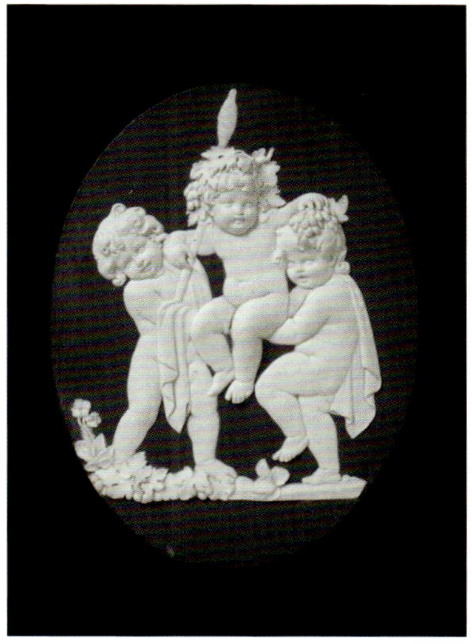

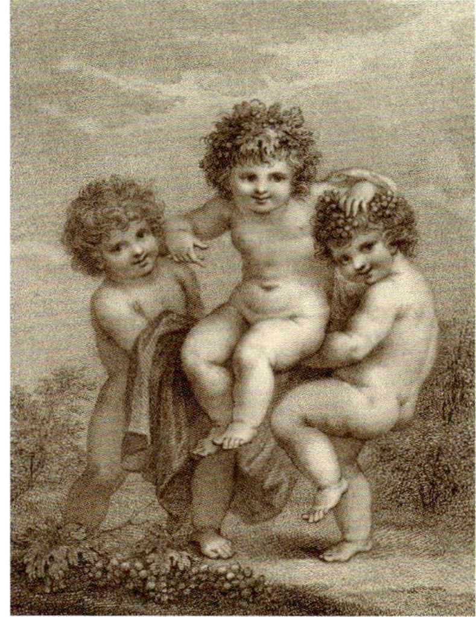

innovation, mercury gilding was identified with gilt bronze furniture mounts as a way to achieve a smooth gold finish without the need for a solid gold body. Hampton's process for applying mercury gilding to ceramics at Worcester became a signature feature of this prestigious centre of porcelain production through the nineteenth century (cat. no. 15). Her contributions exceeded making and management, but her position of power and scientific role within a ceramic workshop not owned by a woman were highly unusual.[38]

Working outside the factory grounds at Wedgwood, three female aristocrats—Elizabeth Upton Templetown, known as Lady Templetown (1746–1823; fig. 15; cat. no. 21), Diana Beauclerk (1734–1808; figs. 16 & 17; cat. nos. 19 & 20), and Emma Crewe (1780–1850)—influenced the workshop through artistry. Each provided Josiah Wedgwood with scenes for ceramic decoration, some first made in cut paper, each engraved for reference and publication (fig. 18). These celebrity designers bridge the divide between an amateur—a member of the upper class with an appreciation and skill for artistic production—and a professional artist or craftsperson who identifies creativity as their livelihood. For Wedgwood, the prestige of an aristocratic woman designer appealed to the middle-class market for the factory's wares, as their subjects intertwined classical themes with images of motherhood and sentimentality.[39] These upper-class female designers did not rely on the factory for their livelihood, but their appeal to women's taste enhanced the market for wares made by factory workers.

Working Women

A plate in Diderot's *Encyclopédie* shows the inside of a silversmith workshop. Among the male apprentices and workers, a woman stands, sleeves rolled up, foot pressed hard against the table stretcher, bearing down on a metal plate (fig. 19). This is one of multiple plates in the encyclopedia that reveal that women laboured within workshops and factories. Often, however, they were assigned the less desirable tasks, like burnishing,

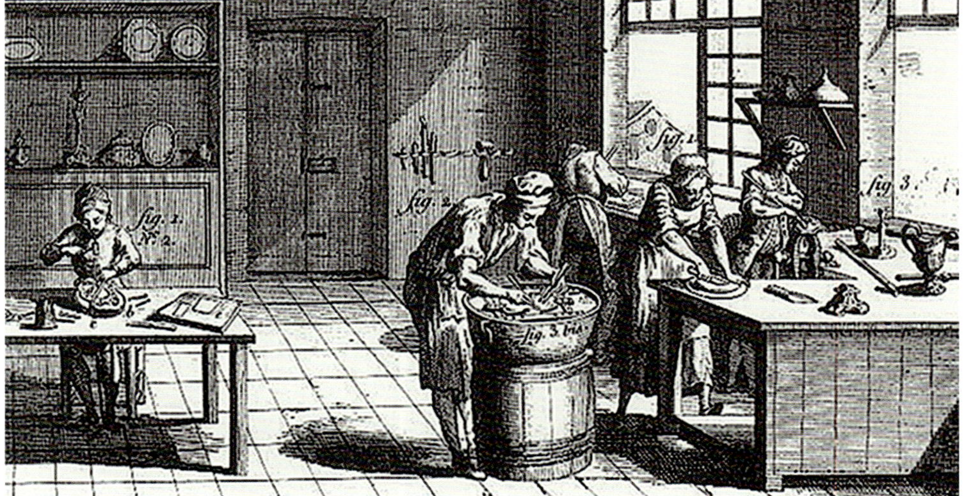

as "the responsibility for the finished piece of silver was widely diffused and many individuals could claim part in its creation from the hammerman (always male), through the raiser, chaser, and engraver (usually male) to the burnisher (often female)."[40] Such a divide was partly the result of less access to education; training in a craft was monitored by guilds or trade organizations, and these official structures often consisted solely of male members prior to 1800, with rare or medium-specific exceptions. To become a member, a craftsperson completed requisite years as an apprentice to earn the status of journeyperson, who could then be employed at a variety of workshops. If financially able, the journeyperson could register his or her own mark as a workshop owner. A guild's exclusion of women—which varied by location, medium, and century—was the most direct form of suppressing education, financial gain, and recognition for women's productivity.

Legal documents also reveal unnamed women's involvement in industry. In the competitive English ceramic market, male painters at the Chelsea-Derby factory petitioned for the exclusion of women china painters based on their gender, warning of "the many injuries done to the trade by employing Women in Painting of China, &c., Particularly not being employ'd in London in any Painting or Gilding Shop whatsoever."[41] Clearly, the skill of women painters was encroaching on male workers' security in this example of men attempting to maintain male domination in manufacturing.

Fig. 19 • Detail: Denis Diderot and Jean le Rond d'Alembert, *Silversmith [Argenteur]*, plate 1 in *Encyclopédie, ou Dictionnaire raisonné des sciences, des arts et des métiers*, vol. 1, Paris, 1751–1772. Printed book on paper, illustrated with engravings, 43.8 × 29.5 cm. University of Michigan Library. Photo: University of Chicago, the ARTFL Project.

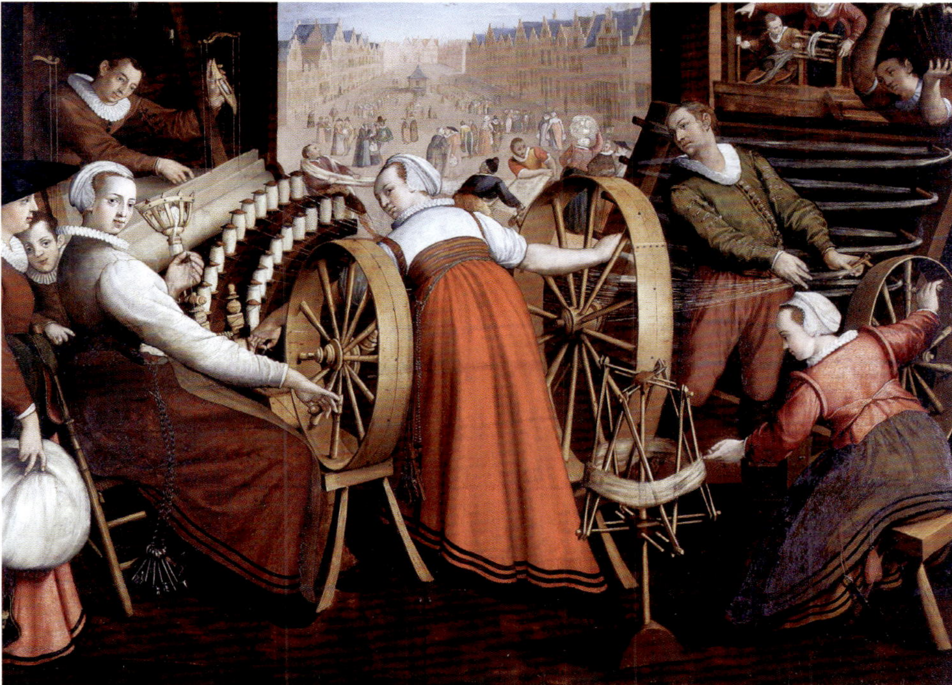

Fig. 20 • Isaac Claesz van Swanenburg, *Spinning, Shearing the Warp, and Weaving*, c. 1594–1596. Oil on panel, 137.5 × 196 cm. Museum De Lakenhal, Leiden, Acquired 1867, inv. no. S 421.

Even in fields dominated by craftswomen, like the urban upholstery and sewing industry, government recognition took until the seventeenth century, when, in 1675, seamstresses in Paris were granted an exclusively female guild that included thousands of members.[42] In Lyon, women were always present in the textile and other trade industries, but their employment was not legalized until a government decree to that effect came into force in 1786.[43] By the 1780s, there were already some thirty-nine hundred wives of manufactory masters engaged in production, as well as over a thousand paid women workers, who were not given the honour of the "journeyman" title and received inferior wages. Women and children were "the true proletariat of the Lyon factory," and Lyonnaise silk exists because of their skilled labour.[44]

Some unnamed, female-powered workshops are evident through representations of families at work. Isaac Claesz van Swanenburg's painting *Spinning, Shearing the Warp, and Weaving* (fig. 20) shows women, men, and children spinning wool in a family workshop beside Leiden's textile market. Women are at the centre of this painting and its related works in a series about saye, a foundational material for utilitarian and decorative textiles. Van Swanenburg's painting was originally installed in Saye Hall, where the lightweight wool material was traded. The prominent placement of women in the city's economic centre, and the location of the series in the meeting room for the city governors, foregrounds women's labour and suggests its wide acceptance in Dutch sixteenth-century culture. Similarly, a printed textile known as *The Activities of the Factory* [*Les Travaux de la Manufacture*], produced by the Oberkampf manufactory near Versailles (founded 1759), animates the work of women, men, and children in the preparation of copperplate-printed furnishing fabrics called *toiles de Jouy* (fig. 21). The Oberkampf manufactory employed an estimated one thousand workers, one-third to one-half of whom were women.[45] Women printers are reflected in the textile through the drawing of designs, dyeing of fabrics, and finishing of colours and details. They are joined by their families, who all worked on the factory site.

Likewise, large ceramic factories in Stoke-on-Trent included studios, kilns, and tenant housing that mimicked a miniature city. Compensation records at the Wedgwood ceramic factory reveal that women comprised about one-third (around eighty people) of the pottery manufactory workforce around 1785.[46] They were employed in roles both unskilled—like pigment grinding—and skilled, such as decorating, but never earned more than two-thirds the salary of men in equivalent positions.[47] The composition of this factory arguably provides a blueprint of integrated male and female factory production applicable across the industry for many factories.

The interconnectivity of weavers, subcontractors, suppliers, and agents was recently the subject of a data-based study on Flemish tapestries that sheds light on the importance of women as intermediaries of the workshop industry. In 2016, the digital art history project MapTap (Mapping the Antwerp-Brussels-Oudenaarde Tapestry Complex via Network Analysis) published the results of analyzing fourteen hundred identified women working in tapestry workshops between 1620 and 1720.[48] To illustrate the collaborative connections between workshops, the MapTap team added the names and family relationships for married, unmarried, and widowed women, as well as for men active within their study parameters. Through this inclusive framework, the women who conducted business trips or managed finances, like Anne Claudine de Breière (active by 1640), Isabella Maria Cocqueel (1649–1705), and Barbara Wauters (1658–1723), receive equal recognition for their workshop productions.[49] With these key additional names and kin groups, explanations for overlapping techniques and the exchange of designs between manufactories appear at unprecedented scale. The Flemish tapestry world is dependent on understanding how individual women were integral to the craft industry, and large industries in early modern Europe were often synonymous with working, skilled families.

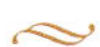

Where are women in the history of European decorative arts between 1400 and 1800? As this overview demonstrates, women artists contributed at all levels of producing objects, textiles, and furniture, including design, preparation, production, direction, and retail. Beyond highlighting the mere existence of women workshop owners or leaders, this essay confirms the competitive, successful entrepreneurship of women across the glass, metal, ceramic, textile, and furniture industries. These female workshop owners, in turn, worked alongside female specialists who commanded leadership roles within large-scale factories or founded independent studios to practise their artistry. Beyond named female figures, the study of communal production in urban and rural municipalities, and the factory complexes that imitated them, shows that Europe consisted of hundreds of thousands of craftswomen whose hands moulded, burnished, glazed, wove, and carved. The pervasiveness of women's engagement with decorative arts, craft, and design histories reveals that the objects and furniture of early modern courts, businesses, and residences were always interconnected, in some form, with the knowledge of expert craftswomen.

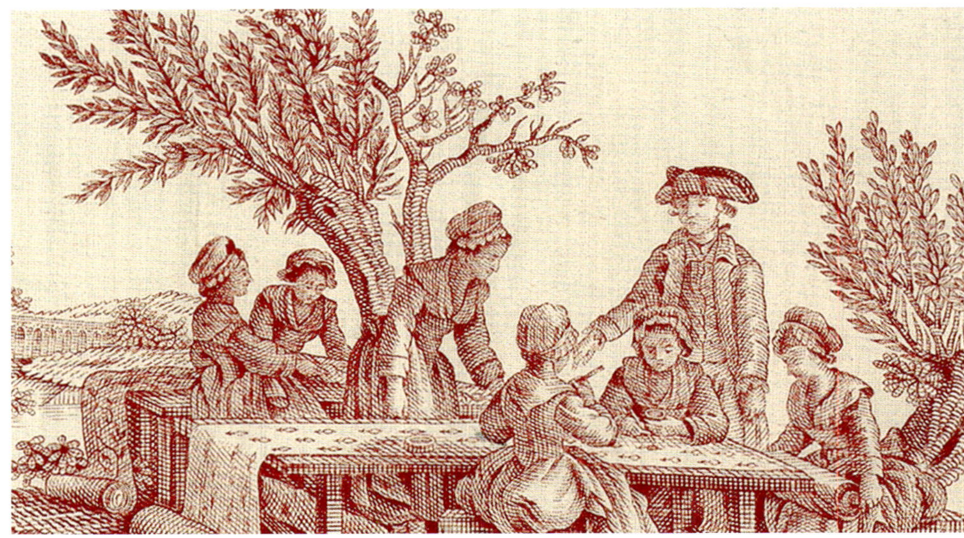

Fig. 21 • Detail: Unknown textile makers at the Oberkampf manufactory, *The Activities of the Factory* [*Les Travaux de la Manufacture*], c. 1790s. Plain weave cotton, printed, 91.4 × 96.5 cm. The Cleveland Museum of Art, Gift of I.T. Frary, inv. no. 1946.156.

Notes

1 I would like to thank Dr. Andaleeb Badiee Banta and Dr. Alexa Greist for the invitation to contribute to this publication, Dr. Theresa Kutasz Christensen for her research and collegiality, the editorial team at the Art Gallery of Ontario, the curators, conservators, collectors, and gallerists who lent their knowledge and time to discussing the history of women and craft, and, most sincerely, to this exhibition.

2 I would like to acknowledge that the terms "woman" and "female" refer to cis-gender identification. The craftswomen in this essay were chosen based on female-identifying pronouns in primary and secondary sources, and it was not possible to confirm that each self-identified as female.

3 For example, two major museum surveys of women artists in the last fifty years, *Women Artists: 1550–1950* (Los Angeles County Art Museum, 1976) and *By Her Hand: Artemisia Gentileschi and Women Artists in Italy, 1500–1800* (Wadsworth Atheneum, 2021), largely limited their scope to two-dimensional works. Exhibitions have identified women makers in specific media, such as *Printing Women: Three Centuries of Female Printmakers, 1570–1900* (New York Public Library, 2016) and *Women Silversmiths from the NMWA Collection* (National Museum of Women in the Arts, 2012), productively investigating women's advancement of materials but not necessarily conveying the wide span of women artisans working across media and centuries.

4 Alice Irma Prather-Moses, *The International Dictionary of Women Workers in the Decorative Arts: A Historical Survey from the Distant Past to the Early Decades of the Twentieth Century* (Metuchen, NJ: Scarecrow Press, 1981).

5 See Ann Christensen, "Merchant Wives, Agency, and Ambivalence in Early Modern Studies," *Early Modern Women* 3 (2008): 217–23, and Clare Haru Crowston, *Credit, Fashion, Sex: Economies of Regard in Old Regime France* (Durham, NC: Duke University Press, 2013).

6 See Rosalind Savill, *Everyday Rococo: Madame de Pompadour and Sèvres Porcelain* (Norwich, UK: Unicorn

Press, 2021); Cynthia Miller Lawrence, ed., *Women and Art in Early Modern Europe: Patrons, Collectors, and Connoisseurs* (University Park, PA: Penn State University Press, 1997); and Erin Griffey, ed., *Sartorial Politics in Early Modern Europe: Fashioning Women* (Amsterdam: Amsterdam University Press, 2019).

7 See Mark Laird and Alicia Weisberg-Roberts, eds., *Mrs. Delany & Her Circle* (New Haven and London: Yale Center for British Art and Sir John Soane's Museum, in association with Yale University Press, 2009).

8 *Mémoires de la Société Historique et Littéraire de Tournai*, vol. 22 (Tournai, Belgium: Société historique et archéologique de Tournai, 1891), 232.

9 Suzanne de Court's ewer (Metropolitan Museum of Art, 1975.1.1234) depicts the Roman goddess Ceres in the upper register and a scene of Moses and the daughters of Jethro from the Book of Exodus.

10 Rosa Barovier Mentasti, Luciano Borrelli, and Cristina Tonini, "Venetian Conical Goblets of the Renaissance," *Journal of Glass Studies* 61 (2019): 160, jstor.org/stable/26862833, accessed April 13, 2023.

11 Luigi Zecchin, "Maria Barovier e le 'Rosette,'" *Journal of Glass Studies* 10 (1968): 105–09.

12 Luke Syson and Dora Thornton, *Objects of Virtue: Art in Renaissance Italy* (London: British Museum, 2004), 191–92.

13 Syson and Thornton, *Objects of Virtue*, 197.

14 Rachele Scuro, "Shaping Identity through Glass in Renaissance Venice," in *Materialized Identities in Early Modern Culture, 1450–1750: Objects, Affects, Effects*, ed. Susanna Burghartz, Lucas Burkart, Christine Göttler, and Ulinka Rublack (Amsterdam: Amsterdam University Press, 2021), 99–134. In addition, the distribution of glass, if not its direct manufacture, was also supported by women like Cristina Brunoro in Milan, who was carrying at least seventeen thousand pieces of glass in her stock in the 1650s.

15 R.J. Charleston, "Glass in the Gambier-Parry Collection," *Burlington Magazine* 109, no. 768 (1967): 162–66, jstor.org/stable/875190, accessed December 12, 2022; see Kate Round, *Sarah Worrall, 1722–1799, Glassmaker!*, kateround.com/2020/06/08/sarah-worrall-1722-1799-glassmaker, accessed December 12, 2022.

16 See Martine van Elk, "Female Glass Engravers in the Early Modern Dutch Republic," *Renaissance Quarterly* 73, no. 1 (2020): 165–211.

17 Joanna Woodall, "'Thus Am I Accustomed to Treat Friends': Engaging with a Roemer Engraved by Maria Roemers Visscher," *Nederlands Kunsthistorisch Jaarboek* 70 (2020): 213.

18 Gherardi Fiocco, "Renaissance Majolica from the Strozzi Sacrati Collection," in "Masterpieces of Maiolica from the Strozzi Sacrati Collection," ed. Gian Carlo Bojani and Francesco Vossilla (Florence, 1998), 20, maiolicaitaliana.com/pubblicazioni/carola-fiocco-gabriella-gherardi/strozzi-sac/.

19 In the Netherlands, Jannetje Wemmersz Hoppestein (active seventeenth century) led the Het Mariaenshooft factory from around 1671 to 1686. The French immigrant and widow G.P. Varion (active late eighteenth century) owned an earthenware workshop in Este, Parma, in the late eighteenth century. L.M. Solon and William Burton, *A History and Description of Italian Majolica* (London: Cassell and Company, 1907), 163.

20 Aronson Gallery, "De Grieksche A (The Greek A) Factory," aronson.com/de-grieksche-a-the-greek-a-factory, accessed March 4, 2023.

21 Roger Massey, "Independent China Painters in 18th Century London," *English Ceramic Circle Transactions* 19, no. 1 (2005): 158. Sarah Wilcox, one of the foremost decorators for Wedgwood & Bentley's Chelsea manufactory, was the daughter of a well-known male ceramicist, confirming that women in craft workshops often learned from parents and then developed their own partnerships.

22 Jeffrey H. Munger, Eric M. Zafran, Anne L. Poulet, Robert D. Mowry, Ellenor M. Alcorn, Vivian S. Hawes, and Joellen Secondo, *The Forsyth Wickes Collection in the Museum of Fine Arts, Boston*, cat. no. 198 (Boston: Museum of Fine Arts, Boston: 1992), 240–42.

23 Amanda Dunsmore, *Hester Bateman: An Eighteenth-Century Entrepreneur*, National Gallery of Victoria, ngv.vic.gov.au/essay/hester-bateman-an-eighteenth-century-entrepreneur, April 9, 2020.

24 Dunsmore, *Hester Bateman*.

25 In eighteenth-century London, less than 1 percent of furniture-making "masters" and apprentices were women. Women achieved greater prosperity in the upholstery trade, and the highest apprentice fee charged by a maker in the eighteenth century was by the upholsteress Sarah Goodchild. See Pat Kirkham, "The London Furniture Trade, 1700–1870," *Furniture History* 24 (1988): 4, jstor.org/stable/23406689, accessed April 14, 2023.

26 Kirkham, "The London Furniture Trade," 4.

27 Adam Bowett and Laurie Lindey, "Labelled Furniture from the White Swan Workshop in St Paul's Churchyard (1711–35)," *Furniture History* 39 (2003), 71–98.

28 Bowett and Lindey, "Labelled Furniture," 72.

29 Bowett and Lindey, "Labelled Furniture," 71.

30 Helen Jacobsen, Rufus Bird, and Mia Jackson, *Jean-Henri Riesener: Cabinetmaker to Louis XVI & Marie Antoinette* (London: Philip Wilson, 2020), 4–6.

31 See Alvar González-Palacios, *Nostalga e invenzione, Arredi e arti decorative a Roma e Napoli nel Settecento* (Milan: Skira, 2010), and Fausto Calderai and Alan Chong, *Furnishing a Museum: Isabella Stewart Gardner's Collection of Italian Furniture* (Berkshire, UK: Periscope, 2012), 246.

32 Calderai and Chong, *Furnishing a Museum*, 246.

33 I am indebted to the research of Dr. Theresa Kutasz Christensen on the history of the Karlberg manufactory. See also John Böttiger and Gaston Levy-Ullmann, *Svenska Statens Samling Af Väfda Tapeter: Historik Och Beskrifvande Förteckning, af Dr. John Böttiger* […] (Stockholm: Fröléen & comp., 1895).

34 On the manufacture and series, see Koenraad Brosens, "Charles Le Brun's Meleager and Atalanta and Brussels Tapestry c. 1675," *Studies in the Decorative Arts* 11, no. 1 (2003): 5–37.

35 Getty Museum Collection, "Katharine Ghuys, the Widow Guillaume Werniers," getty.edu/art/collection/person/103M33, accessed May 15, 2023.

36 Antoine d'Albis, "The Secret of Gravant or the Privilege of Vincennes," *Bulletin of the Society of Friends of Vincennes*, no. 38 (1987): 7.

37 Carl Christian Dauterman, *Sèvres Porcelain: Makers and Marks of the Eighteenth Century* (New York: Metropolitan Museum of Art, 1986), 22.

38 Misty Flores, "Hidden Hands: Untold Stories of the Object," Rienzi Symposium, Museum of Fine Arts Houston, November 6, 2021, mfah.org/visit/rienzi/rienzi-symposium, accessed May 15 , 2023.

39 Alexia Petsalias-Diomidis, "Pottery Workers, 'the Ladies' and 'the Middling Class of People': Production and Marketing of 'Etruscan and Grecian Vases' at Wedgwood c.1 760–1820," in *The Classical Vase Transformed: Consumption, Reproduction, and Class in Eighteenth- and Nineteenth-Century Britain*, ed. Alexia Petsalis-Diomidis and Edith Hall (London: Institute of Classical Studies, School of Advanced Study, University of London, 2020), 36.

40 Philippa Glanville and Jennifer Faulds Goldsborough, *Women Silversmiths, 1685–1845: Works from the Collection of the National Museum of Women in the Arts* (London: Thames and Hudson, 1990), 15–17. In the silver-plating industry, which emerged in the mid-eighteenth century to provide cost-effective alternatives to silver for a growing middle class, women were assigned to finishing work, like burnishing or polishing.

41 Massey, "Independent China Painters," 158.

42 See Clare Haru Crowston, "Women, Gender, and Guilds in Early Modern Europe: An Overview of Recent Research," *International Review of Social History* 53 (2008): 19–44. All-female seamstress guilds were also found in Rouen, Le Havre, and Cologne.

43 Maurice Garden, "Ouvriers et artisans au XVIIIe siècle: L'exemple lyonnais et les problèmes de classification," in *Un historien dans la ville*, ed. René Favier and Laurence Fontaine (Paris: Éditions de la Maison des sciences de l'homme, 2008), 5.

44 Garden, "Ouvriers et artisans," 5.

45 The Met, "Les Travaux de la Manufacture," metmuseum.org/art/collection/search/221839, accessed May 15, 2023.

46 Petsalis-Diomidis, "Pottery Workers," 43.

47 Petsalis-Diomidis, "Pottery Workers," 43. On the Wedgwood factory site, women are recorded as the primary tenants of a home, signalling independence at home and at work. The names of women do appear in this archive, allowing for statistical analysis.

48 Koenraad Brosens, Klara Alen, Astrid Slegten, and Fred Truyen, "MapTap and Cornelia: Slow Digital Art History and Formal Art Historical Social Network Research," *Zeitschrift für Kunstgeschichte* 79, no. 3 (2016): 321.

49 Brosens et al., "MapTap and Cornelia," 322.

WOMEN AND THE ART OF SCIENCE

Virginia Treanor

The rise in realism in art—that is, the quest to depict objects as close to reality as possible—paralleled the advent and growth of modern scientific investigation during the Scientific Revolution in Europe, broadly defined here as the period between 1400 and 1800.[1] As the printing press allowed for the greater dissemination of knowledge and increase in subsequent discoveries, the need for imagery to accurately render plants, animals, insects, and the human body became crucial to these burgeoning areas of study. According to Pamela H. Smith, who has studied the intersection of art and science in the early modern period, "naturalistic representation formed much more than a visual practice; it was a mode of investigating, understanding, and knowing nature."[2] While today we tend to view the fields of art and science at opposite ends of the spectrum (if on the same spectrum at all), the relationship between the two in the early modern period was much more interdependent and symbiotic. The role of artists who were actively engaging with the scientific discourses of the day—and who were participating not only in the *sharing* of knowledge but also in the *creation* of it through their work—is a topic that has received growing attention over the past few decades.[3]

In an effort to fully understand the role of art in relation to science and natural history, it is essential that the work of women who operated at the conjunction of these fields be considered and their contributions acknowledged.[4] This essay examines some of the ways in which women's artistic work dovetailed with, or was an intrinsic part of, the scientific discourses of their respective eras. Further, it demonstrates the depths of their knowledge, the breadth of their impact, and, above all, their consistent presence and participation in the nascent fields of botany, entomology, and anatomy, among others.

Flora and Fauna

The practical uses of plants for their restorative and curative properties have long been under the purview of women across cultures, sometimes leading to suspicion and charges of witchcraft. In art history, the supposed proclivity of women for still-life painting and botanical illustrations is an oft-repeated trope. This association of women artists with the floral arts has been attributed to their purported superior manual dexterity and attention to detail, or their exclusion from the professional training necessary to practise "higher genres" of art, including drawing from a nude model. While this larger topic is outside of the scope of this essay,[5] these claims are somewhat challenged by the fact that male artists also specialized and excelled in floral still-life painting and botanical illustration, and that women artists both executed large-scale history paintings and made use of male and female nude bodies alike.[6]

With the advent of the Scientific Revolution, the desire of the social and intellectual elite (typically men) to label, classify, and systematize everything in the natural world—an instinct born out of colonial expansion and domination—led to the gathering and recording of data that could then be codified. This interest in studying objects went hand in hand with collecting them; initially the pastime of kings and princes, the collection and possession of items from the natural world within so-called "cabinets of curiosities" was an impulse that eventually filtered down to others who sought to convey their interest in and knowledge of the scientific discoveries of the day.[7] Such collections consisted of all manner of things—not only those from the natural world (*naturalia*) but also those created by humans (*artificialia*). Sometimes, these two classifications intersected in the work of artists who represented natural objects such as flowers, insects, and shells, thereby providing collectors with

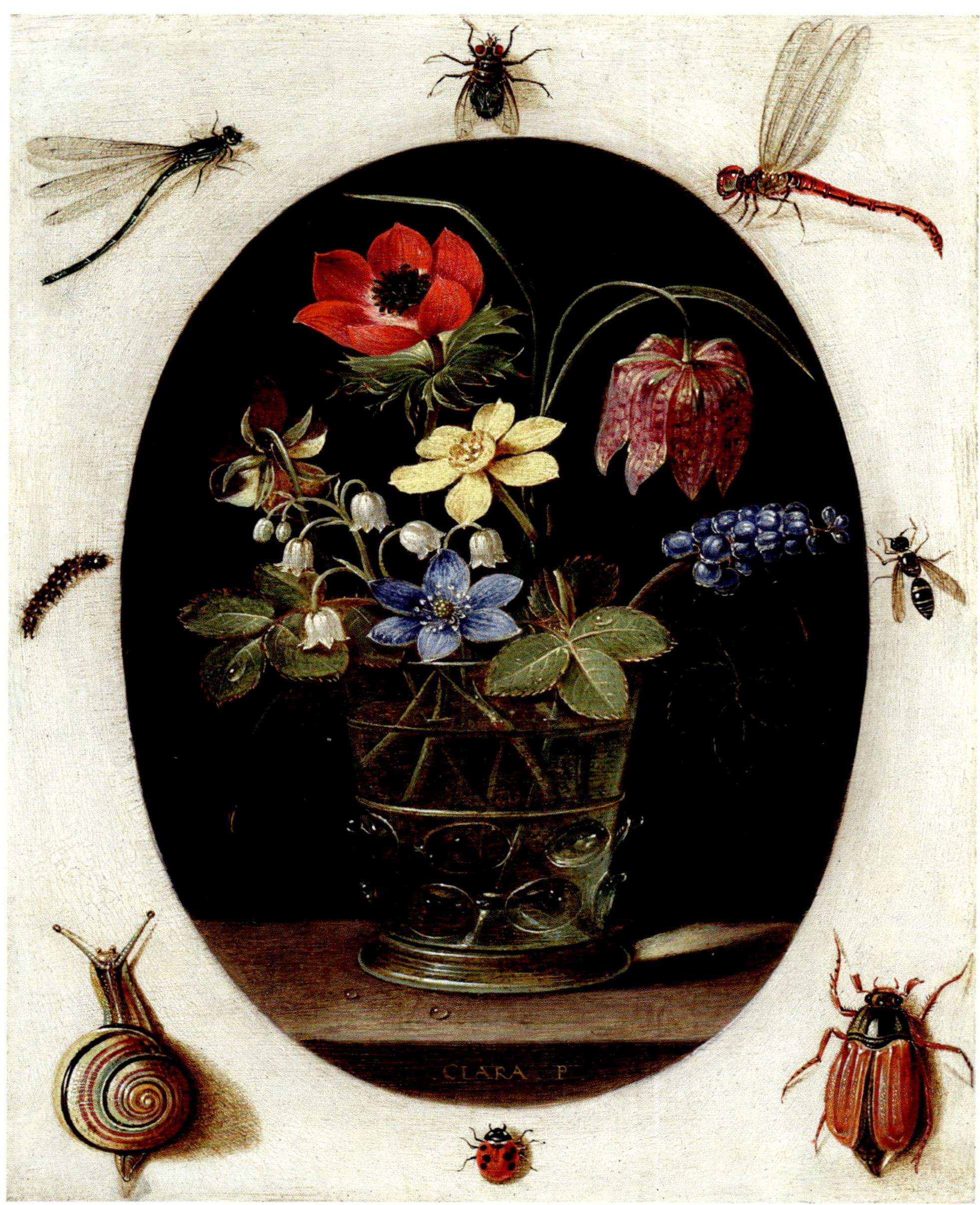

Fig. 1 · Clara Peeters, *Still Life with Flowers Surrounded by Insects and a Snail*, c. 1610. Oil on copper, 16.6 × 13.5 cm. National Gallery of Art, Washington, The Lee and Juliet Folger Fund, inv. no. 2018.144.1.

artificialia that rivalled the natural specimens they possessed or, perhaps, functioned as stand-ins for objects they did not.

It is within this context that many still-life paintings may have functioned, particularly floral still lifes, whose carefully arranged painted blooms would never wilt or fade, thereby providing collectors with a means to represent living specimens within their cabinets. In the early seventeenth century, such images were still a relatively new genre, stemming in part from an interest in examining nature as a subject worthy in and of itself.[8] Beginning in the second half of the sixteenth century, Antwerp became the veritable hub of scientific publications, many of which were accompanied by illustrations of their subject matter. An early work by the Flemish artist Clara Peeters (c. 1587–after 1636), one of the earliest artists to devote herself to the genre of still life, seems to crystallize the interconnectedness of these didactic illustrations, collections of specimens, and the art of painting (fig. 1). Proudly signed by Peeters along the ledge on which a small bouquet in a clear glass sits, *Still Life with Flowers Surrounded by Insects and a Snail* may have originally been part of a larger cabinet-like structure that housed specimens from the natural

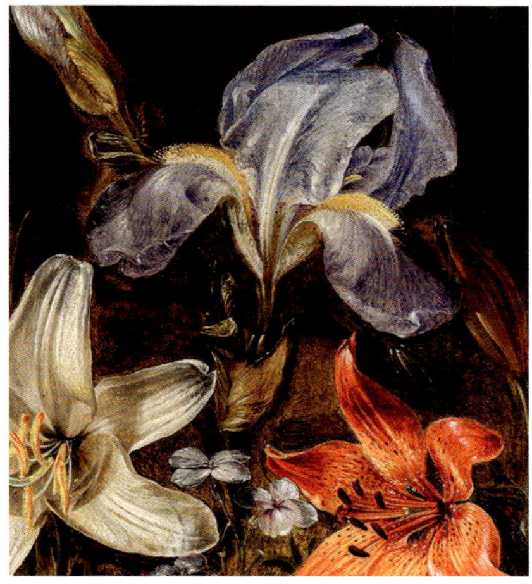

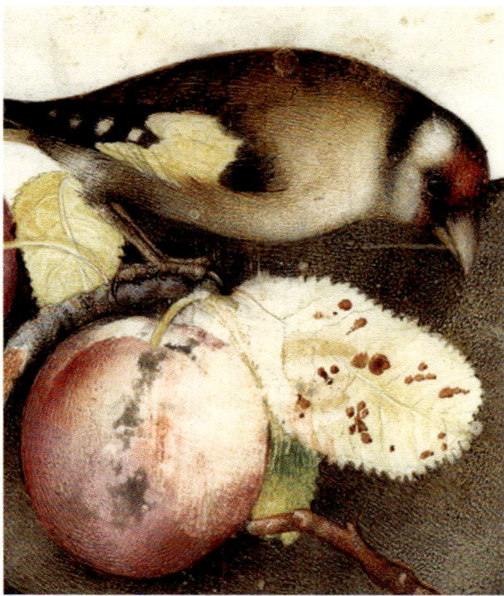

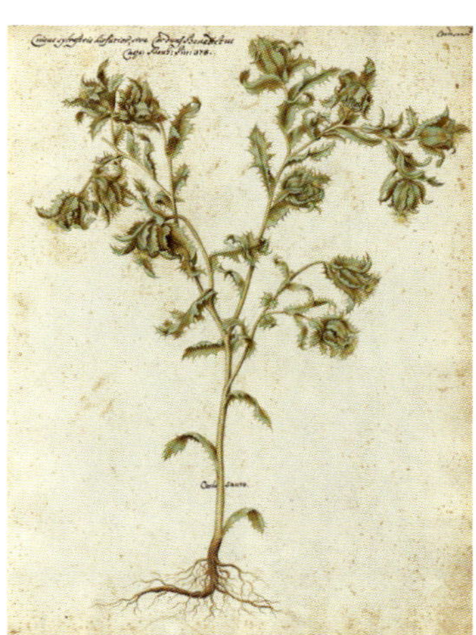

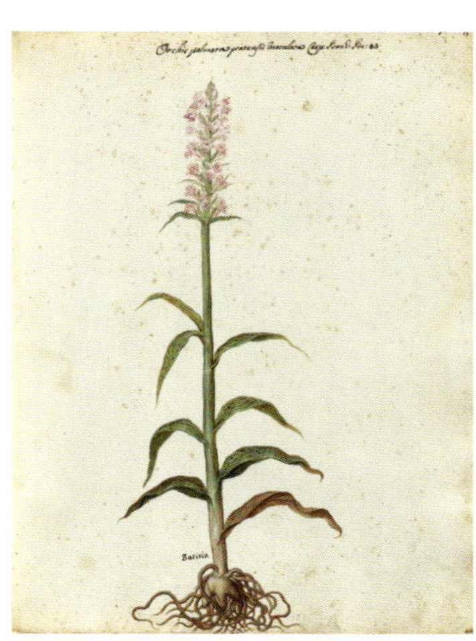

Above (left to right)

Fig. 2 · *Detail*: Clara Peeters, *A Still Life of Lilies, Roses, Iris, Pansies, Columbine, Love-in-a-Mist, Larkspur and Other Flowers in a Glass Vase on a Table Top, Flanked by a Rose and a Carnation*, c. 1610. Oil on panel, 49.5 × 33.7 cm. National Museum of Women in the Arts, Washington, DC, Gift of Wallace and Wilhelmina Holladay, inv. no. 2016.30. Photo: Lee Stalsworth.

Fig. 3 · *Detail*: Giovanna Garzoni, *Still Life with Birds and Fruit*, c. 1650. Watercolour with graphite, heightened with lead white, on vellum, 25.7 × 41.6 cm. The Cleveland Museum of Art, Bequest of Mrs. Elma M. Schniewind in memory of her parents, Mr. and Mrs. Frank Geib, inv. no. 1955.140.

Fig. 4 · Giovanna Garzoni, *Piante varie*, c. 1630–1632. Watercolour on paper, 49.5 × 38 cm. Dumbarton Oaks Research Library and Collection, Trustees for Harvard University, Washington, DC, inv. no. G-3-3.

Openings illustrated:

Fig. 4a · *Cardo Santo* (folio 5)

Fig. 4b · *Satirio* (folio 15)

world.[9] The preciseness with which Peeters articulates each bloom against the dark background is similar to the way that flowers are presented in the illustrations included in the published *florilegia* of the day.[10] Based in Antwerp, Peeters was well placed to benefit from the availability of published studies of flora and fauna.[11] She seems to have used the work of Joris Hoefnagel in particular to inform her own work. The similarities in presentation, particularly in the *trompe l'oeil* effects of the insects, point to the influence of Hoefnagel's *Archetypa Studiaque patris Georgii Hoefnagelii*, which was published in 1592.[12] Didactic illustrations that accompanied text based on an observation of the subject in question—be it animal or vegetal, though they could be quite detailed—tended to be presented frontally, with minimal overlapping of specimens. Peeters's use of such illustrations to inform her own compositions seems plausible if, as is supposed, her still lifes were intended for collectors who were interested in having examples of multiple blooms in one image (fig. 2; cat. no. 114).[13] Utilizing such illustrations would have ensured that an artist could keep working from a static image that was not prone to changing position over time because of wilting. However, as the flowers in this arrangement and other early bouquets were grown in Europe at the time, Peeters may have nevertheless looked to live specimens for colour and texture.

In Italy, too, a deep interest in the genre of still life took hold during the seventeenth century. Giovanna Garzoni (1600–1670) spent time in several major cities in Italy, and a large part of her wide-ranging oeuvre included still lifes of fruits and flowers, often accompanied by shells, birds, insects, and the occasional gastropod (fig. 3; cat. no. 155). Garzoni's many still lifes of fruit done for elite patrons, such as the Medici family, attest to a strong desire among collectors in these circles to possess images of natural beauty as captured through the ingenuity of human artifice.[14] Like Peeters before her, Garzoni realistically rendered different materials and textures in paint within her works, which became objects to be collected and displayed in and of themselves. Also like Peeters, Garzoni was aware of the scientific developments of the time. While in Rome during the early 1630s, Garzoni gained access to the Accademia dei Lincei, a scientific institution founded in 1603 by Federico Cesi, who had a particular passion for botany. Here, Garzoni saw the *Syntaxis Plantaria*, a mammoth compendium of drawings of plants, fungi, and algae native to the region, which would have introduced her to the latest taxonomic distinctions as well as the standardized way specimens were illustrated.[15] This knowledge served her well as she embarked on creating her own series of watercolours featuring plants known as *Piante varie*, which was intended as an aid for plant identification (fig. 4; cat. no. 156). Garzoni's dependence on already published illustrations for her own imagery served an important

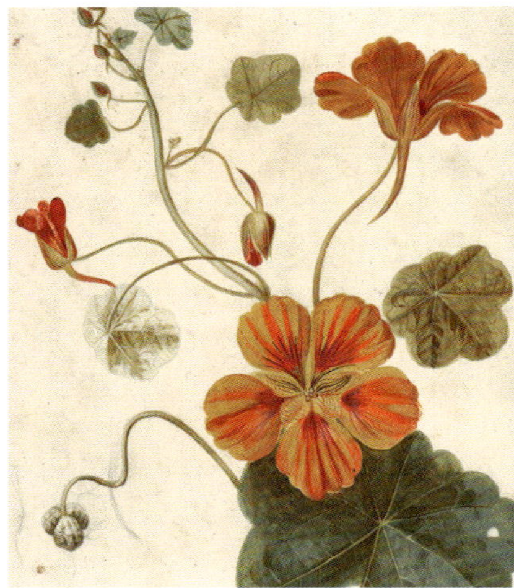

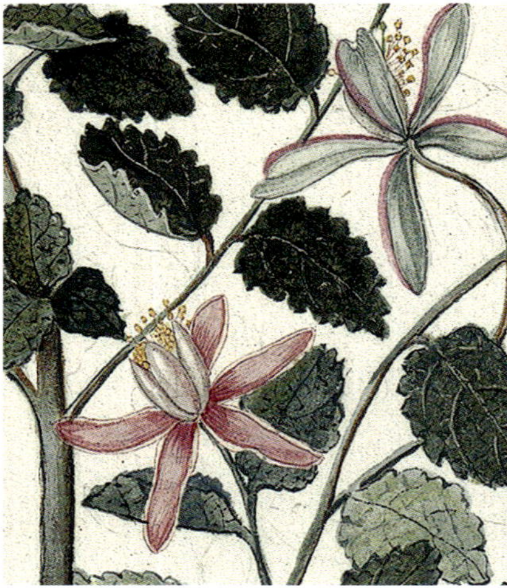

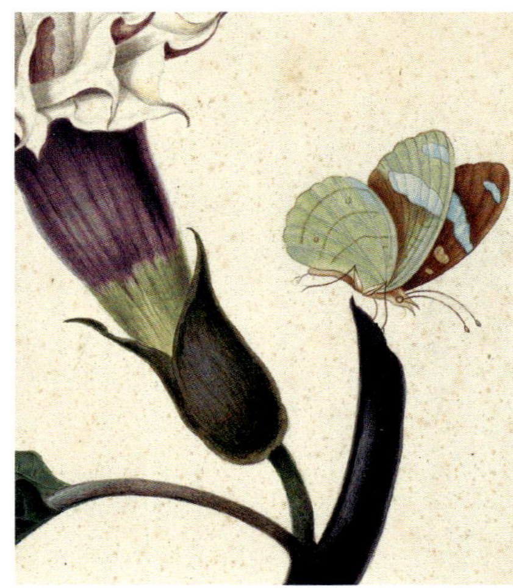

Fig. 5 (left) · *Detail:* Alida Withoos, *Nasturtium*, c. 1675–1715. Watercolour and opaque watercolour over black chalk on paper, 39.6 × 25 cm. The Morgan Library & Museum, New York, Bequest of Charles Ryskamp, inv. no. 2010.179. Photo: The Morgan Library & Museum, New York.

Fig. 6 (middle) · *Detail:* Maria Moninckx, *Study of a Plant with Red-Purple Flowers [Sebastiana africana purpurea]*, 1695. Opaque watercolour and watercolour over graphite on paper, 35.8 × 24.7 cm. Lent by The Metropolitan Museum of Art, New York, Frits and Rita Markus Fund, 2013, inv. no. 2013.147.

Fig. 7 (right) · *Detail:* Maria Sibylla Merian and Willem de Heer, *Datura with Butterflies*, 1679/1695. Watercolour and opaque watercolour, with traces of gum arabic, over graphite on paper, 33.3 × 21 cm. The Morgan Library & Museum, New York, Bequest of Charles Ryskamp, inv. no. 2010.160. Photo: The Morgan Library & Museum, New York.

function: the dissemination of relatively standardized images that aided in the correct identification of plant species was a necessity, especially when trying to ascertain the toxicity of a plant. Furthermore, Garzoni's details of surface texture and colour gradations added greatly to the specificity of each plant and furthered their reliability as didactic aids.[16]

As the century progressed, both still-life painting and scientific illustration grew popular with practitioners, both male and female. The two realms remained closely linked as budding scientists and artists frequently worked for the same patrons. Amsterdam, in particular, became a locus of intense scientific study and publication as well as a booming art market. The colonial exploitation carried out by the Dutch East and West India Companies ensured a nonstop stream of items from around the globe, which collectors were eager to possess. These included plants from abroad that were then cultivated in Dutch soil, a climate that proved challenging for more tropical specimens. Agnes Block (1629–1704) was one of the first botanical enthusiasts in Europe, and the first in the Dutch Republic, to successfully grow a pineapple, a plant indigenous to South America.[17] In her garden outside of Amsterdam, Block grew hundreds of plant and flower species that had originated from all over the world. She obtained seeds directly from Asia and the Americas and also obtained specimens through exchanges with botanists like Paul Hermann in Leiden and Lelio Trionfetti, professor of botany in Bologna. Block also knew Jan Commelin, a founder of the Amsterdam Hortus Botanicus, one of the oldest botanical gardens in Europe that cultivated both domestic and foreign plants.[18]

To document her extraordinary collection of living specimens, Block commissioned artists to make drawings of them, including Alida Withoos (c. 1662–1730), Maria Moninckx (c. 1673–1757), Maria Sibylla Merian (1647–1717), and Merian's daughter, Johanna Helena Herolt-Graff (1668–c. 1723). Images like Withoos's *Nasturtium* (fig. 5; cat. no. 163) capture the different stages of the nasturtium's development (following the standard practice of the day), and would have provided a lasting record of the plants that Block cultivated. Withoos was also commissioned by Block to portray her prized pineapple, an image that is unfortunately no longer extant.[19] Block's own notations have been found on the back of some of the drawings done for her (figs. 6 & 7; cat. nos. 165 & 164), indicating when they bloomed and from where they originated, and, sometimes, even identifying the artist.[20] While Block also commissioned male artists to execute works for her, the women she hired were involved together in another botanical project for the Amsterdam Hortus Botanicus. Withoos, Moninckx, and Herolt-Graff contributed illustrations to the so-called "Moninckx Atlas," named for Maria's father, Jan Moninckx, who received a commission to record the plants, both

Fig. 8 (above, right) • Detail: Maria Sibylla Merian, *Dissertatio de Generatione et Metamorphosibus Insectorum Surinamensium...* [*Metamorphosis of the Insects of Suriname*], Amsterdam, 1719. Bound volume of hand-coloured engravings, 54 × 38.1 × 4.8 cm. Oak Spring Garden Foundation, Upperville, Virginia. Opening illustrated: *Caterpillars, Butterflies, and Flowers* (plate 11).

Fig. 9 (below, left) • Detail: Maria Sibylla Merian, *Convolvulus and Metamorphosis of the Convolvulus Hawk Moth*, c. 1670–1683. Watercolour with touches of opaque watercolour over black chalk or graphite on vellum, 29 × 37.2 cm. The Cleveland Museum of Art, John L. Severance Fund, inv. no. 2019.9.

Fig. 10 (below, right) • Detail: Maria Sibylla Merian, *Der Raupen wunderbare Verwandelung und sonderbare Blumen-Nahrung* [*The Wondrous Transformation of Caterpillars and their Curious Diet of Flowers*], Nuremberg, Frankfurt, and Leipzig, 1679–1683. Bound volume with hand-coloured engraved illustrations, 20.6 × 17.1 × 4.1 cm. Oak Spring Garden Foundation, Upperville, Virginia, inv. RB1030. Opening illustrated: *Grossularia alba vulgaris, Common white Gooseberry* (plate 31).

foreign and domestic, grown at the Hortus Botanicus. Out of the original 420 watercolours produced for this compendium, 223 were published as folio engravings in Jan and Caspar Commelin's two-volume *Horti medici Amstelodamensis*, published between 1697 and 1701. These volumes were, in turn, used later in the eighteenth century by Carl Linnaeus, who based a number of his taxonomies on the illustrations contained therein.[21] Thus, the involvement of women in botanical illustration during a time when plants were first being classified and sorted inevitably led later scholars and scientists, like Linnaeus, to depend and build upon their work.

Linnaeus also relied on the work of Maria Sibylla Merian, particularly her most ambitious publication, *Dissertatio de generatione et metamorphosibus insectorum Surinamensium* [*Metamorphosis of the Insects of Suriname*], for which she travelled from Amsterdam to the Dutch colony in South America (fig. 8; cat. no. 153). So detailed were Merian's illustrations, based on her first-hand observations, that Linnaeus consulted her images rather than actual specimens for his work.[22] Many of the specimens she collected while in Suriname were preserved in Frankfurt where they were subsequently used by entomologist

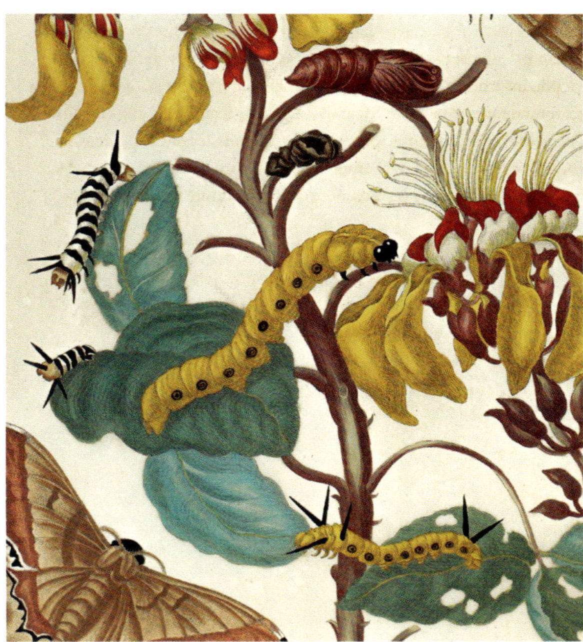

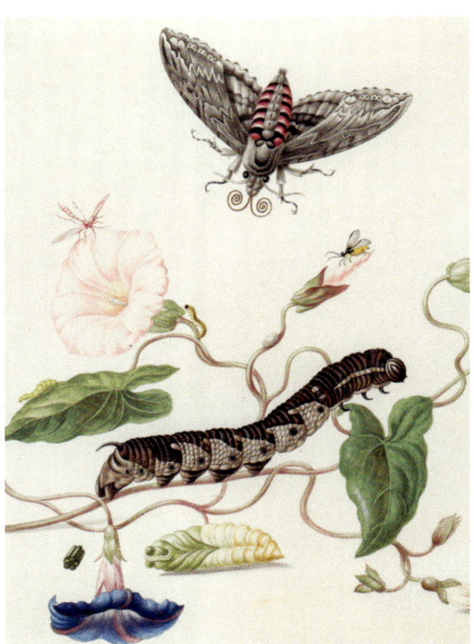

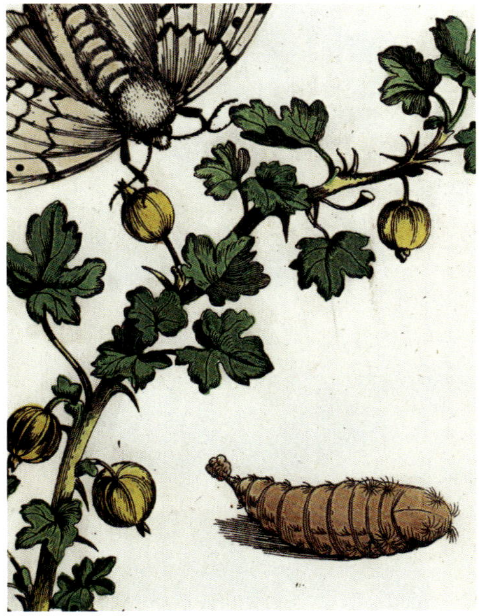

Eugen Johann Christoph Esper.[23] Merian trained as an artist with her stepfather but was drawn to the study of insects and plants through her own desire to understand them (fig. 9; cat. no. 167). In 1679, she published her first study on the metamorphosis of caterpillars, *Der Raupen wunderbare Verwandelung und sonderbare Blumen-Nahrung* [*The Wondrous Transformation of Caterpillars and their Curious Diet of Flowers*] (fig. 10; cat. no. 168), which was replete with text and images based on her own observations about the diet and life cycles of these insects that she raised in her home in Nuremberg.

Long before Merian's lifetime, Nuremberg was the site of robust investigation into the natural world, continuing a tradition that had been established during the Renaissance in both artistic and scientific circles.[24] Throughout the eighteenth century, Nuremberg continued to be a centre of scientific investigation through the visual arts, with women like sisters Barbara Regina Dietzsch (1706–1783) and Margaretha Barbara Dietzsch (1726–1795) operating within this nexus. Working in the family atelier, which included their father and brothers (four of whom also specialized in floral and vegetal still lifes), both women painted "plant portraits," with the elder, Barbara, the principal

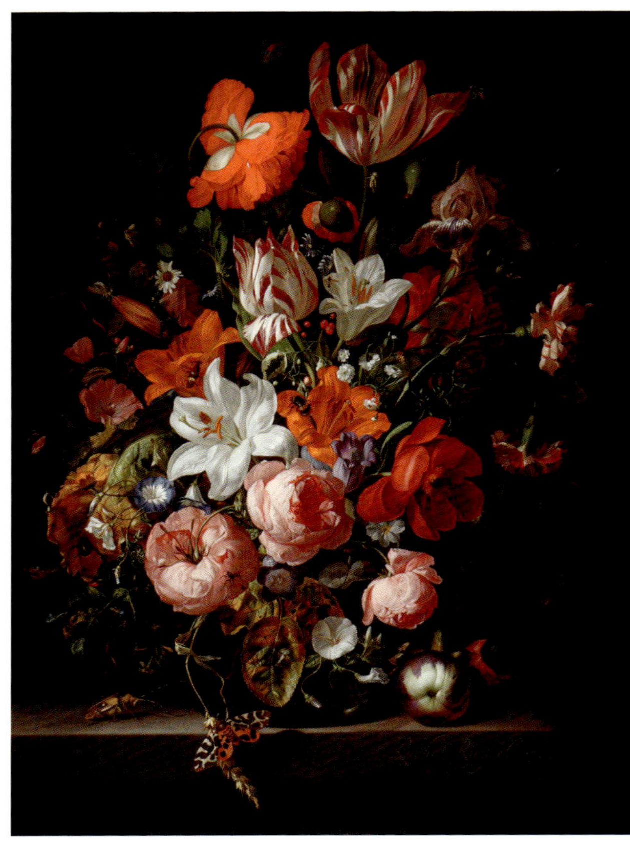

Fig. 11 • Rachel Ruysch, *Flowers in a Glass Vase*, 1704. Oil on canvas, 83.8 × 67 cm. Detroit Institute of Arts, Founders Society Purchase, Robert H. Tannahill Foundation Fund, Joseph M. de Grimme Memorial Fund, et al., inv. no. 1995.67.

flower painter in the family, teaching the younger Margaretha.[25] While their works—particularly those of Barbara—were collected for their decorative appeal, they also functioned as carefully detailed studies of the plant in question (cat. nos. 178 & 179). Noted Nuremberg physician Christoph Jakob Trew invited both sisters to contribute their illustrations to be engraved for inclusion in his 1750 *Hortus Nitidissimis*.[26] Additionally, the distinctive dark backgrounds employed by Barbara, reminiscent of Dutch flower painting of the seventeenth century, were recommended by Trew to the renowned botanical illustrator Georg Dionysius Ehret to make his illustrations clearer.

Despite Nuremburg's favourable conditions for an artist and scientist like Merian, she left after separating from her husband and eventually settled in the Dutch Republic. In Amsterdam, Merian was well-connected to the scientific community of the day, through Agnes Block as well as through her association with Frederick Ruysch, who was, among other things, an anatomist and botanist. Ruysch was also connected with the Hortus Botanicus in Amsterdam, a site where Merian undoubtedly spent much time observing the living specimens grown there.

Through Frederick Ruysch, Merian likely knew his daughter, Rachel Ruysch (1664–1750), who was on her way to becoming the greatest floral still-life painter of her generation. Ruysch's complex floral arrangements were the Baroque fulfillment of the more restrained works of her artistic predecessors earlier in the seventeenth century (fig. 11). While Ruysch trained in the art of painting with preeminent still-life artist Willem van Aelst, her education in observation came from her father; during her youth, he encouraged her to aid with preparations of human anatomical specimens for his renowned collection, the Museum Ruyschiana.[27] Ruysch's immersion in the scientific explorations of her father, which included the use of magnifying lenses to examine a range of specimens, would have attuned her to the importance of empirical observation at a minute level. This familiarity with the power of looking closely at nature is reflected in the painstaking details found in Ruysch's paintings, as the inclusion of plants and animals were often entirely new to still-life painting.[28] Marianne Berardi traces

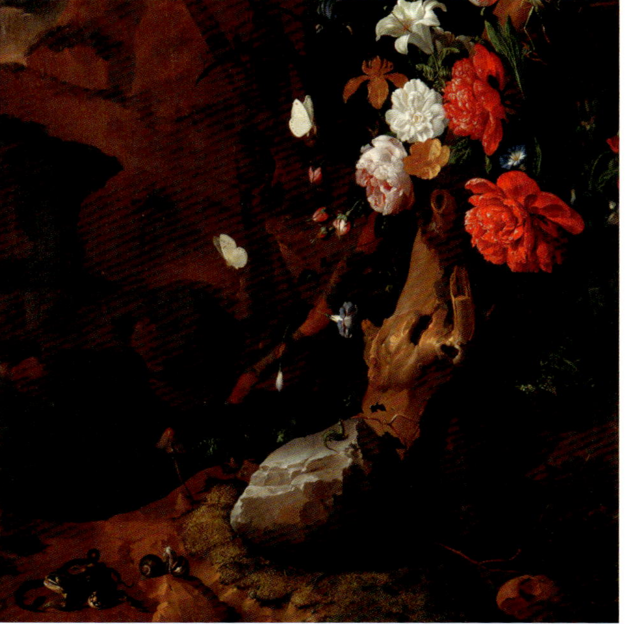

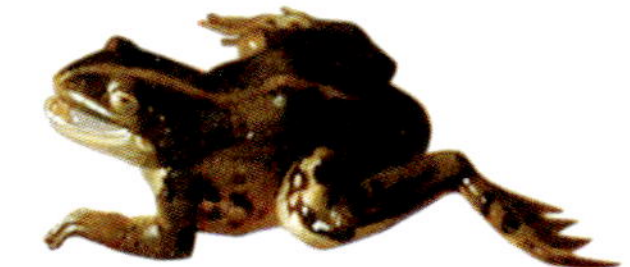

Fig. 12 • Details: Rachel Ruysch, *Floral Still Life*, 1686. Oil on canvas, 114.6 × 87.3 cm. Memorial Art Gallery of the University of Rochester: Acquired with contributions made in memory of Brenda Rowntree by her friends, through the Acquisition Fund of the Women's Council, and the Marion Stratton Gould Fund, inv. no. 1982.9.

the appearance of "scientific motifs" in Ruysch's works from the late 1680s onward to the artist's engagement with her father's reorganization of his specimen collection in 1691 and his role in editing, annotating, and publishing the *Horti medici Amstelodamensis rariorum plantarum historia* between 1692 and 1697 (the same work that, in turn, relied on many of the images from the Moninckx Atlas). Non-native species such as succulents and even amphibians appear scattered throughout Ruysch's still lifes (fig. 12) around the time she was likely assisting her father with his work.[29]

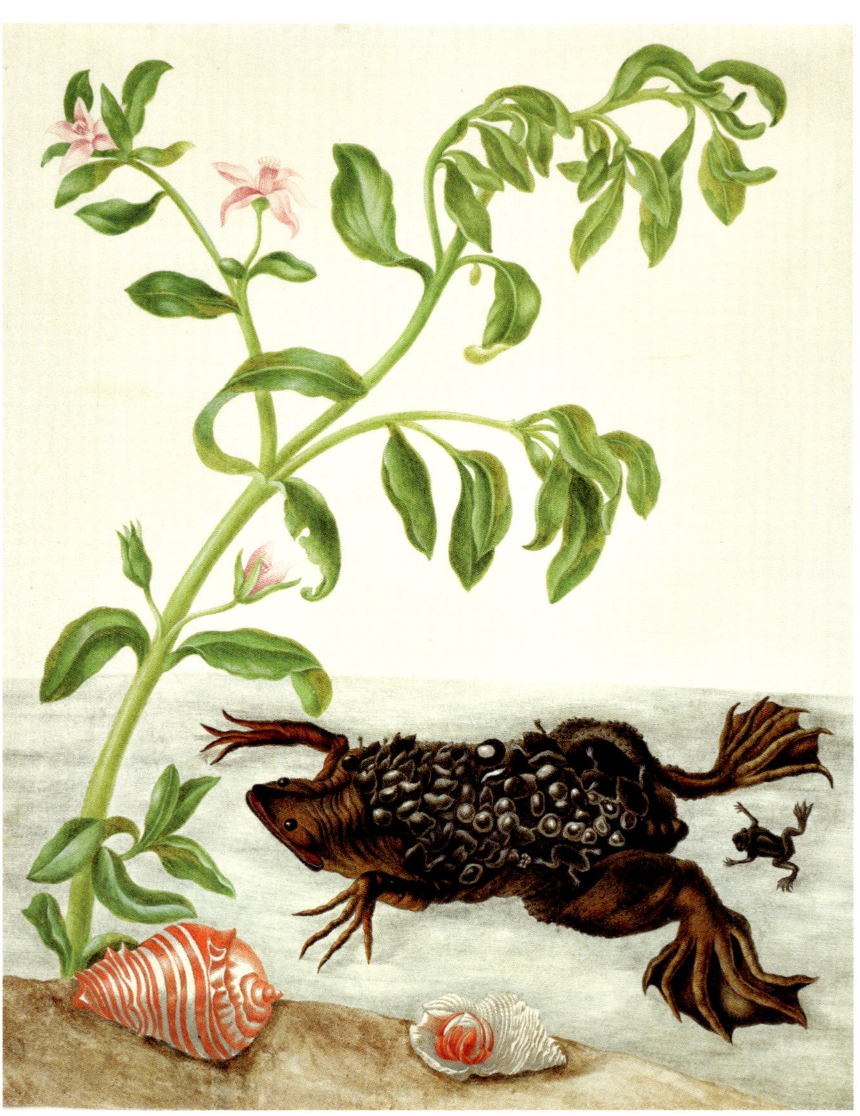

Fig. 13 · Maria Sibylla Merian, *Shoreline Purslane and Suriname Toad*, 1702–1703. Watercolour and opaque watercolour with gum arabic over lightly etched outlines on vellum, 36.1 × 29.1 cm. Royal Collection Trust, inv. no. RCIN 921217. Image: Royal Collection Trust / © His Majesty King Charles III 2023.

Shells

Unlike Ruysch, Merian was able to observe species from life during her travels and was the first to publish an image of a Suriname toad in her *Metamorphosis* (fig. 13). She depicts it swimming in the water and included shells in her illustration, writing in the accompanying description: "I had these shells brought up from the bottom of the sea in order to see what kind of creatures live in them … I pulled a number out with force and established they were a variety of crab."[30] Like the toad she observed from life, Merian was able to inspect shells and their inhabitants in their natural environment while in Suriname. This was in itself a rare opportunity, as most Europeans at the time experienced such shells as rarities in cabinets or through illustrations of them.

Obtaining and possessing shells from across the globe was foundational to any self-respecting collector's cabinet of rarities.[31] As a direct result of European colonial expansion, the shell became a symbol of Western control over lands and people that most collectors would never see in person. Not surprisingly, the trajectory of the fervour surrounding shells grew conjointly with the rise of colonialism and fields of scientific inquiry. The study of shells from a scientific standpoint, historically called "conchology," can be traced back to the Englishman Martin Lister, who published the first comprehensive study in 1678—featuring over one thousand illustrations—with additional publications in 1685 and 1696. Lister engaged his own teenage daughters, Anna Lister (1671–1700) and Susanna Lister (later Knowler) (c. 1670–1738), to create drawings and etchings made from direct observation of specimens (figs. 14–16). Instructed by their father in the art of draughtsmanship and engraving, as well as in careful observation, Anna and Susanna produced a multitude of detailed visual references designed to convey as much information as possible. They were aided in their efforts by the use of a microscope, likely making them among the first women to use the instrument.[32]

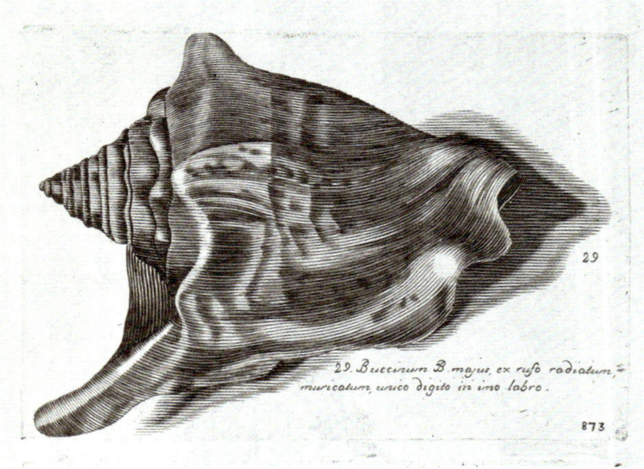

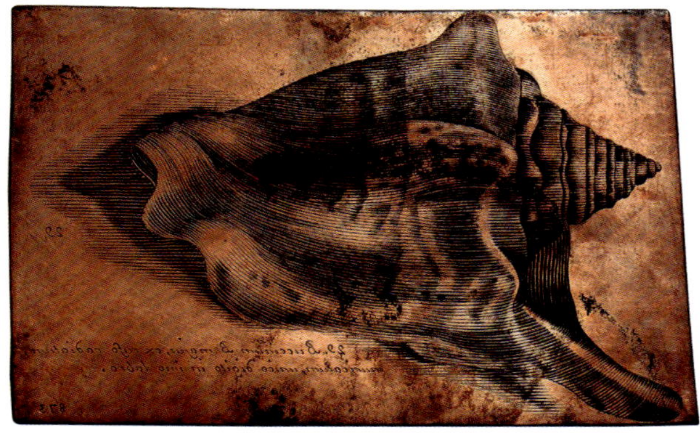

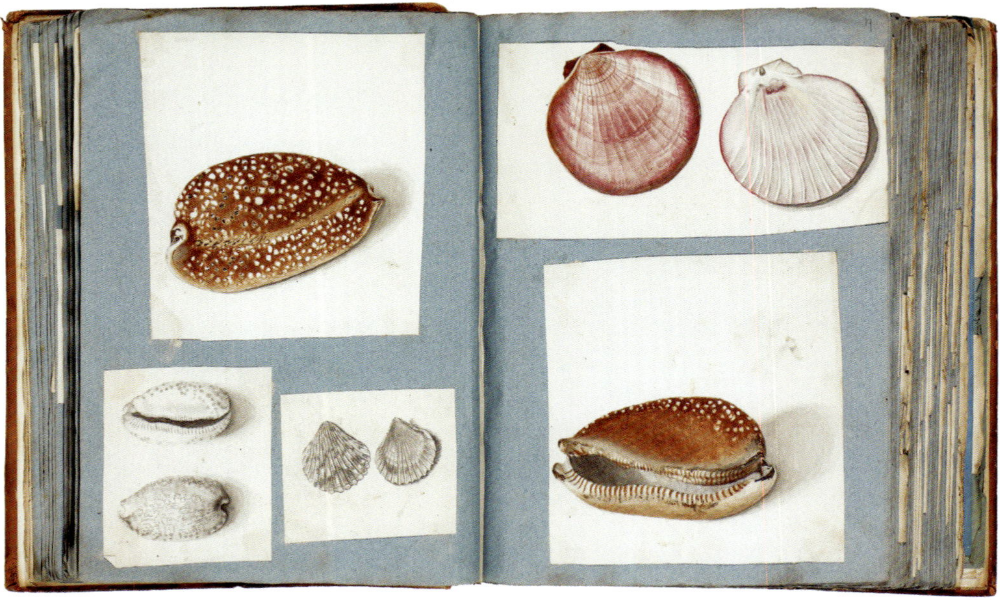

In addition to their function as records of observation and information, books like Lister's were used by collectors to aid in the identification of the shells in their cabinets. His tome, greatly enriched by the illustrations drawn and engraved by his daughters, found its way to Cosimo III de' Medici, Grand Duke of Tuscany, a collector of immense influence.[33] The need for such resources grew apace of the impulse to collect and catalogue the *naturalia* and *artificialia* of the known world as the eighteenth century progressed. Even in the seemingly sentimental and romanticized work of eighteenth-century French artists, the threads of scientific investigation, observation, and art were closely interwoven.

Anne Vallayer-Coster (1744–1818), who was admitted into the Académie Royale de Peinture et de Sculpture in 1770, was well regarded during her lifetime—above all, for her masterfully composed and executed still-life paintings. For her debut at the Salon of 1771, Vallayer-Coster exhibited two still-life pendants, one of which is now lost. The one that survives is a complex and artfully arranged composition of various shells and coral (fig. 17). The presence of shells in still-life painting can be seen in earlier works such as those by Clara Peeters and Giovanna Garzoni, usually lying at the base of the central element of a floral bouquet or other arrangement.[34] Like those earlier works, Vallayer-Coster's painting hung, for a time, in a collection—belonging to Louis-François-Joseph de Bourbon, Prince de Conti—that included a massive array of items, organized and displayed in dedicated rooms. While the prince did not commission the works (he purchased them about five years after Vallayer-Coster first exhibited them), their subject matter—shells and coral in the extant work, and minerals and crystals in the lost one—reflected perfectly the contents of his collection.[35] In fact, Conti did not hang Vallayer-Coster's paintings in his gallery dedicated to French paintings but, instead, in the room devoted to exhibiting his shell collection.[36] Such a pairing of the illusionistic rendering of shells with actual specimens,

Fig. 14 (above, left) • *Detail:* Anna Lister and Susanna Lister Knowler, in Martin Lister's *Historiae sive synopsis methodicae Conchyliorum: Quorum Omnium Picturae, ad vivum delineata, exhibetur Liber Primus, qui est de Cochleis Terrestribus, &c.*, book 4, 1688. Bound volume of engravings, page: 32 × 23 cm. The Bodleian Libraries, University of Oxford, Bodleian Library, BOD: Lister D 49, no. 873. Photo: © The Bodleian Libraries, University of Oxford.

Fig. 15 (below, left) • Anna Lister and Susanna Lister Knowler, *Copperplate, no. 332*, c. 1680–1690. Copper, 9.7 × 14.6 cm. The Bodleian Libraries, University of Oxford. Photo: © The Bodleian Libraries, University of Oxford.

Fig. 16 (above, right) • Anna Lister and Susanna Lister Knowler, album with drawings for Martin Lister's *Historiae Conchyliorum*, before 1692. Watercolours pasted into bound volume on paper, 28.5 × 24.5 × 7 cm. The Bodleian Libraries, University of Oxford, MS Lister 9, opening 18v-19r. Photo: © The Bodleian Libraries, University of Oxford.

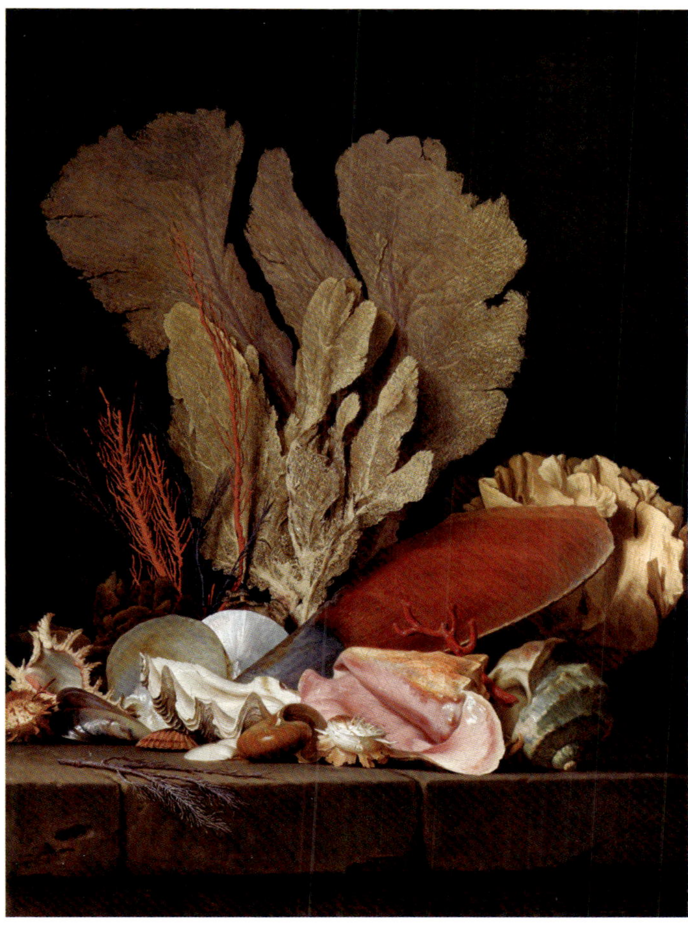

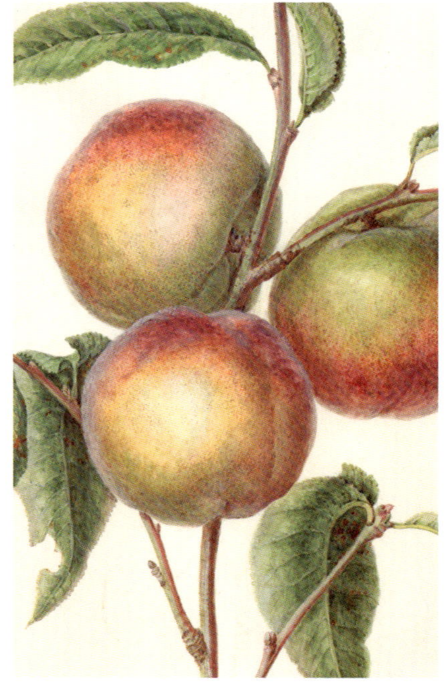

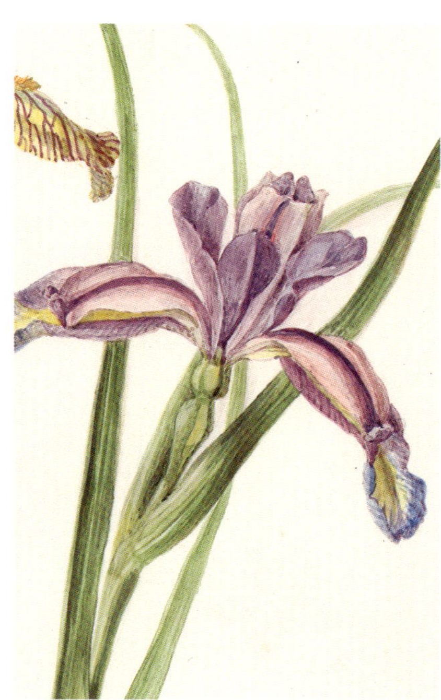

Fig. 17 (left) • Anne Vallayer-Coster, *Still Life with Seashells and Coral*, 1769. Oil on canvas, 160 × 130 cm. Musée du Louvre, Paris, Département des Peintures, RF 1992 410. Photo: © RMN-Grand Palais / René-Gabriel Ojéda / Art Resource, NY.

Fig. 18 (middle) • *Detail*: Madeleine Françoise Basseporte and her circle, *Peaches [Prunus persica]*, c. 1750. Watercolour over pencil on vellum, 40 × 31.1 cm. The Morgan Library & Museum, New York. Gift of Junius S. Morgan and Henry S. Morgan, inv. no. 1952.29:95. Photo: The Morgan Library & Museum, New York.

Fig. 19 (right) • *Detail*: Madeleine Françoise Basseporte and her circle, *Iris germanica (left). Iris xiphium (right).*, c. 1750. Watercolour over pencil on vellum, 40 × 31.1 cm. The Morgan Library & Museum, New York, Gift of Junius S. Morgan and Henry S. Morgan, inv. no. 1952.29:40. Photo: The Morgan Library & Museum, New York.

a common approach as discussed above, must surely have been a partial impetus for Vallayer-Coster to create these works. She was influenced by several French publications on conchology that themselves demonstrated the fluidity between the realms of "aesthetic and scientific discourses" that drove collectors to amass shell specimens.[37]

Vallayer-Coster likely obtained at least part of her artistic training with Madeleine Françoise Basseporte (1701–1780), through whom she may have gained access to shell collections in preparation for her painting and knowledge of contemporary publications on shells. Basseporte, who was appointed official *dessinatrice* at the Jardin du Roi (renamed "Jardin des plantes" during the Revolution) in 1742, interacted with many scientific and intellectual luminaries of the era.[38] Jean-Jacques Rousseau reportedly exclaimed that "nature gives plants their existence," but "Mademoiselle Basseporte gives them their preservation."[39] Carl Linnaeus was enamoured with Basseporte upon their meeting in 1737, and the two maintained a regular correspondence afterward. Although Basseporte was a botanical artist, a genre in which Vallayer-Coster also specialized, her wider associations with the scientific discourses of the time and her access to royal collections would have been important to her putative pupil (figs. 18 & 19; cat. nos. 174 & 175).[40]

Given Basseporte's especially close relationship with Linnaeus, it is not surprising to see his influence in the work of Vallayer-Coster. Pointing out the unmistakably fleshy, vulva-like appearance of the centrally placed conch in her painting, Kelsey Brosnan suggests that this is evidence of Vallayer-Coster's knowledge of Linnaeus's tenth edition of his *Systema Naturae* (1758), in which he labelled various parts of one bivalve shell with names taken from female anatomy. This allusion to the Linnaean description would have also satisfied collectors of shells (and images of them), who undoubtedly would have had copies of Linnaeus's cutting-edge classifications and new binomial nomenclature, along with other resources to help them identify their specimens.[41]

Body of Evidence

As with flora and fauna, art and the study of the human body go hand in hand. The ability to realistically articulate the human form was a quintessential skill artists developed during their professional training. The importance of the mastery of the human form—foundationally in drawing—was, quite simply, understood as the underpinning of artistic achievement. For women, this requirement was fraught because of their active exclusion from such training in some instances as well as wider social mores that made looking at a nude male model unacceptable. However, as mentioned, these factors, undoubtedly relevant in many cases, have become so oft-repeated in art historical scholarship that they threaten to obscure evidence to the contrary and impede our understanding of the circumstances women created for themselves to study and depict nudes. For women, access to female nudes was not as problematic; their own bodies were available to them, and getting other women to pose for them was another option—one that carried less stigma for both themselves and their models than was the case with male artists and female nudes.[42]

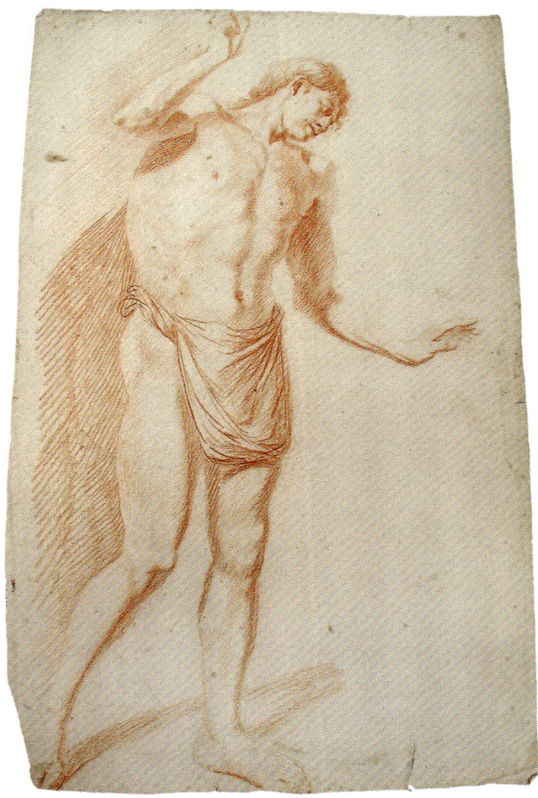

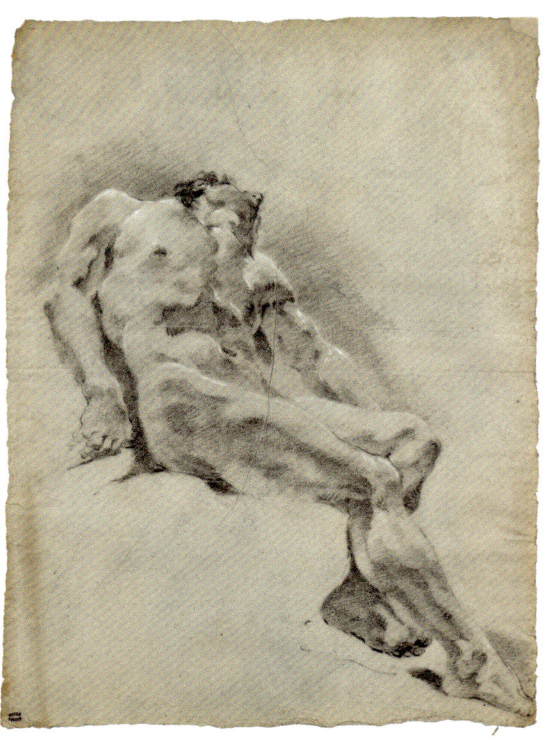

While the male nude presented more difficulties for women, there are examples of studies done by artists including Giulia Lama (1681–1747) and Catharina Backer (1689–1766), which demonstrate their participation in this codified aspect of artistic training. An album of sketches done by Backer in the early eighteenth century is preserved at the Amsterdam Museum and contains sheets with studies of male nudes (fig. 20). Backer, from a very wealthy and influential family (her father had a wide-ranging collection of *naturalia* and *artificialia*), was encouraged in her artistic pursuits by her father and most likely had access to professional training.[43] Whether or not this training included drawing the male nude from life is unclear at this point; however, Backer's numerous images of nudes suggests that, for women, "in the right cultural milieu, models in the form of works of art were quite available."[44] Lama, on the other hand, almost certainly studied the male nude from a living model and, because of this, is considered to be the first known woman artist to do so. Her drawings of nudes demonstrate her prowess in the handling of line, treatment of shadows,

Fig. 20 (above) • Catharina Backer, *Study of a standing man*, 1706–1722. Red chalk on paper, 37.5 × 24 cm. Amsterdam Museum, On loan from the Backer Foundation, inv. no. TB 6533.57. Photo: Amsterdam Museum.

Fig. 21 (below) • Giulia Lama, *Sketch of a man foreshortened*, first half of 18th century. Black chalk and white chalk on paper, 57 × 44 cm. Fondazione Musei Civici di Venezia, Gabinetto dei disegni e delle stampe, Ca' Rezzonico, Inv. Cl. III n. 6994.

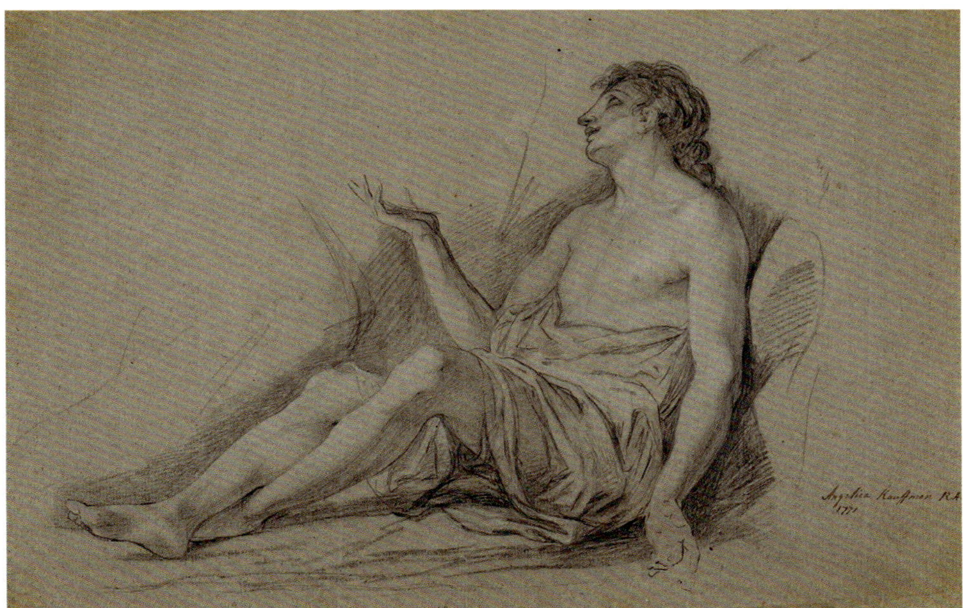

Fig. 22 (above) • Angelica Kauffmann, *An academic study of a young man seated on the ground*, 1771. Black chalk, heightened with white, on grey paper, 30.1 × 48.4 cm. British Museum, Bequeathed by: Richard Payne Knight, 1824, inv. no. Pp,5.151. Image: © The Trustees of the British Museum.

Fig. 23 (below) • Produced under the direction of Marie-Geneviève-Charlotte Darlus Thiroux d'Arconville, plate 4 in Alexander Monro's *Traité d'ostéologie, traduit de l'anglois de M. Monro, professeur d'anatomie...*, vol. 2, Paris, 1759. Bound volume of engravings, closed: 58 × 42.5 × 5 cm; open: 58 × 85 cm. The Institute of the History of Medicine, Johns Hopkins University, CAGE .M7522ay 1759 c. 1.

foreshortening, volumes, and dramatic movement in the figure (fig. 21; cat. nos. 40, 45–49).[45]

The exact circumstances of where and how Backer and Lama made their studies are not fully known, but most likely they executed their drawings in the relative privacy of their own home and/or studios, and not in the company of other (male) artists. This was the case with Angelica Kauffmann (1741–1807), who, despite being a founding member of the Royal Academy of Arts in London in 1768, had to hire her own male model, as women were not permitted to draw from live models at the Academy (fig. 22). The model would come to her home, where her father was always present for the sake of propriety.[46] In France, however, co-ed life drawing classes existed in private studios as early as 1775, well before it was officially tolerated in the rest of Europe and in North America, in the late nineteenth century.[47] Thus, despite societal hand-wringing and admonishments that such exposure would corrupt their virtue, women artists persisted in the face of strong social pressure and did what they felt was necessary to hone their artistic skill in accord with the practicum of the day.

The study and mastery of articulating the human form in art requires close observation and a surface-level understanding of anatomy. A true understanding of the mechanics of the human body was necessary to depict realistic forms and movement. To this end, many artists were de facto anatomists, sometimes going to extreme lengths; Giorgio Vasari describes one Renaissance artist, Bartolomeo Torri, keeping "members and pieces of men" in his house to study from.[48] Like botany and entomology, the growing field of anatomy relied on skilled artists to render accurate images (fig. 23; cat. no. 177). By the early eighteenth century, the Italian city of Bologna was a well-established hotbed of artistic and scientific developments fostered by Enlightenment ideals and the patronage of its native son, Pope Benedict XIV. The practice of using human cadavers to teach anatomy was a particular specialty in Bologna from at least the fourteenth century.[49] In this university city where women, particularly artists, often found success in the public sphere, the participation of women in the study of anatomy was not only accepted but even encouraged.[50] The famed physicist and academician at the University of Bologna, Laura Bassi (1711–1778), for example, regularly attended public anatomy lessons and was well versed in the field.[51]

The use of wax models to aid in the teaching of anatomy became increasingly common throughout the eighteenth century, the substance being prized for

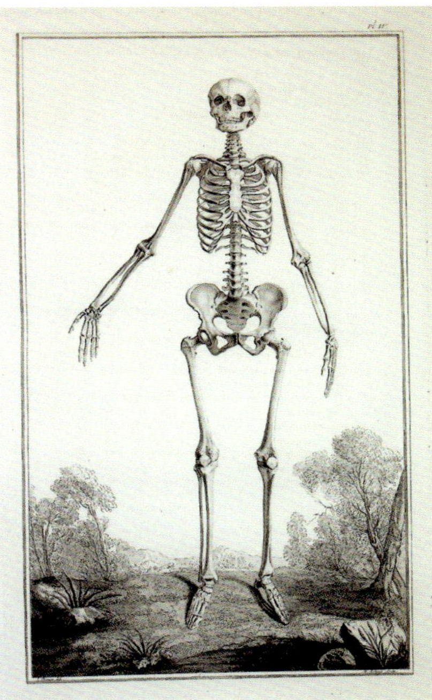

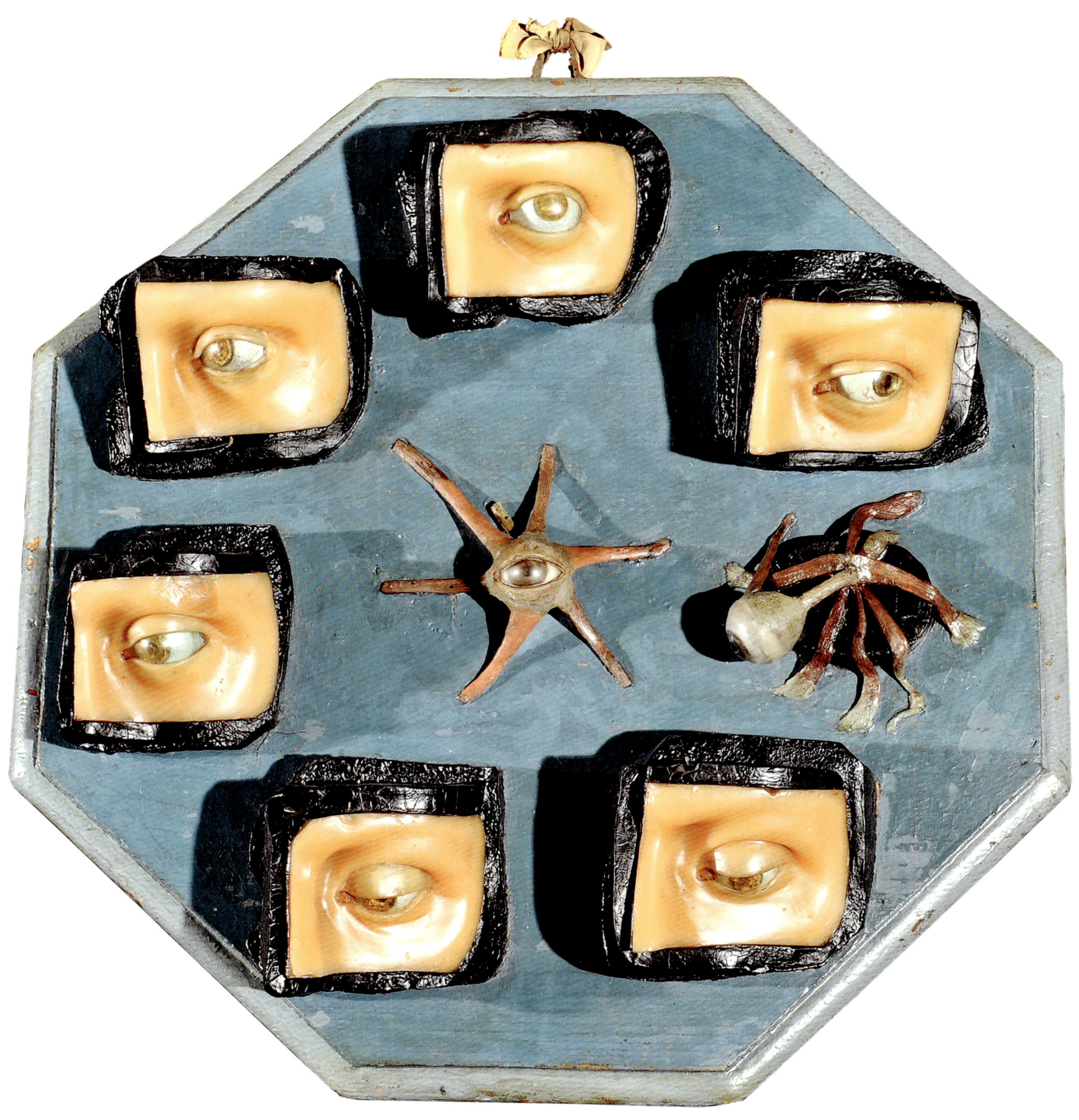

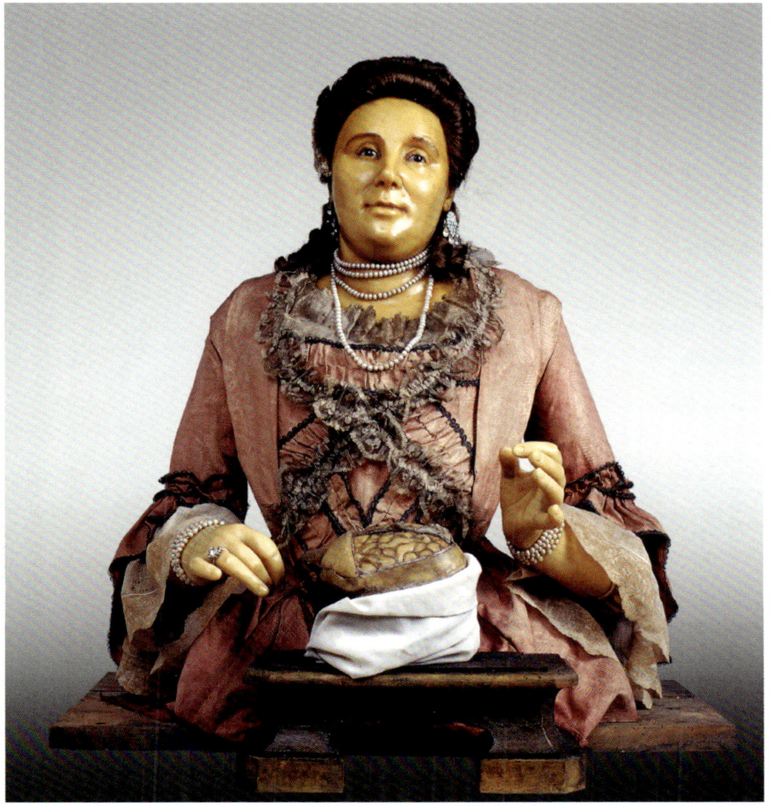

Fig. 24 (facing) · Anna Morandi Manzolini, *Eye Muscles*, 1755. Polychrome anatomical model in wax and wood, 35 × 35 × 7 cm. Courtesy of Alma Mater Studiorum Università di Bologna | Sistema Museale di Ateneo | Museo di Palazzo Poggi. Photo: Fulvio Simoni.

Fig. 25 (above) · Anna Morandi Manzolini, *Self-Portrait Dissecting a Brain*, 1750–1760. Polychrome anatomical model in wax, silk, hair, pearls, and wood, 90 × 82 × 68 cm. Courtesy of Alma Mater Studiorum Università di Bologna | Sistema Museale di Ateneo | Museo di Palazzo Poggi. Photo: Fulvio Simoni.

its malleability and surface resemblance to human tissue. One of the most successful modellers was Anna Morandi Manzolini (1714–1774), who made wax models depicting various human limbs, cavities, and organs that were startlingly lifelike. Morandi worked first alongside her husband, Giovanni Manzolini, and, after his death, by herself out of her home in Bologna. In Morandi's day, the use of wax models to augment the presentations and lectures on anatomy was a growing business, one that Morandi herself came to dominate. Needless to say, an intricate knowledge of the human body was a prerequisite for being able to replicate it in wax form. Morandi gained her knowledge of the human body from first-hand experience dissecting cadavers, as well as from published illustrations that accompanied the anatomical treatises of the day. For her many models of the structure of the eye, Morandi dissected no less than thirty heads and used a microscope to observe minute muscles and ducts (fig. 24).[52] Morandi was familiar with contemporary publications on anatomy, which she cited and sometimes even corrected in her own writings. This was especially true for her studies on the male reproductive system.[53] Morandi's work in wax put her at the forefront of anatomical knowledge of the day, through both her direct observations and her engagement with the work of others in the field (fig. 25). Indeed, Morandi was praised just a few years after her death by a contemporary who noted that her models were "functional to the *creation* and *acquisition* of anatomical knowledge."[54]

Whether detailed paintings of flowers, fruit, or shells—like those by Peeters and Vallayer-Coster that reflected the varied collections in which they hung—or watercolour studies of specimens by Withoos and Merian, reproduced in print form to reach a wide audience, works by women reflected and expanded knowledge in the budding fields of botany and entomology. Women were also engaged with the study of the human body on a scale much larger than is usually recognized. Lama, Backer, and Kauffmann, among other artists, all executed drawings of men's bodies to hone their artistic skills, while Morandi used her talent to greatly advance the field of human anatomy.

The consistent presence of women throughout Europe who were working at the intersection of art and science in the early modern period is well documented in contemporary sources and evidenced by the works they produced. Apart from monographic studies, however, there has been a lacuna in modern scholarship relating to their persistent and innovative contributions to both fields. While commendable and valuable in their own right, these monographic approaches serve to isolate their subjects from the wider narrative and too often rely on the paradigm of exceptionalism.[55] Recognizing the contributions of women, collectively, to their respective areas of expertise allows us to gain a fuller understanding of their place within the histories of art and science, and reveals the influence their work had on their contemporaries and on those who came after them—both male and female.

Notes

1 Pamela H. Smith, "Art, Science, and Visual Culture in Early Modern Europe," *Isis* 97, no. 1 (2006): 91n14.
2 Smith, "Art, Science, and Visual Culture," 95.
3 See especially the work of Pamela H. Smith, *The Body of the Artisan: Art and Experience in the Scientific Revolution* (Chicago: University of Chicago Press, 2004); Smith, "Art, Science, and Visual Culture," in *The Eye of the Lynx: Galileo, His Friends, and the Beginnings of Modern Natural History*, ed. David Freedberg (Chicago: University of Chicago Press, 2002); and Sachiko Kusukawa, *Picturing the Book of Nature: Image, Text, and Argument in Sixteenth-Century Human Anatomy and Medical Botany* (Chicago: University of Chicago Press, 2012).
4 Happily, more scholars are beginning to engage with the topic; see especially Lucia Tongiorgi Tomasi, "'La Femminil Pazienza': Women Painters and Natural History in the Seventeenth and Early Eighteenth Centuries," *Studies in the History of Art* 69 (2008): 158–85.
5 For more on this topic, see Babette Bohn's essay "Designing Women: Drawings by Women Artists in Early Modern Italy" on pages 42–57 of this volume.
6 For a discussion on the "feminization" of still-life painting, see Norman Bryson, *Looking at the Overlooked: Four Essays on Still-Life Painting* (Cambridge, MA: Harvard University Press, 1990), and Charlotte Christensen, "A Look at the Overlooked," *Konsthistorisk Tidskrift* 65, no. 2 (1996): 135–42. For a discussion on the gendering of nature as female, see Mary D. Garrard, *Brunelleschi's Egg: Nature, Art, and Gender in Renaissance Italy* (Berkeley: University of California Press, 2010), 9–30.
7 Throughout this essay, I use the terms "science," "scientist," and "scientific" very broadly and in the most general sense of the term: the study of nature through observation.
8 During this time, many people—artists and scientists included—saw the study of nature as a spiritual exercise, an ever-deepening appreciation of God's creations and wonders. See Eric Jorink, *Reading the Book of Nature in the Dutch Golden Age, 1575–1715* (Leiden: Brill, 2010).
9 Arthur K. Wheelock, *Clouds, Ice, and Bounty: The Lee and Juliet Folger Fund Collection of Seventeenth-Century Dutch and Flemish Paintings* (Washington, DC: National Gallery of Art, 2020), 142–43.
10 Alejandro Vergara has linked the botanical illustrations of Adriaen Collaert published in Antwerp in 1587 to blooms in one of Peeters's still-life elements in a painting at the Prado. Alejandro Vergara, ed., *The Art of Clara Peeters*, trans. Diane Webb (Antwerp and Madrid: Koninklijk Museum voor Schone Kunsten and Museo Nacional del Prado, 2016), 69.
11 For more about the influence of Antwerp-based artists and illustrators on Peeters, see Vergara, *The Art of Clara Peeters*, 29–30.
12 Wheelock, *Clouds, Ice, and Bounty*, 142–43.
13 Walter Liedtke, "Still-Life Painting in Northern Europe, 1600–1800," in *Heilbrunn Timeline of Art History*, Metropolitan Museum of Art, October 2003, metmuseum.org/toah/hd/nstl/hd_nstl.htm.
14 Sheila Barker, "Garzoni's Artworks in a Medici *Wunderkammer*: Vittoria della Rovere's Stanza dell'Aurora," in *"The Immensity of the Universe" in the Art of Giovanna Garzoni*, exh. cat., ed. Sheila Barker (Florence: Gallerie degli Uffizi, 2020), 197.
15 Sheila Barker, "The Universe of Giovanna Garzoni: Art, Mobility, and the Global Turn in the Geographical Imaginary," in Barker, *"The Immensity of the Universe,"* 19. Although most of the artists commissioned to make these drawings are unknown, two women, Elisabetta (or Isabella) Catanea Parasole (c. 1570–c. 1620) and Maddelena Corvino (1607–1664), have been linked with some of the illustrations. See Barker, "The Universe of Giovanna Garzoni," 18n34, and Tomasi, "'La Femminil Pazienza,'" 163–64.
16 Sheila Barker and Anatole Tchikine, "Art in the Service of Botany: Giovanna Garzoni's *Piante varie* at Dumbarton Oaks," in Barker, *"The Immensity of the Universe,"* 42.
17 On Block, see also Catherine Powell-Warren, "Locating Early Modern Women's Participation in the Public Sphere of Botany: Agnes Block (1629–1704) and Networks in Print," *Early Modern Low Countries* 4, no. 2 (2020): 234–58, and Joy Kearney, "Agnes Block, a Collector of Plants and Curiosities in the Dutch Golden Age, and Her Friendship with Maria Sibylla Merian, Natural History Illustrator," in *Women Patrons and Collectors*, ed. Susan Bracken, Andrea M. Gáldy, and Adriana Turpin (Newcastle upon Tyne: Cambridge Scholars, 2012), 67–82.
18 Marloes Huiskamp, "Block, Agneta (1629–1704)," Huygens Institute, *Online Dictionary of Dutch Women*, resources.huygens.knaw.nl/vrouwenlexicon/lemmata/data/Block, September 11, 2017, accessed September 24, 2022.
19 Catherine Powell, "Alida Withoos: Creator of Beauty and of Visual Knowledge," *Art Herstory*, artherstory.net/alida-withoos-creator-of-beauty-and-of-visual-knowledge/, December 5, 2020, accessed September 27, 2022.
20 Sam Segal, "Merian as a Flower Painter," in *Maria Sibylla Merian: Artist and Naturalist, 1647–1717*, ed. Kurt Wettengl (Ostfildern, Germany: Verlag Gerd Hatje, 1998), 80.
21 William T. Stearn, "Carl Linnaeus's Acquaintance with Tropical Plants," *Taxon* 37, no. 3 (1988): 778–79. For specific examples, see D.O. Wijnands, *The Botany of the Commelins: A Taxonomical, Nomenclatural, and Historical Account of the Plants Depicted in the Moninckx Atlas and in the Four Books by Jan and Caspar Commelin on the Plants in the Hortus Medicus Amstelodamensis, 1682–1710* (Rotterdam: A.A. Balkema), 1983.
22 The scholarship on Merian is vast and growing. Works of note include William T. Stearn, Vitor Osmar Becker, and Elisabeth Rücker, *Metamorphosis Insectorum Surinamensium* (London: Pion, 1980); Natalie Zemon Davis, "Metamorphoses," in *Women on the Margins: Three Seventeenth-Century Lives* (Cambridge, MA: Harvard University Press, 1997), 140–202; Katharina Schmidt-Loske, "Maria Sibylla Merian: A Woman's Pioneering Work in Entomology," in *Women and the Art and Science of Collecting in Eighteenth-Century Europe*, ed. Arlene Leis and Kacie L. Wills (New York: Routledge, 2020), 61–77; and Bert van de Roemer, Florence Pieters, Hans Mulder, Kay Etheridge, and Marieke van Delft, eds., *Maria Sibylla Merian: Changing the Nature of Art and Science* (Tielt, Belgium: Lannoo, 2022).
23 Schmidt-Loske, "Maria Sibylla Merian," 72.
24 For more on the scientific community in Nuremburg, see Andaleeb Banta's, "Barbara Regina Dietzsch: Enlightened Flower Painter," *Art Herstory*, September 22, 2021, artherstory.net/barbara-regina-dietzsch-enlightened-flower-painter/, accessed August 29, 2022.
25 For more on the Dietzsch sisters, see Charlotte Brooks, "Botanical Art in the Age of Enlightenment: Barbara Regina Dietzsch and Her Circle," *Occasional Papers from the RHS Lindley Library* 16 (2018): 7–17.
26 Kay Etheridge, *The Flowering of Ecology: Maria Sibylla Merian's Caterpillar Book* (Leiden: Brill, 2020).
27 Marianne Berardi, *Science into Art: Rachel Ruysch's Early Development as a Still-Life Painter* (Pittsburgh: University of Pittsburgh, 1998), 95.
28 Berardi, *Science into Art*, 363
29 Berardi, *Science into Art*, 381. Berardi likens the position of a toad in another of Ruysch's paintings dated to 1690, currently in a private collection, to how an actual specimen might have appeared floating in a jar of preservative. See fig. 49.
30 Merian, *Metamorphosis*, plate 59; translation taken from Julie Harvey, *Maria Sibylla Merian: The Surinam Album* (London: Folio Society, 2006). It is important to note that in this instance, as in others noted throughout *Metamorphosis*, Merian used the labour of enslaved Africans and Indigenous peoples in America to gather specimens. For more on this, see Davis, *Women on the Margins*, 140–202.
31 For the popularity and implication of shell collecting, see Marisa Anne Bass, Anne Goldgar, Hanneke Grootenboer, and Claudia Swan, *Conchophilia: Shells, Art, and Curiosity in Early Modern Europe* (Princeton, NJ: Princeton University Press, 2021).
32 Anna Marie Roos, *Martin Lister and His Remarkable Daughters: The Art of Science in the Seventeenth Century* (Oxford: Bodleian Library, University of Oxford, 2019); Anna Marie Roos, "The Art of Science: A 'Rediscovery' of the Lister Copperplates," *Notes & Records of the Royal Society* 66, no. 1 (2012): 19.
33 Roos, "The Art of Science," 34.
34 For shells in Peeters's work, see Vergara, *The Art of Clara Peeters*, 40. For shells in Garzoni's oeuvre, see Sheila Barker, "Rare, Curious, and Exotic: A Geographical Imaginary on a Global Scale," in Barker, *"The Immensity of the Universe,"* 156.
35 Eik Kahng, Marianne Roland Michel, and Colin B. Bailey, *Anne Vallayer-Coster, Painter to the Court of Marie-Antoinette* (Dallas: Dallas Museum of Art; New Haven, CT: Yale University Press, 2002), 64.
36 Kelsey Brosnan, "Anne Vallayer-Coster's *Still-Life with Sea Shells and Coral*," in Leis and Wills, *Women and the Art and Science of Collecting*, 45.
37 Brosnan, "Anne Vallayer-Coster's *Still-Life*," 45.

38 For more on Basseporte, see Nina Rattner Gelbart, *Minerva's French Sisters: Women of Science in Enlightenment France* (New Haven, CT: Yale University Press, 2021).
39 Laura Auricchio and Jordana Pomeroy, eds., *Royalists to Romantics: Women Artists from the Louvre, Versailles and Other French National Collections* (Washington, DC: National Museum of Women in the Arts, 2012), 55.
40 Although there is no direct evidence of Vallayer-Coster having studied with Basseporte, the botanical watercolours of the former share stylistic similarities with the latter; see Kahng, Roland Michel, and Bailey, *Anne Vallayer-Coster*, 14. Basseporte was also godmother to Vallayer-Coster's younger sister; see Brosnan, "Anne Vallayer-Coster's *Still-Life*," 45.
41 Brosnan, "Anne Vallayer-Coster's *Still-Life*," 49. Brosnan points out that Linnaeus used these terms despite the corresponding parts of the shell having nothing to do with biological function.
42 Sheila Barker, *Artemisia Gentileschi* (London: Lund Humphries; Los Angeles, Getty, 2022), 37.
43 Elizabeth Alice Honig, "The Art of Being 'Artistic': Dutch Women's Creative Practices in the 17th Century," *Woman's Art Journal* 22, no. 2 (2001): 35.
44 Honig, "The Art of Being 'Artistic,'" 35.
45 Liana De Girolami Cheney, "Giulia Lama: A Luminous Painter and a Tenebrist Poet," *Artibus et Historiae* 38, no. 75 (2017): 230n38.
46 "Drawing," Collection Online, museum no. Pp,5.151, British Museum, britishmuseum.org/collection/object/P_Pp-5-151, accessed May 26, 2023.
47 Margaret A. Oppenheimer, "'The Charming Spectacle of a Cadaver': Anatomical and Life Study by Women Artists in Paris, 1775–1815," *Nineteenth-Century Art Worldwide* 6, no. 1 (Spring 2007).
48 Lucia Dacome, *Malleable Anatomies: Models, Makers, and Material Culture in Eighteenth-Century Italy* (Oxford: Oxford University Press, 2017), 112.
49 Giovanna Ferrari, "Public Anatomy Lessons and the Carnival: The Anatomy Theatre of Bologna," *Past & Present*, no. 117 (1987): 53.
50 For the preponderance of women artists in Bologna, see Babette Bohn, *Women Artists, Their Patrons, and Their Publics in Early Modern Bologna* (University Park, PA: Penn State University Press, 2021).
51 Dacome, *Malleable Anatomies*, 104–05.
52 Dacome, *Malleable Anatomies*, 545–46; Rebecca Marie Messbarger, *The Lady Anatomist: The Life and Work of Anna Morandi Manzolini* (Chicago: University of Chicago Press, 2010), 58.
53 Messbarger, *The Lady Anatomist*, 146–47.
54 Dacome, *Malleable Anatomies*, 111. Emphasis mine.
55 For a more in-depth discussion on this topic, see Andaleeb Banta's essay "Not Seen, Not Heard: In Search of the Unexceptional Woman Artist" on pages 14–29 of this volume.

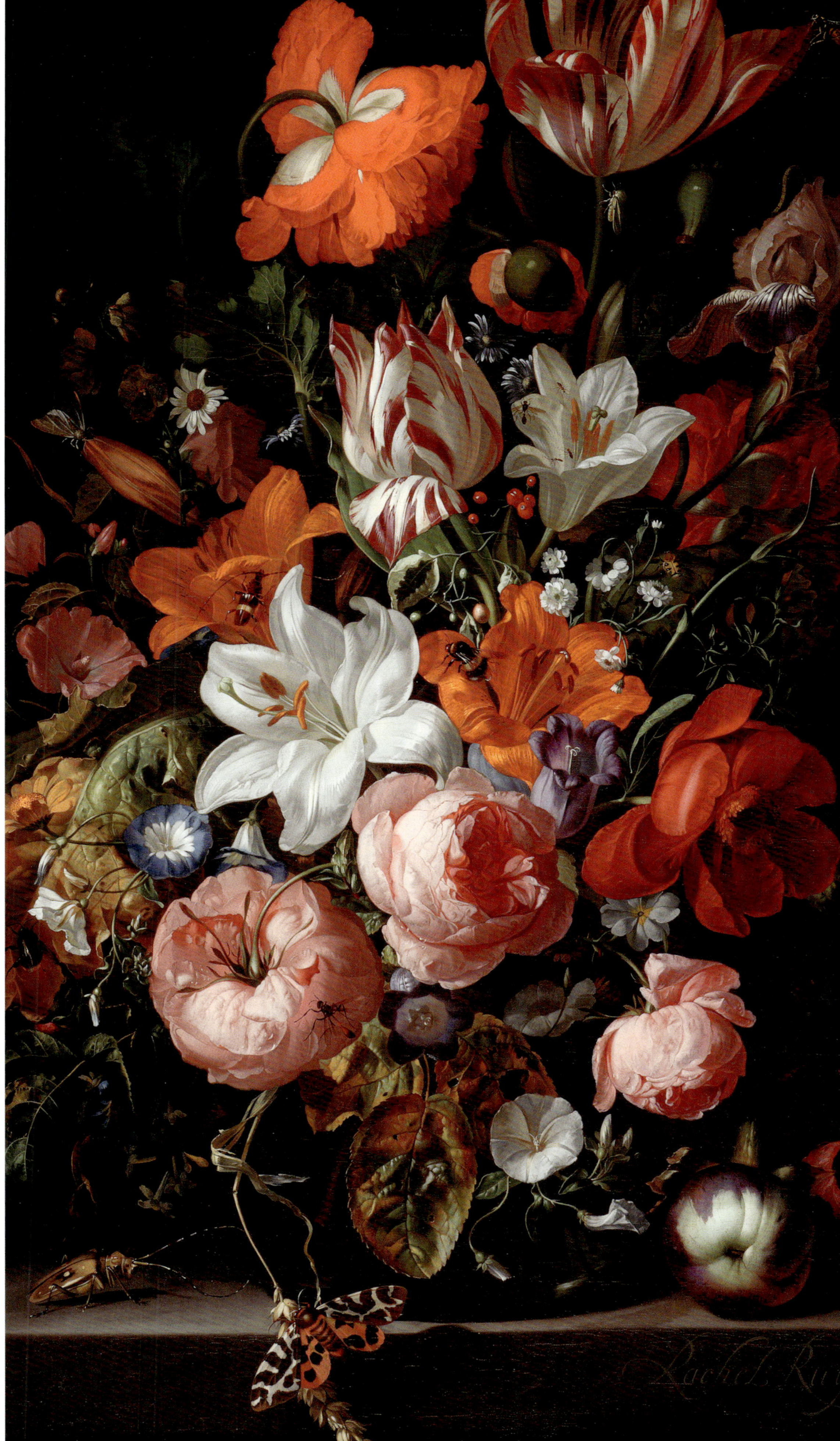

Detail (fig. 11) • Rachel Ruysch, *Flowers in a Glass Vase*, 1704. Oil on canvas, 83.8 × 67 cm. Detroit Institute of Arts, Founders Society Purchase, Robert H. Tannahill Foundation Fund, Joseph M. de Grimme Memorial Fund, et al., inv. no. 1995.67.

ART AND POLITICS

Women Artists and the Rulers of the Revolutionary World

Paris A. Spies-Gans

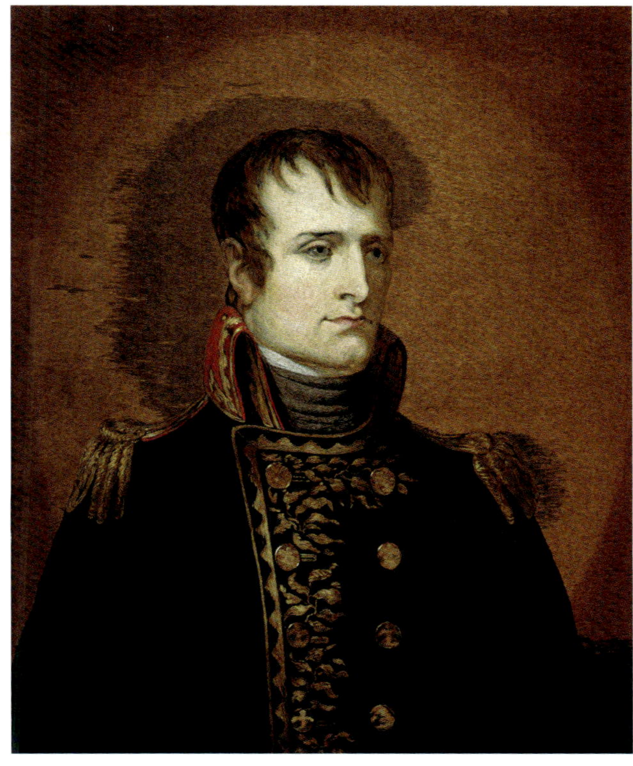

Fig. 1 (and detail on left) • Mary Linwood, *Needlework Portrait of Napoleon Bonaparte*, 1825. Woollen canvas, embroidered in wool, 78.3 × 71.2 cm. Victoria and Albert Museum, London, Bequeathed by Ellen Markland, inv. no. 1438-1874. Image © Victoria and Albert Museum, London.

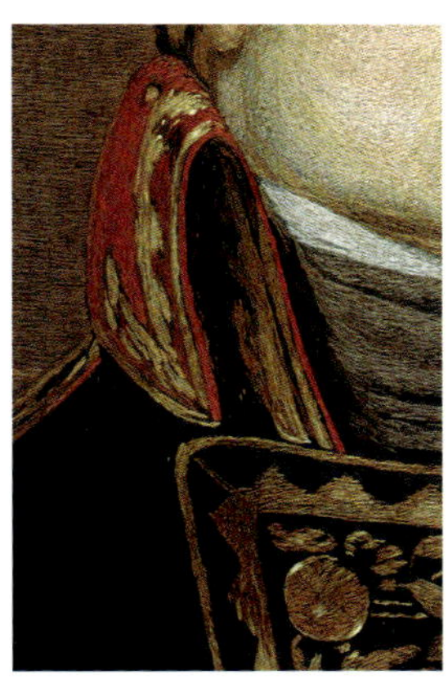

Paris, early 1803. During the first cessation in hostilities between their countries in nearly a decade, the soon-to-be French emperor Napoleon Bonaparte hosted a dinner to which he invited the British artist Mary Linwood (1755–1845). Impressed with Linwood's talent, Napoleon bestowed upon her an honour never before given to a woman: the "Freedom of Paris," and the rare permission to travel, unrestricted, throughout France. What inspired the notoriously dogmatic ruler to allow such an exception for a female artist from Leicester? Linwood specialized in needle paintings—full-scale, intricately sewn wool and silk images made to resemble famous works of art, which she framed and displayed in her own, autonomous exhibitions. Like many before him, Napoleon was captivated; Linwood's oeuvre was unlike any he had ever seen, and he quickly initiated plans for a public display of her art in Paris. Unfortunately, because of the resumption of warfare in May 1803, Linwood's French show never materialized.

Linwood's remarkable Parisian reception pervades descriptions of her work. Her expertly embroidered portrait of Napoleon (fig. 1) is cited as proof of the unusually high esteem this artist inspired in the militaristic First Consul. The image is unique in Linwood's oeuvre, evoking a rare intimacy through her exceedingly detailed portrayal of a famously unapproachable man. Contemporaries extolled its lifelikeness, and she later made a second copy, presumably because of its popularity—the only known work twice painted by her needle.[1]

If only the story were true.

The anecdote appears to be a complete fabrication, seemingly developed most fully upon Linwood's death. Linwood indeed travelled to Paris in 1803 during the brief ceasefire amid two decades of war between Britain and France achieved by the Treaty of Amiens (March 1802–May 1803), as did many other Britons eager to view the city's transformations and Napoleon's growing collection of art.[2] However, by no surviving accounts or records did the First Consul grant Linwood an audience. When, in 1816, Linwood placed her portrait of the former emperor in her London gallery, nowhere did she note that it was taken from life. She made her second copy in 1825, but Napoleon's admiration for her talent did not appear in print until 1832.[3] The full story was first recounted in Linwood's lengthy *Gentleman's Magazine* obituary in 1845,[4] and has anchored nearly every published account of Linwood since.

Among this tale's many noteworthy features, what is perhaps most striking is *not* the fact that the meeting did not take place but rather that it was entirely believable that it did. By the time of Linwood's death, a female needle painter from Leicester had attained such status that she was believed to have had the clout to earn a meeting with Napoleon, the potential to charm him, and the talent to become the sole woman granted the "Freedom of Paris"—also, apparently, a fictitious award. It seemed plausible that this indubitably anti-British ruler, the architect of the Napoleonic Code, with its notorious restrictions on women's public activities, aspired to exhibit Linwood's embroideries in the city where he was assembling the greatest known European works—many of them recently looted—for his own museum, in the Louvre.

Napoleon's supposed patronage of Linwood was so readily devised and accepted because it fit into a phenomenon that had recently transcended cultural spheres across Britain and France, one in which European women artists publicly and remuneratively cultivated the patronage of key political figures of the Revolutionary era. Beginning in the mid-eighteenth century, these women used their artistic practices to establish public reputations as professional artists, earning steady incomes and often significant sums while entering broader civic conversations on women's roles and abilities at pivotal moments of political change. This essay offers a series of windows into their worlds.

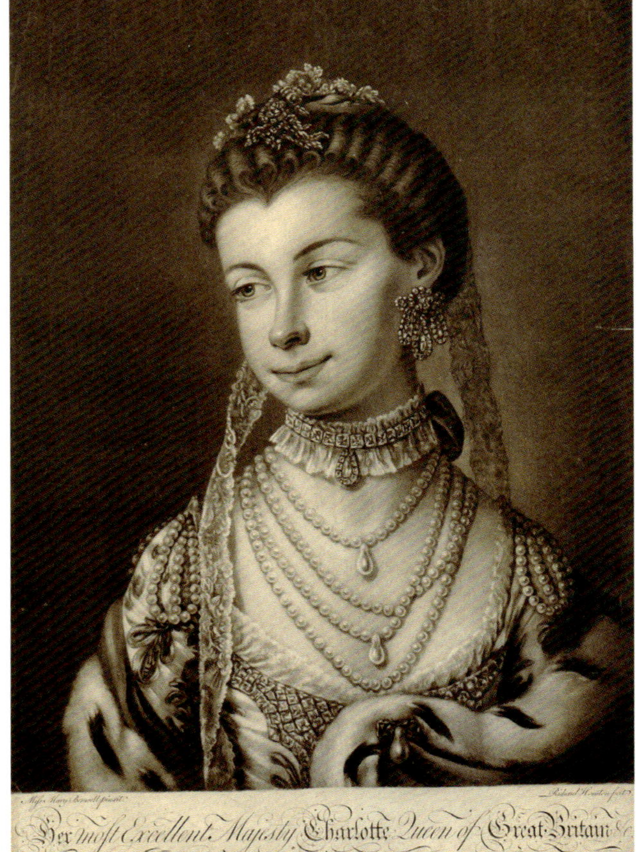

Fig. 2 • Richard Houston, after Mary Benwell, *Her most Excellent Majesty Charlotte Queen of Great Britain*, c. 1766–1775. Mezzotint on paper, 50.3 × 35 cm. British Museum, Purchased from: Hon Christopher Lennox-Boyd, and acquired with the assistance of the National Heritage Memorial Fund, the Friends of the British Museum, the Art Fund, Mrs Charles Wrightsman, the Michael Marks Charitable Trust, and numerous individual donors, 2010, inv. no. 2010,7081.2385. Image: © The Trustees of the British Museum.

Fig. 3 (facing, top) • Self-Portraits installed in the Vasari Corridor at the Uffizi Galleries, Florence. Photo: © Alinari Archives / George Tatge, 1999 / Art Resource, NY.

Facing (below, left to right)

Fig. 4 • Maria Louisa Catherine Cecilia Cosway, *Self-Portrait*, 1778. Oil on canvas, 71 × 57 cm. The Uffizi Galleries, Florence, inv. 1890, no. 5258. Photo: Gabinetto Fotografico delle Gallerie degli Uffizi.

Fig. 5 • Anne Seymour Damer, *Self-Portrait*, 1778. Marble, 59 × 28 cm. The Uffizi Galleries, Florence, inv. 1914, no. 562. Photo: Gabinetto Fotografico delle Gallerie degli Uffizi.

Fig. 6 • Elisabeth Louise Vigée-LeBrun, *Self-Portrait*, 1790. Oil on canvas, 100 × 81 cm. The Uffizi Galleries, Florence, Gift of the artist, 1791, inv. 1890, no. 1905. Photo: Gabinetto Fotografico delle Gallerie degli Uffizi.

Fig. 7 • Angelica Kauffmann, *Self-Portrait*, 1787. Oil on canvas, 128 × 93.5 cm. The Uffizi Galleries, Florence, inv. 1890, no. 1928. Photo: Gabinetto Fotografico delle Gallerie degli Uffizi.

Royals

Our story begins with the induction of two queens: Charlotte of Mecklenburg-Strelitz (r. 1761–1818), Queen of Great Britain from her marriage to King George III in 1760, and Marie Antoinette of Austria (r. 1774–1792), who arrived in France to marry the future Louis XVI in 1770. Ultimately, the ties that women artists established with these royal women provided a foundation for the working relationships they would pursue with a series of political celebrities as the era progressed.

Fortuitously for artists of both sexes, Charlotte's arrival in Britain converged with the development of the nation's public exhibitions. In April 1760, a group of artists hosted London's first commercial art show, using the premises at William Shipley's Society for the Encouragement of Arts, Manufactures and Commerce. It was an unimagined success. Encouraged and excited, competing factions of artists quickly established a series of rival exhibiting societies, each intended to help display and sell their works. This discord culminated with the establishment in 1768 of Britain's Royal Academy of Arts, which explicitly aimed to promote a native British school of art distinct from—and able to match—its more readily celebrated continental rivals. From the outset, women exhibited their art in every single public show on the same terms as men, as both full and honorary exhibitors. Throughout these years in both Britain and France, honorary exhibitors were "amateurs" who created art as a pastime; full exhibitors were "professionals" who made art with commercial aspirations. Full exhibitors declared this professional intent by listing their addresses in exhibition catalogues. In doing so, they invited interested buyers to visit their studios, where they could view, purchase, or commission additional pieces.[5]

Charlotte engaged with this burgeoning cultural sector from the start, becoming a swift and steady sponsor of numerous women artists—painters, engravers, wax modellers, and needle painters—who sought out her public support, a practice in which her husband joined and which her children continued.[6] At first, many of these alliances were initiated by artists themselves. By late 1761, the already distinguished portraitist Katharine Read (1723–1778)—one of two

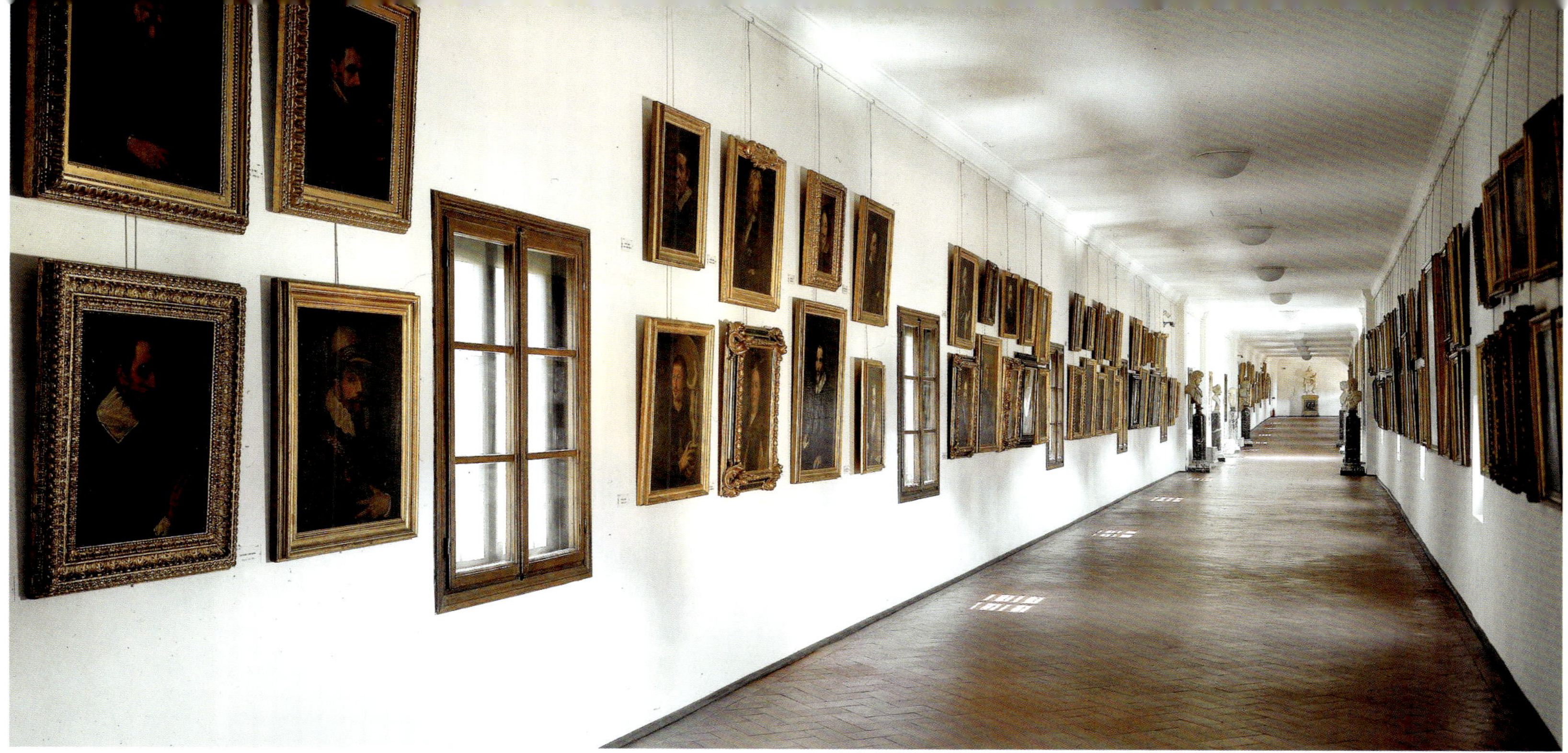

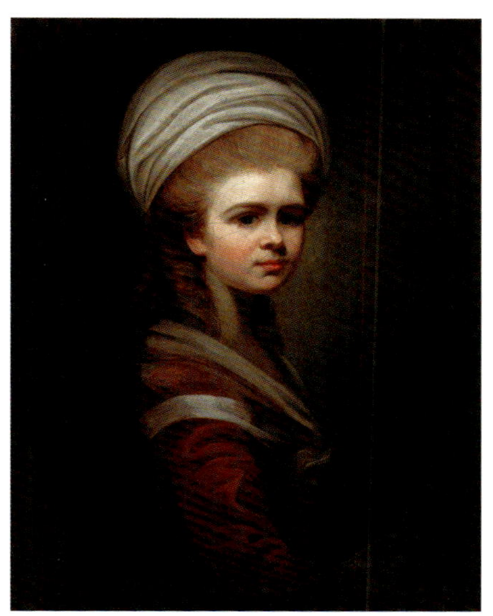

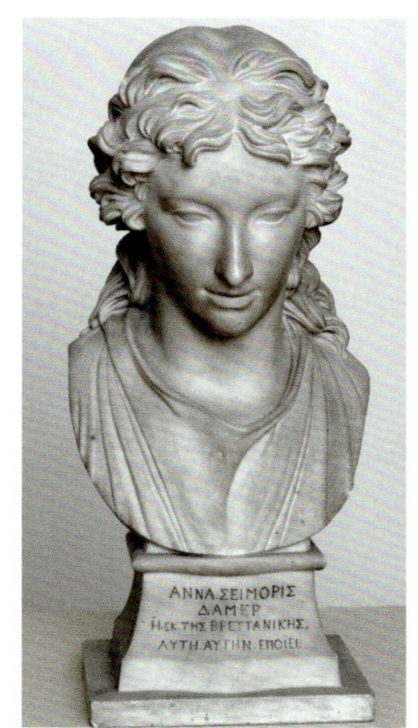

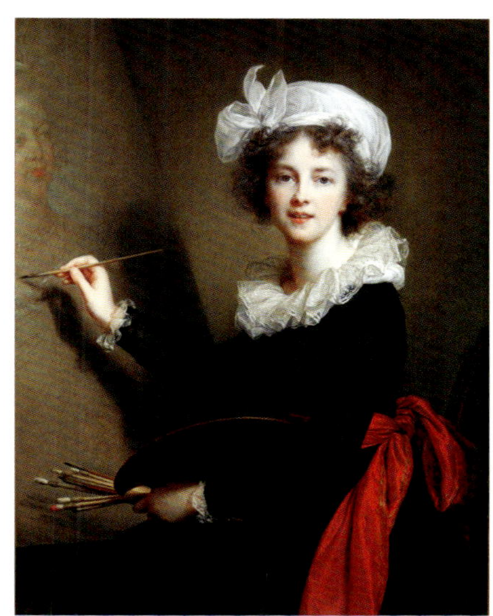

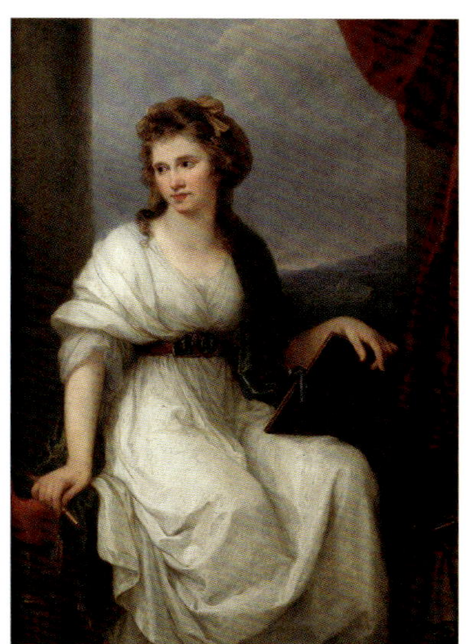

women to have exhibited in London's inaugural 1760 show—had created an unsolicited portrait of Charlotte; so had the pastellist Mary Benwell (1739–1811), who would first exhibit in 1762 (fig. 2).[7] Charlotte purchased both works, and then granted each artist's request for her to sit in person for additional portraits, several of which were then exhibited and reproduced in print—to the clear benefit of each woman.[8] Read's reputation as a society portraitist continued to flourish, while Benwell paved a newly public course for her work. In 1779, the latter presented a self-portrait to the Uffizi's famous Vasari Corridor (fig. 3), where it would soon flank the self-portraits of Angelica Kauffmann (1741–1807; fig. 7), Anne Seymour Damer (1748–1828; fig. 5), Elisabeth Louise Vigée-LeBrun (1755–1842; fig. 6), and Maria Louisa Catherine Cecilia Cosway (1759–1838; fig. 4).

In London, as female artists' exhibition presence rapidly grew (several hundred women would exhibit their art in the British capital through the early nineteenth century), their activity came to centre on the increasingly prestigious Royal Academy (just

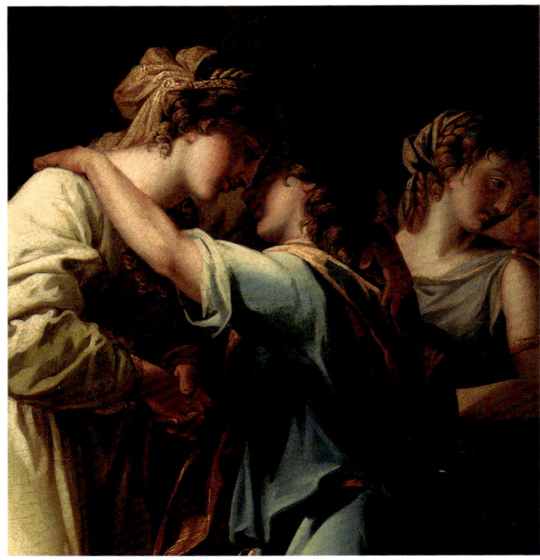

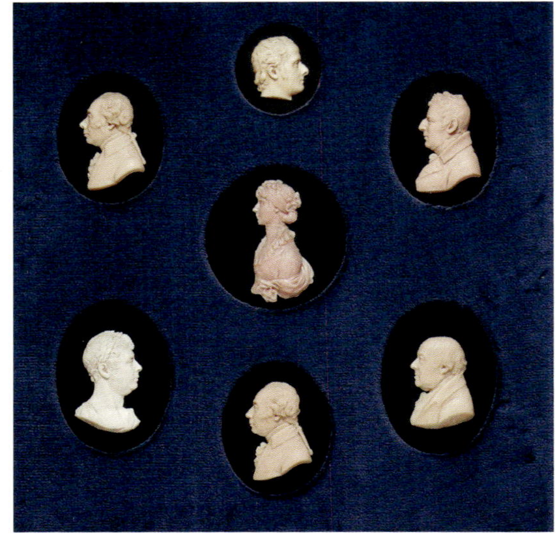

like that of their male peers). They also continued to seek out royal support as both an endorsement and a foundation.[9] Upon arriving in London in 1767, the Swiss Kauffmann—soon to be elected a founding member of the Academy—established profitable connections with several male and female members of the aristocracy and royal family even as she delighted audiences by regularly exhibiting classical and historical works in public shows, such as *Sappho Inspired by Love* (fig. 8; cat. no. 82) and *Telemachus Returning to Penelope* (fig. 9, cat. no. 91).[10] Conversely, several of her peers obtained official endorsements unrelated to specific works of art. In 1785, Caroline Watson (1760/61–1814) earned the title of "Engraver to the Queen."[11] By 1802, Catherine Andras (1775–1860) had gained the title of Charlotte's "Modeller in Wax" (fig. 10), which she appended to her name in most subsequent Academy exhibition catalogues.[12] In the early nineteenth century, Charlotte Jones (1768–1847) and Maria Spilsbury (1776–1820), among others, sold several works to the Prince of Wales; in 1808, Jones further gained the title of "Miniature Painter" to Princess Charlotte of Wales.[13]

Still another set of women, who have received less art historical attention, used royal support to chart pathways that veered away from the Academy's show. This included two needle painters, Mary Linwood and Mary Morris Knowles (1703–1807). In 1771, Charlotte commissioned Knowles to stitch what would be her great artistic triumph: a needle painting of King George III after a painted portrait by Johan Zoffany exhibited at the Academy that year.[14] For Knowles, this would not have been an expected charge. She was a Quaker by birth and, by all accounts, religion kept her from pursuing an exhibiting career.[15] (Although needlework was prohibited at the Academy quite early, artists of both sexes exhibited needle paintings and embroideries at London's other exhibiting societies through the early 1790s, and at Paris's Louvre Salon in 1793.) Instead, Knowles began writing at a young age, advocating for women's education and freedom of choice in matters of religious belief as well as domestic duties and marriage.[16] In 1767, she wed the Quaker apothecary Thomas Knowles; aged thirty-four, she had waited well past a woman's average point of matrimony for the time. Still, she continued to gain a reputation for her needlework and, by early 1771, the American artist and royal favourite Benjamin West, also a Quaker, seemingly facilitated her introduction to Charlotte at court.

Knowles garnered instant recognition for her portrait of the king. On June 4, 1771, the *Birmingham Gazette* lauded, "There is lately finished, by a Lady of this Town, a Portrait of his Majesty, in Needle-Work, allowed by the Connoisseurs to be the greatest Curiosity ever seen of the King, being the closest Likeness of his Majesty,

Fig. 8 (left) · *Detail:* Angelica Kauffmann, *Sappho Inspired by Love*, 1775. Oil on canvas, 132.1 × 145.1 cm. Collection of The John & Mable Ringling Museum of Art, the State Art Museum of Florida, Florida State University, Sarasota, Florida; Bequest of John Ringling, 1936, inv. no. SN329.

Fig. 9 (middle) · *Detail:* Angelica Kauffmann, *Telemachus Returning to Penelope*, c. 1771. Oil on canvas, 96.5 × 122.6 cm. Chrysler Museum of Art, Norfolk, Virginia, Gift of Walter P. Chrysler, Jr., inv. no. 71.665.

Fig. 10 (right) · Catherine Andras, *Portraits depicting Princess Charlotte Augusta of Wales and members of the Royal Family*, 19th century. Wax relief, 8 × 4.2 cm. Victoria and Albert Museum, London, Rupert Gunnis Bequest, inv. no. A.127-1965. Image © Victoria and Albert Museum, London.

and so highly finished, that it has all the Softness and Effect of Painting."[17] While Zoffany's portrait circulated around royal residences, Knowles's needle painting—replicating Zoffany's work exactly in size and closely in form—remained on display at Kew Palace for over two hundred years.[18] Knowles was rewarded highly for the work—£800, described as a "present"—and this seems to have both financed her husband's medical education abroad and led to continuing contact with the royal family.[19] In the following years, as Quakers came under new scrutiny with the onset of the American (1775–83) and then French Revolutionary Wars (1792–1802), she twice defended members of the faith at court.[20] In 1779, she celebrated this valued relationship in a needlework self-portrait (fig. 11).

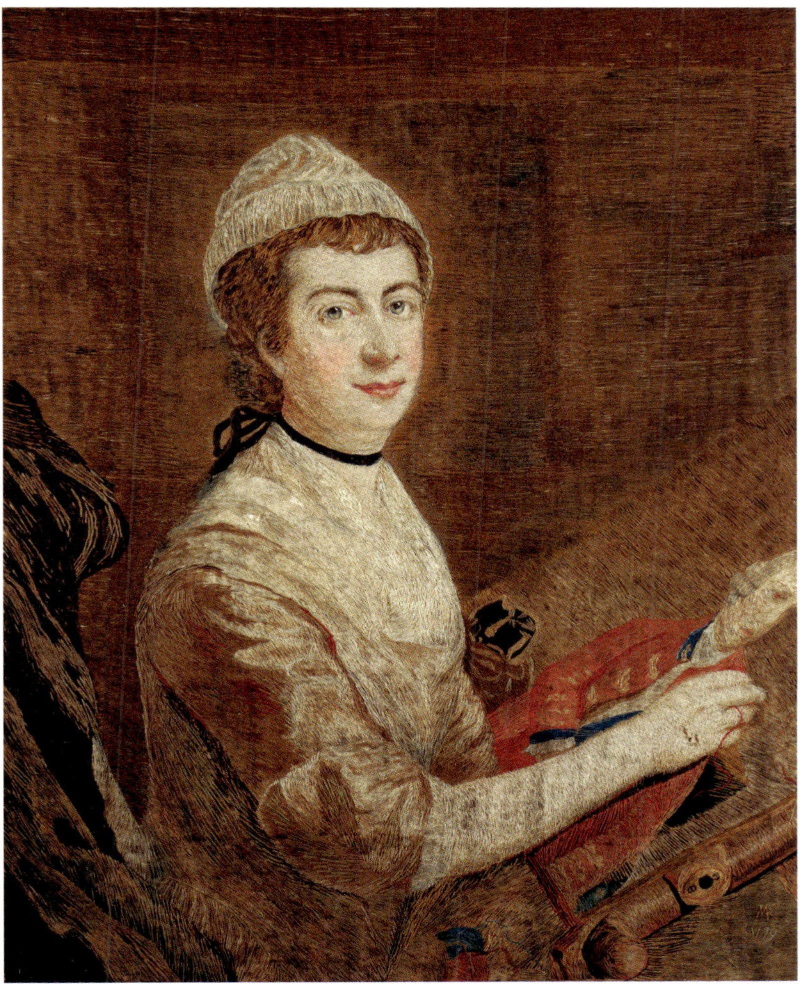

Fig. 11 • Mary Morris Knowles, *Self-Portrait Embroidering the Portrait of King George III*, 1779. Silk, wool, gilt wood, and glass, 89.2 × 84.5 cm. Royal Collection Trust, inv. no. RCIN 11912. Image: Royal Collection Trust / © His Majesty King Charles III 2023.

Coming of age two decades after Knowles, Mary Linwood forged a public-facing career through the meticulous, embroidered replication of paintings of all genres; again, an early royal endorsement proved pivotal. Linwood first exhibited in 1776 and quickly attracted attention.[21] In 1783, contemporary sources recount, Catherine the Great of Russia offered Linwood £40,000 for her entire collection after seeing one of her embroidered canvases. (Linwood reportedly refused but was willing to accept a staggering £7,000 for an individual piece.[22]) Most promisingly, in 1787, with the help of the manufacturer Matthew Boulton (of steam-engine fame), Linwood secured an instrumental reception with Charlotte at court.[23] In a letter to Boulton, Linwood excitedly described the meeting: how she arranged her "pictures" "to the greatest advantage" in the Buckingham House drawing room, and that Charlotte "express'd herself much pleas'd," viewed the canvases for over an hour, and called for her daughters. The princesses "all express'd their approbation, and were sorry the King was so particularly engag'd that he culd not possibly see them that Morn." Perhaps most importantly, Charlotte "express'd her approbation of my intended Exhibition if I culd get a suitable Room," suggesting several "publick ones herself."[24]

This endorsement received attention in the press, and Charlotte's support facilitated Linwood's first solo exhibition that year, showing about thirty of her needle paintings.[25] In London, this seems to have been the first exhibition of its kind. Reviews hailed the "great number of Noblemen and Gentlemen" who visited, reporting that "His Royal Highness the Prince of Wales has been pleased to signify his intention of going to Miss Linwood's Exhibition at the Pantheon," and describing the "character of this work" as belonging to the "elegant arts."[26]

Linwood continued to develop her show while travelling, adding to the works on display and seeking out new venues. In 1798, she leased a space in the Hanover Square Rooms; she had maintained a relationship with the queen, who, as Linwood proudly told Boulton, promised to "visit the Ex—whenever *I wish* it."[27] In June 1806, she took a financial plunge,

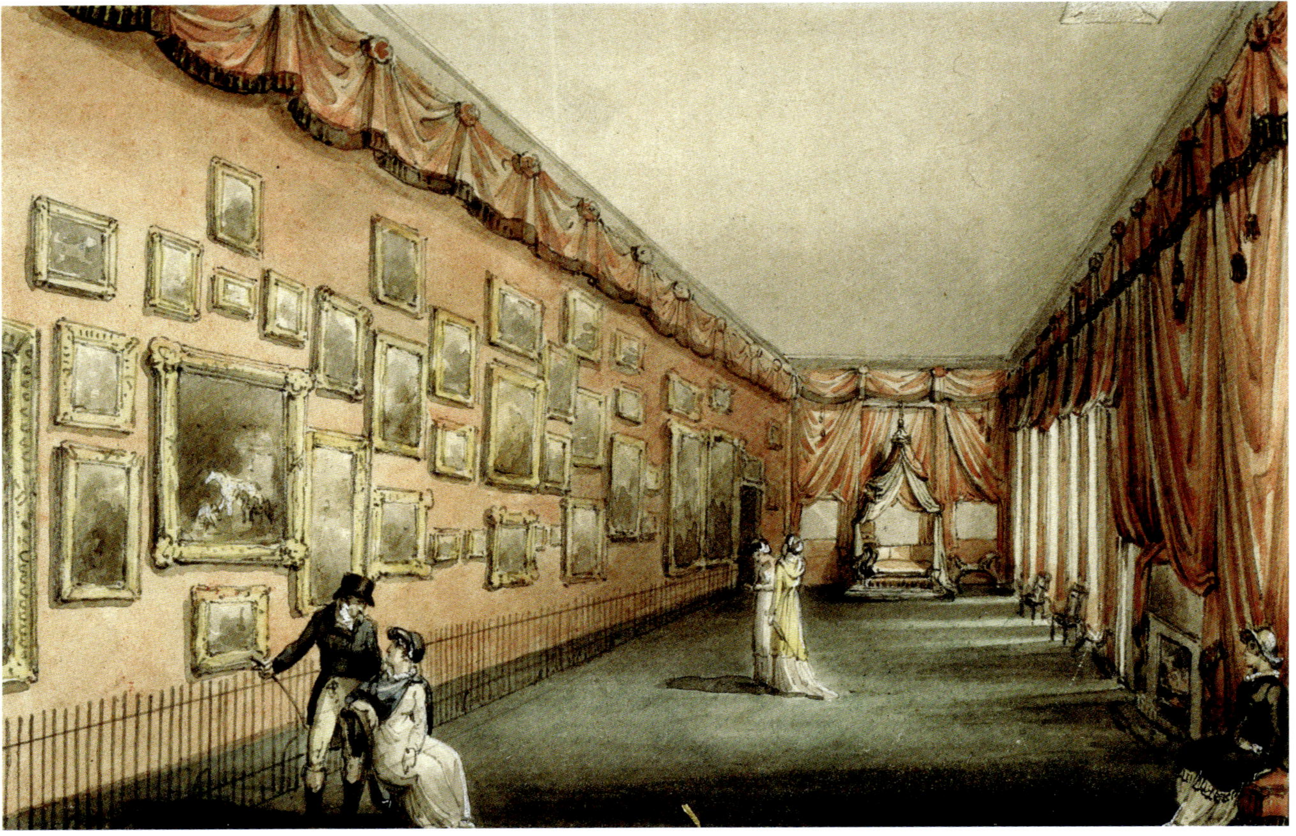

Fig. 12 (above, left) • Unknown maker, *View of Mary Linwood's gallery*, c. 1810. Watercolour on paper, 7.5 × 11.5 cm. Victoria and Albert Museum, London, inv. no. P.6-1985. Image © Victoria and Albert Museum, London.

Fig. 13 (below, left) • Rembrandt van Rijn, *Rembrandt's Mother Reading*, c. 1629. Oil on canvas, 74.4 × 62.7 cm. Wilton House, Wilton, Salisbury, England. Photo: Bridgeman Images.

Fig. 14 (below, right) • Mary Linwood, after Rembrandt van Rijn, *Rembrandt's Mother Reading*, undated. Needlework picture, 104.1 × 88.9 cm. Leicester Arts and Museums Service Collections, inv. no. L.C26.1952.0.0. Photo: © Leicester Arts and Museums Service / Bridgeman Images.

leasing several rooms at Savile House in Leicester Square, London. Her "Gallery of Pictures in Worsted" (fig. 12) would remain at Savile House for forty years, until shortly after her death.[28] She exhibited fifty-five pictures by 1810, and sixty-four by 1822, methodically curated to emphasize their painterly nature (compare figs. 13 & 14; figs. 15 & 16; cat. no. 243). From Dickens to Thackeray, references survive in countless periodicals, journals, letters, and novels, often describing the show as one of the "lions of London."[29]

Across the English Channel, political endorsements proved equally transformative for women painters with professional (i.e., commercial) aspirations in these years. These artists, however, navigated a starkly different environment, one that would soon be upended by decades of revolution. In 1770, when Marie Antoinette settled into her new role as dauphine (wife of the royal heir) of France at the young age of fourteen, *ancien régime* (pre-1789) Paris had long held a reputation as a bellwether of the arts—and, for just as long, provided regular if limited opportunities to excel in these arts for a small number of women. In the French system, leading artists had traditionally procured support through two channels: by forging ties with the aristocracy, with the royal family at its head; and by gaining entry to France's competitive

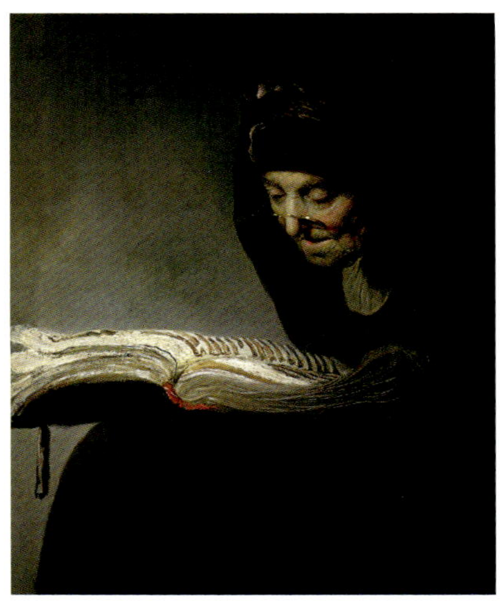

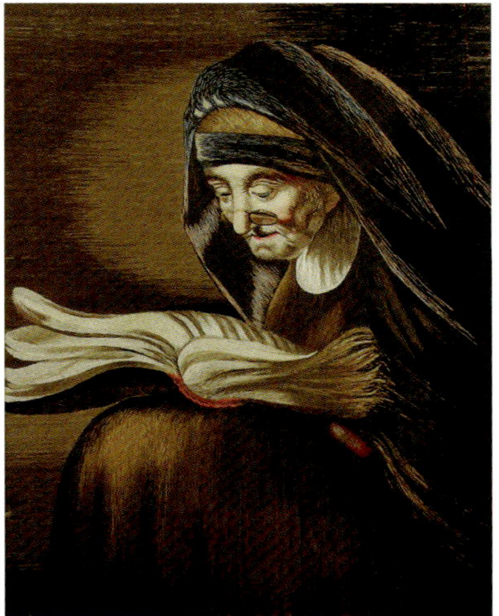

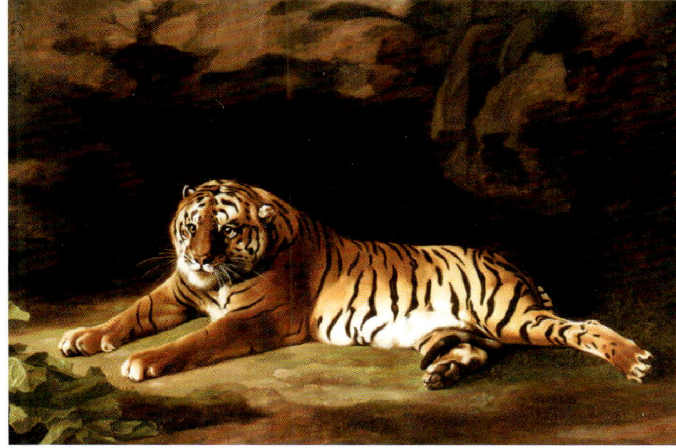

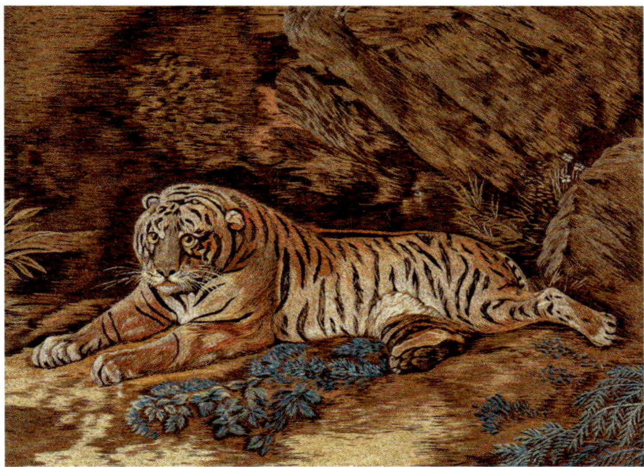

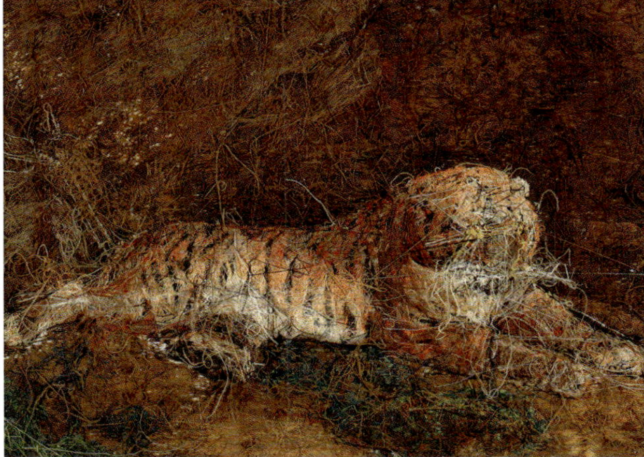

Fig. 15 • George Stubbs, *The Tigress presented by Clive of India to the 4th Duke of Marlborough*, c. 1767–1768. Oil on canvas, 100.4 × 125.7 cm. Blenheim Palace, Oxfordshire. Photo: © Christie's Images / Bridgeman Images.

Fig. 16 (middle and below) • Mary Linwood, after George Stubbs, *Tygress*, c. 1798. Worsted wool needlework, 46 × 59 cm. Yale Center for British Art, Paul Mellon Fund, inv. no. QR.MC 3. Image Courtesy YCBA.

Views illustrated:

Fig. 16a • front view

Fig. 16b • back view

Académie Royale de Peinture et de Sculpture (founded in 1648) and, with it, access to France's most prestigious public exhibition, the biennial Louvre Salon (which first took place in 1737). Until 1791, the Salon displayed the art of Académiciens only; thus, admission to the Académie became the exclusive path to the premier venue for the display of art.

Like their male peers, women learned to pursue both courses for accruing support, often simultaneously. For instance, a royal portrait transformed the career of one of the few female artists from the period whose reputation endures today: Elisabeth Louise Vigée-LeBrun. In 1778, Vigée-LeBrun secured a commission to paint an official portrait of France's new, already controversial queen.[30] The painting was for Marie Antoinette's mother, Maria Theresa of Austria, Holy Roman Empress. At twenty-three years old, Vigée-LeBrun was an apt, if unusual, choice. By this date, she had already begun exhibiting at a few of Paris's smaller, non-Academic venues and had established a name for herself as a society portraitist.[31] Yet the commission was not straightforward. Since 1770, the empress had rejected a series of portrayals, some for being too informal, others for lacking in resemblance; downplaying the prominent Habsburg chin had proved a particularly chronic challenge.[32] Vigée-LeBrun was both the first woman to attempt the queen's portrait, and the first artist whose rendering—a stately if muted depiction of Marie Antoinette in elaborate court attire—satisfied mother and daughter (fig. 17).

Vigée-LeBrun's singular success led to a series of commissions from the royal family as well as to her atypical and somewhat divisive election to France's Académie in 1783. Although women had never been explicitly banned from this august body, in the Académie's entire history—from 1648 until it was disbanded in 1793—it elected only 15 female members, and more than 450 men. In fact, Vigée-LeBrun encountered such strong resistance to her admission that both Marie Antoinette and Louis XVI stepped in.[33] With this royal leverage, Vigée-LeBrun was elected alongside her peer Adélaïde Labille-Guiard (1749–1803) in May 1783; they joined Anne Vallayer-Coster (1744–1818) and Marie-Thérèse Reboul Vien (1728–1805), filling the Académie's recently proposed quota of four female members. Both Vigée-LeBrun and Labille-Guiard advertised their prized status and connections by exhibiting commissioned portraits of members of the royal family at Louvre Salons through 1789.

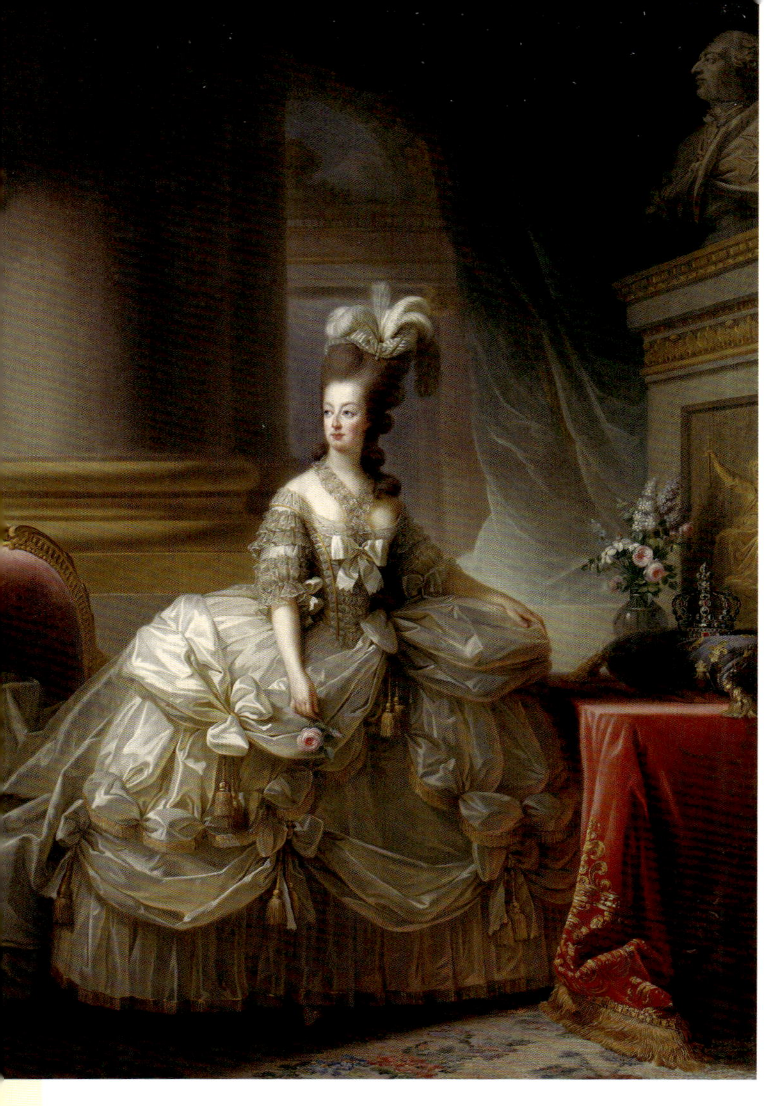

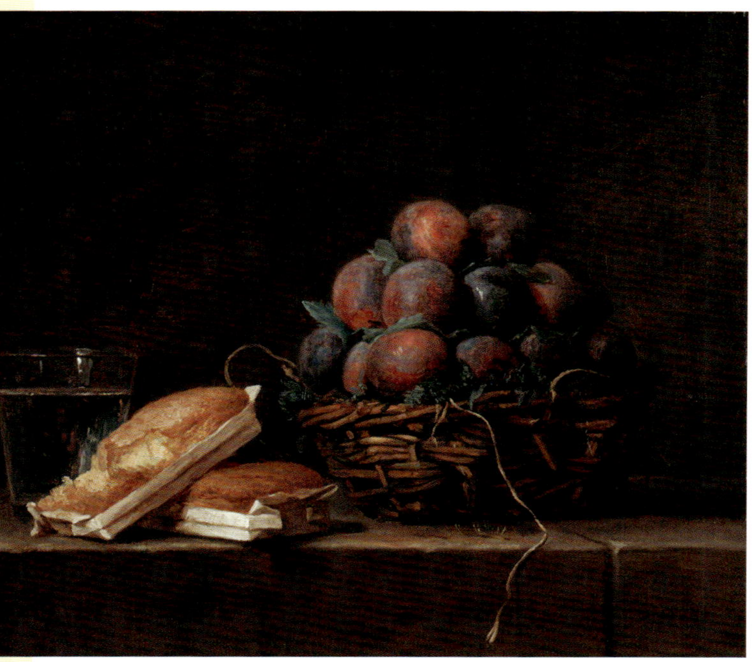

Perhaps inspired by Vigée-LeBrun's quick rise, Vallayer-Coster also expanded her practice to forge ties with members of France's ruling class in the late 1770s. She had joined the Académie in 1771, to minimal objections, and proceeded to exhibit a steady stream of admired still lifes—see *Basket of Plums* (fig. 18)—and often denigrated portraits. Following Vigée-LeBrun, she had secured Marie Antoinette's support by 1779, when she exhibited a painting of a vestal crowned with roses at the Salon, announcing in the *livret* (printed exhibition catalogue) that the painting belonged to the queen. Marianne Roland Michel has speculated that this was a gift of appreciation—in 1780, Vallayer-Coster became the sole female artist to possess one of the Louvre's coveted artists' studios, owing in large part to Marie Antoinette's persistent advocacy.[34] As Vallayer-Coster secured commissions from other female members of the royal family—painting portraits of the Mesdames Tantes, Louis XVI's aunts, in 1779 and 1780 (Labille-Guiard, too, would paint the Mesdames Tantes later in the decade)—she also maintained her relationship with the queen.[35] The educational writer Henriette Campan later recalled that, in 1791, before the royal family's failed attempt to escape Revolutionary Paris, Marie Antoinette asked her to find someone "financially independent and wholly devoted to their sovereigns" to keep a "portfolio" safe; Campan consigned it to Vallayer-Coster, who loyally stored it in her Louvre lodging.[36]

Fig. 17 (above) • Elisabeth Louise Vigée-LeBrun, *Archduchess Marie-Antoinette, Queen of France*, 1778. Oil on canvas, 273 × 193.5 cm. Kunsthistorisches Museum, Vienna, Gemäldegalerie (Picture Gallery), inv. no. GG 2772. Photo: © KHM-Museumsverband.

Fig. 18 (below) • Anne Vallayer-Coster, *Basket of Plums*, 1769. Oil on canvas, 38 × 46.2 cm. The Cleveland Museum of Art, Mr. and Mrs. William H. Marlatt Fund, inv. no. 1971.47.

Revolutions

As the American and then French Revolutions transformed their societies, women artists began to initiate connections with a succession of new, rising political figures, many of them men. Using the valuable relationships they had seen their peers forge in the *ancien régime*—often with prominent women—as a foundation and a framework, they cultivated support from *male* leaders of the Revolutionary world.

One year into the outbreak of the American Revolutionary War, Benjamin Franklin travelled to Paris as an American minister. By the time of his departure in 1785, he had secured France's instrumental support for the American cause and helped broker the Treaty of Paris, which ended the war in 1783. He had also become a popular societal figure, developing relationships with, among others, a series of painters and wax modellers.

Franklin first set up a household in Passy, where one of his neighbours was Anne-Rosalie Bocquet Filleul (1752–1794), a portraitist who had been childhood friends with Vigée-LeBrun.[37] Knowledge about Bocquet Filleul's career remains murky. She exhibited publicly only once, at the Académie de Saint-Luc in 1774, showing several portraits in oil and pastel as well as a still life. In 1777, she married.[38] Her husband was the superintendent of a royal château, and she obtained a handful of royal commissions over the next several years.[39] In 1778 or 1779, she painted a portrait of Franklin (fig. 19; cat. no. 99).

Bocquet Filleul's canvas has been little recognized, perhaps because it remained in the possession of her family for the following two centuries.[40] This disregard is, however, starkly at odds with its reception at the time; so popular was her portrait of Franklin that the Académicien Louis Jacques Cathelin rapidly reproduced it in an engraving, which *he* exhibited at the 1779 Louvre Salon. There, it appeared alongside another portrait of Franklin—the quickly iconic canvas by Joseph Siffred Duplessis, also painted in 1778 (now at the Metropolitan Museum of Art). As this was Cathelin's sole submission to that year's show, Melissa Hyde has argued that this was "a significant work for him," and the print was soon advertised as available for purchase in local periodicals.[41] Viewing the canvas, one can perhaps see why. Compared with Duplessis's portrayal, Bocquet Filleul presents a more vibrant, intimate, and inviting Franklin. Wrapped in a loose-fitting dressing gown, he points to a map of Philadelphia, precisely painted spectacles resting on the paper's edge—the polymath, it feels, as she would have encountered him herself.

Bocquet Filleul was one of several French women to render the well-liked American's likeness. Also in 1778, the painter Marguerite Gérard (1761–1837)—only three years into her training in the Louvre studio of her brother-in-law, Jean-Honoré Fragonard—etched a large allegorical tribute to Franklin's genius, after a drawing by Fragonard (fig. 20; cat. no. 147). Gérard would go on to become one of the most collected painters of her day. A decade later, after Franklin's departure, his friend Marie-Anne Paulze Lavoisier (1758–1836) roughly copied Duplessis's famed image. She then shipped the canvas to Franklin, back in Philadelphia.[42]

Even earlier, two *other* women had modelled the diplomat's features in wax. Alongside Voltaire, Franklin was one of the first figures sculpted by a young Marie Tussaud (1761–1850), in the 1770s. The wax portrait then appeared, on display, at her teacher Philippe Curtius's popular interactive Salon de Cire (Wax Salon) in the Palais Royale.[43] Likewise, as early as 1772, the *New-York Gazette* reported that the American wax modeller Patience Lovell Wright (1725–1786) had set up a modelled figure of Franklin in her new London studio, near a wax effigy of the contemporary historian and writer Catherine Macauley.[44]

Wright had arrived in London that year and would remain based in the capital through to her death. During this time, she pioneered her own waxworks business while successfully cultivating relationships with Franklin and John Adams as patrons and allies. Fashioning a colourful public persona from the start,

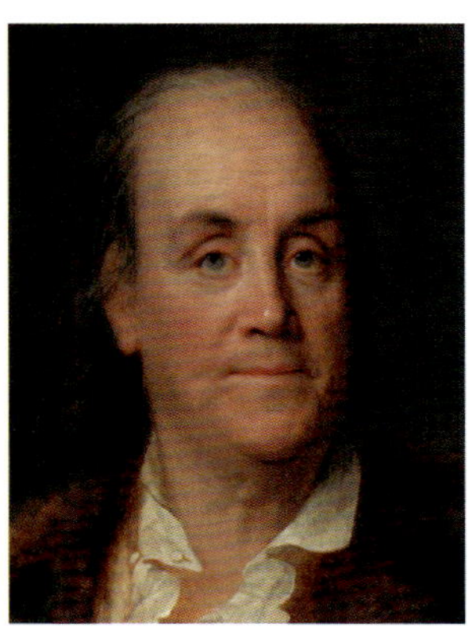

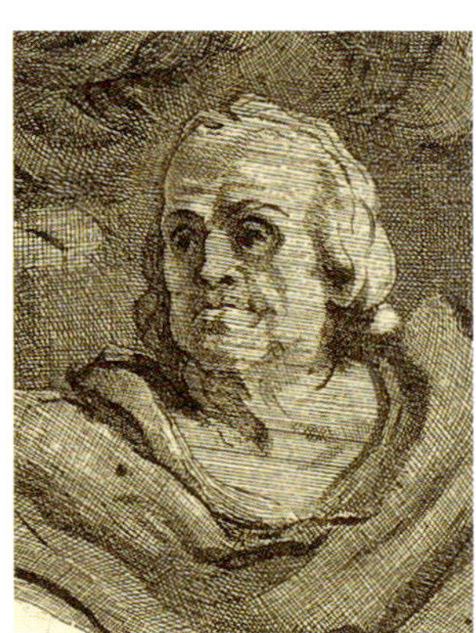

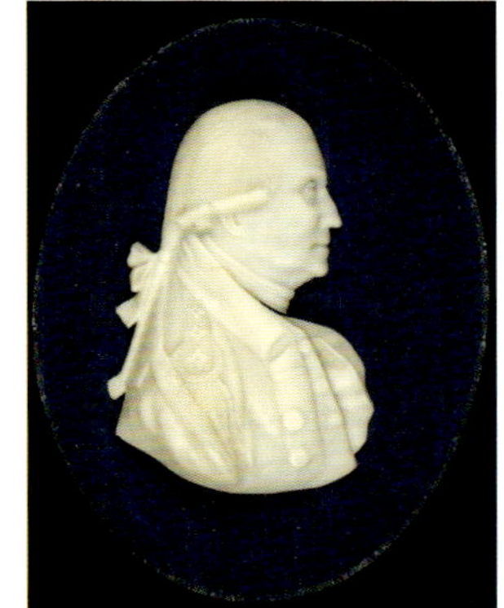

Fig. 19 (left) • *Detail*: Anne-Rosalie Bocquet Filleul, *Portrait of Benjamin Franklin*, 1778 or 1779. Oil on canvas, 91.1 × 72.4 cm. Philadelphia Museum of Art: Gift of the Honourable Walter H. Annenberg and Leonore Annenberg and the Annenberg Foundation, 2007, inv. no. 2007-13-2.

Fig. 20 (middle) • *Detail*: Marguerite Gérard, after Jean-Honoré Fragonard, *The Genius of Franklin [Au Génie de Franklin]*, 1778. Etching printed in brown, image: 47.8 × 37.3 cm; plate: 55.1 × 42.2 cm; sheet: 62 × 44.5 cm. National Gallery of Art, Washington, Rosenwald Collection, 1964, inv. no. 1964.8.867.

Fig. 21 (right) • *Detail*: Attributed to Patience Lovell Wright, *Portrait of George Washington*, c. 1775. Wax, 38.7 × 30.5 × 6.6 cm. On loan from Old Barracks Museum.

Wright endeavoured to use her artistic enterprise to mould herself into an influential political player at the height of the American Revolution. More than a dozen letters to Franklin survive in which she attempted to apprise him of British activities and assert her political worth as a woman. In 1778, for instance, she wrote that she aspired "to Bring about the grand and most Extrordary Revolutions by the most unlikly means … [and] Bring on the Glorious Cause of sivil and religious Liberty."[45] In a letter from March 1777—which enclosed a political pamphlet on King George III and a newspaper printing of a recent speech by the radical writer and politician John Wilkes—Wright shared a "dream" that "this [year] 1777 will Bring the ways of god more Clear to MAN and Prove that women are usful and may be admitted into the Bond of usful Friendship wher the good of all men are Concernd."[46]

Conscious of the limitations she faced owing to her sex and profession, Wright revelled in her change of status with the Revolution's close. "I now no longer the old Mad Woman," she wrote to Franklin in 1783, "but Madam Wright or 'the Ingenous Mrs Wright from America who told us TRUTH'—Now I have a feild for my Politicall genis Joynd with My Wax Work which will do me Some Credit if I Keep Within proper bounds."[47] Later that year, she initiated contact with George Washington, expressing her "Wish and desire…to moddel" his likeness (fig. 21; cat. no. 199). Washington's response—prized and kept by her daughter for years after Wright's death—must have marked a pinnacle of her career; after referring to Wright's "celebrated Genii," he enthused,

> If your inclination to return to this Country should overcome other considerations, you will, no doubt, meet a welcome reception from your numerous friends: among whom, I should be proud to see a person so universally celebrated; & on whom, nature has bestowed such rare & uncommon gifts.[48]

In 1785, aged sixty, Wright continued to seek out new ties. That August, she wrote to Thomas Jefferson, once more using art to launch a conversation. She proposed a series of statues depicting "those *five* gentlemen, who assisted at the signing the treaty of peace, that put an end to so bloody and dreadful a war."[49] Offering to come to Paris to model Jefferson herself, Wright attempted to cement this final link by proposing a project by which her known "genii" could serve political ends: statues of the men whose acknowledgement had so impacted her own career and sense of purpose.[50] This project was never realized; Wright died in March 1786, the result of a fall while walking home from John and Abigail Adams's London residence.

~

John Adams returned to the United States in 1788, followed by Jefferson two years later, just as another set of Revolutionary episodes began to unfold. In July 1789, the storming of Paris's Bastille prison precipitated a series of episodes that became known as the French Revolution and shook much of the Western world to its core; it would also transform the artistic sphere for women. In August 1791, France's new National Assembly declared the Louvre Salon open to all artists, regardless of their sex or Academic status. When the first "open" Salon took place two weeks later, twenty-two women exhibited sixty works of art: thirty-eight portraits, twelve narrative scenes, three landscapes, three sculptures, three pieces in enamel, and three non-identifiable works.

Artists with former royal ties had to approach these quickly evolving political events with extreme caution. Vigée-LeBrun fled to Italy in October 1789, as part of the first wave of *émigrés.* She would spend the next decade in exile, travelling through Italy, Germany, and Russia, and securing financial support and new celebrity while depicting aristocratic sitters, such as in her *The Countess von Schönfeld with Her Daughter* (fig. 22) and *Princess Anna Alexandrovna Galitzin* (figs. 23 & 24; cat. nos. 37 & 110). Along the way, she wrote a travel narrative, titled *Souvenirs* (1835–37), that became the first autobiographical memoir published by a female artist. Vallayer-Coster remained in France but spent time away from Paris, maintaining a quieter

Fig. 22 (facing, above, left) • Elisabeth Louise Vigée-LeBrun, *The Countess von Schönfeld with Her Daughter*, 1793. Oil on canvas, 134 × 97.8 cm. Collection of the University of Arizona Museum of Art, Tucson; Gift of Samuel H. Kress Foundation, inv. no. 1961.013.028.

Fig. 23 (facing, above, middle) • Elisabeth Louise Vigée-LeBrun, *Princess Anna Alexandrovna Galitzin*, c. 1797. Oil on canvas, 135.9 × 100.3 cm. Baltimore Museum of Art: The Mary Frick Jacobs Collection, 1938.192. Photo: Mitro Hood.

Fig. 24 (facing, above, right) • Elisabeth Louise Vigée-LeBrun, *Princess Anna Alexandrovna Galitzin*, c. 1797. Black chalk and white chalk with stumping on paper, 28.2 × 23.4 cm. Baltimore Museum of Art: Stiles Tuttle Colwill Acquisitions Fund, and Marion Tuttle Colwill Memorial Fund, 2016.2. Photo: Mitro Hood.

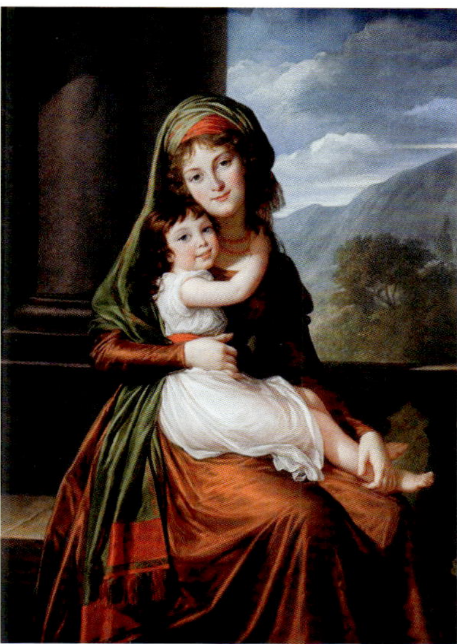

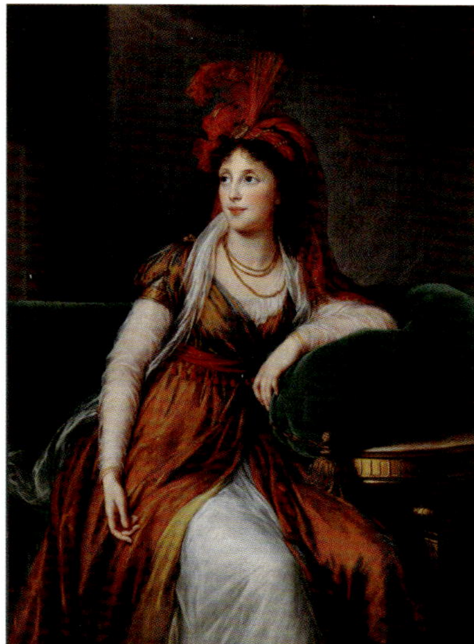

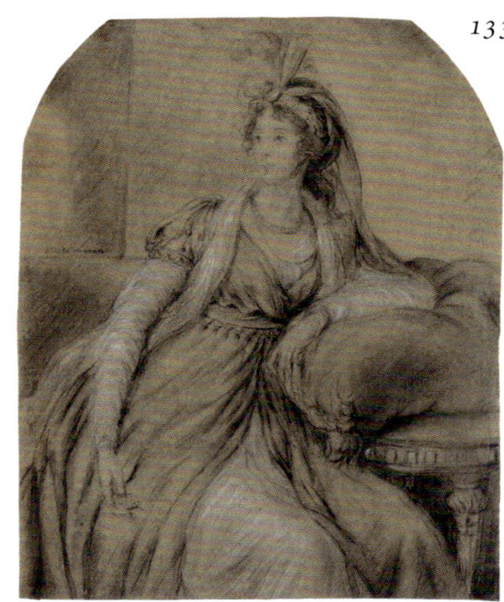

Fig. 25 (below, left) • Adélaïde Labille-Guiard, *Portrait of a Woman (Presumed Portrait of the Marquise de Lafayette)*, 1793–1794. Oil on canvas, 78.1 × 62.9 cm. National Museum of Women in the Arts, Washington, DC, Gift of Wallace and Wilhelmina Holladay, inv. no. 2001.145. Photo: Lee Stalsworth.

Fig. 26 (below, right) • Marie-Nicole Vestier Dumont, *The Author at Her Occupations*, c. 1791. Oil on canvas, 54 × 44 cm. Musée de la Révolution française, Domane de Vizille, Département de l'Isère, inv. no. MRF 2017-5. Image: © Coll. Musée de la Révolution française – Département de l'Isère.

profile while sporadically exhibiting and selling works to those in power, including the Empress Josephine.[51]

Yet for women (and men) without royal associations, the legislation of the early Revolution would have seemed to hold great promise. Women never received many of the fundamental rights granted to men at this time, including the ability to vote. But still, from 1790 through 1792, the National Assembly and its successor, the Legislative Assembly, abolished primogeniture (a law in which inheritance passed to the firstborn male, bypassing female offspring), instituted egalitarian inheritance laws, newly allowed women to enter contracts, lowered the age of majority to twenty-one, secularized marriage, and legalized divorce. Unlike her peer Académiciennes, Labille-Guiard joined a wave of women whose practices embraced the exciting new politics at hand. In 1790, leveraging this republican spirit, she advocated for the Académie to abolish its quota on women—a motion that was quickly approved, overturned, and then essentially moot.[52] More publicly, beginning with the 1791 Salon, she emphatically shirked her royal ties in the nine portraits in oil and pastel she submitted for display: seven depicted National Assembly deputies, including Maximilien Robespierre.[53] Recognizing her political realignment, one critic remarked, "Madame Guyard attaches her reputation to that of the great men of our century."[54] She also infused these civic changes into her visual choices, developing a more muted, simpler aesthetic, which we can see in her *Portrait of a Woman (Presumed Portrait of the Marquise de Lafayette)* (fig. 25; cat. no. 98).

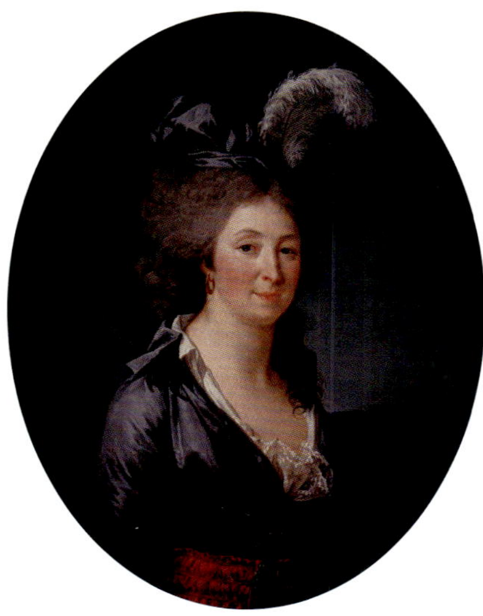

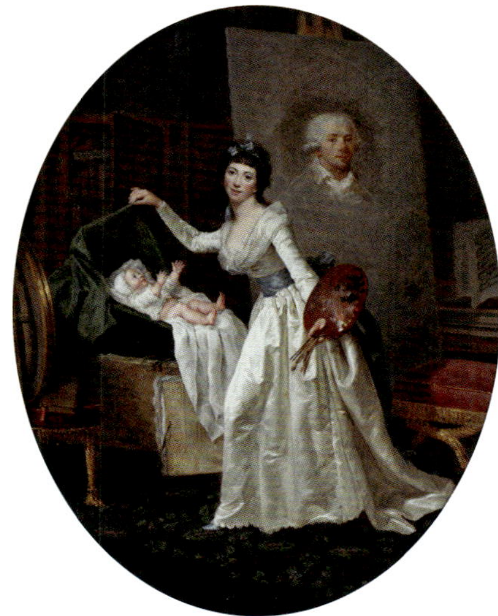

Although we rarely hear about other prominent female artists from this time, Labille-Guiard was far from alone. At the exact moment women found themselves allowed to exhibit in France's most prestigious venue, they promptly and shrewdly suffused their canvases with Revolutionary styles and themes. In 1791, Anna Gault de Saint-Germain (1760–1832) also showed a portrait of the National Assembly deputy Charles Lameth; in 1793, Marie-Nicole Vestier Dumont

(1767–1846) visualized the new rhetoric of motherhood and citizenship in *The Author at Her Occupations* (fig. 26); and in 1793–1794, Jacques-Louis David's student Nanine Vallain (1767–1815) painted a large, steely-gazed *Liberty* that was not exhibited publicly—yet it hung in the Jacobin Club (the political group headed by Robespierre and responsible for the bloody events of the Terror) at the height of its noxious polemic against women. In 1799, Marie-Guillemine Benoist (1768–1826)—another David student—exhibited a portrait of a woman, wrapped in a shawl; if this is the piece now at the San Diego Museum of Art (fig. 27; cat. no. 111), she clad her subject in classically inspired attire. These works hint at the complex ways in which women may have been reconceptualizing their own civic roles.

British women, too, embraced this new wave of figures and ideals. In one case among many, the Sharples family travelled to America (the first of two trips) in the mid-1790s; en route, they were captured by a French privateer as prisoners of war. Upon finally arriving in Philadelphia, Ellen Sharples (1769–1849) began copying her husband James's portraits of American and French political figures, including George and Martha Washington, John Adams, Thomas Jefferson, James and Dolley Madison, Charles Maurice de Talleyrand-Périgord, Alexander Hamilton, Aaron Burr, and the Marquis de Lafayette. Back in England, when Sharples debuted at the Royal Academy in 1807, she exhibited a portrait of Washington and two of the political theorist Joseph Priestley.[55]

Most unexpectedly, as the era closed, Napoleon, his administration, and his family became consistent supporters of numerous female artists who had launched their careers in the Revolutionary Salons. Some, like Marguerite Gérard and Pauline Auzou (1775–1835), exhibited non-commissioned pieces with Napoleonic subject matter, which the state then acquired on the emperor's behalf; others saw a range of their exhibited works purchased by Bonaparte family members. Some, like Vigée-LeBrun (once returned from exile), secured commissions to paint family portraits; others received state support for specific projects or in the form of annuities and lodging. The ornithologist and ceramic painter Pauline Rifer de Courcelles (1781–1851; fig. 28; cat. no. 25), known as Madame Knip, even used her exhibition activity to complement and advance serial endeavours in print, one of which she dedicated to Empress Marie-Louise—who had received the artist at court after she won a second-class medal at the Louvre Salon of 1810. It is not clear that Napoleon or his administration saw this active support of women artists to be at odds with their broader legislative policies, which imposed severe restrictions on women's activities; with the Napoleonic Code of 1804, women notoriously lost many of the rights gained in the early 1790s, including control of any earnings or inheritance. Instead, women were (re-)subordinated to their fathers and husbands as eternal minors. Many of these gendered aspects of the code lasted well into the twentieth century.

Such draconian policies make it all the more astonishing that, exactly as it implemented these laws, the Napoleonic state seems to have treated women artists as established financial players—and

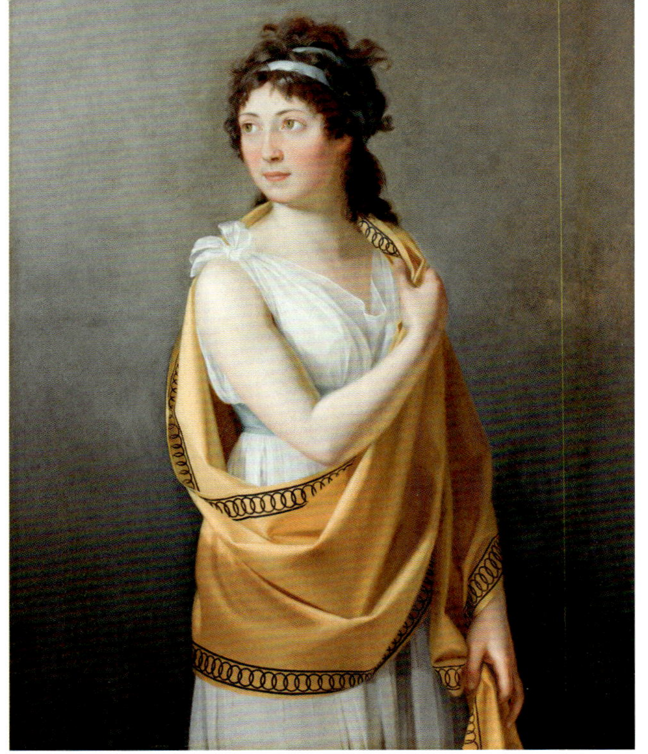

Fig. 27 (above) • Marie-Guillemine Benoist, *Portrait of a Lady*, c. 1799. Oil on canvas, 100.3 × 81.6 cm. San Diego Museum of Art: Gift of Anne R. and Amy Putnam, inv. no. 1946.5.

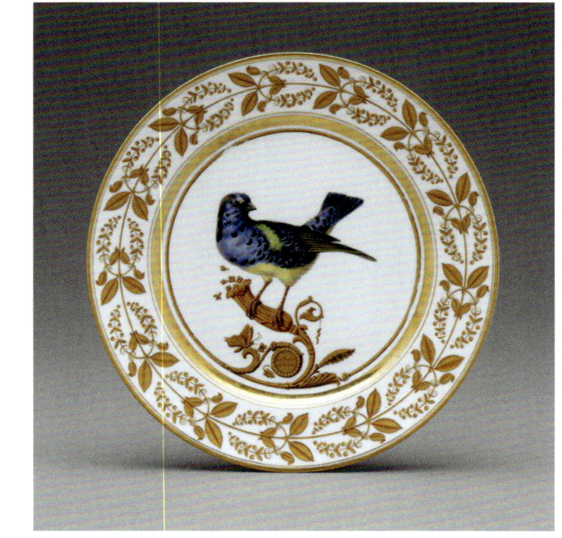

Fig. 28 (below) • Pauline Rifer de Courcelles, known as Madame Knip, decorator for Manufacture Nationale de Sèvres, *Turquoise Tanager [Le Diable enrhumé] plate*, from the series *The South American Birds Service*, 1819–1821. Diameter: 23.5 cm, hard-paste porcelain. On Loan from Hillwood Estate, Museum & Gardens, Bequest of Marjorie Merriweather Post, 1973, inv. no. 24.136.1. Photographed by Edward Owen.

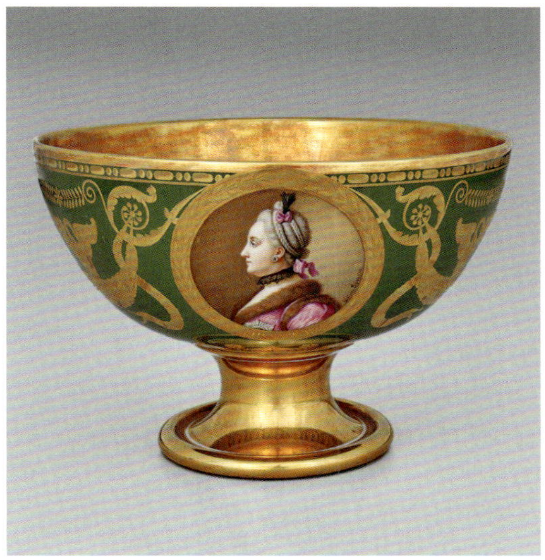

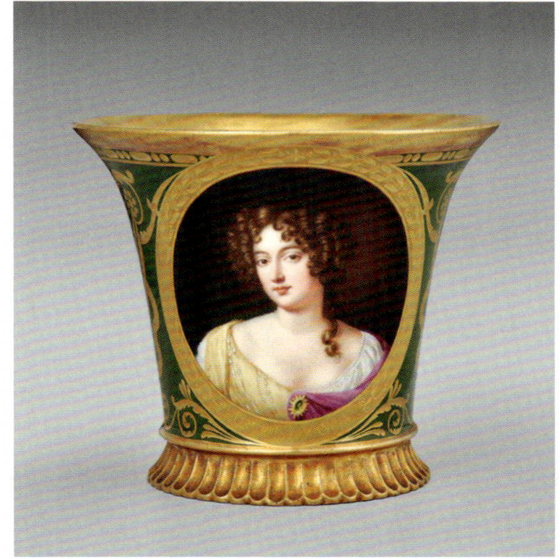

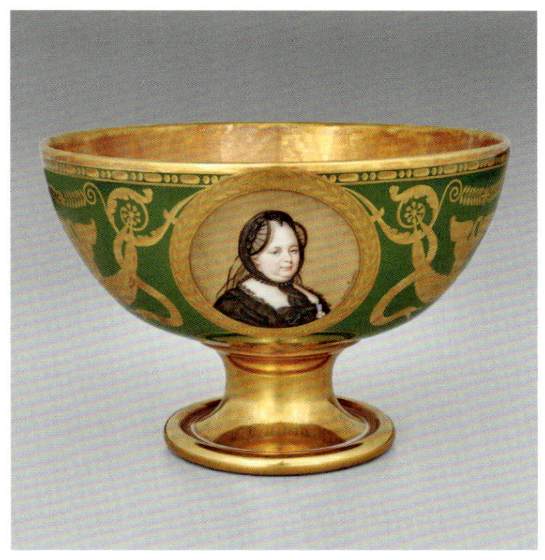

Figs. 29a (left) & 29c (right) • Marie-Victoire Jaquotot, decorator for Manufacture Nationale de Sèvres, *Bowl with portraits of Catherine the Great of Russia (1729–1796), Maria Theresa of Austria (1717–1780), and Blanche of Castille (1188–1252)*, from *Tea Service of Famous Women*, 1811–1812. Hard-paste porcelain, height: 14.6 cm; diameter: 21.9 cm. Clark Art Institute, Williamstown, Massachusetts, USA, Acquired by the Clark, 2021, inv. no. 2021.3.4. Image courtesy Clark Art Institute. clarkart.edu.

Fig. 29b (middle) • Marie-Victoire Jaquotot, decorator for Manufacture Nationale de Sèvres, *Cup with portrait of Hortense Mancini, Duchess de Mazarin (1646–1699)*, from *Tea Service of Famous Women*, 1811–1812. Hard-paste porcelain, 8.7 × 12.2 × 10.3 cm. Clark Art Institute, Williamstown, Massachusetts, USA, Acquired by the Clark, 2021, inv. no. 2021.3.10. Image courtesy Clark Art Institute. clarkart.edu.

as the professionals that they were. Marie-Guillemine Benoist completed at least ten official portraits of Napoleon between 1804 and 1812, including canvases for the towns of Ghent, Brest, Mans, Angers, and Sarthe; the Sarthe portrait alone brought her 3,000 francs, a price commensurate with that paid to Jean-Antoine Gros for similar pieces.[56] Along with Césarine Davin-Mirvault (1774–1844), a student of David and Joseph-Benoît Suvée, and several male artists, Benoist also secured 2,000 francs to paint one of the Marshals of the Empire as part of a series Napoleon commissioned for the Tuileries around 1805; in an 1821 petition to the Restoration arts administration, Davin-Mirvault referred to this commission as evidence of her merit.[57] In 1808, Davin-Mirvault also obtained access to paint the Persian ambassador Askar Khan Afshar on his trip to Paris, and she exhibited this portrait at the following Salon (now at the Château de Versailles).

Additionally, from 1811 to 1812, the porcelain painter Marie-Victoire Jaquotot (1772–1855)—the highest-paid artist at the acclaimed Sèvres porcelain manufactory from 1808 to 1847—completed an exquisite tea service (fig. 29; cat. no. 24) for the emperor, intended to be a gift to his first wife, Josephine.[58] Featuring sixteen prominent women from history, its subjects range from rulers (including Catherine the Great and Maria Theresa of Austria) to luminaries of literature and philosophy who remain little known today—such as Hortense Mancini (1646–1699), the first French woman to publish an autobiography during her own lifetime, under her own name.[59] In 1816, with the restoration of the Bourbon monarchy, Jaquotot earned the title *premier peintre sur porcelaine du Roi* (First Porcelain Painter to the King). Other women artists, too, gained commissions, sales, annuities, titles, and other forms of recognition from the new administration—but that is another chapter of our story.

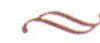

In this often contradictory context of friendships, sittings, commissions, purchases, and private and public engagement across decades of political, religious, and sociocultural shifts, the story of Napoleon sitting for a detailed portrait by Mary Linwood hardly seems implausible. Rather, it would have fit securely into the cultural landscape of the mid-nineteenth-century's art-going public, which had come of age witnessing the prominent place of professional women painters, sculptors, and other makers in popular, prestigious public shows. That such accounts may surprise us today owes largely to the fact that these artists' stories have been omitted from official histories for far too long.

Notes

1 The first woollen canvas is in the New Walk Museum and Art Gallery, Leicester Arts and Museums Service collections, Leicester, L.C398.1951.0.0; the second is in the Victoria and Albert Museum, London, 1438–1874.

2 Britain and France had been at war since 1793 (as part of the French Revolutionary Wars), and would be again until 1815 (the Napoleonic Wars).

3 William Liddiard, *A Three Months' Tour in Switzerland and France* (London: Smith, Elder, and Co., 1832), 31.

4 "Miss Linwood," *The Gentleman's Magazine* (May 1845): 555–57.

5 In London, addresses first appeared in the catalogue for a 1763 show. In Paris, they began to appear in 1791. Most women in both Britain and France listed their addresses while exhibiting through at least the 1820s.

6 See Heidi A. Strobel, *The Artistic Matronage of Queen Charlotte (1744–1818): How a Queen Promoted Both Art and Female Artists in English Society* (Lewiston, NY: Edwin Mellen, 2011), as well as Jane Roberts, ed., *George III & Queen Charlotte: Patronage, Collecting and Court Taste* (London: Royal Collection, 2004).

7 Read listed her address from 1763, Benwell from 1764.

8 Strobel, *Artistic Matronage*, 89.

9 For women's exhibiting numbers, see Paris A. Spies-Gans, *A Revolution on Canvas: The Rise of Women Artists in Britain and France, 1760–1830* (London: Paul Mellon Centre for Studies in British Art in association with Yale University Press, 2022), 17–53.

10 Kauffmann received a portrait commission from Princess Augusta immediately after arriving in London, followed by a studio visit from the princess, signalling her satisfaction with the work. Soon thereafter, Queen Charlotte requested a portrait and then commissioned what became Kauffmann's *Her Majesty Queen Charlotte Raising the Genius of the Fine Arts*. See Angela Rosenthal, *Angelica Kauffman: Art and Sensibility* (New Haven, CT: Paul Mellon Centre for Studies in British Art in association with Yale University Press, 2006), 163–66.

11 For Watson, see David Alexander, *Caroline Watson & Female Printmaking in Late Georgian England* (Cambridge: Fitzwilliam Museum, 2014).

12 Other artists who gained Charlotte's support in these years include Mary Black and Margaret Meen.

13 For Jones, see Annette Peach, "Jones, Charlotte (1768–1847)," *Oxford Dictionary of National Biography* (Oxford: Oxford University Press, 2004), online ed., and Richard Walker, *The Eighteenth and Early Nineteenth Century Miniatures in the Collection of Her Majesty the Queen* (Cambridge: Cambridge University Press, 1992), 343. For Spilsbury, see Charlotte Yeldham, *Maria Spilsbury (1776–1820): Artist and Evangelical* (Surrey, UK: Ashgate, 2010). Later examples include, among others, Emma Kendrick, who became "court miniature painter" to Princess Elizabeth in 1818; in 1831, she was named "miniature painter" to King William IV.

14 For the most complete account of Knowles, see Judith Jennings, *Gender, Religion, and Radicalism in the Long Eighteenth Century: The "Ingenious Quaker" and Her Connections* (Burlington, UK: Ashgate, 2006).

15 For evolving Quaker attitudes toward visual art, see David Sox, *Quakers and the Arts: "Plain and Fancy," an Anglo-American Perspective* (York, UK: Sessions Book Trust, 2000).

16 The work survives in two manuscripts in the Library of the Society of Friends, London, alternatively titled "The Memoirs of M. M. Spinster of This Parish" and "The Pudding-Making Mortal"; both date the composition to 1765. TEMP MSS 28/7 contains "The Memoirs of M. M. Spinster of This Parish"; "The Pudding-Making Mortal" is a title added to TEMP MSS 403/7/15/3/43 c. 1765.

17 *Birmingham Gazette* (June 4, 1771), cited by Jennings, *Gender, Religion, and Radicalism*, 38; newspaper clipping, New Walk Museum, Leicester, UK.

18 One of her husband's fellow students in Edinburgh wrote that Thomas "is come to graduate, & this we suppose is occasioned by his wife having executed such a royal performance as the King's picture in needlework." Jennings, *Gender, Religion, and Radicalism*, 39, citing George Binns, "A Short Account of the Life of Jonathan Binns, M.D.," typescript, Liverpool City Library, 4.

19 The high sum is significant; West normally earned about £150 for his royal portraits, while Sir Joshua Reynolds's highest recorded portrait payment was 200 guineas, for a full-length in 1779. William K. Wimsatt Jr. and Frederick A. Pottle, eds., *Boswell for the Defense, 1769–1774* (London: William Heinemann, 1960), 37; Strobel, *Artistic Matronage*, 133–34; and David Mannings, *Sir Joshua Reynolds: A Complete Catalogue of His Paintings* (New Haven, CT: Yale University Press, 2000), 1:21. Boswell further detailed the transformation in Knowles's life that ensued from this gift: "Her husband was an apothecary; but upon his wife's getting thus a kind of interest at Court, bethought himself of commencing physician and is now actually studying at Edinburgh in order to take his degrees;" Wimsatt and Pottle, *Boswell for the Defense*, 37.

20 Jennings, *Gender, Religion, and Radicalism*, 73–74 and 83–84.

21 Her first public forays occurred in 1776 and 1778, when she exhibited a "Piece of Flowers in Needle-Work," and then a "Landscape in Needlework" in the Society of Artists' London show.

22 Alexander Lanskoy offered this sum on behalf of the empress, which converts to over US$1 million today. Lanskoy died in 1784, and Linwood was never paid—though not for lack of trying. In April 1787, she updated a friend on "intelligence I receiv'd this day from the Russian Court … from Mr Tooke of St Petersburg, who last year was so kind to undertake the enquiry after my picture." Mary Linwood to Matthew Boulton, April 21, 1787, MS 3782/12/32/59, Library of Birmingham.

23 Boulton had sent his daughter to the girls' school that Linwood and her mother, Hannah, ran in Leicester.

24 Mary Linwood to Matthew Boulton, April 21, 1787, MS 3782/12/32/59, Library of Birmingham.

25 It opened on May 5, 1787, at London's Pantheon, an entertainment facility on Oxford Street. The *Morning Post* (April 24, 1787) reported on her reception. The *Public Advertiser*; *Morning Herald*; *St. James's Chronicle: or, British Evening-Post*; *World and Fashionable Advertiser*; *General Evening Post*; and *Morning Post* (May 4, 1787) advertised the opening. See Valerie Hedquist, "How a Lost Painting Endured: Gainsborough's Woodman, Macklin's Poets' Gallery, and Miss Linwood's Needle Painting," *Southeastern College Art Conference Review* 16, no. 3 (2013): 262n53.

26 *Morning Post* (May 12, 1787), and Hedquist, "How a Lost Painting Endured," 264n75, citing *Whitehall Evening Post* (May 22–24, 1787).

27 Mary Linwood to Matthew Boulton, February 6, 1798, MS 3782/12/43/14, Library of Birmingham, emphasis in original.

28 Despite the 1806 purchase, the earliest surviving Savile House exhibition catalogues I have found date back to 1810.

29 This phrase is widely quoted from Countess of Wilton, ed., *The Art of Needle-Work, from the Earliest Ages* (London: Henry Colburn, 1841), 396.

30 Marie Antoinette and Louis XVI ascended to the throne after Louis XV's death in 1774.

31 She had joined the Parisian artists' guild, the Académie de Saint-Luc, in 1774, and married the arts dealer Jean-Baptiste-Pierre Le Brun in 1776.

32 For details, see Mary D. Sheriff, *The Exceptional Woman: Elisabeth Vigée-Lebrun and the Cultural Politics of Art* (Chicago: University of Chicago Press, 1996), 158–65.

33 One ostensible reason voiced by opponents was that her husband was an art dealer, and Académiciens were not supposed to have ties to the commercial world (though several of them did). For detailed analyses of these proceedings, see Laura Auricchio, *Adélaïde Labille-Guiard: Artist in the Age of Revolution* (Los Angeles: J. Paul Getty Museum, 2009), 29–37, and Mary D. Sheriff, *The Exceptional Woman: Elisabeth Vigée-Lebrun and the Cultural Politics of Art* (Chicago: University of Chicago Press, 1996), 73–104.

34 Beginning in March 1779, Marie Antoinette had repeatedly advocated for Vallayer-Coster to receive one of the Louvre's artists' studios. In early April, a letter announced that a studio had been awarded—but there were delays. Marie Antoinette continued to advocate through late June, when a letter from M. Dorival to M. Duperson reiterated, "The Queen, who honors Mlle Vallayer with particular protection, desires that the lodgings be accorded her without delay." See Marianne Roland Michel, "Vallayer in Her Time," in *Anne Vallayer-Coster: Painter to the Court of Marie-Antoinette*, ed. Eik Kahng and Marianne Roland Michel (Dallas: Dallas Museum of Art; New Haven, CT: Yale University Press, 2002), 19, citing Marianne Roland Michel, *Anne Vallayer-Coster, 1744–1818* (Paris: C.I.L., 1970), 260–64. See also "État des logements employés pour le service du Roi dans le Louvre et ses Galeries et dans les maisons appurtenant au Roi," 1790, O/1/1914, Archives Nationales, Paris.

35 Kahng and Roland Michel, *Anne Vallayer-Coster*, cat. nos. 55, 59, 60.

36 Roland Michel, "Vallayer in Her Time," 20, citing Jeanne-Louise-Henriette Campan, *Mémoires de Madame Campan, première femme de chambre de Marie-Antoinette*, ed. Jean Chalon (Paris: Mercure de France,

1988), 342. In 1781, Marie Antoinette also signed Vallayer-Coster's marriage contract.

37 Joseph Baillio, "The Artistic and Social Odyssey of Elisabeth Louise Vigée Le Brun," in Joseph Baillio, Katharine Baetjer, and Paul Lang, *Vigée Le Brun* (New York: Metropolitan Museum of Art, 2016), 5.

38 Her husband, Louis Filleul, invited Franklin to the blessing of their marriage. "To Benjamin Franklin from Louis Filleul: A Wedding Invitation [on or before 30 September 1777]," *Founders Online*, National Archives, founders.archives.gov/documents/Franklin/01-24-02-0438. [Original source: *The Papers of Benjamin Franklin*, vol. 24, *May 1 through September 30, 1777*, ed. William B. Willcox (New Haven, CT: Yale University Press, 1984), 571–72.]

39 This included a group portrait of the children of the comte d'Artois, the king's brother: *Les Enfants du comte et de la comtesse d'Artois*, 1781, Château de Versailles.

40 Melissa Hyde, "Femmes-Artistes and America from the Early Republic to the Gilded Age," in Yuriko Jackall, Phillippe Bordes, Jack Hinton, Melissa Hyde, Joseph H. Rishel, and Pierre Rosenberg, *America Collects Eighteenth-Century French Painting* (Washington, DC, and London: National Gallery of Art in association with Lund Humphries, 2017), 84n96.

41 Such as the *Journal des sçavans*. Hyde, "Femmes-Artistes," 84.

42 It had arrived by October 1788, the date of his letter of acknowledgement.

43 Pamela Pilbeam, *Madame Tussaud and the History of Waxworks* (New York: Hambledon and London, 2003), 29, and Pauline Chapman, *Madame Tussaud in England: Career Woman Extraordinary* (London: Quiller Press, 1992), 10.

44 A letter to the printer in the *New-York Gazette*, November 9, 1772, cited by Charles Coleman Sellers, *Patience Wright, American Artist and Spy in George III's London* (Middletown, CT: Wesleyan University Press, 1976), 52n15. See Sellers for the most complete treatment of Wright. More recent treatments include Wendy Bellion, "Patience Wright's Transatlantic Bodies," in *Shaping the Body Politic: Art and Political Formation in Early National America*, ed. Maurie McInnis and Louis Nelson (Charlottesville: University of Virginia Press, 2011); and Jennifer A. Kokai, "Molding a Heroine: Patience Wright and Transatlantic Notions of American Female Patriotism," *Journal of American Drama and Theatre* 21, no. 2 (Spring 2009): 49–66. Franklin had been working as an American representative in the British capitol for the past several years.

45 "To Benjamin Franklin from Patience Wright, 29 March 1778," *Founders Online*, National Archives, founders.archives.gov/documents/Franklin/01-26-02-0140. [Original source: *The Papers of Benjamin Franklin*, vol. 26, *March 1 through June 30, 1778*, ed. William B. Willcox (New Haven, CT: Yale University Press, 1987), 190–92.]

46 "To Benjamin Franklin from Patience Wright [after 7 March 1777]," *Founders Online*, National Archives, founders.archives.gov/documents/Franklin/01-23-02-0291. [Original source: *The Papers of Benjamin Franklin*, vol. 23, *October 27, 1776, through April 30, 1777*, ed. William B. Willcox (New Haven, CT: Yale University Press, 1983), 447–50.]

47 "To Benjamin Franklin from Patience Wright, 19 March 1783," *Founders Online*, National Archives, founders.archives.gov/documents/Franklin/01-39-02-0208. [Original source: *The Papers of Benjamin Franklin*, vol. 39, *January 21 through May 15, 1783*, ed. Ellen R. Cohn (New Haven, CT: Yale University Press, 2008), 357–58.]

48 "From George Washington to Patience Wright, 30 January 1785," *Founders Online*. [Original source: *The Papers of George Washington*, Confederation Series, vol. 2, *18 July 1784–18 May 1785*, ed. W.W. Abbot (Charlottesville: University Press of Virginia, 1992), 299–300.]

49 "To Thomas Jefferson from Patience Wright, 14 August 1785," *Founders Online*. [Original source: *The Papers of Thomas Jefferson*, vol. 8, *25 Feb.–31 Oct. 1785*, ed. Julian P. Boyd (Princeton, NJ: Princeton University Press, 1953), 380–81.] Emphasis in original.

50 No responses from Jefferson to Wright survive; yet he corresponded for decades with the Italian-born British painter Maria Cosway (1759–1838), from the 1780s (when they met in Paris) through the 1820s. The letters between Jefferson and Cosway offer a rare window into a woman artist's views on her own visual practice, and Jefferson's powerful support of this work. For one example, see "From Thomas Jefferson to Maria Cosway, 27 July 1788," *Founders Online*, National Archives, founders.archives.gov/documents/Jefferson/01-13-02-0311. [Original source: *The Papers of Thomas Jefferson*, vol. 13, *March–7 October 1788*, ed. Julian P. Boyd (Princeton, NJ: Princeton University Press, 1956), 423–24.]

51 She welcomed the Bourbon Restoration of 1815; in 1817, her final Salon showing included her *Still Life with Lobster* (cat. no. 121), advertised as already in the collection of the restored king and complete with a conspicuous fleur-de-lis—a nod to the past and present royal dynasty.

52 Auricchio, *Adélaïde Labille-Guiard*, 70.

53 The others were Alexandre de Beauharnais (Empress Josephine's first husband), Adrien Duport, Charles Maurice de Talleyrand-Périgord, the duc d'Aiguillon, Emmanuel-Armand de Richelieu (one of the first nobles to ally himself with the Third Estate), and the brothers Alexandre and Charles Lameth.

54 My translation, *Sallon de peinture de 1791*, transcribed by Neil Jeffares, "Labille-Guiard, Adélaïde," *Dictionary of pastellists before 1800*, online ed.

55 Another of her portraits may include *Mrs. Robert Eglesfeld Griffith (Maria Thong Patterson)* (cat. no. 56). All three of the Sharples's children, including their daughter Rolinda Sharples (1794–1838), pursued artistic careers.

56 Marie-Juliette Ballot, *Une Élève de David: La Comtesse Benoist, "L'Emilie de Demoustier," 1768–1826* (Paris: Plon, 1914), 270. In 1803, Jean-Antoine Gros received 3,000 francs each for portraits of Napoleon painted for the towns of Lyon, Rouen, and Lille. Other artists commissioned to paint full-length portraits of Napoleon that year included Ingres, Greuze, Lefèvre, Meynier, and Vien the younger. Margaret A. Oppenheimer, *The French Portrait: Revolution to Restoration* (Northampton, MA: Smith College of Art, 2005), 8, citing Marie-Anne Dupuy, Isabelle Le Masne de Chermont, and Elaine Williamson, eds., *Vivant Denon, Directeur des Musées sous le Consulate et l'Empire: Correspondence, 1802–1815* (Paris: RMN, 1999), 1:114, and Gary Tinterow and Philip Conisbee, eds., *Portraits by Ingres: Image of an Epoch* (New York: Metropolitan Museum of Art, 1999), 46–48.

57 O/2/847, Archives Nationales, and Césarine Davin-Mirvault to the Marquis de Lauriston, Ministre de la Maison du Roi, January 5, 1821, O/3/1391. This seems to be Benoist's *Portrait du Marechal Brune* (1805, Musée de l'Armée) and Davin-Mirvault's *Portrait de Francois-Joseph Lefebvre, Duc de Danzig, Marechal* (1807, Château de Versailles) executed for either the Salles des Marichaux or the Galerie de Diane in the Tuileries Palace (accounts conflict); see Margaret A. Oppenheimer, "Women Artists in Paris, 1791–1814" (PhD diss., New York University, 1996), 156–57, and Amy M. Fine, "'Portrait of Bruni' and Other Works by a Student of David," *Woman's Art Journal* 4, no. 1 (Spring–Summer 1983): 18.

58 Oppenheimer, *Women Artists in Paris*, 206. For Jaquotot, see Anne Lajoix, *Marie-Victoire Jaquotot, 1772–1855: Peintre sur Porcelaine* (Troyes, France: Librairie Le Trait d'Union, 2006).

59 The intended recipient, former empress Josephine, rejected the set, and it was regifted by the new empress, Marie-Louise, to a friend in 1813. In 1814, Napoleon bought another four-piece porcelain *déjeuner* by Jaquotot for his Marie-Louise, valued at 7,270 francs—"the most valuable lot" on "a list of porcelains that Napoleon and Marie-Louise chose to give as New Year's gifts in 1814." Oppenheimer, *Women Artists in Paris*, 58, citing O/2/202, Archives Nationales, Paris.

WOMEN OF THE WORLD

European Women Makers in a Global Context

Andaleeb Badiee Banta
Theresa Kutasz Christensen

It is ironic that there continues to be a commonly held assumption that at least half the population of Europe had little to no engagement with the wider world during a period of history marked by unparalleled European expansionism, colonialism, and exponential increase in the global trade of ideas, objects, and resources, namely from around 1500 to 1800. This determination that men engaged with the external world by exploring, dominating, and transacting while women stayed home to tend to family and household is reflected in the 1747 pamphlet *The Art of Governing a Wife*. Men were encouraged "to go abroad and get [their] living ... to manage all things without doors," and women were instructed "to lay up and save ... look to the house ... talk to few ... take care of all within."[1] Despite significant contemporary evidence to the contrary, this persistent dichotomous myth of exteriority versus interiority continues to colour our general understanding of this era. Even more perplexing is that, despite a pronounced turn toward a global framework in pre-modern studies,[2] European women visual artists and makers of the period continue to be overlooked or infrequently considered as active participants in international or global exchange.[3]

The majority of existing literature and scholarship on European women's creative and intellectual reach outside the home during the pre-modern era focuses on their significant contributions in the fields of literature, poetry, political dissent, science, or other nonvisual arts.[4] Travel writing, in particular, has been an area of feminist focus that explores women's increased geographic circulation and engagement with an expanding world. Scholarship has proliferated in the last decade or so in regard to a pronounced increase in the publication of women's travelogues during the eighteenth century, in addition to imagined journeys presented through literary vehicles.[5] Closely tied to this subject was a growing European settler presence, in which women participated as part of the resident expatriate communities as well as consumers and recipients of the extraction economy that encouraged and perpetuated colonial expansion within Africa, Asia, and the Americas.

Relatively less examination has been invested in the reach and reception of women's visual creations across national and continental boundaries, with only a few exceptional examples of visual artists—such as Giovanna Garzoni (1600–1670) and Maria Sibylla Merian (1647–1717)—as the subjects of detailed study.[6] Surviving works made by women in preindustrial Europe indicate the rich and complex relationships they developed between the domestic and worldly spheres, complicating the dominant narrative that women were relegated to an impermeable domestic bubble or that they were only on the receiving end of marvels and materials coming from abroad. Moreover, diverse catalysts—from architectural trends to the changing geopolitical landscape of Europe—during this era impacted women's mobility and individual freedoms, further challenging the notion of separately gendered public and private spheres.[7] A general review of the numerous and often less straightforward ways that women's artistic accomplishments reflected and inflected their engagement with the broader world is missing from the robust scholarship currently being produced on early modern global material culture.[8] In light of these factors, we propose reframing the question to investigate the many different international paths that women artists actively sought or that were made available to them during this period—either as a lived experience centred on travel or as a virtual one, translated through the objects they made and acquired for their homes and produced for others. It is our hope that this brief overview—limited in scope though it must be—will provide intriguing examples of women's direct and virtual encounters with the wider world in their creative practices, and stimulate further investigations into the topic.

This essay addresses the question of how visually creative women of the past engaged with the broader world in two primary ways. First, we look at the experiences of women makers who were able to travel. Extended travel was overwhelmingly understood as a male activity during this period; women who travelled risked their safety, their virtue, and their established, located identity. Despite this gendered dimension to travel, there are standout examples of women artists who voyaged far and often alone, building international reputations. Second, we examine how the global turn was manifested in the work that women produced in their own spaces without having experienced extensive travel. For most women charged with running a household, that environment was their primary locus of identity-building and exploration, but it was also one increasingly filled with access to so-called "exotic" materials, plants, patterns, and flavours. Although many women across socioeconomic boundaries were unable to directly experience travel, they instead received virtual interpretations of foreign lands through the performing, literary, and visual arts, as well as through traded goods that provoked, inspired, and informed creative productions for their personal worlds and their local communities.

Making Her Mark Abroad

Women makers gained access to broader arenas and accomplished recognition beyond their local spheres in many ways. For women born into artistic families, or into families that supported or promoted their creative accomplishment in a professional capacity, their opportunities to engage with a wider range of worldly perspectives were perhaps easier to come by than for their less-well-connected counterparts. This degree of access was necessarily affected by the social class into which these women were born. Those in the social strata above the lower working class could choose to provide for their daughters an education that might include advanced literacy, basic arithmetic, and training in socially determined gender-appropriate pursuits such as music, drawing, and embroidery; some were fortunate to receive further education in fundamental humanistic subjects, such as rhetoric, poetry, philosophy, and foreign languages.[9] It is also significant that this period witnessed intensive and changing debates about the education of girls and women, which increasingly included knowledge about geography, trade routes, and political borders.[10]

Within the professional artistic world, perhaps the most accessible paths toward mobility available to aspiring daughters of established artists were the connections they could pursue through their family's acquaintances and colleagues. We know of several instances where fathers' professional contacts contributed to the promotion of their daughters' artistic education or reputation. In 1521, the Netherlandish miniature painter Susanna Horenbout (c. 1500–c. 1554) reportedly sold one of her drawings to the great German polymath artist Albrecht Dürer when he came to visit her father in Ghent, where the family had a thriving workshop patronized by Margaret of Austria (1480–1530).[11] Although not an artist, Amilcare Anguissola used his status as a minor Cremonese noble to ensure that his daughter Sofonisba Anguissola (c. 1535–1625) would receive proper training from prominent local artists, pursuing an epistolary relationship with significant cultural figures, including Michelangelo Buonarroti, as a means to promote his daughter's work.[12] Efforts to secure a daughter's artistic education outside the home was not without its perils. This is evidenced by the traumatic violation of Artemisia Gentileschi (1593–after 1654) by her teacher and father's colleague Agostino Tassi; the possibility of such an event surely contributed to female artists-in-training remaining in the family home workshop to a greater degree than their male counterparts—and thus potentially missing opportunities for self-promotion and wider recognition.[13] Mothers also played a role—still not widely explored in scholarship—in promoting their daughter's work. We know from letters belonging to the lauded eighteenth-century pastellist Rosalba Carriera (1673–1757) that her mother, Alba Foresti, herself talented in the arts of lacemaking and

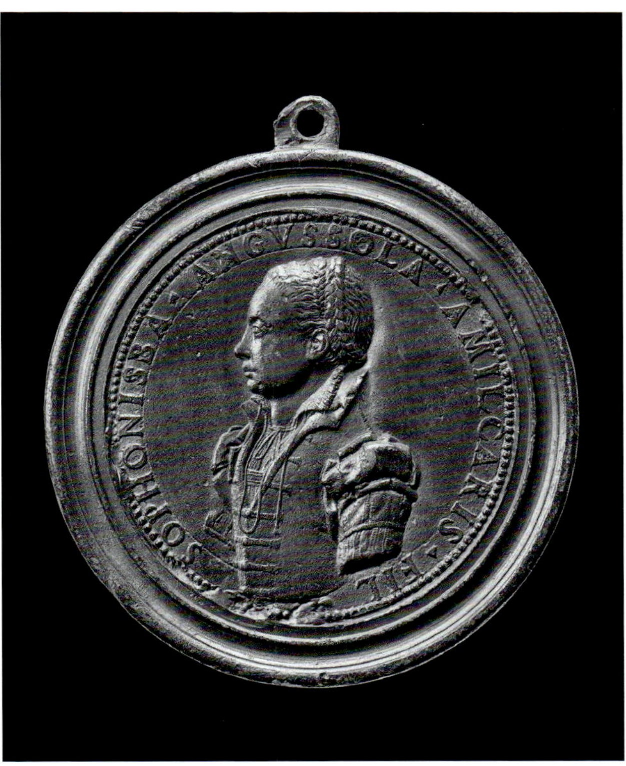

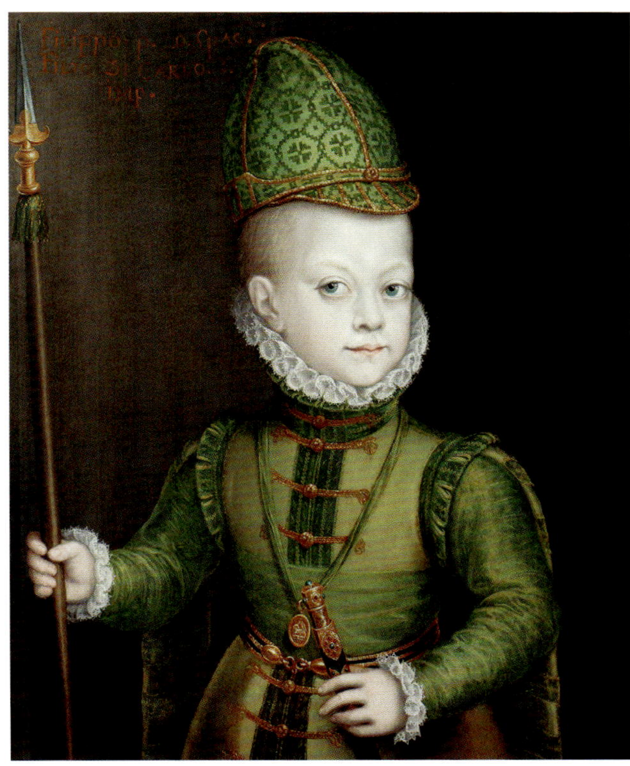

Fig. 1 (left) · Unknown maker, *Bust of Sofonisba Anguissola facing left, wearing a gown, a chemise, and braided hair*, 1559. Cast lead medal, inserted into lead frame, diameter: 8.7 cm, 81.5 g. British Museum, Purchased from: Christie's (presented by Sir George Hill), 1925, inv. no. 1925,0310.44. Image: © The Trustees of the British Museum.

Fig. 2 (right) · Sofonisba Anguissola, *Portrait of a Spanish Prince*, c. 1573. Oil on canvas, 59.1 × 48.3 cm. San Diego Museum of Art: Gift of Anne R. and Amy Putnam, inv. no. 1936.58.

embroidery, actively promoted her daughter's artistic abilities to potential clients through the exchange of gifts and letters, and hosted receptions in their home and abroad.[14] The international reputation of painter and illustrator Maria Louisa Catherine Cecilia Cosway (1759–1838) was due in large part to her mother's decision to relocate the family to London, in 1779 after her husband's death, in order to give Maria access to the opportunities available in that cosmopolitan centre.[15] There, the young artist met Swiss history painter and portraitist Angelica Kauffmann (1741–1807), who encouraged Cosway's artistic production and participation in Royal Academy exhibitions.

For women artists who had the opportunity and desire to become professional painters operating at the highest echelons of patronage—at royal courts or for the church—their careers often depended on their ability and willingness to travel.[16] Having a male family member to forge the path abroad was particularly useful, as in the case of Horenbout's relocation with her father and brothers to the English Tudor court, where she found favour as a manuscript illuminator under Henry VIII.[17] In the case of Anguissola, her family's aristocratic status facilitated her acquisition of skills that would earn her a position as a lady-in-waiting to Queen Isabel de Valois (1545–1568) at the Spanish Hapsburg court, an appointment commemorated with a medal of her likeness struck in 1559 (fig. 1).[18] She arrived in Spain at the apex of her career, living there for fourteen years and producing portraits of the royal family—such as the striking presentation of a young Spanish prince, possibly Prince Don Fernando (fig. 2; cat. no. 103)—until her marriage to a Genoese nobleman and departure from court in 1573.[19] About a century later, the Spanish sculptor Luisa Roldán (1652–1706), having already established herself in Seville and Cádiz as a preeminent designer of devotional polychrome wood-and-terracotta sculptures (fig. 3; cat. nos. 195–197), relocated to Madrid to serve the Hapsburg court (fig. 4) for the second half of her career.[20]

Royal and noble courts throughout the principalities of early modern Europe not only offered financial support and professional validation for

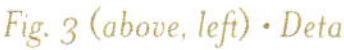

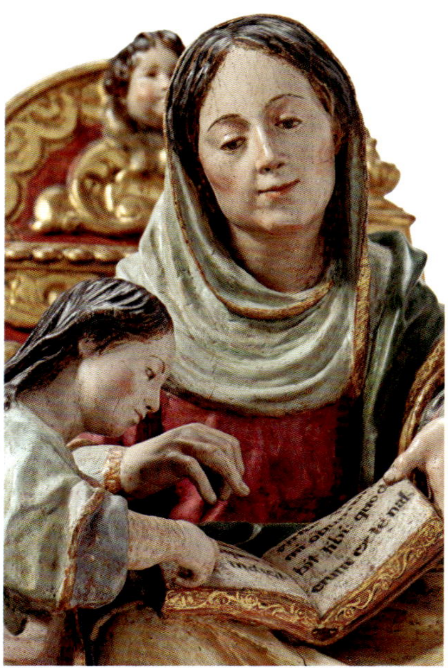

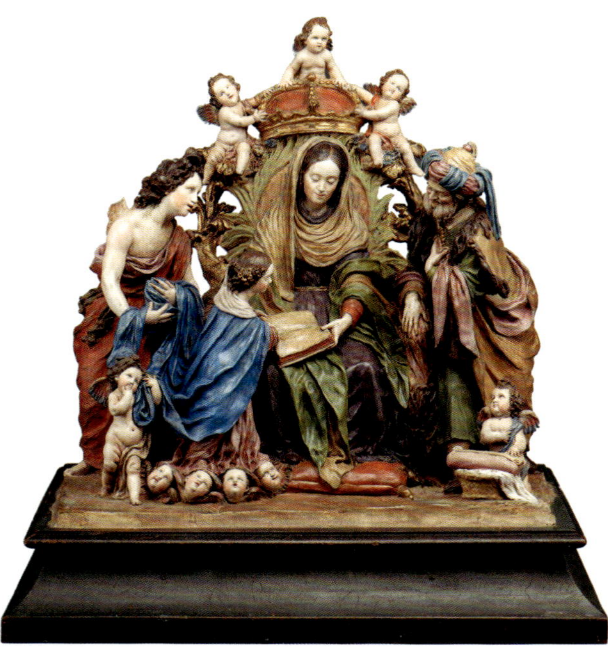

Fig. 3 (above, left) • *Detail:* Luisa Roldán, *The Education of the Virgin*, 1680s. Polychrome paint and wood, 76 × 63 × 43 cm. Los Angeles County Museum of Art, Gift of the 2019 Collectors Committee with additional funds from Linda Borick and Bill Davidson on behalf of the Louis L. Borick Foundation, inv. no. M.2019.235.

Fig. 4 (above, right) • Luisa Roldán, *Education of the Virgin*, 1689–1706. Polychrome terracotta, 43 × 45 × 36 cm. Blanton Museum of Art, The University of Texas at Austin, The Suida-Manning Collection, 2017, inv. no. 2017.1346.

an artist, they also provided access to intellectual developments, clientele, and objects from around the world. The accomplished seventeenth-century still-life painter, portraitist, and natural history illustrator Giovanna Garzoni began her career in the cosmopolitan international port city of Venice and subsequently worked at the courts in Florence, Turin, Naples, Paris, and London. Her circulation through these courts provided her the opportunity to meet fellow artists, such as Jacopo Ligozzi, Artemisia Gentileschi, Anna Maria Vaiani (active c. 1627–died c. 1655), Stefano della Bella, needle-artist Arcangela Paladini (1599–1622), and possibly the still-life painter Louise Moillon (c. 1610–c. 1696). It also afforded her access to courtly collections of artistic and natural examples from around the world.[21] The Medici court, which Garzoni visited between 1618 and 1621 and again from 1642 to 1651, had long been a repository for exotic plant specimens, objects from Spanish colonies in Central and South America, and porcelain from China, examples of which appear in Garzoni's still lifes.[22] Rome was the stage for Garzoni's engagement with the famed collector and naturalist Cassiano dal Pozzo, who likely introduced her to the community of the Accademia dei Lincei—famed for its scientific investigations—and ultimately informed her pursuit of botanical illustrations of native and exotic plants, such as those found in her *Piante varie* manuscript (fig. 5; cat. no. 156).[23] While at the Savoy court in Turin, Garzoni painted a miniature portrait of the African visitor Zaga Christ, who claimed ties to the Ethiopian throne, shown wearing an impressive collar of Venetian needle lace (fig. 6).[24] Likely commissioned by either the Duke of Savoy or by the sitter himself in 1635,

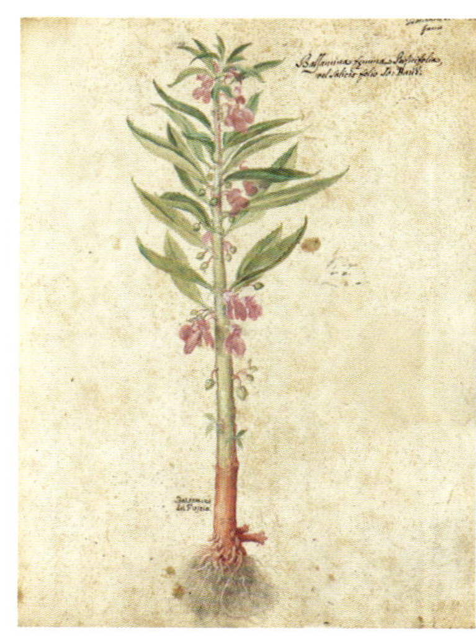

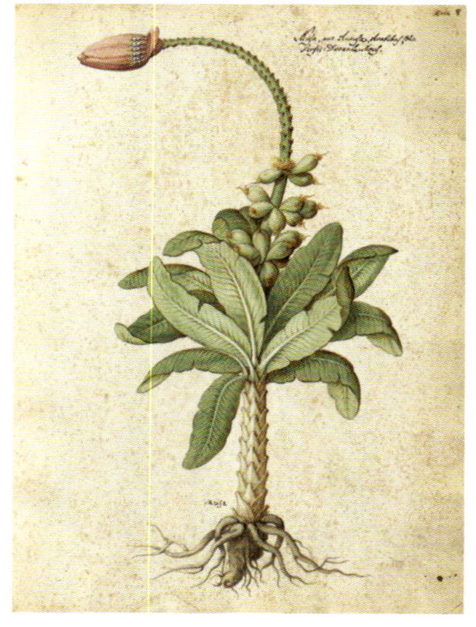

Fig. 5 (below) • Giovanna Garzoni, *Piante varie*, c. 1630–1632. Watercolour on paper, 49.5 × 38 cm. Dumbarton Oaks Research Library and Collection, Trustees for Harvard University, Washington, DC, inv. no. G-3-3.

Openings illustrated (left to right):

Fig. 5a • *Impatiens balsamina* (folio 22)

Fig. 5b • *Musa* (folio 8)

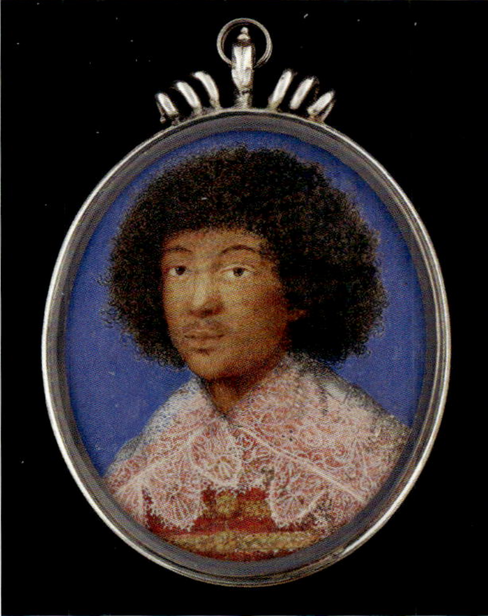

Fig. 6 • Giovanna Garzoni, *Portrait of Zaga Christ [Ṣägga Krastos]*, 1635. Watercolour and opaque watercolour on vellum mounted on card; silver frame is later, oval: 5.7 × 4.8 cm; framed: 7.1 × 5.2 × 0.5 cm. Allen Memorial Art Museum, Oberlin College, Oberlin, Ohio, Museum Friends Fund, inv. no. 2021.21. Image: Philip Mould & Company.

this may be the earliest European portrait miniature to depict a named African individual.

Associations with royal courts, however, could prove to be a double-edged sword. For Elisabeth Louise Vigée-LeBrun (1755–1842), her close connection with the French court of Marie Antoinette (r. 1774–1792) resulted in her rushed relocation out of Paris in 1789 to avoid revolutionaries. This departure started her on a twelve-year peripatetic career, visiting other royal and noble courts throughout Europe, including Florence, Naples, Vienna, St. Petersburg, and Berlin, and building an international reputation as a portraitist (cat. nos. 37, 108–110). Similarly mobile was Angelica Kauffmann, the daughter of a court painter to the Prince-Bishop of Chur, who received an education in music and painting, areas she excelled at so much that her father toured her around the courts of Northern Italy to perform for princes in a manner not dissimilar to Mozart's earliest years.[25] Her repeated exposure to classical sources and sites in Italy informed and shaped the neoclassical aesthetic for which she would become best known (cat. nos. 82 & 91).[26] Her professional identity was amplified by her international status so much so that several national schools claim her as their member, particularly the British, for whose Royal Academy of Arts she was a founding member.

The age of the Grand Tour, from the mid-seventeenth century through the end of the eighteenth, saw a significant circulation of people and artistic goods around the European continent, as visitors—primarily English gentry—sought to improve their education and erudition by taking in the marvels of the Italian peninsula. Despite the majority of travellers on the Grand Tour circuit being elite men, this increased exchange resulted in meaningful encounters for women. The tour exposed travelling women artists to historic sites, art collections of antique and exotic objects, and other women travellers. Vigée-LeBrun's encounters near Naples with the actress and model Emma Hart (Lady Hamilton) (1765–1815) resulted in her depiction of several of the lady's classical poses or "attitudes," including a portrait of the Englishwoman as a bacchante, posed before Mount Vesuvius (fig. 7), reflecting the act of experiencing classical and contemporary Italy that occurred during the Grand Tour itself.[27] Katharine Read (1723–1778), a Scottish portraitist who gained significant notoriety in her lifetime, travelled to Paris, Rome, Florence, and Venice before returning to London, where she established a studio.[28] While in Rome, a letter to her brother refers to her completion of a painting depicting a group of

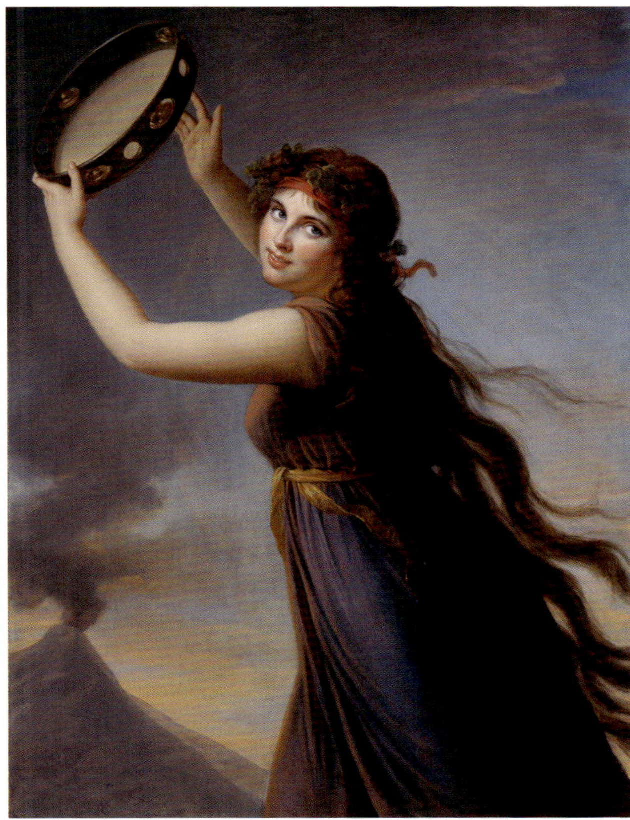

Fig. 7 • Elisabeth Louise Vigée-LeBrun, *Lady Hamilton as a Bacchante*, c. 1790–1792. Oil on canvas, 132.5 × 105.5 cm. National Museums Liverpool, Lady Lever Art Gallery, Purchased by William Hesketh Lever for the Lady Lever Art Gallery in 1903, inv. no. LL 3527.

male tourists at the ancient ruins in 1751, ostensibly the conversation piece now in the Yale Center for British Art's collection (fig. 8; cat. no. 107).[29] During her travels, Read found patrons in other British visitors as well as Italian aristocrats and ecclesiastics, and made connections with fellow artists, as documented in her visit with Rosalba Carriera, by then blind and of advanced age.[30] Angelica Kauffmann hosted one of the most important Salons in Rome, attended by leading literati, antiquarians, connoisseurs, and artists. The poet and author Giovanni Gherardo De Rossi, a regular attendee, referred to it as a "temple of female glory," noting that it was a particularly hospitable environment for women engaged in the literary and visual arts.[31]

Travel around the continent was not the only means of international exposure for European women artists and makers. Although exchange and encounters between the continents of Asia, Africa, and Europe existed since antiquity, opportunities to engage with people, plants, animals, goods, and ideas from the world beyond Europe proliferated at an unforeseen rate once trade routes incorporated the Atlantic World during the age of European exploration. Travel pathways between heretofore largely unconnected areas of the world were established or deepened through motivations of curiosity, conquest, and profit, creating a global dynamic that increasingly affected all parts of the world in complex and enduring ways.[32] These exchanges did not exclude women: some were active and willing participants, while others—whose stories remain understudied or were never recorded—were relocated forcibly or without consultation. Typically, only those creative women with economic means and specific personal circumstances were able to travel outside Europe during this period; the visual records they made during their travels provide a glimpse of their role within Europe's engagement with the Americas, Africa, and Asia. The bravery of these women to undertake adventurous and potentially perilous journeys is impressive but is nevertheless couched within a colonialist dynamic that must be considered part and parcel of their achievements.

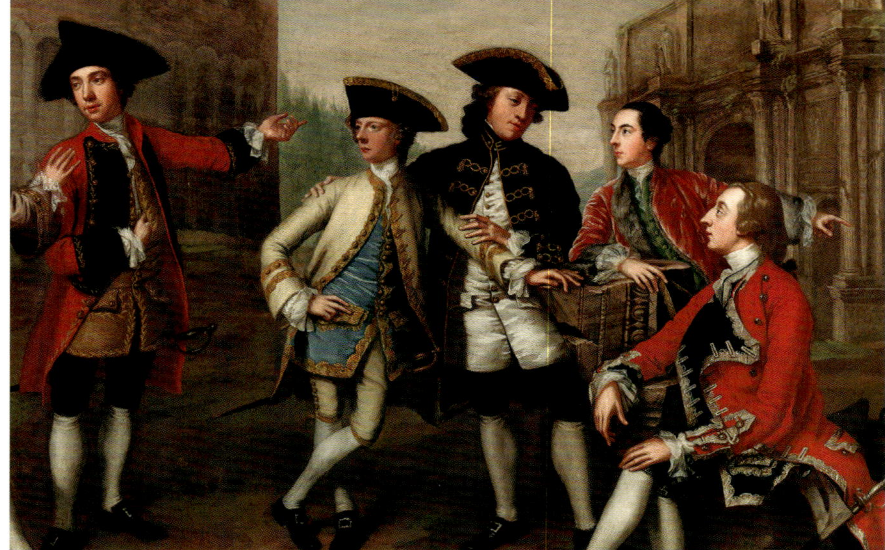

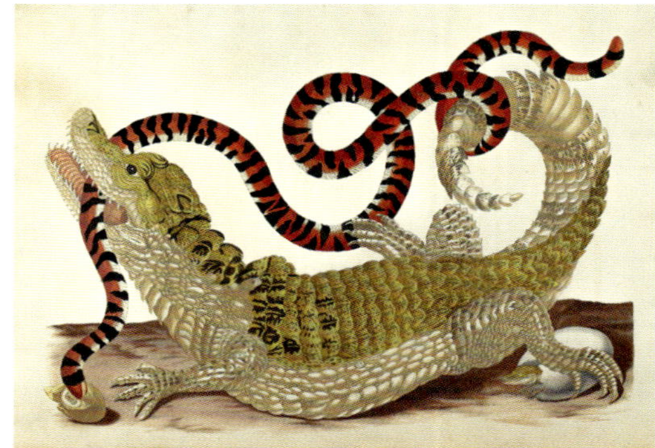

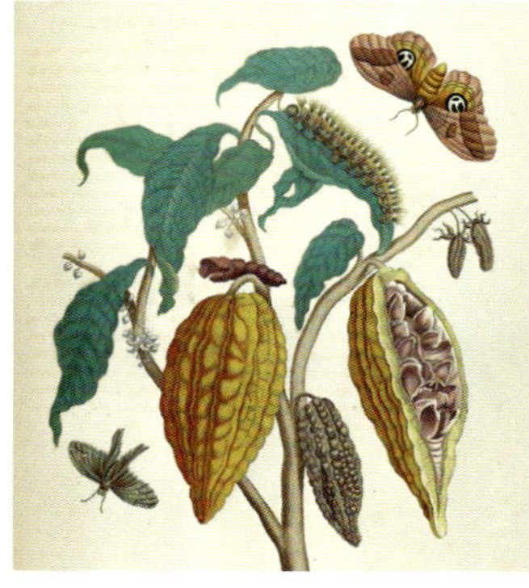

Perhaps best known among the women artists who had agency over their travels is the German-born natural illustrator Maria Sibylla Merian, who voyaged with her daughter Dorothea Maria Merian Graff (1678–1743) to Suriname in 1699, then under Dutch control. Although the marvellous and influential studies of native plant and insect life that she later published resulted in significant contributions to the Western history of entomology, botany, and natural history illustration (fig. 9; cat. no. 153), they conveyed little of the realities of Dutch brutality to the people under their subjugation.[33] While no evidence currently indicates that Merian herself owned enslaved people, she nevertheless benefitted from this dynamic, as she used enslaved African and Indigenous women as guides during her visit: "Because the forest is so densely grown with thistles and thorns, I had to send my slaves ahead of me with axes to hack out an opening for me, to get through it all, which was still very troublesome."[34] These women's knowledge of local plants and their medicinal uses is also conveyed through Merian's commentary

Fig. 8 (above) · *Detail:* Attributed to Katharine Read, *British Gentlemen in Rome*, c. 1750. Oil on canvas, 94.6 × 134.6 cm. Yale Center for British Art, Paul Mellon Collection, inv. no. B1981.25.272. Image Courtesy YCBA.

Fig. 9 (below) · *Details:* Maria Sibylla Merian, *Dissertatio de Generatione et Metamorphosibus Insectorum Surinamensium...* [*Metamorphosis of the Insects of Suriname*], Amsterdam, 1719. Bound volume of hand-coloured engravings, 54 × 38.1 × 4.8 cm. Oak Spring Garden Foundation, Upperville, Virginia.

Openings illustrated (left to right):

Fig. 9a · *Common or Spectacled Caiman with South American False Coral Snake*

Fig. 9b · *Cocoa Tree with Southern Armyworm Moth*

on the individual entries in her published text within *Metamorphosis Insectorum Surinamensium* (1705). In one instance, she references the plant *Flos pavonis* that Indigenous women used to induce abortions when they became pregnant while enslaved.[35] In many ways, Merian's expedition reflected the colonialist, specimen-collecting practices of her male contemporaries such as Hans Sloane and later James Cook. Her resulting publication created a scientific iteration of the long-standing tradition of prioritizing the concept of the "marvel" or "wonder" that framed encounters with the unfamiliar throughout the early modern age of exploration.[36] That these observations and their highly aesthetic interpretations were published by a woman made their acceptance in her lifetime by the prevailing male-dominated scientific community all the more remarkable.[37] It is also worth noting that Merian's decision to travel to Suriname was motivated by scientific curiosity as much as it was by entrepreneurial factors. She intended to transform her carefully rendered observations into a lavishly produced publication—as she had done with her earlier ventures *Blumenbuch* (1675–1680) and *Der Raupen* (1679–1683, cat. no. 168)—that would provide income to cover her travel costs.[38]

Financial factors doubtlessly played a role in women artists' decision to move to non-European locales, where colonial communities represented a rich potential market. For the unmarried and independent Katharine Read, the decline in the popularity for her pastel and painted portraits in London may have precipitated her choice to join her niece Helena Beatson in sailing to Madras in 1777, where Read's brother William and nephew Alexander had posts with the East India Company.[39] Despite receiving positive attention for her work from the provincial governor, Read's time in India was cut short by declining health; she returned with her brother by ship in 1778 and died during the journey home. The expatriate colonial community in India also attracted the miniaturist Diana Dietz Hill (c. 1760–1844), who needed to support her two children following her husband's death. Upon her arrival in 1786, her brother-in-law John Hill helped her secure clients among Calcutta's colonial ruling society. Surviving miniatures by her indicate that she had access to members of the British military stationed in India (fig. 10) as well as to their wives and daughters (fig. 11).[40] Her success as a portraitist there was such that fellow miniaturist Ozias Humphry expressed professional jealousy at what he perceived as her special status as a young widowed woman painter.[41] She continued to paint until her second marriage in 1788 and remained in India until 1806. Read's and Hill's talents as pastel and miniature portraitists may have been especially suited to the situation among the British elite in India; small, portable works that could be sent to loved ones

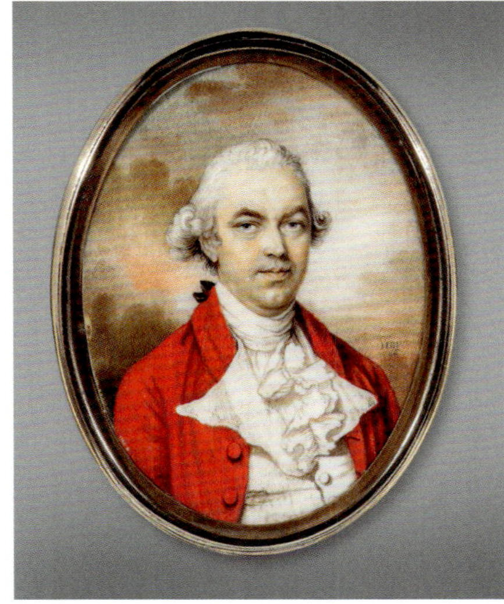

Fig. 10 (left) • Diana Dietz Hill, *Charles Cornwallis, 1st Marquess Cornwallis*, 1786. Watercolour on ivory, lacquered copper alloy, and glass, 10.5 × 8.3 × 0.5 cm. Courtesy of Mount Vernon Ladies' Association, Gift of Katherine Merle-Smith Thomas, 2010 Conservation courtesy of The Founders, Washington Committee Endowment Fund, inv. no. H-4912. Photo: Gavin Ashworth.

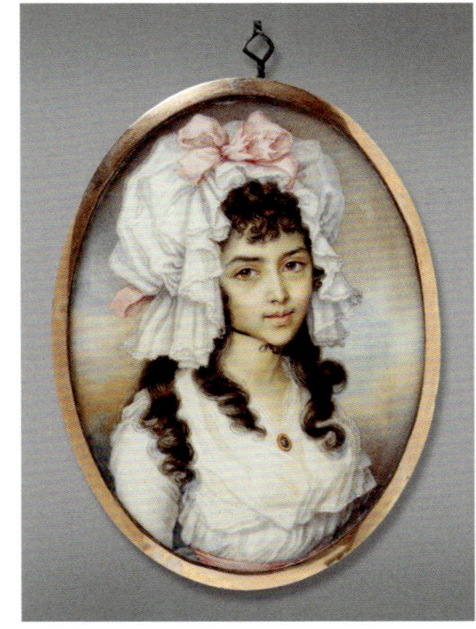

Fig. 11 (middle) • Diana Dietz Hill, *An unknown girl*, c. 1785–1790. Watercolour on ivory, 9.2 × 7 cm. Victoria and Albert Museum, London, inv. no. P.139-1929. Image © Victoria and Albert Museum, London.

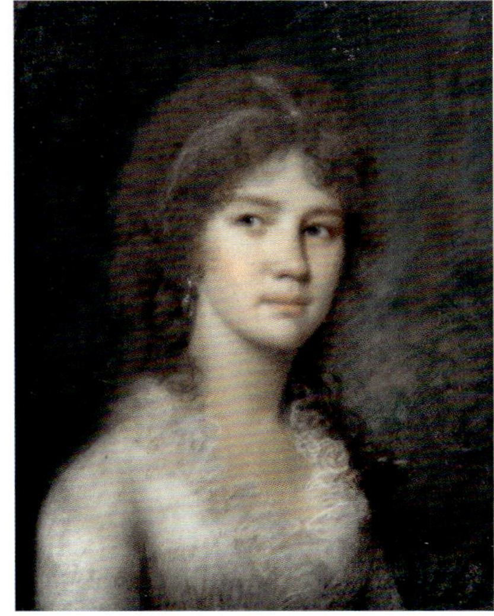

Fig. 12 (right) • Attributed to Ellen Sharples, *Mrs. Robert Eglesfeld Griffith (Maria Thong Patterson)*, c. 1793–1797. Pastel on brown paper, 21.6 × 17.2 cm. Baltimore Museum of Art: Purchase with exchange funds from Gift of Edgar William and Bernice Chrysler Garbisch, Gift of Mrs. C. Oliver Iselin, Gift of Blanchard Randall, and Gift of Andrew Speir; and W. Clagett Emory Bequest Fund, in Memory of his Parents, William H. Emory of A and Martha B. Emory, 1986.117. Photo: Mitro Hood.

back home had a certain niche market in the expatriate circle. In the newly established United States, the recently emigrated British pastellist Ellen Sharples (1769–1849) and her husband, James, developed an itinerant family art business, providing portraits in oil and pastel, such as *Maria Thong Patterson* (fig. 12; cat. no. 56), to a growing clientele in burgeoning cities like New York, Philadelphia, and Washington, DC, until their return to England in 1801.[42]

Whether motivated by fame, family, or finances, European women artists had greater mobility than often recognized. While we have seen that many diverse circumstances instigated their travel, not all women artists had the necessary connections, opportunities, or desire to leave home. Likely a far more common situation was that they navigated channels of access that brought the world to them, or the works they produced travelled in their stead.

Making Her Mark from Home

Even if women never left their home territories, their creativity had an enduring effect on artistic production throughout the global trade network, from religious sculpture and texts to furniture, silverwork, and garments. Not surprisingly, prints provided a ready conduit for the distribution of compositional and iconographic models around and beyond the European continent. Significant scholarship has focused on the circulation of European prints as a source—at times indirect but pervasive all the same—for imagery that developed as part of the colonial expansion of Spain and Portugal into the Americas and Asia.[43] To date, however, there has been no sustained consideration of the role that prints executed by women might have played in this global dynamic. Some illustrative examples are offered here in the hope that it stimulates further research.[44]

The widespread use of prints in the Catholic Church's conversion program is well documented, but less so is the implication of women's devotional graphic imagery in the development of religious art within a colonial setting. *The Savior Seated on a Heart* (fig. 13; cat. no. 134) by Diana Mantuana (c. 1547–1612)—an image considered by many scholars to be a reproduction of Flemish printmaker Thomas de Leu's undated contemporary engraving of the same subject—illustrates the layered global trajectory that characterized the circulation of prints by women engravers. Certain details diverge from de Leu's version and argue for Mantuana's creative intervention, namely the ring of clouds and the wooden logs beneath the flames.[45] These same details appear in another version of this subject on the title page of a Spanish translation of the devotional treatise *Legatus Divinae Pietatis* [*Herald of Divine Love*] by Saint Gertrude of

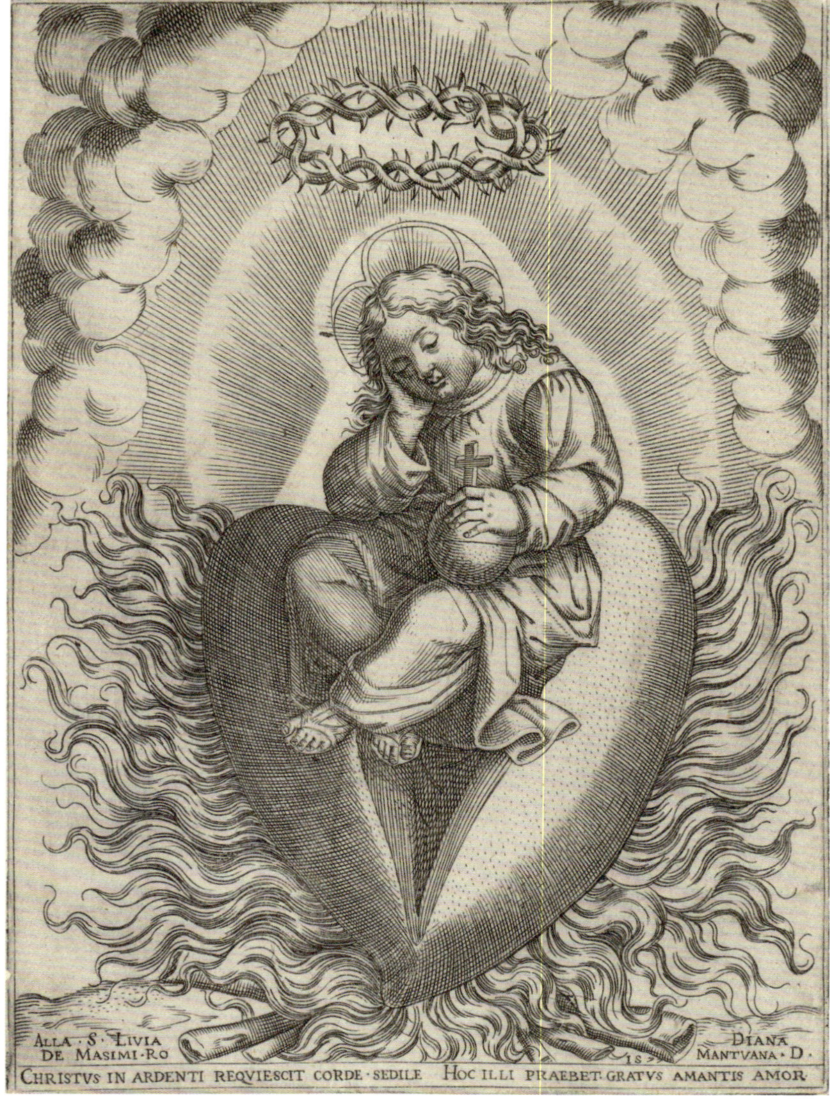

Fig. 13 (above) · Diana Mantuana, *The Savior Seated on a Heart*, 1577. Engraving, 18.5 × 13.8 cm. Baltimore Museum of Art: Garrett Collection, 1946.112.4636. Photo: Mitro Hood.

Fig. 14 (facing, above, left) · Unknown Brazilian maker, *The Christ Child Jesus as The Good Shepherd slumbering on a heart*, 17th century. Ivory, 34 × 11 × 6 cm. The Sacred Art Museum of the Federal University of Bahia (MAS-UFBA Museu de Arte Sacra, Universidade Federal da Bahia), inv. no. M-650. Photo: Sergio Benutti.

Fig. 15 (facing, above, right) · Detail: Unknown Filipino maker, *The Christ Child sleeping on a heart*, 1587–1604. Relief on wood. Museo de San Agustin (Convent Museum), Manila, Philippines.

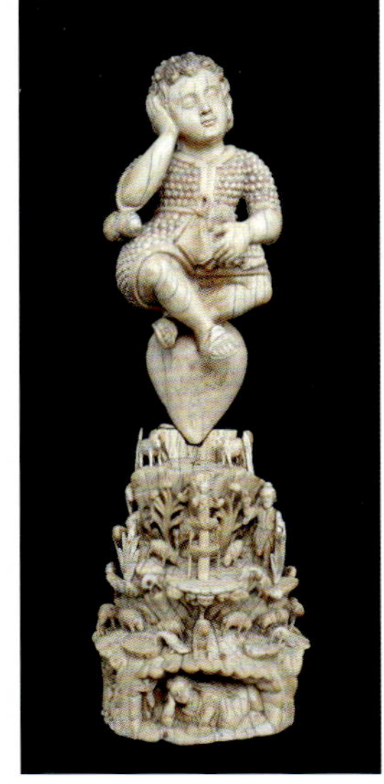

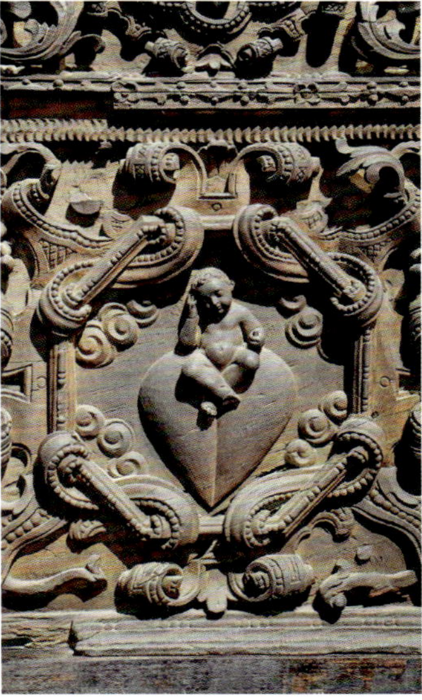

Below (left to right)

Fig. 16 • Detail: Magdalena van de Passe, after Maarten de Vos, *The Lighthouse of Alexandria*, from the series *The Seven Wonders of the World*, 1614. Engraving, sheet: 24.1 × 28.6 cm; plate: 21.7 × 25.5 cm; image: 19.1 × 25 cm. Baltimore Museum of Art: Garrett Collection, 1946.112.4036. Photo: Mitro Hood.

Fig. 17 • Unknown Cuzco School maker, *A builder takes instructions from King Ptolemy [Le Phare de Messine]*, from the series *The Seven Wonders of the Ancient World*, 17th or 18th century. Oil on canvas, dimensions unknown. Formerly Christie's, Lot 67b, Sale 7676 (May 18, 1993). Present location unknown, likely a private collection.

Fig. 18 • Detail: Magdalena van de Passe, after Maarten de Vos, *The Pyramids of Egypt*, from the series *The Seven Wonders of the World*, 1614. Engraving, sheet: 24.3 × 28.5 cm; plate: 21.2 × 25 cm; image: 18.7 × 24.3 cm. Baltimore Museum of Art: Garrett Collection, 1946.112.4037. Photo: Mitro Hood.

Fig. 19 • Unknown Cuzco School maker, *King Khufu admires the Pyramid of Giza [Les Pyramides d'Egypte]*, from the series *The Seven Wonders of the Ancient World*, 17th or 18th century. Oil on canvas, dimensions unknown. Formerly Christie's, Lot 67c, Sale 7676 (May 18, 1993). Present location unknown, likely a private collection.

Helfta (1256–1302), published in Salamanca in 1603, suggesting that Mantuana's image, rather than that of de Leu, served as its pictorial model. This connection is further supported by the inscription of "Rome" in the Spanish frontispiece image, as Mantuana published her print while in the papal city. Having made its way from Rome to Spain, Mantuana's engraved model seems to have continued its journey, inspiring numerous sculptural interpretations of the subject of the sleeping Christ Child *(Niño Dormido)* by artists active in Spanish and Portuguese colonial centres from Peru and Brazil to Goa and Manila (figs. 14 & 15).[46]

Similarly, engravings by Magdalena van de Passe (1600–1638) of the *Libyan Sibyl*, translated in reverse by the French engraver Élie Dubois,[47] and her scenes of *The Lighthouse of Alexandria* and *The Pyramids of Egypt* from the series *The Seven Wonders of the World* (figs. 16 & 18), re-engraved by Jacques Picart, served as models for colonial visual production. The scenes from the *Seven Wonders* inspired a series of paintings of the same subject by the Cuzco School (figs. 17 & 19).[48] Picart's translation of van de Passe's *Sibyl* appears to have informed at least two examples of late-eighteenth-century imagery found in churches in Diamantina within the region of Minas Gerais, Brazil—then the largest centre of diamond mining and production in the Western Hemisphere.[49] The propagandistic engraving of *The Eucharistic Mission of the Habsburgs*, created in 1640 by Maria Eugenia de Beer (died c. 1562) as the title-page image for a Jesuit publication on the sacrament in Madrid, appears transformed with a pronounced papal distinction in a text translated from Spanish to Guarani for the purpose of propagating the mission of the Society of Jesus in Paraguay.[50] While connections between images engraved by these female printmakers and the resulting versions they inspired do not always offer a direct correlation, they point to the global circulation and reception of their art and inspire further questions about the reach of European women artists of the pre-modern era.

Prints after women's painted works also facilitated their translation into the visual lexicon of the early American context. Angelica Kauffmann's international fame was perpetuated both by prints she made after her painted compositions and by reproductive prints made by others. These same graphic interpretations of her paintings found their way to the British colonies in North America and became a mainstay of women's

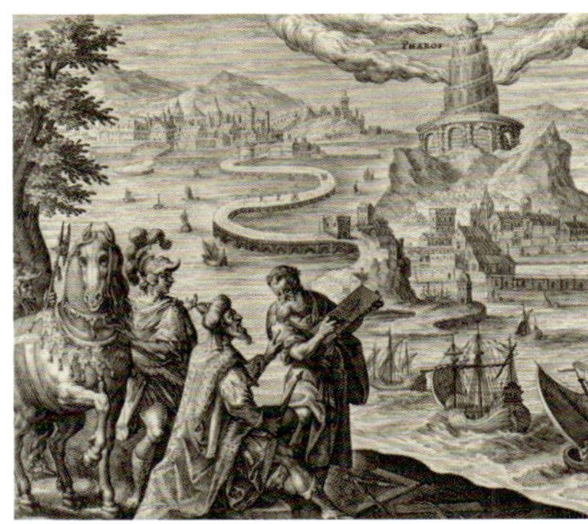

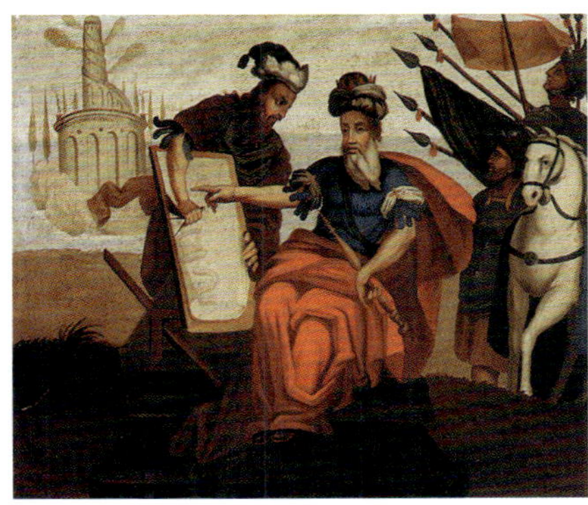

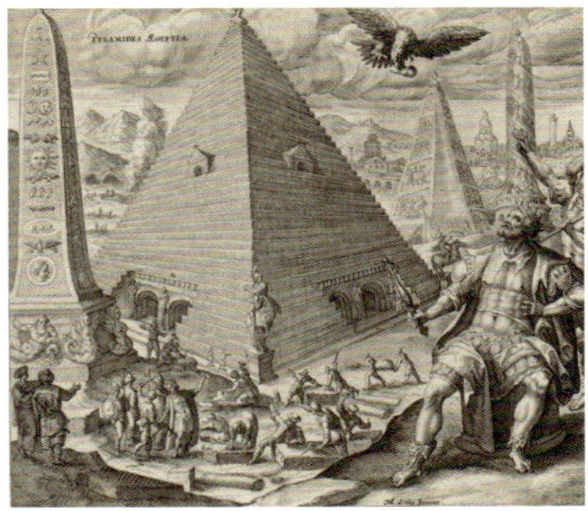

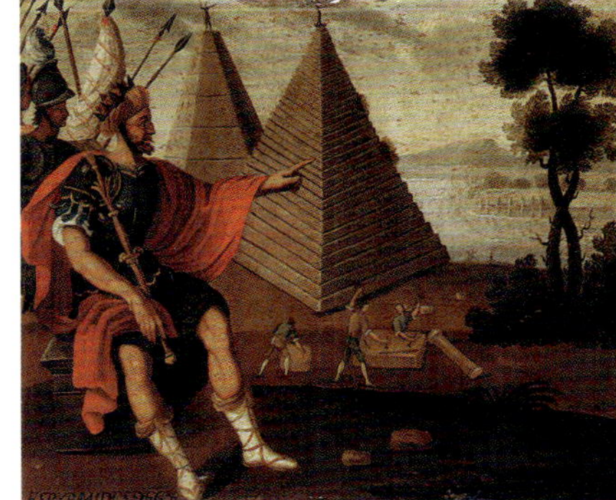

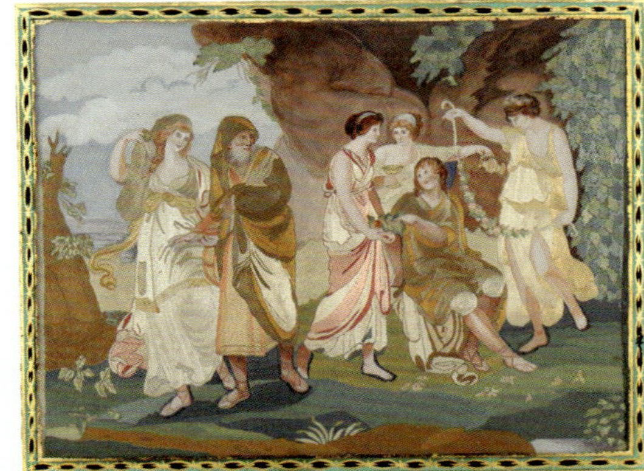

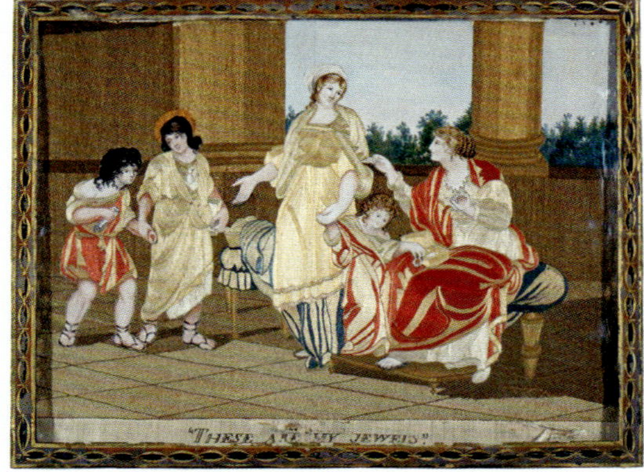

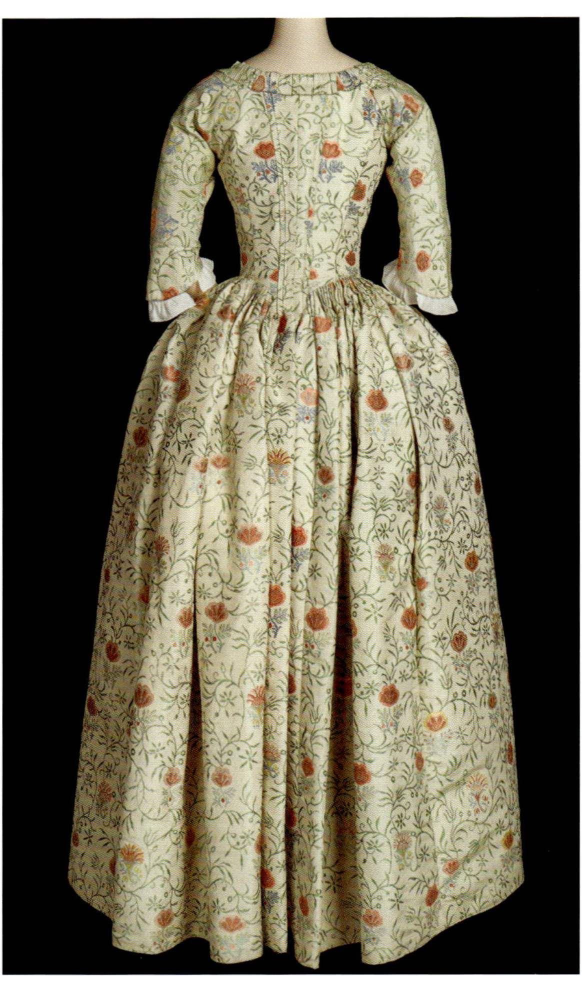

Fig. 20 (above, left) • Frances Mecia Campbell, after Angelica Kauffmann, *Telemachus and Mentor in the Island of Calipso*, 1807. Silk ground, silk embroidery threads, and watercolour, 45.7 × 52.1 cm. Baltimore Museum of Art: Purchase with exchange funds from Gift of Mr. and Mrs. James R. Herbert Boone; Gift of Maria Lovell Eaton and Mrs. Charles R. Weld; Gift of J. Gilman D'Arcy Paul; Bequest of John Henry Scarff; Gift of Florence Hendler Trupp; and Gift of the Women's Eastern Shore Society, 1989.352. Photo: Mitro Hood.

Fig. 21 (below, left) • Lydia Bowles Austin, after Angelica Kauffmann, *These Are My Jewels*, c. 1803–1824. Silk, 26.7 × 39.1 cm. National Museum of American History, Smithsonian Institution, Gift of Mrs. Robert B. Stephens, inv. no. 1996.0125. Photo: Division of Home and Community Life, National Museum of American History, Smithsonian Institution.

Fig. 22 (right) • *Back view:* Anna Maria Garthwaite, *Gown*, 1726–1728 (textile); 1775–1785 (gown). Silk "lampas" brocaded with silk; linen bodice and sleeve lining, length: 137.2 cm, waist: 55.9 cm, textile width: 53.3 cm, vertical repeat: 45.7 cm. Courtesy of The Colonial Williamsburg Foundation, Museum Purchase, accession #1951-150,1.

education in embroidery during the first decades of the newly established United States. Several of Kauffmann's paintings of subjects inspired by Greco-Roman antiquity, such as *Telemachus and the Nymphs of Calypso* (1782, Metropolitan Museum of Art) and *Cornelia, Mother of the Gracchi, Pointing to Her Children as Her Treasures* (c. 1785, Virginia Museum of Fine Arts) were rendered in stipple etching by Francesco Bartolozzi in the 1780s and printed by London publishers.[51] These prints after Kauffmann's paintings in turn served as models for silk embroidered pictures made at Mrs. Saunders and Miss Beach's Academy in Dorchester, Massachusetts, in the early 1800s (figs. 20 & 21). The moralizing subjects, neoclassical style, and artist's gender all likely contributed to the selection of Kauffmann's works as models for young women growing up in early America.[52]

Textiles, like prints, could travel with relative ease, resulting in the perpetuation of European designs within the context of a colonial setting. The prevalence of British culture in the North American colonies meant that many early American homes exhibited aspects of English decor and fashion. Garments made from silk patterns designed by Anna Maria Garthwaite (1688–1763), a prolific Spitalfields designer who specialized in floral patterns based on botanical species from both Europe and Asia, enjoyed significant popularity in the American colonies (fig. 22; cat. no. 223). Surviving portraits of American-born colonialists wearing Garthwaite silk designs speak to a complex narrative of creativity, knowledge, commerce,

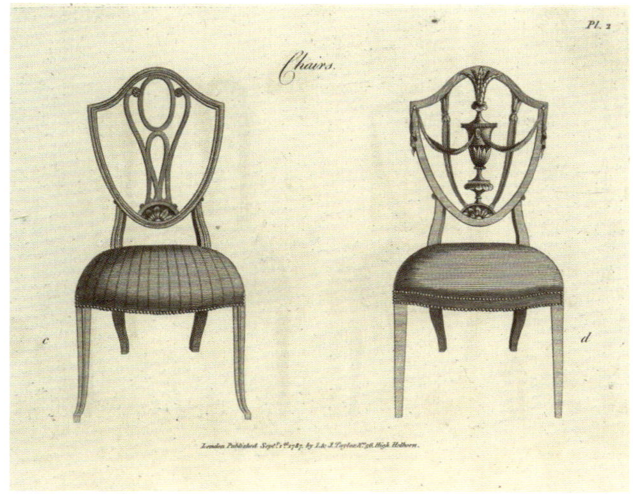

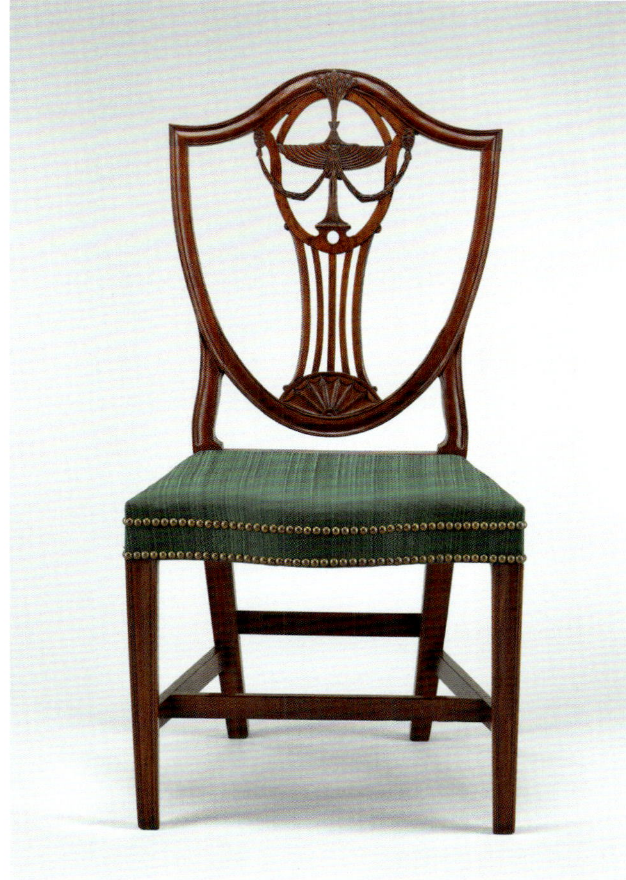

Fig. 23 (above) · Alice Hepplewhite and Co., *The Cabinet-Maker and Upholsterer's Guide; or Repository of Designs for Every Article of Household Furniture, in the Newest and Most Approved Taste*, 1794. Bound volume of engravings, 38 × 25 cm. The George Peabody Library, The Sheridan Libraries, Johns Hopkins University, 749.223 H529 1794 QUARTO c. 1. Photo: Digitization Services Unit, Johns Hopkins University.

Fig. 24 (below) · Designed by Alice Hepplewhite, and manufactured by John Carlile and Sons, *Side chair*, 1789–1803. Mahogany, black walnut, white oak, maple, haircloth upholstery, and replacement brass nails, 99.4 × 53.3 × 50.8 cm. Baltimore Museum of Art: Friends of the American Wing Fund, 1983.6. Photo: Mitro Hood.

social hierarchy, slavery, gender norms, and identity in the British Atlantic.[53] Within this context, Garthwaite's designed silks worn by an American colonist could be read as the textile embodiment of a shifting hybrid identity that was facilitated by the global circulation of her artistic production.[54]

Several successful British widows led craft workshops that developed global reputations through exportation of their products, translating and interjecting European tastes into colonial settings. After her husband's death, Rebecca Emes (active 1808–1829) developed a successful partnership with Edward Barnard in 1808, running a major silver manufacturing firm in London that produced pieces for export to British colonies in North America and India.[55] The publication of designs by Alice Hepplewhite (active eighteenth century) for furniture produced by the cabinetmaking workshop she continued to run after her husband George's death in 1786 ensured the popularity of these designs in North American colonial homes (fig. 23; cat. no. 61). North American furniture makers produced chairs based on Hepplewhite designs, ensuring her business's global reach (fig. 24).[56]

Concurrent with the circulation of European women-made objects outside the continent was the importation of foreign, "exotic" objects and documents that came into the hands of European women makers. This engagement with a virtual version of the world beyond occurred for most women through objects that arrived in their homes and marketplaces because of colonial expansion, trade and scholarly networks, and the established global import economies.[57] Women of all social classes served active roles in the increasingly global economy of things and played an integral part in the ever-evolving European project of documenting and cataloguing the wider world. The earliest documented work by Venetian nun and illustrative engraver Elisabetta (later Isabella) Piccini (1644–1734), known for her portraits and religious illustrations, is an allegorical frontispiece to a book on historical and contemporary international maritime law made when she was still a teenager, before she took the veil. It features a nude woman and a lion, possibly representing the rulership of the Sea, drawn on a cart behind a wildman, possibly representing Land.[58] Even after taking vows, Piccini supported her family and convent by illustrating historical texts, such as Antonio de Solís's *Istoria della conquista del Messico* [*History of the Conquest of Mexico*], for which Piccini produced portraits of Hernán Cortéz and

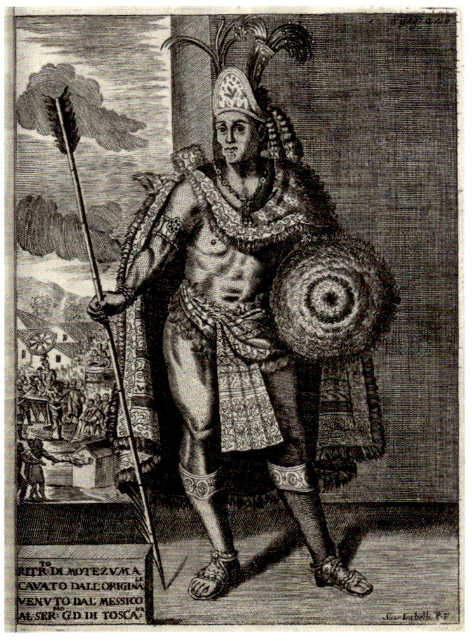

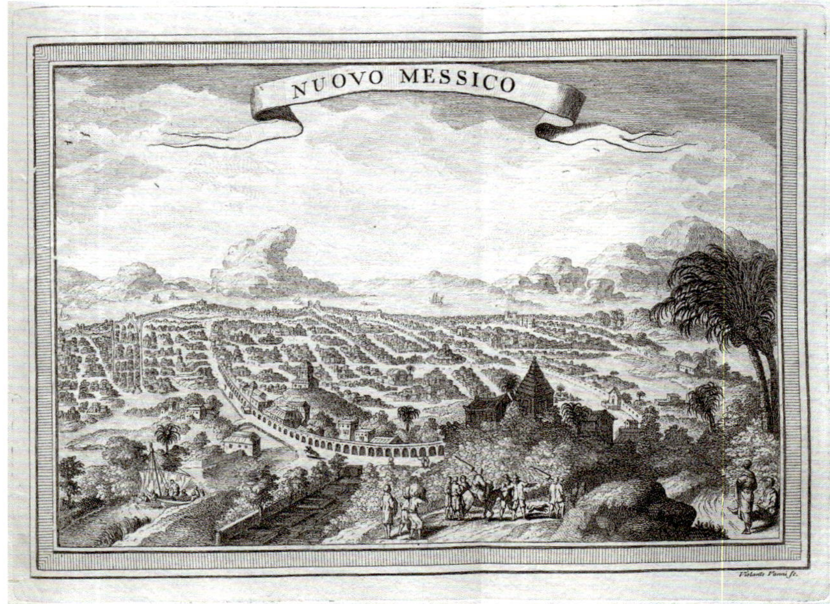

Fig. 25 (above, left) • Elisabetta (Isabella) Piccini, *Portrait of Moctezuma* in Antonio de Solís's *Istoria della conquista del Messico della popolazione, e de' progressi nell' America Settentrionale conosciuta sotto nome di Nuova Spagna* [*History of the Conquest of Mexico*], 1715. Engraving, page: 22 × 16.5 cm; image: 19 × 14 cm. Special Collections, Princeton University Library, inv. no. N-001866. Image: Courtesy of Princeton University Library.

Fig. 26 (above, right) • Violante Vanni, *Nuovo Messico* in *Il Gazzettiere Americano...* [*The American Gazetteer*], vol. 2, 1763. Engraving, 23.9 × 31.8 cm. Universitat de Barcelona, Biblioteca Patrimonial Digital.

Fig. 27 (below, left) • Pauline Rifer de Courcelles, known as Madame Knip, decorator for Manufacture Nationale de Sèvres, *Euphonia Violacea* [*Euphone téité*] *plate*, from the series *The South American Birds Service*, 1819–1821. Hard-paste porcelain, diameter: 23.5 cm. On Loan from Hillwood Estate, Museum & Gardens, Bequest of Marjorie Merriweather Post, 1973, inv. no. 24.136.2. Photographed by Edward Owen.

Fig. 28 (below, right) • Pauline Rifer de Courcelles, known as Madame Knip, decorator for Manufacture Nationale de Sèvres, *Paradise Tanager* [*Septicolour*] *plate*, from the series *The South American Birds Service*, 1819–1821. Hard-paste porcelain, diameter: 23.5 cm. On Loan from Hillwood Estate, Museum & Gardens, Bequest of Marjorie Merriweather Post, 1973, inv. no. 24.136.3. Photographed by Edward Owen.

the Aztec ruler Moctezuma (fig. 25). Without access to Moctezuma himself, Piccini copied his glorified likeness from a painting by the Mexican artist Antonio Rodríguez that had recently been acquired by the Medici Grand Duke.[59] The documentation of the history, exploration, and exploitation of the Americas was similarly captured in illustrations of native species and landscapes as well as in maps by engraver Violante Vanni (1732–1775/76), who likely never personally saw the locations and animals in the text but who nevertheless illustrated them (fig. 26).[60]

For many women, their ability to access foreign materials and subjects was essential to their personal and professional success, appealing to an elite clientele base that collected and catalogued such exotica. For her work on Saverio Manetti's *Storia naturale degli Uccelli* [*A Natural History of Birds*], Vanni was given access to specimens owned by the Marchese Giovanni Gerini. Still-life painters, such as Maria van Oosterwijck (1630–1693) and Rachel Ruysch (1664–1750), or Merian and Barbara Regina Dietzsch (1706–1783), had access to prominent scientists and botanical gardens in major university cities like Amsterdam and Nuremberg. Their highly detailed and botanically accurate works reflected the tradition of collecting rare and foreign specimens to form essentially an encyclopedic botanical museum.[61] The accomplished bird painter Pauline Rifer de Courcelles (1781–1851), known as Madame Knip, navigated herself into the protection of royal patronage by Empress Marie-Louise (r. 1814–1847) and a position with the Sèvres porcelain manufactory. With this support came access to prized subjects such as the South American birds she drew from specimens in the Musée d'Histoire Naturelle for *The South American Birds Service* (figs. 27 & 28; cat. no. 25), an eighty-four-piece service produced by Sèvres and presented to the Duchess of Angoulême (1778–1851), the only surviving daughter of Louis XVI and Marie Antoinette.[62]

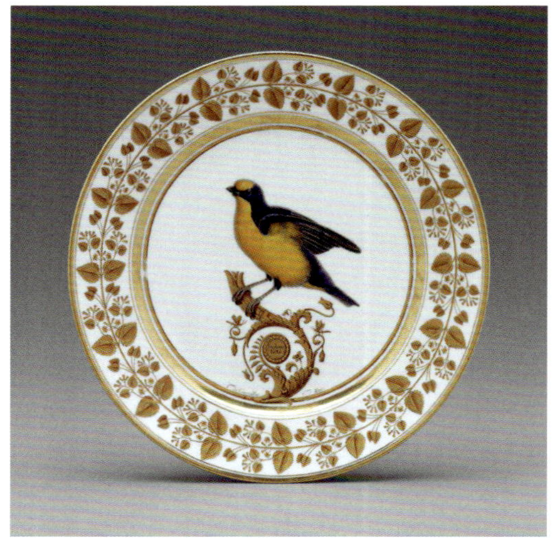

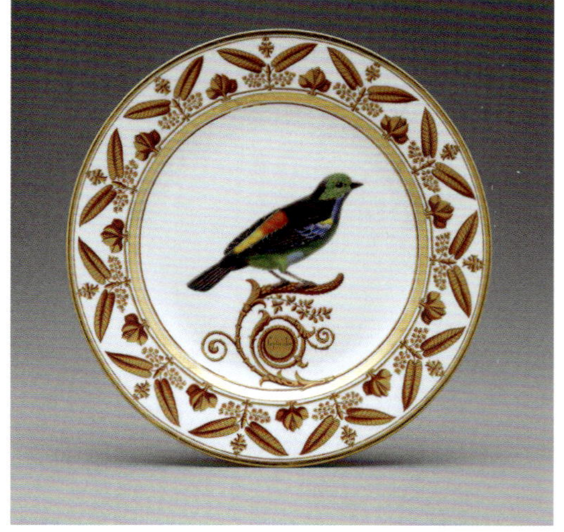

Fig. 29 (above) • Anna Lister and Susanna Lister Knowler, *Mirabilistrombus listeri* [*Lister's snail*], plate 855, in Martin Lister's *Historiae sive synopsis methodicae Conchyliorum*..., Oxford, 1770. Etching and engraving, 39.4 × 26.7 × 10.8 cm. Kislak Center for Special Collections, Rare Books and Manuscripts, University of Pennsylvania Libraries, Folio QL431 .L57 1770 Peachey copy.

Women artists' ability to portray the constantly expanding world of ethnographic material and biodiversity relied directly on the colonial extractive economy that trafficked both living and preserved specimens.[63] Sisters Susanna Lister Knowler (c. 1670–1738) and Anna Lister (1671–1700) created drawings and engravings based on physical specimens for their father's influential text on molluscs and shells, the *Historiae Conchyliorum*, produced from 1685 to 1692 (fig. 29; cat. no. 184).[64] While Lister owned a shell collection, many of the examples the Lister sisters studied came from Hans Sloane, who had used the labour of enslaved West African men and women and the profits from his wife's family plantation in Jamaica to build his hugely influential collection.[65] While still a teenager, artist Sarah Stone (c. 1760–1844) was engaged by Ashton Lever to document his museum of ethnographic and natural specimens. Now dispersed, Lever's extensive collections featured taxidermied birds from around the world (fig. 31; cat. no. 189) as well as an array of ethnographic material, including musical instruments and accessories (fig. 30) from the Americas, Asia, and the Arctic that came to the collection through the travels of Lever's associate Captain James Cook.[66]

One of Cook's contemporaries, the British naturalist Joseph Banks became known in scientific circles following his 1766 expedition to present-day Newfoundland and Labrador.[67] In addition to natural specimens, Banks brought back to England articles of clothing, artifacts, and accessories made by Indigenous populations. Angelica Kauffmann came into contact with these Inuit items and was either hired to document what she saw or was moved to depict them in a pair of paintings, *Woman in Inuit Clothing from Labrador* and *Man in Inuit Clothing*, dateable between 1768 and 1772 (figs. 32 & 33).[68] While the clothes and natural specimens brought back by Banks brought him fame, the forced appearance in London in 1768 of an abducted Inuk woman named Mikak (c. 1740–1795) and her son Tutauk, along with another boy named Karpik, caused a sensation.[69] They were popular subjects for British artists, including Katharine Read, who is documented to have produced a pastel portrait of Mikak and her son, which she exhibited at the Society of Artists in 1769.[70] Although Kauffmann is known for her portraits, there is no indication that the figures, set within simple, idealized landscapes, represent historical individuals such as Mikak; the works could instead be considered portraits of the clothing. This reading is supported by the appearance of a second adult figure in the background of the painting of the woman who is facing away from the viewer, allowing

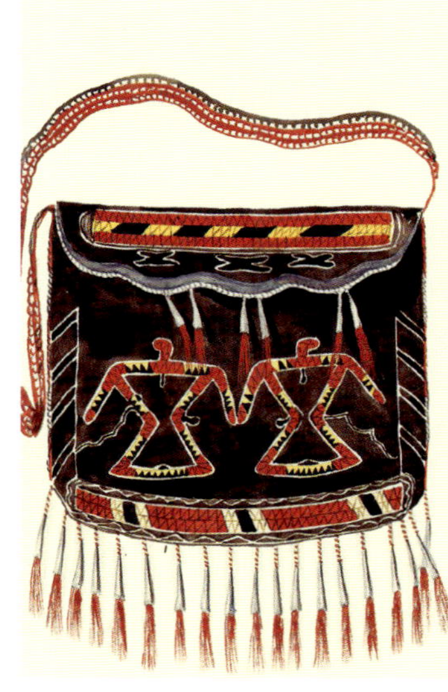

Fig. 30 (below, left) • Sarah Stone, *Bandolier bag with Thunderbird motifs*, from *Drawing Album (made for Sir Ashton Lever)*, 1780. Watercolour on paper, 33.5 × 21 cm. British Museum, Purchased, 2006, inv. no. Am2006,Drg.53. Image: © The Trustees of the British Museum.

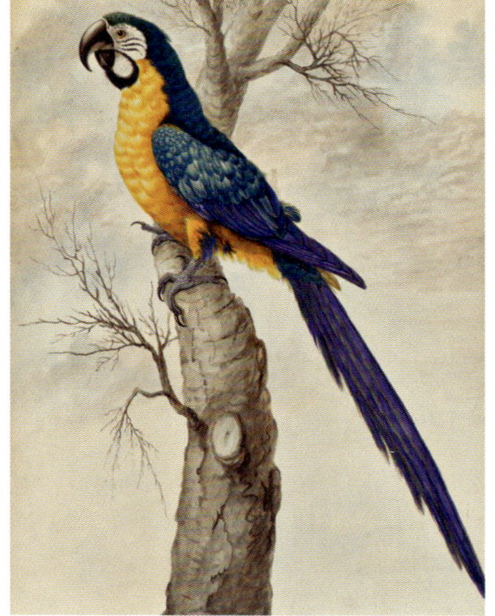

Fig. 31 (below, right) • Sarah Stone, *A Blue and Yellow Macaw*, c. 1789. Watercolour heightened with opaque watercolour and glazes, with a black ink border on paper, 44.1 × 33.9 cm. Art Gallery of Ontario, Purchase, with funds from the Marvin Gelber Fund, and the Master Print & Drawing Society of Ontario, 2022/7043. Photo: Craig Boyko, AGO.

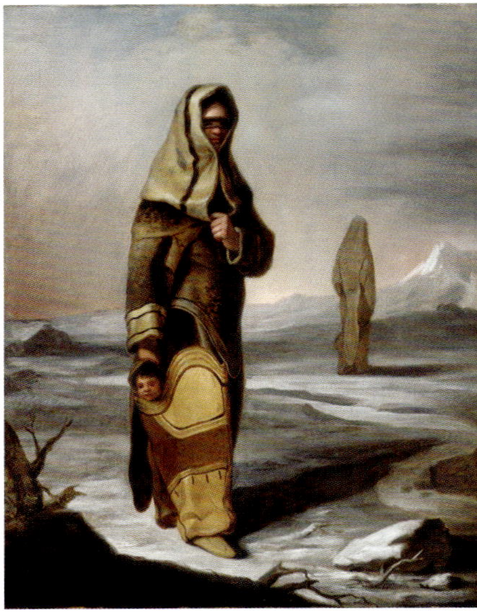

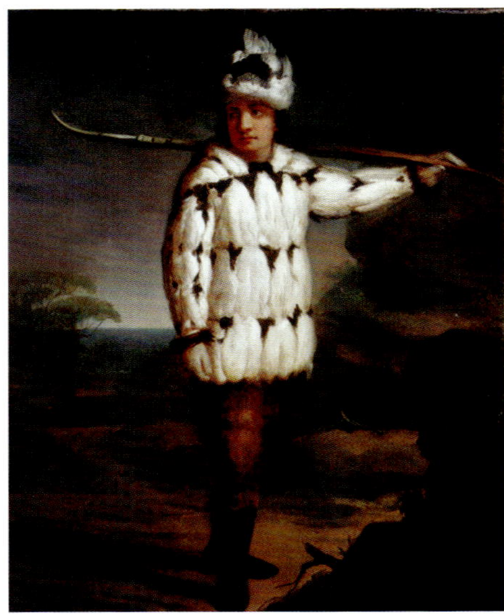

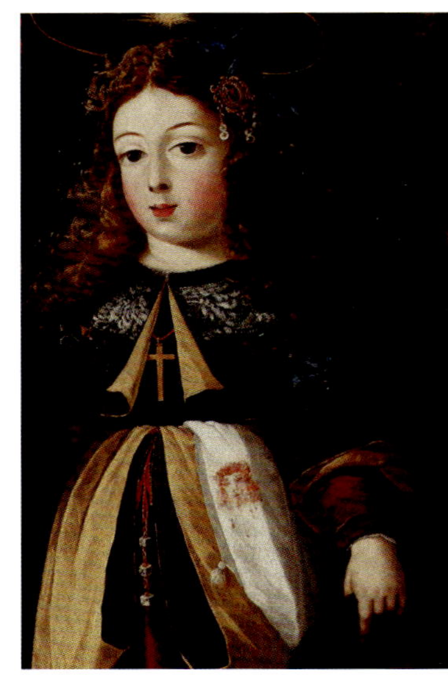

Fig. 32 (left) · Angelica Kauffmann, *Woman in Inuit Clothing from Labrador*, c. 1768–1772. Oil on canvas, 76.5 × 63.5 cm. Library and Archives Canada, acc. no. 1978-23-1.

Fig. 33 (middle) · Angelica Kauffmann, *Man in Inuit Clothing*, c. 1768–1772. Oil on canvas, 76.5 × 63.5 cm. Library and Archives Canada, acc. no. 1978-23-2.

Fig. 34 (right) · *Detail:* Josefa Ayala, *The Christ Child as Pilgrim*, 1676. Oil on canvas, 108 × 83 cm. The Gaudium Magnum Collection – Maria and João Cortez de Lobão, Lisbon. Photo: Jorge Simão.

Fig. 35 (facing, above, left) · *Detail:* Unknown French embroiderer(s), *Bed hanging*, 18th century. Linen ground, wool, and silk embroidery threads, 275.6 × 82.6 cm. Baltimore Museum of Art: Gift of Judge Irwin Untermyer, 1952.148b. Photo: Mitro Hood.

Fig. 36 (facing, above, right) · *Detail:* M.K. Herbert, *Crewelwork bed curtain*, 1692. Linen (warp) and cotton (weft) ground; wool, silk, and cotton embroidery threads, 246.4 × 111.8 cm. Baltimore Museum of Art: Gift of Judge Irwin Untermyer, New York, 1956.151a. Photo: Mitro Hood.

for the documentation of both the front and back of the garment type.

The transmission of garments as well as textile techniques, motifs, and materials connected women makers across a spectrum of class structures—from court productions to professional workshops and domestic makers—with the global exchange network. The exquisite work of Portuguese painter Josefa Ayala (c. 1630–1684) highlights her access to materials obtained through Portugal's influential role in extractive trade in West Africa and India, including some of the copper on which she painted (cat. no. 80), as well as her personal ownership of a collection of Portuguese silks and taffeta from India that she studied for the garments on her painted figures (fig. 34; cat. no. 89).[71] Additionally, many popular motifs, such as the tree of life, on domestic textiles made in both professional workshops and the home reflect awareness of patterns originating outside Europe. In Portugal, tapestries embroidered by women in Castelo Branco represent a rich tradition that began in the sixteenth century.[72] The works, locally specific in their style of stitching, often incorporate stylized Asian flora such as lotus blossoms as well as non-native fauna. Appearing in both the Old and New Testaments of the Christian Bible, the tree of life held both philosophical and religious meanings to European audiences, with the added appeal of playing into the period's fascination with empire, both natural and national. An interpretation of this theme appears in two examples of bed curtains in the Baltimore Museum of Art's collection—one likely produced in a professional French workshop and featuring animals from the continents of Africa and Asia, including elephants and rhinoceroses (fig. 35; cat. no. 224), and one produced by M.K. Herbert (active seventeenth century), possibly with the help of her maids at home, featuring East- and Southeast Asian–inspired imagery (fig. 36; cat. no. 245). Many extant examples of amateur-made embroidered bed curtains indicate the intercontinental transport of both patterns and materials that mirrored the exchange of designs and fabric patterns being produced in professional manufactures, facilitating women's direct participation in the creation of a global domestic aesthetic.[73]

The popularity of motifs with Asian flora and fauna in European household decorative arts and furniture was ubiquitous in the seventeenth and eighteenth centuries. Chinoiserie, a fantastical Western interpretation of Chinese themes, relied largely on the aesthetic influence of imported wares as well as on cultural stereotypes often taken from the writings of Jesuit missionaries, such as the encyclopedic compilation *The General History of China* by French Jesuit scholar Jean-Baptiste Du Halde.[74] As the arbiters of taste for many homes and the creators of household

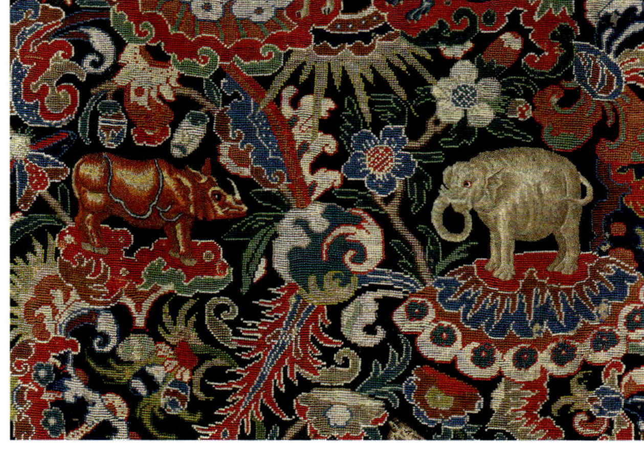

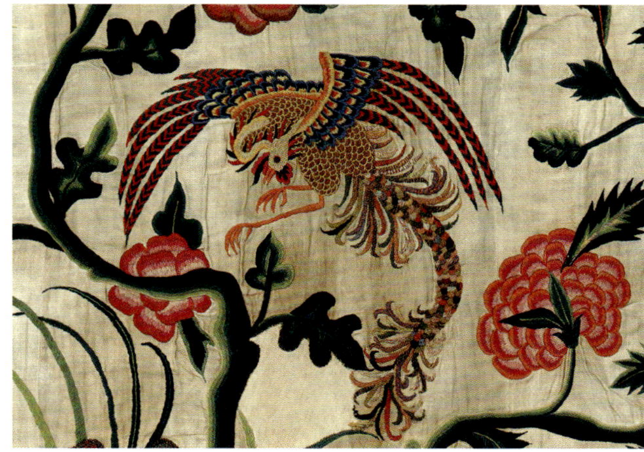

Below (left to right)

Fig. 37 • Detail: Anne Allen, after Jean Pillement, plate from the series *New Suite of Notebooks of Chinese Designs for the Use of Designers and Painters*, c. 1796–1798. Colour etching inked *à la poupée*, sheet: 25.6 × 23.1 cm; plate: 19.5 × 13.8 cm. Baltimore Museum of Art: Blanche Adler Memorial Fund, 2011.114.2. Photo: Mitro Hood.

Fig. 38 • Detail: Pierette Candelot, workshop director of Manufacture de la Veuve Perrin, *Lobed round plate with Chinoiserie*, c. 1750–1800. Tin-glazed earthenware and petit feu enamels, diameter: 25 cm. Gardiner Museum, Toronto, Canada, The Pierre Karch and Mariel O'Neill-Karch Collection, inv. no. G14.4.6.

Fig. 39 • Detail: Probably Anna Elizabeth Auffenwerth Wald, and possibly Sabina Auffenwerth Hosennestel, decorators for Meissen Porcelain Factory, *Tureen and stand*, c. 1725. Hard-paste porcelain with overglaze enamels and gilding, 17.8 × 22.9 × 22.9 cm. Gardiner Museum, Toronto, Canada, Gift of George and Helen Gardiner, inv. no. G83.1.0717.1-.3. Photo: Toni Hafkenscheid.

Fig. 40 • Detail: Elizabeth Godfrey, *Tea canister set*, 1754–1755. Silver, largest canister: 14 × 10.2 × 10.2 cm; two smaller canisters: 13.3 × 10.2 × 7.6 cm. Saint Louis Art Museum, Funds given by Lewis and Amanda Smith; and gift of John M. Harney in memory of Florence M. Warfield and Charlotte W. Harney, funds given by Joseph Pulitzer in memory of his wife, Elinor Wickham Pulitzer, and funds given in honour of Joseph Pulitzer II, by exchange, inv. no. 4:2010.1a,b-.3a,b.

items, women were major contributors to the development of Europe's visual obsession with the East. Patterns featuring flowers and small vignettes—like the hand-inked prints by Anne Allen (c. 1749/50–after 1808) in the *New Suite of Notebooks of Chinese Designs for the Use of Designers and Painters* (fig. 37; cat. no. 152)—were in high demand, as was chinaware reflecting similarly exoticized decoration (fig. 38; cat. no. 9). East Asian designs also appeared on tea, coffee, and chocolate services, such as those manufactured by Meissen and decorated by the German *hausmalers* Anna Elizabeth Auffenwerth Wald (born 1696) and her sister Sabina Auffenwerth Hosennestel (1706–1782), often echoing the exotic origins of the container's contents and creating a signature style that appears across diverse forms (fig. 39; cat no. 10).

The seventeenth-century development of afternoon tea into a convention presided over by women led to the creation of a broad spectrum of objects designated for the service in various media and at a wide range of price points. Rituals of tea and coffee largely transcended rigid class structures, and women were both primary consumers and heavily involved producers of accoutrements for its service.[75] These works ranged from hand-rolled paper-filigree tea caddies (cat. no. 65) made by women for their own services to the exquisitely produced silver examples of tea canisters featuring orientalized designs by Elizabeth Godfrey (active c. 1720–1758) (fig. 40; cat. no. 208). The permeation of exoticized imagery and the socialized rituals based on extractive trade goods were part of a larger cultural shift, particularly on the part of colonial powers, to build national pride and reliance on continued expansionism.

It was within this framework of national pride that young girls growing up in homes that featured

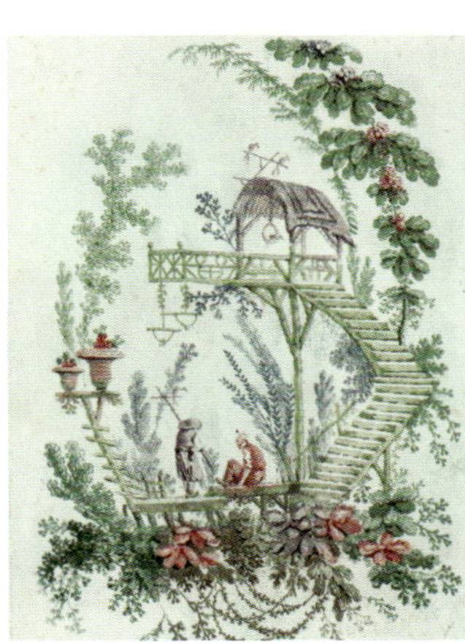

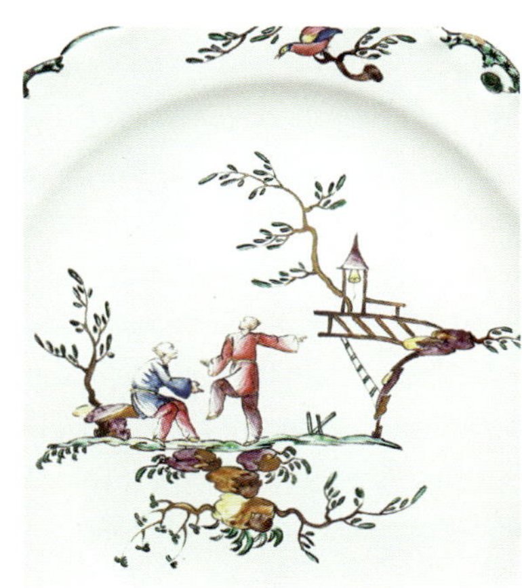

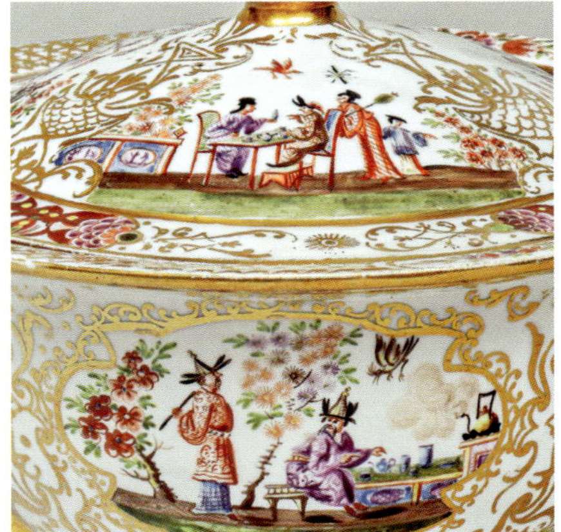

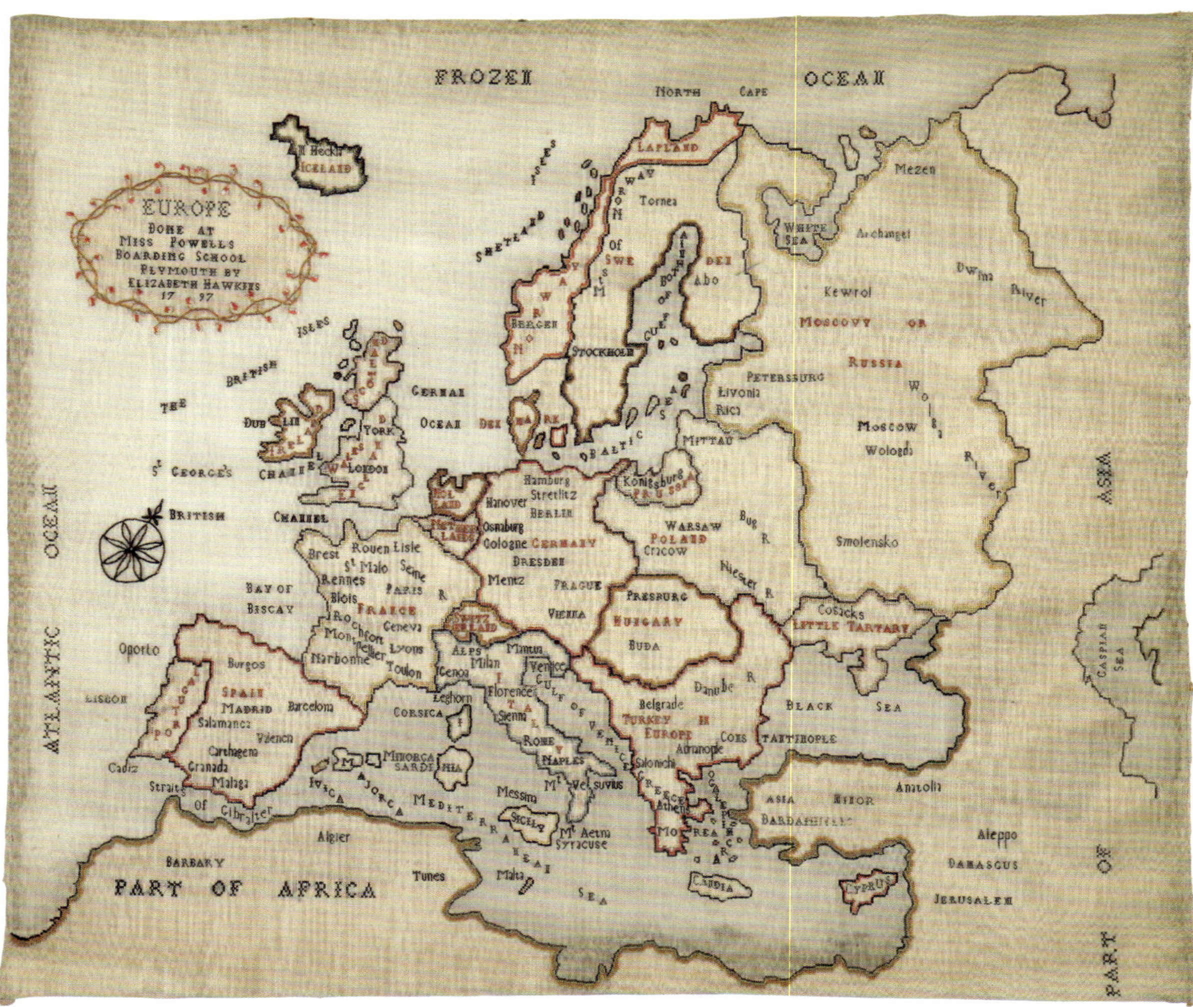

Fig. 41 · Elizabeth Hawkins, *Map sampler*, 1797. Woollen sampler embroidered in silks, 48.5 × 58.5 cm. Victoria and Albert Museum, London, Given by Miss A.P. Rean, inv. no. T.165-1959. Image © Victoria and Albert Museum, London.

imported flora and fauna, diverse teas, and japanned furniture began to be formally trained in geographic sciences.[76] By the late seventeenth century, geography primers for children were available for English-speaking audiences, making the world more accessible to literate households; geography was the first science in which girls were regularly educated.[77] Embroidery was already a pan-European staple in the education of young girls, and its utility beyond darning is evident in the frequent presence of teaching parables, religious verses, alphabets, and exotic animals adorning samplers produced by girls in early adolescence (cat. nos. 235, 240, 242). It is no coincidence then that, by the final decades of the eighteenth century, map samplers became a staple of many young British and American women's domestic education.[78] Embroidered maps depicting everything from local county lines to Europe in its entirety or intricate depictions of the globe were popular tools that could be displayed in the home to promote continued geographical learning. This access allowed women in a domestic context to expand their personal worlds beyond the borders they embroidered (fig. 41; cat. no. 241).

The value of women's labour as both makers and consumers driving and contributing to the mechanism of colonialism and the preindustrial economy has only relatively recently begun to be recognized, supplanting a traditional male-centred view of women-made objects and their roles in the market for things.[79] The difficulty of neatly or comprehensively summarizing women's material and aesthetic contributions to the global turn in European culture is due, in part, to the multifaceted effects of race, class, and gender that obscure the impact of the individual in the process of manufacture. As demonstrated here, many European women makers who travelled to expand their market, access new subject matter, attract new patrons, or further their skills found the means to do so through their attachment to courts, family connections, colonialist networks, and established routes of travel and exchange.

For women of the lower classes, the large amounts of labour that went into maintaining a household—whether they were running their own house or whether they were employed in domestic service for someone else—would point toward a life of relative confinement.[80] Women trained by family members in a trade and employed in a workshop setting often found this space of work inextricably tied to that of the domestic, both physically and mentally. Not unlike the work-at-home experiences of many twenty-first-century women, their creative labour was expected to be in addition to domestic duties, not in lieu of them. Upper-class women who were not completing all the physical tasks of homemaking themselves were still in charge of managing the teams of labourers that kept grand houses running. These daily tasks—combined with social restrictions that inhibited their ability to move freely throughout society or travel alone in the same way as men—created a restrictive environment which, on the surface, would seem to support the traditional assertion that women's experience and influence was largely contained to domestic spaces. What this narrative fails to consider, however, is the extent to which women who largely remained within their local communities were able to work within established patriarchal structures to be active participants in mapping, documenting, collecting, and designing the full scope of the globalized European pre-modern experience.

Notes

1 *The Art of Governing a Wife; with Rules for Batchelors* (London: J. Robinson, 1747), 29.

2 Selected studies on the global turn include Pamela H. Smith and Paula Findlen, eds., *Merchants and Marvels: Commerce, Science, and Art in Early Modern Europe* (New York: Routledge, 2002); Mary D. Sheriff, ed., *Cultural Contact and the Making of European Art since the Age of Exploration* (Chapel Hill: University of North Carolina Press, 2010); Daniela Bleichmar and Peter C. Mancall, eds., *Collecting across Cultures: Material Exchanges in the Early Modern Atlantic World* (Philadelphia: University of Pennsylvania Press, 2011); Paula Findlen, ed., *Early Modern Things: Objects and Their Histories, 1500–1800* (New York: Routledge, 2013); and Benjamin Schmidt, *Inventing Exoticism: Geography, Globalism, and Europe's Early Modern World* (Philadelphia: University of Pennsylvania Press, 2015).

3 Recent scholarship on the global scope of textiles provides models for seeking out women makers' contributions and global involvement. See Danielle C. Skeehan, *The Fabric of Empire: Material and Literary Cultures of the Global Atlantic, 1650–1850* (Baltimore: Johns Hopkins University Press, 2020); Zara Anishanslin, *Portrait of a Woman in Silk: Hidden Histories of the British Atlantic World* (New Haven, CT: Yale University Press, 2016); and Amelia Peck, ed., *Interwoven Globe: The Worldwide Textile Trade, 1500–1800* (New York: Metropolitan Museum of Art, 2013).

4 See Lisa Walters and Brandie R. Siegfried, eds., *Margaret Cavendish: An Interdisciplinary Perspective* (Cambridge: Cambridge University Press, 2022); Martine van Elk, *Early Modern Women's Writing: Domesticity, Privacy, and the Public Sphere in England and the Dutch Republic* (London: Palgrave Macmillan, 2017); Katharine Gillespie, *Domesticity and Dissent in the Seventeenth-Century: English Women Writers and the Public Sphere* (Cambridge: Cambridge University Press, 2004); Marilyn J. Boxer and Jean H. Quataert, eds., *Connecting Spheres: European Women in a Globalizing World, 1500 to the Present*, 2nd ed. (New York: Oxford University Press, 2000).

5 Misty Krueger, ed., *Transatlantic Women Travelers, 1688–1843* (Lewisburg, PA: Bucknell University Press, 2021), 14–17; see also Katrina O'Loughlin, *Women, Writing, and Travel in the 18th Century* (Cambridge: Cambridge University Press, 2018); Katherine Turner, *British Travel Writers of Europe, 1750–1800: Authorship, Gender, and National Identity* (Farnham, UK: Ashgate, 2001).

6 See Sheila Barker, ed., *"The Immensity of the Universe" in the Art of Giovanna Garzoni*, exh. cat. (Florence: Gallerie degli Uffizi, 2020); Bert van de Roemer, Florence Pieters, Hans Mulder, Kay Etheridge, and Marieke van Delft, eds., *Maria Sibylla Merian: Changing the Nature of Art and Science* (Tielt, Belgium: Lannoo, 2022).

7 See Anne Jacobson Schutte, Thomas Kuehn, and Silvana Seidel Menchi, eds., *Time, Space, and Women's Lives in Early Modern Europe* (University Park, PA: Penn State University Press, 2002); Amanda Flather, *Gender and Space in Early Modern England* (Rochester: Boydell, 2007); Helen Hills, *Architecture and the Politics of Gender in Early Modern Europe* (New York: Routledge, 2001).

8 An important exception is the subject of women as patrons of art. See Elizabeth A. Sutton, ed., *Women Artists and Patrons in the Netherlands, 1500–1700* (Amsterdam: Amsterdam University Press, 2019); Katherine A. McIver, ed., *Wives, Widows, Mistresses, and Nuns in Early Modern Italy: Making the Invisible Visible through Art and Patronage* (Farnham, UK: Ashgate, 2012); Susan Bracken, Andrea M. Gáldy, and Adriana Turpin, eds., *Women Patrons and Collectors* (Newcastle upon Tyne: Cambridge Scholars, 2012); Jennifer Milam and Melissa Hyde, eds., *Women, Art and the Politics of Identity in Eighteenth-Century Europe* (Milton Park, UK: Routledge, 2003); Sheryl Riess and David Wilkins, eds., *Beyond Isabella: Secular Women Patrons of Art in Renaissance Italy* (Kirksville, MO: Truman State University Press, 2001).

9 Alessandra Franco, "Malleable Youth: Forging Female Education in Early Modern Rome," in *The Youth of Early Modern Women*, ed. Elizabeth Storr Cohen and Margaret Louise Reeves (Amsterdam: Amsterdam University Press, 2018), 217–34.

10 See Rebecca Messbarger, "The Italian Enlightenment Reform of the Querelle des Femmes," in *The Contest for Knowledge: Debates over Women's Learning in Eighteenth-Century Italy*, ed. and trans. Rebecca

Messbarger and Paula Findlen (Chicago: University of Chicago Press, 2005), 1–22; Judith A. Tyner, *Stitching the World: Embroidered Maps and Women's Geographical Education* (Milton Park, UK: Routledge, 2015).

11 Susan E. James, "The Horenbout Family Workshop at the Tudor Court, 1522–1541: Collaboration, Patronage and Production," *Cogent Arts & Humanities* 8, no. 1 (2021), tandfonline.com/doi/full/10.1080/23311983.2021.1915933.

12 Michael Cole, *Sofonisba's Lesson: A Renaissance Artist and Her Work* (Princeton, NJ: Princeton University Press, 2019), 21 and 100–101.

13 On Gentileschi's assault, see Elizabeth S. Cohen, "The Trials of Artemisia Gentileschi: A Rape as History," *Sixteenth Century Journal* 31, no. 1 (2000): 47–75.

14 Angela Oberer, *The Life and Work of Rosalba Carriera (1673–1757): The Queen of Pastel* (Amsterdam: Amsterdam University Press, 2018), 28–29.

15 Diane Boucher, "Maria Cosway: A Commentator on Modern Life," *British Art Journal* 18 (Winter 2017–18): 78.

16 See Christina Strunck, "Female Court Artists: Women's Career Strategies in the Courts of the Early Modern Period," in *Women Artists in the Early Modern Courts of Europe, c. 1450-1700*, ed. Tanja L. Jones (Amsterdam: Amsterdam University Press, 2021), 35–69.

17 See James, "The Horenbout Family Workshop at the Tudor Court, 1522-1541."

18 Jorge Sebastián Lozano in *A Tale of Two Women Painters: Sofonisba Anguissola and Lavinia Fontana*, exh. cat., ed. Leticia Ruiz Gómez (Madrid: Museo Nacional del Prado, 2019), 130.

19 Almudena Pérez de Tudela, "Sofonisba Anguissola at the Court of Philip II," in *A Tale of Two Women Painters: Sofonisba Anguissola and Lavinia Fontana*, exh. cat., ed. Leticia Ruiz Gómez (Madrid: Museo Nacional del Prado, 2019), 156–57.

20 See Catherine Hall-van den Elsen, *Luisa Roldán* (Los Angeles: Getty Publications, 2021).

21 Sheila Barker, "The Universe of Giovanna Garzoni: Art, Mobility, and the Global Turn in the Geographical Imaginary," in Barker, *"The Immensity of the Universe,"* 16–29. For more on Paladini, see Lisa Goldenberg Stoppato, "Arcangela Paladini and the Medici," in *Women Artists in Early Modern Italy*, ed. Sheila Barker (Turnhout: Brepols, 2016), 81–97.

22 See Detlef Heikamp, "American Objects in Italian Collections of the Renaissance and Baroque: A Survey," in *First Images of American: The Impact of the New World on the Old*, ed. Fredi Chiappelli, vol. 1 (Berkeley: University of California Press, 1976), 455–82; Lia Markey, *Imagining the Americas in Medici Florence* (University Park, PA: Penn State University Press, 2016); Francesco Morena, "An Exotic Liaison: China, the Medici and Giovanna Garzoni," in Barker, *"The Immensity of the Universe,"* 88–95.

23 Sheila Barker and Anatole Tchikine, "Art in the Service of Botany: Giovanna Garzoni's *Piante varie* at Dumbarton Oaks," in Barker, *"The Immensity of the Universe,"* 36–45; Lucia Tongiorgi Tomasi, "Giovanna Garzoni at the Crossroads of Art and Science: Floral and Floristic Aspects of the Cultural Landscape of Her Times," in Barker, *"The Immensity of the Universe,"* 78–87.

24 Alexandra Letvin, "Giovanna Garzoni's Portrait of Zaga Christ (Ṣägga Krəstos)," *Art Herstory*, August 17, 2021, artherstory.net/giovanna-garzonis-portrait-of-zaga-christ-%E1%B9%A3agga-kr%C7%9Dstos/; Hilda Groen, "Giovanna Garzoni (Ascoli Piceno 1600 – Rome 1670): Portrait of Zaga Christ," in Barker, *"The Immensity of the Universe,"* 128.

25 Bettina Baumgärtel, "'The Whole World Is Angelicamad,'" in *Angelica Kauffman*, ed. Bettina Baumgärtel (Munich: Hirmer, 2020), 10.

26 See Wendy Wassyng Roworth, "'The Residence of the Arts': Angelica Kauffman's Place in Rome," in *Italy's Eighteenth Century: Gender and Culture in the Age of the Grand Tour*, ed. Paula Findlen, Wendy Wassyng Roworth, and Catherine M. Sama (Stanford: Stanford University Press, 2009), 151–71.

27 Paula Findlen, "Gender and Culture in Eighteenth-Century Italy," in Findlen et al., *Italy's Eighteenth Century*, 21.

28 Neil Jeffares, "Katherine Read," *Dictionary of pastellists before 1800*, London, 2006; online edition, updated May 15, 2023, pastellists.com/articles/Read.pdf, accessed December 5, 2022.

29 Margery Morgan, "British Connoisseurs in Rome: Was It Painted by Katherine Read (1723–78)?" *British Art Journal* 7, no. 1 (2006): 40–44.

30 See Jeffares, "Katherine Read."

31 Maria Pia Donato, "The Temple of Female Glory: Female Self-Affirmation in the Roman Salon of the Grand Tour," in Findlen et al., *Italy's Eighteenth Century*, 75.

32 Elizabeth Horodowich and Lia Markey, eds., *The New World in Early Modern Italy, 1492–1750* (Cambridge: Cambridge University Press, 2017), 3–4.

33 Julie Hochstrasser, "Remapping Dutch Art in Global Perspective: Other Points of View," in *Cultural Contact and the Making of European Art since the Age of Exploration*, ed. Mary D. Sheriff (Chapel Hill: University of North Carolina Press, 2010), 60–62.

34 Marieke van Delft, "Maria Sibylla Merian and the People of Suriname," in van de Roemer et al., *Maria Sibylla Merian: Changing the Nature of Art and Science* (Tielt, Belgium: Lannoo, 2022), 125. There is mention of an Indigenous woman returning with Merian on the voyage to the Dutch Republic, but it is unclear whether she was enslaved or a servant.

35 Hochstrasser, *Remapping Dutch Art in Global Perspective*, 61. For more on Merian's interaction with the Indigenous and enslaved populations of Suriname, see Natalie Zemon Davis, "Metamorphoses: Maria Sibylla Merian," in *Women on the Margins: Three Seventeenth-Century Lives* (Cambridge, MA: Harvard University Press, 1995), 172–202.

36 Diana Epelbaum, "'Little Atlas': Global Travel and Local Preservation in Maria Sibylla Merian's *Metamorphosis of the Insects of Surinam*," in Krueger, ed., *Transatlantic Women Travelers*, 23–47.

37 For a feminist reading of Merian's travels, see Davis, "Metamorphoses."

38 Elisabeth Rücker, "Maria Sibylla Merian: Businesswoman and Publisher," in *Maria Sibylla Merian, 1647–1717: Artist and Naturalist*, ed. Kurt Wettengl (Berlin: Hatje Cantz, 1998), 254–61.

39 Jeffares, "Katherine Read," 2; Joanna Frew, "Scottish Background and Indian Experiences in the Late Eighteenth Century," *Journal of Scottish Historical Studies* 34, no. 2 (2014): 167–98.

40 Cornwallis's portrait, executed in the year of Hill's arrival, may have been commissioned to commemorate the general's appointment as governor-general and commander-in-chief of India; see Philip Mould and Co., London: philipmould.com/exhibitions/23-pioneers-500-years-of-women-in-british-art/works/artworks5536/.

41 William Foster, "British Artists in India, 1760–1820," *Walpole Society* 19 (1930–31): 39; Marjorie E. Wieseman in *Perfect Likeness: European and American Portrait Miniatures from the Cincinnati Art Museum*, ed. Julie Aronson and Marjorie E. Wieseman (New Haven: Yale University Press, 2006), 209.

42 See Kathryn Metz, "Ellen and Rolinda Sharples: Mother and Daughter Painters," *Woman's Art Journal* 16 (Spring–Summer 1995): 3–11.

43 Almerindo Ojeda, "El Grabado Como Fuente del Arte Colonial: Estado de la Cuestión," Project on the Engraved Sources of Spanish Colonial Art (PESSCA), University of California, Davis, 2017, colonialart.org/essays/el-grabado-como-fuente-del-arte-colonial-estado-de-la-cuestion; see also Cécile Michaud and José Torres Della Pina, eds., *De Amberes al Cusco: El grabado europeo como fuente del arte virreinal* (Lima: Impulso Empresa de Servicios, 2009).

44 Project on the Engraved Sources of Spanish Colonial Art (PESSCA), directed by Almerindo E. Ojeda, has identified several correspondences between prints by European women artists and the artistic production of Spanish and Portuguese colonial artists. The examples cited here come from PESSCA's digital compendium: colonialart.org/. Many thanks to Aaron Hyman for bringing this valuable resource to the authors' attention.

45 Research conducted by Rachel Young, a PhD candidate at Johns Hopkins University, suggests that Mantuana's composition may have been, at least in part, her own invention, signified by her inclusion of a "D." (standing for *delineata* or *delineavit* [has drawn]) after her signature on the plate, the only known instance of her using such a designation. For discussion of Diana Mantuana's career, see Evelyn Lincoln, *The Invention of the Italian Renaissance Printmaker* (New Haven, CT: Yale University Press, 2000).

46 Further supporting this connection is the fact that Saint Gertrude, whose attribute is the flaming heart, has been a figure of significant and long-standing Catholic veneration in colonial Spanish territories, especially Peru. Gertrude Casanova, "St. Gertrude the Great," *The Catholic Encyclopedia*, vol. 6 (New York: Robert Appleton Co.), *New Advent*, newadvent.org/cathen/06534a.htm, accessed February 20, 2023.

47 For Dubois's image, see Séverine Lepape, *Gravures de la rue Montorgueil* (Paris: Bibliothèque Nationale de France, 2015), no. 458.

48 PESSCA 2200A/2200B, colonialart.org/archives/locations/united-kingdom/city-of-london/christies-london#c2200a-2200b; the paintings were sold at Christie's London on May 18, 1993, as lot 67.

49 A *Libyan Sibyl*, likely painted by Silvestre de Almeida Lopes, is in the vault of the Igreja do Senhor do Bonfim dos Militares, Diamantina; another *Libyan Sibyl* appears on a fragment of a Lenten veil, attributed to Caetano Luiz de miranda, for Igreja de Nossa Senhora do Carmo, Diamantina. See PESSCA 2108A/2108B, colonialart.org /archives/subjects/old-testament/kings-prophets-and -sibyls/sibyls#c2108a-2108b.

50 Gauvin Alexander Bailey, *Art on the Jesuit Missions in Asia and Latin America, 1542–1773* (Toronto: University of Toronto Press, 1999), 173 and 253. See also PESSCA 2255A/2255B, colonialart.org/archives/locations/ paraguay/antigua-mision-jesuita-no-identificada/ antigua-imprenta-no-identificada#c2255a-2255b.

51 One of the London publishers was Mary Ryland, who took over her husband's printshop after he was executed for counterfeiting with intent to defraud the East India Company; see "William Wynne Ryland," *Oxford Dictionary of National Biography*, vol. 50 (1897): 58–59. For the paintings, see Bettina Baumgärtel, ed., *Angelica Kaufman* (Munich: Hirmer, 2020). For the prints, see David Alexander, "Chronological Checklist of Singly Issued English Prints after Angelica Kauffman," in *Angelica Kauffman: A Continental Artist in Georgian England*, ed. Wendy Wassyng Roworth (London: Reaktion Books, 1992), 179–89.

52 Paula Bradstreet Richter, *Painted with Thread: The Art of American Embroidery* (Salem, MA: Peabody Essex Museum, 2000), 66.

53 See Anishanslin, *Portrait of a Woman in Silk*.

54 For the interpretation of the body as an emblem of cultural difference and a point of negotiation between cultures, see O'Loughlin, *Women, Writing, and Travel*, 22.

55 Reference to the export aspect of their business is found here: collections.vam.ac.uk/item/O96396/taperstick -emes-and-barnard/.

56 *The Cabinet-Maker and Upholsterer's Guide* [...] was reissued two more times in the following five years.

57 For virtual understanding as a form of discovering a foreign place, see Horodowich and Markey, *The New World in Early Modern Italy*, 16.

58 Giovanni Palazzi, *De Dominio Maris, Libri Duo: Serenissimae Venetae Reipublicae dicati* (Venice: Combi & La Nou), 1663.

59 Piccini's work appears in both Italian and Spanish editions of the volume. Kevin Terraciano, "Canons Seen and Unseen in Colonial Mexico," in *Canons and Values*, ed. Larry Silver and Kevin Terraciano (Los Angeles: Getty Research Institute, 2019), 172–73.

60 *Il Gazzettiere Americano Continente un Distinto Ragguaglio di Tutte le Parti Del Nuovo Mondo Americana* [*The American Gazetteer: Containing a Distinct Account of All the Parts of the New World*], Livorno, 1763; *Atlante dell'America contenente le migliori carte geografiche, e topografiche delle principali citta, laghi, fiumi e fortezze del nuovo mondo* [*Atlas of America containing the best geographical and topographic maps of the main cities, lakes, rivers and fortresses of the new world*], Livorno, 1777.

61 See Paula Findlen, *Possessing Nature: Museums, Collecting, and Scientific Culture in Early Modern Italy* (Berkeley: University of California Press), 155–93. In relation to Vanni, see Christies, Printed Books and Manuscripts from Longleat, lot 180, June 13, 2002, christies.com/en/lot/lot-3934726.

62 For more on Knip, see Ann Bermingham, *Learning to Draw: Studies in the Cultural History of a Polite and Useful Art* (New Haven, CT: Yale University Press, 2000); Paris Spies-Gans, *A Revolution on Canvas: The Rise of Women Artists in Britain and France, 1760–1830* (London: Paul Mellon Centre for Studies in British Art in association with Yale University Press, 2022), 271–73.

63 Apurba Chatterjee, "A Memsahib's 'Natural World': Lady Mary Impey's Collection of Indian Natural History Paintings," in *Women, Collecting, and Cultures beyond Europe*, ed. A. Leis (New York: Routledge, 2023), 103; see also Richard Drayton, *Nature's Government: Science, Imperial Britain, and the "Improvement" of the World* (New Haven, CT: Yale University Press, 2000); Lucille Brockway, *Science and Colonial Expansion: The Role of the British Royal Botanic Gardens* (London: Yale University Press, 2002).

64 For more on the Lister sisters' contributions to the history of conchology, see Anna Marie Roos, *Martin Lister and His Remarkable Daughters* (Oxford: Bodleian Library, 2019).

65 Original drawings and copperplates for the project are in the Bodleian Library at Oxford University. For Sloane's collections, see Michael Hunter, Arthur MacGregor, and Alison Walker, *From Books to Bezoars: Sir Hans Sloane and His Collections* (London: British Library, 2012).

66 Many thanks to Wanda Nanibush, Curator of Indigenous Art at the Art Gallery of Ontario, for aiding with the identification of the thunderbird bag, likely made by an Anishinaabe woman and later documented by Stone. On Stone, see Christine E. Jackson, *Sarah Stone: Natural Curiosities from the New World* (London: Merrell, 2003).

67 Banks financed many of Cook's expeditions that collected specimens to bring back to England. On the Arctic voyages, see James C. Hamilton, *Captain James Cook and the Search for Antarctica* (Yorkshire: Pen and Sword History), 2020.

68 The paintings are in the collection of the Canadian Government. Kauffmann may have gained access to these articles through their public display, through Banks himself, or through his sister Sarah Sophia Banks. Sarah was a patron of Kauffmann's and an avid collector of objects from around the world. See Marilyn Bailey Ogilvie, *Women in Science Antiquity through the Nineteenth Century: A Biographical Dictionary with Annotated Bibliography* (Boston: MIT Press, 1990), 35. On Sarah's collections, see Arlene Leis, "Sarah Sophia Banks: Femininity, Sociability and the Practice of Collecting in Late Georgian England" (PhD diss., University of York, 2013).

69 While Kauffmann's image is from the same period, the baby in her painting is too young to have been Tutauk. The Inuit trio were brought to England by Captain Francis Lucas, who was on the same frigate as Banks in 1766. In 1767, Lucas took a group of Inuit women and children, including Mikak and her son, after a skirmish that left an estimated twenty Inuit dead. On Mikak's life, see Maryanne Stopp, "Eighteenth Century Labrador Inuit in England," *Arctic* 62, no. 1 (March 2009): 45–64.

70 Listed as "174. The Esquimeaux Woman and Child; in Crayons," *Royal Society of Artists, The Society of Artists of Great Britain, 1760–1791* (London: G. Bell and Sons, 1911). See also Jeffares, "Katherine Read," 12.

71 Copper as a support medium not only made Josefa Ayala's paintings more valuable though its portability and luminosity, it also situated her works in the Atlantic trade economy of goods like pepper, textiles, ivory, and slaves. Carmen Ripolles, "Precious Inventions: The Copper Paintings of Josefa de Obidos," (paper presented at the College Art Association Annual Conference, February 18, 2022).

72 This tradition of making is primarily continued by women today. See "Embroideries of Castelo Branco," Center of Portugal, centerofportugal.com/article/ embroideries-of-castelo-branco.

73 Panels with pre-drawn patterns were used in eighteenth-century Europe and the Americas for making embroidered crewelwork bed curtains and matching seat covers. Ann Pollard Rowe, "Crewel Embroidered Bed Hangings in Old and New England," *Boston Museum Bulletin* 71, nos. 365/366 (1973): 106. On the exchange of textile patterns and designs, particularly between Southeast Asia and Europe, see Peck, *Interwoven Globe*, 230–32, particularly cat. no. 74B.

74 Jean-Baptiste Du Halde, *The General History of China*, Paris, 1735. This text discussed the production of popular materials such as silkworm cultivation and porcelain manufacture, along with cultural customs.

75 Elizabeth Kowaleski-Wallace, *Consuming Subjects: Women, Shopping, and Business in the 18th Century* (New York: Columbia University Press, 1997), 19–52.

76 Widely regarded in the seventeenth and eighteenth centuries as a feminine pastime, japanning was a popular style of surface finishing on furniture or decorative items, meant to imitate East Asian lacquerware. Many European women japanned items based on designs such as those circulated by Jean-Baptiste Pillement, husband and collaborator of Anne Allen, in his *Ladies Amusement: Or, The Whole Art of Japanning Made Easy*, published in London in 1760. See Ariane Fennetaux, "Female Crafts: Women and Bricolage in Late Georgian Britain, 1750–1820," in *Women and Things, 1750–1950: Gendered Material Strategies*, ed. Maureen Daly Goggin and Beth Fawkes Tobin (Farnham, UK: Ashgate, 2009), 91–108.

77 The first text published specifically naming young women as the target audience was produced in the Americas in 1784. Robert J. Mayhew, "Geography in Eighteenth-Century British Education," *Paedagogica Historica* 34, no. 3 (1998): 731–69.

78 See Judith Tyner, *Stitching the World*. Caitlin Dempsy, "Teaching Geography through Map Samplers," April 2019, geographyrealm.com/map-samplers/.

79 See Jan de Vries, *The Industrious Revolution: Consumer Behavior and the Household Economy, 1650 to the Present* (Cambridge: Cambridge University Press, 2008), and Alexandra Shepard, "Crediting Women in the Early Modern English Economy," *History Workshop Journal* 79, no. 1 (Spring 2015): 1–24.

80 See Tim Meldrum, *Domestic Service and Gender, 1660–1750: Life and Work in the London Household* (New York: Routledge, 2000).

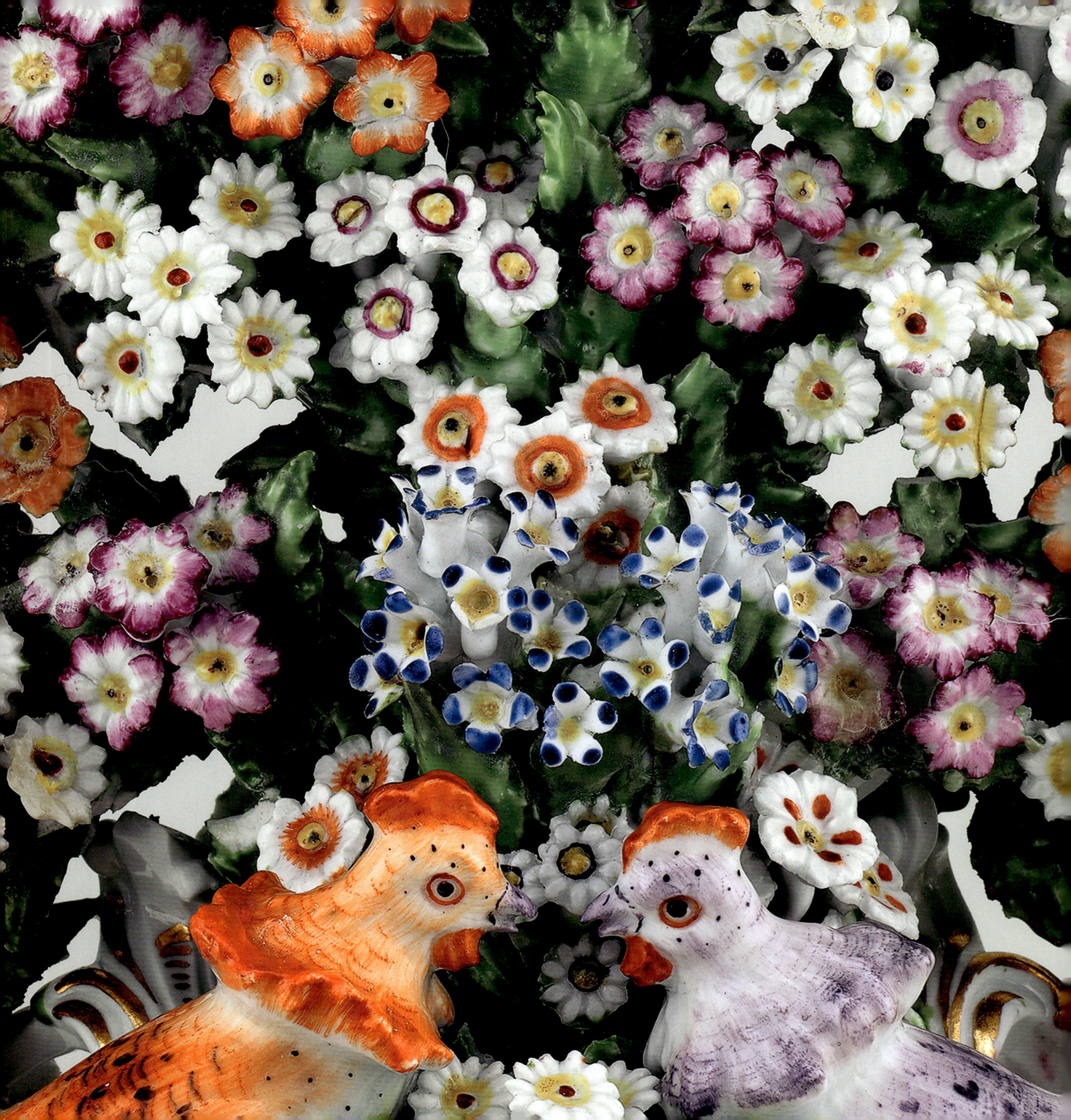

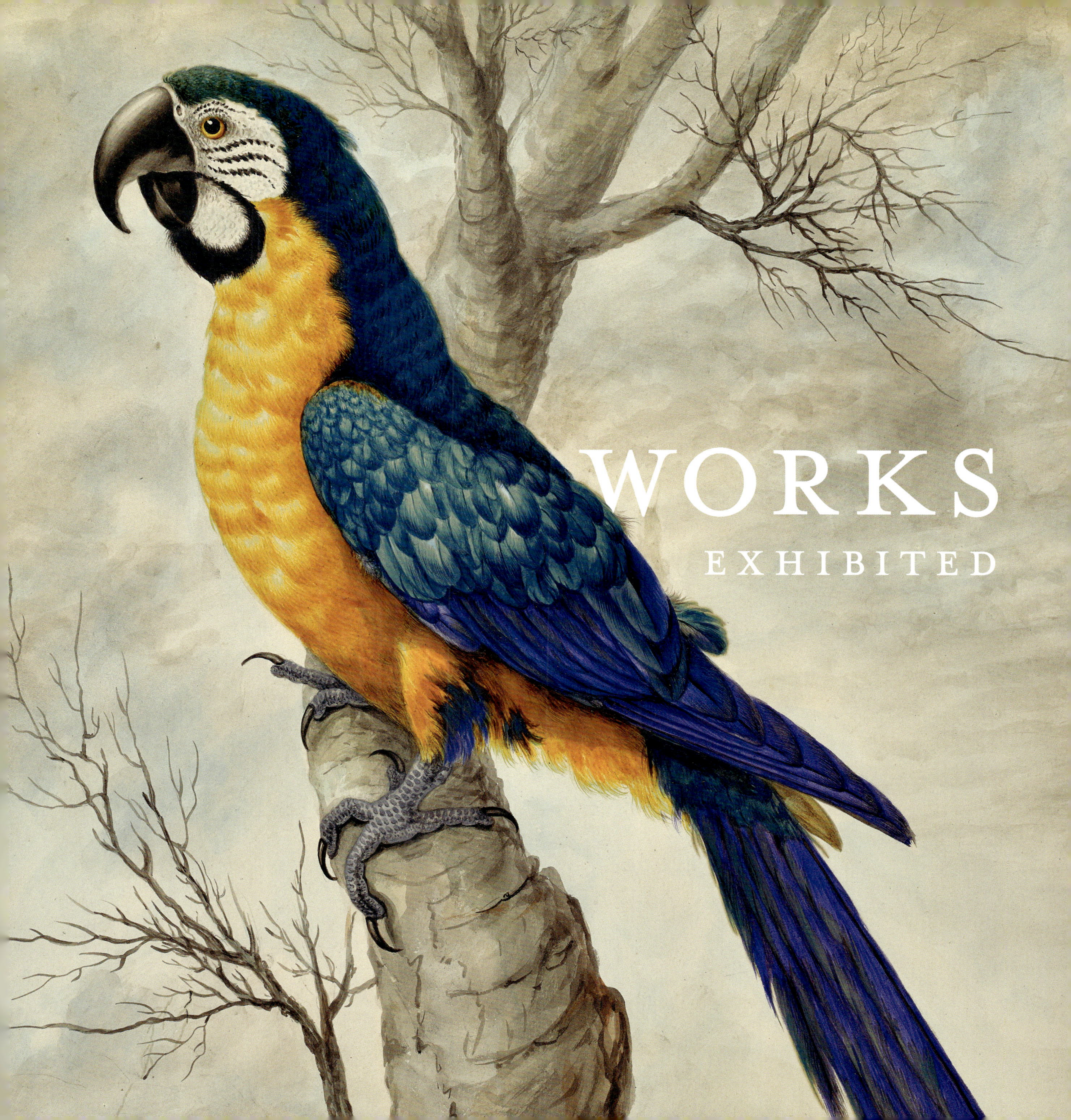
WORKS
EXHIBITED

Book Arts and Publishing

Alexa Greist

Women have a long and rich history in the European book trade, as in the world of manuscript illumination and hand-copied manuscription. Not long after metal movable type came into use in Germany, the first printed books appeared south of the Alps. In Florence, nuns at the Dominican Convent of San Jacopo di Ripoli worked as typesetters on the first books printed in that city. From 1476 to 1484, their press printed around one hundred books, only half of which were religious in nature. As with manuscript illumination, the nuns received payment for their work (recorded in the convent's *diario* or daybook) that went toward supporting the convent.[1] One of the earliest books from the press was Pseudo-Petrarch's *Incominciano Le uite de pontefici et imperadori Romani* (1478), a work detailing the history of popes and Roman emperors (cat. no. 1). The copy presented here is incomplete, as it is untrimmed and lacks its coloured initials. Its marginalia more than makes up for this, in particular the detail of the manicule pointing exuberantly to the name of the ninth-century woman pope, Joan.[2]

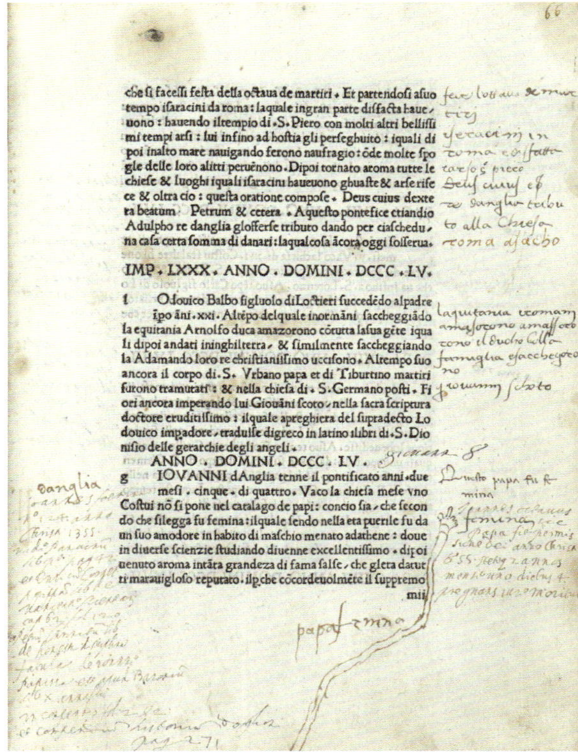
che si facessi festa della octaua de martiri. Et partendosi asuo tempo isaracini da roma: laquale ingran parte disfacta haueuono: hauendo iltempio di .S. Piero con molti altri bellissimi tempi arsi: lui infino ad hostia gli perseghuito: iquali dipoi inalto mare nauigando ferono naufragio: õde molte spogle delle loro alitti peruẽnono. Dipoi tornato aroma tutte le chiese & luoghi iquali isaracini haueuono ghuaste & arse risece & oltra cio: questa oratione compose. Deus cuius dextera beatum Petrum & cetera. Aquesto pontefice etiandio Adulpho re danglia glofferse tributo dando per ciaschedu-na casa certa somma di danari: laqualcosa ãcora oggi sosserua.

IMP. LXXX. ANNO. DOMINI. DCCC. LV.

l Odouico Balbo figluolo di Lottieri succedẽdo alpadre ĩpo ãni. xxi. Altẽpo delquale inormãni saccheggiãdo la equitania Arnolfo duca amazorono cõtutta lasua gẽte iquali dipoi andati ininghilterra, & similmente saccheggiando la Adamando loro re christianissimo uccisono. Altempo suo ancora il corpo di. S. Vrbano papa et di Tiburtino martiri furono tramutati: & nella chiesa di. S. Germano posti. Fiori ancora imperando lui Giouãni scoto, nella sacra scriptura doctore eruditissimo: ilquale apreghiera del supradecto Lodouico impadore, tradusse digreco in latino ilibri di. S. Dionisio delle gerarchie degli angeli.

ANNO. DOMINI. DCCC. LV.

g IOVANNI dAnglia tenne il pontificato anni. due mesi. cinque. di quattro. Vaco la chiesa mese vno Costui nõ si pone nel catalago de papi: concio sia, che secondo che silegga fu femina: ilquale sendo nella eta puerile fu da un suo amodore in habito di maschio menato adathene: doue in diuerse scienzie studiando diuenne excellentissimo. dipoi uenuto aroma intãta grandeza di fama salse, che gle ra datutti marauiglioso reputato. il pche cõcordeuolmẽte il suppremo mii

Women who worked in the book trade—and several other workshop-based artistic productions—are often hidden behind the names of the men in their lives, such as their fathers or husbands, who were the public and legal heads of family businesses. Widows proved the exception, as their names are recorded in archives and on title pages as heads of publishing workshops after the death of their husbands. Although not permitted to establish an independent publishing venture, widows could continue to operate existing businesses, which they often already had experience running before their husband's deaths. They would typically remarry within the trade—a smart business decision—or keep the enterprise running until a son was old enough to assume official ownership. Some scholars viewed a widow's short-lived proprietorship or management of book publishing firms as evidence that women were unsuccessful at running shops because they lacked experience. The very survival of these businesses after a husband's death instead suggests that women in book publishing families were often deeply involved in the financial and practical aspects of the business while their husbands lived.

In sixteenth-century France, Yolande Bonhomme (c. 1490–1557) was one of a number of widows who successfully ran book publishing enterprises. In a fantastic example of such women working together to advance their livelihoods, Bonhomme is documented as having worked with printer Charlotte Guillard and others to bring a lawsuit against the papermakers' guild, protesting the quality of the paper they were

CAT. NO. 1 (facing)
Printer & Publisher: Nuns of the Convent of San Jacopo di Ripoli
Pseudo-Petrarch's *Incominciano Le uite de pontefici et imperadori Romani* [*The Early Stories of the Popes and Roman Emperors*], vol. 2
Florence, 1478
Printed handset type text
28.4 × 21.7 × 2.5 cm
Lisa Unger Baskin Collection, David M. Rubenstein Rare Book & Manuscript Library, Duke University
BX953 .V584 1478 8vo c.2

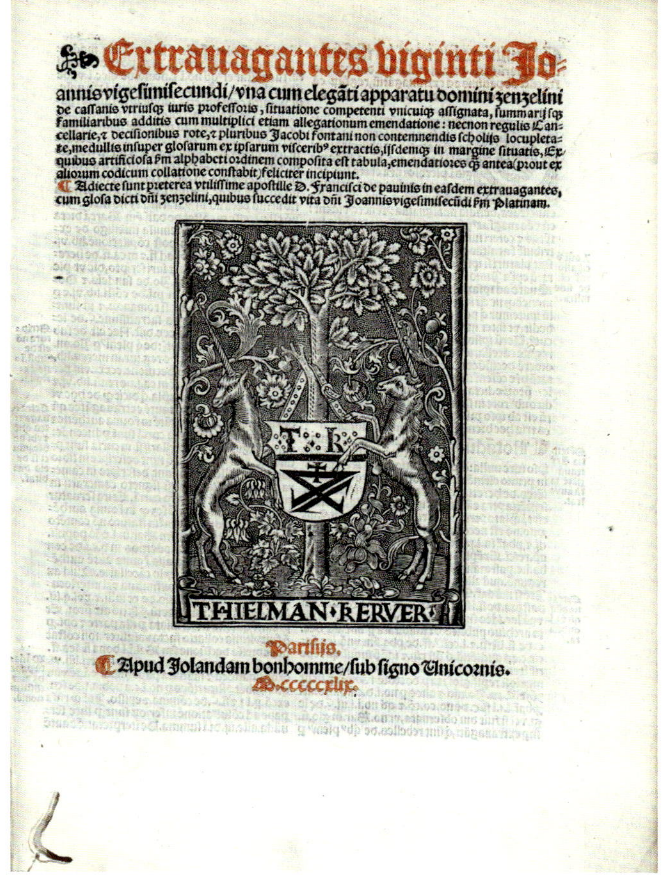
Extrauagantes viginti Jo-
annis vigesimisecundi/vna cum elegāti apparatu domini zenzelini
de cassanis vtriusq3 iuris professoris, situatione competenti vnicuiq3 assignata, summarijs q3
familiaribus additis cum multiplici etiam allegationum emendatione: necnon regulis Cancellarie, z decisionibus rote, z pluribus Jacobi fontani non contemnendis scholijs locupletate, medullis insuper glosarum ex ipsarum visceribus extractis, ijsdemq3 in margine situatis, Ex
quibus artificiosa sm alphabeti ordinem composita est tabula, emendatiores q3 antea (prout ex
aliorum codicum collatione constabit) feliciter incipiunt.
Adiecte sunt preterea vtilissime apostille D. Francisci de pauinis in easdem extrauagantes,
cum glosa dicti dñi zenzelini, quibus succedit vita dñi Joannis vigesimisecūdi sm Platinam.

THIELMAN·KERVER·

Parisijs.
Apud Jolandam bonhomme/sub signo Unicornis.
M.cccccxlix.

CAT. NO. 2
Publisher: Yolande Bonhomme
Pope John XII's *Extravagantes viginti Joannis Vigesimisecundi una cum elega[n]ti apparatu Domini Zenzelini de Cassanis utriusq[ue] juris professoris...* [*The Extravagant Twenty of John the 22nd along with an elegant appendix by Lord Zenzelinus De Cassanis, Professor of Laws...*]
Paris, 1549
Bound volume of woodcut text and illustrations
23.4 × 17 cm
Collection of Lisa Unger Baskin
Photo: Stephen Petegorsky

provided. Bonhomme grew up in a book-printing family before marrying Thielmann Kerver, a successful printer in her hometown of Paris. After becoming widowed in 1522, she took over the business and never remarried. She eventually published under her own name, continuing the firm's successful specialization in illustrated Books of Hours, with over two hundred editions issued under her management. Bonhomme maintained relationships with powerful patrons, including the Catholic Church and, in 1526, she became the first woman to publish an edition of the Bible. In the frontispiece for *Extravagantes viginti Joannis Vigesimisecundi...*, an ecclesiastical text produced by Bonhomme in 1549 (cat. no. 2), the publisher's trademark used by her husband features a pair of unicorns and is accompanied with text below indicating it was made by "Yolande Bonhomme / under the sign of the unicorn." This inscription maintained the workshop's history and identity while also recognizing Bonhomme's authority.

The use of a well-established publisher's trademark could help a widow's business maintain its marketability, but the creation of a new emblem could help build a unique identity for a women-run press. The nuns at the Augustinian monastery of Santa Maria Maddalena in Venice selected for their publishing trademark the Penitent Magdalene, her body covered in her own hair, to reflect the other name for their monastery, *le Convertite* (the Converted)—an order made up primarily of reformed sex workers. From 1557 to 1561, the nuns' press printed twenty-five titles and sold its products through a bookshop located in the nearby square of Santa Maria Formosa. The production and dissemination of volumes like the *Resolutorium Dubiorum Circa Celebrationem Missarum Occurrentium* (cat. no. 3) was considered an active part of the sisters' devotional practice. It was discovered shortly after this period of productivity that the rector was sexually abusing the nuns, resulting in his public execution and the closure of the press.[3]

Supplying printed illustrations for books was a lucrative aspect of printmaking that brought women engravers, etchers, and woodblock cutters into contact with book publishing through family printing businesses or by commission. Geronima Cagnaccia Parasole (c. 1569–1622) was one of two women active in the Parasole family of Rome who signed both single prints and book illustrations. Although she did not sign any of the woodcut illustrations in certain texts, Geronima likely cut the woodblocks for the lace manuals designed by her sister-in-law Elisabetta (or Isabella) Catanea Parasole (c. 1570–c. 1620), such as the *Teatro delle Nobili et Virtuose Donne* (cat. no. 70) as well as illustrations for an herbal.[4] In contrast, Geronima Parasole signed two of the woodcuts with her initials and a woodblock cutter's tool in the illustrations to *Dialoghi di Don Antonio Agostini arciuescouo di Tarracona intorno alle medaglie, inscrittioni et altre antichità* (1592), a text on medals (coins), inscriptions, and other antiquities of Rome (cat. no. 4). Her presence in the volume is stated unmistakably on the title page and on an impressive three-quarter-page woodcut of architectural ruins.

Catharina Sperling-Heckel (1699–1741) was likewise trained within a family workshop—in her case, a family of goldsmiths and miniature painters. She was active in Augsburg as a miniature painter, etcher, and engraver alongside her husband, Hieronymus Sperling. Both their names are recorded as engravers in the ambitious *Kupfer-Bibel, in welcher die Physica Sacra, oder geheiligte Natur-Wissenschaft derer in Heil. Schrifft vorkommenden Natürlichen Sachen, deutlich erklärt und bewährt* (cat. nos. 6 & 7) published in 1731. This lushly illustrated, multi-volume encyclopedic work represents Swiss scientist

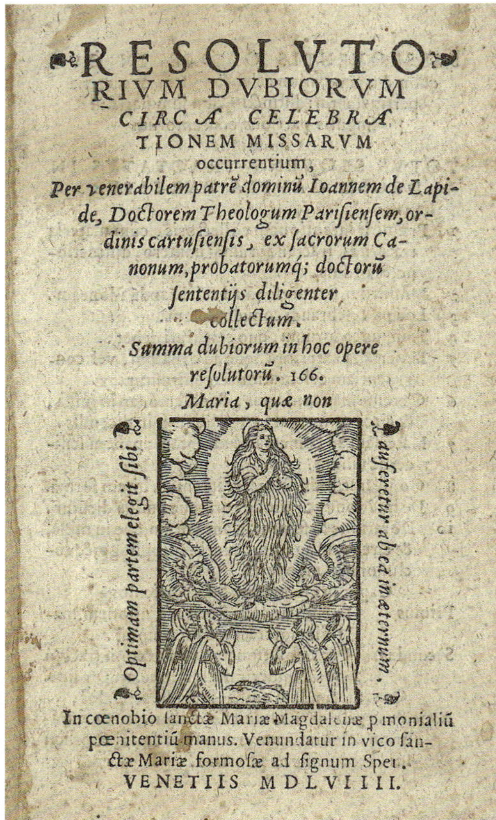
RESOLVTORIVM DVBIORVM CIRCA CELEBRATIONEM MISSARVM occurrentium,

Per venerabilem patrē dominū Ioannem de Lapide, Doctorem Theologum Parisiensem, ordinis cartusiensis, ex sacrorum Canonum, probatorumq; doctorū sententijs diligenter collectum.

Summa dubiorum in hoc opere resolutorū. 166.

Maria, quæ non

Optimam partem elegit sibi

auferetur ab ea in æternum.

In cœnobio sanctæ Mariæ Magdalenæ p monialiū pœnitentiū manus. Venundatur in vico sanctæ Mariæ formosæ ad signum Spei.

VENETIIS MDLVIIII.

CAT. NO. 3
Printer & Publisher: Nuns of the Convent of Santa Maria Maddalena
Resolutorium Dubiorum Circa Celebrationem Missarum Occurrentium…
[The Solution of the Doubts about the Celebration of the Masses]
Venice, 1559
Printed handset type text
14.2 × 9.7 × 3 cm
Special Collections, The Sheridan Libraries, Johns Hopkins University, Rare Books and Manuscripts, Women of the Book Collection, Bib#7595990
Photo: Digitization Services Unit, Johns Hopkins University

Johann Jacob Scheuchzer's attempt to explain Old Testament events through science and thus prove the existence of God. His approach is illustrated through the studiously rendered examples of plants, animals, and human anatomy that feature in the framing of biblical events. For example, in the engraving related to the seventeenth chapter of Exodus, Moses is shown in prayer with arms outstretched, a position he had to hold for the entire battle against the Amalecites in order for the Israelites to prevail. The anatomically accurate depiction of an outstretched arm—with the muscles exposed and labelled—above the scene accompanies a description of the physical stresses Moses would have endured during this feat of endurance.

Elisabetta (later Isabella) Piccini (1644–1734) also worked in book illustration, and received her training in engraving and etching from her father, printmaker Giacomo Piccini, before entering the Venetian convent of Santa Croce. She signed a number of her prints "Suor Isabella Piccini," including a plate depicting the birth of the Virgin in the *Officium B. Mariae Virginis* (1727), a publication for which she engraved six plates and numerous details (cat. no. 5). Working without any assistants, Piccini engraved illustrations for books and single prints for almost seventy years. The many commissions she undertook from the busy Venetian book publishing trade went to support both her convent and her family—for example, paying the dowry of her sister.

Widely unrecognized until recently, women played essential but often silent roles in book production. In sixteenth-century England, women and girls living in extreme poverty supported themselves and their families by collecting rags that were then used by paper mills to make paper.[5] Women running publishing houses fought legal battles over paper quality to protect their businesses. Working as illustrators, publishers, typesetters, writers (cat. no. 130), consumers, or translators (cat. no. 177), they were active agents in the creation of printed books in Europe since the days of the earliest examples, incunabula. As seen in these assorted selections, women's contributions were both secular and religious, and are recorded in archives, business agreements, trademarks, and signatures that confirm the varied roles they played in the history of the printed book.

Resources Consulted

Conway, Melissa. *The Diario of the Printing Press of San Jacopo di Ripoli, 1476–1484: Commentary and Transcription*. Florence: L.S. Olschki, 1999.

Farmer, Alan B. "Widow Publishers in London, 1540–1640." In *Women's Labour and the History of the Book in Early Modern England*. Edited by Valerie Wayne. London: Bloomsbury, 2020.

Lincoln, Evelyn. "Models for Science and Craft: Isabella Parasole's Botanical and Lace Illustrations." *Visual Resources* 17, no. 1 (2001): 1–35.

Trevisan, Luca, and Giulio Zavatta. *Incisori itineranti nell'area veneta nel Seicento: Dizionario bio-bibliografico*. Verona: Università di Verona, 2013.

Two of the most relevant sources for further reading are online records of two exhibitions and collections held at libraries: "Fifty Women" at the Bridwell Library at Southern Methodist University, accessible at bridwell.omeka.net/exhibits/show/fiftywomen/earlyprinters, and the "Women of the Book" collection in the Sheridan Libraries at Johns Hopkins University, accessible at archive.org/details/wotb-collection-illustrated-portfolio-jhu-2021.

Notes

1 Katrina Martin, "Women at Work: The Nuns of the Ripoli Press," *The Devil's Tale: Dispatches from the David M. Rubenstein Rare Book and Manuscript Library*, Duke University, March 10, 2016, blogs.library.duke.edu/rubenstein/2016/03/10/women-at-work-the-nuns-of-the-ripoli-press/.

2 Although most scholars since the seventeenth century believed Joan to have been apocryphal, in the fifteenth century she was a staple in Dominican teaching. She has long been used as a divisive character who was able to deceive the Church and become elected as pope, only to be betrayed by her own womanly body when she was found to be pregnant. For additional reading, see Craig M. Rustici, *The Afterlife of Pope Joan: Deploying the Popess Legend in Early Modern England* (Ann Arbor: University of Michigan Press, 2006).

3 "Women of the Book Collection Catalogue," Internet Archive, Sheridan Libraries, Johns Hopkins University, archive.org/details/copy-of-wotb-word-doc-catalogue-8.18.21:, Bib# 7595990.

4 For a list of lace manuals designed by Elisabetta (or Isabella) Catanea Parasole, see Arthur Lotz, *Bibliographie der Modelbücherbeschreibendes Verzeichnis der Stick- und Spitzenmusterbücher des 16. und 17. Jahrhunderts* (Leipzig: Hiersemann, 1933). For the herbal text, see Castore Durante, *Herbario novo di Castore Durante medico, et cittadino Romano. Con Figure, che rappresentano le vive Piante, che nascono in tutta Europa, & nell' Indie Orientali, & Occidentali* (Venice, appresso li Sessa, 1602).

5 On women's varied roles in early book production, see Heidi Craig, "English Rag-Women and Early Modern Paper Production," in *Women's Labour and the History of the Book in Early Modern England*, ed. Valerie Wayne (London: Bloomsbury, 2020), 29–46.

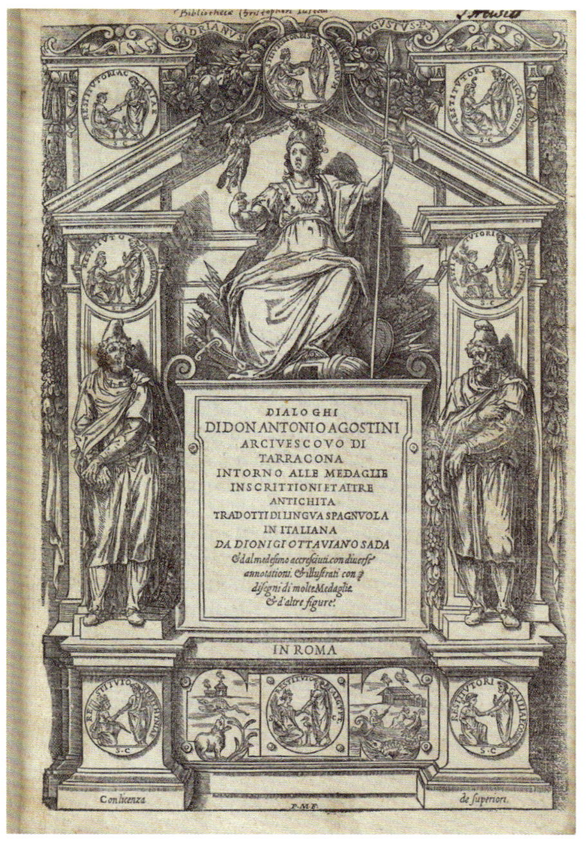

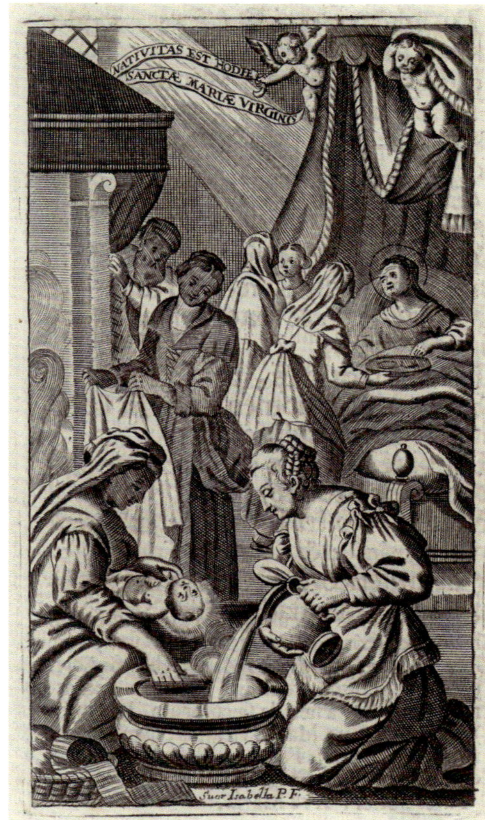

CAT. NO. 4 (left)
Geronima Cagnaccia Parasole
Frontispiece in Antonio Agustín's *Dialoghi di Don Antonio Agostini arciuescouo di Tarracona intorno alle medaglie, inscrittioni et altre antichità* [*Dialogues of Don Antonio Agostini, Archbishop of Tarracona on medals, inscriptions and other antiquities*]
Rome, 1592
Bound volume of woodcuts on paper
32.2 × 23.5 × 3.2 cm
Lisa Unger Baskin Collection, David M. Rubenstein Rare Book & Manuscript Library, Duke University
CJ5595 .A38716 1592 4to c.2

CAT. NO. 5 (right)
Elisabetta (Isabella) Piccini
Nativity of the Virgin Mary in *Officium B. Mariae Virginis : S. Pii C. Pontificis max. jussu editum, et ab. Urbano VIII…* [*Engraved illustrations for the Offices of the Virgin Mary*]
Venice, 1727
Bound volume of engravings
Page: 20 × 10 cm
Harvard University, Houghton Library, Gift of Philip Hofer
TYP 725.27.262
Exhibited at AGO only

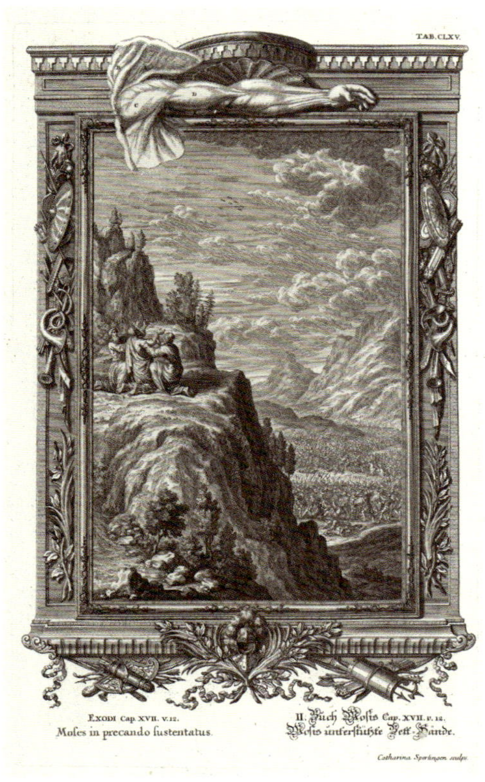

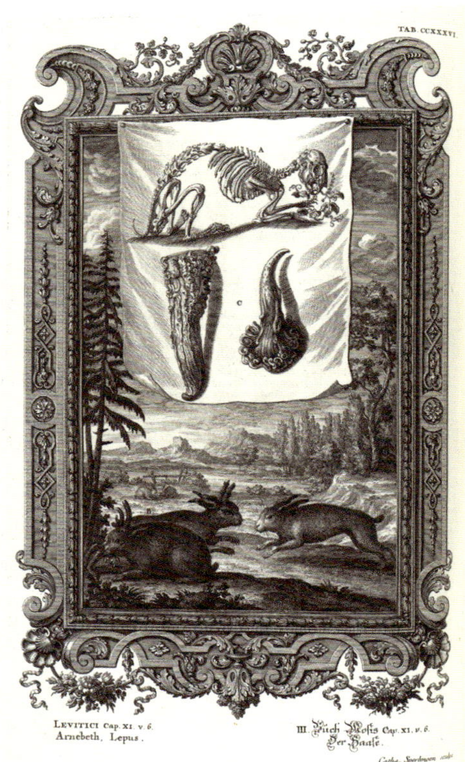

CAT. NO. 6
Catharina Sperling-Heckel, after Johann Melchior Füssli and Johann Daniel Preissler
Moses's arms grow heavy as he prays for the victory of the Israelites over the Amalecites in Johann Jakob Scheuchzer's *Kupfer-Bibel, in welcher die Physica Sacra, oder geheiligte Natur-Wissenschaft derer in Heil. Schrifft vorkommenden Natürlichen Sachen, deutlich erklärt und bewährt* [*Copper Bible – in which the Physica Sacra or sacred natural science of natural things that appear in Holy Scripture are clearly explained and proven*], vol. 1
Augsburg and Ulm, 1731
Bound volume of engravings
Page: 38.3 × 24.4 cm;
book: 39.1 × 26.5 × 6.5 cm
National Gallery of Art, Washington, Epstein Family Fund, 1987
1987.26.1

CAT. NO. 7
Catharina Sperling-Heckel, after Johann Melchior Füssli and Johann Daniel Preissler
The hare [*Arnebeth lepus*] in Johann Jakob Scheuchzer's *Kupfer-Bibel, in welcher die Physica Sacra, oder geheiligte Natur-Wissenschaft derer in Heil. Schrifft vorkommenden Natürlichen Sachen, deutlich erklärt und bewährt* [*Copper Bible – in which the Physica Sacra or sacred natural science of natural things that appear in Holy Scripture are clearly explained and proven*], vol. 2
Augsburg and Ulm, 1731
Bound volume of engravings
Page: 38.3 × 24.4 cm;
book: 39 × 26.5 × 7 cm
National Gallery of Art, Washington, Epstein Family Fund, 1987
1987.26.2

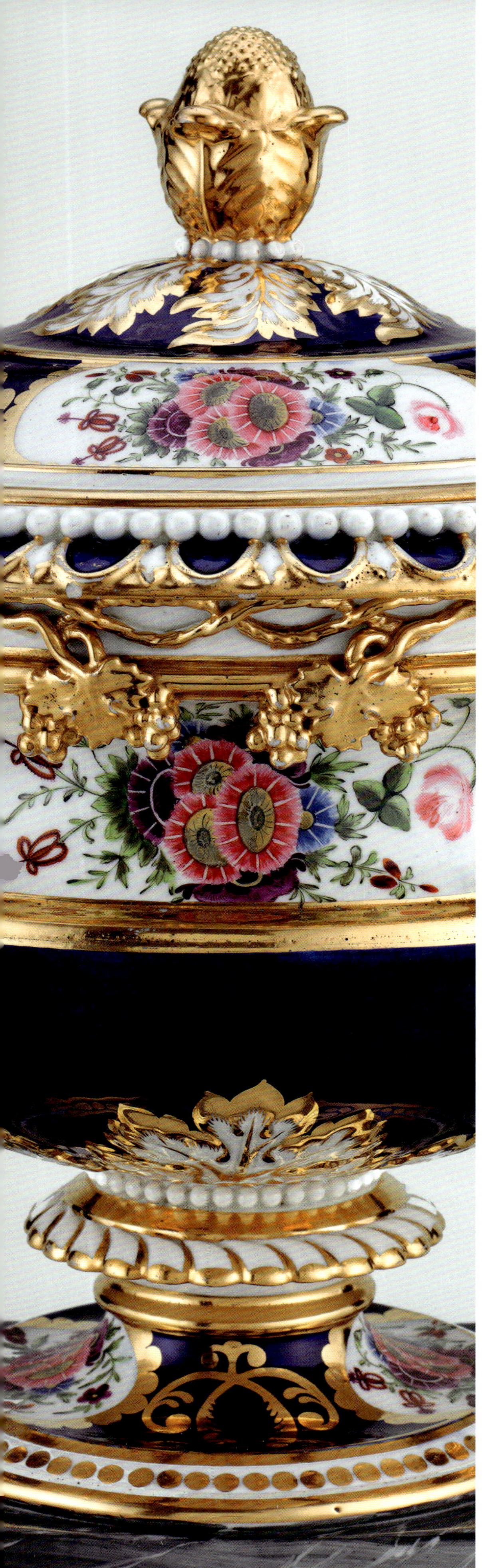

Ceramics

Brittany Luberda and Theresa Kutasz Christensen

> Mrs. Wilcox was a brave and valiant woman. She brought her pencils and brushes tied in a bundle, carefully preserved from the tread of the wagon folk. She brought her tools, but still more important, she brought herself. Her husband always admitted that she was much greater than he himself was. She long worked for [Josiah] Wedgwood, and, indeed, died in his service.
>
> —Samuel Smiles[1]

Women at the wheel and workbench made and decorated pottery for a wide range of contexts, including utilitarian purposes and royal commissions, throughout pre-modern Europe. Between the 1400s and 1800s, pottery-making took place in domestic workshops with a single wheel and homemade kiln, as well as in large-scale factories where subject-matter experts in modelling and decoration produced ceramics fired in massive kilns yielding twenty thousand or more pieces. Women are found at each stage of production, employed in both family workshops and global enterprises. Their roles ranged from the largely anonymous labour of the preparation of clay to the modelling of forms, painting of surfaces, and the ownership of factories. Women ceramicists worked with all clay forms, types, and glazes. Their names and hands are intertwined with the histories of porcelain in Germany, Prussia, and France and of tin-glazed earthenware in Italy, France, and the Netherlands, and with the profusion of ceramics fired by eighteenth-century English potteries, among other geographies.

The emergence of porcelain factories in Europe during the 1710s expanded opportunities for women's involvement in the production and decoration of ceramics for upper-class patrons. Vessels and objects from the Meissen manufactory in Germany—the first European factory to produce a clay akin to Asian porcelain factories—were adorned with enamel and gold by Anna Elizabeth Auffenwerth Wald (born 1696) and Sabina Auffenwerth Hosennestel (1706–1782). These sisters ran separate *hausmaler* (home painter) decorating studios, where they painted on either blanks or seconds—products with minor defects—for the Meissen factory or private clients. The white surface of porcelain offered a consistent backdrop for the sisters' distinctive decorations. A service for coffee and tea painted by one or more of the sisters, now split between the collections of the Museum of Fine Arts, Boston, and the Smithsonian, features chinoiserie scenes depicting exoticized figures drinking coffee and tea or smoking (cat. nos. 11 & 12). It is possible that sets like this were used in the coffee house owned by Sabina's husband. While the sisters are best known for their beverage services, they worked on a range of tableware, including a tureen and matching stand in the collection of the Gardiner Museum (cat. no. 10) that feature the sort of elaborate, multicoloured strapwork in which Elizabeth and Sabina are known to have often hidden their initials, though none have been identified in the Gardiner examples.

The Vincennes Porcelain Factory in France, established by royal investors under Louis XV (r. 1715–1774), prospered under the direction of Marie-Henriette Gravant (active mid-1700s). From 1745 to 1755, Gravant led a workshop of women flower makers at Vincennes. Historically, the narrative around their involvement in the floral workshop has included the trope that the formation of the delicate petals required the nimbleness of thin female fingers. While this seems a highly gendered generalization about the women who worked in these porcelain manufactories, they were indeed able to produce remarkably fine and botanically accurate studies of roses, carnations, lilies, and other florals, each an example of *trompe l'oeil* par excellence. In 1748, Gravant's studio was

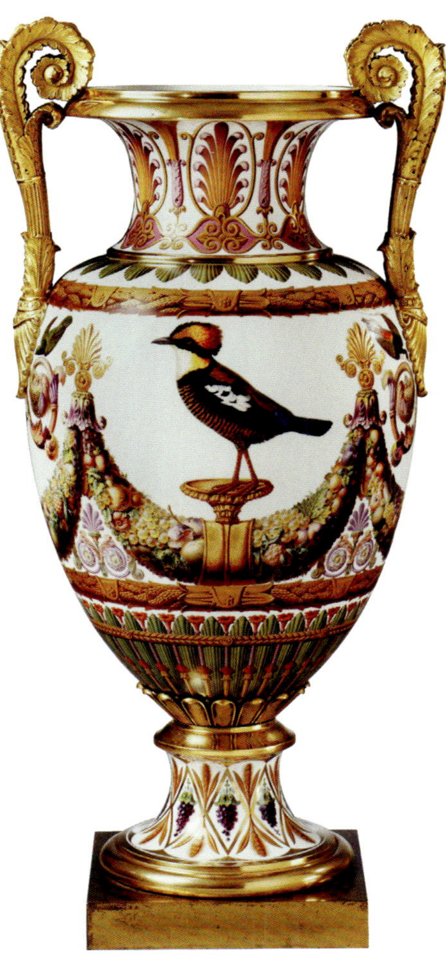

CAT. NO. 8 (left)
Decorator: Pauline Rifer de Courcelles, known as Madame Knip
Manufacturer: Manufacture Nationale de Sèvres
Vase with African Birds
1822
Porcelain, ormolu, and bronze
71.8 × 36.2 × 32.4 cm
On Loan from Hillwood Estate, Museum & Gardens,
Bequest of Marjorie Merriweather Post, 1973
24.181
Photographed by Edward Owen

CAT. NO. 9 (below)
Workshop director: Pierette Candelot
Manufacturer: Manufacture de la Veuve Perrin
Lobed round plate with Chinoiserie
c. 1750–1800
Tin-glazed earthenware and petit feu enamels
Diameter: 25 cm
Gardiner Museum, Toronto, Canada,
The Pierre Karch and Mariel O'Neill-Karch Collection
G14.4.6

listed as having employed forty-five women who modelled and painted lifelike flowers attached to the factory's productions or that were sold to *marchands-merciers*, art dealers who affixed the loose florals (cat. no. 16) to clocks, vases, and sculpture. In subsequent centuries, these pieces were often reworked according to changing fashions, resulting in assemblages like a nineteenth-century flower arrangement that mimics the form of an edged garden full of flowers (cat. no. 17). Following in the tradition of the flowers produced by Vincennes, women across Europe produced detailed flowers for porcelain manufacturers of the type found at Chelsea-Derby, which was active in England between 1770 and 1784. On a pair of candlesticks (cat. no. 13) emblematic of that manufacture, lively birds and chickens fill the Rococo base in front of a towering floral bocage.

After the Vincennes factory relocated to Sèvres, women continued to innovate, particularly in painting on porcelain. Geneviève Taillandier (active 1774–1798) was a painter of flowers credited with designing the *oeil-de-perdrix* pattern widely found on dinnerware and furniture with plaques in the 1770s and '80s. Spanning multiple stylistic periods at the factory, her painting ranges from Rococo florals to neoclassical motifs, as seen on the scrolls and flowered border of her tea service with tray and sugar bowl (cat. no. 23). Women painters were so significant to the production process that the Sèvres factory established a designated studio, the *atelier des desmoiselles*, for women painters and gilders, where figures such as Sophie Chanou Binet (active 1779–1798) and Geneviève-Louise Bouillat (active 1776–1798) adapted textiles and pearls into patterns on porcelain (cat. no. 22).

Bridging art and science, Pauline Rifer de Courcelles, known as Madame Knip (1781–1851), painted birds on Sèvres porcelain, displaying her ability to accurately render nature on ceramic. For women makers of flowers and painters on porcelain, the natural sciences were integral to artistic practice. For example, to prepare for a major commission, such as a vase covered in African birds (cat. no. 8), or a set of plates featuring South American birds ringed in flora native to their habitat (cat. no. 25), Knip studied specimens on display at the Musée d'Histoire Naturelle in Paris. An exploration of the role of women in the material-science side of ceramic manufacture yields similarly impressive contributions by innovators such as Charlotte Hampton (active after 1789). Hired by Flight's factory in Worcester to head the decorating department, Hampton introduced a new technique for mercury gilding to Worcester, which created the bright, highly polished gilding seen on the Baltimore Museum of Art's ice pail with lid (cat. no. 15).

In the seventeenth and eighteenth centuries, large ceramic factories across Europe like Sèvres and the Royal Prussian porcelain manufactories functioned as maker-complexes that included clay mines, pottery studios, kilns, and tenant housing. Whole families lived and worked together at these miniature cities, which also included the English potteries in Stoke-on-Trent owned by Josiah Wedgwood. At Wedgwood, women living on site were employed in the preparation of clay, the painting of ornamental details, and the production of new designs. For the *Frog Service*—a royal commission from Catherine II of Russia (often called Catherine the Great; r. 1762–1796) consisting of 952 pieces of creamware painted with scenes of England and a green frog crest—at least six women painted borders and central landscapes (cat. no. 14). At the London manufactory producing the service, Sarah Wilcox is listed in the inventories as the highest-paid female painter for the commission; however, she received only half the amount per

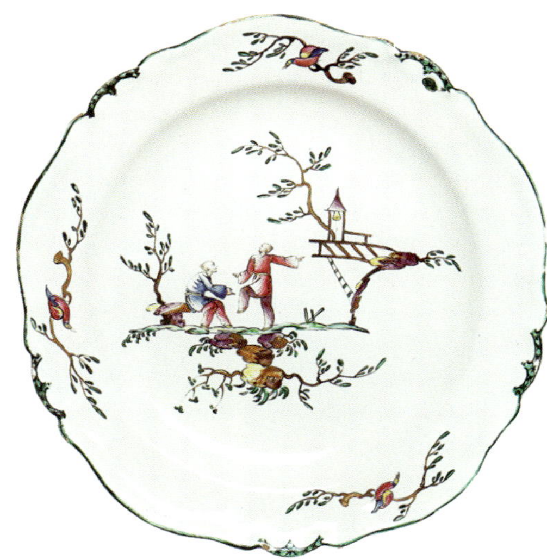

week as the top-earning male painter, indicating gender bias.[2] Outside the factory's locations in London and Stoke-on-Trent, Wedgwood engaged aristocratic artists Elizabeth Upton Templetown, known as Lady Templetown (1746–1823), Diana Beauclerk (1734–1808), and Emma Crewe (1780–1850), who had the luxury of working from home studios. They designed motifs and scenes of women and children deemed appealing to middle-class female markets. Lady Templetown's figures appear in period jewellery (cat. no. 18) set in the newly fashionable and relatively affordable medium of cut steel, as well as on elegant decorative vases made for domestic spaces (cat. no. 21). A playful design featuring a chubby young Bacchus by Beauclerk can be seen both in black on a red stoneware jug (cat. no. 20) and in white relief on a plaque (cat. no. 19), demonstrating the varied applications of her designs across Wedgwood products.

In France, competition with Wedgwood's tableware for an upper-class domestic clientele came from the faience industry, which included factories owned by women like Pierette Candelot (1709–1794). Candelot, or the Veuve (widow) Perrin, as she was known, operated the Veuve Perrin factory in the bustling port city of Marseilles from 1748, when her husband died, until her own death in 1794. The manufacture specialized in *petit feu* enamels in which a tin-based glaze is applied to earthenware, creating creamy, glossy, off-white and cream works that were visually comparable to popular and much more expensive porcelain services. Considered an affordable option for a toilette service or dinnerware, Perrin's pieces were recognized for their quality in design and decoration, which ranged from landscapes and veristic flowers to fashionable interpretations of Asian ceramic decoration. The latter can be seen in a plate from the Gardiner Museum's collection (cat. no. 9), which was part of a set made in the style of the popular chinoiserie designs produced by Anne Allen (c. 1749/50–after 1808) and her husband Jean-Baptiste Pillement (cat. no. 152).

The prominence of women in early modern European ceramics comes to full fruition in the *Tea Service of Famous Women* (cat. no. 24), painted at Sèvres by Marie-Victoire Jaquotot (1772–1855), a renowned portraitist on porcelain. In this service, originally designed for Empress Josephine, Jaquotot paid homage to historically prominent female politicians, soldiers, authors, and philosophers, including Elizabeth I, queen of England (r. 1558–1603); Christina, Queen of Sweden (r. 1632–1654); Catherine the Great, empress of Russia (r. 1762–1796); Joan of Arc (c. 1412–1431); and Madame de Sévigné (1646–1705). These figures span centuries of female enlightenment and entrepreneurship parallel to the consistent presence and expanding recognition of women as leaders in European ceramics.

Whether turning a wheel to produce pottery for a regional town market in the fifteenth century or imitating ikat fabrics on porcelain at the close of the eighteenth century, women experts crafted ceramics, in shape or decoration, continuously pushing the limits of form and glaze. As Victorian biographer Samuel Smiles attested of Wilcox, one of the most respected decorators at the Wedgewood factory, "she brought her tools, but still more important, she brought herself."

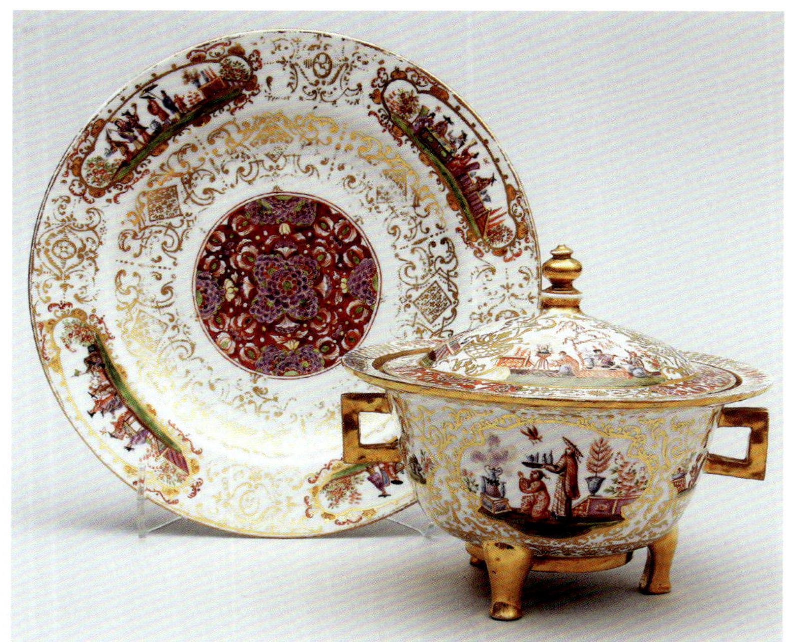

CAT. NO. 10
Decorators: Probably Anna Elizabeth Auffenwerth Wald, and possibly Sabina Auffenwerth Hosennestel
Manufacturer: Meissen Porcelain Factory
Tureen and stand
c. 1725
Hard-paste porcelain with overglaze enamels, and gilding
17.8 × 22.9 × 22.9 cm
Gardiner Museum, Toronto, Canada, Gift of George and Helen Gardiner
G83.1.0717.1-.3

Resources Consulted

Dauterman, Carl Christian. *Sèvres Porcelain: Makers and Marks of the Eighteenth Century*. New York: Metropolitan Museum of Art, 1986.

Petsalis-Diomidis, Alexia. "Pottery Workers, 'the Ladies,' and 'the Middling Class of People': Production and Marketing of 'Etruscan and Grecian Vases' at Wedgwood, c.1760–1820." *Bulletin of the Institute of Classical Studies* 63, no. 1 (2020): 34–53.

Raeburn, Michael. *The Green Frog Service*. London and St. Petersburg: Cacklegoose Press in association with the State Hermitage, 1995.

Savill, Rosalind, and Karen Wilks. *Everyday Rococo: Madame de Pompadour and Sèvres Porcelain*. Norwich: Unicorn Press, 2021.

Vincentelli, Moira. *Women Potters: Transforming Traditions*. Oxford: Rutgers University Press, 2004.

Young, Hilary. *English Porcelain, 1745–95: Its Makers, Design, Marketing and Consumption*. London: V&A, 1999.

Notes

1 Samuel Smiles, *Josiah Wedgwood F.R.S, His Personal History* (London: Harper & Brothers, 1895), 23.

2 Sophie Guiny, "Artists, Workers and Tastemakers: Wedgwood and Women," *All Things Georgian*, May 7, 2019, georgianera.wordpress.com/2019/05/07/artists-workers-and-tastemakers-wedgwood-and-women-a-guest-post-by-sophie-guiny/, accessed June 16, 2023.

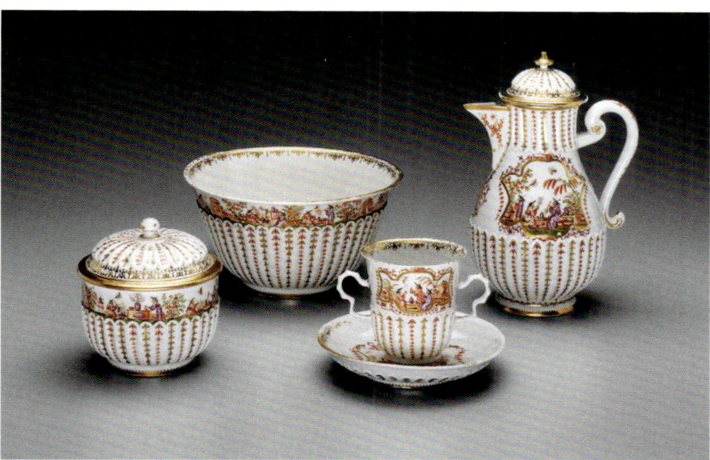

CAT. NO. 11
Decorators: Probably Anna Elizabeth Auffenwerth Wald, and possibly Sabina Auffenwerth Hosennestel
Manufacturer: Meissen Porcelain Factory
Partial coffee service
c. 1723, decorated c. 1725–1730
Hard-paste porcelain with coloured enamel and gilded decoration
Coffee pot: 19.6 × 13.6 × 10.6 cm; cup: 7.8 × 10.7 × 7.3 cm; saucer: 2.7 × 13.2 cm; covered sugar bowl: 10.4 × 10.2 cm; waste bowl: 9.1 × 17.9 cm
Museum of Fine Arts, Boston, Bequest of Forsyth Wickes—The Forsyth Wickes Collection
65.2076a-b, 65.2077a-b, 65.2079a-b, 65.2080
Photograph © 2023 Museum of Fine Arts, Boston

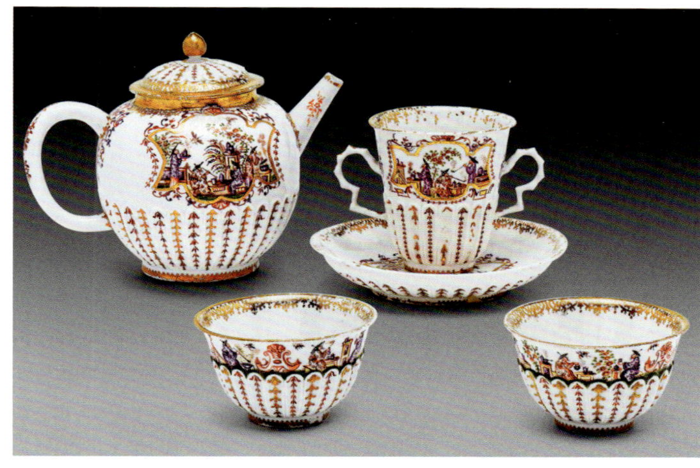

CAT. NO. 12
Decorators: Probably Anna Elizabeth Auffenwerth Wald, and possibly Sabina Auffenwerth Hosennestel
Manufacturer: Meissen Porcelain Factory
Partial tea service
1730
Hard-paste porcelain with polychrome and gold
Tea bowl: 4.5 × 7.6 cm; chocolate cup: 8 cm; saucer: 31.1 cm; teapot: 12.7 × 16.8 cm
National Museum of American History, Smithsonian Institution
1987.0896. 34 A,B; 36 a,b; 37 a,b
Photo: Division of Home and Community Life, National Museum of American History, Smithsonian Institution
Exhibited tea bowl and teapot only

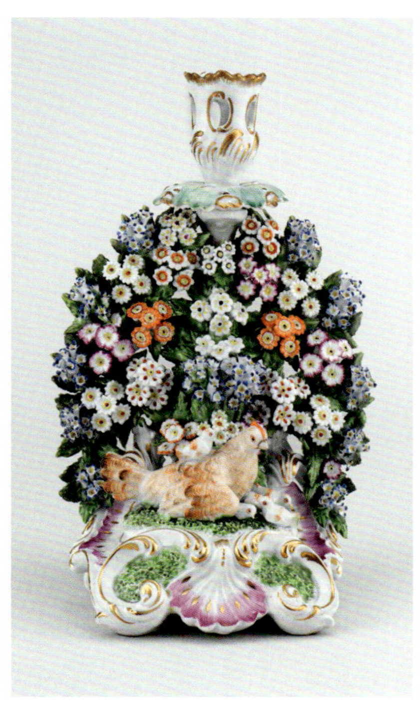

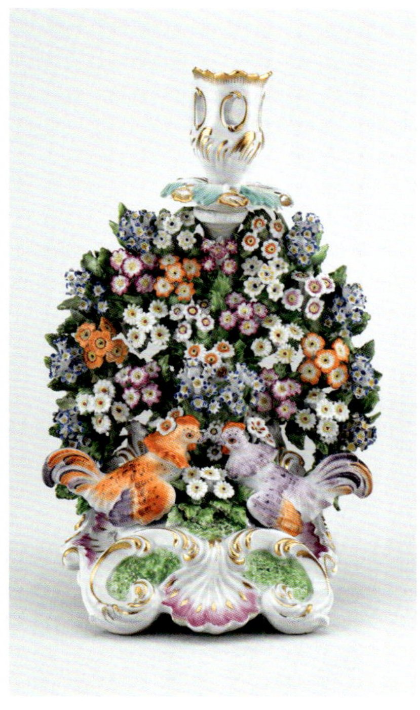

CAT. NO. 13
Manufacturer: Chelsea-Derby Porcelain Factory
Pair of candlesticks
c. 1770–1775
Soft-paste porcelain, painted with overglaze enamels, and gold
A (left): 23.5 × 15.2 × 13 cm; B (right): 23.5 × 15.9 × 13.3 cm
Baltimore Museum of Art: Gift of Mr. and Mrs. Kenneth S. Battye, Baltimore, 1971.24.1a-b
Photo: Mitro Hood

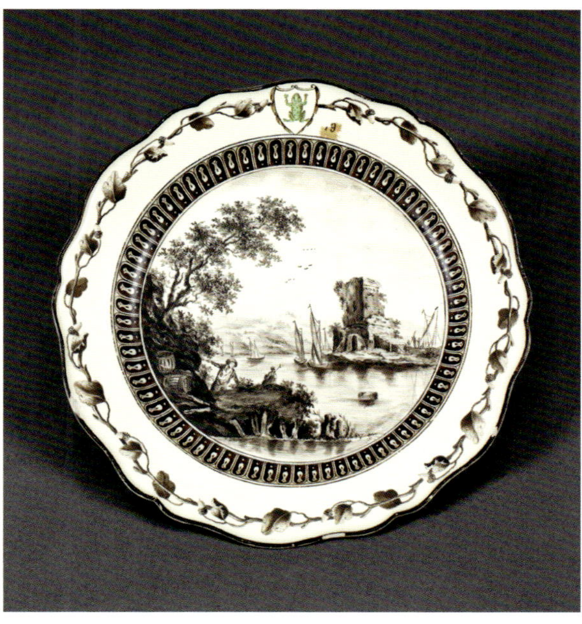

CAT. NO. 14
Service decorators: Sarah Wilcox, Catherine Dent, Bernice Glisson, Ann Mills, Anne Pars, and others
Manufacturer: Wedgwood
Dinner plate from the *Frog Service*
1773–1774
Glazed earthenware with enamel
Diameter: 22.9 cm
Saint Louis Art Museum, Gift of Mr. and Mrs. Milton L. Zorensky, by exchange
511:2018

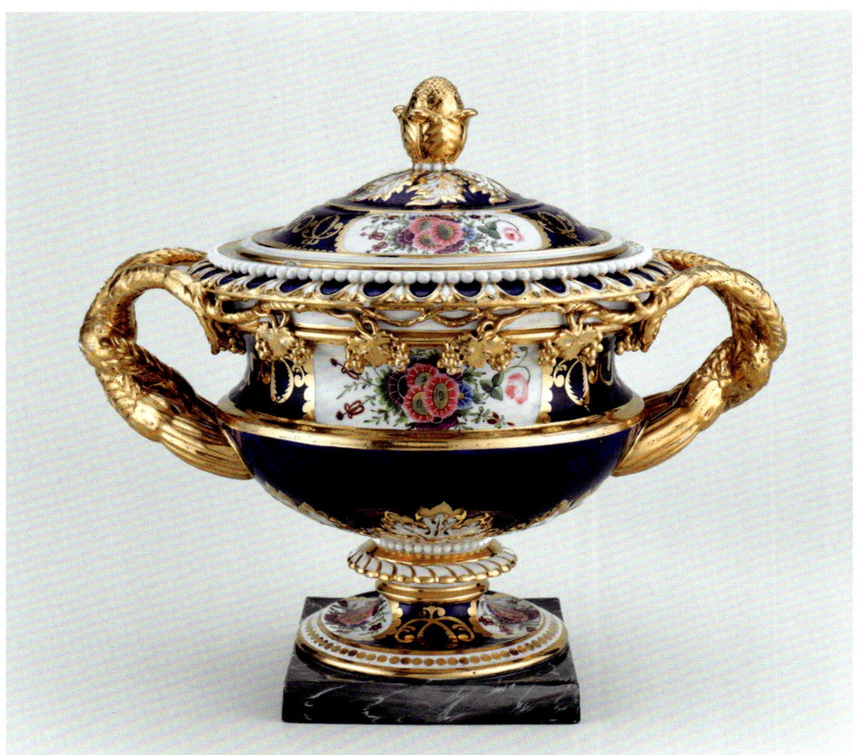

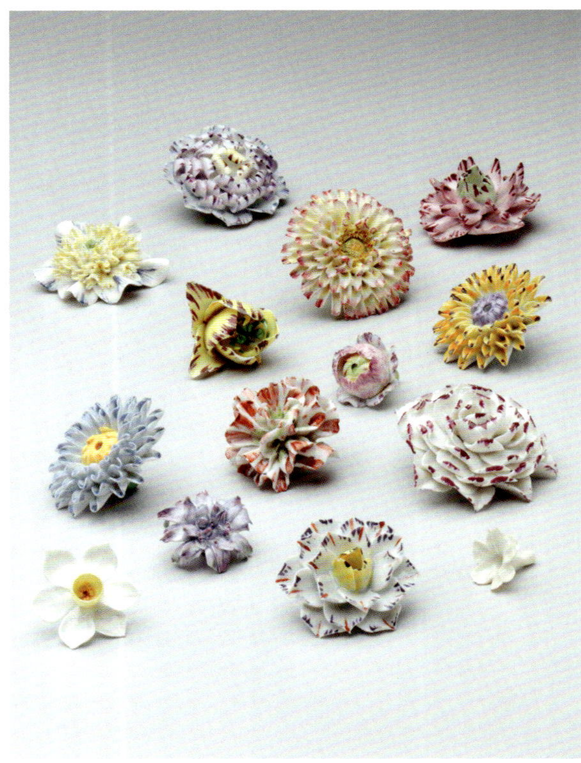

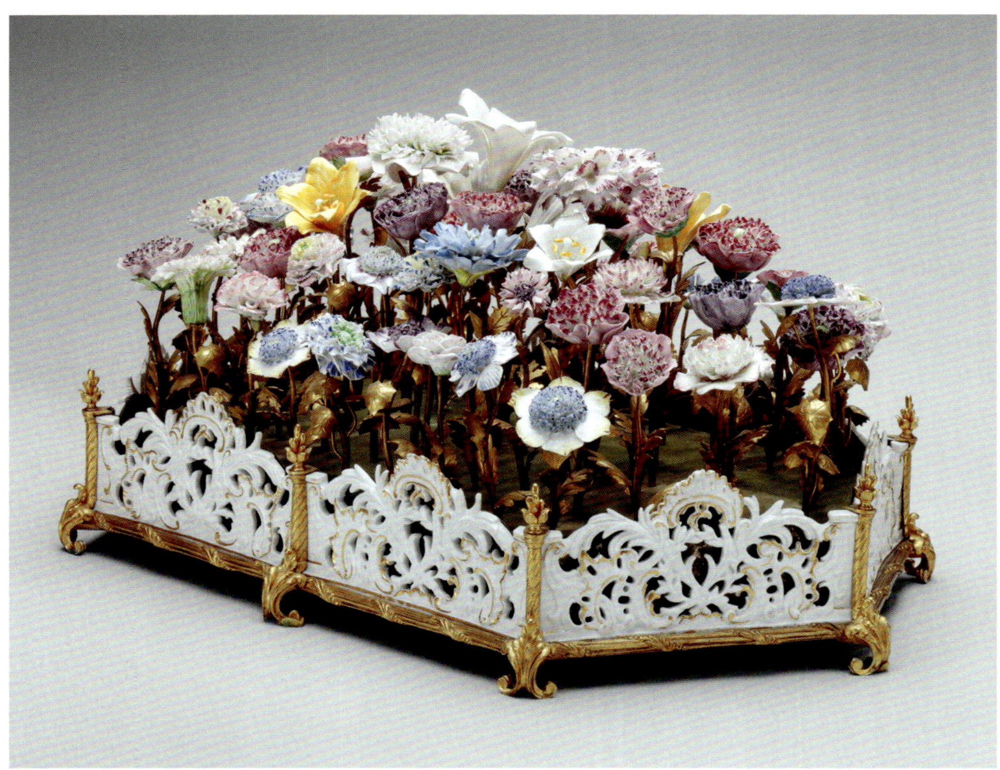

CAT. NO. 15 (above, left)
Manufacturer: Chamberlain's (later The Royal Worcester Porcelain Co., Ltd.)
Ice pail with cover and liner
1810–1820
Porcelain, painted with underglaze blue, overglaze enamels, and gold
31.1 × 34.9 × 24.8 cm
Baltimore Museum of Art: Gift of Mrs. Francis White, from the Collection of Mrs. Miles White, Jr., 1973.76.26.2
Photo: Mitro Hood

CAT. NO. 17 (below, left)
Workshop director: Marie-Henriette Gravant
Manufacturer: Manufacture Nationale de Sèvres
Flower arrangement
c. 1748
Porcelain
59.7 × 37.5 × 30.5 cm
Courtesy of Michele Beiny Harkins
Photo: Richard Goodbody

CAT. NO. 16 (above, right)
Workshop director: Marie-Henriette Gravant
Manufacturer: Manufacture Nationale de Sèvres
Individual flowers
c. 1748
Soft- and hard-paste porcelain
Sizes vary, approx. life-size; smallest flower: 1.9 × 1.9 × 1.3 cm; largest flower: 5.7 × 5.7 × 3.2 cm
Courtesy of Michele Beiny Harkins
Photo: Richard Goodbody

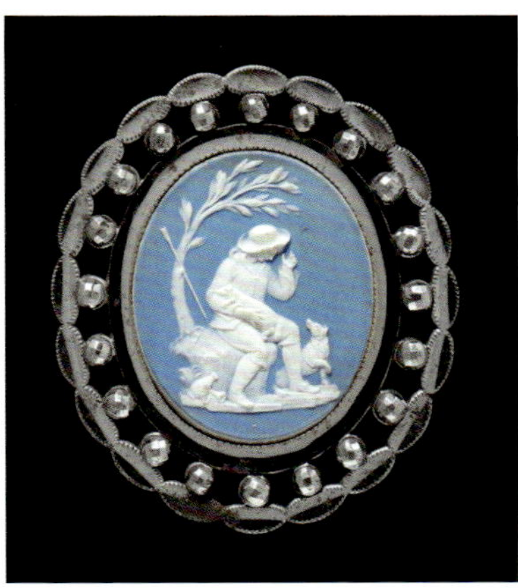

CAT. NO. 18
Designer: Possibly Elizabeth Upton Templetown, known as Lady Templetown
Manufacturer: Wedgwood
Bourbonnais Shepherd Jasperware brooch
c. 1780–1800
Steel, cut and polished, and mounted with a plaque of blue Jasper-dip with a white cameo
7.6 × 6.4 cm
Victoria and Albert Museum, London, Given by Lady Charlotte Schreiber
414:1286-1885
Image © Victoria and Albert Museum, London

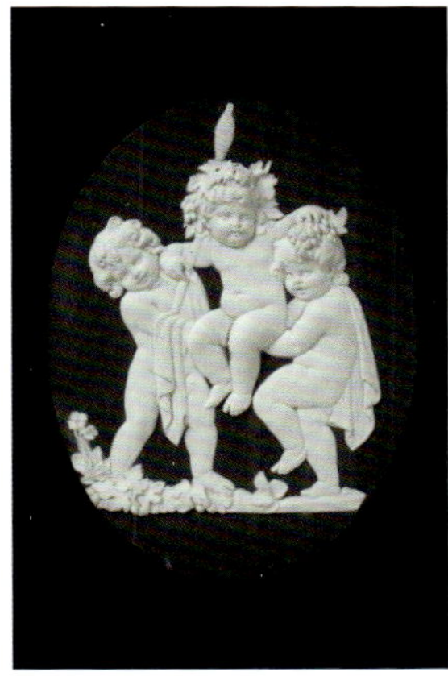

CAT. NO. 19
Designer: Diana Beauclerk
Manufacturer: Wedgwood
Plaque
c. 1789–1800
White Jasperware with black dip and applied white bas relief
14.6 × 10.5 cm
Victoria and Albert Museum, London
3506-1855
Image © Victoria and Albert Museum, London

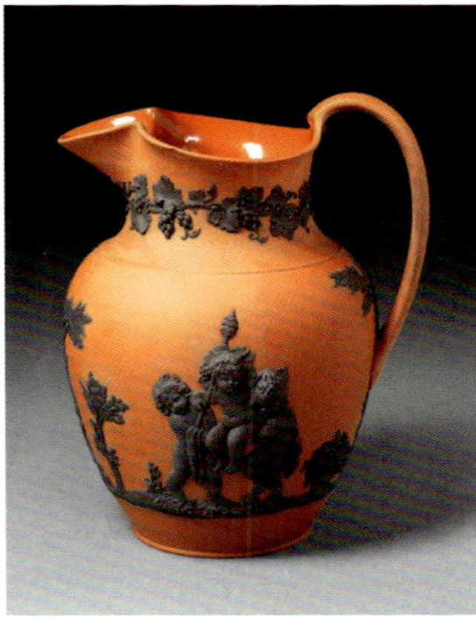

CAT. NO. 20
Designer: Diana Beauclerk
Manufacturer: Wedgwood
Jug
c. 1800–1810
Red stoneware with applied black basalt reliefs and glazed interior
23.5 × 17.8 cm
Victoria and Albert Museum, London
3480-1855
Image © Victoria and Albert Museum, London

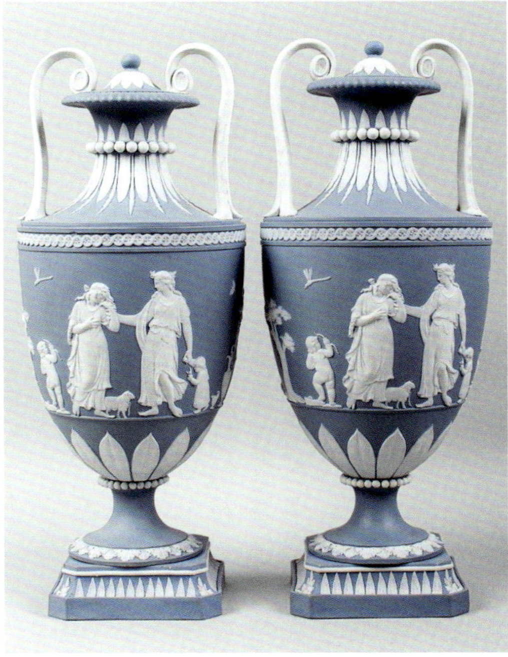

CAT. NO. 21
Designer: Elizabeth Upton Templetown, known as Lady Templetown
Manufacturer: Wedgwood
Pair of two-handled vases and covers
c. 1790
Jasperware
25.4 cm each
Collection of Sophie Guiny and Charles Bushman

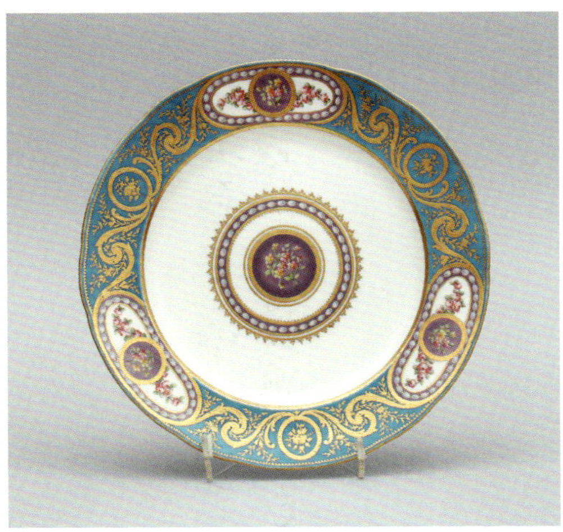

CAT. NO. 22
Decorator: Possibly Geneviève-Louise Bouillat
Manufacturer: Manufacture Nationale de Sèvres
Plate
1784
Soft-paste porcelain, overglaze enamels, and gilding
Diameter: 24 cm
Gardiner Museum, Toronto, Canada, Gift of Dr. William Johnston
G13.6.1

CAT. NO. 23 (right)
Decorator: Geneviève Taillandier
Manufacturer: Manufacture Nationale de Sèvres
Tea service with tray and sugar bowl
1787–1790
Soft-paste porcelain
Tray: 5.6 × 27.9 × 22.9 cm; sugar bowl and cover: 9.5 × 7.3 cm; teapot and cover: 8.7 × 6.8 cm; cup: 6 cm, diameter: 5.6 cm, with handle: 7.6 cm; saucer: 3 × 11.7 cm
Clark Art Institute, Williamstown, Massachusetts, USA, Acquired by Sterling and Francine Clark before 1955
1955.1343.1-5
Image courtesy Clark Art Institute. clarkart.edu

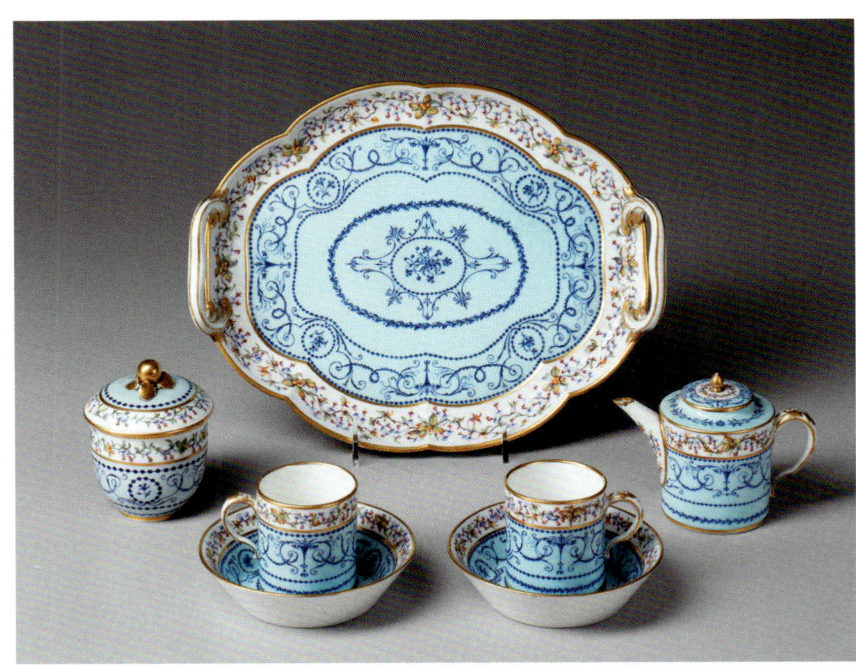

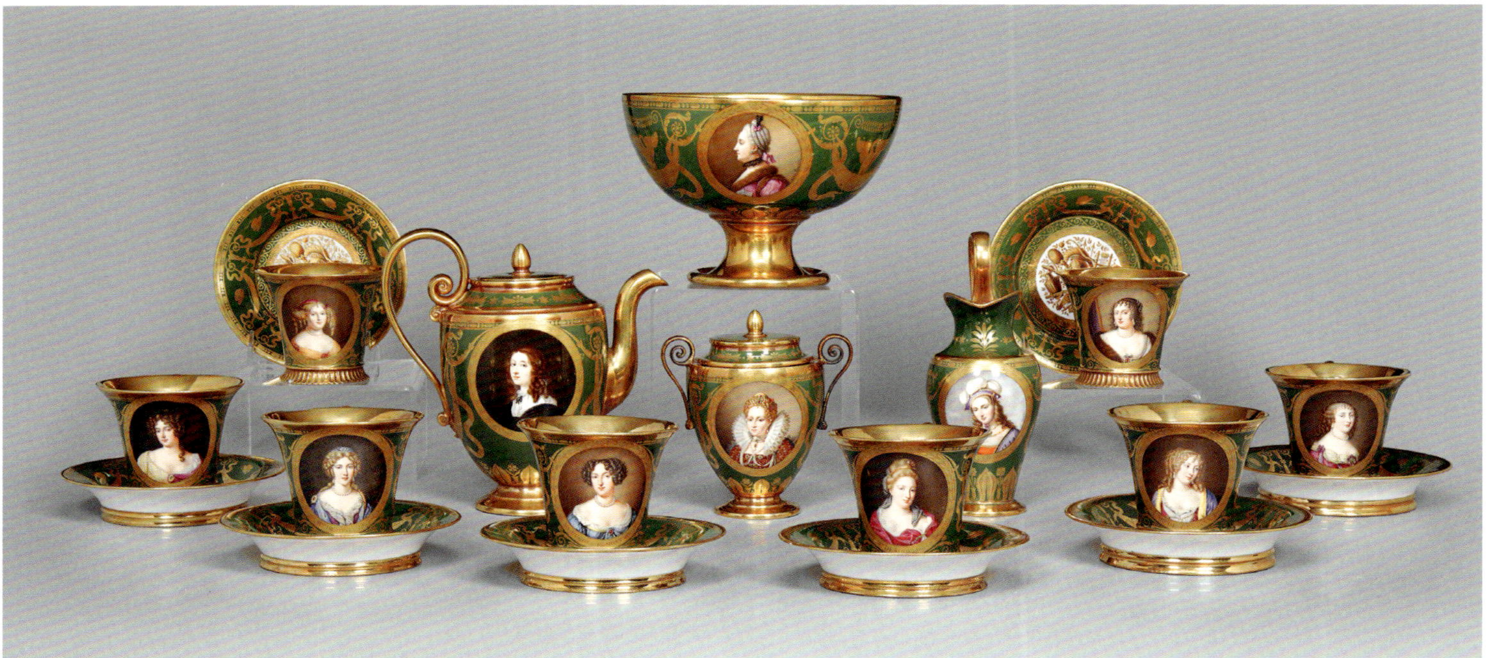

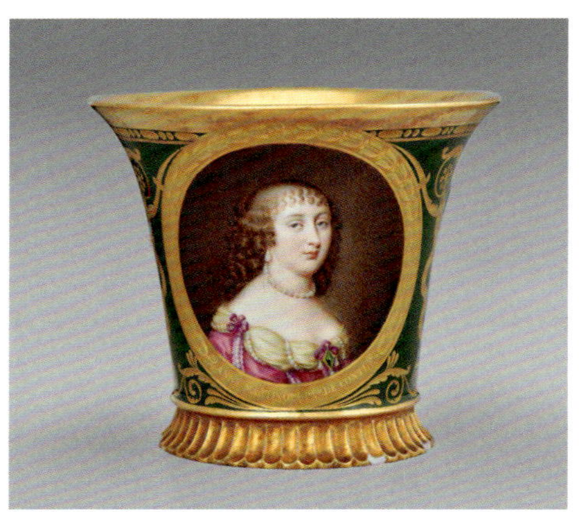

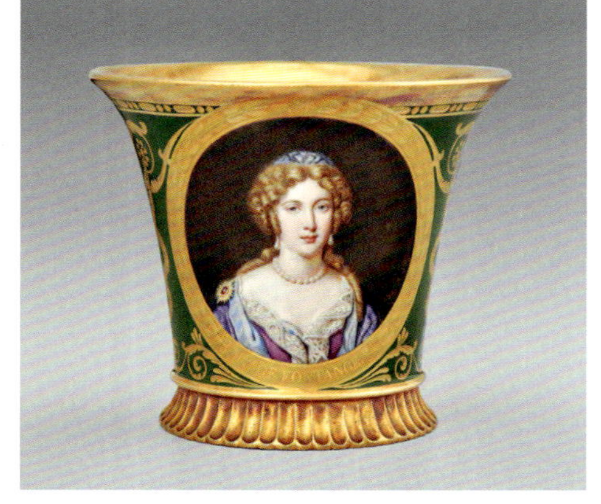

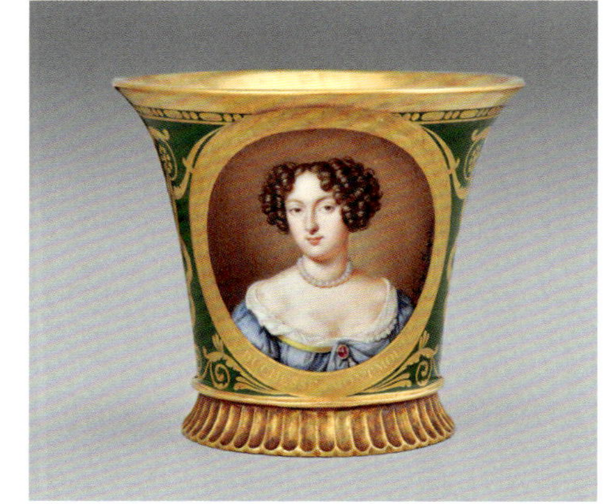

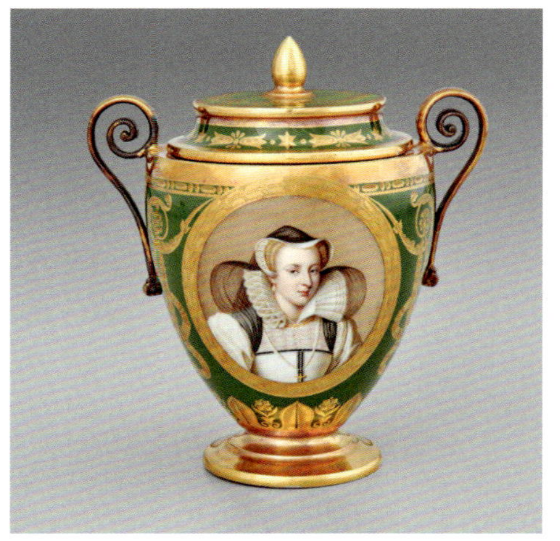

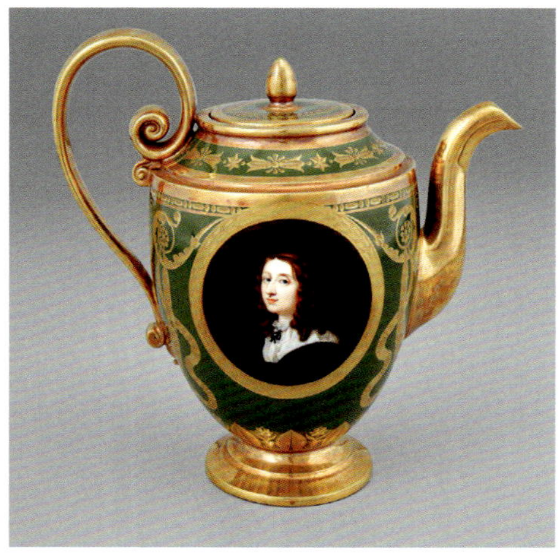

CAT. NOS. 24 A–L

Decorator: Marie-Victoire Jaquotot
Manufacturer: Manufacture Nationale de Sèvres
Tea Service of Famous Women
1811–1812
Hard-paste porcelain
Clark Art Institute, Williamstown, Massachusetts, USA, Acquired by the Clark, 2021
2021.3.1a-b-20
Images courtesy Clark Art Institute. clarkart.edu

*A: *Teapot and cover with portraits of Anne of Austria (1601–1666) and Christina of Sweden (1626–1689)*, teapot: 20.5 × 21 × 12.4 cm; cover: 3.8 × 6.4 cm, 2021.3.1a-b

B: *Milk jug with portrait of Joan of Arc (c. 1412–1431)*, 20.3 × 10.8 × 8.4 cm, 2021.3.2

*C: *Sugar bowl and cover with portraits of Elizabeth I (1533–1603) and Mary, Queen of Scots (1542–1587)*, overall: 14.8 × 14 × 10.2 cm; sugar bowl: 13.2 × 14 × 10.2 cm; cover: 4.1 × 8.6 cm, 2021.3.3a-b

D: *Bowl with portraits of Catherine the Great of Russia (1729–1796), Maria Theresa of Austria (1717–1780), and Blanche of Castille (1188–1252)*, Height: 14.6 cm; diameter: 21.9 cm, 2021.3.4

E–L: *Cups with portraits*, average size: 8.8 × 12 × 10.3 cm
**Anna Scott, Duchess of Monmouth (1651–1732)*, 2021.3.5
**Marie Angélique de Scorailles, Duchess of Fontanges (1661–1681)*, 2021.3.6
"La Princess Palatine," 2021.3.7
Antoinette du Ligier de la Garde Deshoulières (1638–1694), 2021.3.8
**Anne Marie Martinozzi, Princess of Conti (1637–1672)*, 2021.3.9
Hortense Mancini, Duchess de Mazarin (1646–1699), 2021.3.10
Françoise-Marguerite de Sévigné, Comtesse de Grignan (1646–1705), 2021.3.11
Marie de Rabutin-Chantal, Madame de Sévigné (1626–1696), 2021.3.12

*Individually illustrated on this page

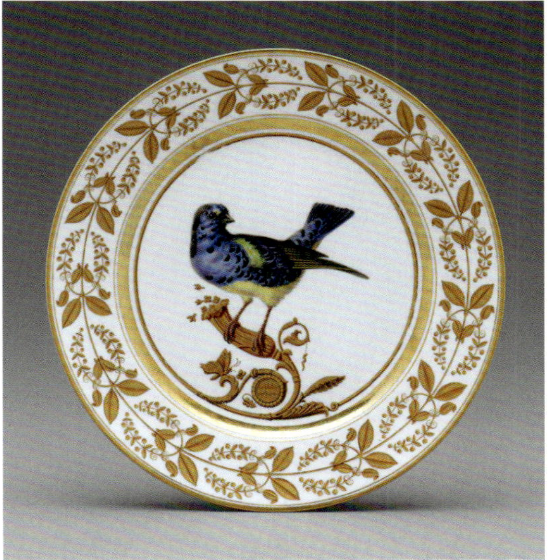

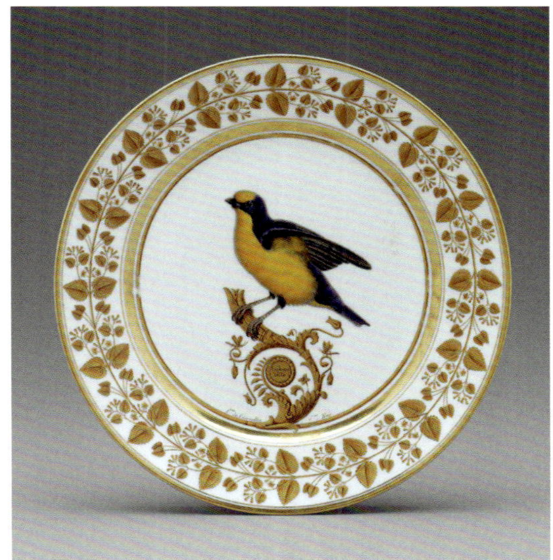

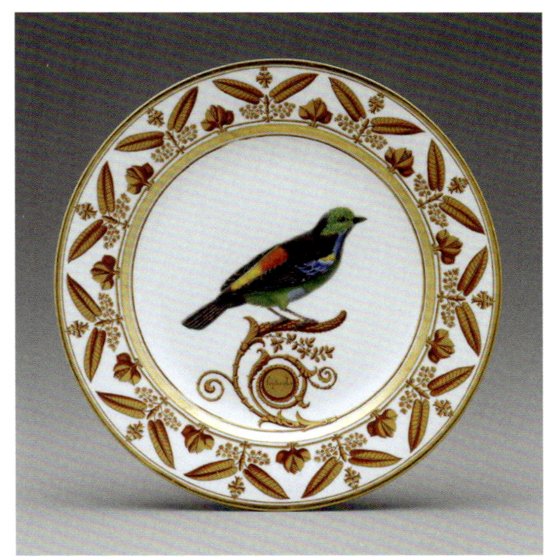

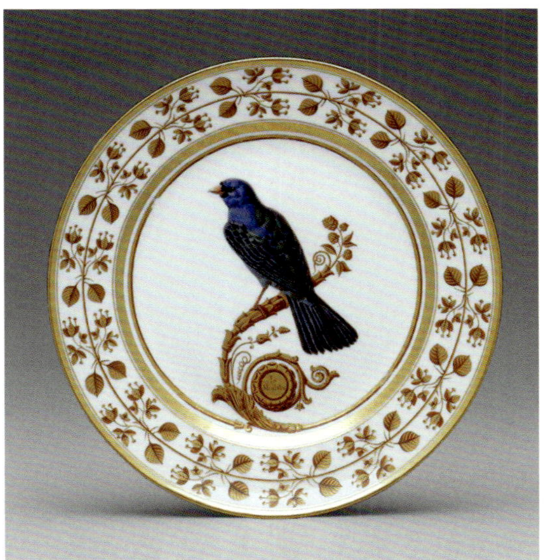

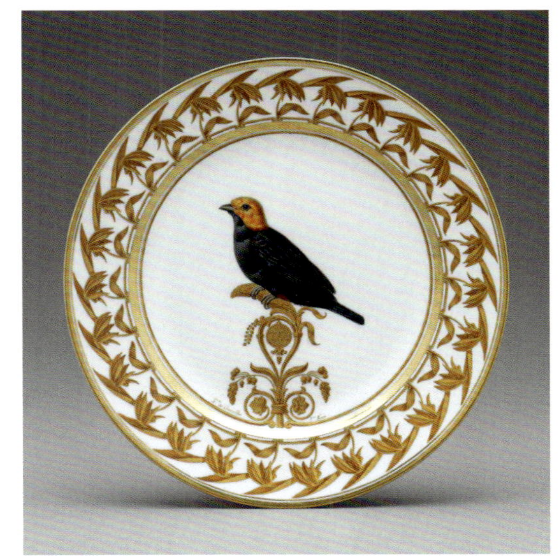

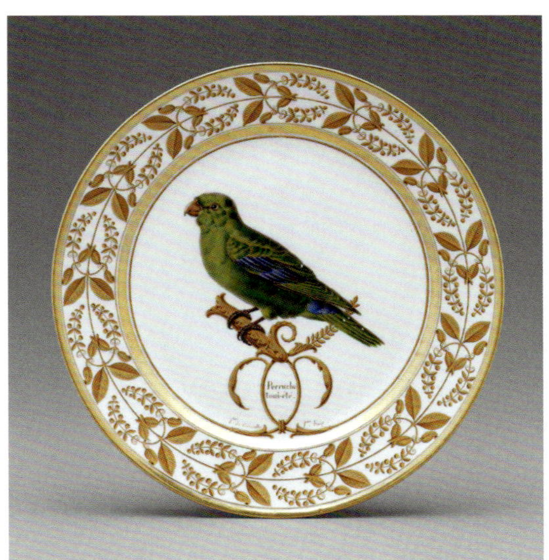

CAT. NOS. 25 A–F
Decorator: Pauline Rifer de Courcelles, known as Madame Knip
Manufacturer: Manufacture Nationale de Sèvres
The South American Birds Service
1819–1821
Diameter: 23.5 cm each
Hard-paste porcelain
On Loan from Hillwood Estate, Museum & Gardens,
Bequest of Marjorie Merriweather Post, 1973
24.136.1-4, 24.136.6, 24.136.8
Photographed by Edward Owen

Left to right, above then below:
A: *Turquoise Tanager [Le Diable enrhumé] plate,* 24.136.1
B: *Euphonia Violacea [Euphone téite] plate,* 24.136.2
C: *Paradise Tanager [Septicolor] plate,* 24.136.3
D: *Indigo Bunting [Le Ministre] plate,* 24.136.4
E: *Golden-headed Manakin [Manakin à Tête d'or] plate,* 24.136.6
F: *Green-rumped Parrotlet [Perruche toui-été] plate,* 24.136.8

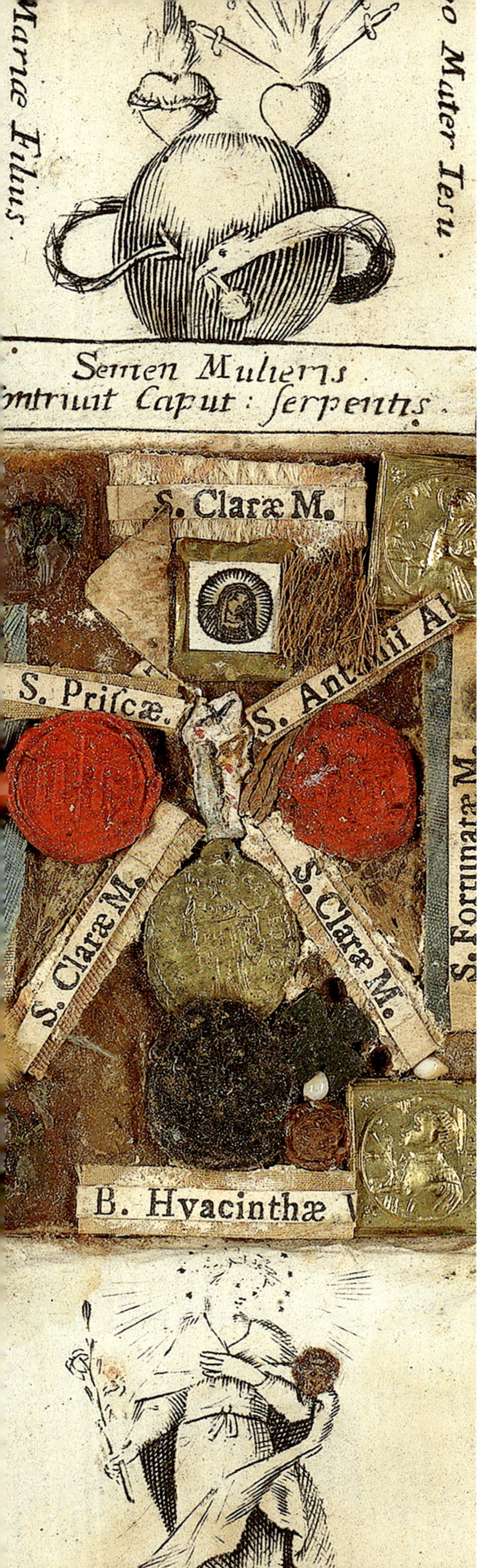

Cloister Work

Theresa Kutasz Christensen

In many ways, the relationship of cloistered women to the manufacture and use of material goods in their daily lives closely mirrored that of their secular counterparts. Skills typical of young women's education and production in the home—such as needlework, drawing, lacemaking, and cooking—were easily transferable to support both their personal needs and those of the convent. Many women who, in their lives as wives and mothers, had run households and already worked in media such as embroidery or paper rolling joined religious communities as widows, bringing with them their expertise in handicrafts. Also like their secular counterparts, women in conventual communities made works that ranged from small, amateur productions to commissioned pieces of the highest quality. Many convents were sites of making even for those who were not nuns. Women and girls who did not take vows often lived and worked in conventual communities or contributed to their decoration. This was the case of Portuguese painter Josefa Ayala (c. 1630–1684), who produced some of her earliest professional work while boarding in an Augustinian convent as a teenager. Much of the work featured in this essay falls into a category of objects often referred to as *klosterarbeiten* or "cloister work," a term that intones a certain handmade quality to the items, often created from affordable materials readily available within the confines of a nunnery.

In the wake of the dissolution of their monasteries at the close of the fifteenth century, the nuns of the Bridgettine order in England travelled abroad in search of safety and protection. After several attempts to resettle, the order found a welcoming home in Lisbon, Portugal, where the community lived in exile for nearly three centuries. A work bag and box made to hold equipment for needlework was made by a member of this community composed of expatriate Bridgettine women in Lisbon around 1787 (cat. no. 26). While certainly not the only order to produce ecclesiastical textiles, the

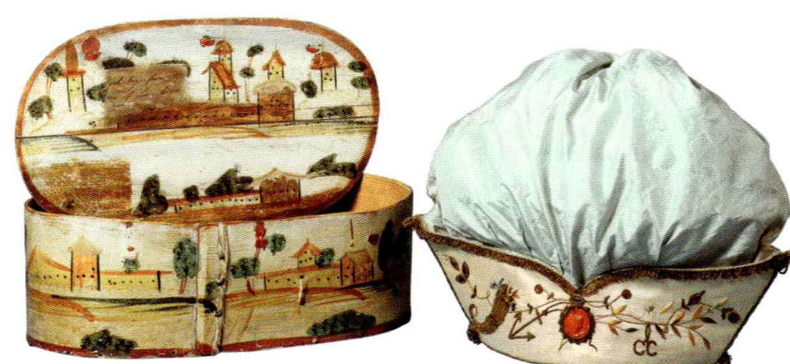

Bridgettines have become somewhat synonymous with needlework due to the large number of extant textiles produced by women at their motherhouse at Vadstena in Sweden (now in the collection of the Historiska museet in Stockholm; see page 37, fig. 10). While vows of poverty may have affected the ownership of luxury objects by some religious women, the spangles, polished red stones, and finely worked silk and gold thread on the work bag indicate that many orders found no issue with producing fine works. Elements such as the embroidered initials and wax stamps with heraldic devices of both the Cotton family of England and the nuns of Syon House give the work bag a personal meaning, as it was likely commissioned by Admiral Sir Charles Cotton Baronet for his wife, Philadelphia, before their wedding. The wooden work box is similarly personal, featuring a simply painted landscape and an image possibly depicting the sisters' Syon House abbey in Lisbon, which had recently been reconstructed following its partial destruction in the earthquake of 1755, an event which all of the Bridgettine sisters miraculously survived.[1]

Nuns from wealthy households who had been afforded an education often contributed their skills in reading and writing, and engaged in popular middle- and upper-class domestic crafts such as drawing and paper filigree. From 1645 to 1831, the nuns of the Discalced Mercedarians in Écija, an Andalusian town near Seville, maintained a *lybro de profesyones* (cat. no. 27) that documented the wom-

CAT. NO. 26 (facing)
Bridgettine nuns of Syon House, Lisbon, Portugal
Work bag and box
c. 1787
Silk and gold embroidery, sequins, paste stones, wax seals, anc painted wood
Bag: 40.6 × 39.4 × 12.1 cm;
box and lid: 13.3 × 39.7 × 21.9 cm
Los Angeles County Museum of Art, Gift of Mr. and Mrs. Michael Laykin
M.81.94a-c

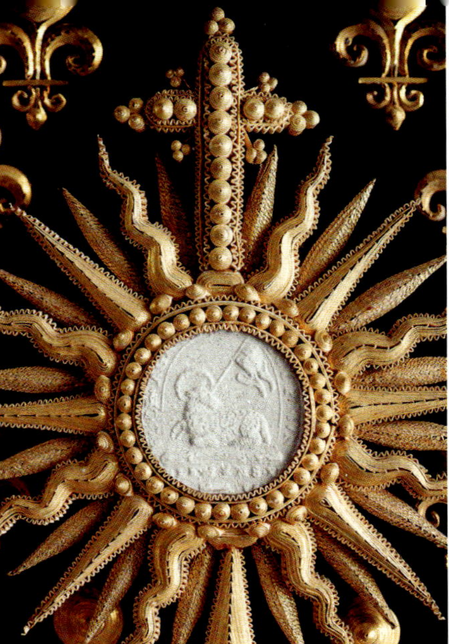

Detail (cat. no. 30):
Unknown French (?) Ursuline nuns
Quilled Agnus Dei Reliquary
17th or 18th century?

en who matriculated into the Convent of the Incarnation. The pages of the text contain a static set of information but vary widely in their calligraphy and the decorative borders, suggesting that numerous women in the convent contributed to its creation. In a reliquary holding a blessed host, produced by a seventeenth- or eighteenth-century Ursuline maker likely in France (cat. no. 30), gilded strips of paper are carefully rolled into fleurs-de-lis.[2] This use of common materials to mimic expensive metal filigree was popular in conventual settings where the sisters often had ready access to books with gilded foredges that could be carefully cut down to produce works like this one. For many sisters, their creative contributions were not only pastimes but also opportunities for quiet contemplation where both the elaborate act of making and the use of the objects served private devotional purposes. The meditative quality of rolling paper was not exclusive to nuns and was also popularly used by secular women, who could purchase kits and dyed papers to create small works for domestic decoration and devotion. An eighteenth-century framed example featuring intricate vases and flowers made of rolled paper surrounding a small image of the Madonna and Child was valued enough by the family of its maker that it accompanied them when the family relocated across the Atlantic (cat. no. 31).

The use of affordable materials can be seen in objects that served a wide variety of essential functions within the family life of a religious community. A holy water stoup (cat. no. 28) made of woven straw was likely used in the private devotional practice of a French Visitandine nun within her cell. The face of the work is covered in meticulously woven floral designs; a fountain of life at the top references the utility of the object as a vessel for holy water, and two flaming hearts at the base align with the watercolour of a sacred heart at centre. The image of the sacred heart gained significant popularity in late-seventeenth-century France. A heart-shaped reliquary on a stand, likely produced by Ursuline makers in France (cat. no. 29), displays similar simplified floral designs. When used in communal devotion, the tightly coiled metal wire covering the reliquary would have glistened in the candlelight, echoing the light and flame emblematic of imagery associated with the sacred heart.

The manufacture of small works in inexpensive materials was also completed by women in communities located on pilgrimage routes; they were able to support their church through the production of tokens and talismans that pilgrims could then purchase. For a group of early-eighteenth-century German nuns, this included the creation of carefully constructed "book amulets," or *breverls* (cat. no. 32). The object was worn for the general purpose of warding off evil, from protecting against deceptions to preventing torment by demons through a blessing or indulgence attached to the object. The amulet, a multimedia assemblage of printed and found materials, was not intended to be opened by the owner and contained carefully arranged images, prayers, and small objects, including a German pilgrimage medallion of a Venetian church, a dried flower, a coloured woodcut, and the letterpress names of mainly female saints arranged on small slips of silk.

Similar to the amulet, a Rose of Viterbo contact relic (cat. no. 34) was imbued with religious power through its proximity to the remains of the saint, and was likely made by a nun to be sold to pilgrims at Rose of Viterbo's burial site in Italy. Shaped like a glove, the contact relic is made of silk with silver embroidery and is attached by silk strings and the monastery's seal to a print depicting the saint. Below the printed image is a certificate of authenticity signed by the abbess of the church where Rose of Viterbo's remains are located. The text reads, in part, "I, the undersigned Abbess of the Ven. Monastery of S. Rosa of Viterbo, certify that the hand annexed to this sheet bound with a rose-colored silk ... was above the sacred body of S. Rosa Vergine Viterbo, which is preserved in this city of Viterbo, original and incorrupt in a chapel."[3] Although relatively few examples survive due to their fragile materials and their tactile use as talismans, items of protection and veneration like these were made in the thousands by nuns across Europe and would have constituted a significant portion of cloistered material output.

The enormity of the time and resources spent venerating objects within the context of the cloister can be seen in a spectacular account book (cat. no. 33) written over the period between 1739 and 1770. The Italian nun Metilde Benvenuti (died 1772) was tasked with keeping this *libbro di memorie* to document the care of a *presepio*, or nativity scene, kept in the cloister for use by her Augustinian sisters. The payments recorded in the book outline the regular purchase of cloth and other materials utilized by her fellow nuns in a near constant cycle of updating and refreshing the clothing on the figures. Instances are also recorded of the nuns paying women outside the convent for their skills in needlework to complete garments for the crèche figures.[4] While in select instances the documents indicate that figures were brought out for public veneration, this lifetime of work by Benvenuti and her sisters was purely for the benefit of their own devotional practice. Although the building of crèches in Italy has long been associated with workshops run by men, documents of their upkeep, like the books of memories, indicate a long tradition of women's involvement—particularly in the making of the textiles that dressed the figures, a topic ripe for additional scholarship.

Many members of religious orders were afforded the ability to spend their time creating incredibly detailed devotional works for the benefit of themselves and their communities; for others, their labour closely resembled a full-time occupation carried out for the primary financial benefit of those above them in the Church hierarchy. The personal experiences and skills of cloistered makers was as varied as the types of works they produced.

Resources Consulted

Agnelli, Marella. *Quilling: Devotional Creations from Cloistered Orders.* Milan: Coraini, 2012.

Bernasconi, Gianenrico. "Pour Une Histoire Technique de l'artisanat Conventuel: Fabrication et Échange Des *Klosterarbeiten* (XVIIIe-XIXe Siècles)." *Archives de Sciences Sociales des Religions* 63, no. 183 (2018): 143–66.

Dunn, Marilyn. "Convent Creativity." In *The Ashgate Research Companion to Women and Gender in Early Modern Europe.* Edited by Jane Couchman and Allyson M. Poska. London: Routledge, 2013.

Hamburger, Jeffrey F. *Nuns as Artists: The Visual Culture of a Medieval Convent.* Berkeley: University of California Press, 1997.

———. *The Visual and the Visionary: Art and Female Spirituality in Late Medieval Germany.* Princeton, NJ: Zone, 2009.

Johns Hopkins University Library. Women of the Book Collection Catalogue. Accessed July 4, 2023, archive.org/details/womenofthebook.

Notes

1 University of Exeter, "Remarkable Letter Reveals Earthquake Drama for Nuns in Exile," March 12, 2019, news-archive.exeter.ac uk/featurednews/title_708245_en.html.

2 Founded in 1639, the Ursulines of Quebec formed the earliest European institution for women's education in North America, teaching domestic crafts such as paper rolling, embroidery, and drawing to both European settlers and the Indigenous populations they were working to convert.

3 "Attesto io sottoscritta Abbadessa del Ven. Monastero di S. Rosa di Viterbo che la mano annessa in questo foglio, e legato con settuccia di seta color di rose unita nelle sue estremita, e sigillata con cera di Spagna con il Sigllo del Ven. Monasterio, e statosopra il Sagro Corpo di S. Rosa Vergine Viterbese, che si conserva in questa citta di Viterbo, iniero ed incorrotto in una Capella vestita dell Abito Monacale di S. Chiari in questo Monasterio di S. Rosa. In sede di che ho sottoscritto la presente, e munita del solito Sigllo di questo Ven. Monasterio. This 20th of May, 1824," trans. Theresa Kutasz Christensen, catalyst.library.jhu.edu/permalink/01JHU_INST/1lu78g9/alma9910c9125979707861.

4 A special thank-you to Kelsey Champagne for sharing her research and for bringing these entries to the author's attention.

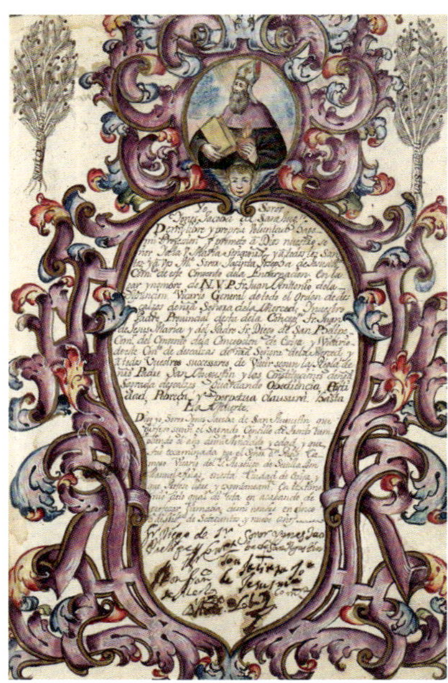

CAT. NO. 27
Nuns of the Discalced Mercedarians, Écija, Spain
Lybro de Profesyones deste Convento de la Encarnacyon Descalças de la M[erce]... [Book of Professions of the Convent of Incarnation of the Discalced Mercedarians]
1645–1831
Watercolour and ink on paper, with gold-tooled goatskin binding
Folio: 30 × 20 cm
Special Collections, The Sheridan Libraries, Johns Hopkins University, Rare Books and Manuscripts, Women of the Book Collection, Bib# 7522662
Photo: Digitization Services Unit, Johns Hopkins University

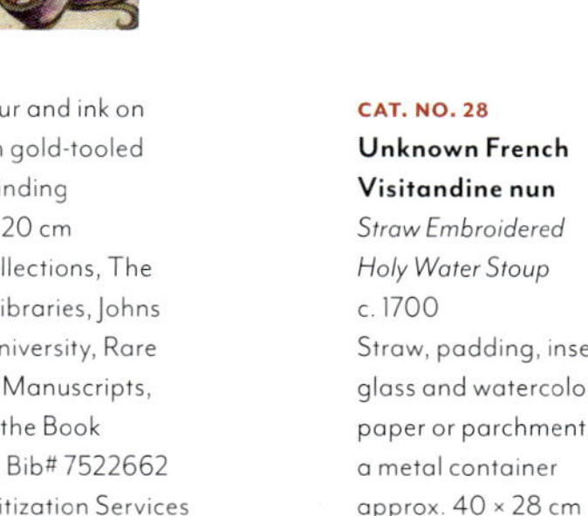

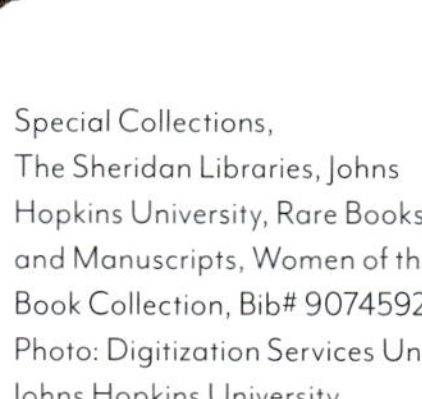

CAT. NO. 28
Unknown French Visitandine nun
Straw Embroidered Holy Water Stoup
c. 1700
Straw, padding, inset with glass and watercolour on paper or parchment, and a metal container
approx. 40 × 28 cm
Special Collections, The Sheridan Libraries, Johns Hopkins University, Rare Books and Manuscripts, Women of the Book Collection, Bib# 9074592
Photo: Digitization Services Unit, Johns Hopkins University

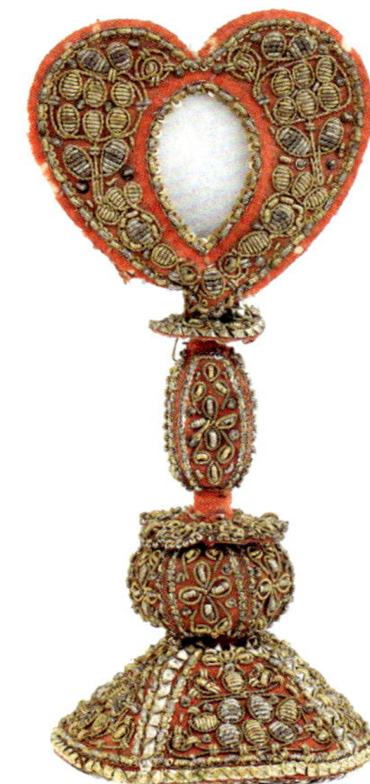

CAT. NO. 29
Unknown French (?) Ursuline nuns
Reliquary in the Shape of a Heart
17th century
Cardboard, velvet, gold, and silver
22.1 × 11.5 × 9.9 cm
Collections | Pôle culturel du Monastère des Ursulines (Quebec, Canada)
1995.2166

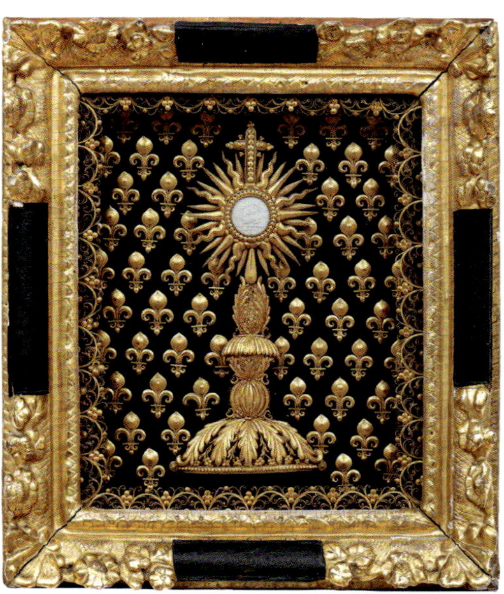

CAT. NO. 30
Unknown French (?) Ursuline nuns
Quilled Agnus Dei Reliquary
17th or 18th century?
Wood, paper, glass, sealant, gold, and silver
39.3 × 35 × 8.5 cm
Collections | Pôle culturel du Monastère des Ursulines (Quebec, Canada)
1995.2199

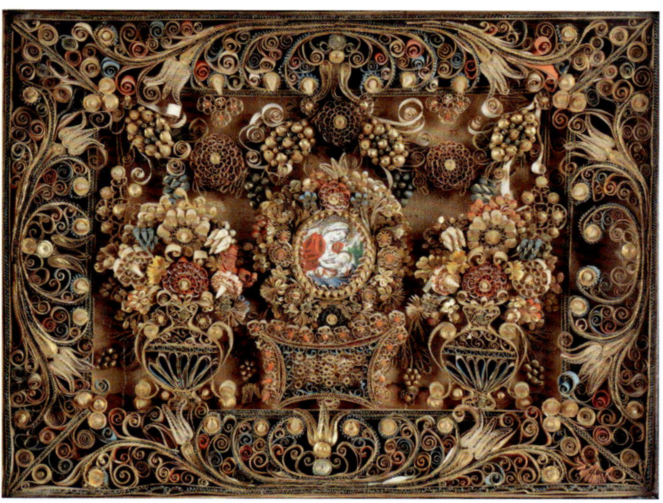

CAT. NO. 31

Unknown European maker

Quillwork (paper filigree) picture with Madonna and Child

18th century

Rolled paper, gilding, paint, wood, and glass

27.3 × 35.6 × 5.4 cm

Peabody Essex Museum, acquired before 1919

109453

Image courtesy of the Peabody Essex Museum

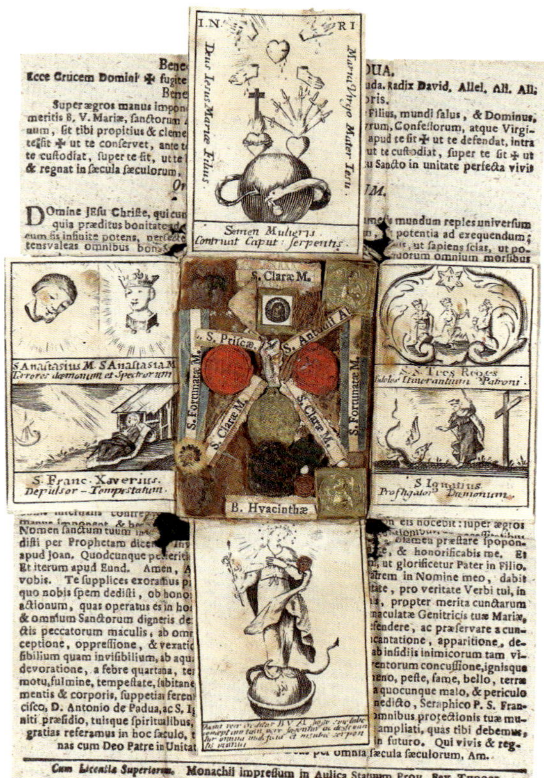

CAT. NO. 32

Unknown cloistered maker, likely German

Book amulet, or breverl

c. 1712

Letterpress on paper decorated with embossed metal seals and medallion, red wax seals, and a dried flower

Open: 20 × 14.5 cm

Special Collections, The Sheridan Libraries, Johns Hopkins University, Rare Books and Manuscripts, Women of the Book Collection, Bib# 9381889

Photo: Digitization Services Unit, Johns Hopkins University

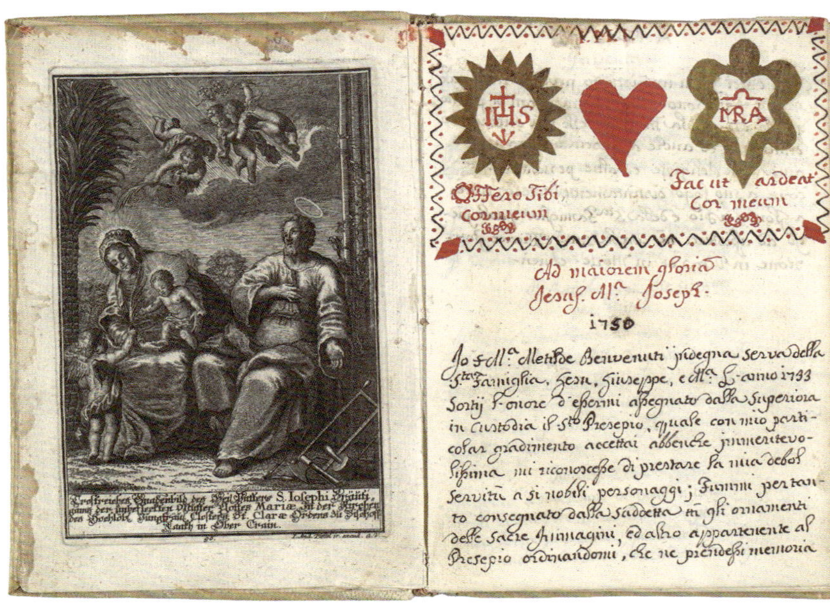

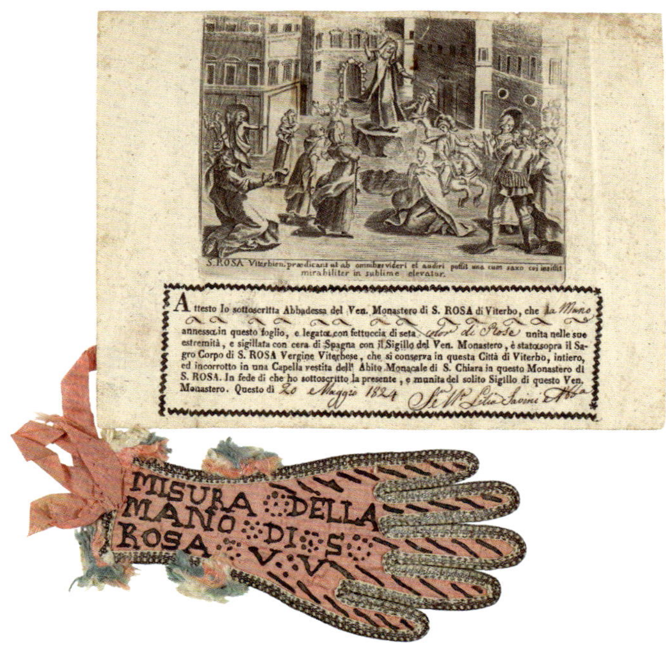

CAT. NO. 33

Metilde Benvenuti

Libbro di Memorie Appartenenti al Presepio

[The Book of Memories Pertaining to the Holy Crib]

1739–1770

Ink on paper, bound in vellum

17.4 × 12.5 cm

Special Collections, The Sheridan Libraries, Johns Hopkins University, Rare Books and Manuscripts, Women of the Book Collection, Bib# 6815273

Photo: Digitization Services Unit, Johns Hopkins University

CAT. NO. 34

Nuns of the Convent of Saint Rose of Viterbo

Contact Relic for the Hand of St. Rose of Viterbo with Certificate of Authenticity

1824

Engraving on paper, silk ribbon and silk fabric, white cotton, and silver embroidery

Sheet: 18 × 25 cm; glove: 8 × 18.5 cm

Special Collections, The Sheridan Libraries, Johns Hopkins University, Rare Books and Manuscripts, Women of the Book Collection, Bib# 9844820

Photo: Digitization Services Unit, Johns Hopkins University

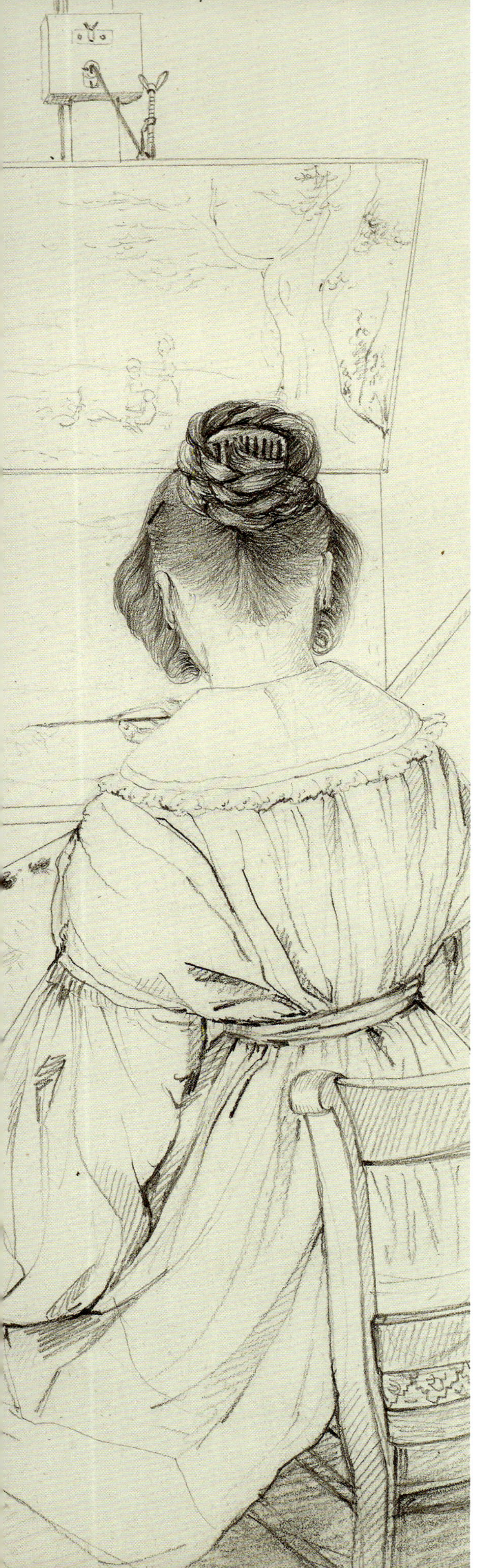

Drawings, Pastels, and Watercolours

Andaleeb Badiee Banta and Joanna Karlgaard

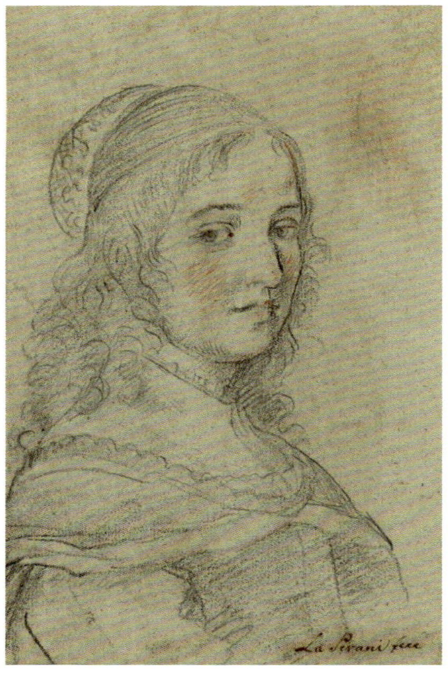

CAT. NO. 35
Elisabetta Sirani
Self-Portrait
c. 1658
Black chalk, red chalk, and white chalk on paper
22.9 × 15.4 cm
Purchased with the Diane A. Nixon, class of 1957, Fund, and the gift of the Almathea Charitable Foundation, Smith College Museum of Art, Northampton, Massachusetts
SC 2020.7.1

In Giorgio Vasari's foundational 1550 text *The Lives of the Most Excellent Painters, Sculptors, and Architects* (revised 1568), he characterized drawing, especially of the human form from direct observation, as a fundamental skill necessary for all other visual arts. This primacy of drawing had decidedly gendered implications, as official avenues for formal artistic training in pre-modern Europe—namely the academy or studio where models posed for groups of male artists—were officially unavailable to the majority of aspiring women artists until the eighteenth century. That is not to say that women did not learn to draw or that when they drew they avoided the human figure; graphic, sculpted, and painted visual evidence included in this exhibition points to the contrary. Rather, what we know about women's engagement with the act of drawing remains obscured by patriarchal priorities imposed upon our understanding of artistic processes and production of the past. Whether as a pedagogical exercise, a component of their working process, or as pleasurable pursuit, drawings by pre-modern women implemented the same formal practices established by and expected of male artists. What makes the drawn output of these women remarkable is how it functions within a shifting continuum of gendered restriction and opportunity throughout the centuries. Drawings by women during the pre-modern era not only reflect their achievements and connections but also provide a sense of the changing attitudes toward women as artists during this period.

For women born into artistic families, witnessing the role of drawing during the creative process was part of their daily experience. A seventeenth-century sketchbook in the Fitzwilliam Museum contains drawings attributed variously to Carlo Dolci, court painter to the Medici, and to his daughter Agnese (1659–1686). Carlo presumably shared this collection of drawings with Agnese as she learned to draw. In its compilation of copies after other artists' works and studies from life by both father and daughter, the sketchbook (cat. no. 44) illustrates the ways that daughters gained competence in conversation with their fathers' practice. Presumably, Agnese acquired drafting skills she could use in her independent practice, though recognition for her contributions has been overshadowed by her father's reputation.

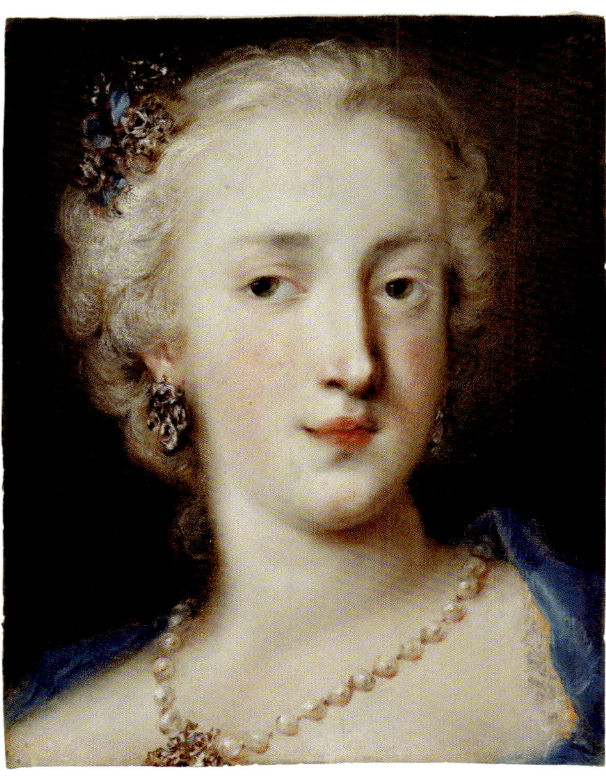

CAT. NO. 36
Rosalba Carriera
Portrait of a Woman
c. 1720s
Pastel on blue paper
31 × 25 cm

Art Gallery of Ontario,
Purchased as a gift from
Mrs. Walter Gordon, 1995
94/308
Photo: AGO
Exhibited at AGO only

Without familial access to artistic education, female makers often relied upon copying other artists' works—something male artists did as well—or other indirect means of learning outside the studio setting. A popular practice was to copy drawing exercises found in printed instructional manuals that circulated widely and frequently in lieu of live teaching. The study sheets of noses and tongues (cat. nos. 52 & 53) by Anna Helena Alströmer (1764–1792) come from a sketchbook that bears the inscription "All my drawings which I have drawn for Mr Schöberg," suggesting that the repetitive formation of facial aspects was part of the private, aristocratic artistic education she received.

Women who received formalized artistic training and pursued professional careers as artists engaged in drawing modes that reflected the prevailing practices of the time. Using chalk, pen, brush, and ink, they mapped out compositions, explored details observed from life, and honed their craft. In the case of the Bolognese painter Elisabetta Sirani (1638–1665), her considerable graphic output, documented by contemporary biographers and inventories alike, explains why she is regarded as one of the most prolific of seventeenth-century Italian women artists despite her short life span. A drawn self-portrait (cat. no. 35) from her early career follows the graphic idiom of the celebrated Guido Reni, another artistic star of Bologna, in its use of black and red chalk to produce a strikingly fresh and keenly observed portrayal of an artist intent on placing herself in the same legacy as her famous predecessor. Later in her career, Sirani's assured handling of the brush technique—diluted ink applied with a brush—became one of her hallmarks, as seen in her study (cat. no. 43) for the painting *Virgin and Child* (cat. no. 85). Using red chalk, brush, and a grey wash, Sirani sketched out the composition as an exploration of form and light, with special attention given to the points of physical and psychological contact between mother and son that made her paintings popular among Bolognese nobles and to whom this humanized interpretation of doctrine appealed.

Whereas Sirani's brush drawing established a model for a subject she repeated numerous times to entice potential clients, a study for the portrait of Princess Anna Alexandrovna Galitzin (cat. nos. 37 & 110) by Elisabeth Louise Vigée-LeBrun (1755–1842) was created for a specific commission. After hastily departing Paris on the cusp of a revolution that violently unseated the French monarchs for whom she had worked, Vigée-LeBrun embarked on a twelve-year-long exile circuit of European courts, supporting herself and her daughter Julie through portrait commissions. Her talent at presenting aristocratic sitters, such as this member of the Russian royal court, in a seemingly casual but carefully orchestrated manner, contributed to the great demand for her services. Since the act of painting a portrait was a time-consuming and frequently boring experience for the sitter, Vigée-LeBrun's facility with chalk on paper would allow her to capture the main details of likeness and costume that she could later work up in a studio.

By the mid-eighteenth century, women's access to formalized institutions of education had shifted profoundly. Especially in France and England, women were increasingly able to pursue professional careers and acquire the artistic training that they had been denied in earlier centuries. Yet official study of the human body continued to be heavily regulated for most women, particularly in more conservative societies in Italy and Spain. Antique sculptures, wax and plaster moulds, and mannequins of the human body were resources throughout the early modern era, used by male and female student artists alike, but women's access to the live nude male model still was officially prohibited. The remarkable drawings of male (cat. nos. 45–49) and female nudes (cat. no. 40) attributed to the Venetian artist Giulia Lama (1681–1747) indicate that women found ways around these strictures. These dramatically yet sensitively depicted studies of musculature, form, and light rendered in red, black, and white chalks exhibit a degree of uninhibited

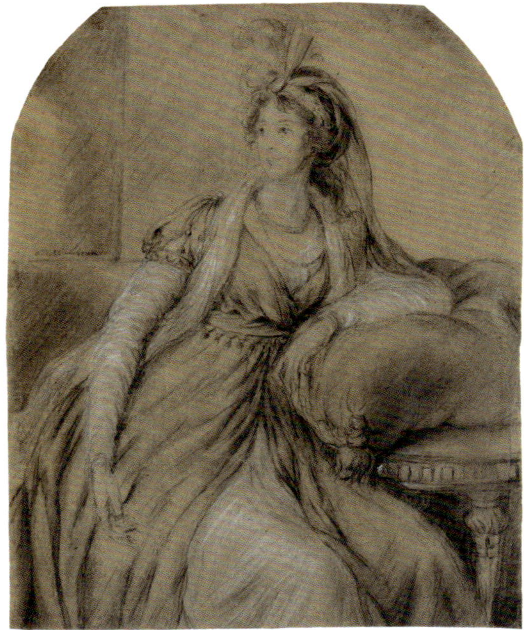

CAT. NO. 37
Elisabeth Louise Vigée-LeBrun
Princess Anna Alexandrovna Galitzin
c. 1797
Black chalk and white chalk with stumping on paper
28.2 × 23.4 cm

Baltimore Museum of Art:
Stiles Tuttle Colwill Acquisitions Fund, and Marion Tuttle Colwill Memorial Fund, 2016.2
Photo: Mitro Hood

immediacy that suggests they were observed from life. They are currently the only examples of male nudes drawn from life attributable to an Italian woman artist before 1800. In London, the only two female founding members of the Royal Academy of Arts, Mary Moser (1744–1819) and Angelica Kauffmann (1741–1807), produced studies of male and female nudes as part of their training and preparatory processes—albeit not alongside their male colleagues. Kauffmann, in particular, used such studies for her historical narrative compositions, but Moser, who was best known for her still-life paintings and watercolours (cat. no. 38), particularly for Queen Charlotte, also evidently engaged in the practice of drawing from the live model (cat. no. 51). Her awareness of the practice of drawing models likely started early, as her father, director of the St. Martin's Lane Academy, was an advocate for including both male and female models in the classroom.

The depiction of a woman in the act of drawing (cat. no. 55) by Anne Guéret (1760–1805) conveys several important aspects of a woman's status as an artist by the end of the eighteenth century. As her debut work exhibited at the Salon of 1793, this drawing—possibly a self-portrait—importantly shows an artist, with her *porte-crayon* poised and attention directed outside the picture frame, engaged in the act of drawing a nude, male figure.[1] Further, it shows a woman artist at ease in the act of drawing and promotes her ability to portray the human body and classicizing narratives, a theme underscored by her ancient Greek–inspired empire-waist dress.[2] While it is not clear whether she is drawing from a live model, this assured representation of a young woman artist aligns with the fact that, by the late eighteenth century, women artists began to populate spaces once reserved for men.

Due in large part to relaxing social restrictions, this shift also speaks to the trailblazing efforts of professional women artists from the generation before, such as Adélaïde Labille-Guiard (1749–1803) and Anne Vallayer-Coster (1744–1818) in France, and Angelica Kauffmann and Mary Moser in England, who used their positions of professional achievement to train the next generation of female students and normalize women's participation in official Salons and exhibitions. One such example of this female pedagogical genealogy is the deep and abiding relationship between Labille-Guiard and her student Marie Gabrielle Capet (1761–1818). A touching tribute to their dynamic is a portrait that Capet made of her teacher's husband, François-André Vincent (cat. no. 42). Capet had become a member of the artistic couple's household, staying on after Labille-Guiard's passing to take care of the elder Vincent.

Women's drawings also played an integral role in literary illustration. Several women artists, professional and amateur alike, circulating in London during the late eighteenth century participated in a complex social and artistic network that gave them access to established cultural figures who promoted and published their work. A British noblewoman in the circle of the writer and antiquarian Horace Walpole, Diana Beauclerk (1734–1808) created a series of five sizable watercolours illustrating scenes from Edmund Spenser's 1590 Renaissance epic poem "The Faerie Queene" that she likely intended to have translated into print and more broadly distributed. Her large-scale watercolours (cat. no. 39) not only evoke an exoticized place through architectural detail but also demonstrate an interest in portraying historical female characters from the text.

By contrast, some women artists' illustrations took on a decidedly contemporary tone, as in the imagery of Maria Louisa Catherine Cecilia Cosway (1759–1838) for Mary Darby Robinson's 1800 poem "The Wintry Day." Born to an English father and an Italian mother, Cosway arrived in London in 1779, bringing her into contact with the city's cultural elite, among them Robinson (1757–1800), a lauded writer, actress, and former mistress of the Prince of Wales. Cosway's drawings for "The Wintry Day" were translated into an aquatint by Caroline Watson (1760/61–1814), engraver to Queen Charlotte and widely considered the first professional British woman engraver. One of "The Wintry Day"

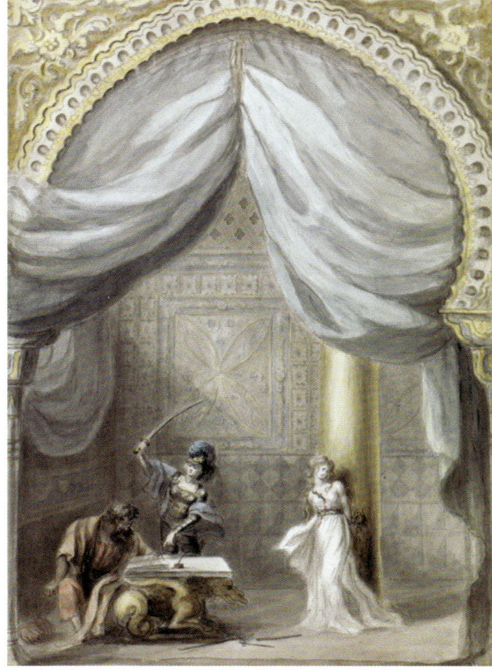

CAT. NO. 39
Diana Beauclerk
Drawing for Book III, Canto XII, 30–33 of Edmund Spenser's Faerie Queene
c. 1781
Watercolour on paper
78.2 × 57.3 cm
Courtesy of The Lewis Walpole Library, Yale University
Drawer Drawings B373 no. 10 +

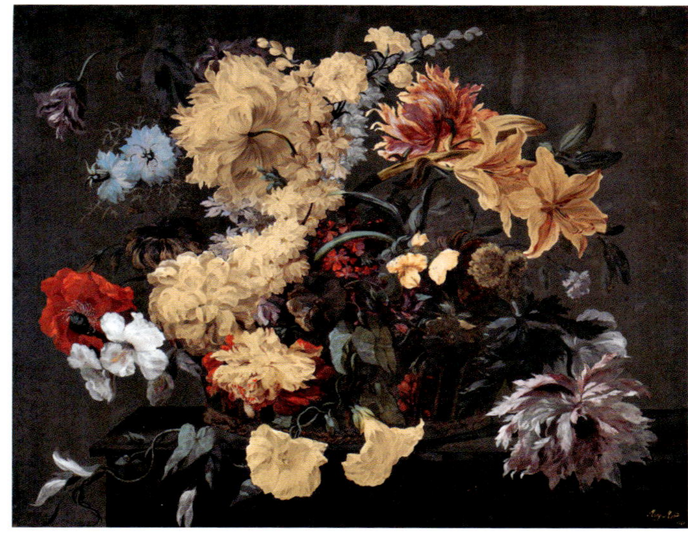

CAT. NO. 38
Mary Moser
Flowers in a Basket: chrysanthemums, lilies, nigella, convolvulus, delphiniums
1765
Opaque watercolour and watercolour on paper
42 × 58.4 cm
Victoria and Albert Museum, London.
The Lady Bettine Abingdon Collection.
Bequeathed by Mrs T.R.P. Hole.
P.22-1987
Image © Victoria and Albert Museum, London

illustrations, Cosway's vignette *Home Industry* (cat. no. 57), portrays a destitute family engaged in acts of making—sewing, weaving, and spinning—in a dilapidated cottage unable to withstand the cold. *Home Industry* reflects the daily hardships of less fortunate members of rural society, whose labour and best efforts could not compete with the rise of industrial urban manufacturing.[3] Cosway also used her drawing skills to create moralizing imagery in her later years that supported progressive movements addressing girls' education and women's rights.

The materials and format of women's drawings had gendered and commercial implications as well. Despite male artists' avid production of watercolours and pastels throughout this period, these techniques have been intrinsically linked with their historical perception as feminine.[4] Watercolour and pastel media were viewed as cleaner (no offensive odour of oil paints), quicker to complete, of lower cost to produce, diminutive in scale, not requiring great physical exertion or strength, and overall, more pleasant and appropriate for women. However, these very attributes also meant that these types of works, and the materials needed to create them, were easily transportable, offering freedom from a conventional studio space and flexibility to work in various locations; the shorter production time also offered an economic advantage. By the eighteenth century, specialty suppliers produced commercially available pastel sticks and watercolour cakes or pans, along with wooden work boxes with fitted compartments for holding pigments, brushes, and other tools (cat. no. 244).[5] The support for watercolours and pastels was most often paper, although vellum, ivory, and marble were also used for miniatures.

Portraits became popular subject matter for works executed in watercolour and pastel by women artists, often stemming from commissions. Venetian-born Rosalba Carriera (1673–1757) is best known for her innovative contributions in pastel, popularizing the medium for portraits and allegorical figures in eighteenth-century Europe, and becoming one of the most successful international artists of the century while remaining unmarried. She accepted commissions for portraits not only at her studio in Venice but also throughout Europe, including travels to Paris and Vienna, where she received patronage from royal courts. *Portrait of a Woman* (cat. no. 36) and *Allegory of Painting* (cat. no. 50), both on blue paper, illustrate the hallmarks of her exceptional work in pastel: the use of soft colours, bust-length format, and unique layering of the pastel medium using both wet and dry pigments, sometimes with the use of a brush, to create a velvety, powdery appearance—particularly in depicting skin—which appealed to contemporary notions of beauty.[6]

A portrait attributed to the British artist Ellen Sharples (1769–1849) (cat. no. 56) reflects the far-reaching influence of Carriera's use of the pastel medium for commissioned portraits. At the age of seventeen, she took drawing lessons from painter and pastellist James Sharples, later becoming his wife. Both James and Ellen eventually became known for their pastel portraits, first in England and then in America, where a newly forged national identity had created a robust market for commissioned portraits of politicians and distinguished citizens. Their use of standard-size papers and a physiognotrace instrument allowed for each of their pastel portraits to be completed in only a few hours.[7] In America, mainly Philadelphia and New York, Ellen's artistic career and reputation expanded greatly, progressing from making copies of portraits made by her husband (resulting in uncertain attributions between the two artists) to producing works that were entirely her own.[8] Often perceived as diminutive and merely for the amusement of ladies, the mediums of watercolour and pastel allowed for the commercial, social, and technical advancement of many women artists in Europe and beyond.

Closely related to women's engagement with drawing is the topic of the amateur. Historically treated as separate from the activities of fine artists and inaccurately cast as a gendered label reserved

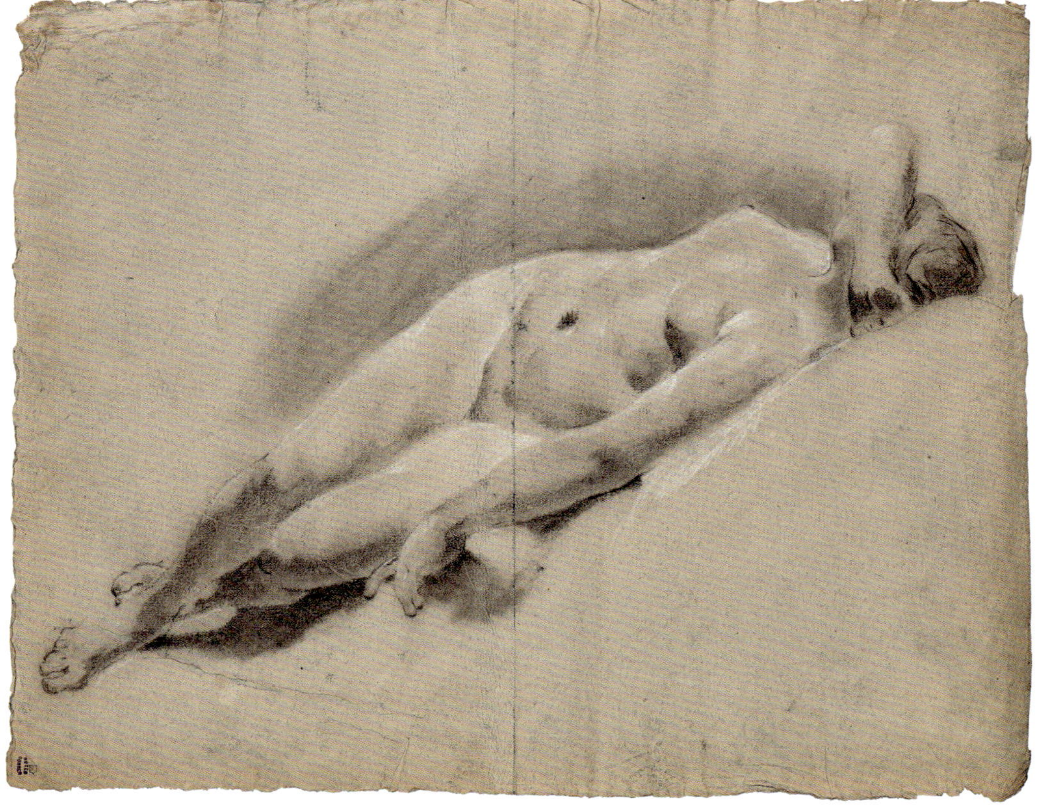

CAT. NO. 40
Giulia Lama
Sketch of a woman reclining
first half of 18th century
Black chalk and white chalk on paper
45.1 × 57 cm

Fondazione Musei Civici di Venezia, Gabinetto dei disegni e delle stampe, Ca' Rezzonico
Inv. Cl. III n. 6987
Exhibited at AGO only

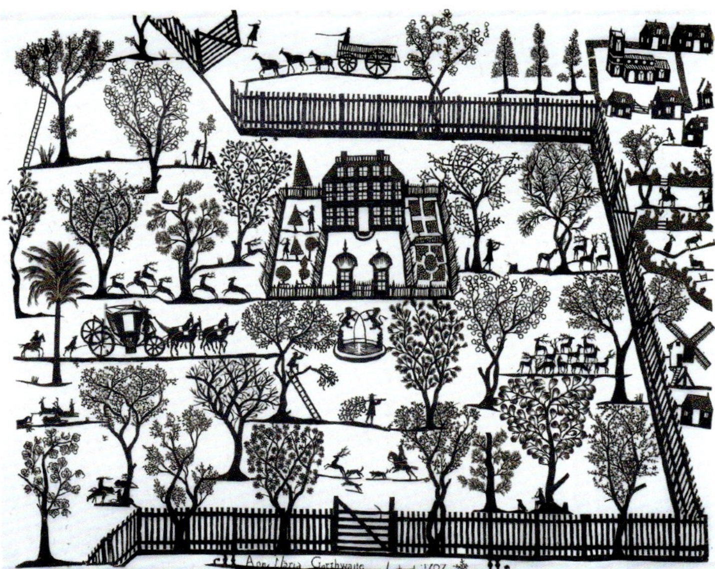

CAT. NO. 41
Anna Maria Garthwaite
English manor house and gardens
1707
Knife-cut cut-paper work, with pin pricking and collage, paper, and ink on a vellum backing
32.5 × 40 cm
Victoria and Albert Museum, London
E.1077-1993
Image © Victoria and Albert Museum, London

for women of means, the term "amateur" technically refers to someone who creates art for which they do not receive payment. By that standard, many artists in history could be labelled as amateurs, since many strove throughout the sixteenth and seventeenth centuries to prove the intellectual basis for their art by not openly pursuing payment that would cast it as mere trade or craft. Yet over time, the complicating factors of class and gender have derogatorily coloured the term as a decidedly unintellectual or untalented status even though historically amateur practitioners were often highly educated and accomplished, and had the financial security to explore all manner of artistic formats.[9] Such arts as watercolour, calligraphy, and paper-cutting have been dismissed as mere crafting pastimes or curiosities, despite their long history of being received as legitimate artistic pursuits by both men and women around the world. One of the most famous European woman papercut artists was the seventeenth-century Dutch Mennonite Johanna Koerten (1650–1715), who was lauded by contemporaries and received international attention and significant compensation for her works.[10] An impressively detailed cut-paper landscape (cat. no. 41) by Anna Maria Garthwaite (1688–1763), produced when she was just nineteen years old, indicates the widespread popularity of the practice. In her delicate application of two-toned paper that activates the composition, Garthwaite previews her dexterous facility with design, line, and detailed natural forms that would inform her later prodigious and lucrative production of floral patterns for silk clothing fabrics (cat. nos. 233 & 234).

The social component of drawing among the so-called amateur arts is also an important contextual factor to consider. By the late eighteenth century, mothers and daughters of the aristocratic or burgeoning middle classes were encouraged to engage in domestic crafts as a means to occupy their time; one writer in 1774 noted to his daughters that such tasks "enable you to fill up, in a tolerable agreeable way, some of the many solitary hours that you must necessarily pass at home."[11]

A collection of graphite drawings by the noblewoman Fanny Guillaume de Bassoncourt, Baronne de Molaret (1820–1888), indicates, however, that the hours at home were not necessarily spent alone. Her closely studied portrayals of women—presumably members of the artist's family or inner circle of friends—engaged with paint brushes or needles suggest a sociable creative atmosphere (cat. nos. 58 & 59). Activities like embroidery, drawing, paper-quilling, japanning, and quilting lent themselves to collaborative productions (cat. nos. 66 & 239) that commemorated specific family groups or social circles. Drawing also contributed to the practice of gifting, as in a booklet of drawings by Sarah Ponsonby (1755–1831) detailing the Welsh cottage she shared with her life partner, Lady Eleanor Butler (1739–1829) (cat. nos. 54 A–C). Delicately rendered in ink on vellum, the drawings are dedicated on the title page to Lady Frances Douglas (1750–1817) as "Memorandums of A Cottage Whose Inhabitants are proud to boast The Obligations Her Friendship has Conferred." The drawings inside convey the community that the so-called Ladies of Llangollen created independent of male-centred societal expectations. Presented with an embroidered and monogrammed booklet cover and a woven silver purslet, Ponsonby's handcrafted gift chronicled the experience for visitors invited into their private world. Lady Eleanor's diary describes a quiet day in their idyllic life, in which drawing plays a central role: "Up at Seven. From nine 'till one writing. My Beloved drawing Pembroke Castle—from one to three read to her—after dinner Went hastily around the gardens ... from Four 'till Ten reading to my Sally—She drawing—from ten 'till Eleven Sat over the Fire Conversing with My beloved. A Silent, happy Day."[12]

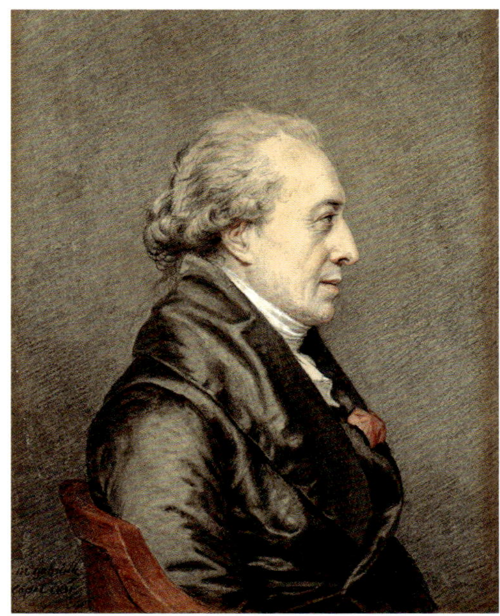

CAT. NO. 42
Marie Gabrielle Capet
Portrait of the Painter François-André Vincent
1811
Black chalk, red chalk, and white chalk on paper
20.2 × 16.1 cm
Katrin Bellinger Collection
2021-024
Photo: Matthew Hollow

Resources Consulted

Bohn, Babette. *Women Artists, Their Patrons, and Their Publics in Early Modern Bologna*. University Park, PA: Penn State University Press, 2021.

Boucher, Diane. "Maria Cosway (1760–1838): A Commentator on Modern Life." *British Art Journal* 18 (Winter 2017–18): 78–86.

Butler, Kim. *"A Noble Art": Amateur Artists and Drawings Masters, c. 1600–1800*. London: British Museum Press, 2000.

D'Anza, Daniele, and Alberto Craievich, eds. *Giulia Lama, Nudi*. Venice: Editrice Eidos, 2018.

Gower, Hazel. *Painted Out of History: The Story of Ellen and Rolinda Sharples*. Bristol: Redcliffe Press, 2021.

Honig, Elizabeth. "The Art of Being 'Artistic': Dutch Women's Creative Practices in the 17th Century." *Woman's Art Journal* 22 (2001–02): 31–39.

Metz, Kathryn. "Ellen and Rolinda Sharples: Mother and Daughter Painters." *Woman's Art Journal* 16, no. 1 (Spring–Summer 1995): 3–11.

Oberer, Angela. *The Life and Work of Rosalba Carriera: The Queen of Pastel*. Amsterdam: Amsterdam University Press, 2020.

Oppenheimer, Margaret A. '"The Charming Spectacle of a Cadaver': Anatomical and Life Study by Women Artists in Paris, 1775–1815." *Nineteenth-Century Art Worldwide: A Journal of Nineteenth-Century Visual Culture* 6, no. 1 (Spring 2007). 19thc-artworldwide.org/spring07.

Roman, Cynthia. "The Art of Lady Diana Beauclerk: Horace Walpole and Female Genius." In *Horace Walpole's Strawberry Hill*. Edited by Michael Snodin and Cynthia Roman. New Haven, CT: Yale University Press, 2009, 155–59.

Spies-Gans, Paris A. *A Revolution on Canvas: The Rise of Women Artists in Britain and France, 1760–1830*. London: Paul Mellon Centre for Studies in British Art in association with Yale University Press, 2022.

Notes

1. Stephen Ongpin Fine Arts, *Master Drawings* (London: SOFA, 2008), cat. no. 22.
2. Paris A. Spies-Gans, *A Revolution on Canvas: The Rise of Women Artists in Britain and France, 1760–1830* (London: Paul Mellon Centre for Studies in British Art in association with Yale University Press, 2022), 188.
3. According to the publisher's introduction for the poem, the illustrations were intended to "contrast the evils of poverty with the ostentatious enjoyment of opulence," the latter represented by Cosway's illustrations of fashionable women relaxing, shopping, or attending social gatherings.
4. Furio Rinaldi, *Color into Line: Pastels from the Renaissance to the Present* (San Francisco: Fine Arts Museums of San Francisco; Atglen, PA: Schiffer, 2021), 22–23; Alison Smith, ed., *Watercolour* (London: Tate Publications, 2011), 14–17.
5. Smith, *Watercolour*, 24–25.
6. Thea Burns, *The Invention of Pastel Painting* (London: Archetype, 2007), 84, and Thea Burns, "Making Up the Face: Technique and Meaning in the Pastels of Rosalba Carriera," in *The Broad Spectrum: Studies in the Materials, Techniques, and Conservation of Color on Paper*, ed. Harriet K. Stratis and Britt Salvesen (London: Archetype, 2002), 17–22.
7. Rinaldi, *Color into Line*, 20.
8. Later in life, Sharples secured the education of future generations of women artists by donating funds to establish the Bristol Academy for the Promotion of Fine Arts, now the Royal West of England Academy (RWA). Upon its founding in 1844, the Academy's exhibitions sought to show equality between male and female artists; in 1845, life drawing classes were offered to women students.
9. Elizabeth Honig, "The Art of Being 'Artistic': Dutch Women's Creative Practices in the 17th Century," *Woman's Art Journal* 22 (2001–02): 31.
10. Martha Moffitt Peacock, "Paper as Power: Carving a Niche for the Female Artists in the Work of Johanna Koerten," *Netherlands Kunsthistorisch Jaarboek* 62 (2012): 238–65.
11. Dr. John Gregory, *A Father's Legacy to His Daughters* (Dublin, 1774), 30. Cited in Clive Edwards, "'Home Is Where the Art Is': Women, Handicrafts, and Home Improvements, 1750–1900," *Journal of Design History* 19 (Spring 2006): 11–21.
12. "Eleanor Butler, Thursday 22 September 1785," in *Eleanor Butler: Diary, 1784*, National Library of Wales, NLW MS 22968A, archives.library.wales/index.php/eleanor-butler-journal-6.

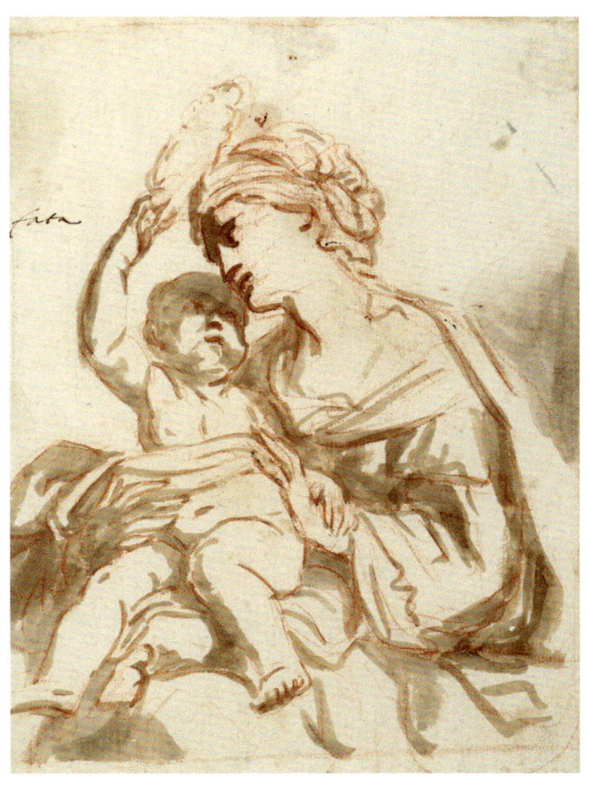

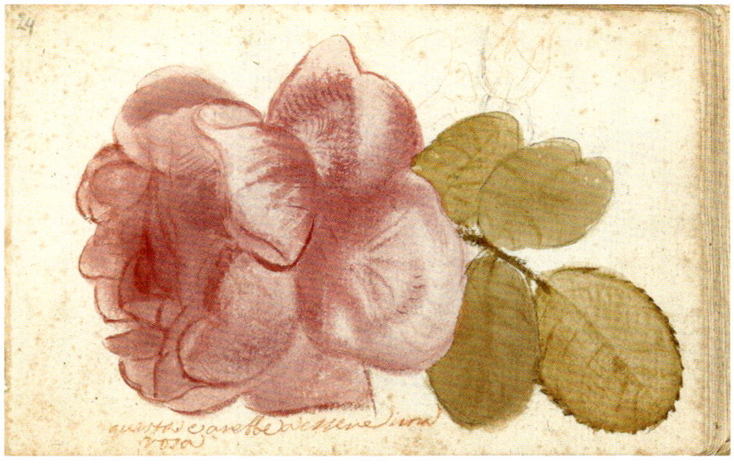

CAT. NO. 43 (left)
Elisabetta Sirani
The Virgin Crowned by the Christ Child with Roses
1663
Red chalk and grey wash on paper
21 × 16.5 cm
National Museums Liverpool, Walker Art Gallery, Purchased from the Trustees of the Weld Heirlooms Settlement with the assistance of the National Heritage Memorial Fund, Art Fund, Sir Denis Mahon and British Nuclear Fuels, in 1995
WAG 1995.76

CAT. NO. 44 (right)
Agnese Dolci and Carlo Dolci
Sketchbook
1667–1670
Red and green wash, and traces of red chalk and black chalk on paper
Sheets: 9.3 × 14.8 cm;
closed volume: 11.2 × 16.7 × 2.9 cm
The Syndics of the Fitzwilliam Museum, University of Cambridge
904*3
Image © The Fitzwilliam Museum, Cambridge

Opening illustrated: *Rose with a leaf* (folio 25r)

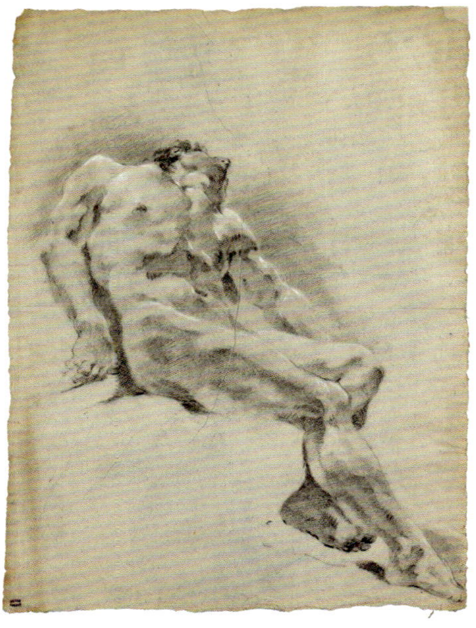

CAT. NO. 45
Giulia Lama
Sketch of a man foreshortened
first half of 18th century
Black chalk and white chalk on paper
57 × 44 cm
Fondazione Musei Civici di Venezia, Gabinetto dei disegni e delle stampe, Ca' Rezzonico
Inv. Cl. III n. 6994
Exhibited at AGO only

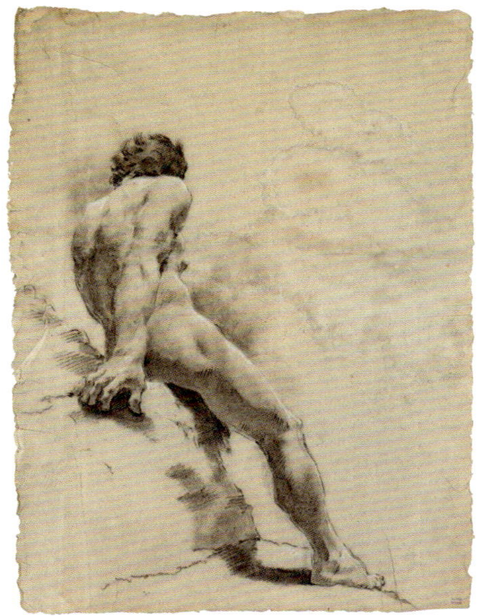

CAT. NO. 46
Giulia Lama
Sketch of a man seen from behind, leaning back on a rock
first half of 18th century
Black chalk and white chalk on paper
57.5 × 44 cm
Fondazione Musei Civici di Venezia, Gabinetto dei disegni e delle stampe, Ca' Rezzonico
Inv. Cl. III n. 6989
Exhibited at BMA only

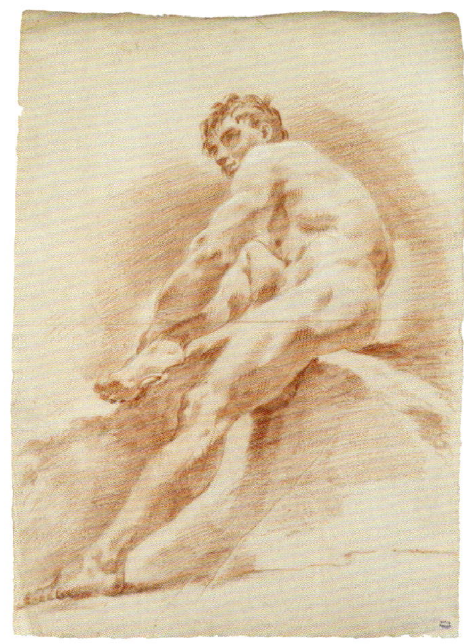

CAT. NO. 47
Giulia Lama
Sketch of a man seen from behind, seated and looking to his left
first half of 18th century
Red chalk and white chalk on paper
59 × 43.1 cm
Fondazione Musei Civici di Venezia, Gabinetto dei disegni e delle stampe, Ca' Rezzonico
Inv. Cl. III n. 6995
Exhibited at AGO only

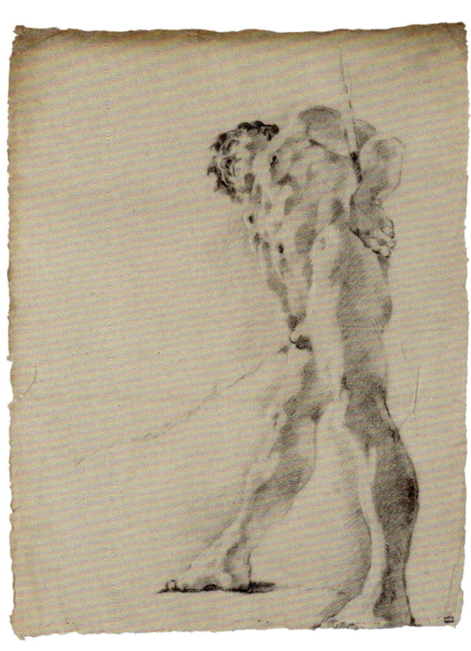

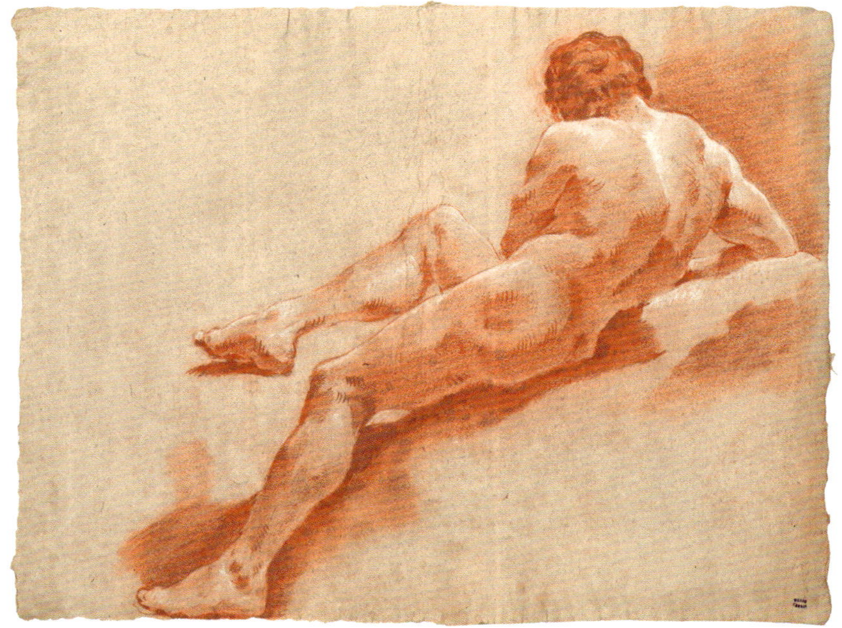

CAT. NO. 48 (left)
Giulia Lama
Sketch of a man standing, possibly urinating
first half of 18th century
Black chalk and white chalk on paper
62 × 44 cm
Fondazione Musei Civici di Venezia, Gabinetto dei disegni e delle stampe, Ca' Rezzonico
Inv. Cl. III n. 6997
Exhibited at BMA only

CAT. NO. 49 (right)
Giulia Lama
Sketch of a man seen from behind, reclining
first half of 18th century
Red chalk and white chalk on paper
43 × 57 cm
Fondazione Musei Civici di Venezia, Gabinetto dei disegni e delle stampe, Ca' Rezzonico
Inv. Cl. III n. 6993
Exhibited at BMA only

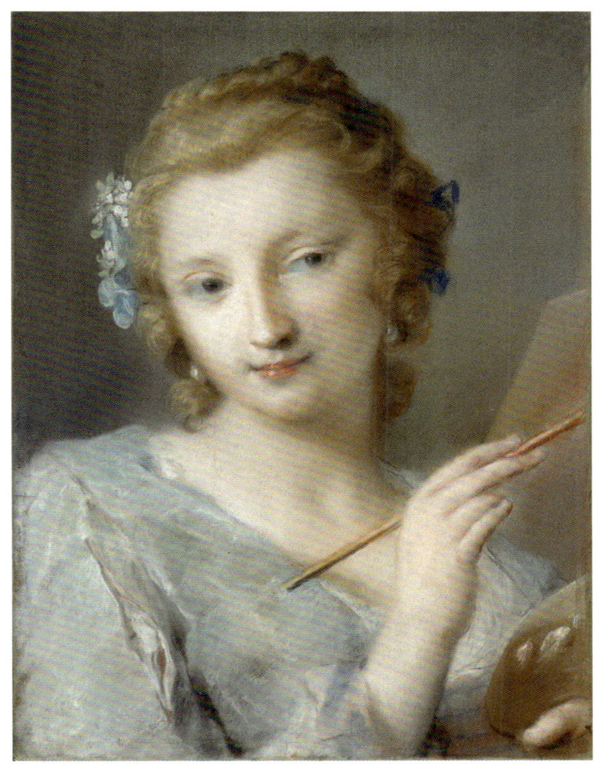

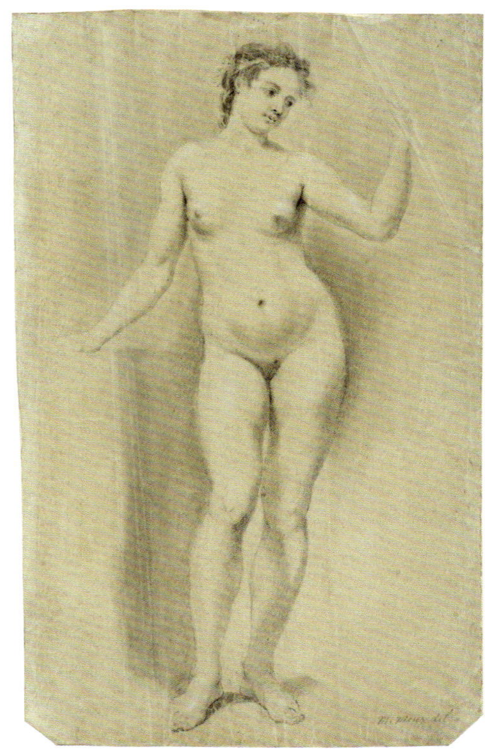

CAT. NO. 50 (left)
Rosalba Carriera
Allegory of Painting
1730s
Pastel and red chalk on blue paper, mounted on canvas
44.3 × 34.1 cm
National Gallery of Art, Washington,
Samuel H. Kress Collection
1939.1.136
Exhibited at BMA only

CAT. NO. 51 (right)
Mary Moser
Standing female nude
undated
Black chalk and white chalk on grey-green paper
49 × 30.2 cm
The Syndics of the Fitzwilliam Museum,
University of Cambridge
PD.4-1947
Image © The Fitzwilliam Museum, Cambridge

CAT. NO. 52 (left)
Anna Helena Alströmer
Study of noses, no. 3
1775
Red chalk on paper
21.4 × 17.8 cm
Nationalmuseum, Stockholm, Donated
2018 by Lene Marinus Jensen, Stockholm
NMH 28/2018
Photo: Cecilia Heisser / Nationalmuseum
Exhibited at AGO only

CAT. NO. 53 (right)
Anna Helena Alströmer
Study of tongues, no. 5
1775
Red chalk on paper
21.4 × 17.8 cm
Nationalmuseum, Stockholm, Donated
2018 by Lene Marinus Jensen, Stockholm
NMH 24/2018
Photo: Cecilia Heisser / Nationalmuseum
Exhibited at BMA only

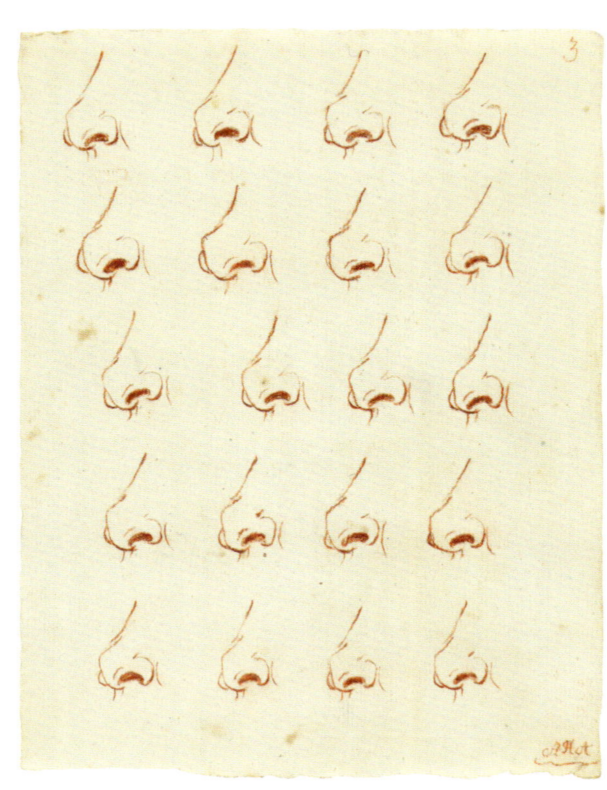

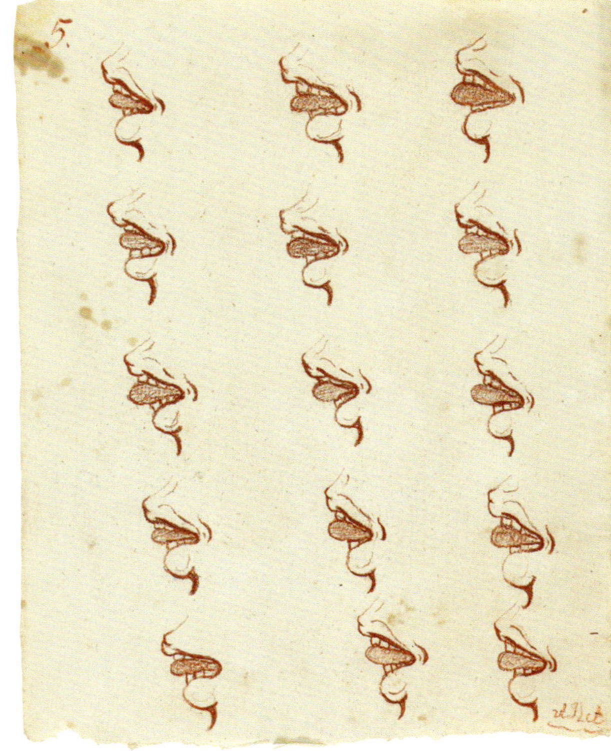

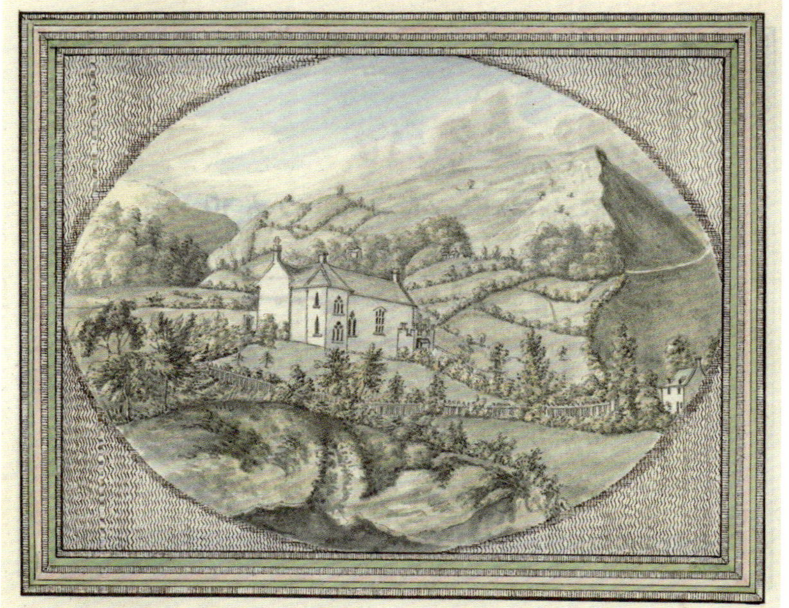

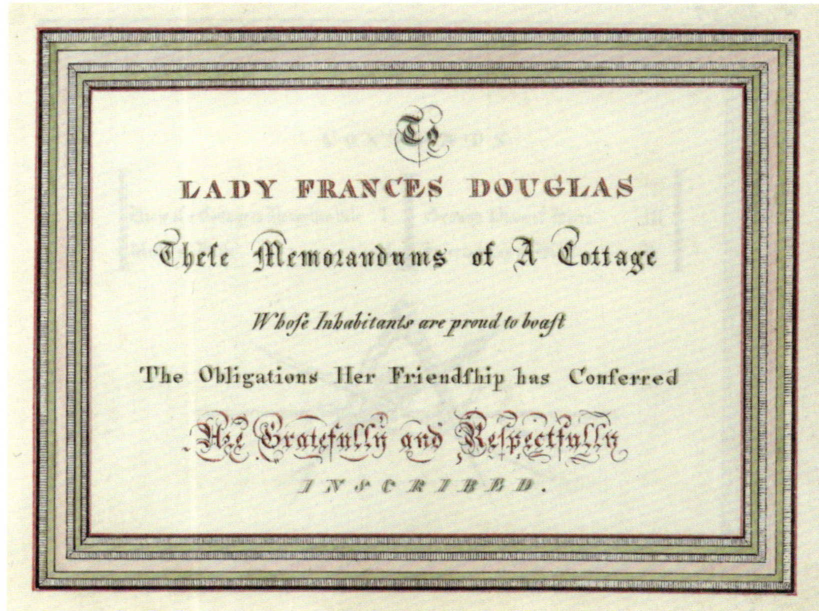

To

LADY FRANCES DOUGLAS

Theſe Memorandums of A Cottage

Whoſe Inhabitants are proud to boaſt

The Obligations Her Friendſhip has Conferred

Are Gratefully and Reſpectfully

INSCRIBED.

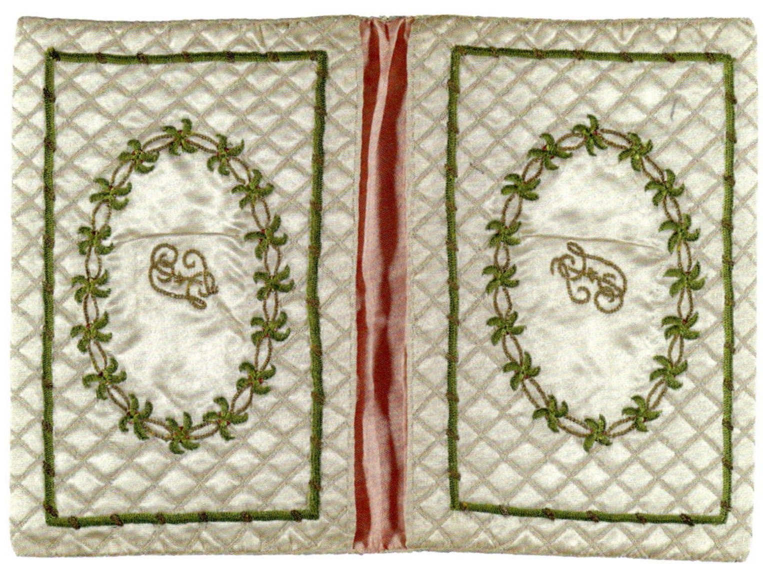

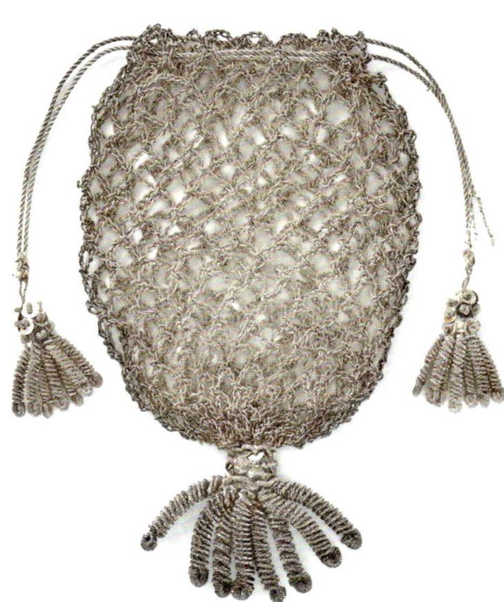

CAT. NOS. 54 A–C
Sarah Ponsonby
To Lady Frances Douglas: These Memorandums of A Cottage Whose Inhabitants are proud to boast The Obligations Her Friendship has Conferred
1788
Booklet of watercolours on vellum, bound in a quilted silk cover; embroidered double pocket silk pouch; drawstring netted purse woven with silver-wrapped cotton threads with silver tassels
Book (closed): 8.7 × 12.4 × 0.3 cm; book (open): 17.4 × 12.4 × 0.3 cm; purse: 11 × 7 cm
Harvard University, Houghton Library, Purchased with the Amy Lowell fund, 1964
MS ENG 1225
Exhibited at BMA only

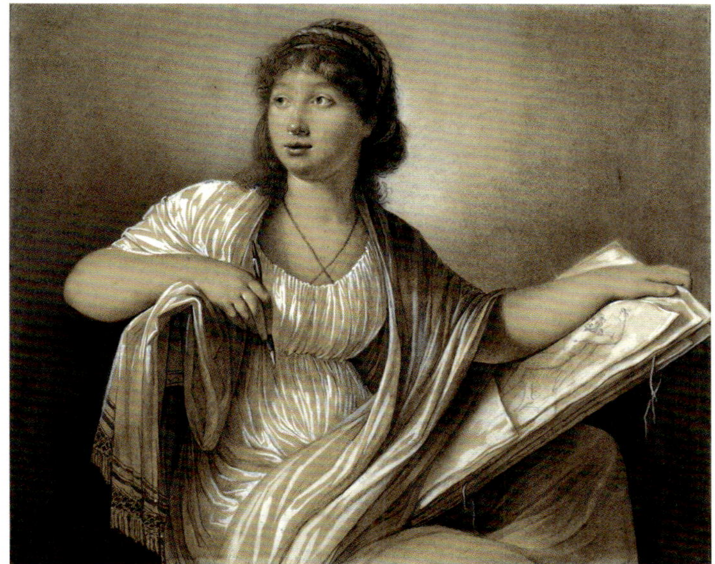

CAT. NO. 55 (left)
Anne Guéret
Portrait of an Artist with a Portfolio (Self-Portrait?)
c. 1793
Black chalk, pen and grey ink, and wash, heightened with white gouache on paper
32 × 40.4 cm
Katrin Bellinger Collection
2008-012
Photo: Matthew Hollow

CAT. NO. 56 (right)
Attributed to Ellen Sharples
Mrs. Robert Eglesfeld Griffith (Maria Thong Patterson)
c. 1793–1797
Pastel on brown paper
21.6 × 17.2 cm
Baltimore Museum of Art: Purchase with exchange funds from Gift of Edgar William and Bernice Chrysler Garbisch, Gift of Mrs. C. Oliver Iselin, Gift of Blanchard Randall, and Gift of Andrew Speir; and W. Clagett Emory Bequest Fund, in Memory of his Parents, William H. Emory of A and Martha B. Emory, 1986.117
Photo: Mitro Hood
Exhibited at BMA only

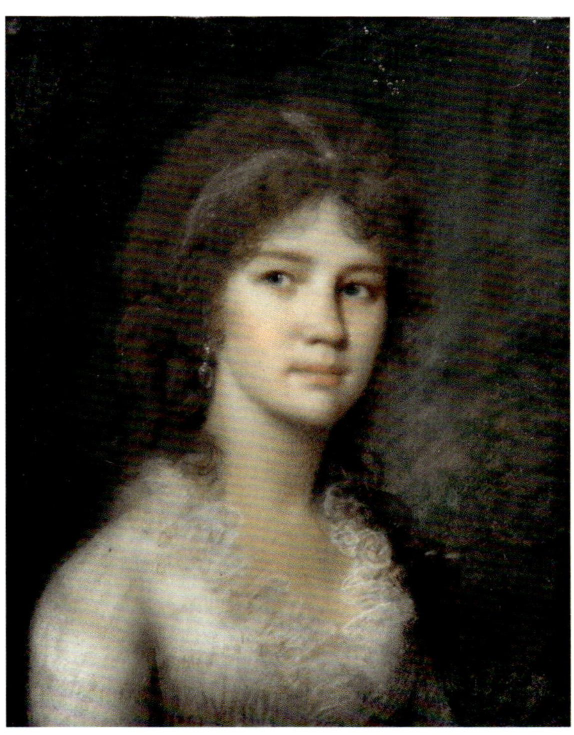

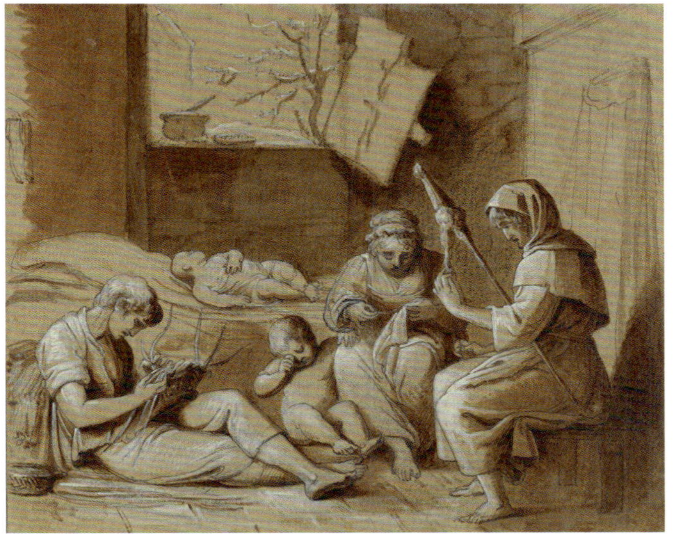

CAT. NO. 57
Maria Louisa Catherine Cecilia Cosway
Home Industry
1800
Pen and ink, wash, and white heightening on paper
23 × 28.7 cm
Gift of Francis Peabody, Print Collection, Miriam and Ira D. Wallach Division of Art, Prints and Photographs, The New York Public Library, Astor, Lenox and Tilden Foundations
Object number 112634

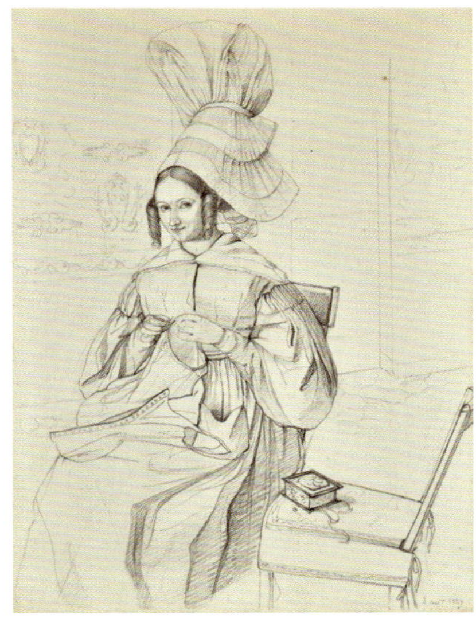

CAT. NO. 58
Fanny Guillaume de Bassoncourt, Baronne de Molaret
Sketchbook
c. 1837
Bound volume of graphite drawings on paper
Closed: 22.2 × 29.7 × 2 cm; open: 22.2 × 60 cm
Katrin Bellinger Collection
2015-017
Photo: Matthew Hollow

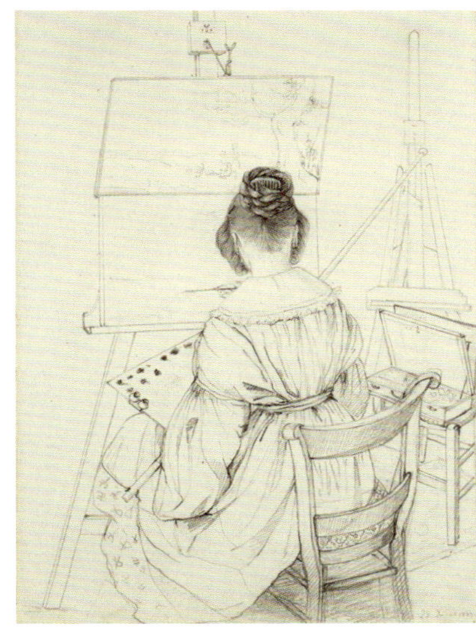

CAT. NO. 59
Fanny Guillaume de Bassoncourt, Baronne de Molaret
Landscape Painter at her Easel
1837
Graphite on vellum paper
27.7 × 21.2 cm
Katrin Bellinger Collection
2015-017
Photo: Matthew Hollow

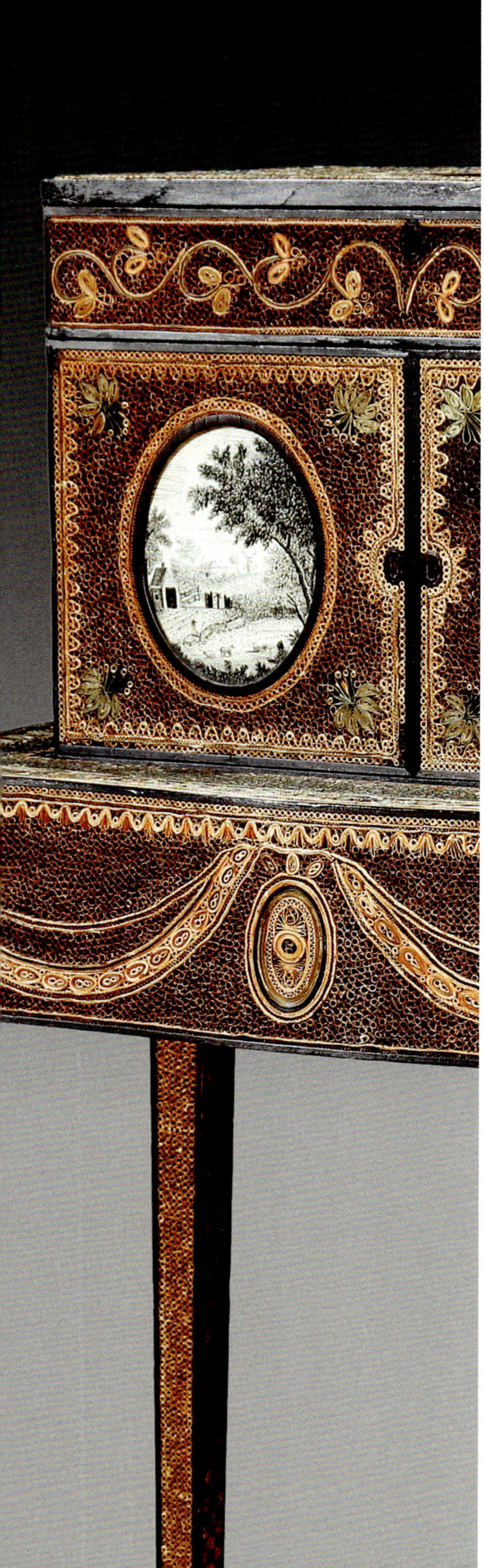

Furniture

Brittany Luberda

Women were instrumental in the physical making, professional retail, and artistic decoration of furniture in early modern Europe. In recent years, a closer reading of furniture manuals, an attention to detail in city archives, and a widened definition of making—that includes expertise honed outside guild guidelines—have provided revelations about women working with wood. The conclusions are expansive and show that female furniture makers were working on a local and global scale, for themselves as well as for middle-class and elite patrons, and, justifiably, at the centre of court cabinetmaking.

For over two centuries, furniture makers from England to Asia to the Americas have taken inspiration from *The Cabinet-Maker and Upholsterer's Guide; or, Repository of Designs for Every Article of Household Furniture, in the Newest and Most Approved Taste*, a collection of almost three hundred furniture designs after drawings by "A. Hepplewhite and Co. Cabinetmakers" (cat. no. 61). Chairs, tables, cellarets (wine cabinets), chests, and other forms with neoclassical elements were marketed to English makers and collectors across the country as well as abroad to "foreigners, who seek a knowledge of English taste in the various articles of household furniture."[1] The producer of this global guide for fashionable furniture was Alice Hepplewhite (active eighteenth century), the owner of a large London cabinetmaking workshop. Hepplewhite was not a member of a London livery company—a guild and trade system—but she inherited ownership of a workshop after the death of her husband, George, in 1786. Women in early modern England could carry on their late husbands' trades because customary law considered the period of their marriage the equivalent of having served the required seven-year apprenticeship.[2] Although the *Guide* was produced by Alice two years after her husband's death, today George Hepplewhite almost ubiquitously receives credit for this internationally recognized eighteenth-century style. But there is no evidence that George had a hand in the designs or the publication, nor is any surviving furniture attributed to the workshop at-large. The legacy of the Hepplewhite vision for a delicate neoclassicism is the book produced under Alice Hepplewhite's guidance; designs produced in England, Asia, and the recently independent United States of America (cat. no. 62) were the result of her initiative.[3]

Preceding Hepplewhite were several women furniture workshop owners. The White Swan was a thriving furniture workshop and retail outlet owned by Grace Coxed (active 1700–1735). Located outside the gates of bustling St. Paul's Cathedral in London from 1704 until roughly 1735, the workshop occupied two premises and produced enough furniture that today "The White Swan" is the most frequently found label on English furniture from the first half of the eighteenth century.[4] In her rise as one of England's preeminent owners, Coxed was involved with the joinery workshop of her first husband, John Mayo, which she relocated to St. Paul's after his death. This district was also home to women like the chair carver Martha Martin (active 1696–1721), and their businesses were just two examples of the 10 to 20 percent of London households and businesses headed by widows.[5] Grace was listed as the principal owner of The White Swan until she married John Coxed, an apprentice likely turned journeyman, in 1708. After John died, Grace's name returned to the business record by 1719; she then partnered with her brother-in-law Thomas Woster to found the co-owned workshop called The White Swan. Continuing her early expansion of the business, this prolific workshop hosted apprentices and journeymen, and supplied veneered furniture for both metropolitan and rural clients. The walnut veneer over oak and pine on the Colonial Williamsburg bureau table (cat. no. 63) reflects the workshop's central output, and

CAT. NO. 60
Mary Ashfield
Fire Judge Frame
c. 1671
Pine
Approx. 316 × 199.5 × 16.5 cm
Arnold Wiggins & Sons
AW13078
Image courtesy of Arnold Wiggins & Sons

its bun feet are a recent replacement by conservators to return the bureau to its form when it left The White Swan. Grace's oversight of the business extended to trade, and her business card lists their furniture as well as imported wares and mirrors:

> G.Coxed and T.Woster ... Makes and Sells Cabinets, Scrutoires [writing desks], Desks and Book-Cases, Buro's, Chests of Drawers, Wisk, Ombre, *Dutch* and *Indian* Tea-Tables; All sorts of Look-ing Glasses, Large Sconces, Dressing Sets, and Wainscot-Work of all sorts ... Old Glasses New polished, and Made up fashionable.[6]

A combination of maker and merchant was common in the early modern period, and Coxed exemplifies the dual role.

While Hepplewhite and Coxed owned large workshops with multifaceted production, women were also specialists in specific stages of making—joinery, turning, japanning, or frame-making—in small, often household, workshops. Between 1671 and 1675, three women frame workers were commissioned by the British royal court to carve elaborate frames in the auricular style for portraits of the London Fire Judges, the committee that settled property disputes after the Great Fire of London in 1666.[7] A report on the progress of the commission delivered on December 14, 1671, identifies Mary Ashfield (active second half of seventeenth century) (cat. no. 60) as one of these three women. John Norris designed the frames, and Ashfield was expected to use her carving skills to fashion eight full-length portrait frames. Each of the frames has an individualized treatment, and confirms that women woodworkers received court commissions in England.

Across the channel in France, too, women were integrated into the furniture trade at the highest levels of quality and commissions. Françoise-Marguerite Vandercruse (1731–1775) was born into a cabinetmaking dynasty and lived in the epicentres of French royal craftsmanship. She was the daughter of François Vandercruse, a successful, independent furniture maker in Paris. Two of her sisters married cabinetmakers, and her brother became a royal cabinetmaker. As a young adult, Vandercruse lived in the Louvre artist studio apartments until around 1754 with her first husband, royal cabinetmaker Jean-François Oeben. Between 1754 and 1756, they lived at the Gobelins manufactory, home to workshops for tapestry, metalsmithing, cabinetmaking, embroidery, and designers. When Oeben died in 1763, Vandercruse inherited the cabinetmaking enterprise, thereafter known as the workshop of the Veuve (widow) Oeben. She oversaw the finances and production, to which she likely had already contributed while Oeben was alive. As a widow, it was her prerogative to either continue ownership independently or to remarry. In 1767, several months pregnant, she married Jean-Henri Riesener, Oeben's former apprentice, and Riesener assumed legal ownership of the workshop. Despite owning the workshop for the period of her widowhood, Vandercruse's name does not appear stamped on the furniture produced under her management, as it does for Oeben and Riesener. However, this "considerable cabinetmaking workshop" was still listed in the *Almanach des marchands* under the widow "Hobenne" until her death in 1775, highlighting her authority over her new husband.[8] A design by Oeben but piece likely executed by Riesener under the direction of Vandercruse, the Wallace Collection's worktable (cat. no. 64) was made primarily to hold women's needlework and other accoutrements. Many such pieces produced under Vandercruse can be identified by the presence of stamps for both Oeben and Riesener, indicating a work was started or designed under one workshop head and finished by another. Both in practice and in the public sphere, then, Vandercruse's leadership is written into the history of the furniture her workshop made for Versailles and other French aristocratic residences.

Paper filigree or quillwork—the application of dyed or metallic rolled paper onto a wooden surface—was practised primarily by women in early modern continental Europe and England and is mostly found on small objects used by women, such as an elegant tea caddy held in the Gardiner Museum (cat. no. 65). Papers for filigree were ordered from specialty craft stores, and period magazines published designs for filigree inlay in the same inspirational spirit as Alice Hepplewhite's guide for furniture makers. A cabinet covered with paper filigree (cat. no. 66) by Sophia Jane Maria Bonnell (c. 1748–1841) and Mary Anne Harvey Bonnell (1763–1853) is one of fewer than ten surviving pieces of furniture decorated in this medium. The designs imitate dyed wood veneers or painted ornamentation, and the Bonnells rendered both classical motifs, like swags, and botanical illustrations in various places. The Bonnells likely ordered the carcass, or wood base, from cabinetmaker George Brookshaw, who also filled an order for painted furniture with scenes after the designs of Angelica Kauffmann (1741–1807) for their estate at Pelling Place, Berkshire, England.

Histories of furniture have previously focused on either individual workshops or specialized skills, such as cabinetmakers, joiners, marquetry makers, or mount makers. When the definition of decoration is expanded to include domestic practices like paper filigree, and the biographies of female makers are read between the lives of those allowed to make a mark, the presence of women in wood resurfaces.

Resources Consulted

Bowett, Adam, and Laurie Lindey. “Labelled Furniture from the White Swan Workshop in St Paul’s Churchyard (1711–35).” *Furniture History* 39 (2003): 71–98.

Jacobsen, Helen, Rufus Bird, and Mia Jackson. *Jean-Henri Riesener: Cabinetmaker to Louis XVI & Marie Antoinette*. London: Philip Wilson, 2021.

Kirkham, Pat. “The London Furniture Trade, 1700–1870.” *Furniture History* 24 (1988): i–219.

Riley, Noël. *The Accomplished Lady: A History of Genteel Pursuits, c. 1660–1860*. Wetherby, UK: Oblong Creative, 2017.

Simon, Jacob. “Women in Picture Framing.” *The Frame Blog*. March 5, 2014. theframeblog.com/tag/fire-judges/.

Notes

1 Preface to *Alice Hepplewhite and Co., The Cabinet-Maker and Upholsterer’s Guide; or, Repository of Designs for Every Article of Household Furniture, in the Newest and Most Approved Taste* (London: I. and J. Taylor, 1788).

2 Laurie Lindey, “Women Working in the Furniture Trade in Early Modern London,” *British and Irish Furniture Makers Online*, July 24, 2019, bifmo.furniturehistorysociety.org/blog/women-working-in-the-furniture-trade-in-early-modern-london.

3 Gloria Breeskin Peck, “Alice and George Hepplewhite’s ‘Cabinet-Maker & Upholsterer’s Guide,’” *Woman’s Art Journal* 8, no. 2 (1987): 25–27.

4 Adam Bowett and Laurie Lindey, “Labelled Furniture from the White Swan Workshop in St Paul’s Churchyard (1711–35),” *Furniture History* 39 (2003): 71.

5 Lindey, “Women Working in the Furniture Trade in Early Modern London.”

6 Bowett and Lindey, *Furniture History*, 96. Emphasis in original.

7 Arnold Wiggins & Sons, “The Fire Judge Frames,” Frame Hangs, January 12, 2017.

8 Helen Jacobsen, Rufus Bird, and Mia Jackson, *Jean-Henri Riesener: Cabinetmaker to Louis XVI & Marie Antoinette* (London: Philip Wilson, 2020), 8.

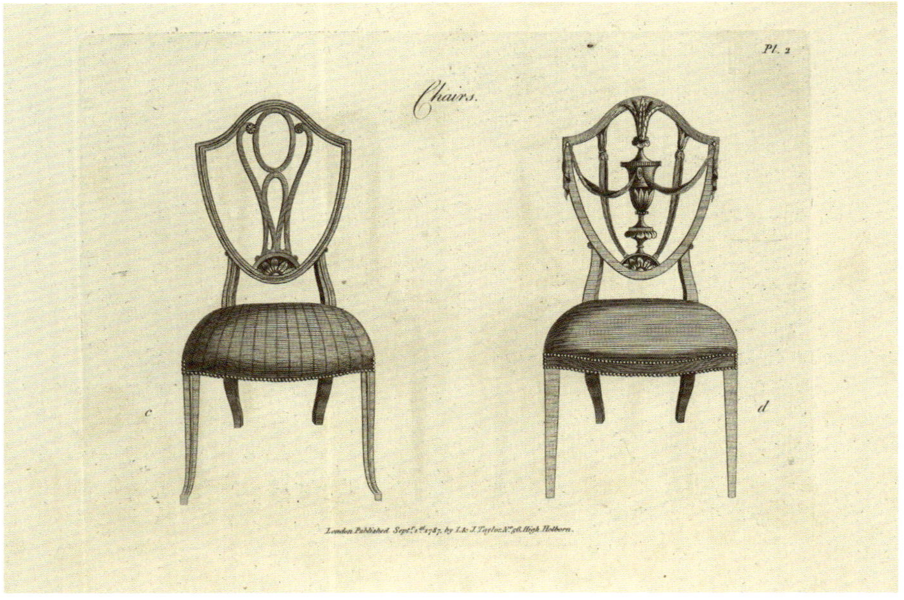

CAT. NO. 61
Alice Hepplewhite and Co.
The Cabinet-Maker and Upholsterer’s Guide; or Repository of Designs for Every Article of Household Furniture, in the Newest and Most Approved Taste
1794

Bound volume of engravings
38 × 25 cm
The George Peabody Library, The Sheridan Libraries, Johns Hopkins University
749.223 H529 1794 QUARTO c. 1
Photo: Digitization Services Unit, Johns Hopkins University

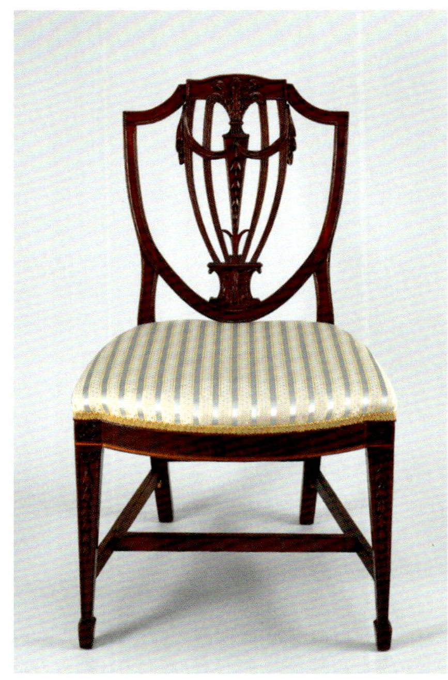

CAT. NO. 62
Designer: Alice Hepplewhite and Co.
Manufacturer: Unknown American chairmaker
Side chair
1795–1810

Mahogany, mahogany veneers, light and dark wood inlays; yellow pine and mahogany secondary woods
92.7 × 53.7 × 55.9 cm
Baltimore Museum of Art: Gift of Dorothea Harper Pennington Nelson, Baltimore, 1979.46
Photo: Mitro Hood

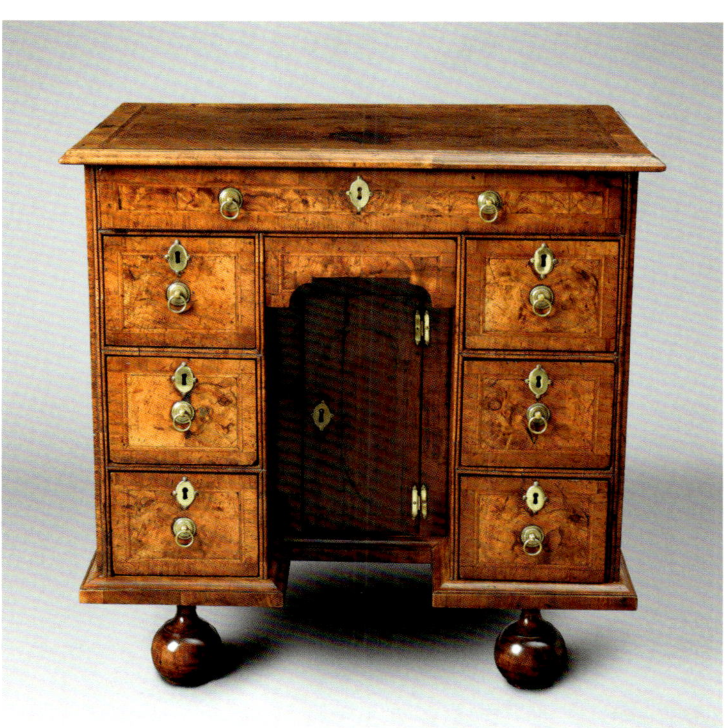

CAT. NO. 63 (left)
Workshop owners: Grace Coxed and Thomas Woster
Manufacturer: The White Swan
Bureau table
1719–1725
Walnut, walnut veneer, oak, and deal
75.6 × 79.4 × 52.1 cm
Courtesy of The Colonial Williamsburg Foundation, Museum Purchase
Accession #1974-169

CAT. NO. 64 (right)
Workshop director:
Françoise-Marguerite Vandercruse
Cabinetmakers: Attributed to
Jean-François Oeben and Jean-Henri Riesener
Work-table
c. 1765
Oak, walnut, tulipwood, stained woods, ebony or ebonized wood, box, and gilt bronze
102 × 41.7 × 29.5 cm
The Wallace Collection, London
Inv. F313
Photo: © The Wallace Collection, London, UK / Bridgeman Images

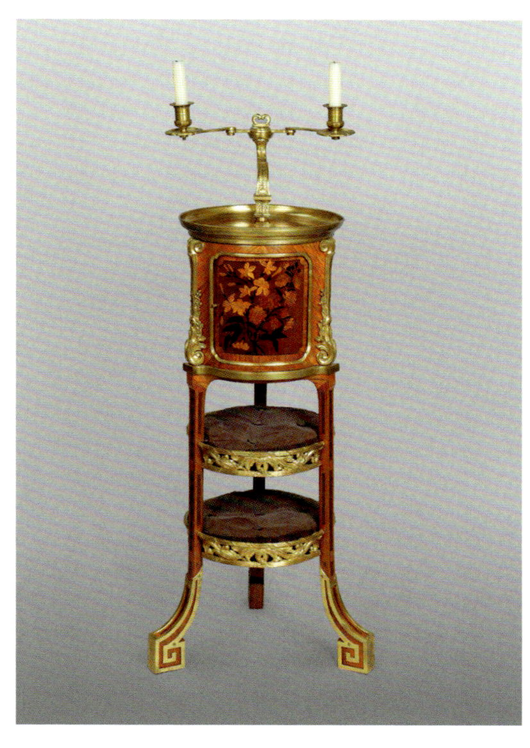

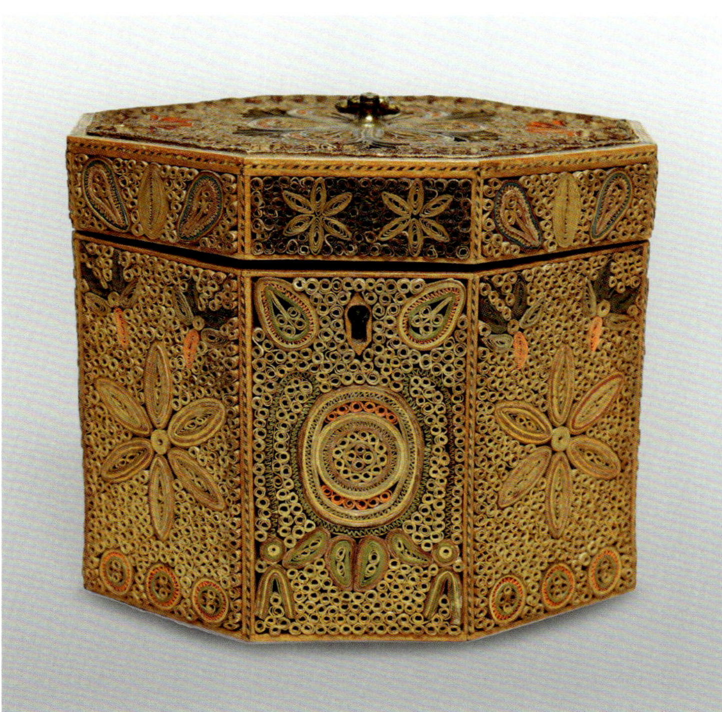

CAT. NO. 65 (left)
Unknown European maker
Tea caddy
late 18th century
Wood and metal with paper inlay
12 × 14.5 × 10 cm
Gardiner Museum, Toronto, Canada, Gift of W.B.G. Humphries
T21.2.358a-b

CAT. NO. 66 (right)
Sophia Jane Maria Bonnell and Mary Anne Harvey Bonnell
Paper filigree cabinet on stand
c. 1789
Wood, paper, metallic paper, silk, hair, and adhesive
105.4 × 58.4 × 39.4 cm
Baltimore Museum of Art: Decorative Arts Acquisitions Endowment established by the Friends of the American Wing, 2022.78
Photography courtesy Carlton Hobbs LLC

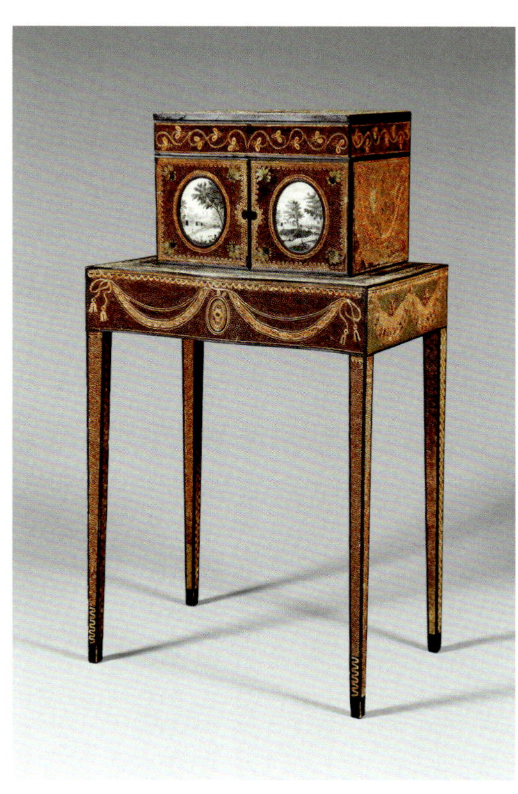

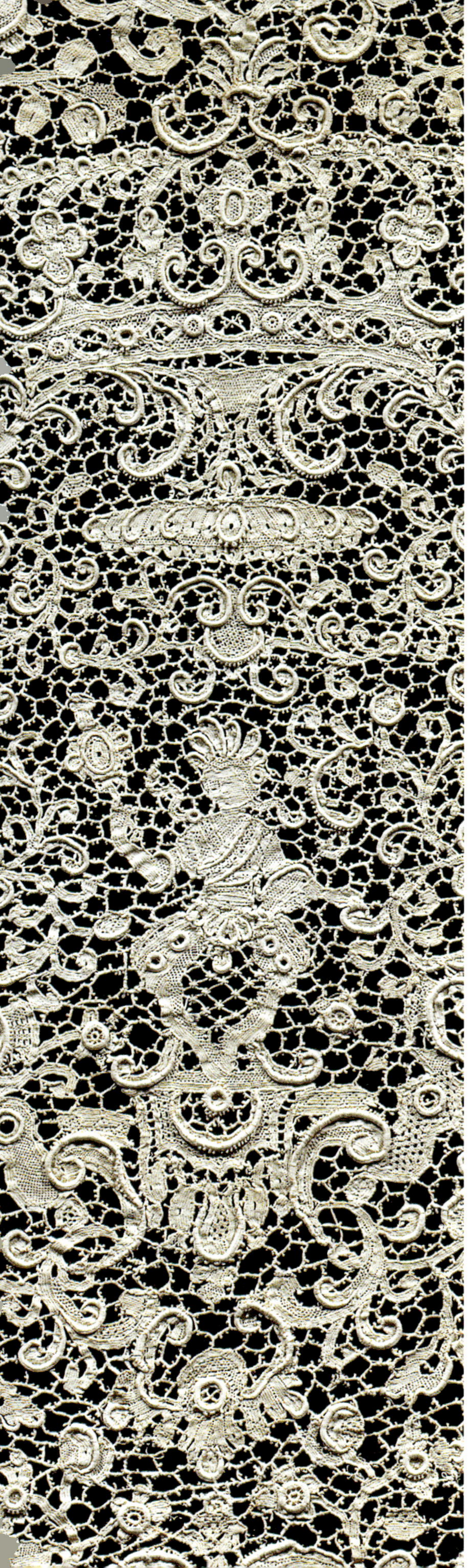

Lace

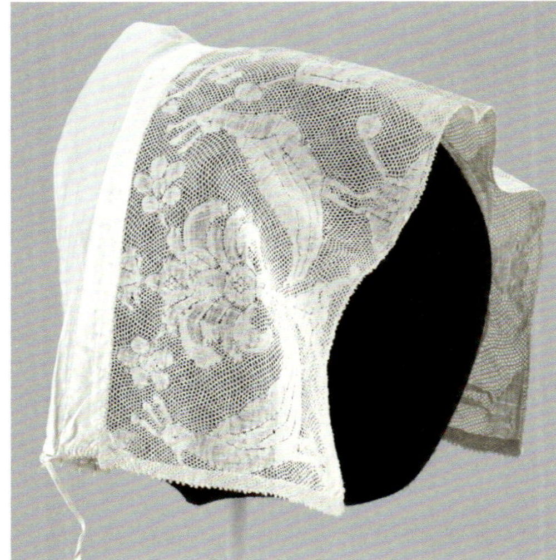

Elena Naomi Kanagy-Loux

How can a piece of lace—described by the seventeenth-century English clergyman Thomas Fuller as "nothing save a little thread descanted upon by art and industry"—reveal the untold stories of women makers?[1] Lacemakers worked outside the male-dominated guild system, and few records of their identities have survived. During its heyday, lace was one of the most valuable textiles in Europe, produced across numerous convents and charitable institutions to adorn the clothing and furnishings of wealthy men and women alike. In the wake of industrialization, handmade lace continued to be treasured and passed down, championed by philanthropists and reformists as an important expression of cultural heritage and feminine creativity.

Lace is a textile in which the pattern is defined by the spaces between the threads, and can be produced using various techniques involving knotting, looping, and interlacing threads. Beginning with their parallel emergence in the early sixteenth century, needle and bobbin lace competed for the mantle of the most fashionable lace in Europe for several centuries, often evolving in imitation of each other. Needle lace developed out of cutwork and drawnwork, in which a pattern would be transferred onto woven linen, threads cut and pulled out according to the design, and buttonhole stitches worked into the voided areas. To create *reticella* (little net), the linen was almost completely cut away, leaving only a skeleton of warp and weft threads. Eventually, the step of using a base fabric was discarded, and the lace was worked directly on the pattern by couching down outline threads and stitching between them in rows without piercing the base, resulting in the first true needle-lace technique, *punto in aria*, or stitches in air.

Bobbin lace, on the other hand, developed out of braiding techniques, which grew increasingly complex until it was necessary to wind the individual threads around cylindrical bobbins made of bone, wood, or lead, and insert a scaffolding of pins between the stitches for support. Pairs of bobbins are crossed and twisted following a pattern pinned to a firm pillow base to create an endless variety of designs. Both bobbin and needle lace were produced in convents, where many Northern Italian girls, for example, were cloistered by their families to avoid the expense of dowries. Milanese bobbin lace is distinct for its patterns of scrolling tapes that are worked in separate parts and later linked by braids or filled in with a mesh ground. The part-lace technique allowed for an exquisitely rendered seventeenth-century Milanese flounce for an alb (a robe worn by clergymen) (cat. no. 74), which depicts Saint Paul and an ecclesiastical coat of arms, to be worked in the round with no seam.

CAT. NO. 67 (above)
Unknown Flemish lacemaker
Cap with bobbin lace brim
18th century
Linen
22.9 × 26.7 cm
Baltimore Museum of Art: The Cone Collection, formed by Dr. Claribel Cone and Miss Etta Cone of Baltimore, Maryland, 1950.2022.267
Photo: Mitro Hood

CAT. NO. 68 (facing)
Unknown Russian lacemaker
Embroidered drawn net bed valance with bobbin lace border
1766–1833
Linen ground and linen embroidery threads
40.6 × 170.2 cm
Baltimore Museum of Art: The Cone Collection, formed by Dr. Claribel Cone and Miss Etta Cone of Baltimore, Maryland, 1950.2010.20
Photo: Mitro Hood

One of the most ancient techniques for producing lace is *lacis*, a knotted net darned with decorative embroidery stitches to create a pattern. A related square net or *filet* lace technique, *buratto* (coarse cloth), was also produced during the Italian Renaissance. *Buratto* uses as its base strips of gauze woven on narrow looms by manually twisting the vertical warp threads and securing them in place with the horizontal weft. Although *lacis* was typically worked in white linen, *buratto* was woven in linen or silk and often embellished with a vibrant array of metal and polychrome silk threads, as in an example from the seventeenth century (cat. no. 69). Comparable designs for scrolling patterns appear in one of the earliest lace pattern books, *Il Burato: Libro de Recami* by Alessandro Paganini, which was published in Bergamo around 1527.[2]

During the heyday of the printed pattern book, in the sixteenth and seventeenth centuries, the circulation of innovative embroidery and lace techniques across Europe exploded. Although lacemaking was predominantly the domain of women, most of the named designers, printmakers, and publishers of pattern books were men, who offered grandiose dedications to the noble matrons for whom their books were intended. One exception was Elisabetta (or Isabella) Catanea Parasole (c. 1570–c. 1620), who was trained in embroidery but likely not woodblock cutting, despite having married into a family of printmakers in Rome. Likely working with her sister-in-law Geronima Cagnaccia Parasole (c. 1569–1622) as engraver and her brother-in-law Leonardo as publisher, Elisabetta is connected with multiple pattern books for elaborate embroidery and lace designs, including her 1616 pattern book *Teatro delle Nobili et Virtuose Donne*. Considered one of her finest works, it was reprinted posthumously with an updated title page and dedication in 1620 (cat. no. 70).

Flanders was an early competitor of the Italian lace industry, and the archives of the powerful Plantin family of print publishers offer insight into the importance of the lace trade in sixteenth-century Antwerp. The lace portion of the business was overseen by teenage sisters Martine Plantin (1550–1616) and Catharina Plantin (1553–1622), and their correspondence indicates the international demand for Flemish lace, which was exported across Europe and to the Americas. As the desire for lace fashion grew, its production became the focus of many Flemish convents and *béguinages*, as well as of orphanages such as the Maagdenhuis in Antwerp. Flemish lace was known for its use of incredibly fine linen thread, which was highlighted by the gossamer effect of continuous bobbin lace designs featuring stylized *potten kant* (flowerpot) and chrysanthemum motifs (cat. no. 72), requiring hundreds of bobbins and many months to produce. By the second half of the eighteenth century, court fashions had once again shifted, but Antwerp bobbin laces continued to adorn regional Dutch headwear (cat. no. 67).[3]

By the time Louis XIV passed a sumptuary edict in 1660 barring French courtiers from draining their fortunes on foreign lace, its popularity had reached a fever pitch, and many resorted to theft and smuggling to obtain the latest styles. Rather than accept defeat, the controller-general of finances, Jean-Baptiste Colbert, established royal lace manufactories across France by enticing Venetian and Flemish lacemakers to train local women. The Venetian Republic regarded this as espionage and decreed that anyone caught practising their craft abroad would be imprisoned or executed, but their French competitors persisted. *Point de France*, as the new style was dubbed, contrasted with heavy, Baroque Venetian needle lace, its miniature motifs in symmetrical designs influenced by the artist Jean Bérain.[4] The royal support of the French industry enabled the production of incredibly fine work on a massive scale, requiring upward of seven hours to produce one centimetre of Alençon needle lace. One wide point de France furnishing flounce (cat. no. 73) that features regal motifs would have been the work of numerous hands.

Given the staggering cost of handmade lace, inventors raced to mechanize its production during the Industrial Revolution, and the increasing sophistication of lace machines in the nineteenth century nearly decimated the handmade lace industry. However, lacemaking survived in small pockets across Europe and around the globe, and by the late nineteenth century many philanthropic organizations focused their attention beyond merely the survival of handmade lace. From John Ruskin, who spearheaded the revival of hand-spun English linen cutwork, to Queen Margherita of Savoy, patroness of Burano needle lace, a new appreciation for handicraft traditions led to the opening of countless lace schools, whose creations were seen by international crowds at expositions from Paris to Chicago.

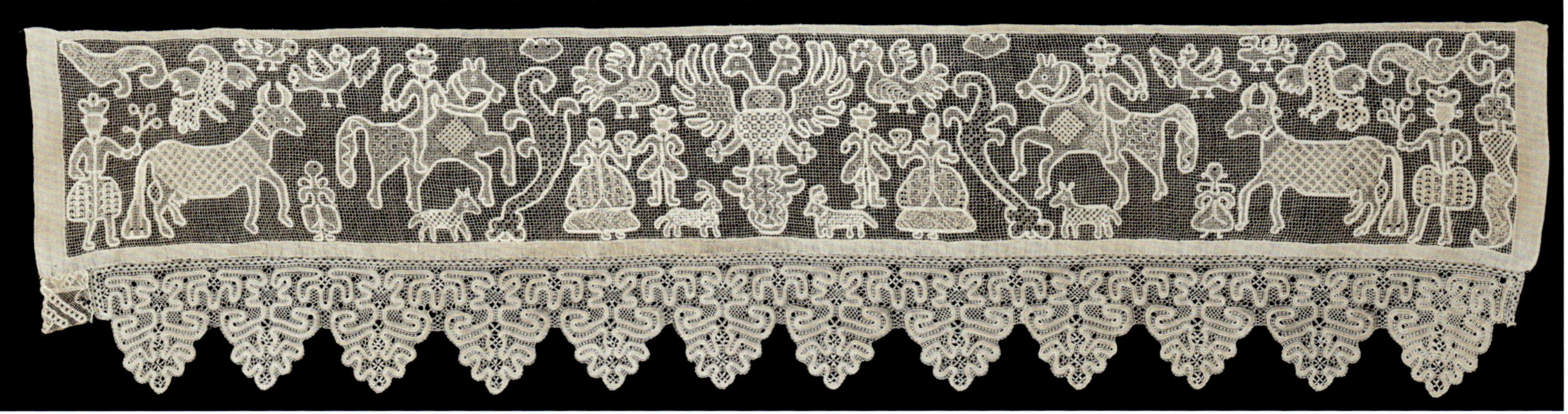

After the abolishment of serfdom in 1861, the Russian lace industry—which dated back several centuries—provided an independent income to rural women. Its importance was championed by the enterprising lacemaker Sofia Davydova (1841–1915), who documented and published lace techniques from across Russia, propelling them to international renown.[5] Eastern European and Russian bobbin lace (cat. no. 68) are identifiable by their narrow, meandering tape—a descendent of the Milanese style—that is used to create elaborate designs with a limited number of bobbins. Russian bobbin lace includes complex fillings made using only two pairs of bobbins, with a distinctive pair of threads outlining the tape in a contrasting hue, and is sometimes paired with cut- and drawnwork.

Alongside the handicraft revival, collecting antique lace became fashionable in the late nineteenth century among high society ladies, who sought to distinguish themselves amid the widespread availability of machine-made laces. A collection of paintings belonging to Etta Cone (1870–1949) and Claribel Cone (1864–1929), now at the Baltimore Museum of Art, is world-renowned, but lesser known is the Cone sisters' affinity for collecting fine laces. Their diaries contain various entries noting the purchases of *point de France*, Russian lace, and two Milanese priest's robes from a lace dealer in Paris, some of which were priced in the thousands. Despite their rarity, popular antique laces—such as the seventeenth-century needle lace *gros point de Venise*—were regularly cut apart and reworked into fashionable new silhouettes (cat. no. 71).

The history of lace is full of contradictions: produced by the poor for the rich, seen as virtuous to make but vain to wear, and the pride of international empires whose makers laboured in anonymity. As one of the most time-consuming textiles in history, the exploitative nature of lacemaking at its pinnacle was not sustainable, and the industry went into decline almost as quickly as lace had risen to the height of fashion. However, the beauty and complexity of extant lace is a testament to the ingenuity of generations of lacemakers whose work inspired espionage, smuggling, and eye-watering prices. Although few of their names are known, we can honour these women by continuing to study and admire the lace that they created during their lives.

Resources Consulted

Cormack, Emma, and Michele Major, eds. *Threads of Power: Lace from the Textile Museum St. Gallen*. New Haven, CT: Yale University Press, 2022.

Dabo, Kaat, Frieda Sorber, and Tessy Schoenholzer. *Lace: P.LACE.S—Looking through Antwerp Lace*. Tielt, Belgium: Lannoo, 2021.

Dye, Gilian, and Jean Leader. *Lace Identification: A Practical Guide*. England: Crowood, 2021.

Hopkin, David, and Nicolette Makovicky, eds. *By the Poor, for the Rich: Lace in Context*. Accessed April 24, 2023. laceincontext.com.

Levey, Santina M. *Lace: A History*. London: V&A, 1983.

Notes

1 Thomas Fuller and John Fuller, *The History of the Worthies of England Who for Parts and Learning Have Been Eminent in the Several Counties: Together with an Historical Narrative of the Native Commodities and Rarities in Each County* (London: Printed by J.G.W.L. and W.G. for Thomas Williams, 1662), 397.

2 Chiara Romano, "Polychrome Nets Italian Lace from the Collection of the Metropolitan Museum of Art," in *Textile Society of America 2014 Biennial Symposium Proceedings*, paper 896, digitalcommons.unl.edu /tsaconf/896.

3 Frida Sorber, "Antwerp, a Center of Lacemaking and Lace Dealing, 1550–1750," in *Threads of Power: Lace from the Textile Museum St. Gallen*, ed. Emma Cormack and Michele Major (New Haven, CT: Yale University Press, 2022), 89–112.

4 Santina M. Levey, *Lace: A History* (London: V&A, 1983), 35–37.

5 Hannah Chuchvaha, "Quiet Feminists: Women Collectors, Exhibitors and Patrons for Embroidery, Lace and Needlework in Late Imperial Russia (1860–1917)," *West 86th: A Journal of Decorative Arts, Design History, and Material Culture* 27, no. 1 (2020): doi.org/10.1086/711189.

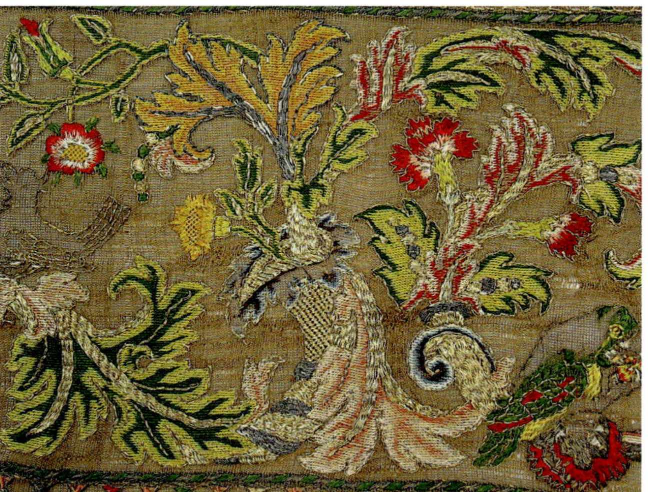

CAT. NO. 69 (left)
Unknown Italian lacemaker
Embroidered buratto lace
1600s
Linen, silk, and metallic thread with a gauze weave
26 × 92 cm
Lent by Museum of Art, Rhode Island School of Design, Providence, Gift of Mr. Richard Greenleaf
52.502
Image courtesy of the RISD Museum, Providence, RI

CAT. NO. 70 (right)
Elisabetta (or Isabella) Catanea Parasole
Teatro delle Nobili et Virtuose Donne [*Theater of Noble and Virtuous Women*]
Rome, 1620
Printed bound volume of engravings
22 × 28 cm
Harvard University, Houghton Library, Gift of Philip Hofer
TYP 625.20.674
Exhibited at AGO only

Opening illustrated: plate 41

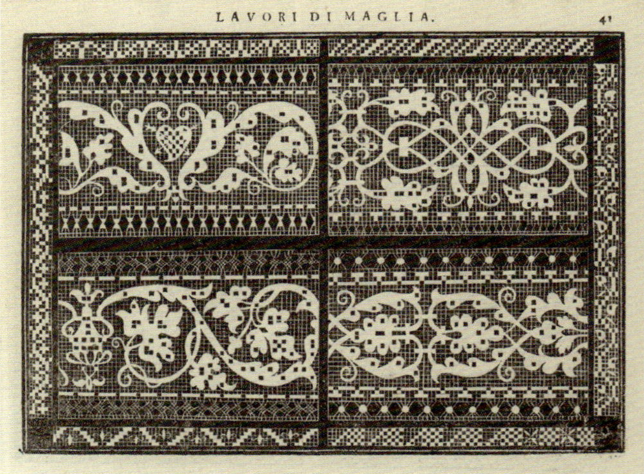

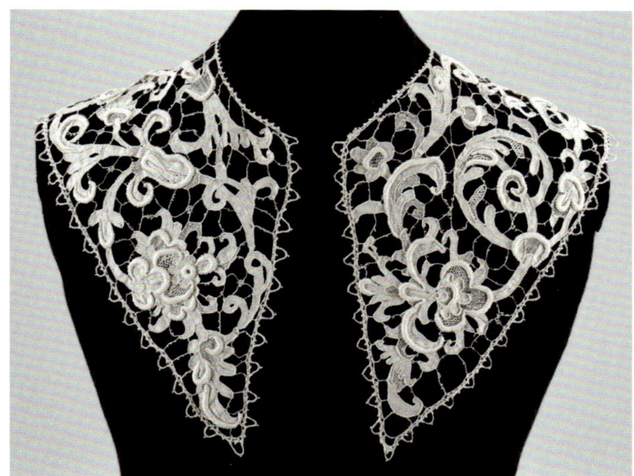

CAT. NO. 71
Unknown French or Italian lacemaker
Gros point de Venise lace collar
17th century
Linen
41.3 × 54 cm
Baltimore Museum of Art: The Cone Collection, formed by Dr. Claribel Cone and Miss Etta Cone of Baltimore, Maryland, 1950.1986.27a
Photo: Mitro Hood

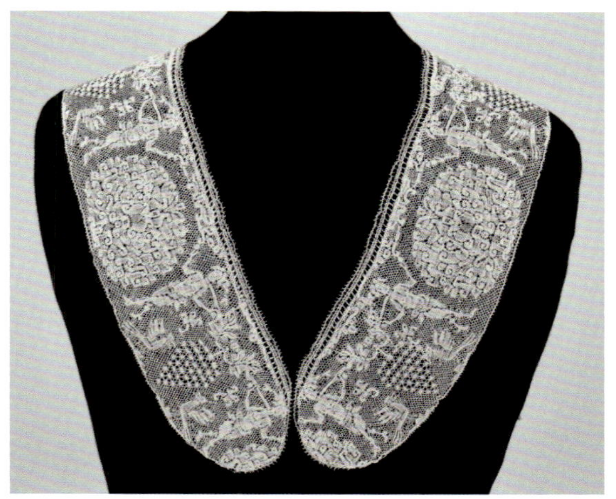

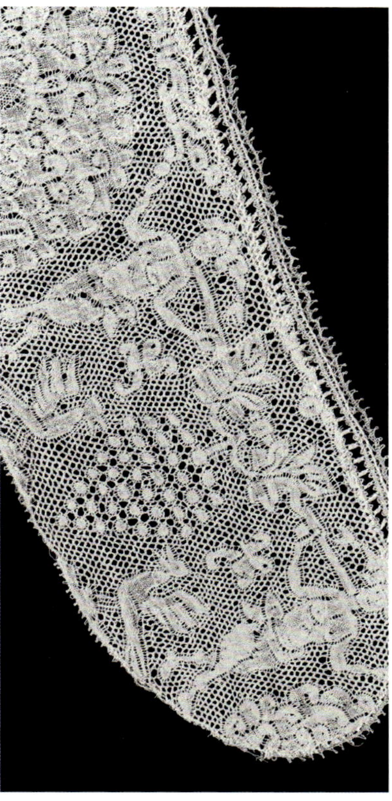

CAT. NO. 72 (above and detail on right)
Unknown Flemish lacemaker
Bobbin lace collar
mid-late 17th century
Linen
71.1 × 7.6 cm
Baltimore Museum of Art: The Cone Collection, formed by Dr. Claribel Cone and Miss Etta Cone of Baltimore, Maryland, 1950.2022.268
Photo: Mitro Hood

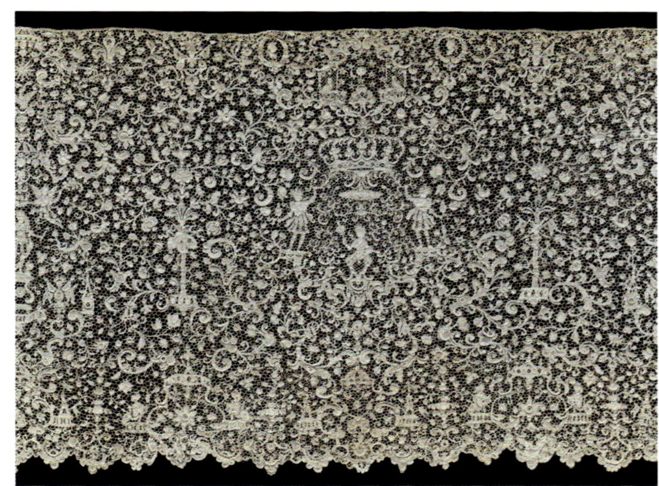

CAT. NO. 73
Unknown French lacemaker
Point de France needle lace furnishing flounce
late 17th century
Linen
58.4 × 266.7 cm
Baltimore Museum of Art: The Cone Collection, formed by Dr. Claribel Cone and Miss Etta Cone of Baltimore, Maryland, 1950.2022.270
Photo: Mitro Hood

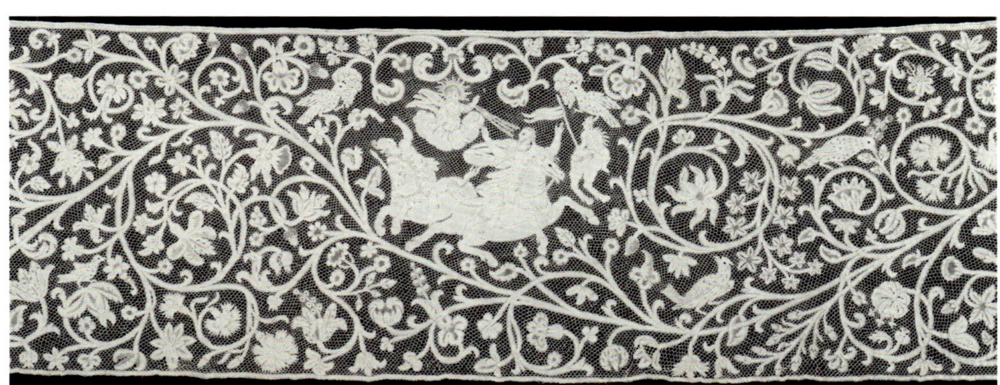

CAT. NO. 74
Unknown Italian lacemaker
Bobbin lace flounce for an alb (clergy vestment)
late 17th–early 18th century
Linen
41.3 × 365.8 cm
Baltimore Museum of Art: The Cone Collection, formed by Dr. Claribel Cone and Miss Etta Cone of Baltimore, Maryland, 1950.2022.269
Photo: Mitro Hood

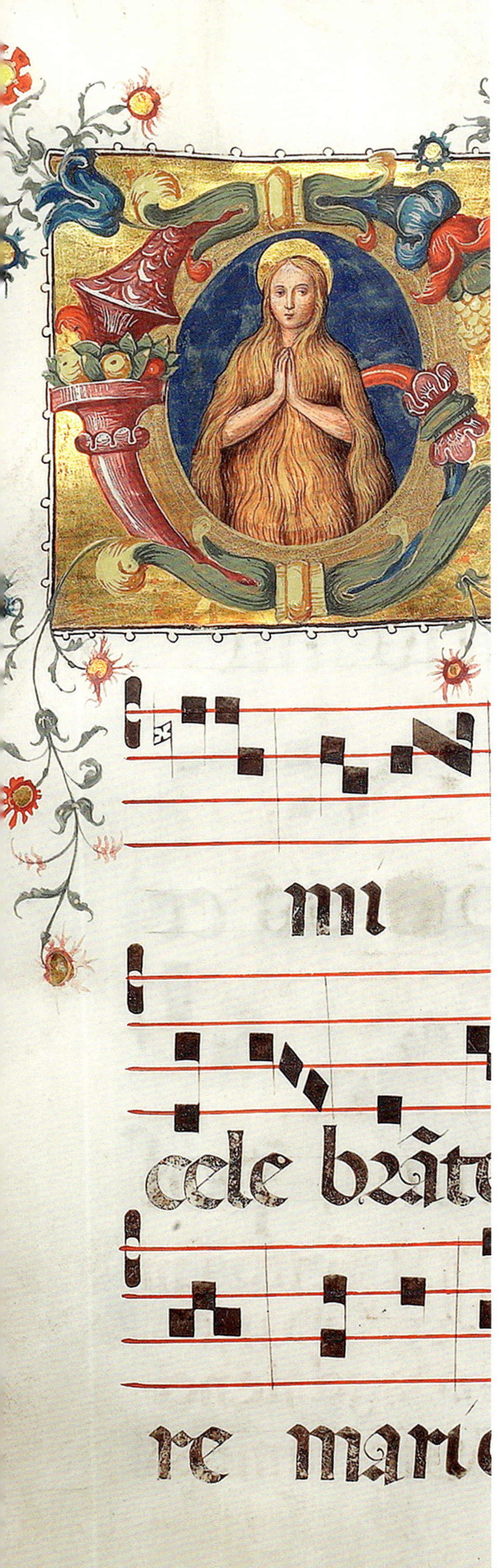

Manuscript Illumination

Alexa Greist

In 2019, researchers discovered the costly pigment lapis lazuli staining the teeth of a woman who had been buried in a convent in Northern Germany between 972 and 1162. They concluded that the lapis came to be present on her enamel through the process of licking a brush to form a fine point necessary for manuscript illumination.[1] Out of humility before God, few religious men or women signed their work during that period; this discovery offers a chance for an individual woman illuminator to partially re-emerge from the annals of history. In Europe, women were known to create illuminated manuscripts—handwritten books with painted embellishments, often including gold and silver pigments—in both secular and religious settings. The Catholic Church considered the copying of religious texts an appropriate activity for cloistered women (as well as men), with some orders, such as the Dominicans, explicitly prescribing the production of manuscripts as part of their devotional practice. While some illuminated texts were made for the convent's use, the works also served as a source of income for religious houses. Before the advent of movable type around 1450, the convent or monastery was a site of artistic training and production outside of the secular structures of workshops but following many of the same models of production.

The manuscripts featured in this exhibition were produced by both cloistered and secular female makers across Europe from the fifteenth through seventeenth centuries. The hands of individual nuns are more readily identifiable than those of women working in commercial settings, where a student, male or female, sought to make their hand indistinguishable from that of the head of the workshop. Additionally, the names of cloistered women survive in the archives of religious houses more often than do those of women in the secular world, where they often vanished behind those of their male relatives. There were notable exceptions, however, such as with the French illuminator Jeanne de Montbaston

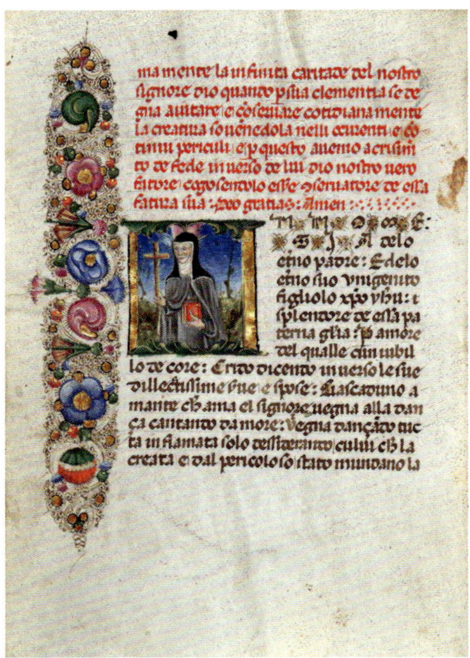

(active 1320–1355), known through fifty-three surviving manuscripts.

Records and surviving works from mid-fifteenth-century Germany indicate that cloistered women, including Sibylla von Bondorf (c. 1450–1524) in Freiburg, were responsible for hundreds of revised editions of Psalters, rules of religious orders, and other popular texts, such as lives of saints that were required to meet doctrinal changes occurring in the Church. In Italy, the nun and scribe Illuminata Bembo (c. 1410–1496) copied a text by Caterina Vigri (1413–1463), *Le Armi Spirituale* (cat. no. 75), at the monastery of Corpus Christi in Ferrara. In her manuscript, she included a portrait of Vigri—later canonized as Saint Catherine of Bologna—an intimate gesture, as Bembo knew her subject personally. Bembo was a devoted follower of the scholarly woman until Vigri's death, three years before the creation of Bembo's copy of *Le Armi Spirituale*. In fact, Bembo stated in the manuscript's colophon

CAT. NO. 75 (facing)
Illuminata Bembo
Saint Catherine of Bologna's *Le Armi Spirituale*
1466
Ink, paint, and gold on parchment
Folio: 14.5 × 10.3 cm; written: 8.6 × 6 cm
The Walters Art Museum, Baltimore, Maryland
W.342
Exhibited at AGO only

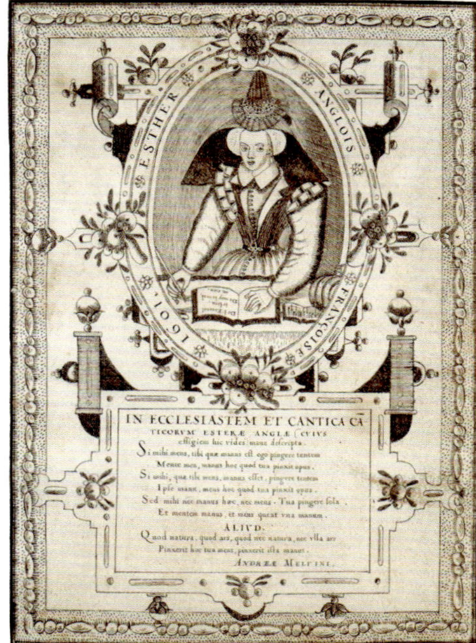

CAT. NO. 76 (right)
Esther Inglis
Self-Portrait within a decorative border in *Le Livre de l'Ecclésiaste*
1601
Pen and ink on paper
17.4 × 13.6 cm
Spencer Collection, The New York Public Library, Astor, Lenox and Tilden Foundations
MS. 8

that she made the volume directly from Vigri's personal copy. In copying her manuscript, Bembo's memorialization of a saintly woman author highlights the tight communal bonds established in convent life. While many copies by other followers of the saint were likely made but are now lost, the personal ties between Bembo and Vigri, as well as the incredibly high quality of this work, likely contributed to its preservation.

Other manuscript examples included antiphonies, which were books containing call-and-response chants called "antiphons." The five antiphonies decorated by Eufrasia Burlamacchi (1482–1548), a Dominican nun living in Prato, Italy, feature psalms written in monumental Gothic minuscule on large vellum sheets, with hundreds of colourful calligraphic lacework initials and twenty gold historiated initials. The large size of Burlamacchi's antiphonies reflects their communal use by women in the cloister during their daily prayers. Burlamacchi was active in the circle of Girolamo Savonarola and heard the fiery preacher speak in Lucca in 1596. She was a joint founder of a new order of cloistered nuns who felt the need for reform within their own ranks. Burlamacchi's illuminations in the antiphonies—today held by the Dominican Sisters in San Rafael, California—place sensitive, portrait-like depictions in the elaborate historiated and inhabited initials to create connection between the saints and the viewer. In the fourth volume, an initial "V" presents a three-quarter-length image of Saint Catherine of Alexandria (died fourth century), the elegantly draped S-curve of her body framing her attributes of a martyr's palm and wheel (cat. no. 77). In Burlamacchi's illumination of the initial "G" from volume five, her delicate flowers wind their way out from the frame, encompassing the figure of Mary Magdalene, whose abundant hair preserves her modesty, her gaze directing the reader gently toward the text that follows (cat. no. 78).

By the close of the sixteenth century, the illuminated manuscript was largely superseded by the printed book. Even communities like the Convent of San Jacopo di Ripoli in Florence, where nuns had previously copied manuscripts, shifted their devotional and commercial practice to the setting of movable type (cat. no. 1). Handwritten volumes like those made for the English court by Esther Inglis (c. 1569–1624) were part of an evolution of the medium into a more academic and luxury tradition, in which their combinations of poetry, calligraphy, and miniature paintings were prized as both gifts and commissions.

Inglis was born in Dieppe to Huguenot parents, who fled shortly after her birth to Scotland to escape persecution. Her mother educated her at home in calligraphy, illumination, and embroidery. Once married, Inglis worked alongside her husband, a clerk at the court of James I. She produced court documents as well as lavish commissions for royalty and English and Scottish nobility, such as the *Argumenta in librum Psalmorum* (cat. no. 79), a handwritten volume of psalms produced by Inglis in 1606 for Thomas Egerton, Baron Ellesmere, lord chancellor of England. The work, now in the Houghton Library at Harvard University, shows the influence of Flemish manuscript traditions with its use of coloured pigments, illuminated flowers on each page, and gold embellishment. *Le Livre de l'Ecclésiaste* (cat. no. 76) is typical of a style of black-and-white work favoured by the artist early in her career, where she copied borders and emblems from print sources so faithfully that they look printed rather than drawn. In her self-portrait contained within the frontispiece, Inglis can be seen at work, looking confidently out at her viewer.

In both religious and secular contexts, women participated in the market for illuminated manuscripts through the production of texts to support their families or convents. Their contributions were present in gift economies, religious and humanistic repositories of knowledge, and intellectual networks. Even if their names are lost to history, their hands are present in centuries' worth of surviving manuscripts.

Resources Consulted

Cyrus, Cynthia J. *The Scribes for Women's Convents in Late Medieval Germany.* Toronto: University of Toronto Press, 2009.

Lähnemann, Henrike. "The Materiality of Medieval Manuscripts." *Oxford German Studies* 45, no. 2 (2016): 121–41.

Morrison, Elizabeth. "Master of Cardinal Wolsey." In *Illuminating the Renaissance: The Triumph of Flemish Manuscript Painting in Europe.* Edited by Thomas Kren and Scot McKendrick, 503–07. Los Angeles: Getty Publications, 2003.

Rouse, Richard, and Mary Rouse. *Manuscripts and Their Makers: Commercial Book Production in Paris, 1200–1500.* Vol. 2. Turnhout, Belgium: Harvey Miller, 2000.

Scott-Elliot, A.H., and Elspeth Yeo. "Calligraphic Manuscripts of Esther Inglis (1571–1624): A Catalogue." *Papers of the Bibliographical Society of America* 84, no. 1 (1990): 10–86.

Vandi, Loretta. "The Eternal Flame: Eufrasia Burlamacchi and Savonarolan Art in the Lucchese Convent of San Domenico." In *Four Essays*, 19–53. Umeå, Sweden: Umeå University Press, 2007.

Winston-Allen, Anne. "Making Manuscripts as Political Engagement by Women in the Fifteenth-Century Observant Reform Movement." *Journal of Medieval Religious Cultures* 42, no. 2 (2016): 224–47.

Notes

1 A. Radini, M. Tromp, A. Beach, E. Tong, C. Speller, M. McCormick, J.V. Dudgeon, et al., "Medieval Women's Early Involvement in Manuscript Production Suggested by Lapis Lazuli Identification in Dental Calculus," *Science Advances* 5, no. 1 (2019), science.org/doi/10.1126/sciadv.aau7126.

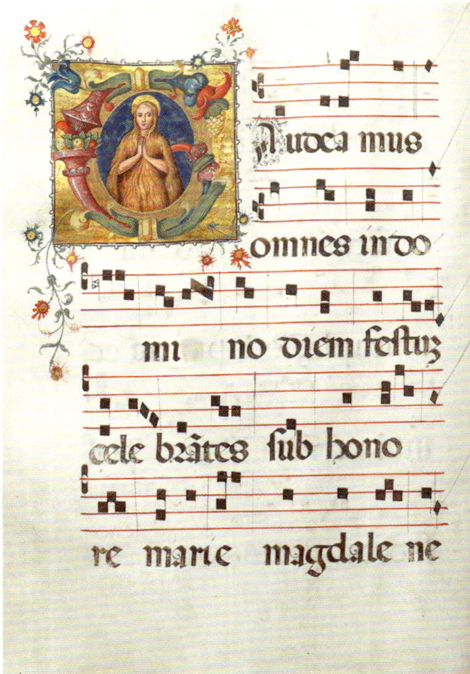

CAT. NO. 77 (left)
Eufrasia Burlamacchi
Saint Catherine in the Initial V
in *Illuminated Antiphonies*, vol. 4
c. 1503–1515
Iron gall ink and red ink, opaque watercolour, gold leaf, and shell gold on vellum with leather binding
53.2 × 38.5 cm
On loan from the archives of the Dominican Sisters of San Rafael

CAT. NO. 78 (right)
Eufrasia Burlamacchi
Mary Magdalene in the initial G
in *Illuminated Antiphonies*, vol. 5
c. 1503–1515
Iron gall ink and red ink, opaque watercolour, gold leaf, and shell gold on vellum with leather binding
53.2 × 38.5 cm
On loan from the archives of the Dominican Sisters of San Rafael

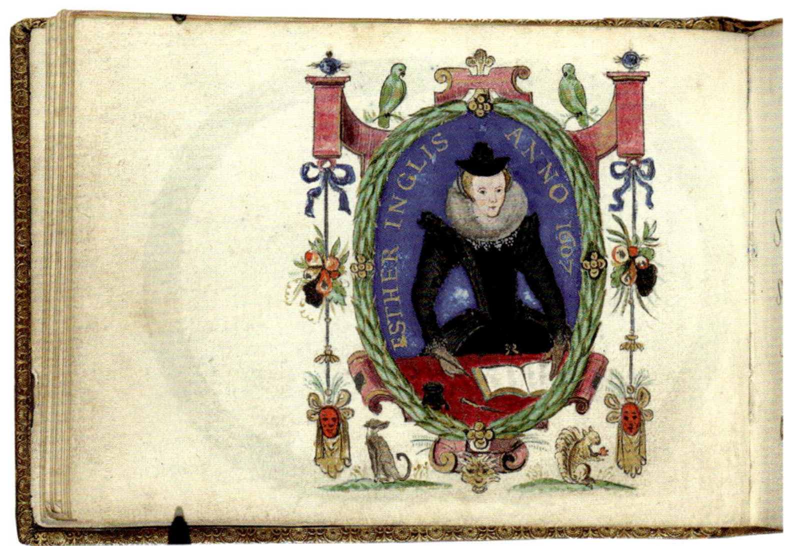

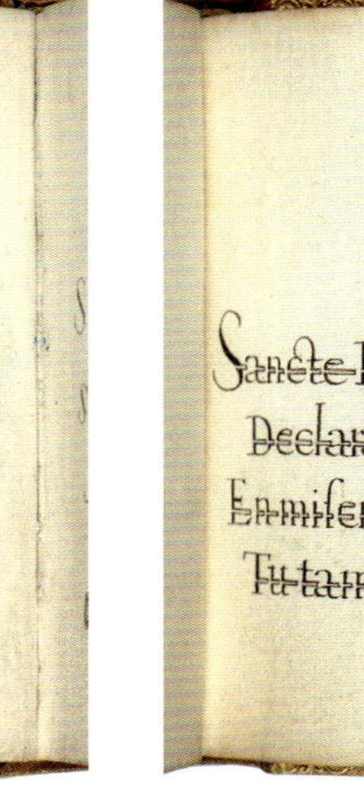

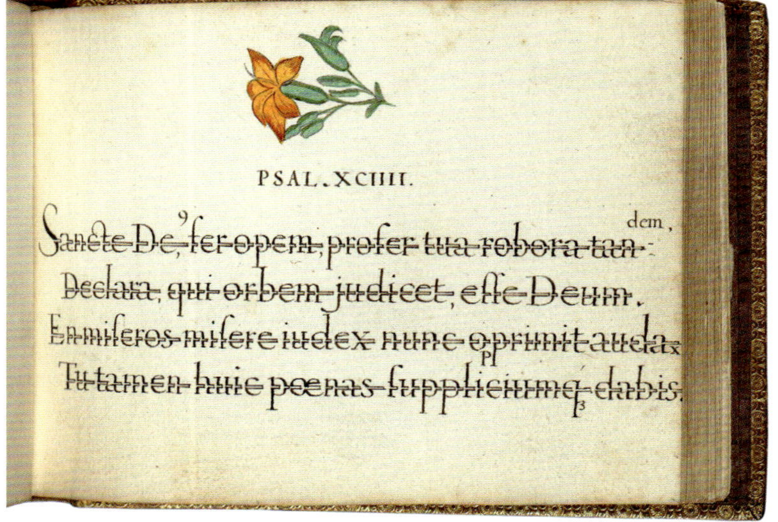

CAT. NO. 79
Esther Inglis
Argumenta in librum Psalmorum [*Arguments on the Book of Psalms*]
1606
Watercolour, opaque watercolour, and gold on paper
Closed: 10.4 × 4.9 × 2.8 cm; open: 20.8 × 14.9 × 2.8 cm
Harvard University, Houghton Library, Gift of Philip Hofer
MS TYP 212
Exhibited at BMA only

Openings illustrated: *Self-Portrait* (left) and *Psal. XCIIII* (right)

Painting ⁜ *History*

Paris A. Spies-Gans

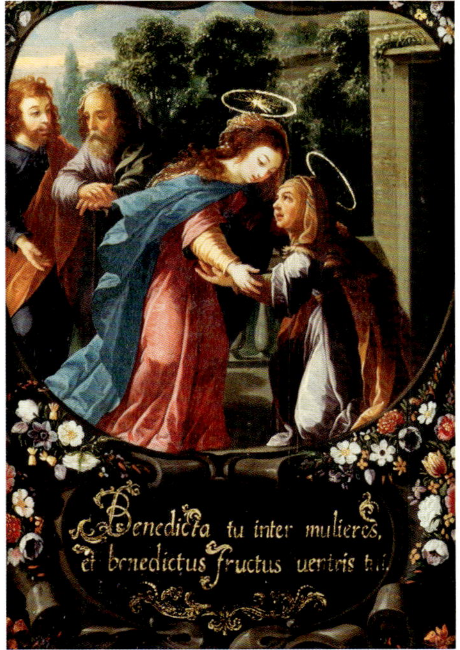

It is one of Western art history's oldest and most tired tropes that during the era covered by this exhibition, history painting was the most prestigious form of fine art—and that this coveted genre was exclusively practised by men. This belief and its corollary—the long-unquestioned assumption that women were unable to become history painters throughout these years—has profoundly influenced our present-day art historical narratives as well as broader understandings of what women were able to achieve as artists in the pre-modern world. Like many clichés honed over time, however, this trope is rooted in rhetoric, not practice. Women have painted historical works for as long as the genre has existed and were, in their own times, widely recognized for their narrative scenes. Why has this biased, inaccurate presumption held so much power, and how can we begin to correct the damage it has caused?

While it is difficult to pinpoint the origins of the male-history-painter myth, we find its vestiges throughout the early modern period. Most frequently, it is tied to what the groundbreaking feminist art historian Linda Nochlin famously labelled the "Question of the Nude": the idea, rooted in early modern theories of artistic education, that aspiring artists should learn to render the human form by studying live nude models before progressing, ultimately and ideally, to large-scale narrative works.[1]

For men, such instruction increasingly took place in formal academies that were off-limits to women, owing (supposedly) to questions of propriety. Thus, it has been argued, women were denied the necessary training to become history painters. Such rhetoric can be traced back to sixteenth-century Florence and Giorgio Vasari's *The Lives*,[2] and by the end of our period, it was in full force. Yet the historical record makes clear to scholars today that women still found ways to become narrative painters throughout these years. They simply learned to depict the human figure in different ways, such as copying drawings and prints, studying plaster casts and sculptures, and sketching live models in private, noninstitutional settings.

Beyond its historical inaccuracy, the assumption that women could not become history painters has reinforced two further, and quite harmful, gendered tropes. First, it was used to bolster the important thesis, championed by Nochlin and other early pioneers of feminist art history, that women could not achieve greatness as artists because they were excluded from key institutional and educational opportunities (especially nude-figure drawing) until the late nineteenth century. Second, it supported a related notion that any woman who *did* manage to forge a successful professional career was an exception who proved the male-artist rule. Although

CAT. NO. 80 (above, left)
Josefa Ayala
The Visitation
c. 1660
Oil on copper
22 × 15 cm
The Gaudium Magnum Collection – Maria and João Cortez de Lobão, Lisbon
Photo: Jorge Simão

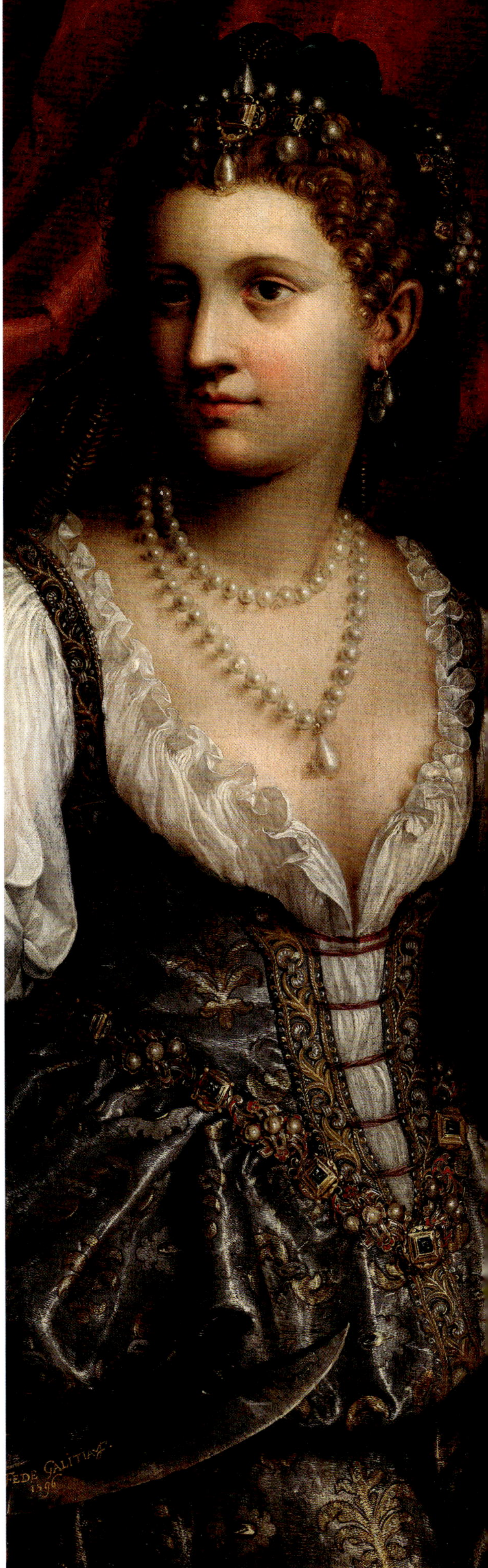

both arguments have indispensably emphasized the structural inequalities women have long faced, they now risk concealing larger patterns of artistic activity, including the ways in which many women regularly navigated institutional obstacles to become history painters and achieve greatness by the standards of their own times.

We need only look to *Danaë* (cat. no. 87) by Artemisia Gentileschi (1593–after 1654) for a paragon of this well- (if carefully) trod path. Painted when Gentileschi was just nineteen years old, the work depicts a subject from classical history that would have signalled high ambitions. Indeed, it launched her career. But we learn still more from her non-idealized portrayal of *Danaë*, who reclines fully unclothed—boasting curves and folds that assert that Gentileschi worked from a live model, likely in the privacy of her own workspace.[3]

Gentileschi was far from alone, following in the steps of many European women who had likewise found themselves drawn to the historical genre and imbued their canvases with the popular visual styles of their times. At the beginning of our period, narrative paintings often took on religious refrains. In Ravenna, Barbara Longhi (1552–c. 1638) completed numerous portraits as well as at least twelve paintings of the Virgin and Child, a popular Counter-Reformation theme. Were they all as subtly limned as her *Virgin Mary and Infant Jesus* (cat. no. 83), with Mary's calm gaze and delicate hands? Her peer Lavinia Fontana (1552–1614), born in nearby Bologna, cultivated an even wider set of skills: she painted both a series of more erotic classical works featuring the goddesses Venus and Minerva in the nude and the *Holy Family with Saints Margaret and Francis* (cat. no. 84), a careful study in mannerism that might have pleased a more modest patron.[4]

In fact, Bologna became an unmatched centre for women in the arts during these years. By the time of her early death at only twenty-seven years old, the Bolognese painter Elisabetta Sirani (1638–1665) had conquered the Baroque, as demonstrated by the deep hues and dramatic chiaroscuro that bring her *Virgin and Child* (cat. no. 85) so convincingly to life. Sirani stressed still other skills in her *Personification of Music* (cat. no. 86), choosing an allegorical representation of music (a popular subject matter) to carry a portrait of a contemporary sitter, enveloped in elaborate seventeenth-century attire and surrounded by exquisitely detailed instruments.

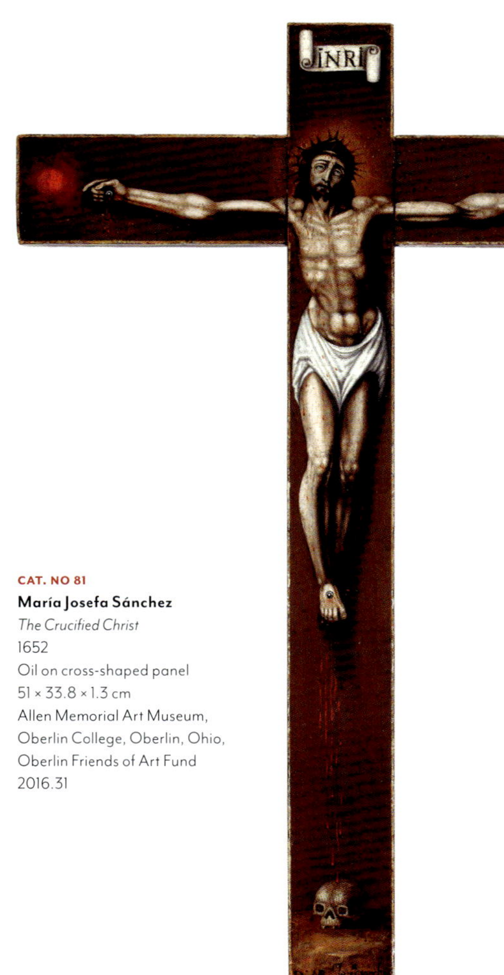

CAT. NO 81
María Josefa Sánchez
The Crucified Christ
1652
Oil on cross-shaped panel
51 × 33.8 × 1.3 cm
Allen Memorial Art Museum, Oberlin College, Oberlin, Ohio, Oberlin Friends of Art Fund
2016.31

Less is currently known about women history painters in other regions of early modern Europe; nevertheless, surviving canvases from the Netherlands, Flanders, Spain, and beyond reveal that these artists, too, painted ambitious narrative scenes.[5] For now, Josefa Ayala (c. 1630–1684) is the only documented independent female painter from seventeenth-century Portugal. She regularly integrated narrative works into her corpus of altarpieces and still lifes (many of them public commissions), painting the elaborate *The Visitation* (cat. no. 80) on copper, an ideal support for minute work.[6] Later in her career, she increasingly concentrated on images of Christ as a child, placing him in a range of elaborate costumes and settings, as with *The Christ Child as Pilgrim* (cat. no. 89).[7] Still, none of Ayala's extant works approach the graphic materiality of several surviving crucifixes by the Spanish María Josefa Sánchez (active mid-seventeenth century).[8] The focus in *The Crucified Christ* (cat. no. 81) is, most of all, her subject's emaciated body, but Sánchez's minutiae also mesmerize—from her own careful signature to the blood that drips, steadily, onto a sinister skull.

Despite a clear and steady market for New Testament works, women hardly limited themselves to its contents. Rather, they quickly and deftly found female subjects to explore in the broader narrative lexicon, selecting stories through which they could highlight their training and individual skills. One favourite story was that of the Jewish widow Judith, who had seduced and beheaded the Assyrian general Holofernes in the sixth century BCE. Female and male artists gravitated to this tale, generally

CAT. NO. 82 (below)
Angelica Kauffmann
Sappho Inspired by Love
1775
Oil on canvas
132.1 × 145.1 cm
Collection of The John & Mable Ringling Museum of Art, the State Art Museum of Florida, Florida State University, Sarasota, Florida; Bequest of John Ringling, 1936
SN329

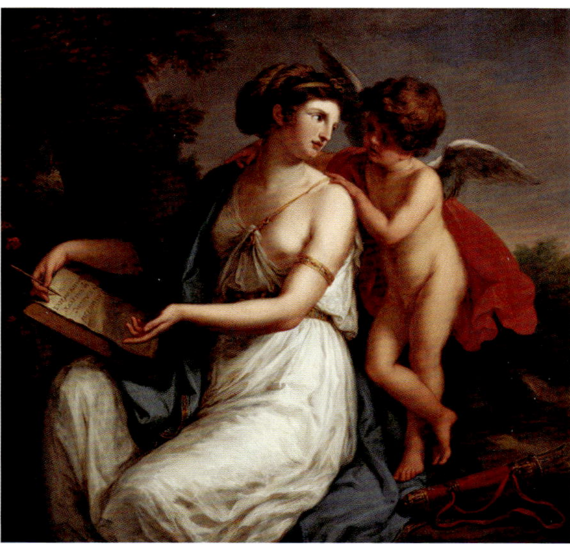

depicting one of two key moments in Judith's journey: the act of the beheading or its aftermath. The Milanese painter Fede Galizia (1578–c. 1630) chose the latter; in her four-foot-tall *Judith with the Head of Holofernes* (cat. no. 88), a calm and meticulously bejewelled Judith holds the severed head.[9] While painting the same moment, Gentileschi took another route. With its deep shadows and minimal use of light, *Judith and Her Maidservant with the Head of Holofernes* (cat. no. 90) is a triumph of Baroque staging and lighting techniques.[10] On other canvases, Gentileschi portrayed the gory moment of the decapitation itself.

Galizia, Gentileschi, and their peers lived at a time in which it was widely accepted that history paintings were the most prestigious works. However, only in 1667—sparked by the founding of France's Académie Royale de Peinture et de Sculpture in 1648—would artists see the codification of an official hierarchy of genres, with history placed firmly at the top.[11] As the French Académie gained prominence and established its biennial Salon—and as Britain followed suit with the Royal Academy of Arts (founded in 1768, with an annual exhibition from 1769)—narrative paintings featuring scenes from European history, classical literature, and contemporary life took on new status.

As these exhibitions grew in importance their reputations spread throughout Europe, and no one was more successful at establishing a correlated, public identity as a history painter than the Swiss-born Angelica Kauffmann (1741–1807), one of the Royal Academy's founding members. She quickly became a point of pride for a British art world that was insecure about its merits in the realm of narrative art. Already in 1772, a print depicting the Academy's 1771 exhibition used Kauffmann's Homerian *Telemachus Returning to Penelope* (cat. no. 91) to exemplify (and satirize) the newly engaged public viewer.[12] In 1775, the year Kauffmann exhibited *Sappho Inspired by Love* (cat. no. 82), a reviewer for one London periodical mentioned the "*Historical* Pieces by West, Signora *Angelica Kauffman,* Mr. Cosway, and Mr. Barry" to hail the "very rapid Progress ... in the Course of a few Years," made by "The Polite Arts," especially in the nation's new "Encouragement for Historical Painting."[13]

Of course, Kauffmann still faced the unique hurdles to artistic success that had plagued women for centuries: despite this consistent praise, she was never allowed to train in the schools of the very Academy of which she was a founding member. But again, this did not stop her from painting the nude. In *Sappho*, she included a fully, deliberately unclothed male body, placed as seamlessly into her composition as her reference to Sappho's own learned writing. Like her predecessors, Kauffmann had found ways to navigate the biases and restrictions of her time, accruing the necessary training and skills to produce historical works, win praise for her craft, and set one more precedent for a new wave of women painters who would join her on this long-revered path as the eighteenth century came to a close.

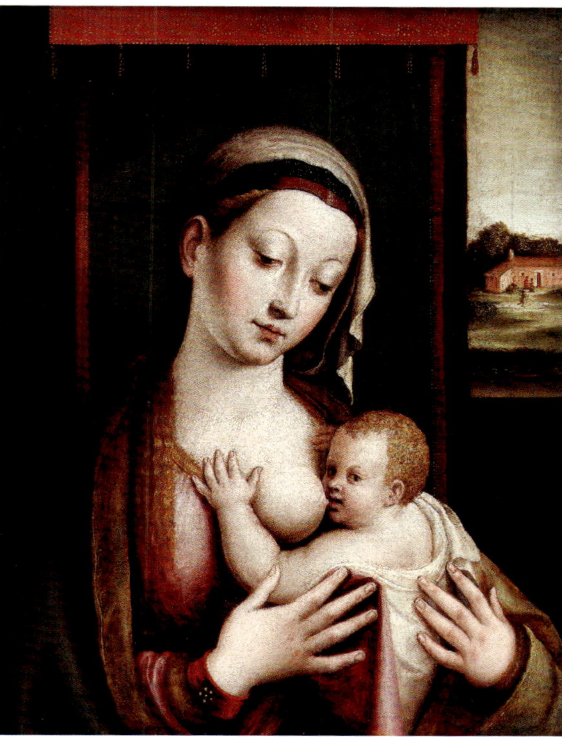

CAT. NO. 83
Barbara Longhi
Virgin Mary and Infant Jesus
c. 1575–1580
Oil on canvas
42.5 × 34 cm
Art Gallery of Ontario, Purchase, with funds from the Gail and Terence Sheard Endowment Fund, 2021
2021/37
Photo: AGO

Resources Consulted

Agosti, Giovanni, Luciana Giacomelli, and Jacopo Stoppa. *Fede Galizia: Mirabile Pittoressa.* Trento, Italy: Museo Castello del Buonconsiglio, 2021.

Barker, Sheila. *Artemisia Gentileschi.* London: Lund Humphries; Los Angeles: Getty, 2022.

Baumgärtel, Bettina, ed. *Angelica Kaufman.* Munich: Hirmer, 2020.

Bohn, Babette. *Women Artists, Their Patrons, and Their Publics in Early Modern Bologna.* University Park, PA: Penn State University Press, 2021.

Cheney, Liana De Girolami. "Barbara Longhi of Ravenna: A Devotional Self-Portrait." *Journal of Literature and Art Studies* 12, no. 1 (2022): 17–37.

Garrard, Mary D. *Artemisia Gentileschi and Feminism in Early Modern Europe.* London: Reaktion, 2020.

Murphy, Caroline. *Lavinia Fontana: A Painter and Her Patrons in Sixteenth-Century Bologna.* New Haven, CT: Yale University Press, 2003.

Rosenthal, Angela. *Angelica Kauffman: Art and Sensibility.* New Haven, CT: Paul Mellon Centre for Studies in British Art in association with Yale University Press, 2006.

Ruiz Gómez, Letizia, ed. *A Tale of Two Painters: Sofonisba Anguissola and Lavinia Fontana.* Madrid: Museo Nacional del Prado, 2019. Exhibition catalogue.

Sheriff, Mary D. *Moved by Love: Inspired Artists and Deviant Women in Eighteenth-Century France.* Chicago: University of Chicago Press, 2003.

Spies-Gans, Paris A. *A Revolution on Canvas: The Rise of Women Artists in Britain and France, 1760–1830.* London: Paul Mellon Centre for Studies in British Art in association with Yale University Press, 2022.

Viroli, Giordano. *I Longhi: Luca, Francesco, Barbara, pittori ravennati (sec. XVI–XVII).* Ravenna, Italy: Angelo Longo Editore, 2000.

Notes

1 Linda Nochlin, "Why Have There Been No Great Women Artists?" *ArtNews* 69, no. 9 (January 1971): 22–39, 67–71.
2 See Andaleeb Badiee Banta's discussion of Vasari's *Lives* in "Not Seen, Not Heard: In Search of the Unexceptional Woman Artist" on pages 14–29 of this volume.
3 Letizia Treves, Sheila Barker, Patrizia Cavazzini, Elizabeth Cropper, Francesca Whitlum-Cooper, Francesco Solinas, and Larry Keith, *Artemisia* (London: National Gallery and Yale University Press, 2020), 121.
4 Liana De Girolami Cheney, "Lavinia Fontana's Nude Minervas," *Woman's Art Journal* 36, no. 2 (2015): 30–40.
5 We also know that, in the mid-sixteenth century, the Flemish Catherina van Hemessen (1528–after 1565), painter of the first self-portrait of an artist at an easel, and the Dutch Mechtelt van Lichtenberg (c. 1520–1598), executed detailed scenes of the life of Christ.
6 Rachel Zimmerman, "Josefa de Óbidos, Christ Child as Salvator Mundi," *Smarthistory*, July 27, 2021, accessed February 7, 2023, smarthistory.org/ayala-obidos-child-salvator-mundi/.
7 Joaquim Oliveira Caetano, *Reading the Fate of the Christ Child: New Masterpiece by Josefa de Ayala (1630–1684)* (Uruguay[?]: Jaime Eguiguren, 2019), 28–29, jaimeeguiguren.com/usr/library/documents/main/cat_josefa-lr.pdf.
8 Entry for *Crucifixion*, María Josefa Sánchez, Art Institute of Chicago, artic.edu/artworks/242449/crucifixion.
9 Eve Straussman-Pflanzer and Oliver Tostmann, eds., *By Her Hand: Artemisia Gentileschi and Women Artists in Italy, 1500–1800* (New Haven, CT: Yale University Press in association with Detroit Institute of Arts, 2021), 94–96.
10 Treves et al., *Artemisia*, 178–81; Straussman-Pflanzer and Tostmann, *By Her Hand*, 108–11.
11 This was promoted in the form of a published lecture by a writer named André Félibien, which he delivered to the Académie in 1667. See André Félibien, *Conférences de l'Académie Royale de Peinture et de Sculpture, pendant l'année 1667* (Paris: Frederic Léonard, 1669). See also Paul Duro, "Imitation and Authority: The Creation of the Academic Canon in French Art, 1648–1870," in *Partisan Canons*, ed. Anna Brzyski (Durham, NC: Duke University Press, 2007), and Susanna Caviglia, "Life Drawing and the Crisis of *Historia* in French Eighteenth-Century Painting," *Art History* 39, no. 1 (February 2016): 40–69.
12 Richard Earlom after Michel-Vincent Brandoin, *The Exhibition of the Royal Academy of Painting, in the Year 1771*, 1772, mezzotint, 46.6 × 55.3 cm, British Museum, London.
13 "ACCOUNT of the Pieces most worthy of Notice at the Exhibition of the ROYAL ACADEMY," *For the Public Advertiser* (1775), bound in *Royal Academy Critiques, 1768–1842*, Royal Academy of Arts, London, vol. 1, 51. Emphasis in original.

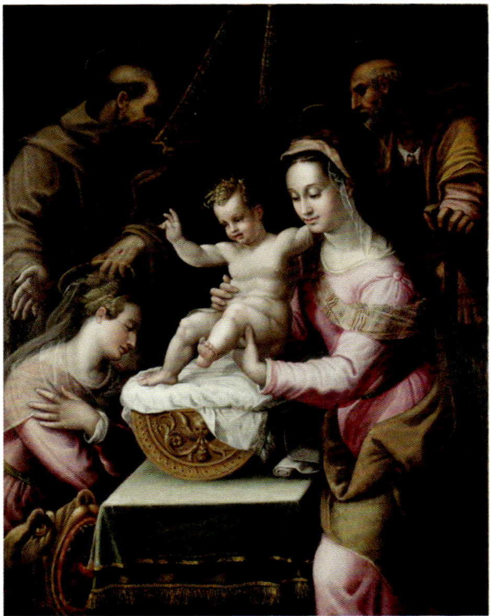

CAT. NO. 84
Lavinia Fontana
Holy Family with Saints Margaret and Francis
1578
Oil on canvas
127 × 104.1 cm
Davis Museum at Wellesley College, Wellesley, Massachusetts, Gift of William and Selma Postar
2001.104

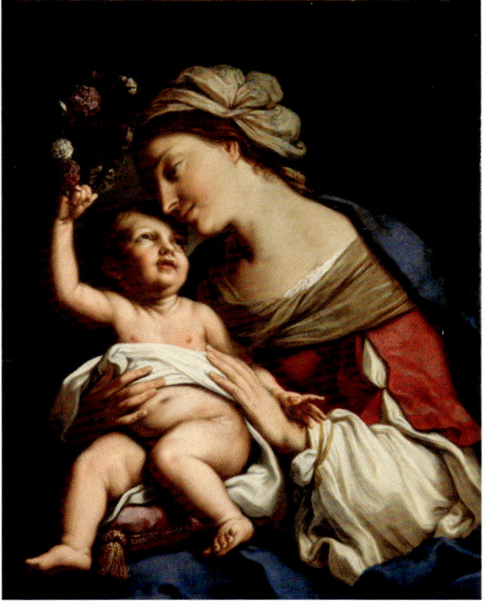

CAT. NO. 85
Elisabetta Sirani
Virgin and Child
1663
Oil on canvas
86 × 68.5 cm
National Museum of Women in the Arts, Washington, DC, Gift of Wallace and Wilhelmina Holladay; Conservation funds generously provided by the Southern California State Committee of the National Museum of Women in the Arts
1986.289
Photo: Lee Stalsworth

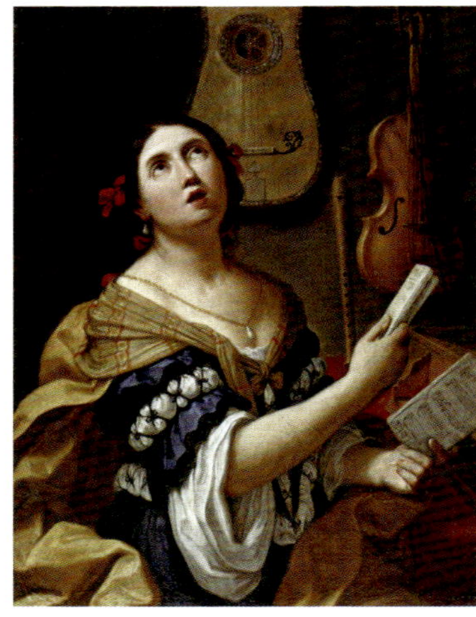

CAT. NO. 86
Elisabetta Sirani
Personification of Music
1659
Oil on canvas
94.6 × 74.3 cm
Private collection

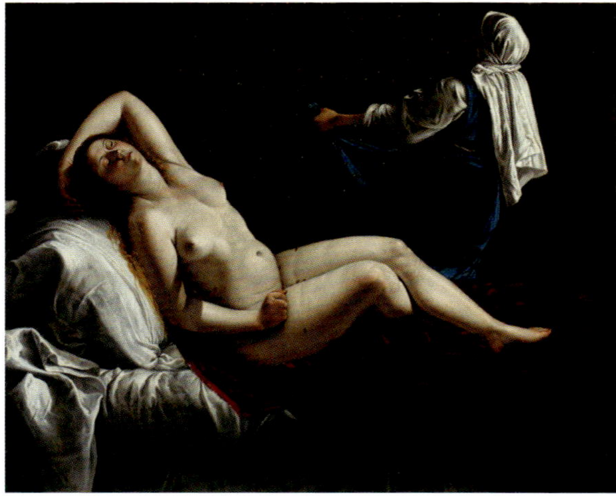

CAT. NO. 87
Artemisia Gentileschi
Danaë
c. 1612
Oil on copper
41.3 × 52.7 cm
Saint Louis Art Museum, Museum Purchase and gift of Edward Mallinckrodt, Sydney M. Shoenberg Sr., Horace Morison, Mrs. Florence E. Bing, Morton D. May in honour of Perry T. Rathbone, Mrs. James Lee Johnson Jr., Oscar Johnson, Fredonia J. Moss, Mrs. Arthur Drefs, Mrs. W. Welles Hoyt, J. Lionberger Davis, Jacob M. Heimann, Virginia Linn Bullock in memory of her husband, George Benbow Bullock, C. Wickham Moore, Mrs. Lyda D'Oench Turley and Miss Elizabeth F. D'Oench, and J. Harold Pettus, and bequests of Mr. Alfred Keller and Cora E. Ludwig, by exchange
93:1986

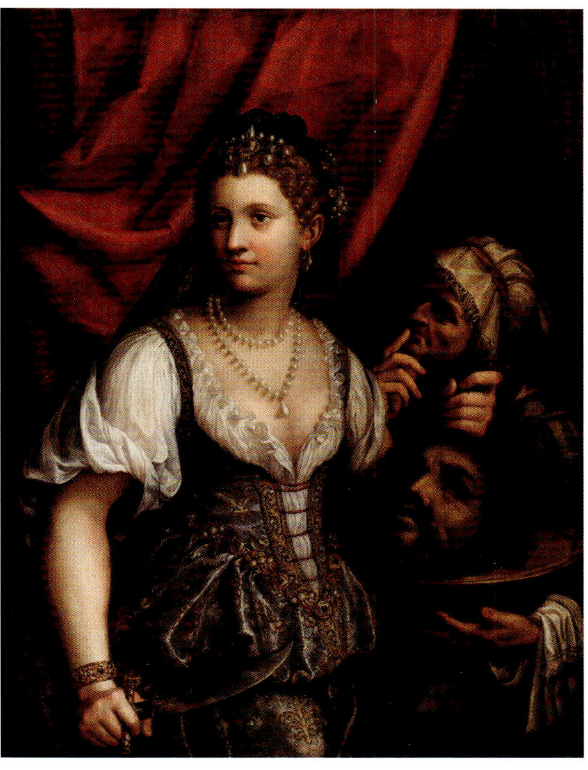

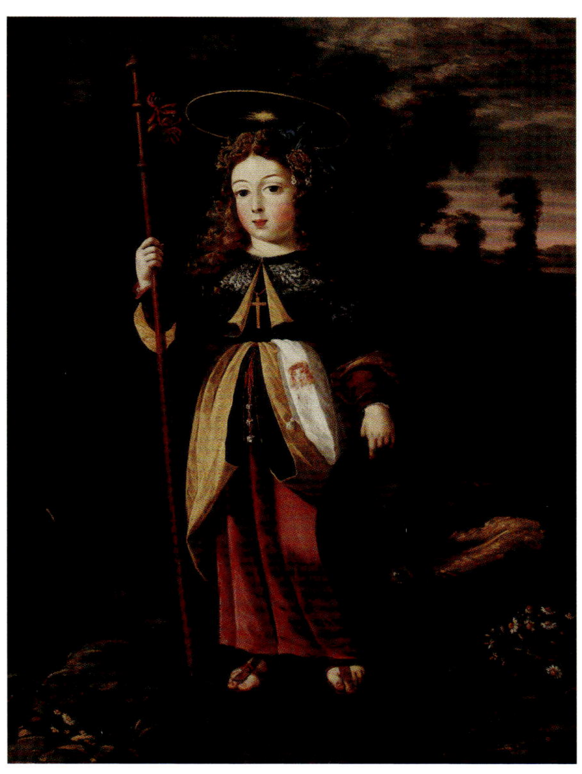

CAT. NO. 88 (left)
Fede Galizia
Judith with the Head of Holofernes
1596
Oil on canvas
120.7 × 94 cm
Collection of The John & Mable Ringling Museum of Art, the State Art Museum of Florida, Florida State University, Sarasota, Florida; Gift of Mr. and Mrs. Jacob Polak, 1969
SN684

CAT. NO. 89 (right)
Josefa Ayala
The Christ Child as Pilgrim
1676
Oil on canvas
108 × 83 cm
The Gaudium Magnum Collection – Maria and João Cortez de Lobão, Lisbon
Photo: Jorge Simão

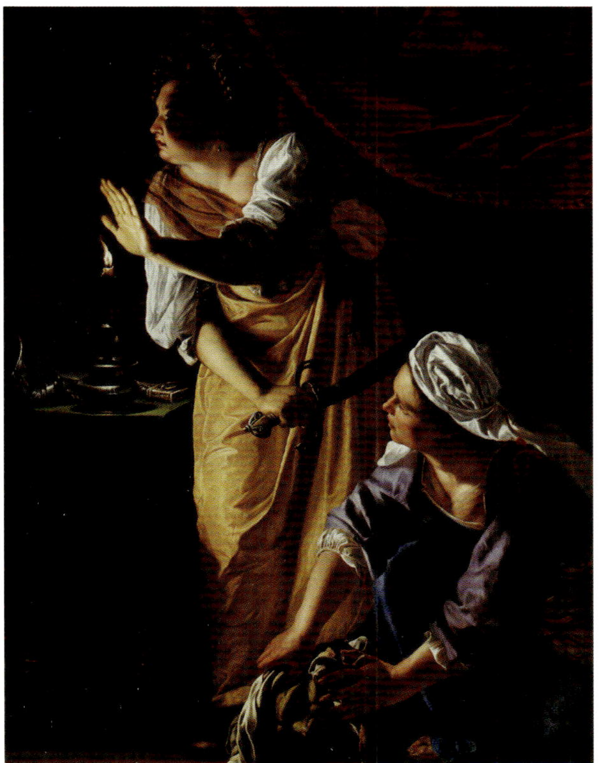

CAT. NO. 90
Artemisia Gentileschi
Judith and Her Maidservant with the Head of Holofernes
c. 1623–1625
Oil on canvas
187.2 × 142 × 3.3 cm
Detroit Institute of Arts, Gift of Mr. Leslie H. Green
52.253

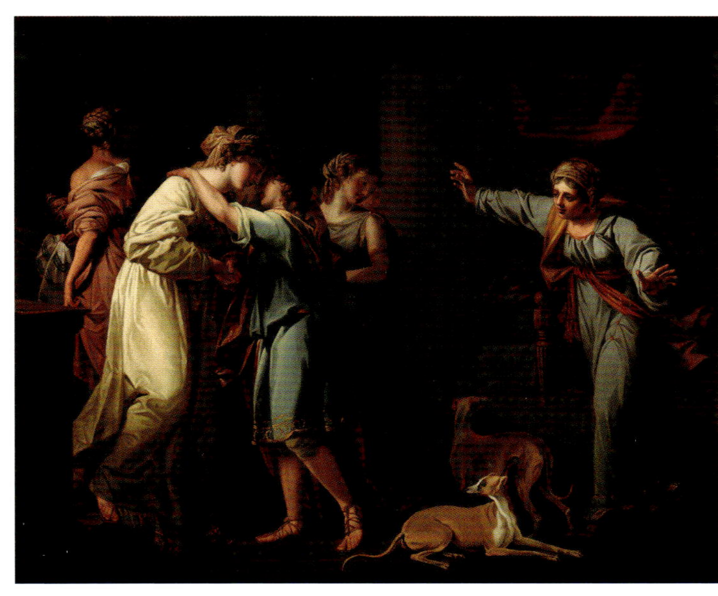

CAT. NO. 91
Angelica Kauffmann
Telemachus Returning to Penelope
c. 1771
Oil on canvas
96.5 × 122.6 cm
Chrysler Museum of Art, Norfolk, Virginia, Gift of Walter P. Chrysler, Jr.
71.665

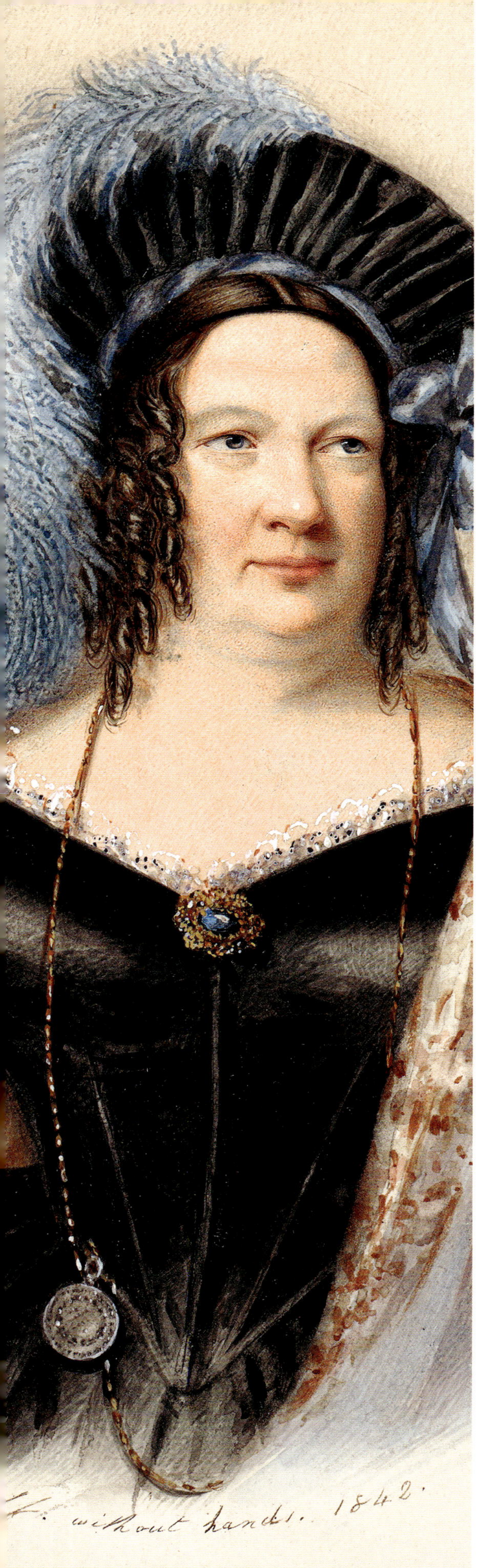

Painting ⁜ *Miniatures*

Andaleeb Badiee Banta and Joanna Karlgaard

Miniature painting was one pathway for women artists to achieve high levels of patronage and professional success outside of competition with artists creating large-scale history subjects or portraiture. Although both male and female artists established careers as miniaturists throughout the pre-modern era, the association of small-scale, delicately rendered portraiture resonated —especially in the nineteenth century—with prevailing gendered assumptions about proper formats, subjects, and media for women. Miniature painting (or limning)—a term generally referring to a manner of painting with watercolour or opaque watercolour on card, vellum, or sometimes ivory—is not always diminutive, but it does assume a degree of fineness of detail and handling that is more akin to traditions of manuscript illumination. In fact, many women miniaturists active in the sixteenth century worked as manuscript illuminators or were trained by them.

Throughout the sixteenth and seventeenth centuries, the English royal court proved a fertile ground for the support of women miniature painters. Documents show that Levina Teerlinc (c. 1510–1576), daughter of the accomplished Flemish manuscript illuminator Simon Bening, arrived in London around 1545 and was hired by queen consort Catherine Parr (1512–1548), receiving an annual payment as painter to the Tudor court. Teerlinc worked at the court until her death in 1576, but there is little consensus around the exact works she made for the courts of Henry VIII and Queen Elizabeth I (r. 1558–1603).

Small-scale portrait miniatures appealed to the court practices of gifting and diplomatic exchange, and reflected interest in using portraiture as a statement of power. Although overpainted at a later point, a 1549 portrait of a lady at court (cat. no. 94)—once thought to be Queen Elizabeth before she took the throne—has been attributed to Teerlinc. While it is impossible to identify definitively the author of this work due to its current condition, it nevertheless provides an example of the type of miniature portraits that Teerlinc made at the Tudor court. A bright (and costly) blue background, established in the work of her predecessors Hans Holbein the Younger, Lucas Horenboult, and Susanna Horenboult (c. 1500–c. 1554), pushes the sitter's likeness forward and emphasizes the jewel-like presentation of her detailed features. The locket-sized object could be worn close to the body, making it at once a highly personal work and a transportable one.

Miniature paintings also serve as records of a painter's engagement with other works of art found in the court setting. A circular watercolour miniature of the *Virgin and Child* (cat. no. 92) by Anna Maria Carew (active 1660s) is the only known work attributed to her. High regard for her work can be gleaned, however, from archival records that document her receipt of a £100 annual pension from King Charles II to create miniature copies of paintings in the Royal Collection. Ten days later, the sum was increased to £200 per year, which equalled the pension from Charles II to the artist Nicholas Dixon, generally regarded as one of the most celebrated miniature painters of the seventeenth century.[1] Although there is no direct link between this work and that specific commission, it is tempting to think that Carew's miniature, signed in gold and based on an oil painting by Anthony van Dyck, may relate.[2] Carew's version includes subtle changes to the composition and colouring, in addition to

CAT. NO. 92
Anna Maria Carew, after Anthony van Dyck
Virgin and Child
c. 1662
Watercolour heightened with gum arabic and gold on vellum
Diameter: 12.1 cm
The Cleveland Museum of Art, Gift of the Painting and Drawing Society of The Cleveland Museum of Art
2008.148

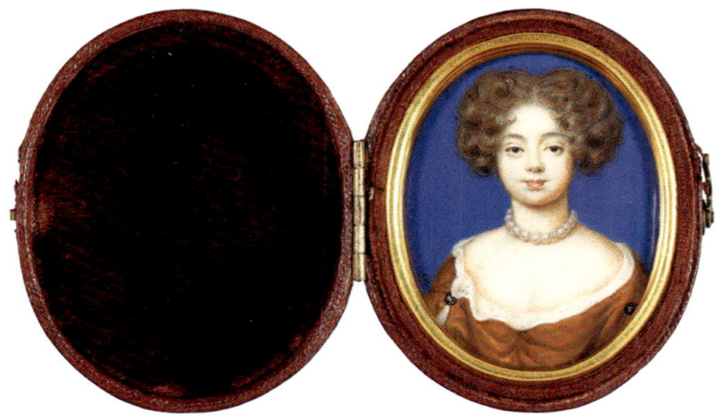

CAT. NO. 93
Susannah-Penelope Rosse
Nell Gwyn
c. 1675?
Watercolour on vellum, mounted on card
4.1 × 3.3 cm
Cincinnati Art Museum, Gift of Mr. and Mrs. Charles Fleischmann in memory of Julius Fleischmann
1990.1790

the obvious changes in format and scale, creating a work that is both a reference to and an original interpretation of van Dyck's painting. A miniature copy by Mary Beale (1633–1699) after Sir Peter Lely's c. 1679 portrait of Lady Elizabeth Percy (1667–1722), exhibits a similar approach (cat. no. 95). Vastly different in scale and colouring from Lely's portrait, Beale's version features fine brushwork and highly pigmented colours that depict the sumptuous costumes and jewellery worn by the aristocratic subject. While she did not have formal training, Beale maintained a friendship with Lely, court painter to Charles II, who offered models for her work. She cleverly adapted characteristics of Lely's work into portraits—miniature and full-size—that she made for a circle of intellectuals, clergymen, and other artists active in post-Restoration London.

Likely acquainted with one another in the thriving artistic community of Covent Garden, Beale and the miniature portraitist Susannah-Penelope Rosse (c. 1655–1700) represent several esteemed professional women artists who worked in partnership with their husbands.[3] Beale established an independent commercial studio, managed and documented by her husband, Charles, and was a prolific artist, obtaining as many as eighty-three commissions in one year.[4] Fewer works by Rosse are known, but her portrait (cat. no. 93) of Nell Gwyn (1650–1687), a celebrated wit, actress, and longtime mistress of Charles II, suggests that Rosse's artistic reputation gave her access to figures of fame and notoriety. Rosse's husband was a jeweller to the royal court and likely produced mounts and frames for many of his wife's miniatures.

The prevalence of the miniature beyond the court setting is due in large part to the innovation of the genre by the Venetian artist Rosalba Carriera (1673–1757). In her early career, she painted watercolour miniatures on ivory, often as decorative lids for snuff boxes produced for the tourist trade, as exemplified by *A Woman Putting Flowers in Her Hair* (cat. no. 97). She was the first to gain international fame for her miniatures on ivory, capitalizing on their popularity among tourists travelling through Venice as part of the Grand Tour circuit. Just as the portability of miniatures satisfied diplomatic requirements of the Tudor court centuries before, Carriera's miniatures appealed to aristocratic travellers wishing to bring home a souvenir of their time abroad, effectively commodifying the miniature format. As international travel became more feasible and affordable, the practice of leaving behind one's miniature likeness or sending it home in one's stead became more widespread.

A remarkably entrepreneurial statement can be found over one hundred years later in a miniature self-portrait (cat. no. 96) by the British artist Sarah Biffin (1784–1850). Of working-class origins, Biffin built her artistic reputation through arduous self-promotion as she toured the circuit of local fairs around England's countryside, providing on-the-spot miniature portraits. Yet this miniature presents Biffin as a professional on par with the old masters of the Renaissance and Baroque periods, wearing fashionable clothes and a silver medal likely bestowed upon her by the Royal Society of Arts. Biffin's achievement is all the more impressive as she was born with phocomelia—or, as described on her baptism record, "born without arms or legs"—and taught herself to use her mouth to write, sew, and paint. Advertising her physical condition and artistic talent, Biffin built a profitable enterprise in miniature painting that earned her invitations for royal patronage in Britain and abroad.[5]

Resources Consulted

Cleland, Elizabeth, and Adam Eaker. *The Tudors: Art and Majesty in Renaissance England*. With contributions by Marjorie E. Wieseman and Sarah Bochicchio. New Haven, CT: Yale University Press, 2022.

Cooper, Tarnya, Aviva Bunstock, Maurice Howard, and Edward Town. *Painting in Britain, 1550–1630: Production, Influences and Patronage*. Oxford: Oxford University Press, 2015.

James, Susan E. *The Feminine Dynamic in English Art, 1485–1603*. Farnham, UK: Ashgate, 2008.

Hunting, Penelope. *My Dearest Heart: The Artist Mary Beale (1633–1699)*. London: Unicorn, 2019.

Korkow, Cory. *British Portrait Miniatures: The Cleveland Museum of Art*. London: D. Giles, 2013.

Oberer, Angela. *The Life and Work of Rosalba Carriera: The Queen of Pastel*. Amsterdam: Amsterdam University Press, 2020.

Rutherford, Emma, and Ellie Smith, eds. *"Without Hands": The Art of Sarah Biffin*. London: Philip Mould, 2022.

Notes

1. Cory Korkow, *British Portrait Miniatures: The Cleveland Museum of Art* (London: D. Giles, 2013), 98; and Mary Anne Everett Green, ed., *Calendar of State Papers, Domestic Series, of the Reign of Charles II, 1661–1662* (London: Longman, Green, Longman, and Roberts, 1861), 270 and 276.
2. It is likely that Carew also studied an engraved copy of the painting; like the engraving, Carew's composition is in reverse of the original. See Korkow, *British Portrait Miniatures*, 98–102, and Erik Larsen, *The Paintings of Anthony van Dyck* (Freren, Germany: Luca Verlag, 1988), 265–66. There are two primary versions of the painting by Anthony van Dyck: one dated 1628, now in the collection of the Fitzwilliam Museum, and a second version from c. 1630–32 in the Dulwich Picture Gallery. An engraved copy of the Dulwich painting was created around 1630 by Paulus Pontius.
3. Rosse learned to paint from her father, Richard Gibson, a court dwarf and painter, and was closely associated with the artistic circle of the miniature painter Samuel Cooper, limner to Charles II. Philip Mould Gallery, "Susannah-Penelope Rosse," accessed June 22, 2023, philipmould.com/exhibitions/23-pioneers-500-years-of-women-in-british-art/works/artworks5457/.
4. "Mary Beale," National Museum of Women in the Arts, nmwa.org/art/artists/mary-beale/.
5. In 1821, she completed commissions for Willem Frederik, Prince of Orange and future king of the Netherlands; in 1830, she became miniature painter to Princess Augusta Sophia (1768–1840), daughter of King George III.

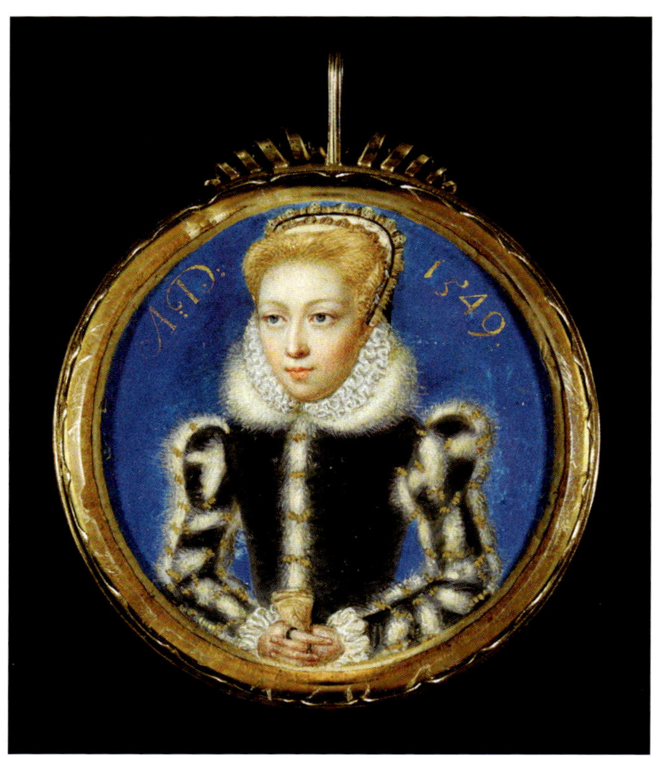

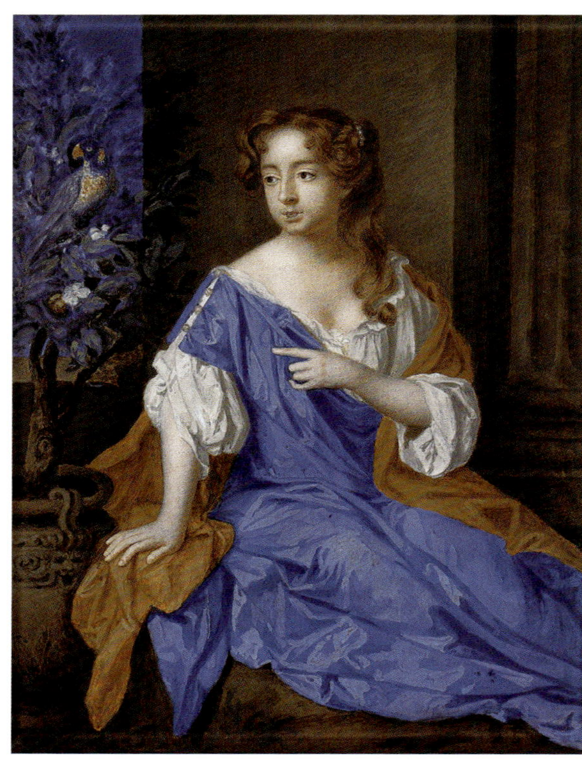

CAT. NO. 94 (left)
Attributed to Levina Teerlinc
Portrait of a Girl, formerly thought to be Queen Elizabeth I
1549
Opaque watercolour on vellum, on card
Diameter: 4.8 cm
Victoria and Albert Museum, London
P.21-1954
Image © Victoria and Albert Museum, London

CAT. NO. 95 (right)
Mary Beale, after Sir Peter Lely
Portrait of Lady Elizabeth Percy, Countess of Ogle and Duchess of Somerset
c. 1679
Watercolour and opaque watercolour on vellum
14.6 × 12.1 cm
Cincinnati Art Museum, Gift of Mr. and Mrs. Charles Fleischmann in memory of Julius Fleischmann
1990.1485

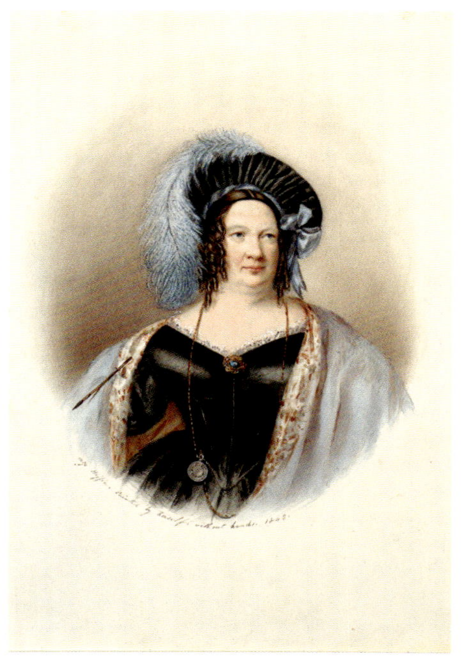

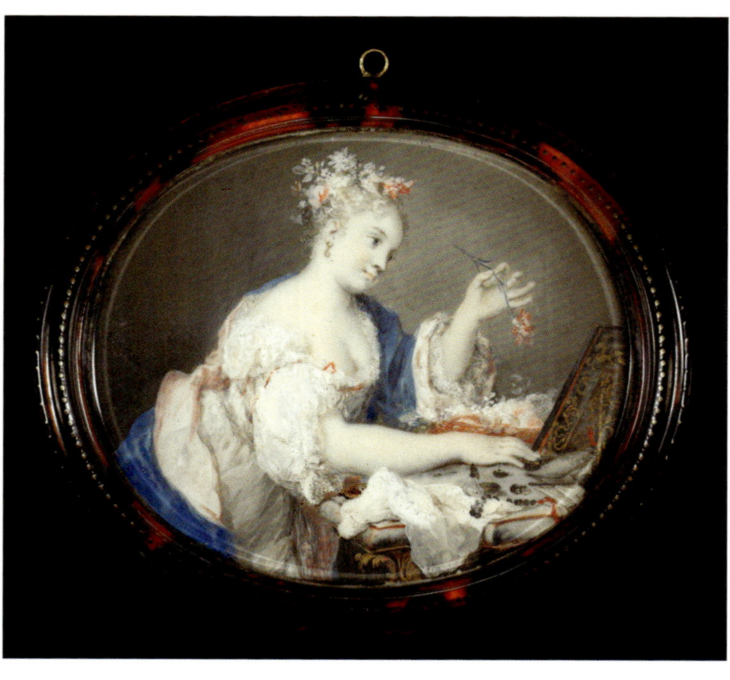

CAT. NO. 96 (left)
Sarah Biffin
Self-Portrait
1842
Watercolour and opaque watercolour on paper
33 x 25.1 cm
Baltimore Museum of Art: Rhoda M. Oakley Prints, Drawings & Photographs Acquisitions Fund, Contemporary Deaccessions Endowment, and The John Dorsey and Robert W. Armacost Acquisition Endowment, 2022.199
Photo: Mitro Hood

CAT. NO. 97 (right)
Rosalba Carriera
A Woman Putting Flowers in Her Hair
c. 1710
Watercolour on ivory in a tortoiseshell pique-point frame
Framed: 10.6 x 12.7 cm;
unframed: 8.6 x 10.5 cm
The Cleveland Museum of Art, The Edward B. Greene Collection
1940.1203
Exhibited at BMA only

Painting ⁂ *Portraiture*

Annelies Verellen and Alexa Greist

For centuries, portraiture was considered one of the most appropriate genres for women artists—both because it could be undertaken within the supervised confines of the home of the artist or sitter, and because it was thought to require little intellectual sophistication or creativity. Prevailing misogynistic theories of human reproduction during the pre-modern period equated women with the passively reproductive qualities of portraiture.[1] Though portraiture was practised by artists of all genders, it offered an arena for financial and professional success for many women painters.

Portraitists do much more than simply observe and slavishly copy their subjects. Through their artistic skill and knowledge of cultural signifiers, they are able to achieve numerous goals for the sitter, including representing physical appearance, solidifying public image, documenting their role in a community, and creating a lasting record of a significant achievement. In her portrait of Girolamo Mercuriale (cat. no. 104), Bolognese artist Lavinia Fontana (1552–1614) placed the Italian physician in a study, surrounded by objects affirming his intellectual virtue through a devotion to medicine. By showing Mercuriale holding Andreas Vesalius's 1542 work on human anatomy, Fontana roots him in the tradition of groundbreaking medical figures. To highlight faithfulness, a virtue highly valued in women, Fontana emphasizes, in her *Portrait of Costanza Alidosi* (cat. no. 100), a noblewoman's chastity and loyalty to her husband through the symbolic presence of a lap dog and juniper blossoms tucked into her bodice. Fontana highlights her sitter's elevated social status by devoting careful attention to her luxurious, gold-embroidered dress and fashionable lace collar, which draws the viewer's eye to the sitter's pearl necklace and the flowers in her bodice. Similarly focused on emphasizing her sitter's virtue, Italian artist Sofonisba Anguissola (c. 1535–1625) created a portrait of one of her sisters (cat. no. 102)—often subjects of the artist's early work—that draws a parallel between the sitter's namesake and Minerva, the pagan goddess of wisdom, who appears in the golden pendant her sister wears. This visual reference may symbolize the sitter's devotion to education and aspirations to acquire wisdom. Minerva Anguissola's coral jewellery, contrasting with her finely woven dress and embroidered chemise, indicates the young woman's innocence, as red coral was thought to protect children against evil influences and illness (cat. no. 204).

Anguissola achieved international success as a portraitist and became an aspirational model for many subsequent women artists. Her early intimate portrayals of her siblings informed her approach to the depiction of children, creating sensitive portraits that endowed her young royal sitters with the appearance of leaders. In Anguissola's first commissioned work, a portrait of nine-year-old Massimiliano Stampa (cat. no. 101), the artist balances the boy's youth with his recent assumption of political responsibilities following his father's death. Armed with a sword and posed like an adult nobleman, the boy's expression is tentative as he leans his right hand on a marble pedestal and looks out at the viewer. Anguissola's ability to portray both the youth

CAT. NO. 98 (above)
Adélaïde Labille-Guiard
Portrait of a Woman (Presumed Portrait of the Marquise de Lafayette)
1793–1794
Oil on canvas
78.1 × 62.9 cm
National Museum of Women in the Arts, Washington, DC, Gift of Wallace and Wilhelmina Holladay
2001.145
Photo: Lee Stalsworth

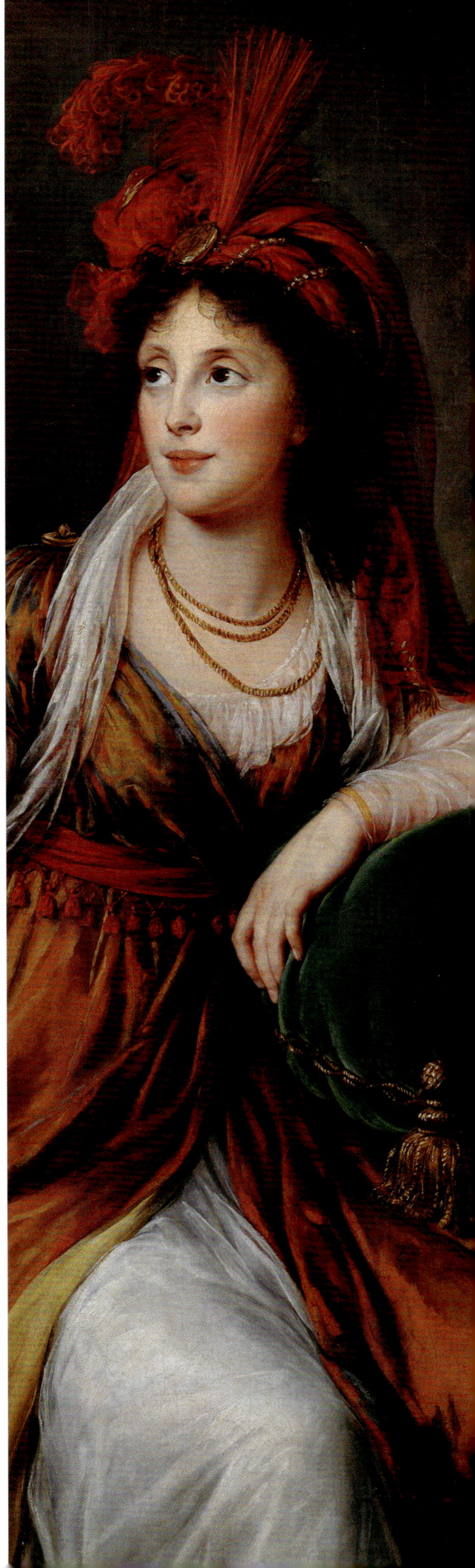

and gravitas of her subject captures the moment of his transition from a child to the leader of a family. While at the Spanish court, where she lived and worked for more than a decade, Anguissola painted another portrait of a young boy in a stunning green silk (cat. no. 103). Although a later Italian inscription identifies the boy as Phillip II, it is more likely a portrait of Ferdinand, Prince of Asturias. Unlike the older Stampa boy, this child gazes directly at the viewer with a leader's steadiness and composure; he is dressed for hunting and holds both a spear and sword, suggesting his destiny as a ruler.

Almost a century later in England, Mary Beale (1633–1699) had a successful career as a portrait painter in London. In *Portrait of a Woman with a Black Hood* (cat. no. 105), the subject is likely a widow, based on her dark clothing. Her age of fifty-five is inscribed in the upper right of the canvas. The sitter's sombre attire and the plain setting are in line with virtues associated with widows at the time. Such half-length portraiture is representative of the majority of Beale's artistic output, a business that allowed her to support her husband and children. A highly prolific painter with contacts at the court of Charles II, Beale instructed students, including women, and she inverted the most typical marital business structure, with her husband serving as her business manager.

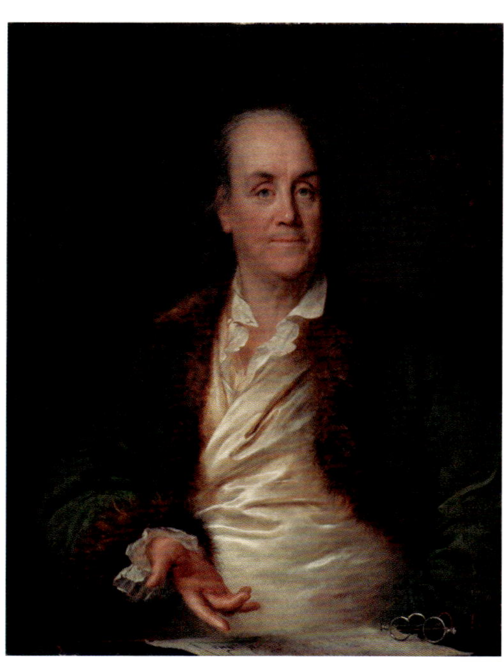

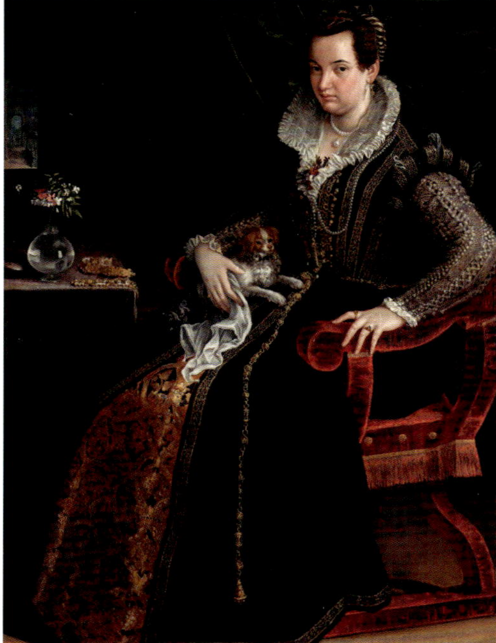

CAT. NO. 99 (below)
Anne-Rosalie Bocquet Filleul
Portrait of Benjamin Franklin
1778 or 1779
Oil on canvas
91.1 × 72.4 cm
Philadelphia Museum of Art: Gift of the Honourable Walter H. Annenberg and Leonore Annenberg and the Annenberg Foundation, 2007
2007-13-2

CAT. NO. 100 (above)
Lavinia Fontana
Portrait of Costanza Alidosi
c. 1595
Oil on canvas
157.5 × 120.3 cm
National Museum of Women in the Arts, Washington, D.C., Gift of Wallace and Wilhelmina Holladay
2002.72
Photo: Lee Stalsworth

Similarly forging her own path to entrepreneurship, Scottish portraitist Katharine Read (1723–1778) travelled for her own education, first to Paris and then Rome, before establishing a profitable portraiture practice in London and participating in its earliest public shows.[2] Although its authorship is debated, *British Gentlemen in Rome* (cat. no. 107) is attributed to Read and immortalizes a group of British connoisseurs conversing among Roman ruins, perhaps a stop on the Grand Tour that was then considered prime cultural edification.[3] While a Grand Tour was out of reach for most women, artists such as Read, Rosalba Carriera (1673–1757), and Elisabeth Louise Vigée-LeBrun (1755–1842) found ways to use the influx of travellers to their own advantage, selling portraits as mementoes and souvenirs.

Vigée-LeBrun—an artist so highly favoured by Queen Marie Antoinette (r. 1774–1792) that the regent influenced the Académie Royale de Peinture et de Sculpture to accept the artist into their ranks—combined her skill at rendering fabrics with creating flattering likenesses of her elite sitters. Vigée-LeBrun's portrait of the Comtesse de Cérès (cat. no. 108) captures her fashionably attired sitter in the privacy of her study upon having just finished writing. Interrupted at this intimate moment, the Comtesse looks up, smiling subtly as she folds a letter. It is not a passive portrayal but rather one that depicts a woman as an active agent in social networks. While Vigée-LeBrun specialized in images of nobility and royalty, her oeuvre features a significant number of portraits celebrating motherly love, including self-portraits with her daughter Julie. In her portrait *The Marquise de Pezay, and the Marquise de Rougé with Her Sons Alexis and Adrien* (cat. no. 109), Vigée-LeBrun effectively captures qualities of tenderness and sweetness that suggest an ideal bond between a mother and her children, and at the same time she celebrates female friendship. Vigée-LeBrun's choice to depict mothers and children in a loving embrace challenges the long-standing tradition of portraying members of aristocratic families in disconnected poses. Instead of emphasizing decorum, stature, and exemplary composure, the noble family is shown as a cohesive institution where the mother is deeply connected and devoted to her children.

From wispy feathers to heavy silks and shining jewels, Vigée-LeBrun created a spectacular combination of idealized yet casual female beauty and luxury that made her popular among elites in France, Russia, and Austria. However, the French Revolution changed the artist's life immensely. Because of her close connection to Marie Antoinette, Vigée-LeBrun fled with the first wave of refugees, finding both safety and lucrative commissions within European courts. In her portrait of Princess Anna Alexandrovna Galitzin (cat. no. 110), made during the artist's years in Russia, Vigée-LeBrun paints her sitter wearing a muslin chemise gown in the style favoured by LeBrun herself and popularized by Marie Antoinette. While her dress pointed to the period's prevailing neoclassical fashion, the princess's elaborate headdress alluded to the sitter's Georgian connections.

On May 31, 1783, along with Vigée-LeBrun, Adélaïde Labille-Guiard (1749–1803) received full membership in the Académie Royale, an opportunity traditionally restricted to men.[4] In her *Portrait of a Woman (Presumed Portrait of the Marquise*

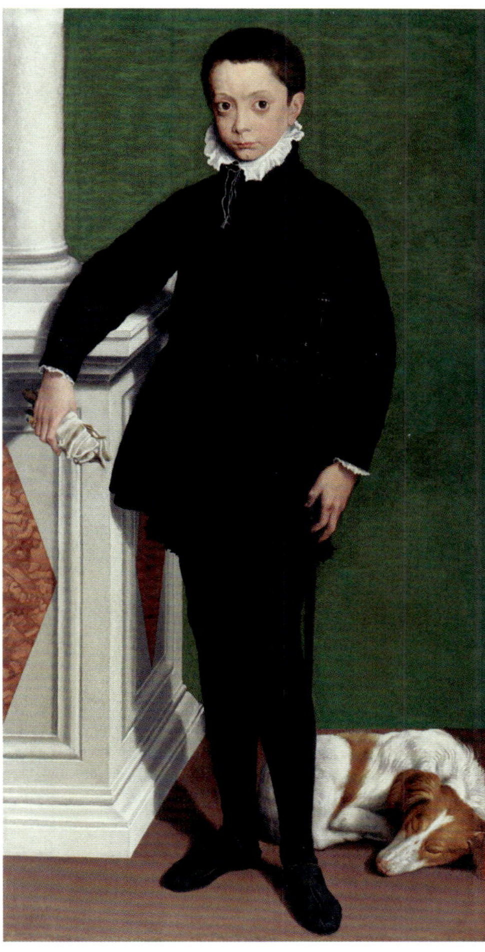

CAT. NO. 101
Sofonisba Anguissola
Portrait of Marquess Massimiliano Stampa
1557
Oil on canvas
134.9 × 71.1 cm
The Walters Art Museum, Baltimore, Maryland
37.1016
Exhibited at AGO only

de Lafayette) (cat. no. 98), Labille-Guiard focuses on textures such as feather, silk, lace, and lightly powdered hair without the distractions of elaborate jewellery or an architectural setting. This shift toward a more casual portrayal of the sitter was initially made fashionable through Vigée-LeBrun's portraits of Marie Antionette and then popularized by her contemporaries like Labille-Guiard. The state-sponsored Académie Royale hosted influential Salons, exhibitions that, as of 1791, allowed non-academic artists—as well as women like Vigée-LeBrun and Labille-Guiard—to show their paintings and promote their works to a wide audience.

In just over a decade of activity, Marie-Guillemine Benoist (1768–1826) exhibited thirty-four paintings at the yearly Salons and received commissions from illustrious patrons, including Napoleon. She was also granted a studio at the Louvre, a lucrative and significant achievement. *Portrait of a Lady* (cat. no. 111) was likely exhibited in the 1799 Salon but for decades was misattributed to her teacher, Jacques-Louis David, a fate similar to that which has befallen many women artists over the centuries. Marie Victoire Lemoine (1754–1820), another woman who exhibited at the Salon, was skilled at capturing the intricate details of her sitters' costume and fashion. Her *Portrait of a Youth in an Embroidered Vest* (cat. no. 106) demonstrates Lemoine's successful rendering of different textile textures. The man's luxurious grey satin jacket and finely embroidered vest likely suggest a close connection with a wealthy family.[5] Despite efforts to identify the sitter, his name remains unknown. Proposed identifications have included the Jacobin revolutionary Zamor, enslaved in the household of Comtesse du Barry, the official mistress of King Louis XV, as well as Scipio or Narcisse, enslaved members of the household of the Duchess d'Orleans, who was a patron of Lemoine. During this period, wealthy Europeans commonly dressed their enslaved servants in finery, presenting the wearer and their clothes as indicators of the owner's wealth.

Another painter working in these circles was Anne-Rosalie Bocquet Filleul (1752–1794), though little is known about her career.[6] She exhibited publicly only once, in 1774, at the Académie de Saint-Luc, though she received a number of royal commissions in the years prior to painting the visiting American statesman Benjamin Franklin (cat. no. 99). Made when the sitter was approximately seventy-two years old, the portrait is a sympathetic rendering of Franklin, then ambassador to France; he seems to invite the viewer to engage in a friendly discussion by opening his hand over a map of Philadelphia. The casual manner of portrayal also hints at the personal relationship between artist and sitter, who were neighbours in Passy, outside Paris.

Whether through personal relationships or by professional reputation, women painters were able to gain commissions and demonstrate their skills in the realm of portraiture during the pre-modern period. Across Europe's cities and courts, these women capitalized on opportunities for successful careers, leaving lasting proof of their talents for expertly rendering likeness in paint.

Resources Consulted

Baillio, Joseph, Paul Lang, and Katharine Baetjer, eds. *Vigée Le Brun*. Ottawa: National Gallery of Canada; New York: Metropolitan Museum of Art, 2016.

Cole, Michael W. *Sofonisba's Lesson: A Renaissance Artist and Her Work*. Princeton, NJ: Princeton University Press, 2022.

Hunting, Penelope. *My Dearest Heart: The Artist Mary Beale (1633-1699)*. London: Unicorn, 2019.

Jacobs, Fredrika H. "(Pro)creativity." In *Defining the Renaissance Virtuosa: Women Artists and the Language of Art History and Criticism*. Cambridge: Cambridge University Press, 1997.

Murphy, Caroline. *Lavinia Fontana: A Painter and Her Patrons in Sixteenth-Century Bologna*. New Haven, CT: Yale University Press, 2003.

Ruiz Gómez, Letizia, ed. *A Tale of Two Painters: Sofonisba Anguissola and Lavinia Fontana*. Madrid: Museo Nacional del Prado, 2019. Exhibition catalogue.

Spies-Gans, Paris A. *A Revolution on Canvas: The Rise of Women Artists in Britain and France, 1760–1830*. London: Paul Mellon Centre for Studies in British Art in association with Yale University Press, 2022.

Notes

1 According to Aristotle's theory of causation, written around 350 BCE, only men possessed the ability to produce and create; women were considered empty vessels who hosted the male's process of creation. While the treatise was reworked and adapted many times over the centuries, this view remained popular well into the early modern period.

2 Read studied with Quentin de La Tour in Paris and Louis-Gabriel Blanchet in Rome.

3 Margery Morgan, "British Connoisseurs in Rome: Was It Painted by Katherine Read (1723–78)?" *British Art Journal* 7, no. 1 (2006): 40–44.

4 Following the double admission of Vigée-LeBrun and Labille-Guiard in 1783, the Academy capped the full membership of women to four. Only fifteen women in total were given full membership between 1648 and 1793, all of whom had their membership revoked in the wake of the Revolution.

5 Scholars contest the attribution of this painting. Joseph Baillio attributed the work to Marie Victoire Lemoine in 1996, while Neil Jeffares attributed the painting to Jacques Antoine-Marie Lemoine in 1999. See Joseph Baillio, "Vie et oeuvre de Marie-Victoire Lemoine (1754–1820)," *Gazette des Beaux-Arts* 127 (April 1996): cat. no. 30, and Neil Jeffares, "Jacques Antoine-Marie Lemoine," *Gazette des Beaux-Arts* (February 1999), 118, cat. no. 138.

6 See Paris A. Spies-Gans's essay "Art and Politics: Women Artists and the Rulers of the Revolutionary World" on pages 122–37 of this volume.

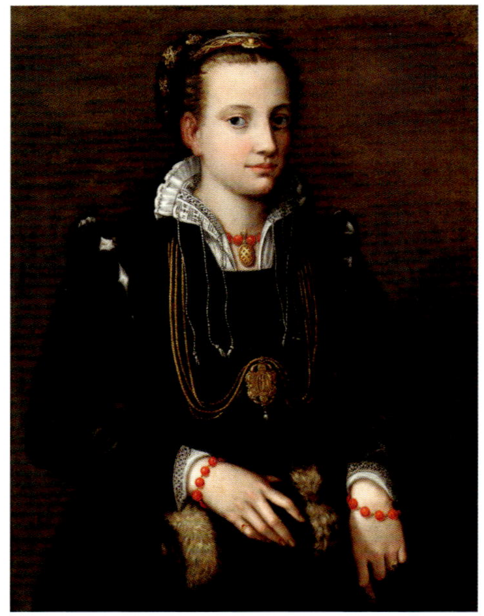

CAT. NO. 102
Sofonisba Anguissola
The Artist's Sister Minerva Anguissola
c. 1564
Oil on canvas
85.1 × 66 cm
Layton Art Collection at Milwaukee Art Museum, Gift of the family of Mrs. Frederick Vogel Jr.
L1952.1
Photo: John R. Glembin
Exhibited at BMA only

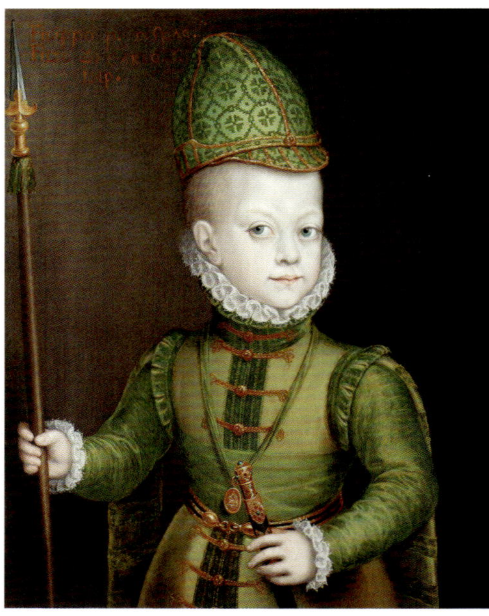

CAT. NO. 103
Sofonisba Anguissola
Portrait of a Spanish Prince
c. 1573
Oil on canvas
59.1 × 48.3 cm
San Diego Museum of Art: Gift of Anne R. and Amy Putnam
1936.58

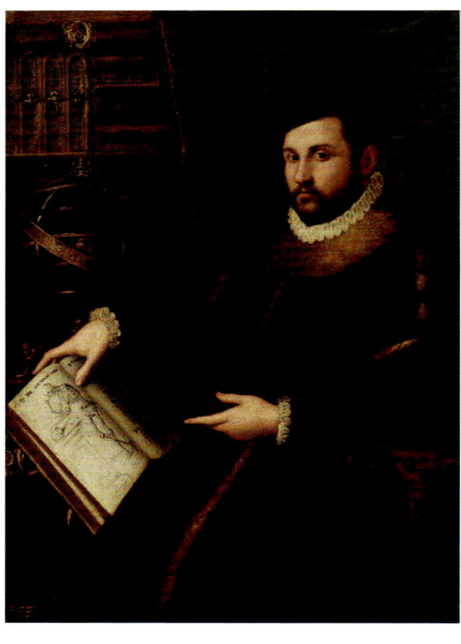

CAT. NO. 104
Lavinia Fontana
Portrait of Girolamo Mercuriale
1588–1589
Oil on canvas
119 × 88.9 cm
The Walters Art Museum, Baltimore, Maryland
37.1106
Exhibited at AGO only

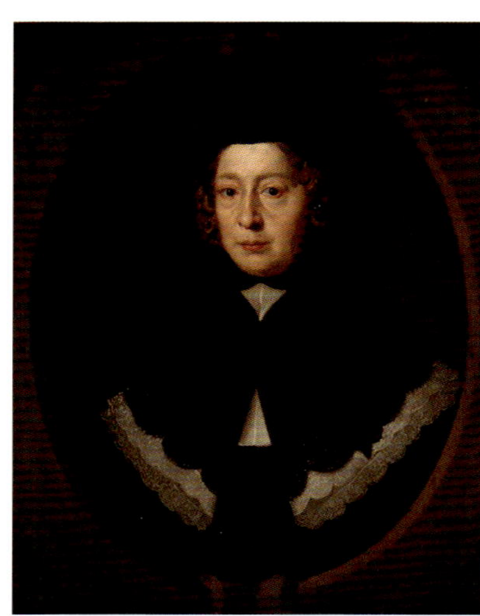

CAT. NO. 105
Mary Beale
Portrait of a Woman with a Black Hood
c. 1660
Oil on canvas
71.8 × 59.7 cm
National Museum of Women in the Arts, Washington, DC, Bequest of John N. and Dorothy C. Estabrook
1988.15
Photo: Lee Stalsworth

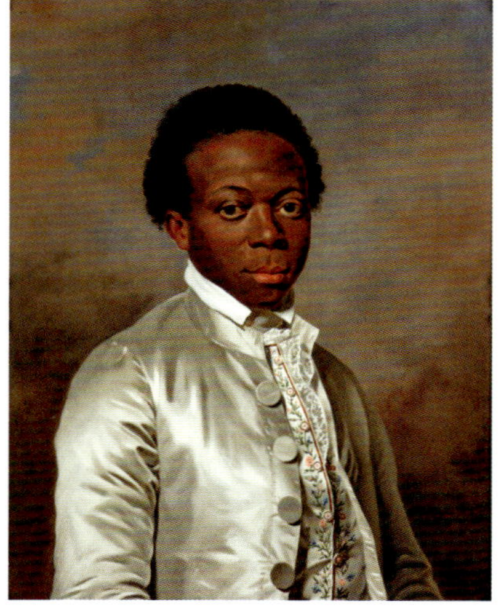

CAT. NO. 106
Marie Victoire Lemoine
Portrait of a Youth in an Embroidered Vest
1785
Oil on canvas
65.1 × 54.6 cm
Purchased with funds from the Cummer Council, Cummer Museum of Art & Gardens, Jacksonville, Florida
AP.1994.3.1
Image: Douglas J. Eng Photography

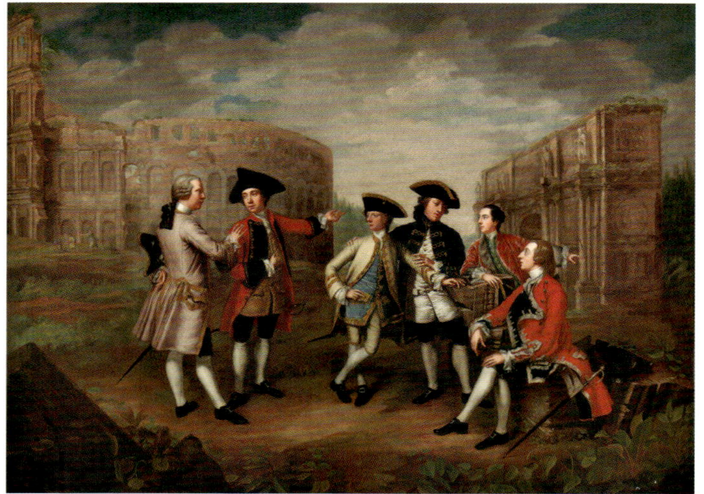

CAT. NO. 107
Attributed to Katharine Read
British Gentlemen in Rome
c. 1750
Oil on canvas
94.6 × 134.6 cm
Yale Center for British Art, Paul Mellon Collection
B1981.25.272
Image Courtesy YCBA

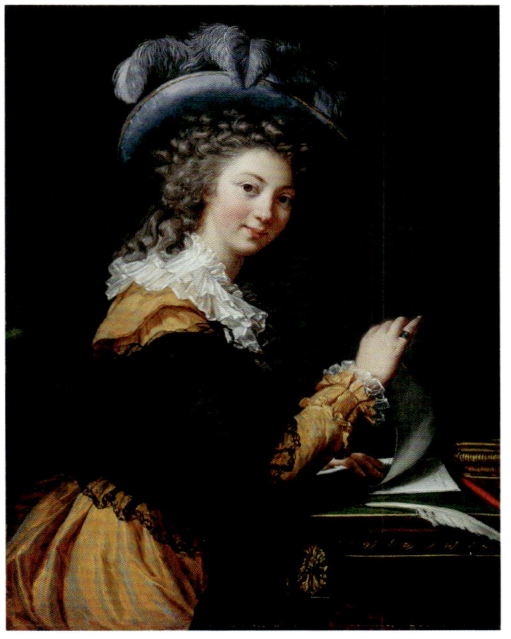

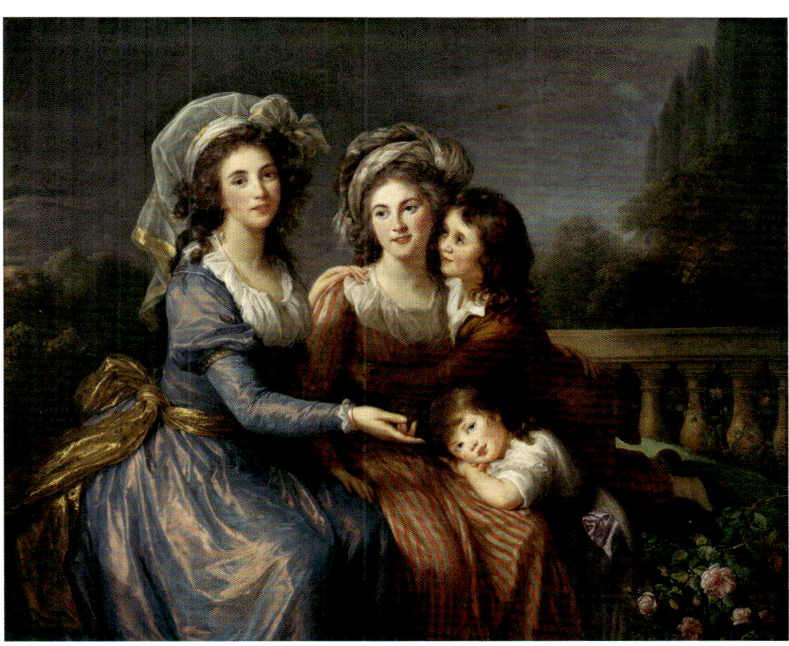

CAT. NO. 108 (left)
Elisabeth Louise Vigée-LeBrun
The Comtesse de Cérès
1784
Oil on canvas
91.4 × 73.7 cm
Toledo Museum of Art, Purchased with funds from the Libbey Endowment, Gift of Edward Drummond Libbey
1963.33

CAT. NO. 109 (right)
Elisabeth Louise Vigée-LeBrun
The Marquise de Pezay, and the Marquise de Rougé with Her Sons Alexis and Adrien
1787
Oil on canvas
123.4 × 155.9 cm
National Gallery of Art, Washington, Purchased as the Gift of the Bay Foundation in memory of Josephine Bay Paul and Ambassador Charles Ulrick Bay
1964.11.1

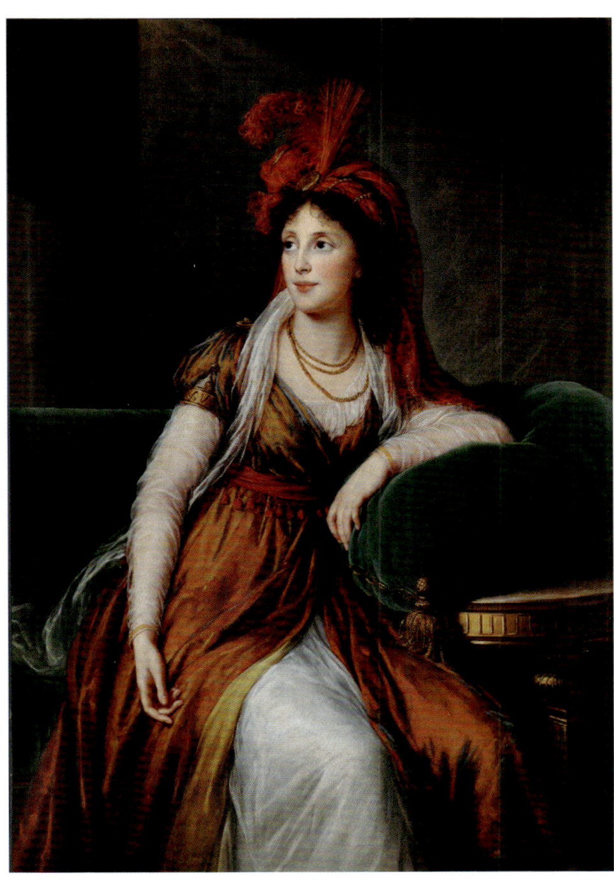

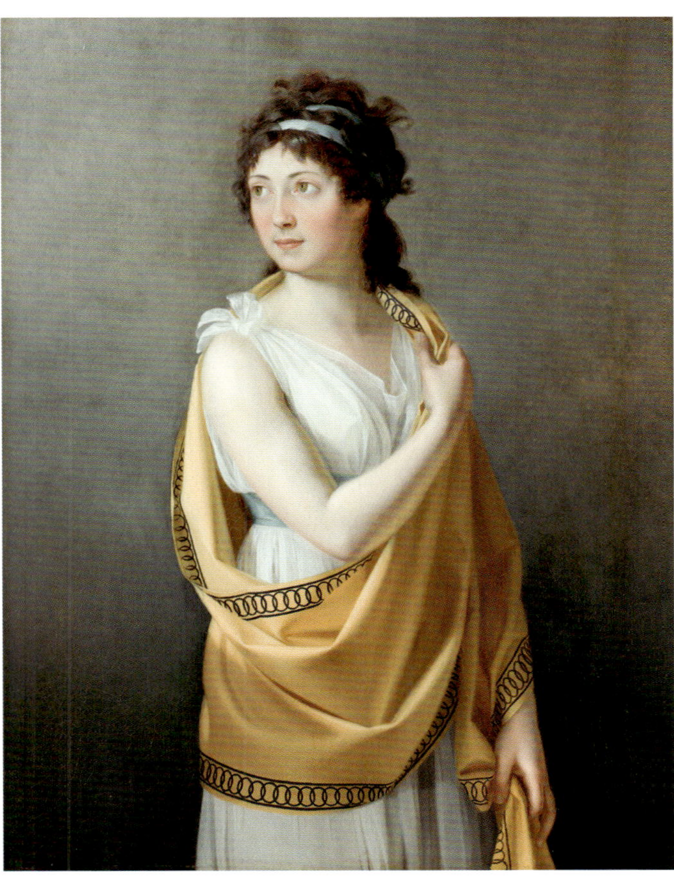

CAT. NO. 110 (left)
Elisabeth Louise Vigée-LeBrun
Princess Anna Alexandrovna Galitzin
c. 1797
Oil on canvas
135.9 × 100.3 cm
Baltimore Museum of Art:
The Mary Frick Jacobs Collection, 1938.192
Photo: Mitro Hood

CAT. NO. 111 (right)
Marie-Guillemine Benoist
Portrait of a Lady
c. 1799
Oil on canvas
100.3 × 81.6 cm
San Diego Museum of Art:
Gift of Anne R. and Amy Putnam
1946.5

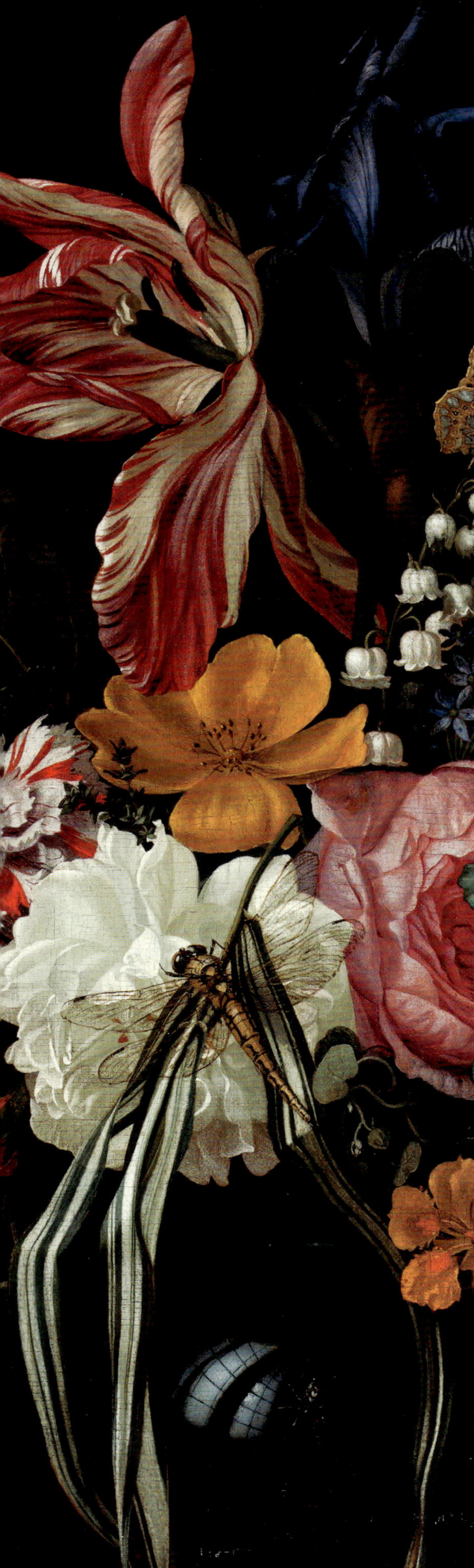

Painting ※ *Still Life*

Lara Yeager-Crasselt

In his *Groot Schilderboek* [*Great Book of Painting*] published in 1707, the Dutch artist and theorist Gérard de Lairesse wrote that no subject was "as feminine, or so suited to a woman" as the flower still life.[1] Willem Goeree expressed a similar sentiment in his handbook on painting in watercolour, *Verlichterie-kunde* [*The Art of Illumination*] in 1670. As Goeree described, while watercolour itself was suited to the young and the old, less challenging subjects like fruit, flowers, and birds were especially fitting for women. Portraits, narratives, and landscapes—those subjects that dealt with the human figure and its noble narratives—were best left to men.[2]

While the gendered views expressed by de Lairesse and Goeree were not uncommon during this period, they reflect broader attitudes toward women artists and still-life painting that existed across early modern Europe—many persisting to this day.[3] The depiction of objects from the natural world, including fruit, flowers, and foodstuffs, was seen as lacking intellect or imagination, and thus fell lower on the hierarchy of genres.[4] Yet far from simply "imitating nature," still-life paintings by artists like Fede Galizia (1578–c. 1630), Clara Peeters (c. 1587–after 1636), and Rachel Ruysch (1664–1750) met a variety of aims and interests: stimulating intellectual discourse, pleasing the eye, and prompting contemplation. The choice of women artists to depict still lifes—in part shaped by issues of accessibility, training, and opportunity—indicates their own sustained interests in this relatively new genre of painting for the time.[5] Women's approach to still life was inventive and diverse, and was met with enormous interest and praise among elite patrons and collectors. Combining sensitive observations of the world around them with an awareness of pressing artistic, cultural, and scientific concerns of the day, women's contributions to still-life painting were critical in the early modern period.

This leading role was certainly true of Galizia, one of the first Italian artists to depict still life at

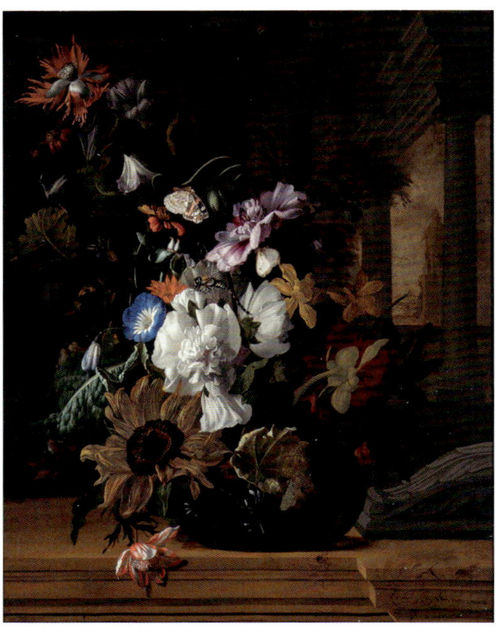

the beginning of the seventeenth century. Fede, who trained with her father, the miniaturist Nunzio Galizia, in Lombardy, transformed humble fruits into scenes of simple elegance. In *Glass Tazza with Peaches, Jasmine Flowers and Quinces* (cat. no. 113), she positions the fruit close to the edge of the stone tabletop and uses the black background to create a sense of sculptural relief. Interspersed with sprigs of jasmine, ripe peaches rest in the glass bowl, while three quinces—one sliced down its centre to reveal seeds and flesh—are displayed at its sides. Galizia carefully renders the fall of light and shadow over the composition, capturing the highlights on the skin of the quinces and the tazza's glass stem. The subject must have been a success on the market, as at least four other versions are known.[6]

While Galizia's success was largely tied to her achievements as a still-life painter—her work found favour both across and beyond Italy, including at the court of Rudolph II in Prague—she also painted portraits and religious subjects. The same can be

CAT. NO. 112 (facing)
Rachel Ruysch
A Vase of Flowers
1689
Oil on canvas
68 × 57.2 cm
San Diego Museum of Art:
Museum purchase with funds from the Gerald and Inez Grant Parker Foundation
1979.25

CAT. NO. 113 (right)
Fede Galizia
Glass Tazza with Peaches, Jasmine Flowers and Quinces
c. 1607
Oil on wood
30.3 × 41.7 cm
The Montreal Museum of Fine Arts,
Gift of Mr. and Mrs. Michal Hornstein
2015.19
Photo: MMFA, Denis Farley

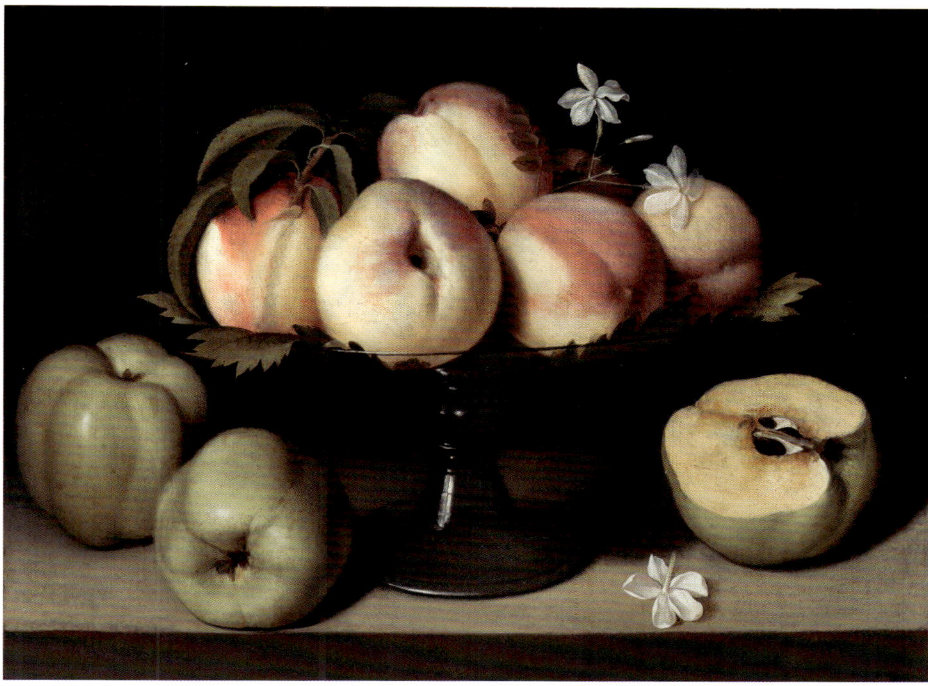

said of Portuguese artist Josefa Ayala (c. 1630–1684), who, working independently from a male family member, produced devotional works and still lifes in the second half of the seventeenth century. She often imbued the latter with religious significance.[7] In her *Still Life with Watermelon and Pears* (cat. no. 118), Ayala renders various fruits and flowers into a densely packed composition, using a muted palette and strong chiaroscuro and eschewing the softer naturalism of her predecessors. In her *Still Life with Fruit, Cardoon, and Carrots* (cat. no. 119), she places ripe oranges in an imported white porcelain bowl atop a finely rendered lace-edged cloth. Like the carrots beside it, the lace hangs illusionistically over the edge of the tabletop. A rotting pear dangles above a silver platter of cardoons, presented before the viewer as if on a sacred altar.

This exacting approach resonates in some ways in the work of Louise Moillon (c. 1610–c. 1696), whose *Still Life with a Basket of Fruit and a Bunch of Asparagus* (cat. no. 115) shows how precisely she captured line, form, and light. Yet her enticing display of foodstuffs—plump peaches and plums, robust cherries, and ripe asparagus—prompts an invitation to eat as much as it does an admiration for her artistry. Moillon, who trained under her father and stepfather in Paris, may have been impacted by the work of Netherlandish artists then circulating in that city, but her work bears a distinctive character of its own.

In the Netherlands, Peeters was among the first generation of still-life painters to achieve enormous success on the open market. The interest in her work represented a shift toward the wealthy class of merchants who emerged in cities like Antwerp, and later Amsterdam. Peeters began painting tabletop scenes with various objects and foodstuffs before turning to flower painting around 1610. In one particular scene of an abundant bouquet, Peeters shows blossoms of various sorts, combining a palette of pinks, oranges, blues, and greens against the dark background (cat. no. 114). To show off her painterly skill, Peeters captured the reflection of an interior window in the glass vase.

By the second half of the seventeenth century, artists working in the Netherlands expanded the motifs and character of flower paintings. Maria-Theresia van Thielen (1640–1706), who was a student of her father, the flower painter Jan Philips van Thielen in Antwerp, incorporated architectural elements into her *Still Life with Parrot* (cat. no. 116). Flowers and grapevines encircle a stone urn in the foreground as the bird greedily eyes the fruit below. The artist's signature and date "carved" into the base of the column proclaim van Thielen's mastery of her subject.

As the century wore on, artists and collectors demonstrated an increasing interest in the intersection of still life and the scientific study of plants and flowers. Abundant flower bouquets painted by Dutch painters such as Ruysch and Maria van Oosterwijck (1630–1693)—who achieved enormous success at home and internationally—demonstrate how their close powers of observation were transformed into expressive and carefully articulated compositions of the natural world. In van Oosterwijck's *Still Life* (cat. no. 117), tulips, carnations, and roses elegantly rise above a marble tabletop in a sinuous line. Insects give life to the bouquet, while some of its wilting petals suggest ideas of transience and temporality, possibly reflecting the impact of van Oosterwijck's upbringing as the daughter of a clergyman in Delft.[8] Van Oosterwijck never married or had children, but she took on her maidservant, Geertje Wyntges, as a pupil, who later became a painter of flower still lifes.[9]

Ruysch's extraordinary career, which included a full family life, stretched nearly seven decades.[10] In *A Vase of Flowers* (cat. no. 112), she sets the bouquet on a marble ledge before a classicizing arcade, full of colour and dramatic lighting. The flowers are arranged asymmetrically in the vase and shown at different stages of blooming and decay. Various insects, including a large butterfly and a bumblebee, animate Ruysch's *Still Life with Flowers* (cat. no. 120), where large petals and textured leaves

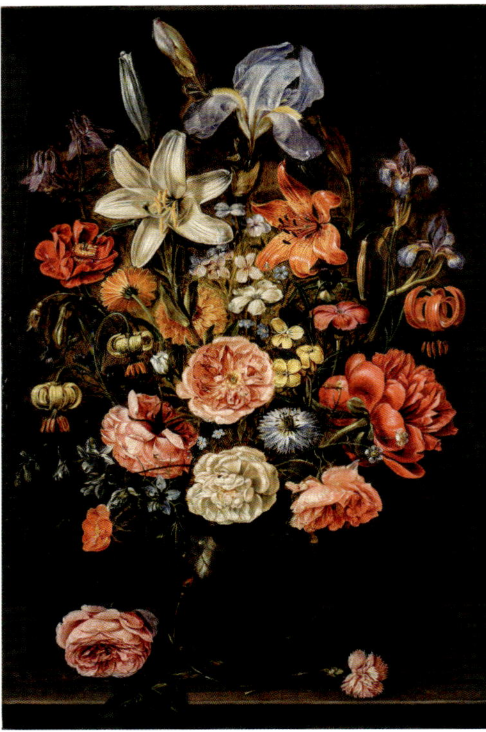

CAT. NO. 114
Clara Peeters
A Still Life of Lilies, Roses, Iris, Pansies, Columbine, Love-in-a-Mist, Larkspur and Other Flowers in a Glass Vase on a Table Top, Flanked by a Rose and a Carnation
c. 1610
Oil on panel
49.5 × 33.7 cm
National Museum of Women in the Arts, Washington, DC, Gift of Wallace and Wilhelmina Holladay
2016.30
Photo: Lee Stalsworth

hover delicately over a stone balustrade. Ruysch's style was both refined and precise, shaped by her training with the celebrated still-life painter Willem van Aelst in Amsterdam, in addition to her early experiences with her father, Frederik Ruysch, a professor of botany and anatomy at the university in Amsterdam. There, Rachel studied specimens in the university gardens, developing a more scientific approach to her subject matter.[11]

Like their Italian predecessors, these northern artists worked for the high end of the market and earned recognition among contemporaries. Van Oosterwijck's work was collected by Prince Cosimo III de' Medici in Florence, whereas Ruysch served as court painter to Johan Wilhelm, the elector Palatine in Düsseldorf, with the privilege to remain in Amsterdam. Professional recognition came for French painter Anne Vallayer-Coster (1744–1818) in 1770, when she became one of only four women elected to the Académie Royale de Peinture et de Sculpture at any one time, an achievement garnered for her admired still-life paintings. Rendered with fluid brushwork and a painterly frankness, Vallayer-Coster's tabletop scenes focus on local produce and foodstuffs. In *Still Life with Lobster* (cat. no. 121), executed the same year she was appointed as painter to the queen of France, she depicts a delicious red lobster beside a silver tureen, salt cellar, and gilded cruet—objects likely crafted by her silversmith father—alongside loaves of bread and a basket of grapes. Her reflection in the tureen shows her commanding artistry, while suggesting an awareness of northern predecessors like Clara Peeters.[12]

The earlier presented statements by de Lairesse and Goeree do not reflect the diversity and artistry of women as still-life painters. De Lairesse's views disparage this subject matter, which had flourished among women and men for well over a century by the time that he composed his treatise. Examined more closely, his sentiments reflect a larger disdain for still life in the hierarchy of genres, rather than specifically for women artists, yet they nevertheless perpetuate old prejudices. As this discussion has shown, however, women artists were not necessarily still-life painters by default; they depicted these rich and complex subjects with ingenuity and energy, balancing the increasingly intertwined worlds of the artistic and the scientific as pioneers of still life.

Resources Consulted

Barker, Sheila, ed. *"The Immensity of the Universe" in the Art of Giovanna Garzoni.* Florence: Gallerie degli Uffizi, 2020. Exhibition catalogue.

Berardi, Marianne. "Science into Art: Rachel Ruysch's Early Development as a Still-Life Painter." PhD diss., University of Pittsburgh, 1998.

Bryson, Norman. "Still Life and 'Feminine Space.'" In *Looking at the Overlooked: Four Essays on Still Life Painting*, 136–78. Cambridge, MA: Harvard University Press, 1990.

Garrard, Mary D. "The Not-So-Still Lifes of Giovanna Garzoni." In *"The Immensity of the Universe" in the Art of Giovanna Garzoni*, 62–77, edited by Sheila Barker. Florence: Gallerie degli Uffizi, 2020. Exhibition catalogue.

Kahng, Eik, and Marianne Roland Michel, eds. *Anne Vallayer-Coster: Painter to the Court of Marie-Antoinette.* Dallas: Dallas Museum of Art; New Haven, CT: Yale University Press, 2002.

Kettering, Alison M. "Watercolor and Women in the Early Modern Netherlands: Between Mirror and Comb." *Women's Art Journal* 42, no. 1 (Spring/Summer 2021): 27–36.

Russell, Margarita. "The Woman Painters in Houbraken's Groote Schouburgh." *Women's Art Journal* 2 (1981): 7–11.

Segal, Sam. "An Early Still Life by Fede Galizia." *Burlington Magazine* 140, no. 1140 (March 1998): 163–71.

Simões de Carvalho, Maria de Lourdes, ed., and Jordana Pomeroy (coord.). *The Sacred and the Profane: Josefa de Obidos of Portugal.* Lisbon: Ministério da Cultura, Gabinete das Relações Internacionais; Washington, DC: National Museum of Women in the Arts, 1997. Exhibition catalogue.

Straussman-Pflanzer, Eve, and Oliver Tostmann, eds. *By Her Hand: Artemisia Gentileschi and Women Artists in Italy, 1500–1800.* New Haven, CT: Yale University Press in association with Detroit Institute of Arts, 2021.

Suchtelen, Ariane van, Fred G. Meijer, Erik A. de Jong, Epco Runia, Charlotte Rulkens, Marya Albrecht, et al. *In Full Bloom.* Translated by Diane Webb. Zwolle, Netherlands: Waanders, 2022.

Tongiorgi Tomasi, Lucia. "The Flowering of Florence: Botanical Art for the Medici." In *The Flowering of Florence: Botanical Art for the Medici.* Edited by Lucia Tongiorgi Tomasi and Gretchen A. Hirschauer, 15–108. Washington, DC: National Gallery of Art, 2002.

Van der Stighelen, Katlijne, and M. Westen, *Elck zijn waeroom: Vrouwelijke kunstenaars in België en Nederland, 1500–1950.* Antwerp: Koninklijk Museum voor Schone Kunsten, 1999–2000.

Vergara, Alejandro. *The Art of Clara Peeters.* Antwerp: Koninklijk Museum voor Schone Kunsten; Madrid: Museo Nacional del Prado, 2016.

Notes

1 Gérard de Lairesse, *Groot Schilderboek* (Amsterdam, 1707), vol. 2, 355.

2 Willem Goeree, *Verlichterie-kunde*, addendum to the 2nd edition of *Inleydinge tot Teyckenkonst* [*Introduction to the Art of Drawing*] (Middelburg, 1670), as cited in Alison M. Kettering, "Watercolor and Women in the Early Modern Netherlands: Between Mirror and Comb," *Women's Art Journal* 42, no. 1 (Spring/Summer 2021), 28–29n10.

3 This phenomenon is also reflected in the relatively low prices that women still-life painters fetch on the art market in comparison to their male peers.

4 See Guido Jansen, "'On the Lowest Level': The Status of Still Life in Netherlandish Art Literature of the Seventeenth Century," in *Still-Life Paintings from the*

Netherlands, 1550–1720, ed. Alan Chong and Wouter Kloek (Zwolle, Netherlands: Waanders, 1999), 51–71.

5 Women's painting of still lifes has been attributed in part to their lack of access to drawing academies, where they would have seen nude models, or professional guilds, thus hindering the degree to which they could paint certain subjects. But many women artists painted still lifes in addition to other subject matter, making the issue more complex than scholars tend to suggest.

6 Galizia's work may have also inspired Giovanna Garzoni (1600–1670), a painter and calligrapher who was active in Naples, Turin, and Rome. Garzoni flourished in her sensitive and original depictions of fruits, flowers, and insects during the seventeenth century, often imbuing her images with an awareness of developments in the botanical sciences.

7 Victor Serrao, Barbara von Barghahn, Ana Hathery, Luis de Mora Sobral, "A Quest for Paradise and 'Dulcedo Dei': Love, Mysticism, and Josefa de Óbidos's Secret Garden of Virtues," in *The Sacred and the Profane: Josefa de Óbidos of Portugal* (Lisbon: Ministério da Cultura; Washington, DC: National Museum of Women in the Arts, 1997), 83–89; 128–35, 160–65. Notably, Ayala is the only known documented Iberian woman to practise her profession independently of a male family member. I would like to thank Andaleeb Badiee Banta for drawing this important point to my attention.

8 See Noud Janssen, "Oosterwijck, Maria van (1630–1693)," Huygens Institute, *Online Dictionary of Dutch Women*, resources.huygens.knaw.nl/vrouwenlexicon/lemmata/data/oosterwijck.

9 See Noud Janssen, "Wyntges, Geertje (1636–1712)," Huygens Institute, *Online Dictionary of Dutch Women*, resources.huygens.knaw.nl/vrouwenlexicon/lemmata/data/wyntges.

10 Ruysch married the portrait painter Juriaen Pool in 1693 and raised ten children.

11 See Luuc Kooijmans, "Ruysch, Rachel (1664–1750)," Huygens Institute, *Online Dictionary of Dutch Women*, resources.huygens.knaw.nl/vrouwenlexicon/lemmata/data/Ruysch,%20Rachel.

12 Peeters's still life discussed earlier in this essay also features a reflection in the glass vase, and in other works she included a knife jutting out from the edge of a tabletop, a quotation that Vallayer-Coster may be directly referencing here. I would like to thank Andaleeb Badiee Banta for making this observation.

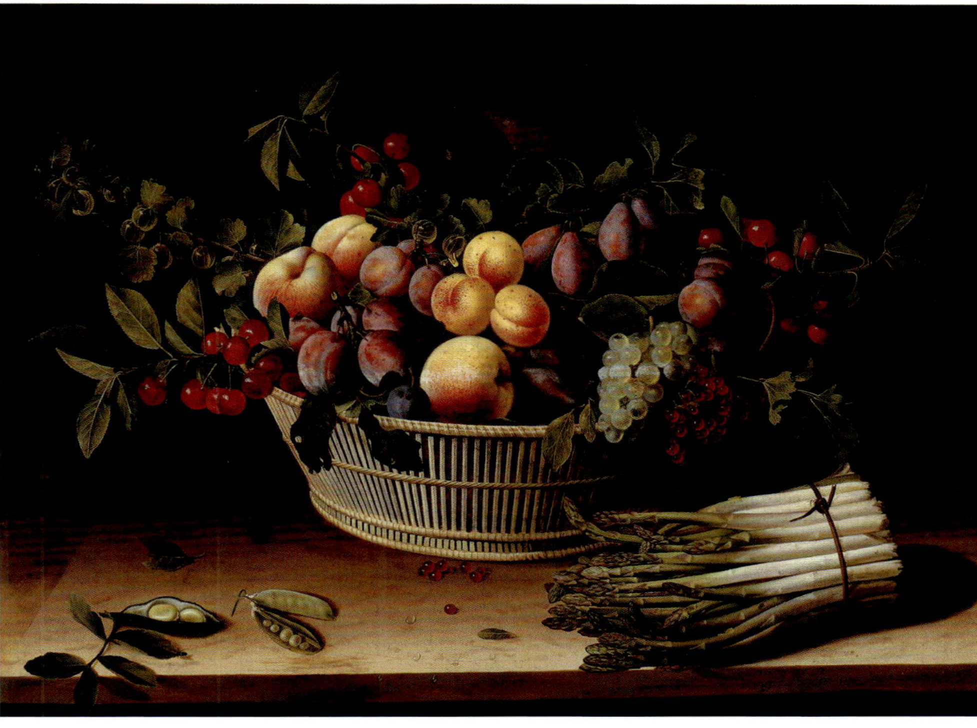

CAT. NO. 115
Louise Moillon
Still Life with a Basket of Fruit and a Bunch of Asparagus
1630
Oil on panel
53.3 × 71.3 cm
Art Institute of Chicago, Wirt D. Walker Fund
1948.78

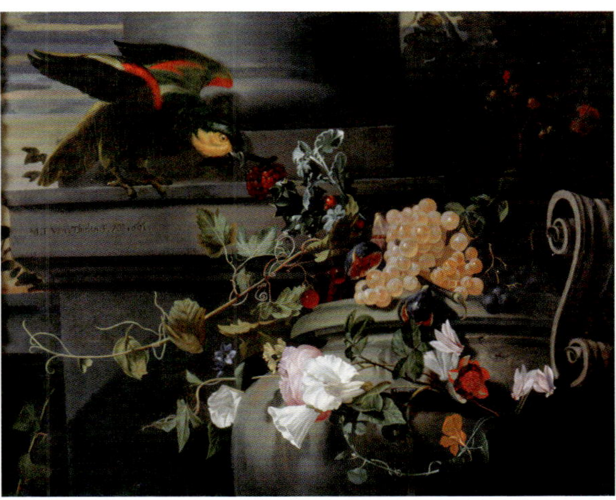

CAT. NO. 116
Maria-Theresia van Thielen
Still Life with Parrot
1661
Oil on canvas
53.3 × 68.6 cm
Milwaukee Art Museum, Gift of Mr. and Mrs. John Schroeder in memory of their parents
M1967.41
Photo: John R. Glembin
Exhibited at BMA only

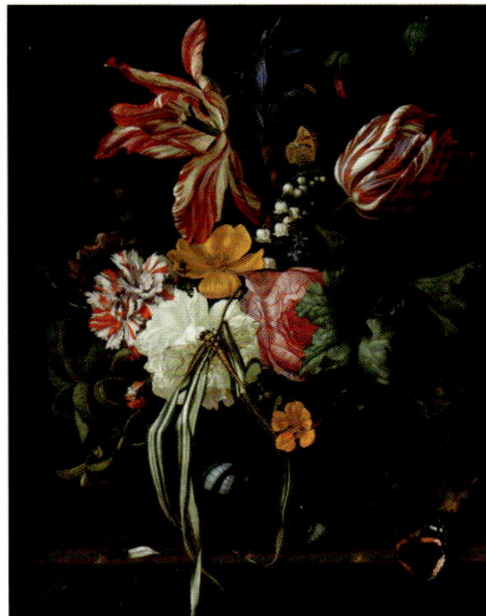

CAT. NO. 117
Maria van Oosterwijck
Still Life
1669
Oil on canvas
46 × 37.1 cm
Cincinnati Art Museum, Bequest of Mrs. L.W. Scott Alter
1988.150

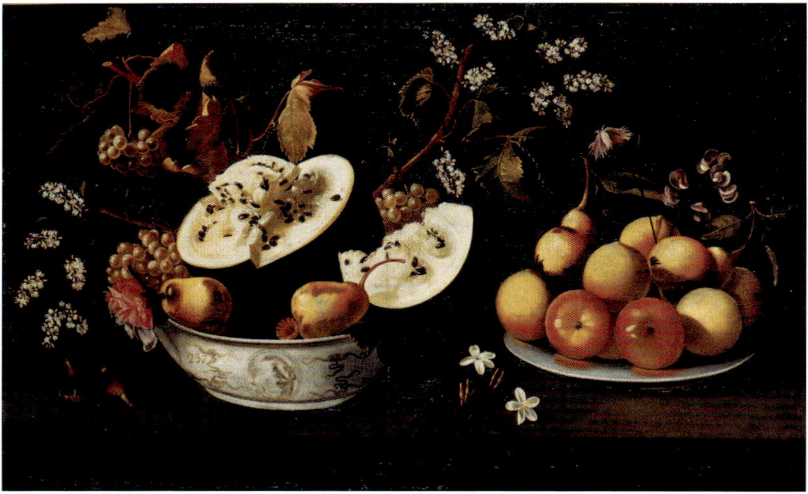

CAT. NO. 118
Josefa Ayala
Still Life with Watermelon and Pears
c. 1670
Oil on canvas
63 × 104 cm
Museu Nacional de Arte Antiga, Lisbon, Academy of the Sciences, Priest Joseph Mayne Collection, 1867
MNAA, INV. 636 PINT
© Photo: José Pessoa, Direção-Geral do Património Cultural / Arquivo de Documentação Fotográfica (DGPC/ADF)

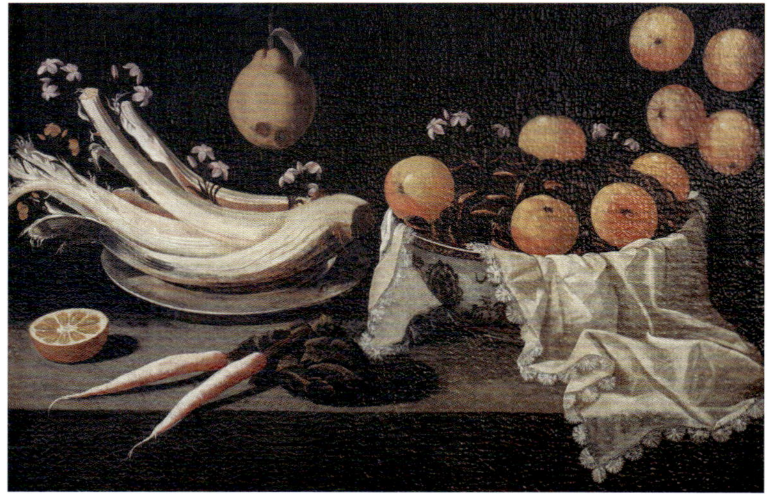

CAT. NO. 119
Josefa Ayala
Still Life with Fruit, Cardoon, and Carrots
c. 1680
Oil on canvas
59 × 91 cm
Collection of the Embassy of Portugal, Washington, DC
Photo: Diogo Almeida

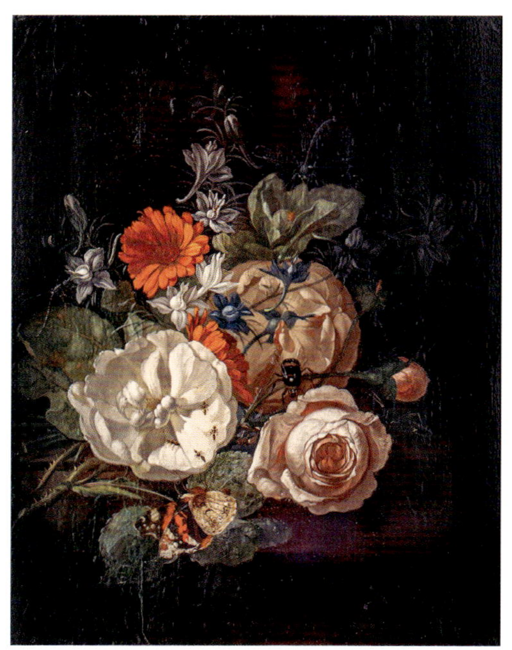

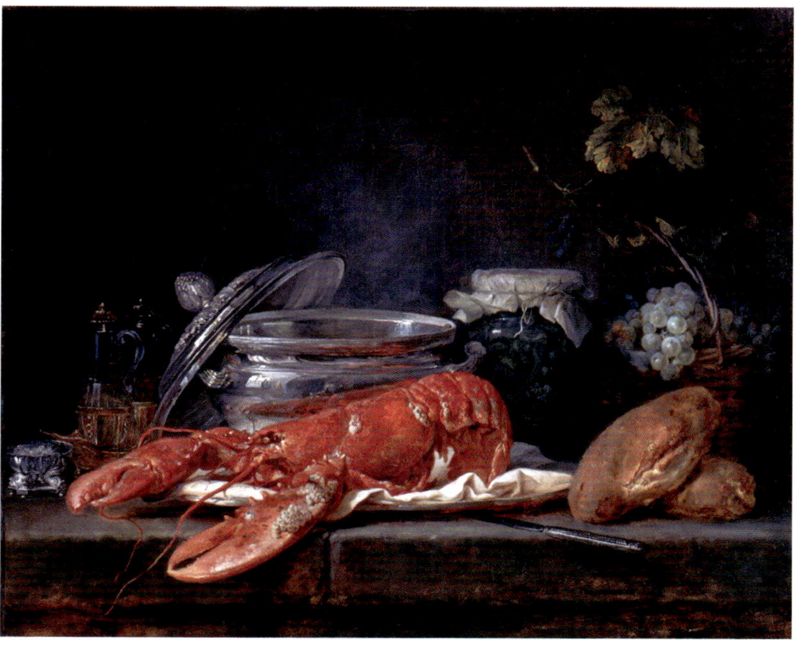

CAT. NO. 120 (left)
Rachel Ruysch
Still Life with Flowers
c. 1700–1750
Oil on panel
32 × 25 cm
George M. and Linda H. Kaufman
Photo: Andrew K. Benjack, Benjack Media

CAT. NO. 121 (right)
Anne Vallayer-Coster
Still Life with Lobster
1781
Oil on canvas
70.5 × 89.5 cm
Toledo Museum of Art, Purchased with funds from the Libbey Endowment, Gift of Edward Drummond Libbey
1968.1A

Painting ⁜ *Women at Work*

Alexa Greist

In pre-modern Europe, the artist's studio was a locus both of creation and identity. When a woman artist portrayed herself within the studio, it served to cement her position in a male-dominated world, advertising her skill, success, learning, and even her virtue. Whether shown in the act of creation or allied with a powerful patron, women painters were intimately aware of how their self-presentation could affect their public reputation. For an artist, a self-portrait was an act of self-promotion that would hopefully result in future commissions as well as a more recognizable public persona as an artist. A woman engaging in a creative pursuit like drawing or embroidery was a way of highlighting her education and skills in gender-appropriate activities, but it could also challenge established norms by occupying a role that typically had been associated with male-dominated notions of genius and artistry.

In what is one of the most famous painted self-portraits in Dutch art, Judith Leyster (1609–1660) looks at the viewer with a relaxed confidence, seemingly interrupted at work at a painting (cat. no. 123). She assertively leans her arm on the back of her chair, in charge of her art, holding a palette full of brushes. On the easel is a reference to a figure from a well-received painting she made around 1629–30 called *Merry Company*. She is richly attired in lace and silk, a costume completely inappropriate for the labour of painting but one that suggests her wealth and place in society, while also advertising her skills as both a portraitist and a painter of genre scenes. Leyster was the first of only two women to gain entrance as a master to the Haarlem painters' guild during the seventeenth century. Although she experienced a great deal of success in her own lifetime, her works were hidden behind the names of male artists until her oeuvre began to be uncovered in the late nineteenth century.[1] The reclamation of Leyster's self-portrait—at times previously attributed to Frans Hals—and the fame it has gained through its frequent exhibition and publication has buoyed the ongoing project of researching and identifying women artists over the last century.

In seventeenth-century Sweden, noblewoman Amalia von Königsmarck (1663–1740) and her sister Aurora had the privileged social connections to train with leading painter David Klöcker Ehrenstrahl. Unlike professional painters such as Leyster, Königsmarck used her well-honed talents in painting as a so-called amateur artist primarily for social gain rather than for strictly professional artistic ambitions. Königsmarck was born in Germany but lived her formative and productive years as an artist in Sweden, where she and her sister were favourites at court. She painted self-portraits at a time when the genre was uncommon in Sweden. In her most ambitious self-portrait, *Allegory with Self-Portrait and Profile Portrait of Ulrika Eleonora the Elder* (cat. no. 122), the artist associates herself with the allegorical figure of Fame, who blows a trumpet both for queen Ulrika Eleonora and for the artist herself. A poet as well as a painter, Königsmarck demonstrated her knowledge of classical themes as part of her self-presentation as a learned, aristocratic artist.

In *The Artist's Painting-Room* (cat. no. 128) by Mary Ann Alabaster (1805–1880), the British artist sits with her back to the viewer, amid the tools of her trade, at the centre of a large, imaginary studio in Britain. Alabaster depicts herself surrounded by paintings from artists of broad international acclaim, including Jusepe de Ribera and Bartolomé Esteban, alongside which she insists her work should be placed. Around the room are also objects for study or for use as models in compositions. Alabaster gazes out at the viewer while painting, the canvas itself functioning as an advertisement for her work. Although her family did not want her to pursue a career in painting, Alabaster eventually succeeded in gaining permission; she trained with

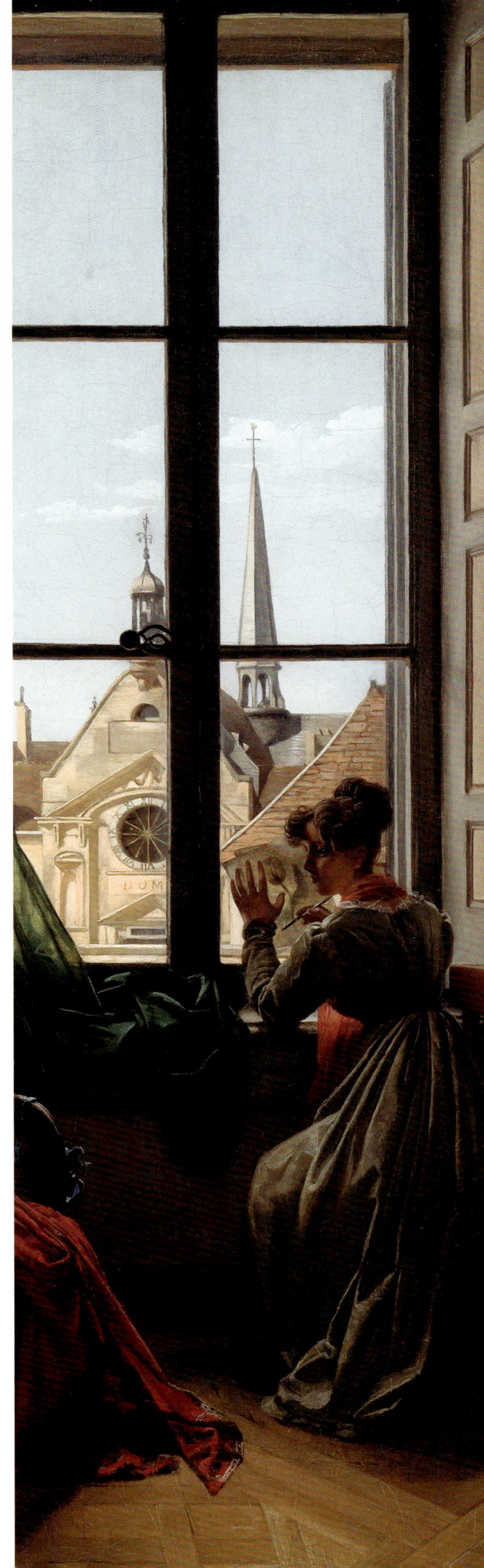

John Hayter, exhibiting and becoming a respected watercolourist later in her career.

Many women artists, both professional and amateur, learned their craft through education provided by male family members formally trained in their trade. It is interesting to note that Leyster, Königsmarck, and Alabaster each became painters despite their not being born into an artistic lineage. It may be tempting, therefore, to see in these three self-portraits a type of self-determination made explicit.

In addition to self-representation, women painters depicted other women at work. The choice of a women painter to highlight the work of other women—whether artistic activity or domestic labour—could be dictated by the commissioning client or by an insightful reading of the art market. Although she never exhibited publicly, Catherine Lusurier (c. 1753–1781), who received her training from her male cousin, was able to support herself and her unmarried sister through private commissions. While the identity of the sitter in *Portrait of a Woman Drawing* (cat. no. 124) is presently unknown, Lusurier presents her subject as an artist. A bust, likely used as a model for drawing, sits behind the woman as she holds her pencil and paper, seemingly ready to start sketching the viewer. For many years, this painting was attributed to Jean Siméon Chardin, but the removal of awkward nineteenth-century overpainting in the 1970s left the work without provenance. Research and comparison with the small, known oeuvre of Lusurier's work identified the hallmarks of her portraits—a delicate colour palette and outward, direct gaze of the sitter—allowing for its reattribution in 2021.

In *Interior with Young Woman Tracing a Flower* by Louise Adéone Drölling (1797–1831) (cat. no. 127), the subject is engaged in faithfully reproducing an image of a flower, an acceptable activity for both professional painters and women of an elevated social class who were not professionals. As explored by Virginia Treanor, Lara Yeager-Crasselt, and Catherine Powell-Warren in this volume, women artists and flowers have a long history—a cultural touch point embraced in this painting when it was exhibited in 1824 at the Salon de les Amies, where it won a gold medal.[2] Drölling, who was taught by her father alongside her older brother, painted a significant number of women engaged in the

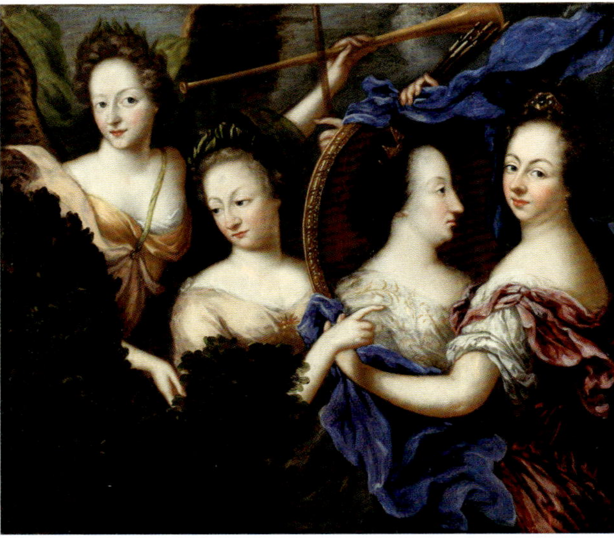

CAT. NO. 122
Amalia von Königsmarck
Allegory with Self-Portrait and Profile Portrait of Ulrika Eleonora the Elder
1689
Oil on canvas, mounted on panel covered with a secondary canvas
101 × 120 cm
Nationalmuseum, Stockholm, Purchase 2009 Hedda and N.D. Qvist Fund
NM 7060
Photo: Erik Cornelius / Nationalmuseum

task of drawing. The seated woman at the centre of the composition uses the light from the window to trace a flower onto a piece of paper against the glass. She is surrounded by objects—such as books, a lute, and a portfolio likely containing drawings—that suggest upper-class accomplishments appropriate for a young woman. Whether or not this is a self-portrait, as has been suggested by some scholars, the work encourages a consideration of the meaning of "amateur" in an era when few women had access to the avenues of training that would have allowed them to pursue art forms, such as oil painting, professionally. A number of Drölling's other paintings show women tracing at a window, and one even shows a woman watching or assisting another woman as she draws. Drölling's women participate in creative activities in a manner that hints at the artificiality of the dichotomy between professional and amateur during the time in which she was painting.

Like Drölling, Marguerite Gérard (1761–1837) exhibited at the Salon. She also took into consideration the state-sanctioned reductions, under Napoleon, in opportunities for women outside of the domestic sphere, focusing on interior domestic scenes as her subject matter of choice. Gérard was the sister-in-law, pupil, and sometimes collaborator of Jean-Honoré Fragonard and was mainly considered a passive member of his studio as result. She never married and thus was able to remain somewhat independent while living with her sister and brother-in-law. The decisions she made about selling her work through the experienced dealers Jean Dubois and Goury de Champgrand as well as capitalizing on her popularity through the creation of prints after her paintings suggest a blueprint for an artist forging her own path. Gérard painted scenes of domestic labour that were in line with the idealized image of women after the French Revolution. In *Motherhood* (cat. no. 125), a mother lovingly holds a healthy infant as a female servant blissfully observes the scene. In *Young Woman Embroidering* (cat. no. 126), the gender-appropriate domestic activity of needlework is highlighted in the hands of a fashionably attired woman. These are not necessarily portraits but rather are more likely depictions of the labour of women by women. They address societal expectations around women's labour at the time they were created, much like the paintings by Drölling or Lusurier, a smart subject matter for the artist to undertake and present to the art market. Gérard painted numerous depictions of women at work, some of which have been suggested to be portraits, while others have been tied to her interest in and reference to Dutch genre scenes of past centuries. Gérard's interiors reflect her own century and national audience, foregrounding her incredible skill in painting the fashionable silks worn by the women in her paintings.

By asserting their skill and education in painting through self-portraiture, or by painting other women in their gender-appropriate occupations, women artists used the conventions of their time and culture to depict work undertaken by women, actual or metaphorical. This subject matter made them worthy of display in public at Salons or in the homes of wealthy patrons. Self-promotion for the woman artist in a world of commissioning patrons and official institutions governing artistic merit—such as the French Salons or Académie Royale de Peinture et de Sculpture—was a vital element of success in the careers of several artists included in this exhibition. While artists often intended these works for an audience made up of family and close social contacts, they nonetheless employed various skills and promoted values that the sitter sought to possess.

Resources Consulted

Blumenfeld, Carole. *Marguerite Gérard: 1761–1837.* Montreuil: Gourcuff Gradenigo; Washington, DC: National Museum of Women in the Arts, 2019.

Borzello, Frances. *Seeing Ourselves: Women's Self-Portraits.* New York: Thames and Hudson, 1998.

Hofrichter, Frima Fox. *Judith Leyster, 1609–1660.* Washington, DC: National Gallery of Art, 2009.

Karlsson, Eva-Lena. "Self-Portrait as Pictura by Amalia von Königsmarck." *Art Bulletin of Nationalmuseum Stockholm* 23 (2016): 117–20.

Peacock, Martha Moffitt. "Mirrors of Skill and Renown: Women and Self-Fashioning in Early-Modern Dutch Art." *Mediaevistik* 28 (2015): 325–52.

Pomeroy, Jordana. *Royalists to Romantics: Women Artists from the Louvre, Versailles, and Other French National Collections.* London: Scala, 2012.

Rewald, Sabine. *Rooms with a View: The Open Window in the 19th Century.* New York: Metropolitan Museum of Art, 2011.

Notes

1. In some cases, this "uncovering" was quite literal, as in the discovery of her signature underneath a spurious Frans Hals signature on the Louvre's *Carousing Couple.*
2. See Treanor's essay "Women and the Art of Science" on pages 106–21, Yeager-Crasselt's text "Painting: Still Life" on pages 210–14, and Powell-Warren's text "Scientific and Natural Illustration" on pages 225–33 of this volume.

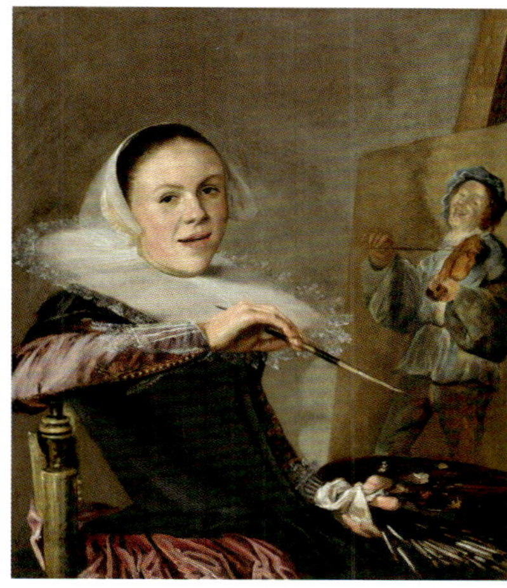

CAT. NO. 123
Judith Leyster
Self-Portrait
c. 1630
Oil on canvas
74.6 × 65.1 cm
National Gallery of Art, Washington,
Gift of Mr. and Mrs. Robert Woods Bliss
1949.6.1

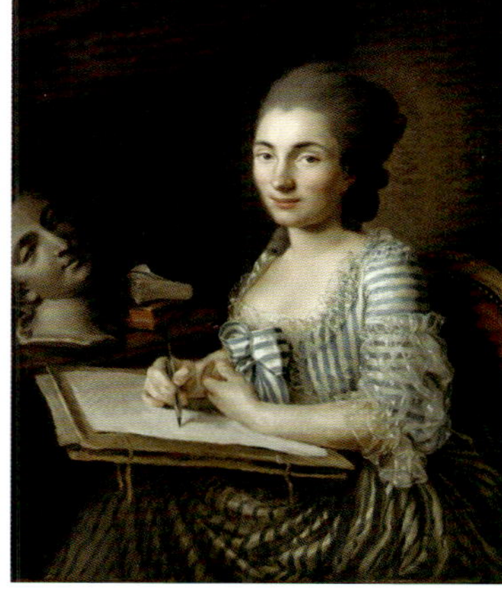

CAT. NO. 124
Attributed to Catherine Lusurier
Portrait of a Woman Drawing
c. 1770–1781
Oil on canvas
92.4 × 74.3 cm
Philadelphia Museum of Art:
John G. Johnson Collection, 1917
Cat. 780

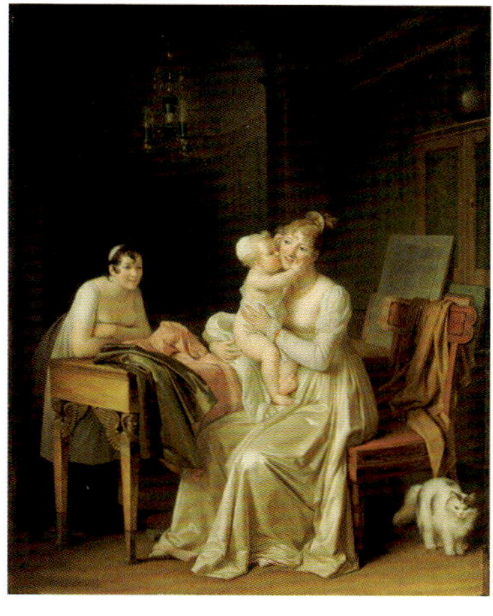

CAT. NO. 125
Marguerite Gérard
Motherhood
c. 1795–1800
Oil on wood panel
61 × 50.8 cm
Baltimore Museum of Art:
Bequest of Elise Agnus Daingerfield,
1944.102
Photo: Mitro Hood

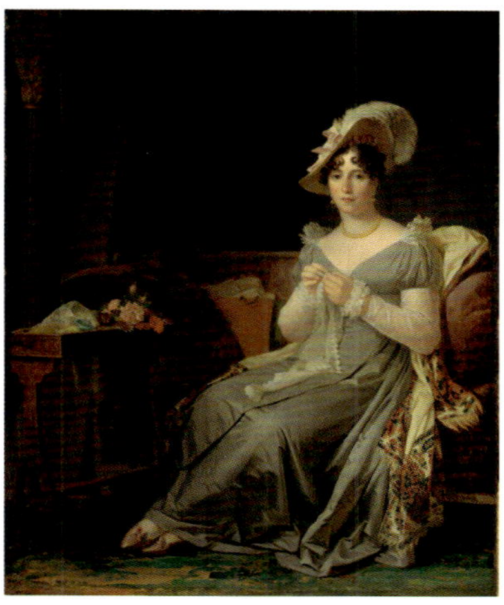

CAT. NO. 126
Marguerite Gérard
Young Woman Embroidering
c. 1815–1820
Oil on canvas
59.7 × 49.5 cm
Baltimore Museum of Art:
Bequest of Elise Agnus Daingerfield,
1944.104
Photo: Mitro Hood

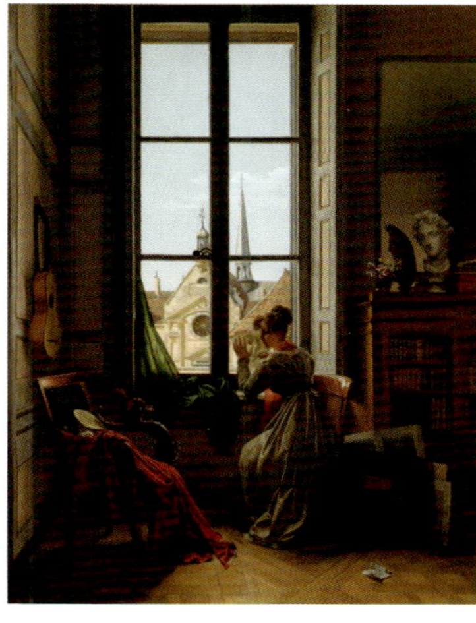

CAT. NO. 127
Louise Adéone Drölling
Interior with Young Woman Tracing a Flower
c. 1820–1822
Oil on canvas
56.5 × 45.4 cm
Saint Louis Art Museum,
Miss Lillie B. Randell by exchange
160:1946

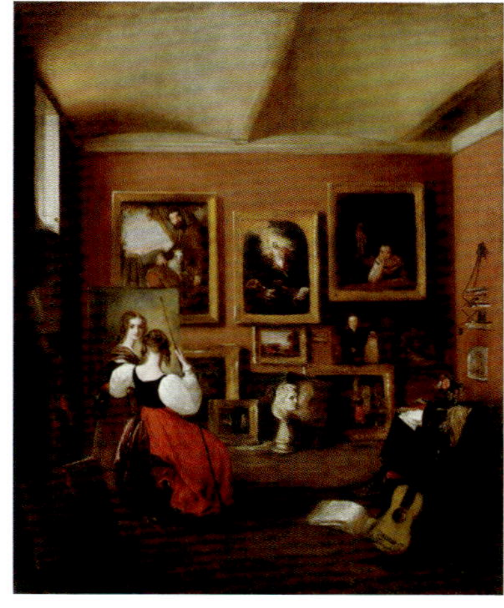

CAT. NO. 128
Mary Ann Alabaster
The Artist's Painting-Room
1830
Oil on canvas
84.5 × 70.4 cm
Art Gallery of Ontario, Gift of Morton Rapp
in memory of Hyman M. Smith, 2008
2008/24
Photo: AGO

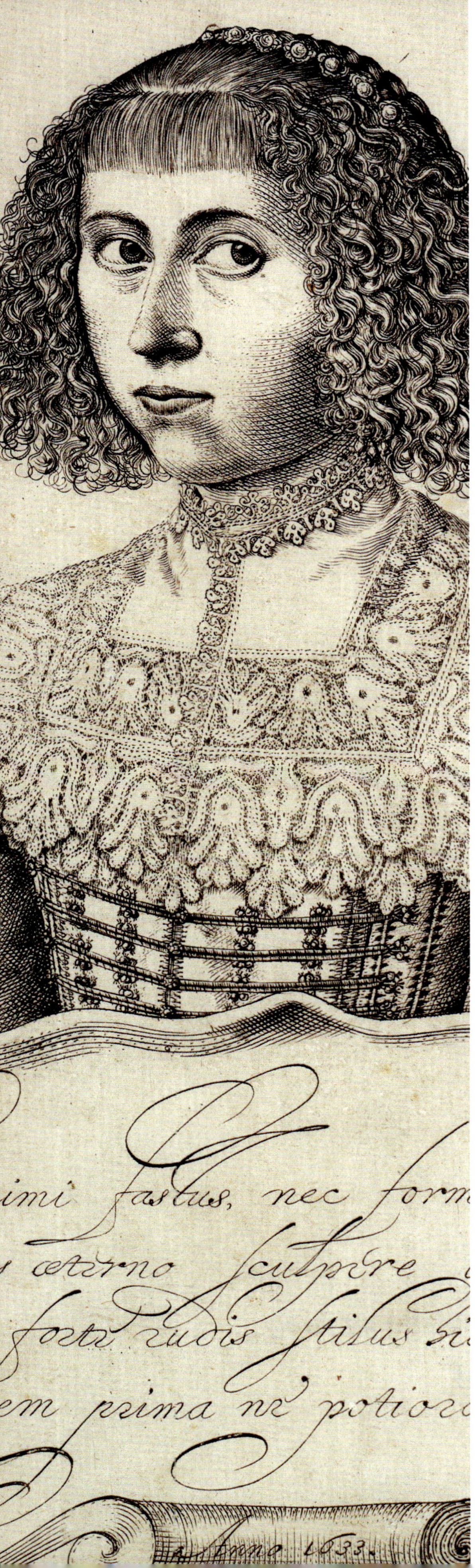

Prints

Madeleine C. Viljoen

The fifteenth-century discovery of a means to produce multiple, identical copies of printed works from a single matrix revolutionized how knowledge was circulated—marking what Francis Bacon would memorably describe as the advent of the modern age. Sold at marketplaces and by itinerant vendors throughout Europe, prints stood apart for being portable, copious, and accessible to consumers of diverse backgrounds and financial means. Aiming to satisfy consumers' wide-ranging tastes and interests, publishers and printmakers depended on a robust supply chain to offer works in a broad variety of subjects. It was consequently a field in which women found opportunities to engage, often in association with close relatives. Well-known female printmakers like Magdalena van de Passe (1600–1638) and Diana Mantuana (c. 1547–1612) were tutored to make prints by their fathers, who recognized the opportunities the medium presented for their daughters to contribute to their families' fortunes. As wives of well-known artists, architects, and designers, Mantuana and later Anne Allen (c. 1749/50–after 1808) (cat. no. 152) would also work closely with their spouses to produce prints after their designs. A large percentage of women simply reproduced the work of men with whom they were neither acquainted nor related, however, and a handful worked autonomously, reproducing designs of their own invention.

While women might be accustomed to hard and physical "male" labour, even implicitly advocating for their capacity to take on the sorts of roles that were traditionally assigned to men—as evidenced in engravings of a female miller (cat. no. 145) and of a young woman hauling a hefty load of wood (cat. no. 146) by Catherine Brandinn (active eighteenth century), for example—the work they undertook as printmakers was not particularly back-breaking in reality. Prized for their industry, fine-motor skills, and natural aptitude for plying small sharp instruments—qualities Geertruydt Roghman (1625–1657) (cat. nos. 141–143) extolls in her etchings of often solitary females engaged in domestic activities, including needlework—women were well suited to perform within the comfort of their own homes the role that was arguably most central to the entire print cycle: the incising of intricate designs into a plate or block.

Early modern women's role in creating copies after men may, from our current vantage point, seem demeaning, even positively disagreeable.

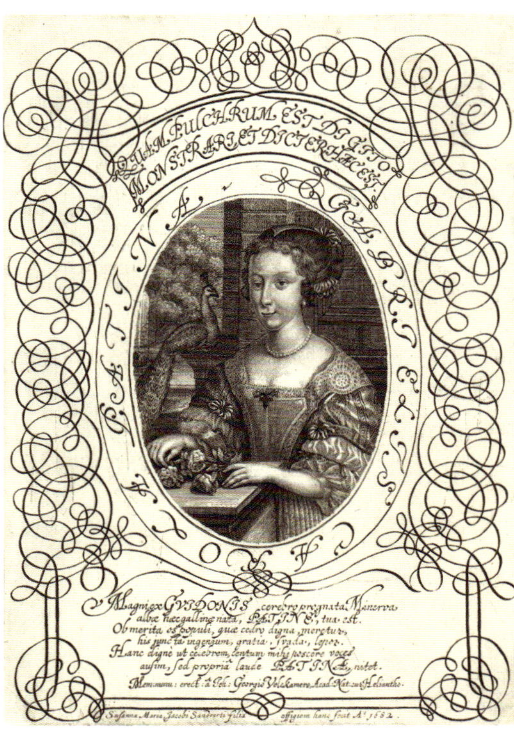

CAT. NO. 129
Susanne Maria von Sandrart
Gabrielle Charlotte Patin
1682
Engraving
24.2 × 17.7 cm
National Gallery of Art, Washington, Rosenwald Collection, 1950
1950.14.966

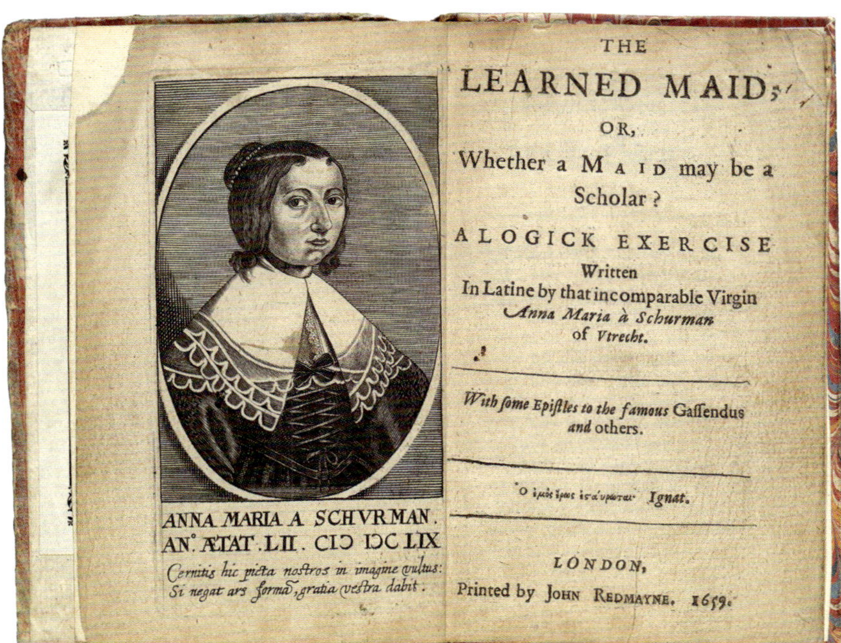
ANNA MARIA A SCHVRMAN.
AN. ÆTAT. LII. CIↃ IↃC LIX
Cernitis hic picta nostros in imagine vultus:
Si negat ars formã, gratia vestra dabit.

THE
LEARNED MAID;
OR,
Whether a MAID may be a
Scholar?
A LOGICK EXERCISE
Written
In Latine by that incomparable Virgin
Anna Maria à Schurman
of *Utrecht.*

With some Epistles to the famous Gassendus
and others.

Ὁ ἐμὸς ἔρως ἐσταύρωται. *Ignat.*

LONDON,
Printed by JOHN REDMAYNE, 1659.

CAT. NO. 130
Anna Maria van Schurman
The Learned Maid; or, Whether a Maid may be a Scholar?: A Logick Exercise
London, 1659
Bound printed volume
Closed: 13.9 × 9.4 × 0.5 cm;
open: 27.8 × 9.4 × 0.5 cm

Harvard University, Houghton Library,
Purchased with the Andrew Preston
Peabody fund, 1938
NC6.Sch867.Eg659b
Exhibited at BMA only

At a time when women had limited occasion to celebrate their accomplishments, however, female printmakers took pride in commemorating their roles in works that not only were widely shared but also informed the world of men. Known for exploring different methods to sign her prints, for example, Mantuana prominently inscribed her name on the grassy promontory on which the sculpture of *Amphion and Zethus Tying Dirce to a Wild Bull (The Farnese Bull)* rests (cat. no. 135). Bolder still, Geronima Cagnaccia Parasole (c. 1569–1622), wife of wood engraver Leonardo Parasole, relegates the identity of the inventor of the design for the *Battle of Lapiths and Centaurs* (cat. no. 131) to a crumpled strap attached to a shield at right, while giving her own name as the print's creator pride of place on a considerably more legible banderole at centre front.

The reproduction of works by male artists had the added virtue of giving women an unprecedented opportunity to be involved in the broadest possible range of printed subject matter. Ranging from conservative devotional prints, like *Virgin of the Immaculate Conception* (cat. no. 144) by Susanna Verbruggen (c. 1684/50–1752) and Mantuana's *The Savior Seated on a Heart* (cat. no. 134), to reproductions after some of the leading artists of the day, including Mantuana's *The Holy Family with St. Elizabeth and St. John* (cat. no. 133) after a composition by Raphael, the output of women printmakers is striking for the manifold opportunities it also provided for portraying the body. Ideals of feminine decorum may have impeded early modern women's access to the study of the nude model—it did not, however, prevent them from *reproducing* it. Indeed, even as loincloths were carefully draped over the offending members of countless well-known sculptures, a practice that was especially common during the Counter-Reformation, Mantuana's engraving after *Amphion and Zethus Tying Dirce to a Wild Bull (The Farnese Bull)* features Dirce naked from the waist up and one of the boys seen from the front completely unclothed. Just less than two centuries later, Maria Catharina Prestel (1747–1794) played a role in reproducing drawings in the cabinet of Paulus Praun, similarly leading her to portray a bare-breasted female personification of Truth subjugating a naked male figure of Envy (cat. no. 149), from whose genital area the menacing head of a phallic serpent surges.

The invention of etching in the early sixteenth century enabled painters for the first time to create their own prints. The innovation is of special consequence for women, for whom until this point the creation of prints had largely been tied to copying the works of men. From this point forward, female printmakers were able to use the medium not just to promote the achievements of men but to flaunt their own. Thanks in part to her success as an etcher, including a stylish portrait of Mary Magdalene (cat. no. 132), the painter-printmaker Anna Maria Vaiani (active 1627–died c. 1655) gained admittance to the prestigious Accademia di San Luca in Rome. Vaiani's career preceded the likes of Angelica Kauffmann (1741–1807), who, a little over a hundred years later, was a founding member of the Royal Academy of Arts in London, creating works after her own inventions, including *Johann Joachim Winckelmann* (cat. no. 148), a portrait of the renowned antiquarian. Like her contemporary Laura Piranesi (1754–1785), who produced views of some of Rome's most famous sights (cat. nos. 150 & 151) after compositions by her celebrated father, Kauffmann's images were favoured as souvenirs among travellers on the Grand Tour. For Kauffmann, the Academy offered useful avenues to promote her art and gain a measure of independence. Those less fortunate to receive this sort of recognition found themselves at a considerable disadvantage. Such was the experience of Marguerite Gérard (1761–1837), who was taught to etch in the household of her brother-in-law Jean-Honoré Fragonard, where she lived for approximately thirty years. Denied membership to the Académie Royale de Peinture et de Sculpture due to rules that limited the number of female artists to four at any one time, she found herself excluded from an important venue for public recognition and display. Without opportunities to present and market her skills, she consequently relied heavily on collaborations with Fragonard. Mostly genre scenes, her prints also included *The Genius of Franklin* [*Au Génie de Franklin*] (cat. no. 147), an over-the-top apotheosis of the popular American statesman that was designed to capture the hearts of French consumers.

Scholar and amateur Anna Maria van Schurman (1607–1678) would use the medium of print not just to advance her reputation as a scholar and intellectual but to convey a sense of her wide-ranging virtuosic talents. In addition to mastering fourteen languages and publishing well-regarded books on

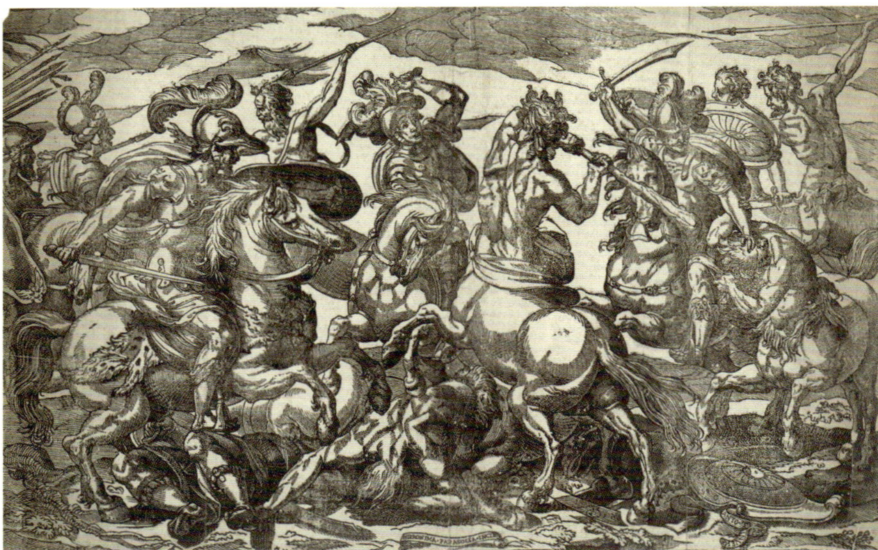

CAT. NO. 131 (left)
Geronima Cagnaccia Parasole, after Antonio Tempesta
Battle of Lapiths and Centaurs
c. 1600
Woodcut
42 × 68 cm
Samuel Putnam Avery Collection, Print Collection, Miriam and Ira D. Wallach Division of Art, Prints and Photographs, The New York Public Library, Astor, Lenox and Tildern Foundations
Grolier 356, Object number 112860

CAT. NO. 132 (below)
Anna Maria Vaiani
Saint Mary Magdalene, Half-Length
1627
Etching and engraving with plate tone
Plate: 18.5 × 14.1 cm; sheet: 19.9 × 15.5 cm
Philadelphia Museum of Art: The Muriel and Philip Berman Gift, acquired from the John S. Phillips bequest of 1876 to the Pennsylvania Academy of the Fine Arts, with funds contributed by Muriel and Philip Berman, gifts (by exchange) of Lisa Norris Elkins, Bryant W. Langston, Samuel S. White 3rd and Vera White, with additional funds contributed by John Howard McFadden, Jr., Thomas Skelton Harrison, and the Philip H. and A.S.W. Rosenbach Foundation, 1985
1985-52-14659

various topics—including the proto-feminist *The Learned Maid; or, Whether a Maid may be a Scholar?* (cat. no. 130), a work on women's learning that in 1659 was translated from Dutch into English—she painted, made elaborate paper cutworks of art, modelled works in wax, and etched on glass. To teach her the art of making prints, Anna Maria's father, Frederik van Schurman, engaged Magdalena van de Passe, a choice that may point to his recognition of the pioneering roles women could play in professions that were commonly associated with men. Van de Passe regularly reproduced compositions by her father, including the series *The Four Seasons* (cat. nos. 136–139), but she also collaborated with her brother on producing sixty-five heads of English scholars, making her an excellent choice to teach van Schurman, who used the medium exclusively for portraiture. Fearless about putting her work into circulation, van Schurman appears to be the first woman to create and share a single-sheet image of her own likeness (cat. no. 140), a gesture that at least one contemporary male scholar considered tantamount to harlotry. The extraordinary nature of van Schurman's print is thrown into relief by a portrait of Gabrielle Charlotte Patin (cat. no. 129). Like van Schurman, Patin excelled as a scholar and was singled out for the honour of receiving a doctorate by the University in Padua, a distinction that was uncommon to her sex. The portrait of Patin was commissioned by Johann Georg Volkamer—a doctor, botanist, and writer from Nuremberg, and friend of the family—who wished to mark her impending doctoral award with an engraving. Avoiding the pitfalls van Schurman experienced when she decided to etch and circulate her own likeness, the image is nevertheless distinctive for being executed by another woman, Susanne Maria von Sandrart (1658–1716), daughter of etcher and bookseller Jacob von Sandrart. Particularly striking, moreover, is the elaborate calligraphic inscription surrounding the portrait. Added to beautify the margins of the print and heap praise on its subject, the elaborate handwriting may also have been intended to draw attention to the gender-busting qualities of its sitter, in whose exceptional status the female printmaker von Sandrart participated by association. While a few women excelled at calligraphy and created prints advertising their expertise in this field, the skill was more commonly considered the work of men. The subject, its creator, and the calligraphic adornments of von Sandrart's print are fitting embodiments of the premise upon which women's involvement in the medium of prints was long predicated.

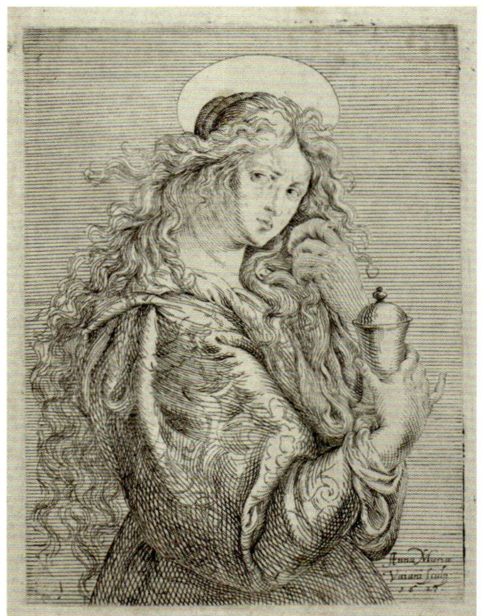

Women might lend a hand with making prints in male-led enterprises and even make prints on their own behalf, but their accomplishments would always be qualified by what it meant for a woman to participate in a forum that, by virtue of its public and peripatetic nature, was still largely regarded as one that belonged to men.

Resources Consulted

Lessmann, Sabina. "Susanna Maria von Sandrart: Women Artists in 17th-Century Nürnberg." *Woman's Art Journal* 14, no. 1 (1993): 10–14.

Lincoln, Evelyn. "Making a Good Impression: Diana Mantuana's Printmaking Career." *Renaissance Quarterly* 50, no. 4 (1997): 1101–47.

Markey, Lia. "The Female Printmaker and the Culture of the Reproductive Print Workshop." In *Paper Museums: The Reproductive Print in Europe, 1500–1800*. Edited by Rebecca Zorach and Elizabeth Rodini, 51–75. Chicago: University of Chicago Press, 2005.

Peacock, Martha Moffitt. "Geertruydt Roghman and the Female Perspective in 17th-Century Dutch Genre Imagery." *Woman's Art Journal* 14, no. 2 (1993): 3–10.

Viljoen, Madeleine C. "Show-Offs: Women's Self-Portrait Prints, c. 1700." In *Female Printmakers, Printsellers and Print Publishers in the Eighteenth Century: The Imprint of Women, c. 1700–1830*. Edited by Cristina S. Martinez and Cynthia E. Roman, 3–16. Cambridge: Cambridge University Press, 2023.

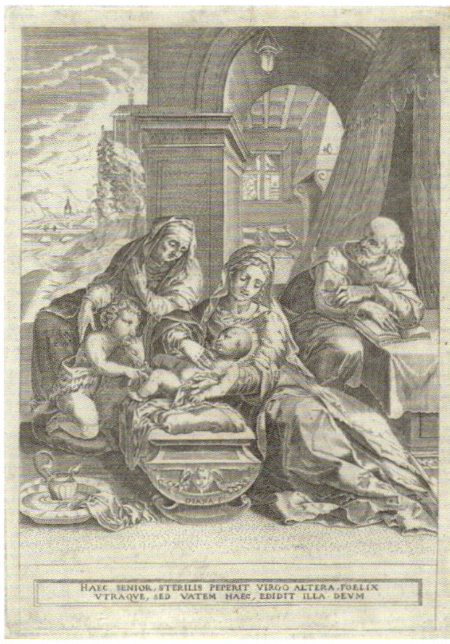

CAT. NO. 133
Diana Mantuana
The Holy Family with St. Elizabeth and St. John
1570s
Engraving
26.7 × 18.7 cm
Baltimore Museum of Art: Garrett Collection, 1946.112.4637
Photo: Mitro Hood

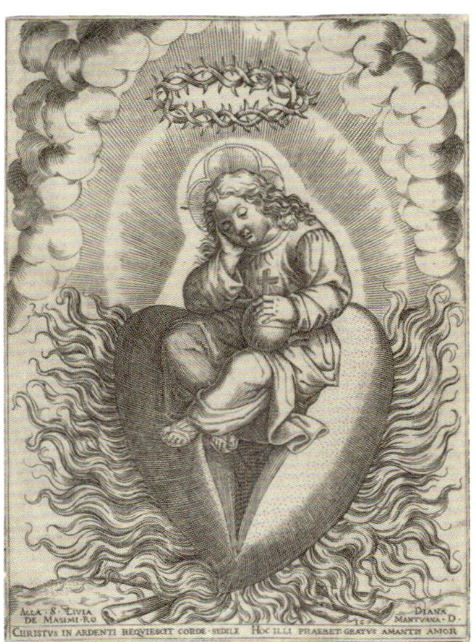

CAT. NO. 134
Diana Mantuana
The Savior Seated on a Heart
1577
Engraving
18.5 × 13.8 cm
Baltimore Museum of Art: Garrett Collection, 1946.112.4636
Photo: Mitro Hood

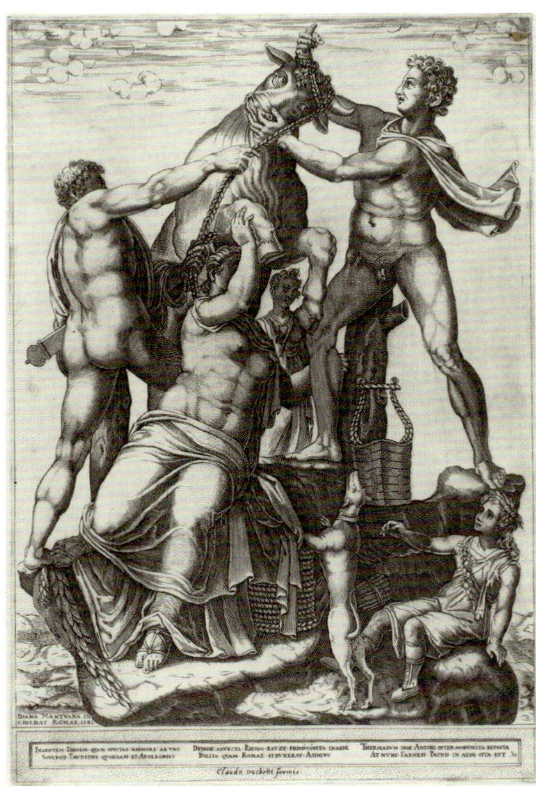

CAT. NO. 135
Diana Mantuana
Amphion and Zethus Tying Dirce to a Wild Bull (The Farnese Bull)
1581
Engraving with plate tone
Plate: 39.5 × 27.2 cm;
sheet: 46.1 × 34.2 cm
Philadelphia Museum of Art: The Muriel and Philip Berman Gift, acquired from the John S. Phillips bequest of 1876 to the Pennsylvania Academy of the Fine Arts, with funds contributed by Muriel and Philip Berman, gifts (by exchange) of Lisa Norris Elkins, Bryant W. Langston, Samuel S. White 3rd and Vera White, with additional funds contributed by John Howard McFadden, Jr., Thomas Skelton Harrison, and the Philip H. and A.S.W. Rosenbach Foundation, 1985
1985-52-32541

CAT. NO. 136
Magdalena van de Passe
Spring
from the series *The Four Seasons*
c. 1614–1634
Engraving
23.3 × 16 cm
Collection of Lisa Unger Baskin
Photo: Stephen Petegorsky

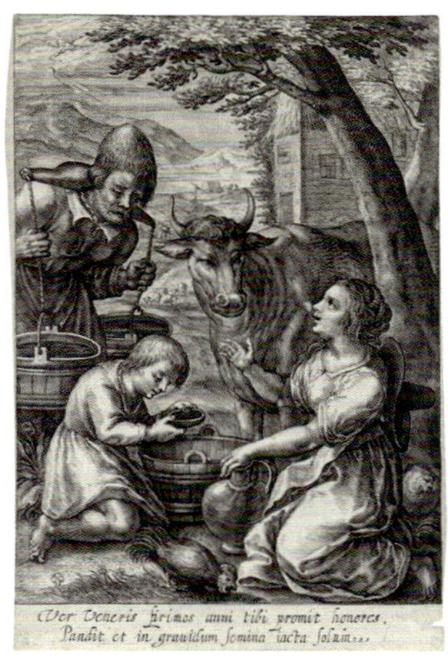

CAT. NO. 137
Magdalena van de Passe
Summer
from the series *The Four Seasons*
c. 1614–1634
Engraving
23.3 × 16 cm
Collection of Lisa Unger Baskin
Photo: Stephen Petegorsky

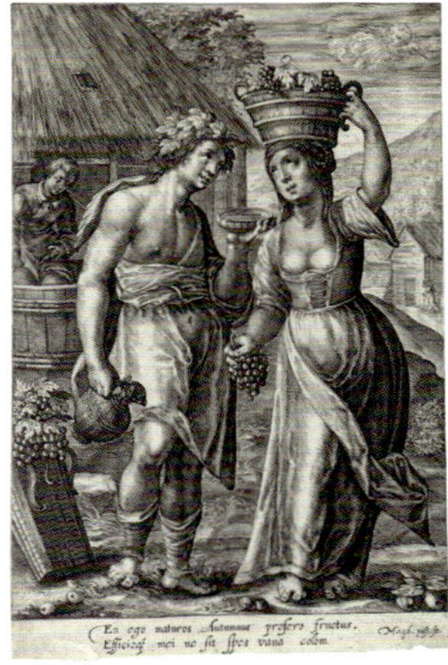

CAT. NO. 138
Magdalena van de Passe
Autumn
from the series *The Four Seasons*
c. 1614–1634
Engraving
23 × 15.8 cm
Collection of Lisa Unger Baskin
Photo: Stephen Petegorsky

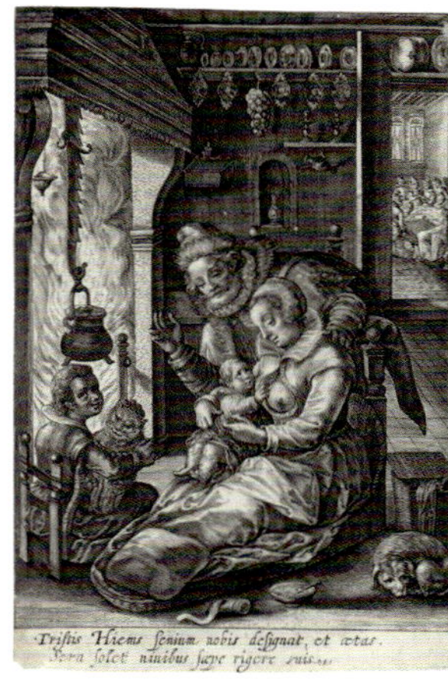

CAT. NO. 139
Magdalena van de Passe
Winter
from the series *The Four Seasons*
c. 1614–1634
Engraving
23 × 15.6 cm
Collection of Lisa Unger Baskin
Photo: Stephen Petegorsky

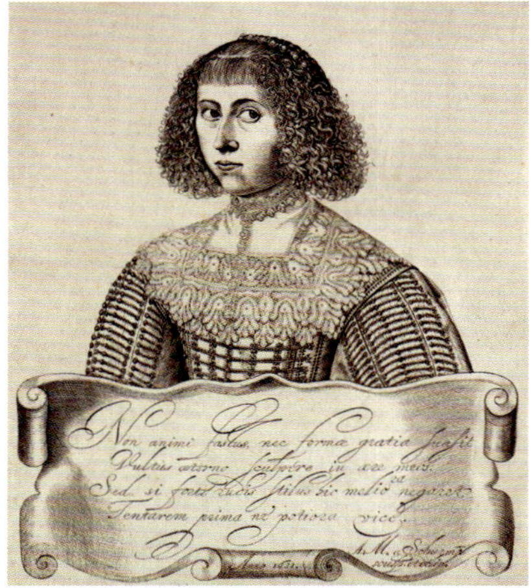

CAT. NO. 140
Anna Maria van Schurman
Self-Portrait
1633
Engraving
16.6 × 15 cm
Lent by Museum of Art, Rhode Island School of Design, Providence, Jesse Metcalf Fund
2002.30
Image courtesy of the RISD Museum, Providence, RI

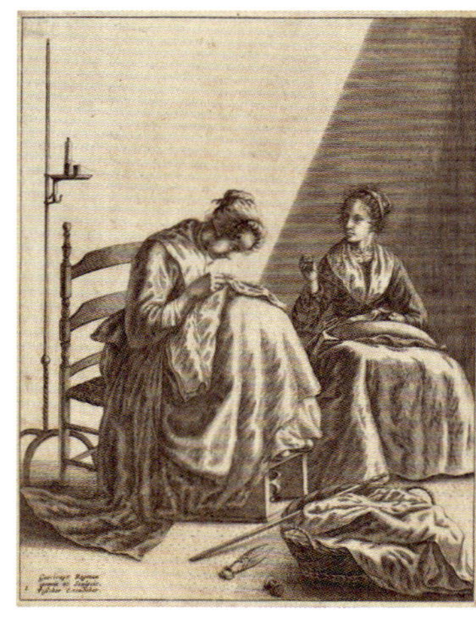

CAT. NO. 141
Geertruydt Roghman
The Dressmakers
from the series *Domestic Occupations*
1640–1647
Engraving
Sheet: 23 × 18.4 cm; plate: 21.2 × 16.8 cm
Baltimore Museum of Art: Garrett Collection, 1946.112.4349
Photo: Mitro Hood

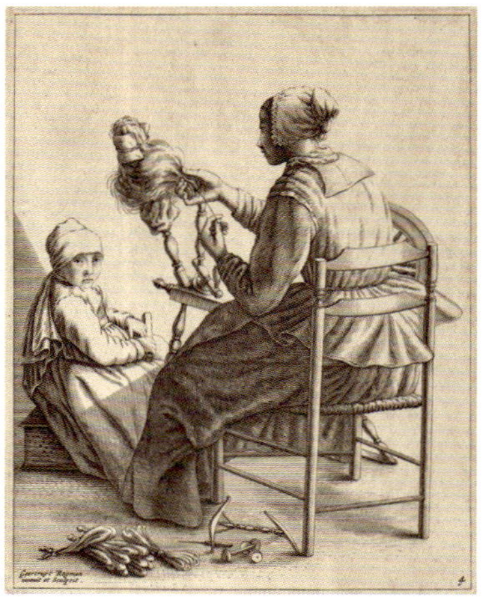

CAT. NO. 142
Geertruydt Roghman
Woman Spinning
from the series *Domestic Occupations*
1640–1647
Engraving
Sheet: 23 × 18.5 cm; plate: 21 × 16.8 cm
Baltimore Museum of Art: Garrett Collection, 1946.112.4352
Photo: Mitro Hood

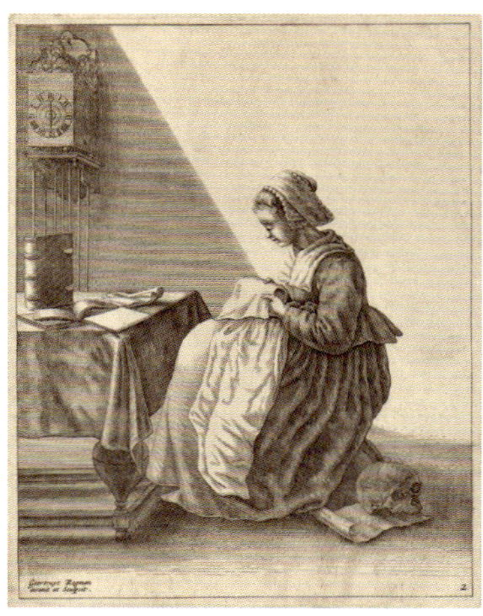

CAT. NO. 143
Geertruydt Roghman
Young Girl Sewing
from the series *Domestic Occupations*
1640–1647
Engraving
Sheet: 22 × 18.3 cm; plate: 20.6 × 16.8 cm
Baltimore Museum of Art: Garrett Collection, 1946.112.4350
Photo: Mitro Hood

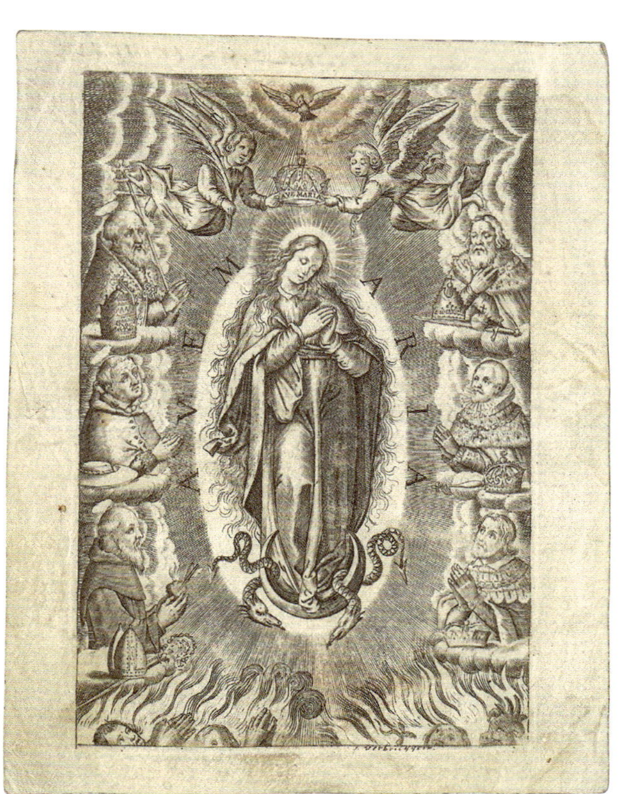

CAT. NO. 144
Susanna Verbruggen
Virgin of the Immaculate Conception
early 18th century
Engraving on vellum
Sheet: 11.8 × 9.6 cm; platemark: 10.6 × 7.3 cm
Special Collections, The Sheridan Libraries, Johns Hopkins University, Rare Books and Manuscripts, Women of the Book Collection, Bib# 9531660
Photo: Digitization Services Unit, Johns Hopkins University

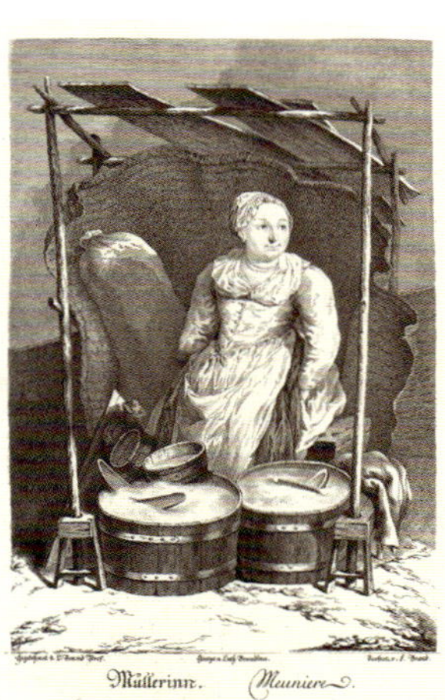

CAT. NO. 145
Catherine Brandinn
Miller [*Müllerinn*]
1775
Engraving
Plate: 36.2 × 25.2 cm; sheet: 47 × 34.4 cm
National Gallery of Art, Washington, Purchased as an Anonymous Gift, 2015
2015.16.13

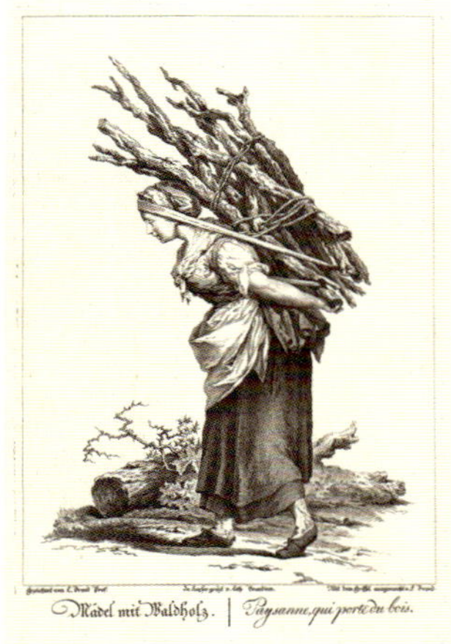

CAT. NO. 146
Catherine Brandinn
Peasant Girl Carrying Wood
[*Mädel mit Waldholz*]
1775
Engraving with etching on paper
Plate: 36.4 × 24.5 cm; sheet: 47 × 34.4 cm
National Gallery of Art, Washington, Purchased as an Anonymous Gift, 2015
2015.16.15

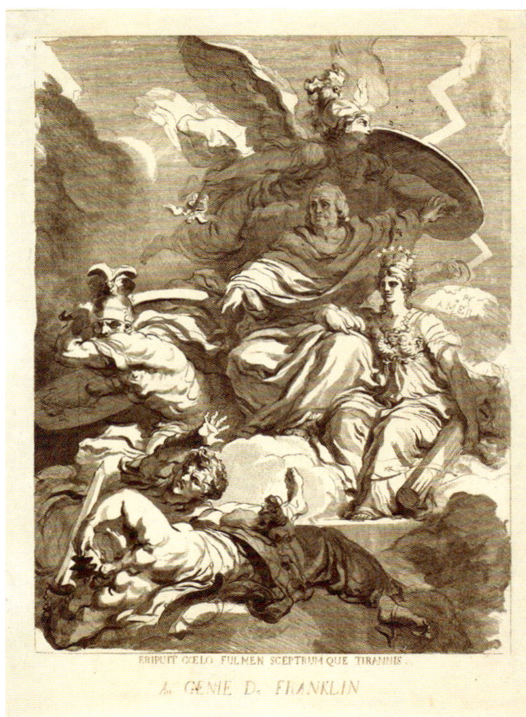

CAT. NO. 147
Marguerite Gérard, after Jean-Honoré Fragonard
The Genius of Franklin
[Au Génie de Franklin]
1778
Etching printed in brown
Image: 47.8 × 37.3 cm;
plate: 55.1 × 42.2 cm;
sheet: 62 × 44.5 cm
National Gallery of Art, Washington, Rosenwald Collection, 1964
1964.8.867

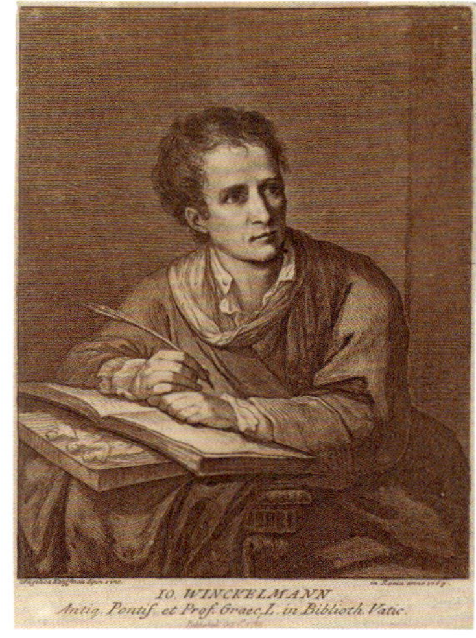

CAT. NO. 148
Angelica Kauffmann
Johann Joachim Winckelmann
1780
Etching and aquatint
Sheet (trimmed within platemark): 21.2 × 15.6 cm;
image: 19.3 × 15.4 cm
Baltimore Museum of Art: Garrett Collection, 1946.112.12358
Photo: Mitro Hood

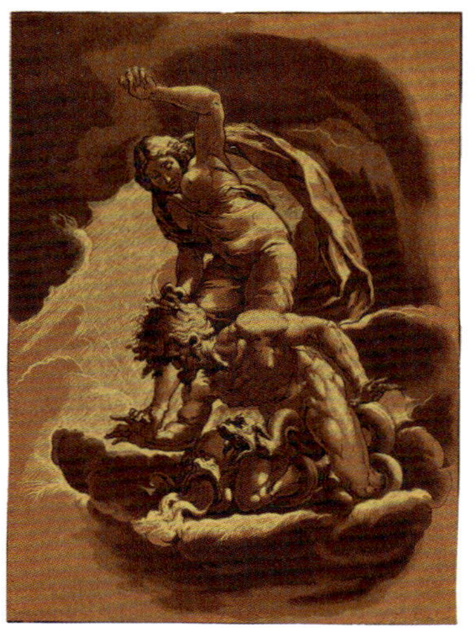

CAT. NO. 149
Maria Catharina Prestel, after Jacopo Ligozzi
Truth Subduing Envy
1781
Colour etching and aquatint
Sheet (trimmed within platemark): 30.7 × 22.8 cm
Baltimore Museum of Art: Garrett Collection, 1984.81.3742
Photo: Mitro Hood

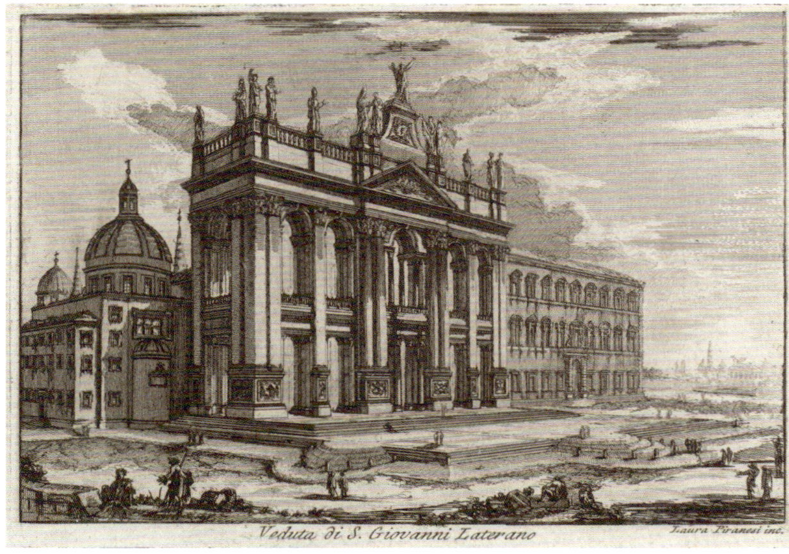

CAT. NO. 150
Laura Piranesi
View of San Giovanni Laterano
c. 1780s
Etching
Sheet: 16.6 × 23.3 cm; image: 13 × 20.1 cm;
plate: 13.9 × 20.5 cm
Baltimore Museum of Art: Purchase with exchange funds from Gift of Alfred R. and Henry G. Riggs, in Memory of General Lawrason Riggs, 2000.50
Photo: Mitro Hood

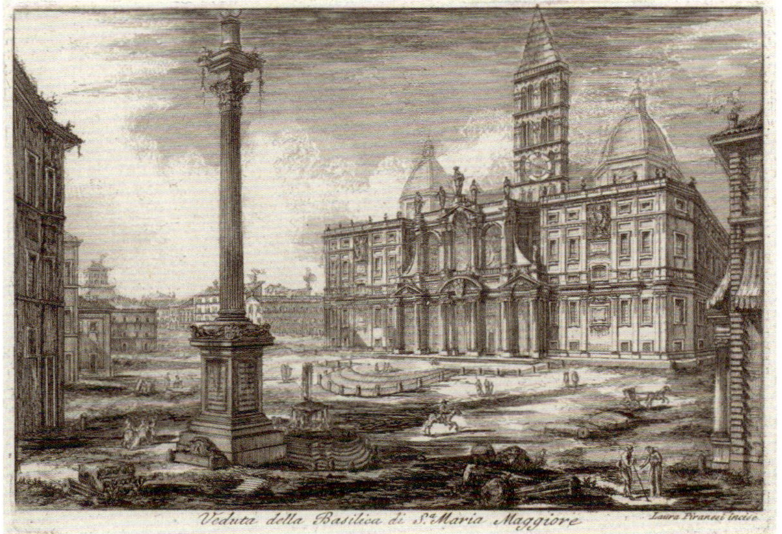

CAT. NO. 151
Laura Piranesi
View of the Basilica di Santa Maria Maggiore
c. 1780s
Etching
Sheet: 16.6 × 23.5 cm; image: 13.3 × 20.2 cm;
plate: 14.2 × 20.5 cm
Baltimore Museum of Art: Purchase with exchange funds from Gift of Alfred R. and Henry G. Riggs, in Memory of General Lawrason Riggs, 2000.51
Photo: Mitro Hood

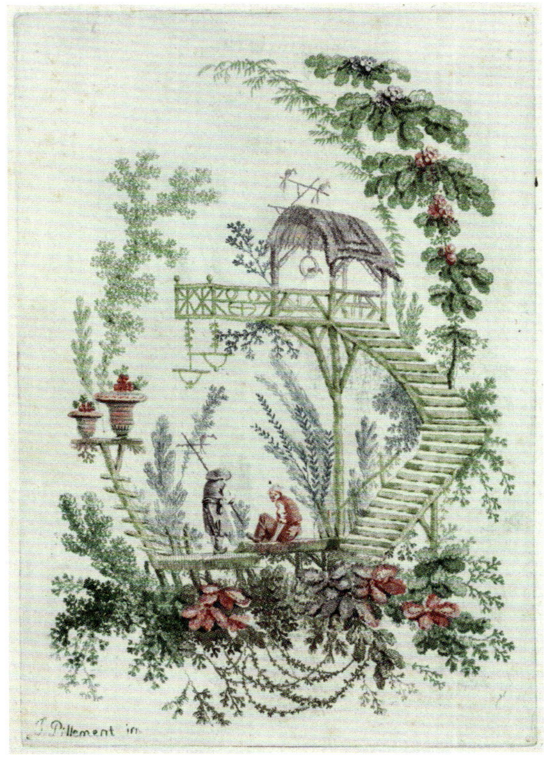

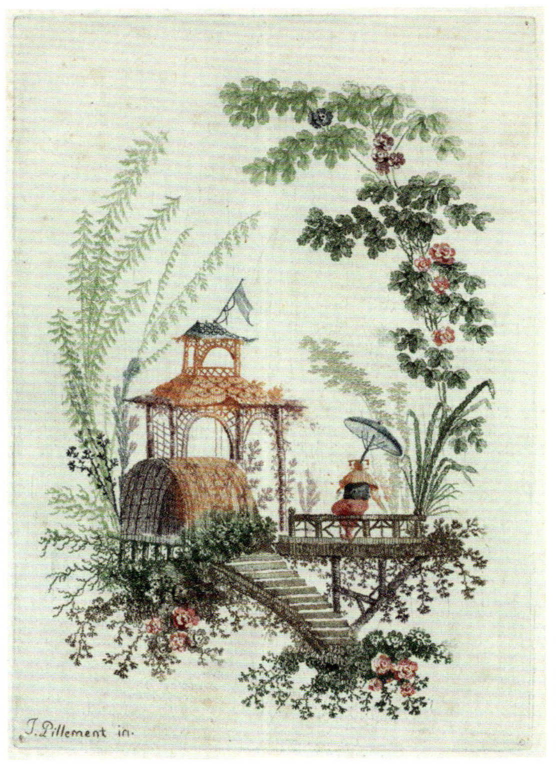

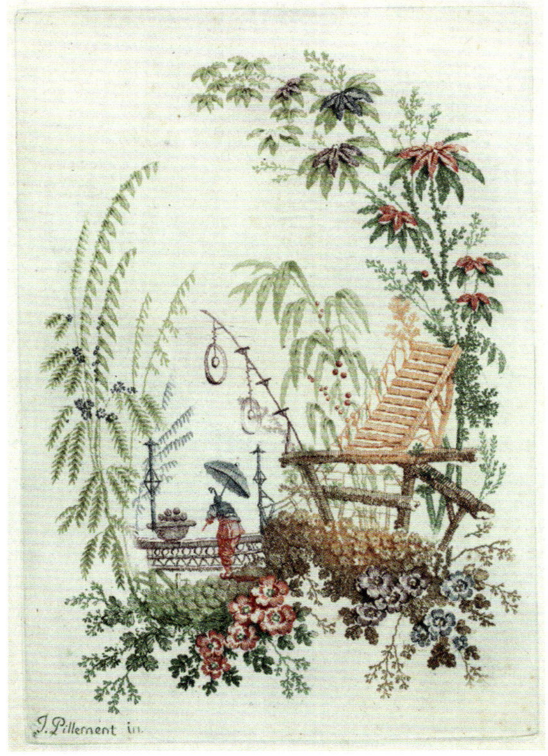

CAT. NOS. 152 A–C

Anne Allen, after Jean Pillement

Three plates from the series *New Suite of Notebooks of Chinese Designs for the Use of Designers and Painters*
c. 1796–1798
Colour etchings inked *à la poupée*
Sheet: 25.6 × 23.1 cm; plate: 19.5 × 13.8 cm each
Baltimore Museum of Art: Blanche Adler Memorial Fund, 2011.114.2, 2011.114.4, 2011.114.5
Photos: Mitro Hood

Scientific and Natural Illustration

Catherine Powell-Warren

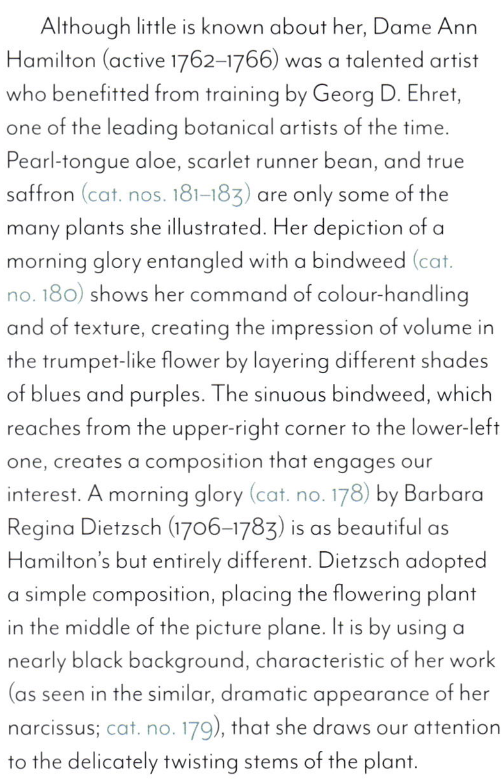

In 1956, Maurice H. Grant, the first modern biographer of the Dutch painter Rachel Ruysch (1664–1750), noted that women were particularly suited to flower painting, in no small part because "this delicate art, to repeat, would be thought to be peculiarly adapted to the feminine eye and paint-brush."[1] As Virginia Treanor points out in this volume, Grant was only repeating old tropes, though his mention of the feminine "paint-brush" is interesting.[2] Indeed, it is consistent with the prejudice that women artists should be limited, not only in relation to subject matter but also with respect to artistic medium. Again, this was nothing new. Some critics writing during Ruysch's time were already dismissive of women artists and of their depiction of nature, stating that fruits, flowers, animals, and insects, in particular, were simple subject matters that required little by way of training, technique, or even intellectual acumen to reproduce.[3]

Notwithstanding the condescension of these male commentators, it is evident that the women of this exhibition elevated the art of watercolour and gouache, and mastered artistic techniques and the use of scientific equipment. Indeed, their illustrations of nature are anything but simple or unchallenging. They are aesthetically complex and scientifically accurate works that demonstrate how women across Europe deployed their skills to illustrate nature to exacting standards, achieving the perfect fusion of art and science.

Although little is known about her, Dame Ann Hamilton (active 1762–1766) was a talented artist who benefitted from training by Georg D. Ehret, one of the leading botanical artists of the time. Pearl-tongue aloe, scarlet runner bean, and true saffron (cat. nos. 181–183) are only some of the many plants she illustrated. Her depiction of a morning glory entangled with a bindweed (cat. no. 180) shows her command of colour-handling and of texture, creating the impression of volume in the trumpet-like flower by layering different shades of blues and purples. The sinuous bindweed, which reaches from the upper-right corner to the lower-left one, creates a composition that engages our interest. A morning glory (cat. no. 178) by Barbara Regina Dietzsch (1706–1783) is as beautiful as Hamilton's but entirely different. Dietzsch adopted a simple composition, placing the flowering plant in the middle of the picture plane. It is by using a nearly black background, characteristic of her work (as seen in the similar, dramatic appearance of her narcissus; cat. no. 179), that she draws our attention to the delicately twisting stems of the plant.

Composition and the manipulation of colour also applied to the rendering of everyday fruits. In a drawing of peaches (cat. no. 175) by an artist in

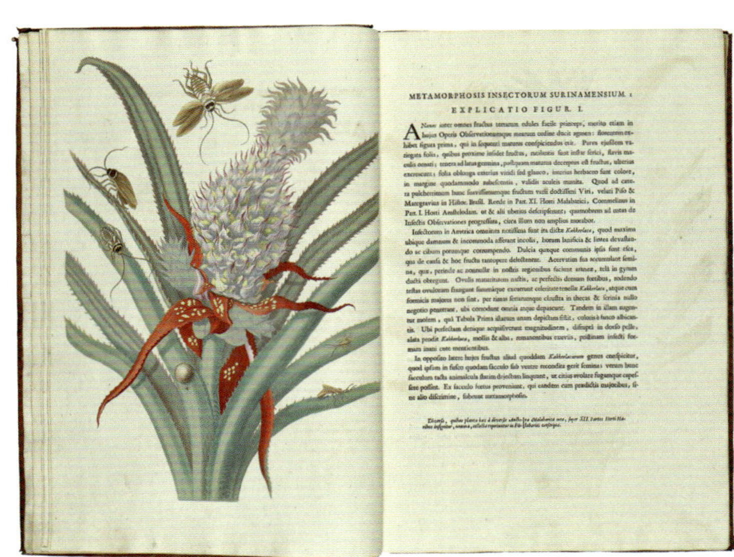

METAMORPHOSIS INSECTORUM SURINAMENSIUM.
EXPLICATIO FIGUR. I.

CAT. NO. 153
Maria Sibylla Merian
Dissertatio de Generatione et Metamorphosibus Insectorum Surinamensium... [Metamorphosis of the Insects of Suriname]
Amsterdam, 1719
Bound volume of hand-coloured engravings
54 × 38.1 × 4.8 cm
Oak Spring Garden Foundation, Upperville, Virginia

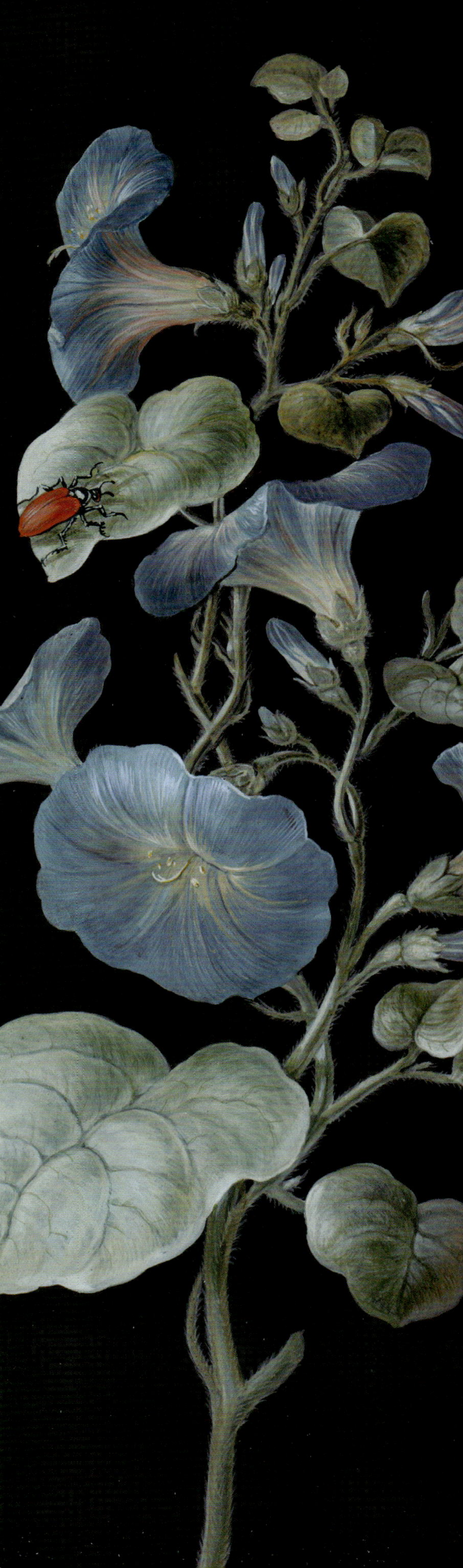

CAT. NO. 154
Elizabeth Pieth Schmitz
Botanical manuscript with 265 drawings of plants
c. 1687

Watercolour and opaque watercolour on paper
25.7 × 33 × 3.2 cm
Oak Spring Garden Foundation, Upperville, Virginia

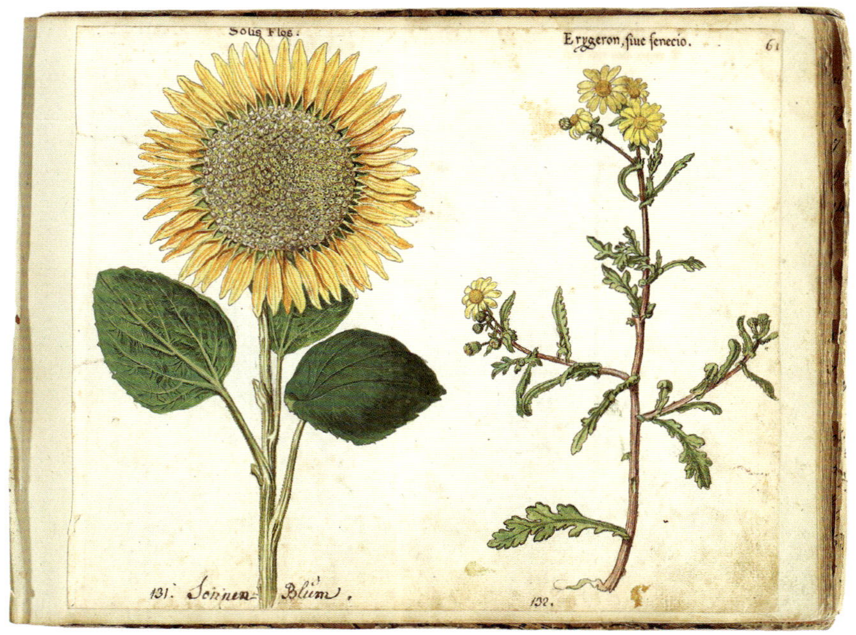

the circle of the French artist Madeleine Françoise Basseporte (1701–1780), which included female students, the fruits are made to appear juicy by dappling small dots of green, yellow, orange, and red watercolour over pencil. In another drawing, delicate irises (cat. no. 174), with their stems that extend beyond the drawn frame, seem to encourage the viewer to pick them up and examine them directly. The Italian Giovanna Garzoni (1600–1670), for her part, chose to play with the transparency of smooth, blended layers of watercolour to convey the ripeness of her peaches, figs, pears, and plums (cat. no. 155).

In the Dutch Republic, Alida Withoos (c. 1662–1730), Maria Moninckx (c. 1673–1757), and Johanna Helena Herolt-Graff (1668–c. 1723) similarly used watercolour to render plant specimens according to sophisticated aesthetic standards. Also noted by Treanor in this volume, all three women produced works for influential patron Agnes Block (1629–1704) and contributed to the so-called "Moninckx Atlas," a prestigious undertaking by the Amsterdam medical garden.[4] It was not a coincidence that Block made a note on the reverse of Moninckx's beautiful branch with star-shaped pink flowers: "Maria Monix faec," meaning "Maria Moninckx made this" (cat. no. 165). As a collector, she was proud of the authorship of the works in her possession. Withoos, Herolt-Graff, and Moninckx were trained by relatives. Nevertheless, their compositions are their own, and the artists were sought for their individual skills. Withoos's *Nasturtium* (or Indian cherry), with its fiery blooms, seems to hover just above the page (cat. no. 163). Herolt-Graff's *Three Mice Nibbling Fruit and Nuts* (cat. no. 166) borrows from a work made by her mother, Maria Sibylla Merian (1647–1717), but incorporates subtle variations that make the drawing her own. This was a common practice in the workshop Merian ran with her daughters. The butterflies Merian added to a drawing of a Datura by Willem de Heer (cat. no. 164), for example, reappear in other pieces by the workshop.

The watercolours in this exhibition were works of art in their own right. A striking blue and yellow macaw (cat. no. 189) by Sarah Stone (c. 1760–1844), for example, with its shaded, detailed plumage against a light cloudy sky, needed no explanation or context to delight. As is the case with the other artworks introduced above, however, nothing in the work's aesthetic quality takes away from its scientific value. Birds and fruits are easily recognizable. For botanical illustrations, the artists emphasized the essential characteristics of the plants, such as the shape and configuration of the leaves, and refrained from including any element that would detract from them, like shadows.[5] The specimens they depict, in addition to being beautifully rendered, are immediately identifiable.

Many women artists were highly knowledgeable in botany and had access to live specimens. Basseporte, for example, trained with Claude Aubriet, the official painter of the French king's garden.[6] While scientific academies in London and Paris restricted membership to men, the Accademia dei Lincei in Rome welcomed artists like Garzoni and Anna Maria Vaiani (active 1627–died c. 1655) into their circles. Vaiani maintained a correspondence with Galileo Galilei and excelled at botanical engravings, among other artforms, as can be seen in the hand-coloured print of a vase of flowers containing hyacinth, narcissuses, tulips, and carnations (cat. no. 158). Garzoni's illustrations of fruits and plants were informed by her knowledge of plant anatomy that she gained in part by consulting Frederico Cesi's *Syntaxis Plantaria* in Rome, which, incidentally, contains illustrations attributed to artists that include two women: Elisabetta (or Isabella) Catanea Parasole (c. 1570–c. 1620) and Maddalena Corvino (1607–1664).[7] In her *Piante varie* (cat. no. 156), Garzoni demonstrated this knowledge with fifty watercolours of plants that diligently record their unique flowers, leaves, and root balls, each labelled with the botanical name at the root of the plant as well as the species identified in the inscription.

Elizabeth Blackwell (1699–c. 1758) compiled her comprehensive *A Curious Herbal* (cat. no. 173) based on her own observations at the Chelsea Physic Garden and with the support of the Society of Apothecaries.[8] Her *Herbal* includes illustrations of seeds and roots to allow readers to readily identify the medicinal parts of common plants, such as the garden radish (cat. no. 169), wood strawberry (cat. no. 171), or peony (cat. no. 170), and more unusual ones, like the yellow asphodel (cat. no. 172), recommended as a diuretic. In compiling *A Curious Herbal*, Blackwell was following in the footsteps of women before her who studied and created remedies and illustrated plants to facilitate their identification and use. Thus, with her carefully illustrated compendium of plant anatomy (cat. no. 154), the German Elizabeth Pieth Schmitz (active c. 1650–1700) could have followed the recipes elaborated by the numerous German women who were recognized as skilful healers, and guided her contemporaries to do the same.[9]

Maria Sibylla Merian's work was similarly empirical. First published in 1679, her book on caterpillars, *Der Raupen wunderbare* (cat. no. 168),

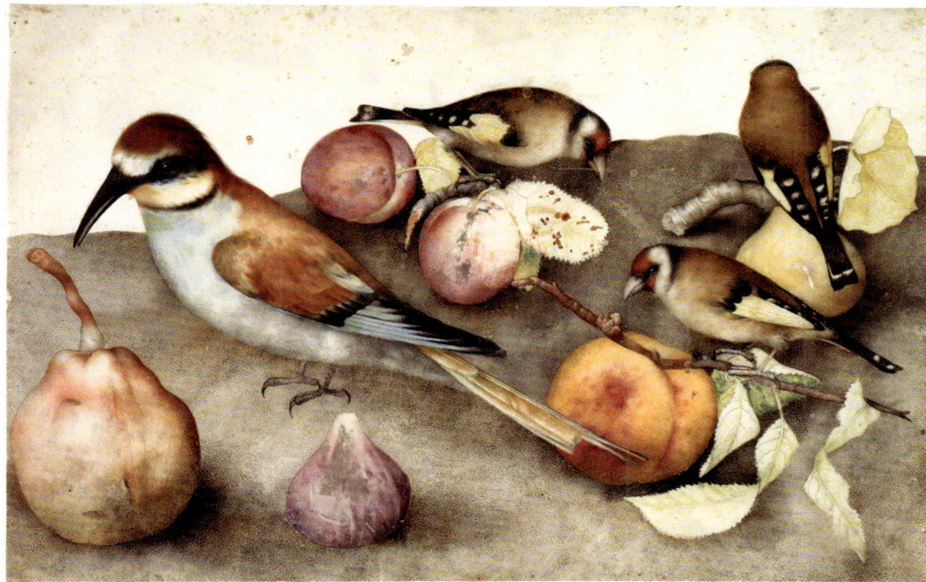

CAT. NO. 155
Giovanna Garzoni
Still Life with Birds and Fruit
c. 1650
Watercolour with graphite, heightened with lead white, on vellum
25.7 × 41.6 cm

The Cleveland Museum of Art, Bequest of Mrs. Elma M. Schniewind in memory of her parents, Mr. and Mrs. Frank Geib
1955.140

relied on her observations of specimens that she collected and nurtured. She taught her daughters, Johanna Helena and Dorothea Maria Merian Graff (1678–1743), how to collect specimens and preserve them, to prepare pigments, to draw, and to paint. The two-volume edition that is included in this exhibition is hand-coloured to appeal to collectors; later editions of the work were similarly overseen and coloured by Dorothea Maria. The *Dissertatio de Generatione et Metamorphosibus Insectorum Surinamensium* (cat. no. 153), the culmination of Maria Sibylla's and Dorothea Maria's trip to Suriname, was a work so monumental that the help of Johanna Helena was required to compile it. The women were organized as a typical artistic workshop and worked together for profit. Their art, which frequently combined the lifecycle of an insect with the plants it relied upon for feeding, was innovative and in great demand. An examination of the study plate for the caterpillar book (cat. no. 167), made on vellum, shows why their works would have appealed to the art collector as much as to the scientifically minded enthusiast. The detailed caterpillars and pupa, and the resulting moths, hovering around delicate morning glories in ethereal pink and cool blue, narrate a fascinating story.

Contrary to what Grant and critics before him implied, the illustration of nature clearly required a great deal of knowledge and intellectual effort, which the women included in this exhibition possessed in abundance. It also necessitated a thorough understanding of artistic techniques and scientific technology, and the ability to use them. In the book of bird etchings that she proudly signed, the Frenchwoman Marie Briot (active seventeenth century) (cat. no. 157), for example, used horizontal lines on the chest of the eagle and cross-hatching on the back of the partridge to create the impression of volume. Almost one hundred and fifty years later, in Rome, Magdalena Bouchard (active c. 1772–1793) was retained to etch plates for the *Hortus Romanus* (cat. nos. 185–188), a collection of eight hundred plates illustrating both European and non-European plants in eight volumes, of which only three hundred copies were printed. Bouchard's contemporary, Barbe Michel Adam Fessard (active c. 1750–1775), was recorded in the Paris archives as a *graveuse en taille-douce*, meaning that she was recognized as possessing the skills necessary for all techniques of printmaking on copper.[10] Philippe-Étienne Lafosse entrusted her to illustrate the minute details of horse anatomy in this treatise on the subject (cat. no. 176). He told his readers that he insisted on using the most exacting images, which caused him to incur "immense costs."[11] Lafosse knew that, without good illustrations, the usefulness of his treatise would be significantly diminished. This was an issue with which the author, translator, and scientist Marie-Geneviève-Charlotte Darlus Thiroux d'Arconville (1720–1805) was familiar, having herself advocated for the thorough and accurate illustration of anatomical treatises such as Alexander Monro's *Anatomy of the Human Bones* (cat. no. 177), which she translated into French.

Learning to manipulate burin and stylus was not all that early modern women achieved. The sisters Anna Lister (1671–1700) and Susanna Lister Knowler (c. 1670–1738), daughters of the naturalist and physician Martin Lister, mastered the technique of drawing with the aid of a microscope. Translating their three-dimensional perceptions into two-dimensional printed illustrations (cat. no. 184) was a complex process that required patience and exceptional powers of observation. While the sisters focused on the wonders of the seas, the German Maria Clara Eimmart (1676–1707) turned her gaze to the sky. At the age of seventeen, she began a series of three hundred and fifty tempera drawings (cat. nos. 159–162) of the phases of the moon, each based on her own observations with a telescope. Each drawing is annotated with the date of her observation, thereby creating a visual scientific record that could be relied upon by astronomers in the following centuries.

From the seventeenth to the nineteenth century, women were key participants in the creation of scientific visual knowledge. Their works fused together artistic sensibility with the sophistication of epistemic images. Throughout Europe, they were sought-after contributors and achieved renown, making their mark on one of the most significant sociocultural and scientific periods in history. Of course, all was not seriousness and business, as shown by the satirical artist Maria Boissier (active 1790s), who combined her knowledge of nature, artistic talents, and biting wit in a whimsical illustration (cat. no. 190) of the life cycle of an eighteenth-century historian, emerging from a Greek vase. A butterfly of exceptional rarity indeed!

Resources Consulted

Curry, Helen Anne, Nicholas Jardine, James Andrew Secord, and Emma C. Spary, eds. *Worlds of Natural History*. Cambridge: University of Cambridge, 2018.

Hunter, Lynette, and Sarah Hutton, eds. *Women, Science, and Medicine: Mothers and Sisters of the Royal Society, 1500–1899*. Stroud: Sutton, 1997.

Ogilvie, Brian. *The Science of Describing: Natural History in Renaissance Europe*. Chicago: University of Chicago Press, 2008.

Powell-Warren, Catherine. "A Strange Attraction: Women Artists and Patrons and the Creatures That No One Can Love." In *Crawly Creatures: Little Animals in Art and Science.* Edited by Jan de Hond, Eric Jorink, and Hans Mulder. Amsterdam: Rijksmuseum, 2022. Exhibition catalogue.

Schiebinger, Londa. *The Mind Has No Sex*. Cambridge, MA: Harvard University Press, 1996.

Notes

1 Maurice H. Grant, *Rachel Ruysch, 1664–1750* (Leigh-on-Sea, UK: F. Lewis, 1956), 19.

2 For Treanor's essay "Women and the Art of Science," see pages 106–21 of this volume.

3 See in particular the discussion of writings by Gerhard ter Brugghen and Willem Goeree in Alison M. Kettering, "Watercolor and Women: Between Mirror and Comb," *Woman's Art Journal* 42, no. 1 (Spring/Summer 2001): 28.

4 See Treanor, "Women and the Art of Science," 110.

5 Lorraine Daston, "Epistemic Images," in *Vision and Its Instruments: Art, Science, and Technology in Early Modern Europe*, ed. Alina Payne (University Park, PA: Penn State University Press, 2015), 20–25.

6 Mary Creed, "Madeline Francoise Basseporte's Hyacinths at the French Court," *Art Herstory*, September 9, 2021, artherstory.net/madeleine-francoise-basseportes-hyacinths-at-the-french-court/.

7 Sheila Barker, "The Universe of Giovanna Garzoni: Art, Mobility, and the Global Turn in the Geographical Imaginary," in *"The Immensity of the Universe" in the Art of Giovanna Garzoni*, exh. cat., ed. Sheila Barker (Florence: Gallerie degli Uffizi, 2020), 18–19.

8 Bruce Madge, "Elizabeth Blackwell: The Forgotten Herbalist?" *Health Information and Libraries Journal* 18, no. 3 (September 2001): 144–52.

9 Alisha Rankin, *Panaceia's Daughters: Noblewomen as Healers in Early Modern Germany* (Chicago: University of Chicago Press, 2013), 10–17.

10 Bibliothèque historique de la ville de Paris, Fonds général 4, Série 30 (III: Histoire générale, fin - Les Parisiens : généalogie, biographies et portraits de Parisiens), fol. 153. ccfr.bnf.fr/portailccfr/jsp/index_view_direct_anonymous.jsp?record=eadcgm:EADC:b1973565.

11 Philippe-Étienne LaFosse, *Cours d'hippiatrique, ou Traité complet de la médecine des chevaux* (Paris: EDME, 1772), x.

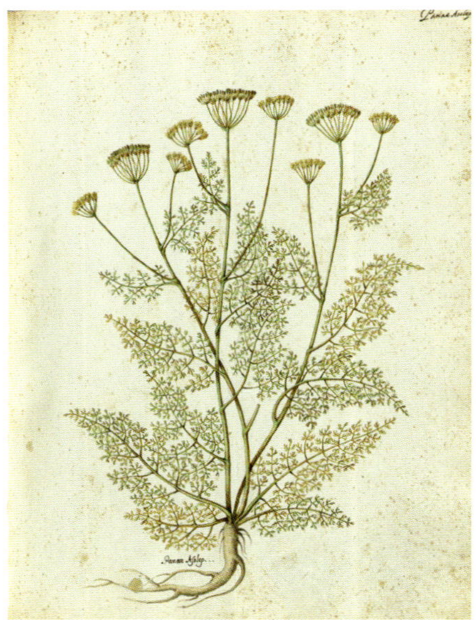

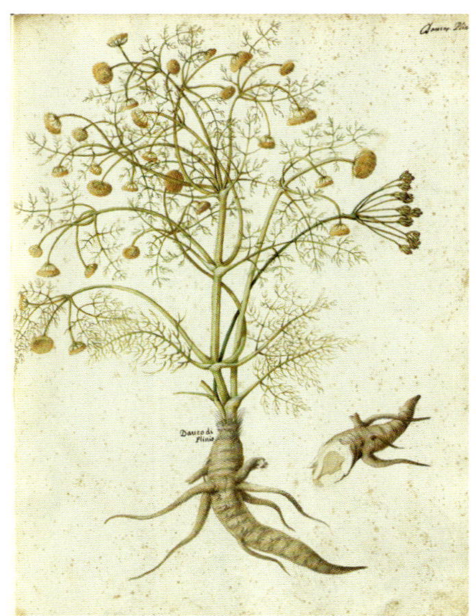

CAT. NO. 156
Giovanna Garzoni
Piante varie
c. 1630–1632
Watercolour on paper
49.5 × 38 cm
Dumbarton Oaks Research Library and Collection, Trustees for Harvard University, Washington, DC
G-3-3
Exhibited at BMA only

Openings illustrated: *Ferulago campestris* (folio 27) and *Ferula communis* (folio 29)

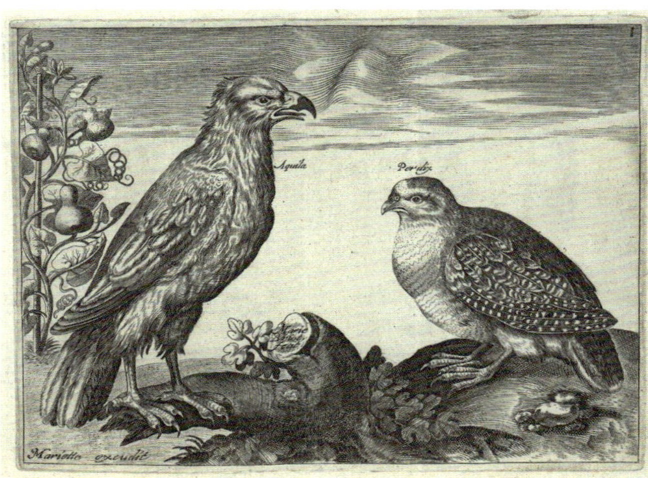

CAT. NO. 157
Marie Briot
Series of fifteen prints representing birds
[Suite de quinze estampes représentant des oiseaux]
Paris, c. 1630–1649
Bound volume of engravings
Plate marks: 13.2 × 19.2 cm or smaller
Lisa Unger Baskin Collection, David M. Rubenstein Rare Book & Manuscript Library, Duke University
NE650.B76 A75 1630 8vo c.1

Opening illustrated: *Eagle and Partridge [Aquila et Perdix]*

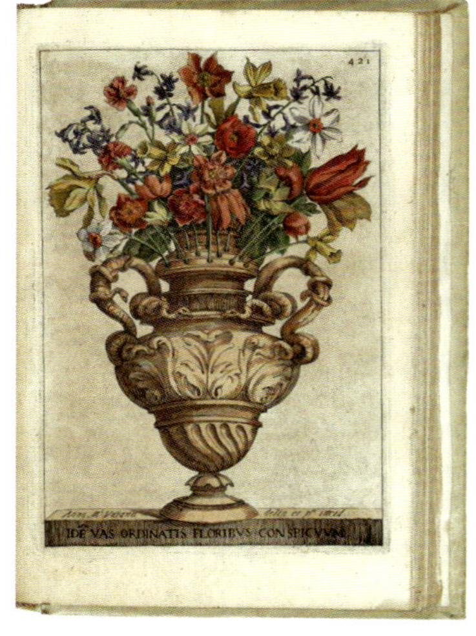

CAT. NO. 158
Anna Maria Vaiani
Vase of Flowers in Giovanni Battista Ferrari's *Flora overo cultura di fiori...*
Rome, 1638
Bound volume of hand-coloured engravings
24.4 × 18.4 × 4.8 cm
Oak Spring Garden Foundation, Upperville, Virginia

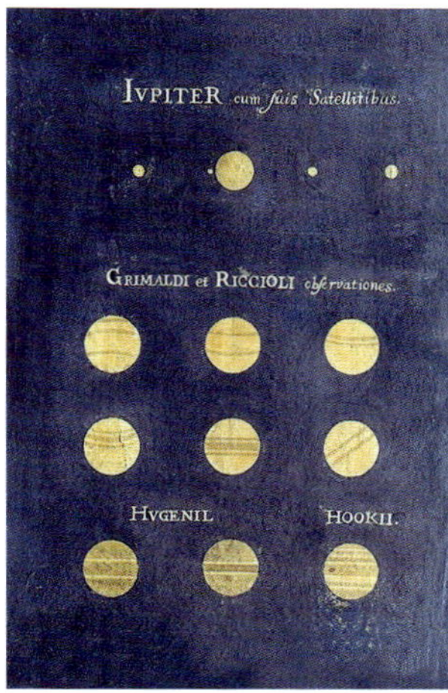

CAT. NO. 159
Maria Clara Eimmart
Aspects of Jupiter [*Jupiter cum fuis Satellitibus*]
from *Depictions of Celestial Phenomena*
1693–1698
Mixed media on paper
64 × 52 cm
Courtesy of Alma Mater Studiorum – Università di Bologna | Sistema Museala di Ateneo | Museo della Specola
Inv. MdS-124i
Photo: Marco Pintacorona

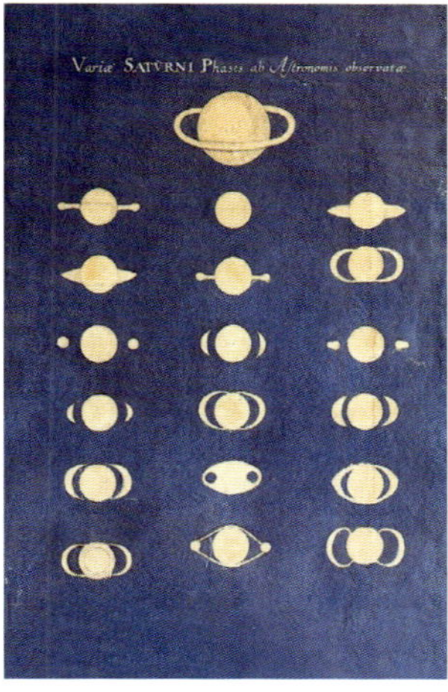

CAT. NO. 160
Maria Clara Eimmart
Aspects of Saturn [*Variae Saturni Phases ab Astronomis observatae*]
from *Depictions of Celestial Phenomena*
1693–1698
Mixed media on paper
64 × 52 cm
Courtesy of Alma Mater Studiorum – Università di Bologna | Sistema Museala di Ateneo | Museo della Specola
Inv. MdS-124l
Photo: Marco Pintacorona

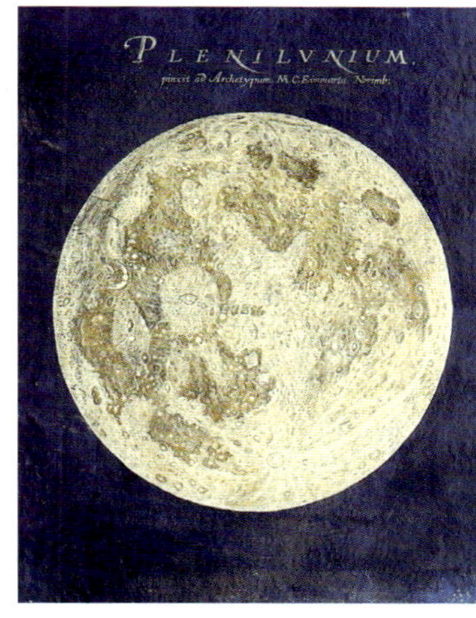

CAT. NO. 161
Maria Clara Eimmart
Full Moon [*Plenilunium*]
from *Depictions of Celestial Phenomena*
1693–1698
Mixed media on paper
64 × 52 cm
Courtesy of Alma Mater Studiorum – Università di Bologna | Sistema Museala di Ateneo | Museo della Specola
Inv. MdS-124c
Photo: Marco Pintacorona

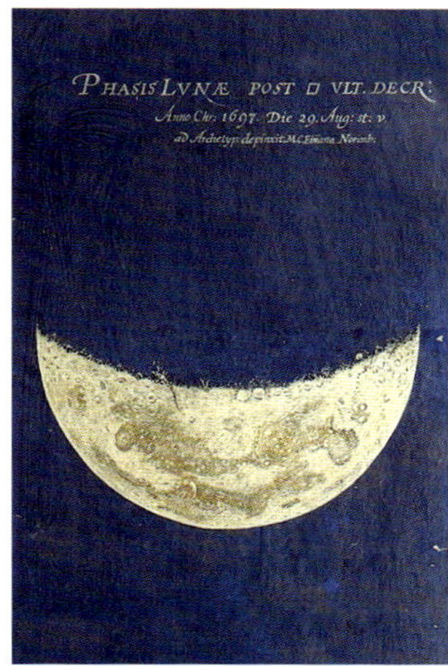

CAT. NO. 162
Maria Clara Eimmart
Lunar phases observed on 29 August 1697 [*Phasis Lunae post ult decr 29 August 1697*]
from *Depictions of Celestial Phenomena*
1693–1698
Mixed media on paper
64 × 52 cm
Courtesy of Alma Mater Studiorum – Università di Bologna | Sistema Museala di Ateneo | Museo della Specola
Inv. MdS-124e
Photo: Marco Pintacorona

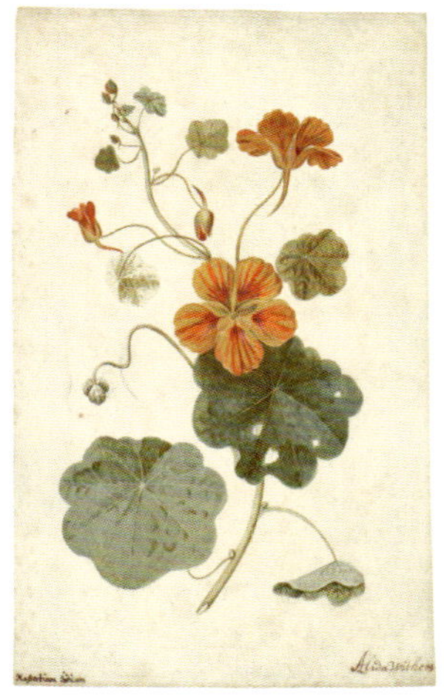

CAT. NO. 163
Alida Withoos
Nasturtium
c. 1675–1715
Watercolour and opaque watercolour over black chalk on paper
39.6 × 25 cm
The Morgan Library & Museum, New York, Bequest of Charles Ryskamp
2010.179
Photo: The Morgan Library & Museum, New York

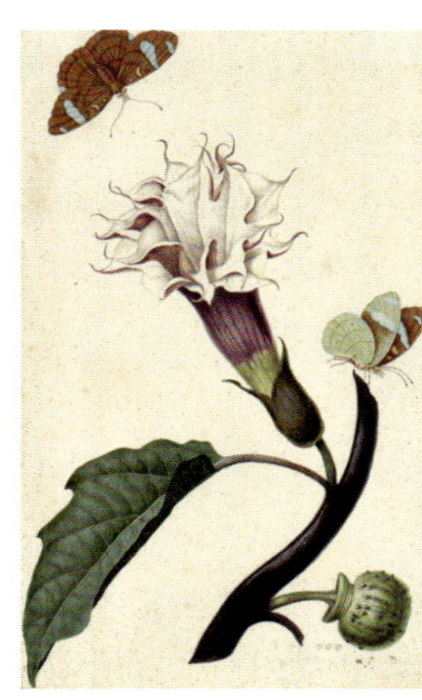

CAT. NO. 164
Maria Sibylla Merian and Willem de Heer
Datura with Butterflies
1679/1695
Watercolour and opaque watercolour, with traces of gum arabic, over graphite on paper
33.3 × 21 cm
The Morgan Library & Museum, New York, Bequest of Charles Ryskamp
2010.160
Photo: The Morgan Library & Museum, New York

CAT. NO. 165
Maria Moninckx
Study of a Plant with Red-Purple Flowers [*Sebastiana africana purpurea*]
1695
Opaque watercolour and watercolour over graphite on paper
35.8 × 24.7 cm
Lent by The Metropolitan Museum of Art, New York, Frits and Rita Markus Fund, 2013
2013.147

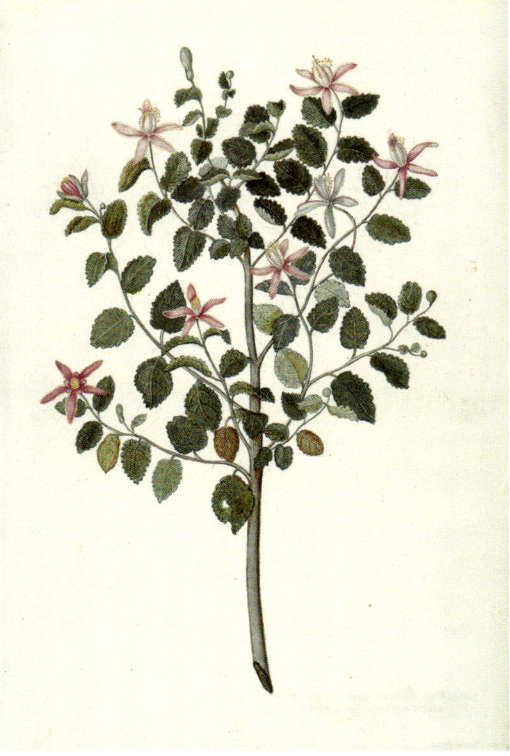

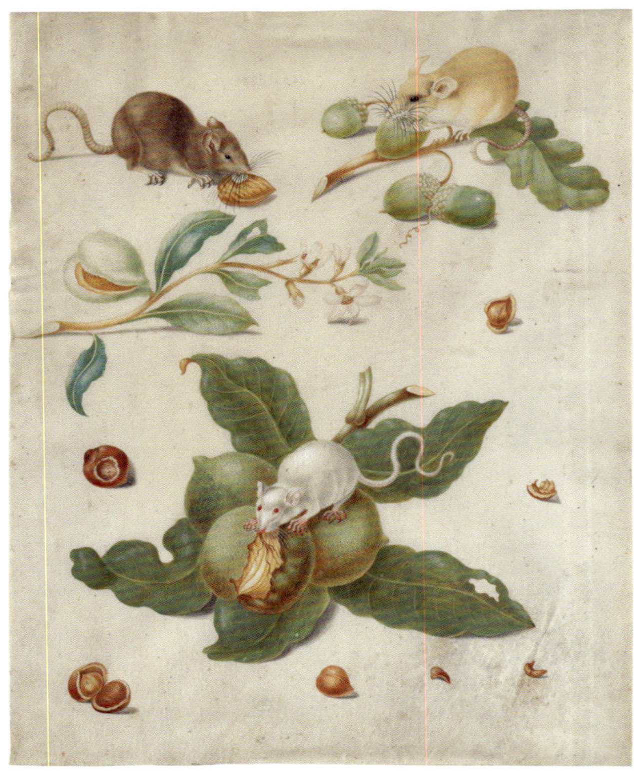

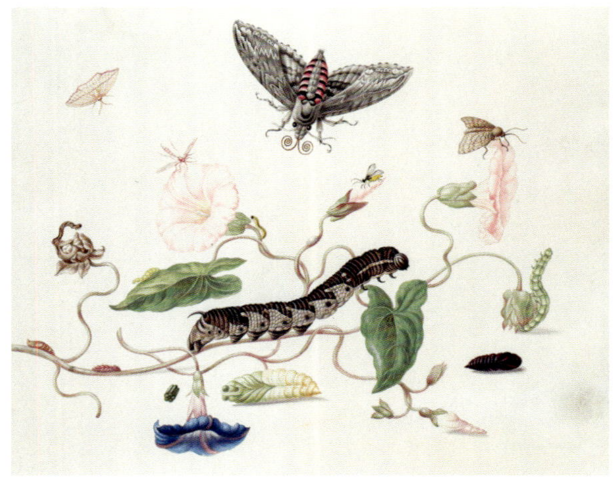

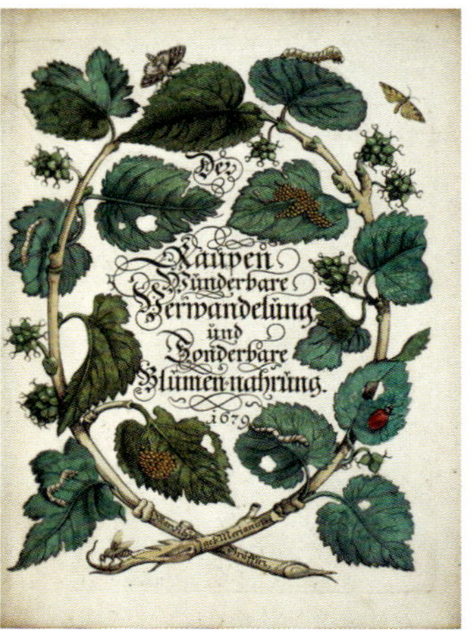

CAT. NO. 166 (left)
Attributed to Johanna Helena Herolt-Graff
Three Mice Nibbling Fruit and Nuts
c. 1690–1710
Watercolour and opaque watercolour on vellum
32.6 × 26.8 cm
The Morgan Library & Museum, New York, Purchased on the Fellows Fund, with the special assistance of Mrs. Carl Stern and Mrs. Lawrence Hughes
1979.37
Photo: The Morgan Library & Museum, New York

CAT. NO. 167 (middle)
Maria Sibylla Merian
Convolvulus and Metamorphosis of the Convolvulus Hawk Moth
c. 1670–1683
Watercolour with touches of opaque watercolour over black chalk or graphite on vellum
29 × 37.2 cm
The Cleveland Museum of Art, John L. Severance Fund
2019.9

CAT. NO. 168 (right)
Maria Sibylla Merian
Der Raupen wunderbare Verwandelung und sonderbare Blumen-Nahrung [The Wondrous Transformation of Caterpillars and their Curious Diet of Flowers]
Nuremberg, Frankfurt, and Leipzig, 1679–1683
Bound volume with hand-coloured engraved illustrations
20.6 × 17.1 × 4.1 cm
Oak Spring Garden Foundation, Upperville, Virginia
inv. RB1030

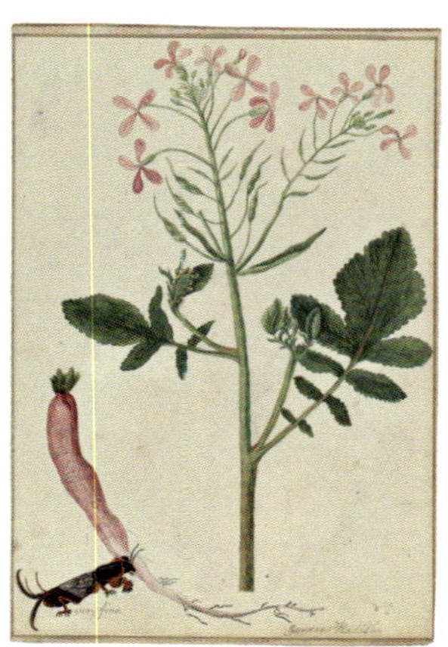

CAT. NO. 169
Elizabeth Blackwell
Garden Radish
c. 1737–1739
Watercolour on paper
28 × 20 cm
Oak Spring Garden Foundation, Upperville, Virginia

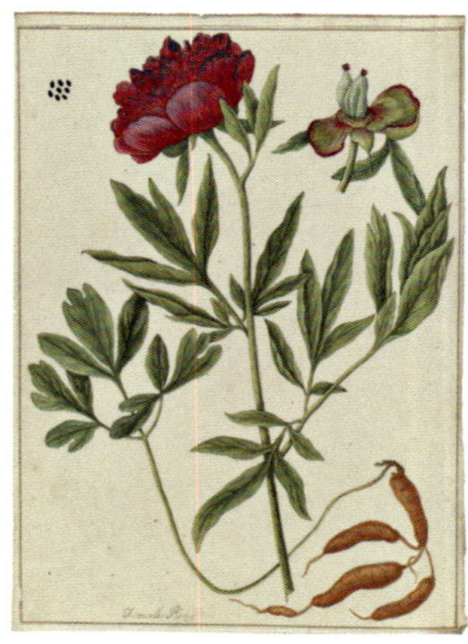

CAT. NO. 170
Elizabeth Blackwell
Peony
c. 1737–1739
Watercolour on paper
28 × 21 cm
Oak Spring Garden Foundation, Upperville, Virginia

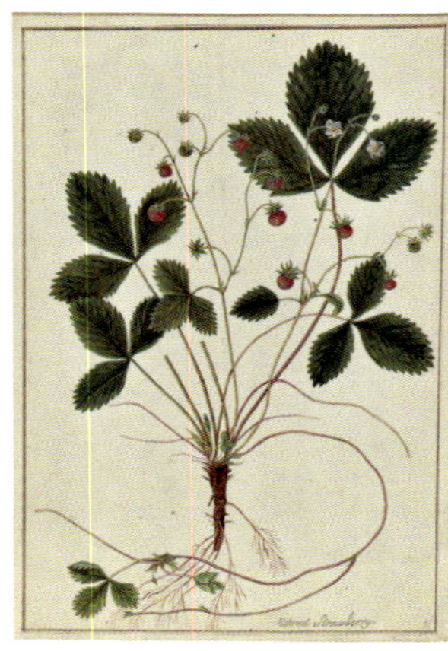

CAT. NO. 171
Elizabeth Blackwell
Wood Strawberry
c. 1737–1739
Watercolour on paper
28 × 20 cm
Oak Spring Garden Foundation, Upperville, Virginia

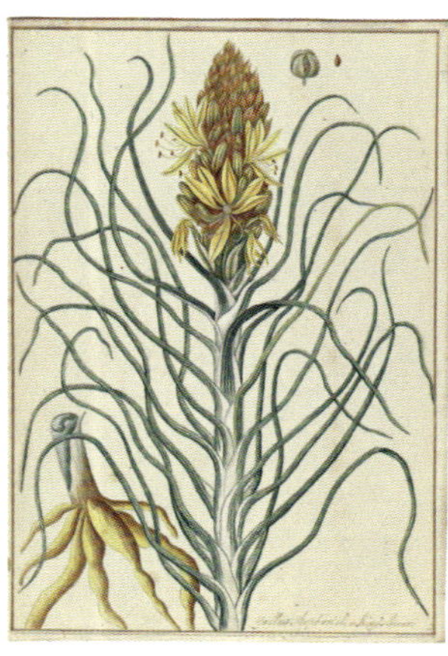

CAT. NO. 172
Elizabeth Blackwell
Yellow Asphodel
c. 1737–1739
Watercolour on paper
28 × 20 cm
Oak Spring Garden Foundation, Upperville, Virginia

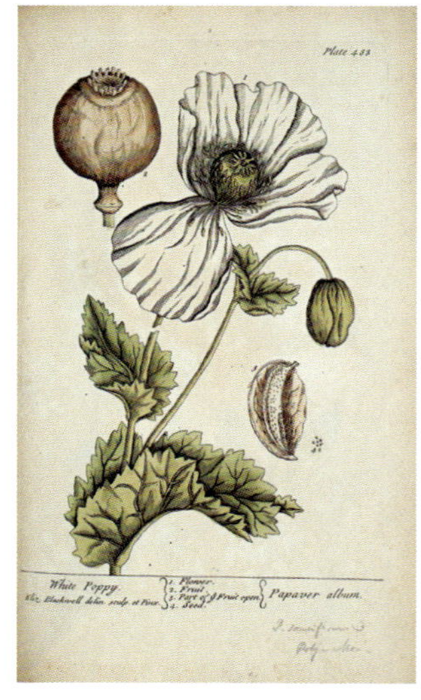

CAT. NO. 173
Elizabeth Blackwell
A Curious Herbal, Containing Five Hundred Cuts, of the most useful plants, which are now used in the practice of physick..., vol. 2
London, 1739
Printed bound volume of hand-coloured etchings and engravings
38.1 × 24.8 × 8.3 cm
Oak Spring Garden Foundation, Upperville, Virginia

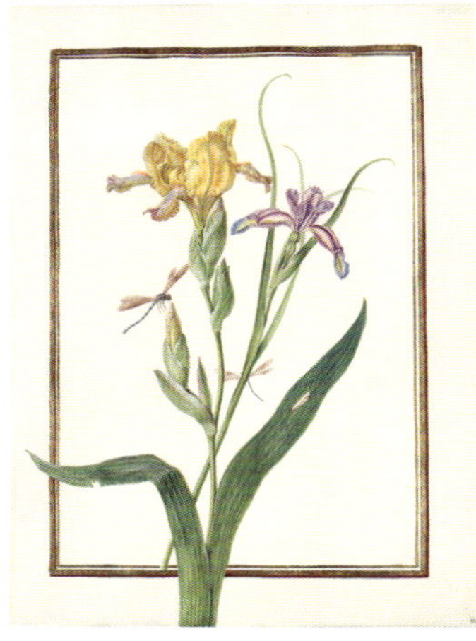

CAT. NO. 174
Circle of Madeleine Françoise Basseporte
Iris germanica (left). Iris xiphium (right).
c. 1750
Watercolour over pencil on vellum
40 × 31.1 cm
The Morgan Library & Museum, New York, Gift of Junius S. Morgan and Henry S. Morgan
1952.29:40
Photo: The Morgan Library & Museum, New York

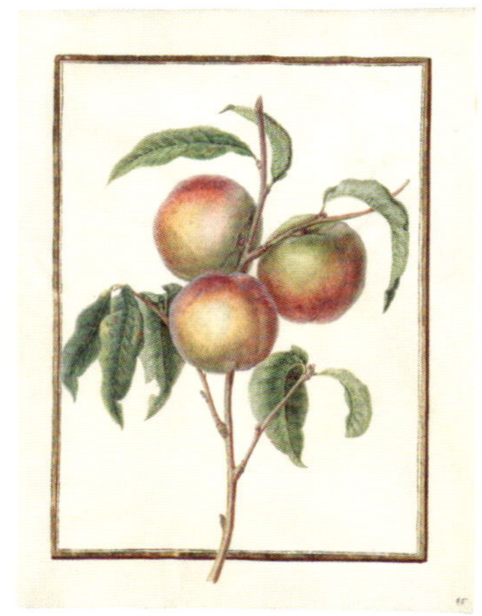

CAT. NO. 175
Circle of Madeleine Françoise Basseporte
Peaches [Prunus persica]
c. 1750
Watercolour over pencil on vellum
40 × 31.1 cm
The Morgan Library & Museum, New York, Gift of Junius S. Morgan and Henry S. Morgan
1952.29:95
Photo: The Morgan Library & Museum, New York

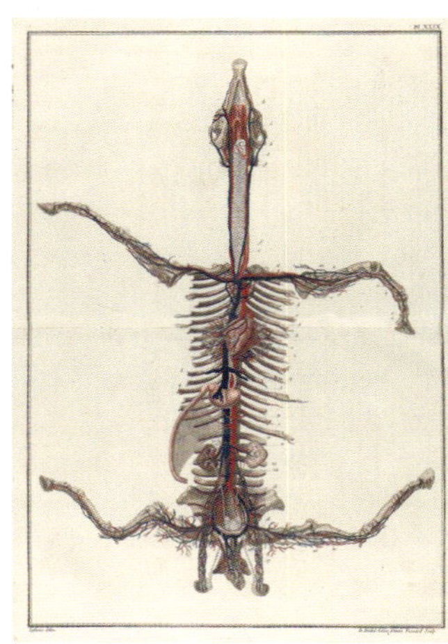

CAT. NO. 176
Barbe Michel Adam Fessard
Plate 29 in Philippe-Étienne Lafosse's *Cours d'hippiatrique, ou Traité complet de la médecine des chevaux...*
Paris, 1772
Bound volume with hand-coloured engraved illustrations
50.2 × 33.3 × 5.1 cm
Yale Center for British Art, Paul Mellon Collection
Folio A 2007 4
Image Courtesy YCBA

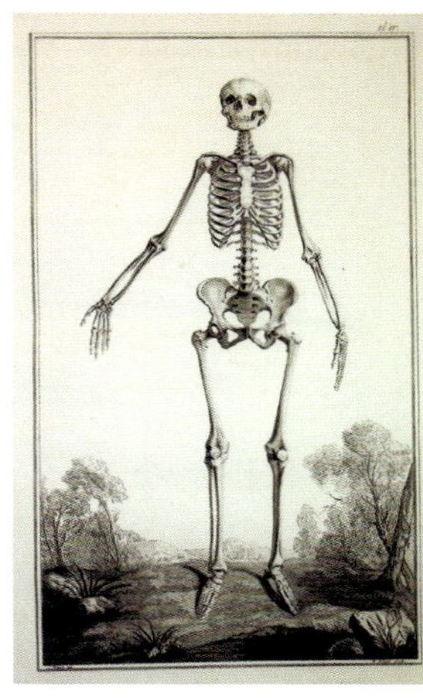

CAT. NO. 177
Translator: Marie-Geneviève-Charlotte Darlus Thiroux d'Arconville
Plate 4 in Alexander Monro's *Traité d'ostéologie, traduit de l'anglois de M. Monro, professeur d'anatomie...*, vol. 2
Paris, 1759
Bound volume of engravings
Closed: 58 × 42.5 × 5 cm; open: 58 × 85 cm
The Institute of the History of Medicine, Johns Hopkins University
CAGE .M7522ay 1759 c. 1

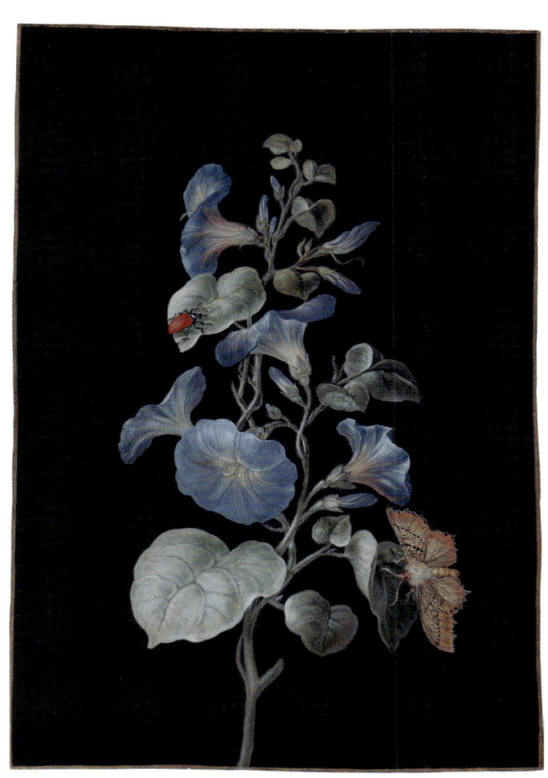

CAT. NO. 178
Barbara Regina Dietzsch
Blue Morning Glory
c. 1760
Watercolour and opaque watercolour on vellum
29.2 × 21 cm
Baltimore Museum of Art: The John Dorsey and Robert W. Armacost Acquisitions Endowment, 2020.3
Photo: Mitro Hood

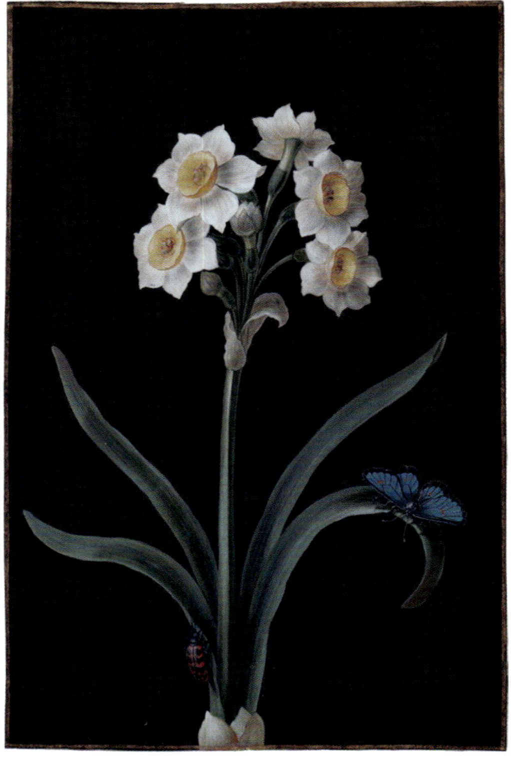

CAT. NO. 179
Barbara Regina Dietzsch
Narcissus
c. 1760
Watercolour and opaque watercolour on vellum
29.2 × 21 cm
Baltimore Museum of Art: The John Dorsey and Robert W. Armacost Acquisitions Endowment, 2020.4
Photo: Mitro Hood

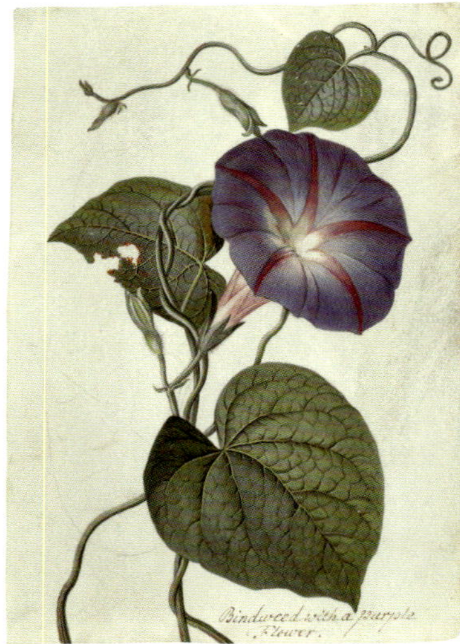

CAT. NO. 180
Dame Ann Hamilton
Bindweed with a Purple Flower
[*Convolvulus purpureus, folio Subrotondo*]
c. 1762–1766
Watercolour and opaque watercolour on vellum
19.1 × 13.7 cm
Oak Spring Garden Foundation, Upperville, Virginia

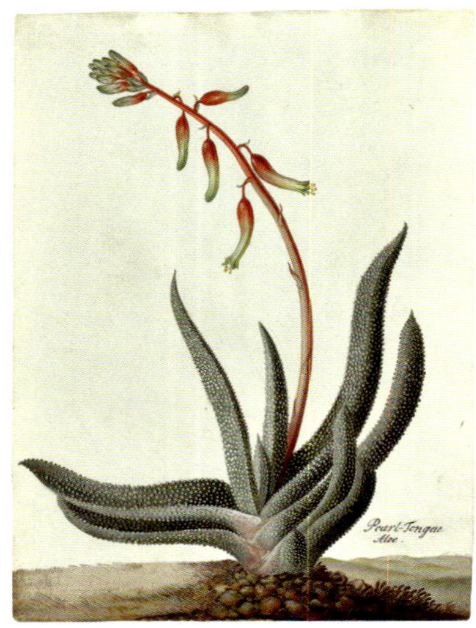

CAT. NO. 181
Dame Ann Hamilton
Pearl-Tongue Aloe [*Aloe Africana foliis longis conjugatis, supra cavis margaritiferis flore rubro elegantissimo*]
c. 1762–1766
Watercolour and opaque watercolour on vellum
21.9 × 16.8 cm
Oak Spring Garden Foundation, Upperville, Virginia

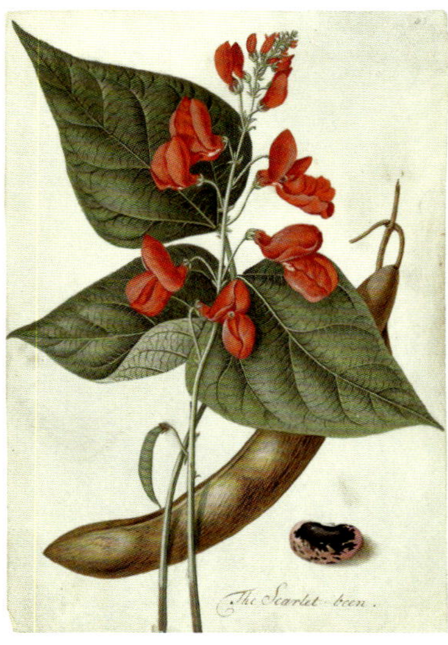

CAT. NO. 182
Dame Ann Hamilton
The Scarlet-been [*Phaeseolus Indicus, flore coccineo seu puniceo*]
c. 1762–1766
Watercolour and opaque watercolour on vellum
19.2 × 13.7 cm
Oak Spring Garden Foundation, Upperville, Virginia

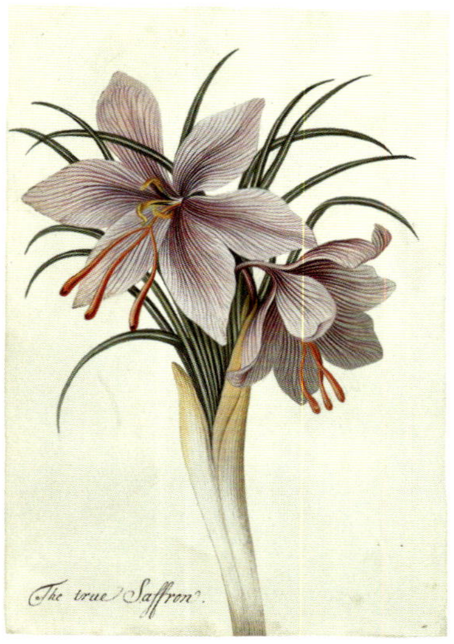

CAT. NO. 183
Dame Ann Hamilton
The True Saffron [*Crocus sativus*]
c. 1762–1766
Watercolour and opaque watercolour on vellum
19.2 × 13.7 cm
Oak Spring Garden Foundation, Upperville, Virginia

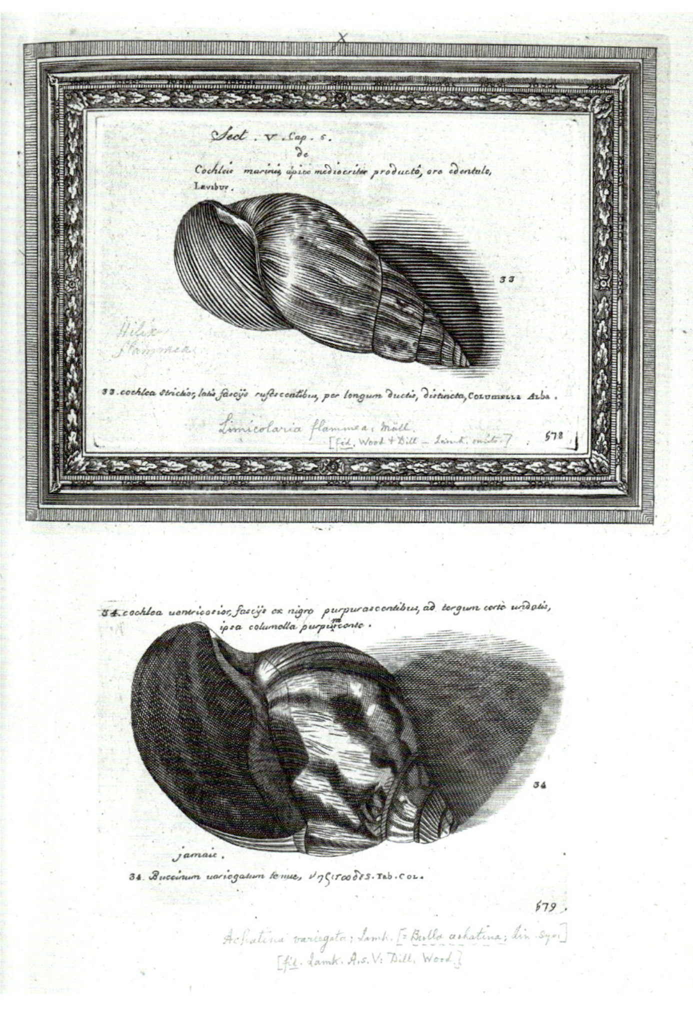

CAT. NO. 184
Anna Lister and Susanna Lister Knowler
Illustrations for Martin Lister's *Historiae sive synopsis methodicae Conchyliorum...*
Oxford, 1770
Etching and engraving
39.4 × 26.7 × 10.8 cm
Kislak Center for Special Collections, Rare Books and Manuscripts, University of Pennsylvania Libraries
Folio QL431 .L57 1770 Peachey copy

Opening illustrated: page 223

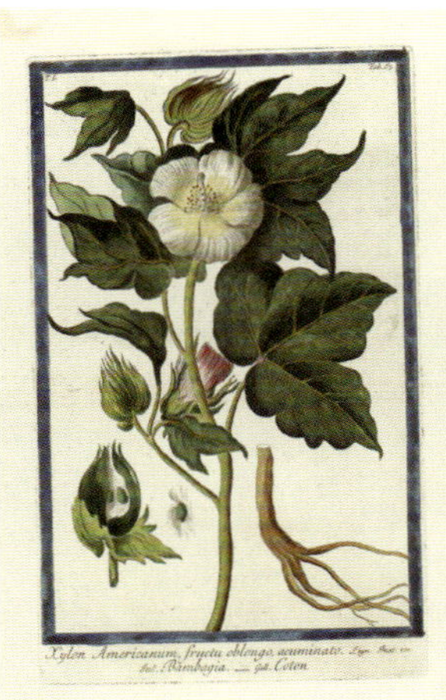

CAT. NO. 185
Magdalena Bouchard, after Cesare Ubertini
Cotton [Xylon Americanum, Fructu Oblongo, Acuminato]
from Giorgio Bonelli's *Hortus Romanus*, vol. 1
Rome, 1772
Hand-coloured engraving
Plate: 36.8 × 22.9 cm; sheet: 54.6 × 39.4 cm
Philadelphia Museum of Art: Gift of Frank and Alice Osborn, 1966
1966-68-100
Exhibited at BMA only

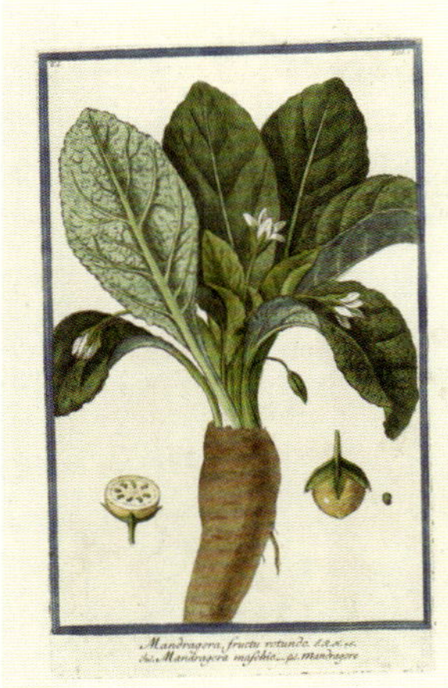

CAT. NO. 186
Magdalena Bouchard, after Cesare Ubertini
Mandrake [Mandragora Fructu Rotundo]
from Giorgio Bonelli's *Hortus Romanus*, vol. 1
Rome, 1772
Hand-coloured engraving
Plate: 36.8 × 22.9 cm; sheet: 54.6 × 39.4 cm
Philadelphia Museum of Art: Gift of Frank and Alice Osborn, 1966
1966-68-74
Exhibited at AGO only

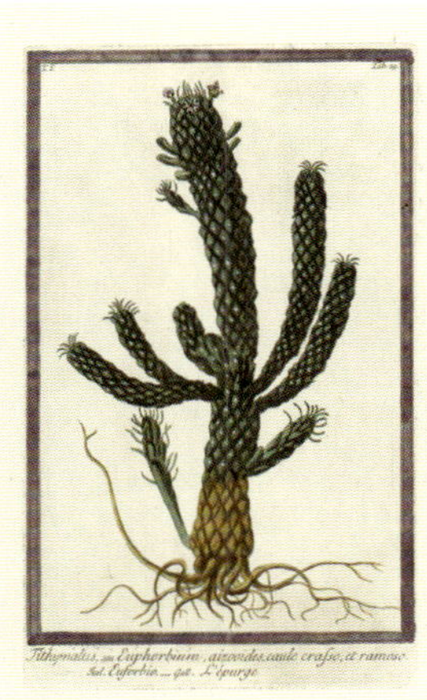

CAT. NO. 187
Magdalena Bouchard, after Cesare Ubertini
Spurge [Tithymalus, Seu Euphorbium, Aizooides, Caule Crasso, et Ramoso]
from Giorgio Bonelli's *Hortus Romanus*, vol. 1
Rome, 1772
Hand-coloured engraving
Plate: 36.8 × 22.9 cm; sheet: 54.6 × 39.4 cm
Philadelphia Museum of Art: Gift of Frank and Alice Osborn, 1966
1966-68-87
Exhibited at AGO only

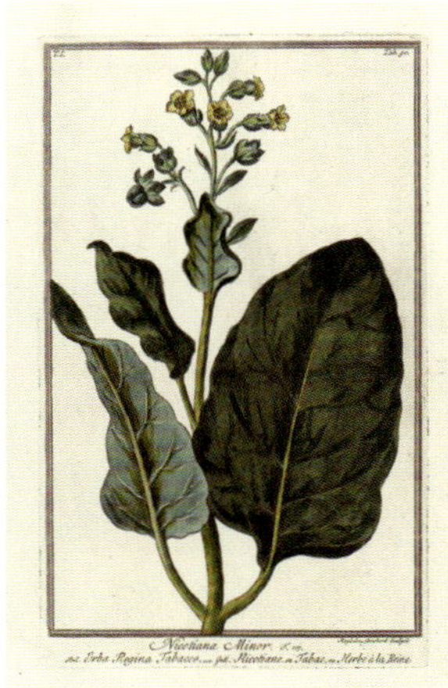

CAT. NO. 188
Magdalena Bouchard, after Cesare Ubertini
Tobacco [Nicotiana Minor]
from Giorgio Bonelli's *Hortus Romanus*, vol. 1
Rome, 1772
Hand-coloured engraving
Plate: 36.8 × 22.9 cm; sheet: 54.6 × 39.4 cm
Philadelphia Museum of Art: Gift of Frank and Alice Osborn, 1966
1966-68-111
Exhibited at BMA only

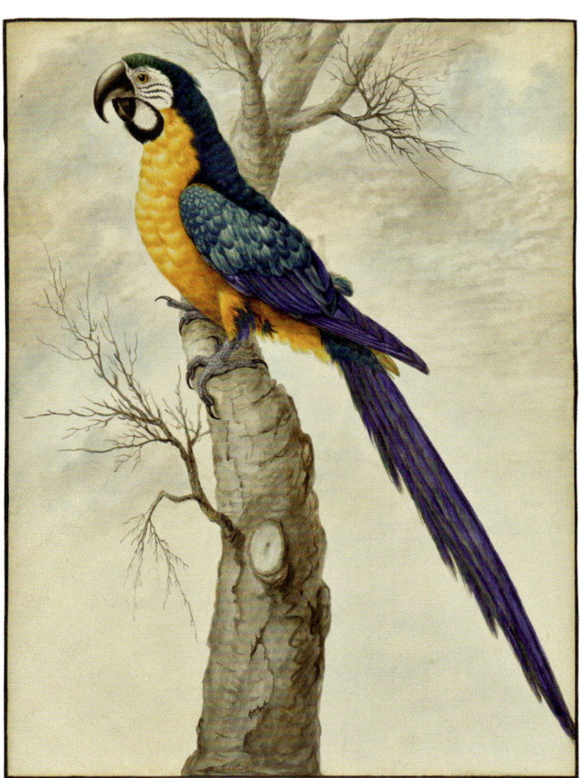

CAT. NO. 189 (left)
Sarah Stone
A Blue and Yellow Macaw
c. 1789
Watercolour heightened with opaque watercolour and glazes, with a black ink border on paper
44.1 × 33.9 cm
Art Gallery of Ontario, Purchase, with funds from the Marvin Gelber Fund, and the Master Print & Drawing Society of Ontario
2022/7043
Photo: Craig Boyko, AGO

CAT. NO. 190 (right)
Maria Boissier
Papill: Graeciensis, mirae raritatas, non nunquam in Insula Capreae repera, ibique vocata CUPIDO MAZZOLANO [Greek butterfly of exceptional rarity, occasionally found on the island of Caprea, where it is called CUPIDO MAZZOLANO]
1790s
Etching and watercolour with ink on wove paper
Plate: 30.4 × 23.6 cm; sheet: 37.1 x 26.9 cm
Art Gallery of Ontario, Purchased as a gift of the Trier-Fodor Fund, 2017
2017/39
Photo: Craig Boyko, AGO

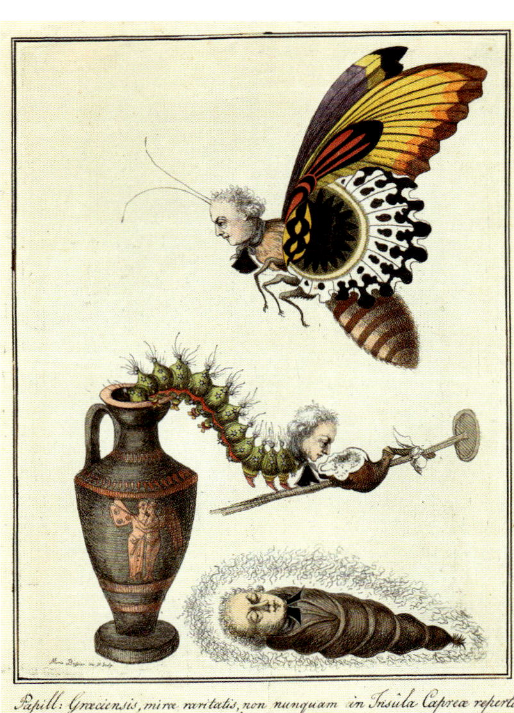

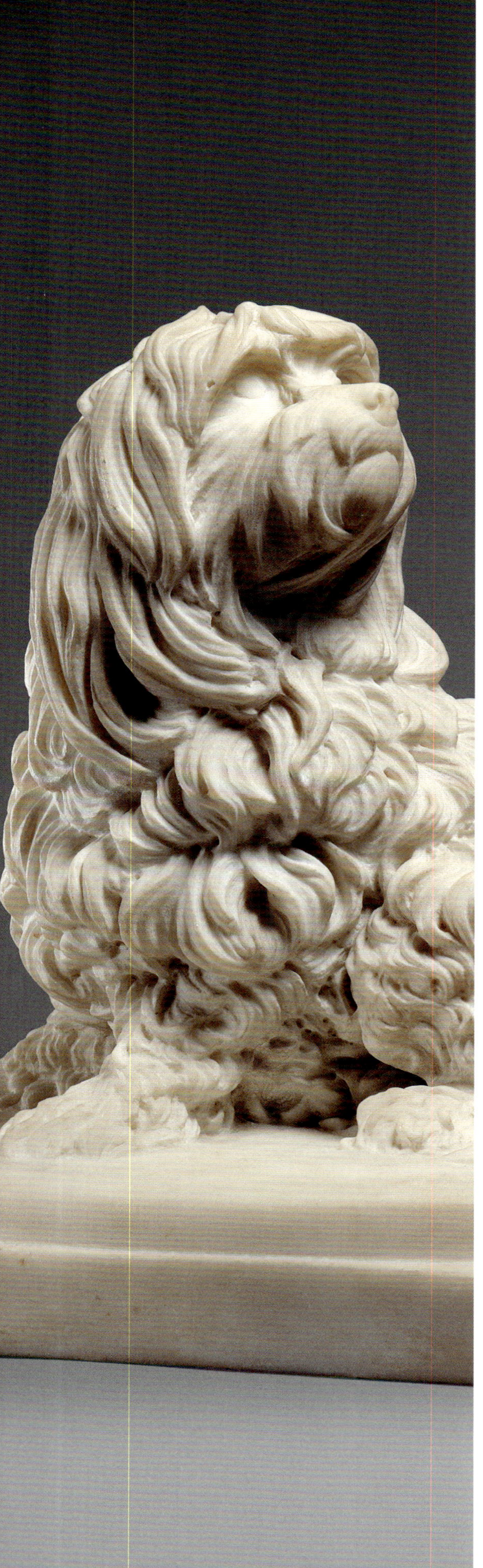

Sculpture

Annelies Verellen and Alexa Greist

In the first edition of Giorgio Vasari's *The Lives of the Most Excellent Painters, Sculptors, and Architects* (1550), the sole biographical entry devoted to a woman was that of sculptor Properzia de' Rossi (c. 1490/91–c. 1530), who was active in the Italian city of Bologna during the 1520s. Vasari's description of the artist purports that despite her "little hands, so tender," she could "brave the roughness of marble and the unkindly chisels." During the Renaissance, women's bodies were not considered suitable for the arduous and messy task of sculpting in marble, whereas men's assumed inherent predisposition for strength suited them to sculpture. Strength aside, a woman who sculpted and engaged in such a physical endeavour did not comply with the ideal characteristics of elegance, composure, and delicacy expected of women.

Despite these societal preconceptions, women made sculpture using an expansive range of materials, including wood, marble, wax, terracotta, bronze, alabaster, and ivory. Carving marble and casting metal require training and access to expensive materials, both generally impediments to women artists during these periods. Consequently, most women working in sculpture before the nineteenth century were either born into aristocratic families that offered more opportunities for education—as was the case for de' Rossi and the British artist Anne Seymour Damer (1748–1828)—or were related to master sculptors, including Maria Faydherbe (1587–1643), Beatrice Hamerani (1677–1704), Anna Felicitas Neuberger (born 1630), and Luisa Roldán (1652–1706). Those who did not have family connections turned to more available or affordable media like wax, or tended to work on a smaller scale.

Throughout the pre-modern period, women created devotional sculptures to be used for private prayer. Polychrome wooden sculptures were often rendered quite realistically in order to enable devotees to feel closer to the holy figure depicted.

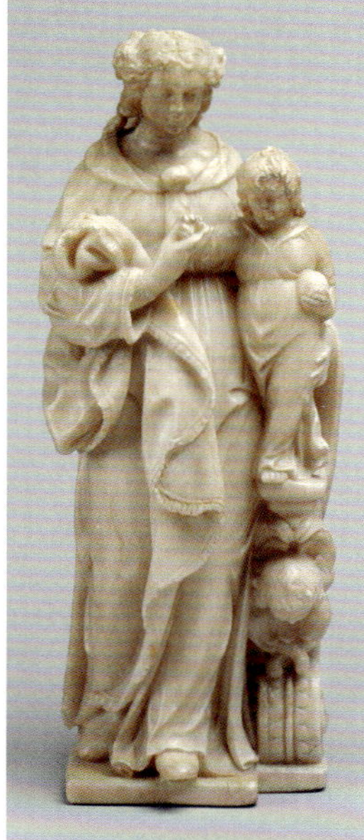

CAT. NO. 191
Maria Faydherbe
Virgin and Child
1630–1640
Alabaster
40 × 16 × 4.5 cm
Victoria and Albert Museum, London, Purchased with the assistance of the Hildburgh bequest and the Murray bequest
A.31-2013
Image © Victoria and Albert Museum, London

Following this tradition, Spanish sculptor Andrea de Mena y Bitoria (1654–1734), who was trained in the family workshop alongside her two sisters, created the *Ecce Homo* (cat. no. 192) and the *Mater Dolorosa* (cat. no. 193). Christ's sunken eyes reveal his intense pain, and he parts his lips as if about to speak to the devout beholder. The highly detailed sculpture creates an arresting degree of naturalism: Christ's skin is painted as flesh, and the drops of blood are raised in the wood. On the face of the mourning Virgin, a single raised, translucent teardrop rolls down her cheek, echoing the blood shed by her son. Three years before making these signed works, de Mena y Bitoria entered the Cistercian abbey of Santa Ana de Recoletas Bernardas in Málaga, which indicates that her talents as a sculptor were appreciated and possibly encouraged within a convent context.

Perhaps the most well-known woman sculptor active in Spain was Luisa Roldán. After training under her father alongside her five sisters and two

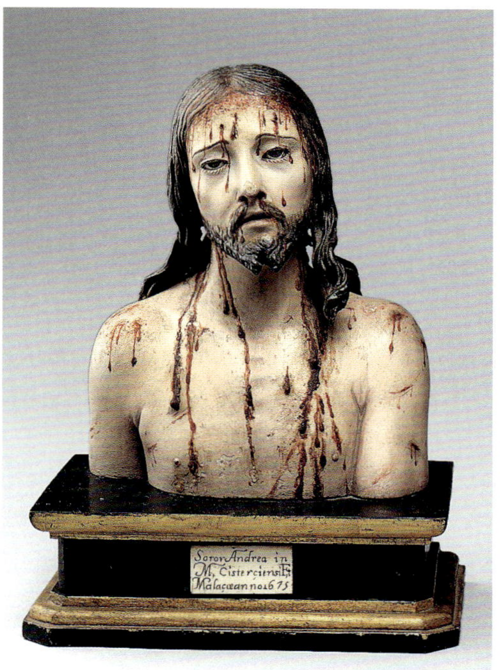

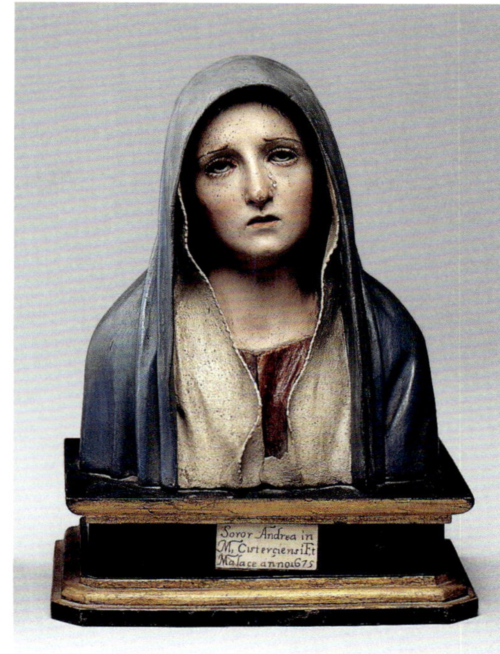

CAT. NO. 192 (left)
Andrea de Mena y Bitoria
Ecce Homo
1675
Wood and polychrome
21 × 16.5 × 9.8 cm
On loan from The Hispanic Society of America, New York, NY
LD1985
Exhibited at BMA only

CAT. NO. 193 (right)
Andrea de Mena y Bitoria
Mater Dolorosa
1675
Wood and polychrome
20.3 × 16.2 × 10.2 cm
On loan from The Hispanic Society of America, New York, NY
LD1987
Exhibited at BMA only

brothers, Roldán established her own workshop with her husband, specializing in biblical subjects for both religious processions and domestic devotion. The Education of the Virgin was a popular subject, and Roldán created numerous versions in both polychromed wood and terracotta. In a version now in the collection of the Los Angeles County Museum of Art (cat. no. 195), she depicted the young Virgin Mary and her mother, Anne, in an everyday moment of maternal education, creating a familiar and intimate portrayal that encourages emotional connection between the depicted figures and the viewer. Similarly emotive, although in an entirely different way, are two polychrome terracotta sculptures Roldán crafted to depict the decapitated heads of saints on chargers. The life-size severed heads of Saint John the Baptist (cat. no. 196) and Saint Paul (cat. no. 197) are presented in alarmingly realistic detail. Recreating post-mortem flesh using green-grey paint, the sculptures convey the excruciating pain of execution, and yet both men open their mouths, seemingly uttering their last words of devotion. Roldán's illusionistic command of material and emotional narration was appreciated in her own lifetime, earning her patronage by the Hapsburg royal court in Madrid, where she served as court sculptor toward the end of her career.

German artist Anna Felicitas Neuberger found similar recognition at court, receiving praise from Holy Roman Emperors Ferdinand III and Leopold I. In a domestically scaled crucifix, she depicts the crucified Christ, combining wood and ivory to create an object for personal devotion (cat. no. 194). Neuberger's subtle depiction of the nude male body in ivory demonstrates her knowledge of human anatomy, suggesting that she was able to study from a nude model or at least from other artworks or drawings of the male body. Like many women artists trained or employed within family workshops, Neuberger did not receive credit for her work, which had been attributed to her father, Daniel Neuberger. Working in the Southern Netherlands, the work of Maria Faydherbe has similarly been obscured by misattributions and the prominence of male family members. Faydherbe seems to have worked entirely within the confines of her brothers' workshop, perhaps the outcome of a rivalrous encounter she had with the local guild. As a result, signed work, such as her touching alabaster *Virgin with Child* (cat. no. 191), is exceedingly rare. It is unknown how many works she may have carved but did not sign, leaving them to be attributed to her brothers.

Unlike ivory or alabaster, wax's highly malleable nature allowed artists to make detailed and lifelike images without the physical effort required to carve a harder material. The use of pigments also resulted in a high degree of naturalism. Wax modelling was used in Europe to create effigies, figures of saints, and other famous figures, as well as in anatomical modelling. Even though the final product is bronze, Beatrice Hamerani's medal of Pope Innocent XII (cat. no. 198) relied upon the manipulation of a wax model, from which the medal was produced. She achieved remarkable recognition as the only woman and the youngest known artist—at the age of seventeen—to design a papal medal. Although her contributions were cut short when she died during childbirth, her family's shop became an important producer of papal medals in seventeenth-century Rome, restriking her medal designs for years.

Many women found fame using wax to create profile busts as well as effigies of powerful figures and celebrities, a tradition that persists today in wax museums like Madame Tussauds. Although little is known about her training, the British sculptor Catherine Andras (1775–1860) achieved success as an official artist for Queen Charlotte. Andras's portrait *Rose Bruce, of Dublin* (cat. no. 201), which survives in two known versions, displays her facility with sculpting in wax to resemble a variety of textures, from the folds in Bruce's dress to her skin. Her formal training similarly hazy, Patience Lovell Wright (1725–1786) was active in the American colonies and later in Britain, where she supported her family as a widow by creating wax portraits of the nobility as well as of the king and queen of

England. Her patriotism and political activism for the American colonies, reflected in her highly detailed wax relief portrait of George Washington (cat. no. 199), were seen as challenging the bounds of the prescribed humble, quiet, and passive feminine behaviour on both sides of the Atlantic.

Active in eighteenth-century England, Anne Seymour Damer was financially independent and enjoyed a successful career sculpting in marble, alabaster, and terracotta with the support of leading cultural figures. Damer received royal commissions from King George III, and she exhibited numerous times at the Royal Academy of Arts. She promoted her sculptures through gifts to powerful institutions, like the Uffizi collection of artists' self-portraits, and produced relief sculptures as well as portrait busts of actresses and writers in her circle of friends. Damer also produced numerous life-size depictions of animals such as a shock dog (cat. no. 200), which highlights her careful attention to detail and ability to bring life to stone. This small dog from the Maltese family—called a "shock dog" because of its rough coat—sits attentively and awaits a command. By including her signature in Greek on the sculpture's base, Damer locates herself within a long history of sculpture, dating back to antiquity.

Pre-modern women artists successfully asserted their skills in a variety of sculptural media, despite sculpture's traditional definition as a masculine art. Whether trained in the workshop of a family member or able to access art education by virtue of elevated social status, these women created three-dimensional works that were both exhibited publicly and treasured in secular and religious settings throughout Europe and beyond.

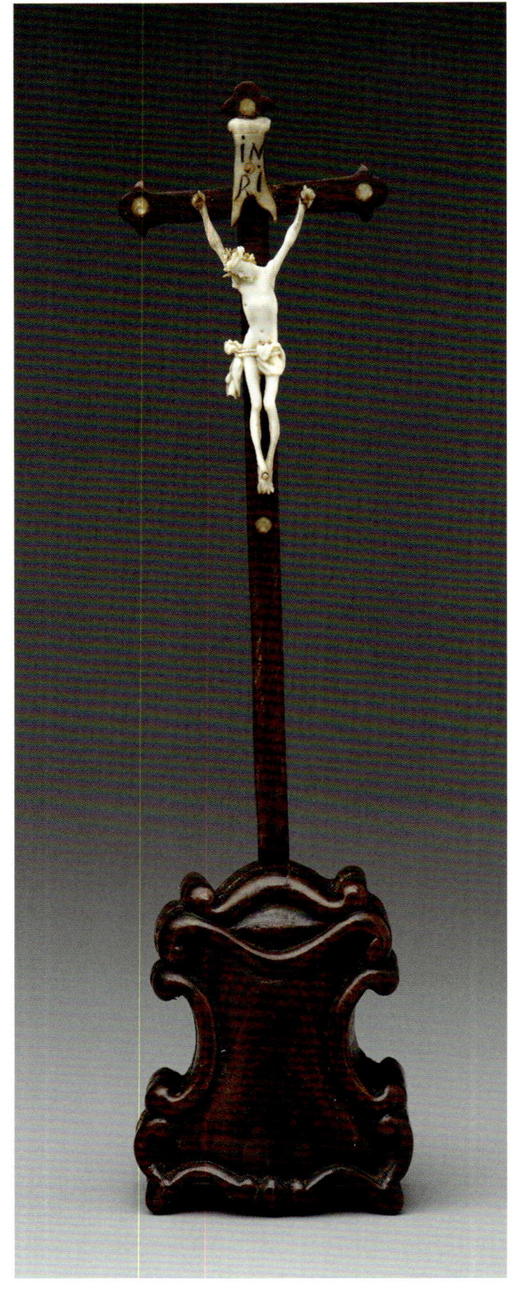

CAT. NO. 194
Anna Felicitas Neuberger
Small Wooden Crucifix with Miniature Ivory Corpus of Christ
late 17th century
Wood and ivory
16.2 × 3.8 × 2.9 cm
The Thomson Collection at the Art Gallery of Ontario
Photo: Craig Boyko, AGO
Exhibited at AGO only

Resources Consulted

Alen, Klara. "Envy and Pride: Maria Faydherbe (Mechelen, 1587–after 1633); A Woman Sculptor in a Man's World." In *Facts & Feelings: Retracing Emotions of Artists, 1600–1800*, edited by Hannelore Magnus and Katlijne Van der Stighelen, 77–99. Turnhout: Brepols, 2015.

Bohn, Babette. *Women Artists, Their Patrons, and Their Publics in Early Modern Bologna*. University Park, PA: Penn State University Press, 2021.

Hall-van den Elsen, Catherine. *Luisa Roldán*. Los Angeles: Getty Publications, 2021.

Kokai, Jennifer A. "Molding a Heroine: Patience Wright and Transatlantic Notions of American Female Patriotism." *Journal of American Drama and Theatre* 21, no. 2 (Spring, 2009): 49–66.

McGrath, Maeve. *Daniel Neuberger the Younger and Anna Felicitas Neuberger: The Ceroplastic Oeuvres 1621–1680 and 1650–1731*. Regensburg: Schnell + Steiner, 2016.

McLintock, John. "'My Colossus, My Overgrown Child': Anne Seymour Damer's Statue of George III in Edinburgh." *Burlington Magazine* 152, no. 1282 (2010): 18–28.

Messbarger, Rebecca. *The Lady Anatomist: The Life and Work of Anna Morandi Manzolini*. Chicago: University of Chicago Press, 2010.

Quin, Sally. "Describing the Female Sculptor in Early Modern Italy: An Analysis of the Vita of Properzia de' Rossi in Giorgio Vasari's Lives." *Gender & History* 24, no. 1 (2012): 134–49.

Trusted, Marjorie. "Maria Faydherbe: A Seventeenth-Century Sculptor in Mechelen." *Burlington Magazine* 156, no. 1331 (2014): 104–06.

Varriano, John L. "Some Documentary Evidence on the Restriking of Early Papal Medals." *Museum Notes (American Numismatic Society)* 26 (1981): 215–23.

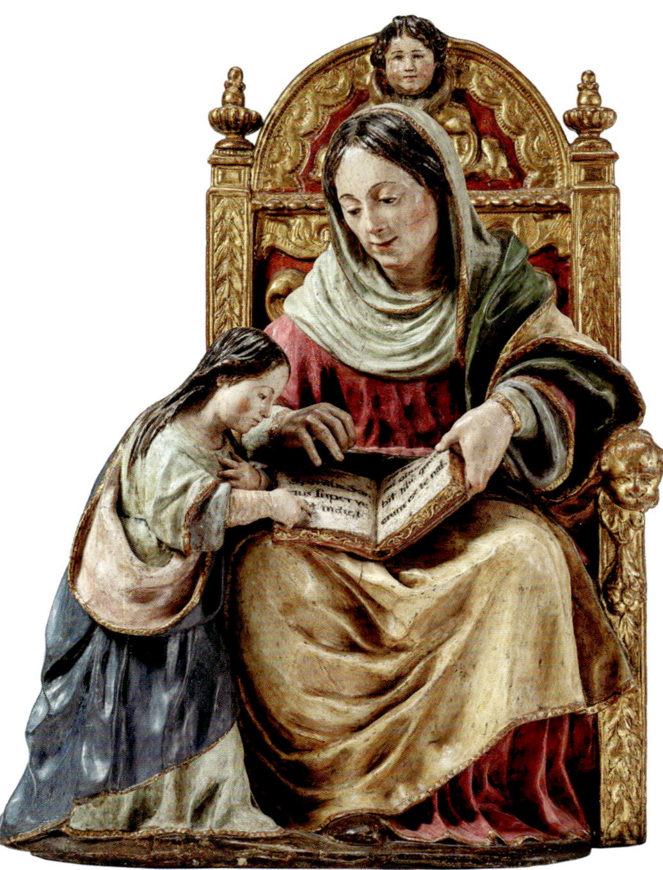

CAT. NO. 195
Luisa Roldán
The Education of the Virgin
1680s
Polychrome paint and wood
76 × 63 × 43 cm
Los Angeles County Museum of Art, Gift of the 2019 Collectors Committee with additional funds from Linda Borick and Bill Davidson on behalf of the Louis L. Borick Foundation
M.2019.235

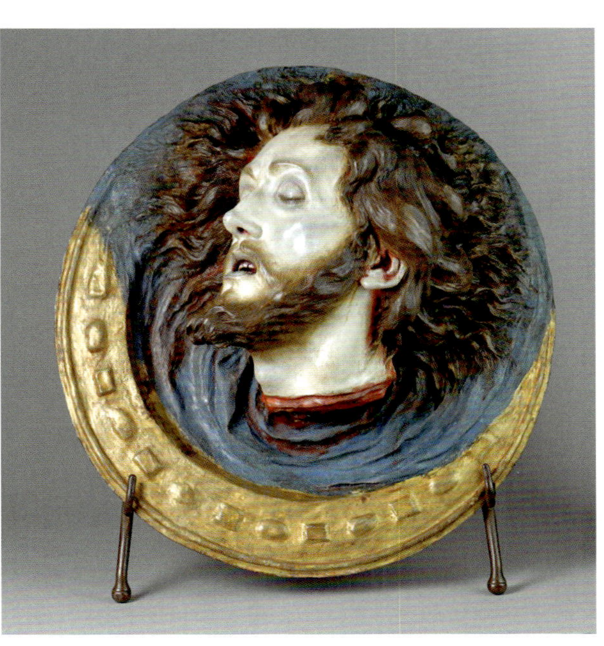

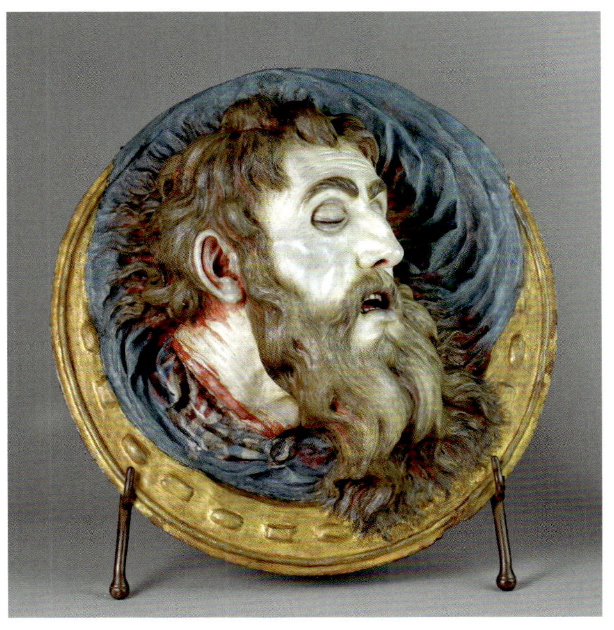

CAT. NO. 196 (left)
Attributed to Luisa Roldán
Head of Saint John the Baptist
c. 1692–1706
Polychrome paint and terracotta
Diameter: 48.5 cm
On loan from The Hispanic Society of America, New York, NY
D823
Exhibited at BMA only

CAT. NO. 197 (right)
Attributed to Luisa Roldán
Head of Saint Paul
c. 1692–1706
Polychrome paint and terracotta
Diameter: 46 cm
On loan from The Hispanic Society of America, New York, NY
D824
Exhibited at BMA only

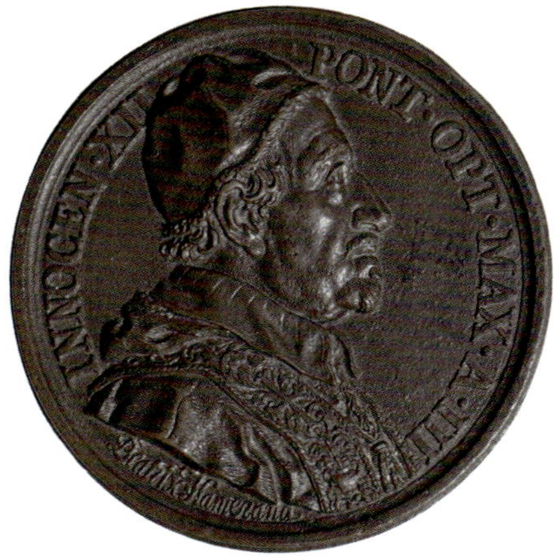

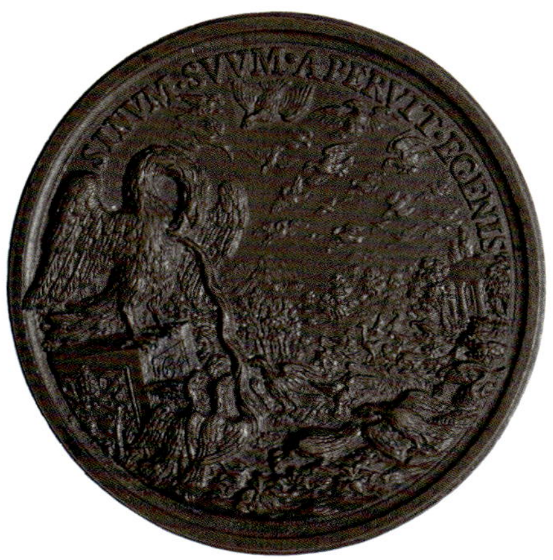

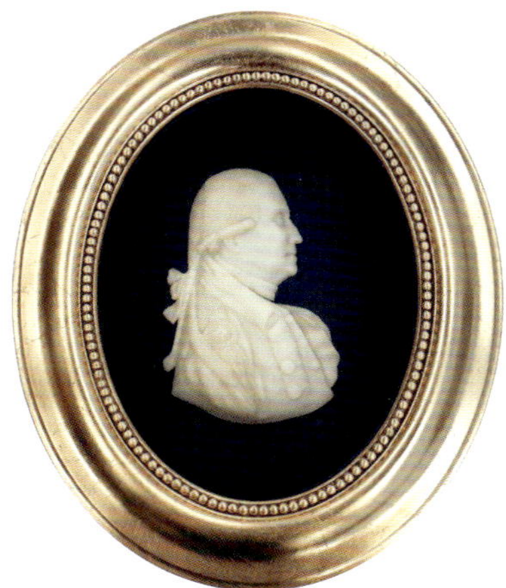

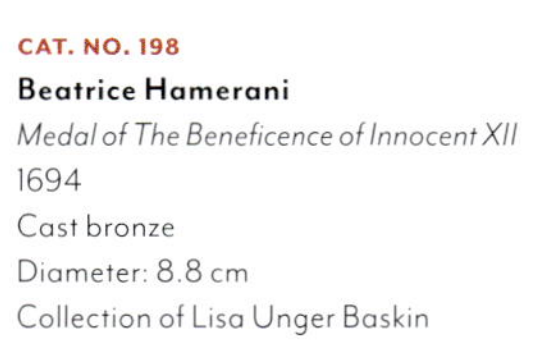

CAT. NO. 198
Beatrice Hamerani
Medal of The Beneficence of Innocent XII
1694
Cast bronze
Diameter: 8.8 cm
Collection of Lisa Unger Baskin
Photo: Stephen Petegorsky

CAT. NO. 199
Attributed to Patience Lovell Wright
Portrait of George Washington
c. 1775
Wax
38.7 × 30.5 × 6.6 cm
On loan from Old Barracks Museum

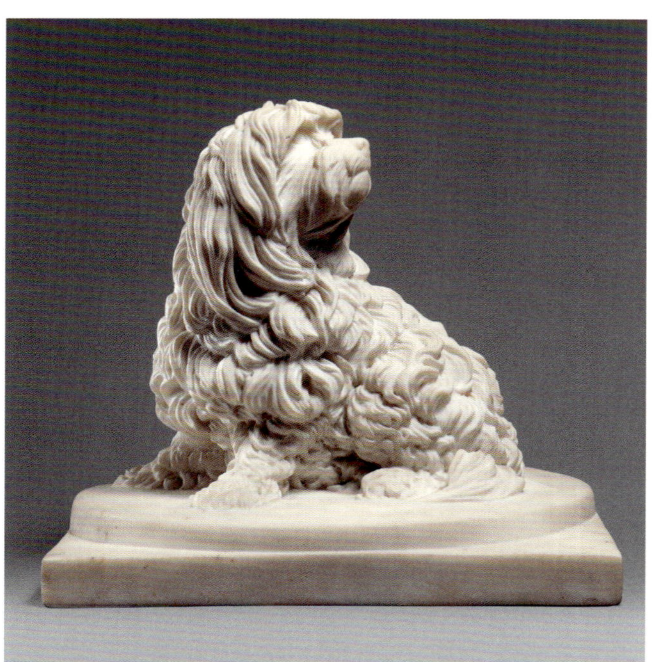

CAT. NO. 200 (left)
Anne Seymour Damer
Shock Dog (nickname for a dog of the Maltese breed)
c. 1782
Marble
33.3 × 38 × 32.1 cm, 34 kg
Lent by The Metropolitan Museum of Art,
New York, Purchase, Barbara Walters Gift,
in honour of Cha Cha, 2014
2014.568

CAT. NO. 201 (right)
Catherine Andras
Rose Bruce, of Dublin
1799
Painted wax
Figure: 18 × 19 cm (at base);
in shadow box: 33 × 28 × 13 cm
Yale Center for British Art, Paul Mellon Fund
RBW.CS 2
Image Courtesy YCBA

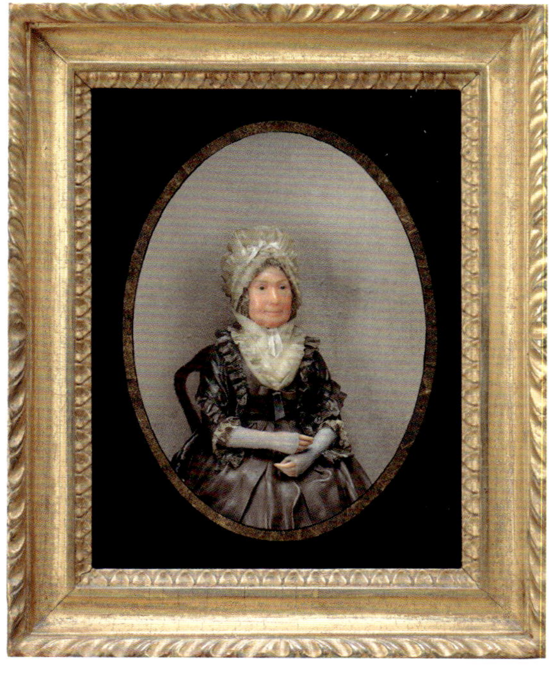

Silver and Enamel

Brittany Luberda and Theresa Kutasz Christensen

The gleam of glass and metal reflected off the tools of women glassmakers and metalsmiths in early modern Europe. Whether fusing heated enamels onto copper or working silver and plated metal into useful objects, women artists created objects with molten materials for decoration, devotion, and domestic purposes. Across Europe, female smiths working in gold, silver, and plate laboured beside male apprentices and journeymen in workshops or, in some cases, owned their own enterprises. Unlike media such as glass, which is often unsigned and therefore underrepresented in histories of known women makers, the registration of metalworkers' maker's marks with assay offices—where the content of precious metal is assessed for authenticity—affirms that women ran successful workshops in competitive city centres like London, Paris, and Amsterdam. While the majority of metalwork produced by women was small and undecorated—for example, thimbles, spoons, and boxes—select workshops led by women produced more refined works for either aristocratic or foreign markets. This widespread industrial craftsmanship led to the representation of silver and enamelled objects associated with women artists between 1400 and 1800 in homes, businesses, synagogues, and churches across Europe.

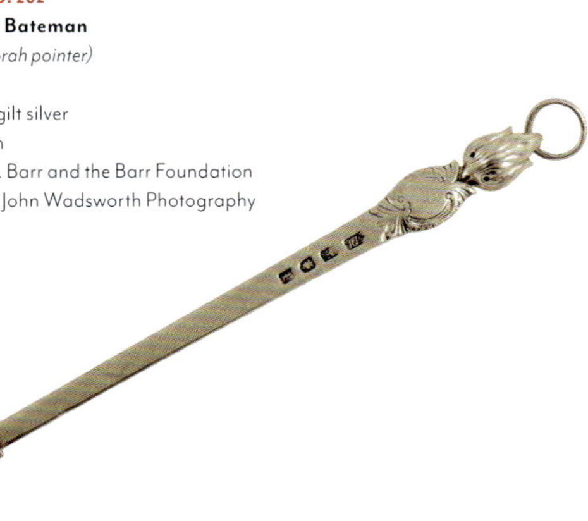

CAT. NO. 202
Hester Bateman
Yad (Torah pointer)
1781
Parcel gilt silver
27.2 cm
Clay H. Barr and the Barr Foundation
Image: John Wadsworth Photography

The small town of Limoges, France, was a centre of enamel production during the Middle Ages and Renaissance. Enamels are glass adhered to metal, made by fusing silica, such as ground sand or quartz, with a fluxing agent and colourful mineral oxides. Although initially associated with goldsmithing, by the sixteenth century Limoges-based enamellers had developed techniques for firing illusionistic portraits and scenes covering the entirety of a metal support. Suzanne de Court (active 1575–1625) was a member of the de Court dynasty of enamellers who received royal patronage; she was an expert in working with silver and gold foil. De Court's opulent pieces are signed "Suzanne Court," "Susanne de Court," or "SC," and she produced an array of forms, including saltcellars, ewers, platters, and caskets decorated with scenes adapted from classical literature and biblical passages, such as on the *Oval plaque with the Annunciation* (cat. no. 203).

The small scale of enamel on metal was well suited for handheld objects. In the eighteenth century, Mademoiselle Duplessis (active c. 1753–1760) was an enamel painter specializing in scenes that were inset in snuffboxes. Her known range of subject matter included pastoral landscapes, children at play, and copies of contemporary paintings by artists like Jean-Baptiste Greuze. In a snuffbox now in the collection of the Metropolitan Museum of Art (cat. no. 209), her polychrome and *grisaille* images of peasants and putti are surrounded by a spectacular diamond-encrusted gold case made by goldsmith Jean Georges (or George). Snuffboxes were made to hold small amounts of tobacco on one's person and were updated each season, and often exchanged as gifts. It was not uncommon for makers to incorporate precious, costly, and socially weighted imported materials such as diamonds, silver, or cowrie shells as a way to flatter the intended owner or reflect that recipient's taste, wealth, and social status. A snuffbox by British silversmith

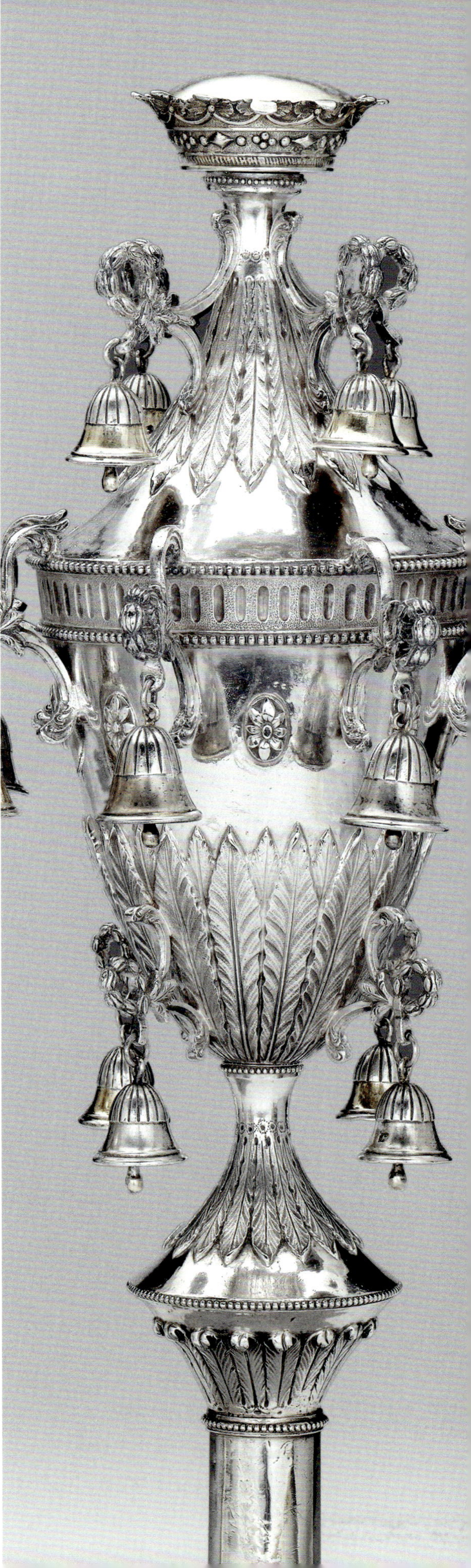

Elizabeth Roker (active from 1776) (cat. no. 216) features a polished silver box topped by a speckled cowrie shell. Belying its simple form, this object would have spoken volumes in eighteenth-century social circles, with each aspect of the work reflecting widespread colonialist trade practices. The sourcing and cleaning of shells, for instance, was typically carried out by enslaved workers in colonial outposts in the Caribbean or Indian Ocean, and cowrie shells were widely used as payment for goods as well as people in the Atlantic slave trade. Although British King George III had strongly rebuked the practice of slavery in the late 1750s, objects like the Roker snuffbox demonstrate the role of women makers in a material and social economy still very much enmeshed in such practices.

During the seventeenth century, large-scale manufacturing of glass began in England, aided by the introduction of a higher lead content, resulting in crystal glass. To produce the thick body glassware that appealed to Baroque tastes, small- and large-scale glassworks emerged across the countryside. In Newcastle upon Tyne, England, the Beilby family specialized in enamelling heraldic symbols on glass vessels from around 1760 to 1778, later relocating to London and Scotland. Their glasses (cat. no. 211) and decanter (cat. no. 210), with the sumptuous crest of King George III, are considered the apex of English enamelling. The Beilby workshop was family-run, and Mary Beilby (1749–1797), the youngest sister, is often credited with enamelling on glass until she had a stroke in the mid-1770s. Her sister Elizabeth Beilby (1738–1813), who lived in London with a husband in politics, was possibly acting as an agent for the enterprise in the workshop's formative years, which explains their many parliamentary-related commissions.[1] Prior to the Beilbys' enamel on glass crests, English heraldry was previously added only to gold and silver, both more expensive materials that inspired many glass forms.

While unmarried women like Mary typically remained in the family workshop, married women often worked alongside their husbands, both in the business of supporting a family workshop and in the process of making—although often under their spouse's mark. Widows, however, were able to register their own marks. English silversmith Rebecca Emes (active 1808–1829) registered her mark along with a partner, likely her late husband's brother William, shortly after the death of her spouse in 1808. The marks found on an egg coddler (cat. no. 217) produced by Emes provide a snapshot of her life as a new widow and manager of the family silversmithing workshop. The pot, where the eggs were boiled, is marked as produced by Emes and William, who remained her partner for only three months. The rack with heating lamp is marked as produced by Emes and Edward Barnes, who became Emes's longtime associate later that year. Together they would register their silverworks under the mark of the firm Emes & Barnes until the end of Emes's career. Like Emes, Louisa Courtauld (1729–1807) had family ties to the silver industry and, in her widowhood, took over her husband's silversmith business and registered her own mark. Her workshop catered to the demand for French-inspired designs as well as the age's love of classical forms, an aesthetic pairing embodied by her monumental, classical vase-shaped hot water urn (cat. no. 212) featuring exuberant Rococo decoration.

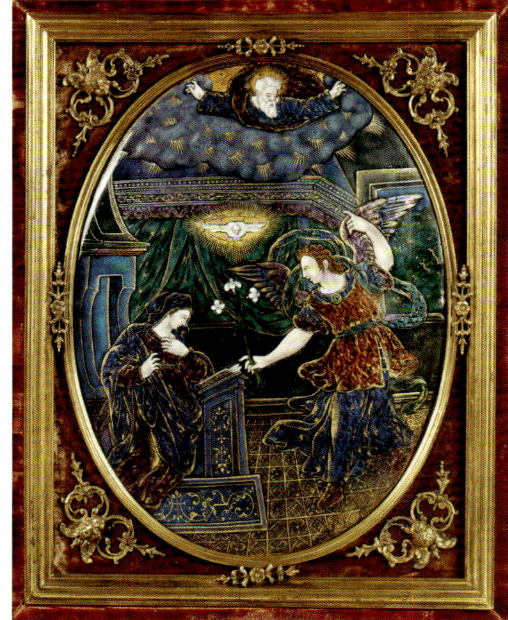

CAT. NO. 203
Suzanne de Court
Oval plaque with the Annunciation
c. 1600
Painted enamel and gilding on copper
18.8 × 13 cm
The Walters Art Museum, Baltimore, Maryland
44.191
Exhibited at AGO only

Many metalworkers seem to have moved in close, family-centred circles, where women learned skills in making and trade from their parents. Born into a distinguished French Huguenot family of silversmiths active in England, Elizabeth Godfrey (active c. 1720–1758) operated under two names as an independent goldsmith. After her first husband died, she registered a mark as Elizabeth Buteux in 1731; after her second husband died, she registered a new mark under "Elizabeth Godfrey" in 1741. Godfrey is unique among London-based women silversmiths in that she was known to have been patronized by a member of the royal family, the Duke of Cumberland. In addition to outstanding quality, her designs show a keen awareness of popular decorative trends that often engaged with global themes. A set of three tea canisters (cat. no. 208) bear images of fantastical Asian-inspired architecture and foreign costumes, while a set of sauce boats (cat. no. 207) exhibit elegantly arched handles and an organic shell motif that reflects the period's fascination with combining nature and artifice.

Godfrey's contributions in quality are matched by the extensive output of another British silversmith, Hester Bateman (1708–1794). Bateman owned a large workshop, which employed her sons and daughter Letitia, as well as a daughter in-law, Ann, along with multiple apprentices and journeymen. Objects with her mark are time capsules of eighteenth-century life, with classic silver designs marketed to a growing class of upper-middle-income buyers, and objects including inkstands (cat. no. 213) and trays to hold cruet sets (cat. no. 215) with clean, simple forms and claw-and-ball feet. Illustrating her engagement across religions as well as cutting-edge design sensibility, Bateman produced works for the Jewish community, including a delicate silver yad, or Torah pointer (cat. no. 202). One of the most elaborate productions to come out of her workshop is a set of neoclassical Torah finials (cat. no. 214) made for the synagogue in Portsmouth, England. An adroit businesswoman, Bateman was one of the first silversmiths in London to capitalize on the technological innovations like plate metal sheets coming out of Birmingham.[2] She even bought a steam engine to produce and sell sheet plates to fellow silversmiths.

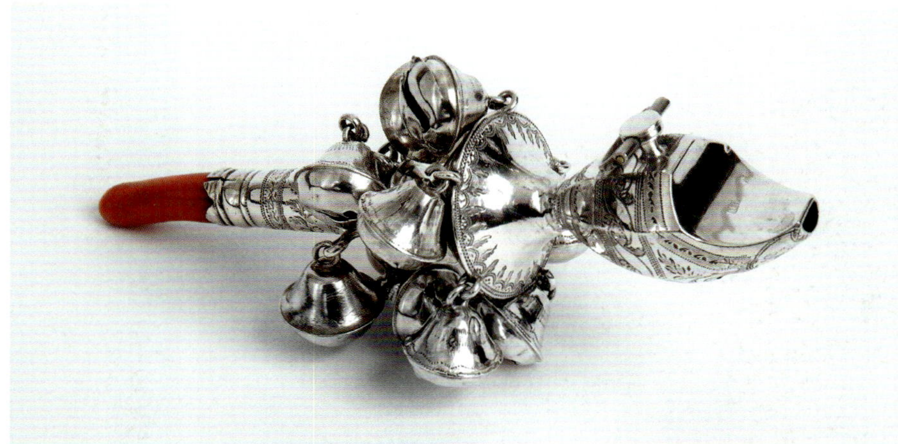

CAT. NO. 204
Attributed to Mary Ann Croswell
Child's rattle
1808
Silver and coral
13.7 × 5.1 × 5.1 cm
National Museum of Women in the Arts, Washington, DC, Silver collection assembled by Nancy Valentine, purchased with funds donated by Mr. and Mrs. Oliver R. Grace
1987.74
Photo: Lee Stalsworth

In 1700, Alice Sheene (active 1700–c. 1714) registered her maker's mark with the London assay office at Goldsmith's Hall. She is one of the earliest named women in the London records, noted as working frequently on small domestic silver such as spoons, casters for imported spices (cat. no. 205), and tankards. Works for women by women are an additional space in which female silversmiths distinguished themselves. Tankards (cat. no. 206) were a traditional gift for new mothers or brides, and it is possible that this example was given on such an occasion. Mary Ann Croswell (died 1830) advertised her expertise in thimbles and objects made with coral out of her London workshop, where she trained multiple male apprentices, including her son, to create pieces generally made for women and children. A finely worked baby rattle (cat. no. 204), likely made in the Croswell workshop, features a whistle on one end, with a ring of delicate silver bells attached at the centre. On the other tip, a long, smooth piece of bright coral reflects the period's belief in the apotropaic power of the material as well as its use in aiding the teething process.

For each named inventor, designer, and proprietor working in silver and enamel, there are countless wives, daughters, and independent women whose identities were never recorded in the assay office records or the patent books. It is clear from surviving examples, however, that enamels as well as metalwork by women were present everywhere, from houses of worship to dining tables and desks of elite residences across early modern Europe.

Resources Consulted

Glanville, Philippa, and Jennifer Faulds Goldsborough. *Women Silversmiths, 1685–1845: Works from the Collection of the National Museum of Women in the Arts*. New York and London: Thames and Hudson, 1990.

Maxwell, Christopher L. *In Sparkling Company: Reflections on Glass in the 18th-Century British World*. Corning, NY: Corning Museum of Glass, 2020.

Rogers, Meyric R. "A Notable Gift of English Silver." *Art Institute of Chicago Quarterly* 49, no. 3 (1955): 44–47.

Wardropper Ian, and Julia Day. *Limoges Enamels at the Frick Collection*. New York: Frick Collection, in association with D. Giles, 2015.

Notes

1 Simon Cottle, "Family Connections: The Formative Years of Beilby Enameled Glass, 1760–1765," *Journal of Glass Studies* 57 (2015): 186.

2 Amanda Dunsmore, "Hester Bateman: An Eighteenth-Century Entrepreneur," National Gallery of Victoria, ngv.vic.gov.au/essay/hester-bateman-an-eighteenth-century-entrepreneur/, accessed April 9, 2020.

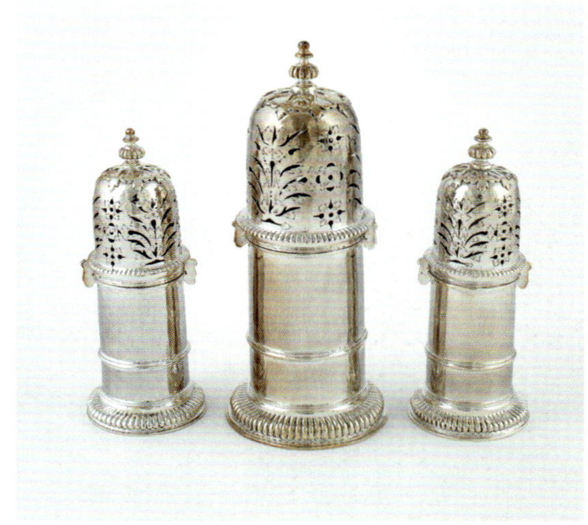

CAT. NO. 205
Alice Sheene
Three casters
1701/02
Silver
A: 19.4 × 7.9 cm; B: 14 × 5.7 cm; C: 14 × 5.7 cm
Art Institute of Chicago, Given in memory of Alice Kimpton Berg
1955.38a-c

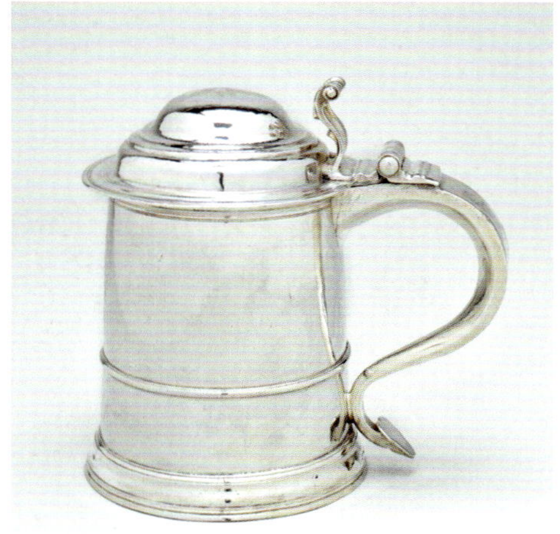

CAT. NO. 206
Alice Sheene
Tankard with cover
1706
Silver
18.4 × 19.4 × 13.7 cm
National Museum of Women in the Arts, Washington, DC, Silver collection assembled by Nancy Valentine, purchased with funds donated by Mr. and Mrs. Oliver R. Grace
1987.148a-b
Photo: Lee Stalsworth

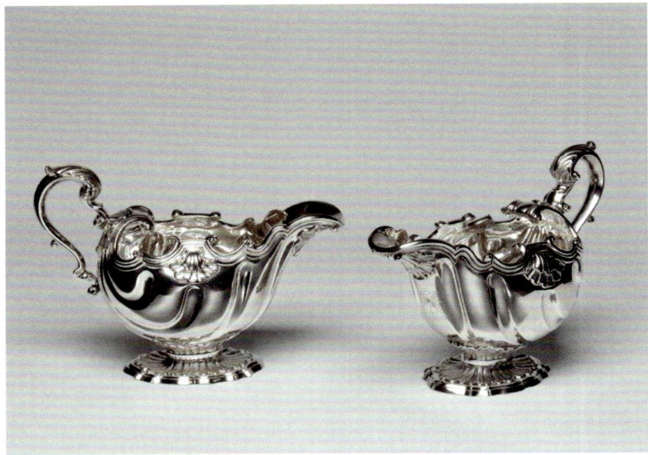

CAT. NO. 207
Elizabeth Godfrey
Sauce boats
1750
Silver
Each: 15.6 × 21 × 11.1 cm
National Museum of Women in the Arts, Washington, DC, Gift of Faith Corcoran
1989.49
Photo: Lee Stalsworth

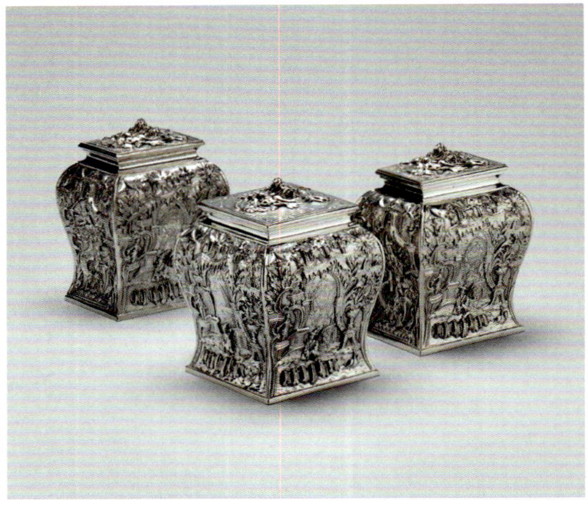

CAT. NO. 208
Elizabeth Godfrey
Tea canister set
1754–1755
Silver
Largest canister: 14 × 10.2 × 10.2 cm; two smaller canisters: 13.3 × 10.2 × 7.6 cm
Saint Louis Art Museum, Funds given by Lewis and Amanda Smith; and gift of John M. Harney in memory of Florence M. Warfield and Charlotte W. Harney, funds given by Joseph Pulitzer in memory of his wife, Elinor Wickham Pulitzer, and funds given in honour of Joseph Pulitzer II, by exchange
4:2010.1a,b-.3a,b

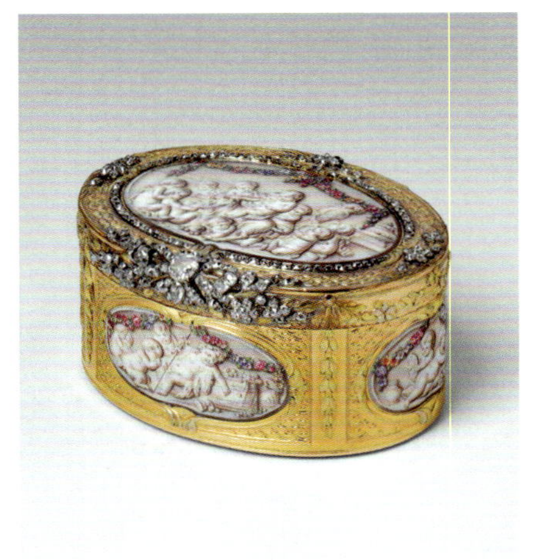

CAT. NO. 209
Enameller: Mademoiselle Duplessis
Goldsmith: Jean Georges (or George)
Snuffbox with six scenes of putti at play
c. 1761–1762
Gold, grisaille enamel, and diamonds
Box: 4.4 × 8.6 × 6.7 cm; miniatures: on cover, 4.3 × 6.5 cm; on bottom, 4.1 × 6.4 cm; on front, 2.4 × 4.8 cm; on back, 2.2 × 4.8 cm; on left side, 2.1 × 3.7 cm; on right side, 2.1 × 3.7 cm
Lent by The Metropolitan Museum of Art, New York, Gift of J. Pierpont Morgan, 1917
17.190.1125

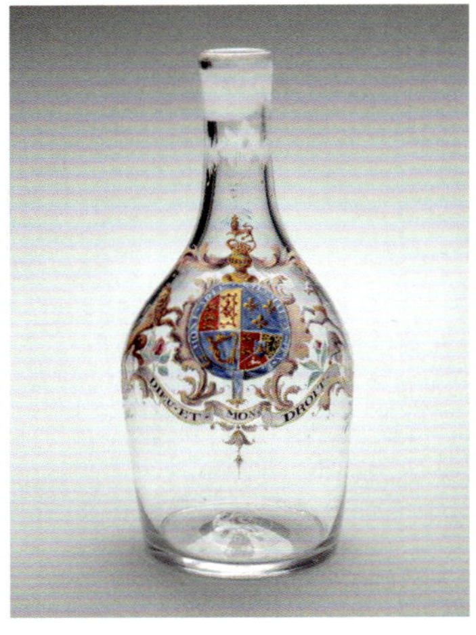

CAT. NO. 210
Beilby Workshop
Decanter
c. 1762
Glass, enamel, and gilding
23.5 × 11.4 × 11.4 cm
Toledo Museum of Art, Purchased with funds from the Libbey Endowment, Gift of Edward Drummond Libbey, 1963
1963.16

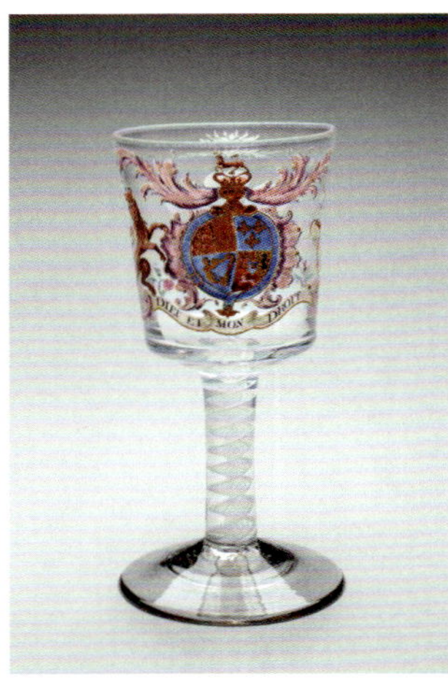

CAT. NO. 211
Beilby Workshop
Goblet with the Royal Arms of George III
c. 1762–1763
Lead glass, enamel, and gilding
22.9 × 11.4 × 11.4 cm
Toledo Museum of Art, Purchased with funds from the Libbey Endowment, Gift of Edward Drummond Libbey, 1954
1954.16

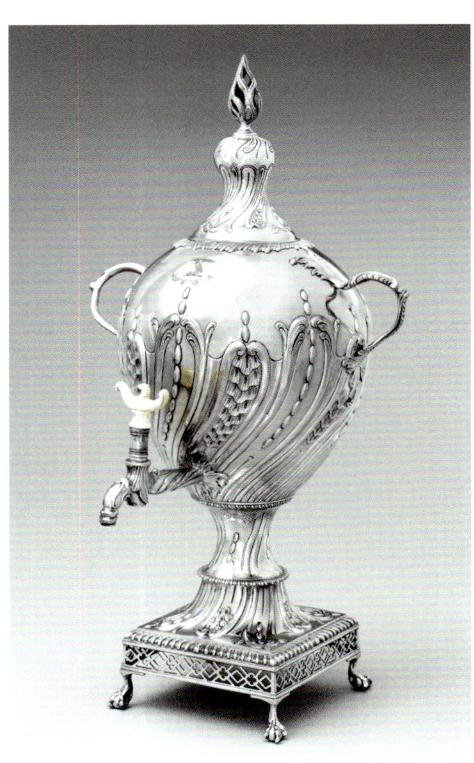

CAT. NO. 212
Louisa Courtauld
Hot water urn
1765–1766
Silver
Urn: 22.2 × 8.1 cm; cover: 17.9 × 8.6 cm; base: 21.3 × 16.8 × 7.9 cm
Lent by The Metropolitan Museum of Art, New York, Gift of Madame Lilliana Teruzzi, 1966
66.192.1a-c
Image copyright © The Metropolitan Museum of Art / Image source: Art Resource, NY
Exhibited at BMA only

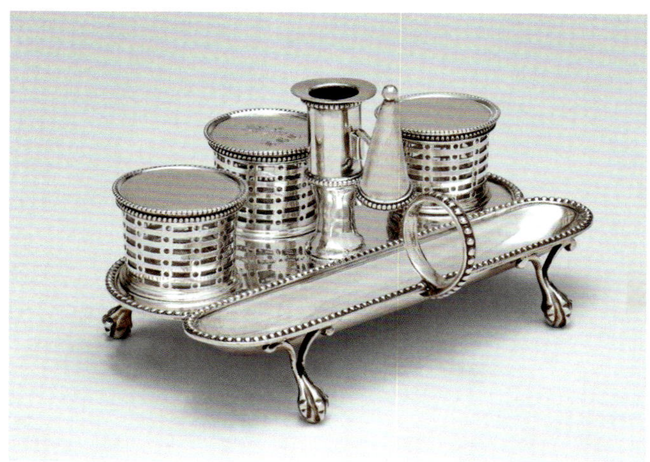

CAT. NO. 213
Hester Bateman
Inkstand
1780–1781
Silver
8.3 × 8.7 × 14.9 cm
Philadelphia Museum of Art: The Israel Corse Collection, Gift of Mrs. Lena Cadwalader Evans Webb, 1936
1936-30-10a--f

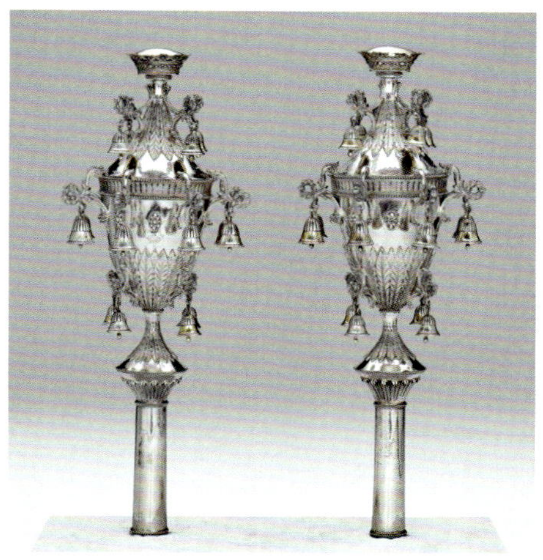

CAT. NO. 214
Hester Bateman with Thomas Evans and Jacob Levi
Pair of Torah Finials (Rimmonim)
1784
Silver
Height: 43.2 cm; 2,208 g
North Carolina Museum of Art, Raleigh, Purchased in memory of B. Elmo and Hannah P. Scoggin with funds from the bequest of Hannah P. Scoggin and the Judaic Art Fund, 2021
2021.22/a-b

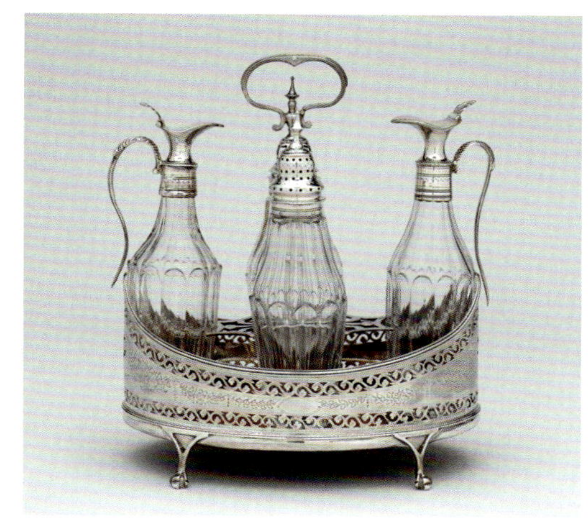

CAT. NO. 215
Hester Bateman
Cruet stand
1784–1790
Silver and mahogany
22.5 × 20.3 × 12.7 cm
Baltimore Museum of Art: Gift of Elizabeth F. Cheney, Oak Park, Illinois, 1981.103.1-.5
Photo: Mitro Hood

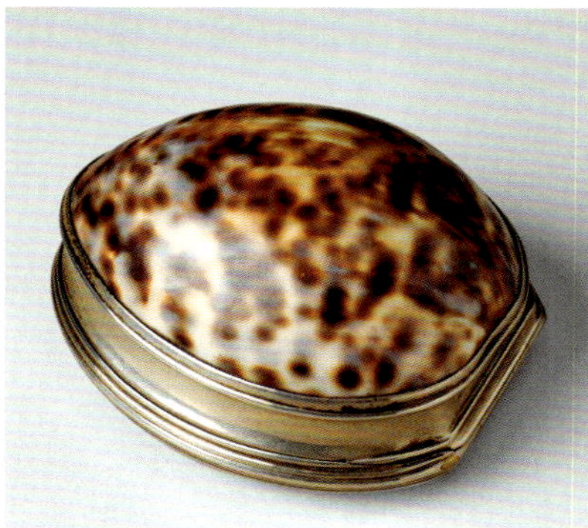

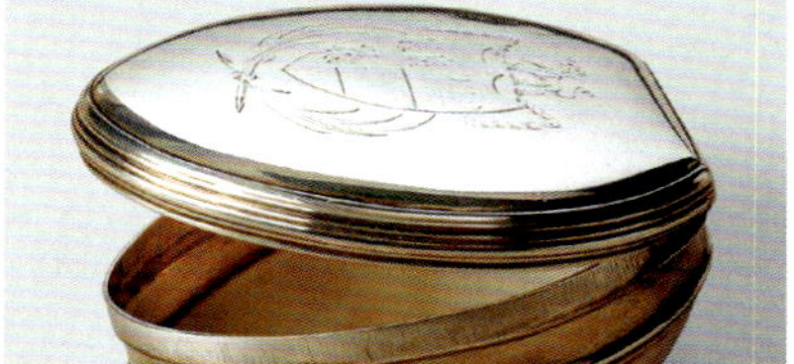

CAT. NO. 216
Elizabeth Roker
Snuffbox
1786
Parcel gilt silver and shell
3.6 × 5.5 × 6.5 cm
Clark Art Institute, Williamstown, Massachusetts, USA, Gift of Marilyn Grossman, 2008
2008.4
Image courtesy Clark Art Institute. clarkart.edu

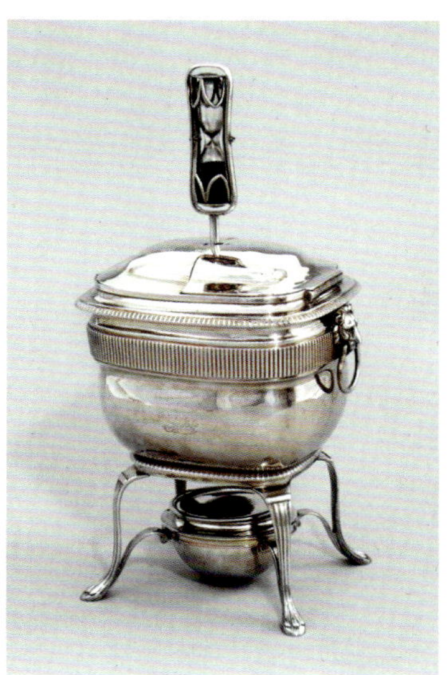

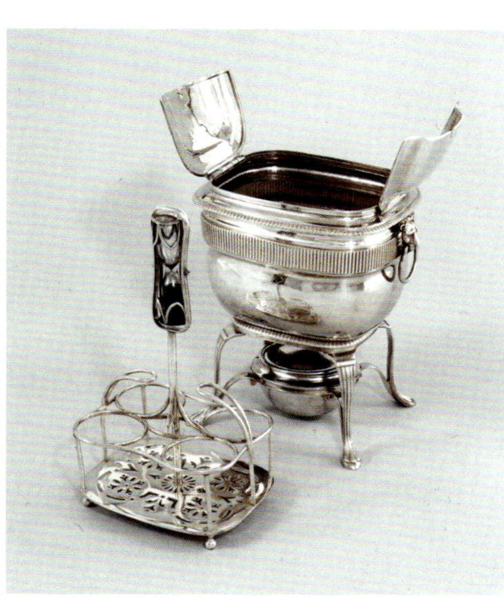

CAT. NO. 217
Rebecca Emes
Egg coddler on lampstand
1808
Silver
23.5 × 16.5 × 13.7 cm
National Museum of Women in the Arts, Washington, DC, Silver collection assembled by Nancy Valentine, purchased with funds donated by Mr. and Mrs. Oliver R. Grace
1987.73a-b
Photo: Lee Stalsworth

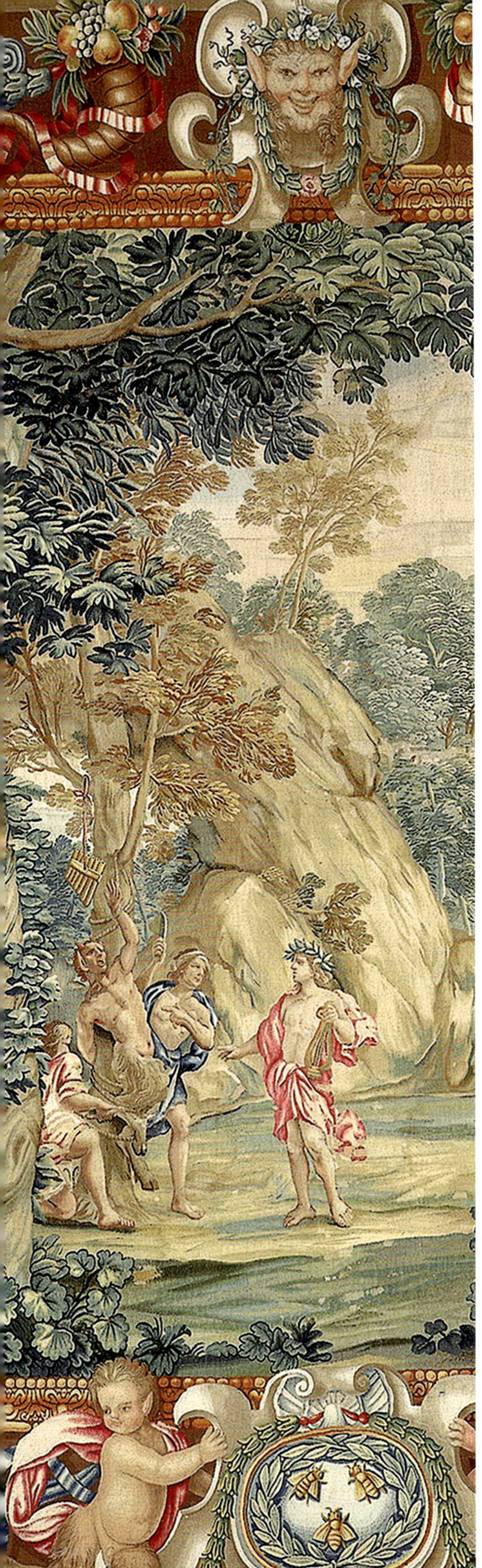

Tapestry, Woven Fabrics, and Embroidery

Isabella Rosner and Theresa Kutasz Christensen

Every stage of a textile's life, in its journey from design to production to use, is an ever-changing landscape of gendered labour and consumption. Professional weaving needlecraft were historically the work of both sexes. The presence of women at the drawing board, in the workshop, and at the shop counter complicates the simplistic understanding that European women in the early modern period were strictly homemakers. Although many women were indeed limited to the domestic sphere, these objects testify to their movement both within and beyond those spaces.

Much of the invisible labour that went into the creation of pre-modern textiles—including the procurement, dyeing, and spinning of wool, the making of glass beads, the care and processing of silkworms, and the design of secondary patterns—likely would have been carried out by women of the lowest classes whose names have not been preserved. While women's involvement in textile-making has been assumed on some level, their specific impact, particularly as professional makers, and the broader influence of their labour on the economy, remains understudied. What we know about women in the textile arts comes from ongoing material and archival study of extant examples, which have been selectively and unevenly preserved because of their utilitarian nature, fragility, and light sensitivity.

Women across Europe are documented in nearly every aspect of tapestry manufacture between the fifteenth and eighteenth centuries. The account books of Sainte-Madeleine of Troyes from 1425 to 1430 document the production of a now lost set of Saint Mary Magdalene choir tapestries. Payments to Poinsète, a seamstress, and an unnamed chambermaid indicate they stitched the base for the cartoons, lined the finished tapestries, and finished them with cord and thread for hanging. Also included are line items that document food and wine consumed by men as they discussed progress and direction. The heavy physical involvement of Poinsète despite the absence of her documented presence in the socialized aspects of creation underscores the difficulties professional women faced in navigating male-dominated economies of production. In Scandinavia, weaving was among the tasks taken up by women of the lower classes outside major cities where there was a long tradition of woven textiles, often featuring a narrative component. In Sweden, there was also a history of high-quality Renaissance tapestry manufacture that included the 1688 royal establishment of a women-led, women-patronized, woman-founded tapestry manufacture that trained orphaned girls in the palace at Karlsberg. Similarly, in the 1680s in France, Françoise-Athénaïs de Rochechouart,

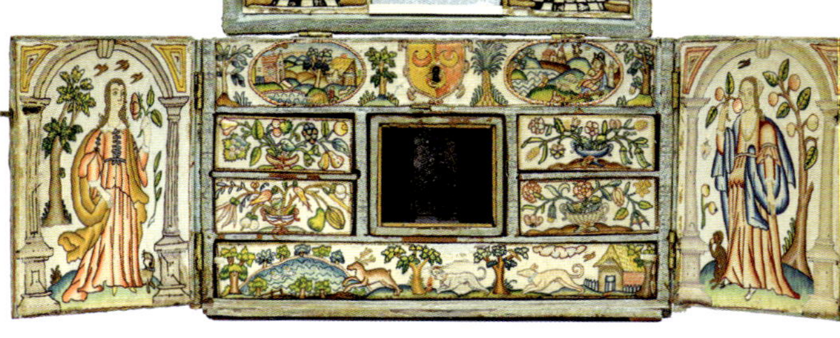

CAT. NO. 218
Susanna Perwich
Embroidered cabinet
1645–1655
Linen plain weave and silk satin with silk embroidery, metallic braid, silk plain weave, and mirrored glass with metal and wood
26 × 30.8 × 20 cm
Los Angeles County Museum of Art,
Gift of Mr. and Mrs. John A. McCone
M.79.39.3a-g

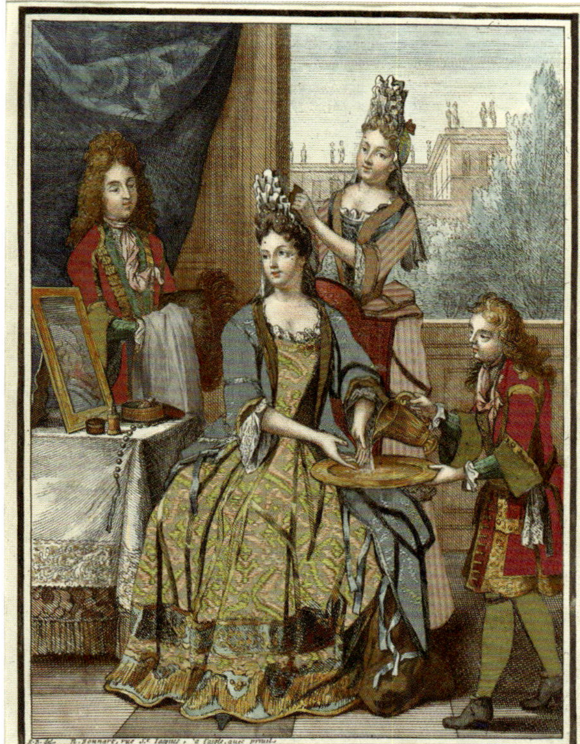

CAT. NO. 219
Unknown European maker
Engraver: Robert Bonnart
A Woman of Quality at Her Toilette [*Dame de qualité à sa toilette*]
Originally printed c. 1690–1710, altered c. 1750
Hand-coloured engraving, faced on reverse with fabrics
26.2 × 18.9 cm
The Morgan Library & Museum, New York
2002.31
Photo: The Morgan Library & Museum, New York

Marquise de Montespan, notably patronized the Parisian convent of the Filles de Saint-Joseph, which trained orphan girls in embroidery and tapestry weaving for royal projects. Women at the French court were additionally involved in the documentation of prestigious tapestry series. The engravings of Johanna Sibylla Küsel (c. 1650–1717) (cat. no. 220) document one of the first sets of tapestries produced by the Gobelins manufactory, featuring the elements and the seasons, and designed by Charles Le Brun. Over the past several decades, long-held assumptions about women's roles in tapestry production have shifted due to the location of women in archival sources as well as popular depictions, such as author Tracy Chevalier's fictionalized account of women involved in every step of the making of the Unicorn Tapestries.

In seventeenth-century Italy, a notable group of women ran the Barberini Tapestry Workshop, one of Rome's most prestigious manufactures. The tapestries they produced played a major role in public life, displayed in churches, residences, and on streets during celebrations. The Barberini were among the most powerful families in the city, engaging leading architects and artists and running their own tapestry manufacture, which produced an average of one panel every ten months for over fifty years, on subjects ranging from biblical scenes to mythological and historical subjects. Founded by Cardinal Francesco Barberini with the assistance of Flemish weaver Giacomo della Riviera, the manufacture was referred to by at least one contemporary as the "*arrazo delle donne*" (women's tapestry workshop). An extraordinary series of twelve tapestries that feature the life of Christ (cat. no. 221), now in the collection of the Cathedral of St. John the Divine, was on the looms at the manufacture when the management of the workshop passed from della Riviera's successor and son-in-law, Gaspare Rocci, to a series of women in the family—including Caterina della Riviera (active 1648–1653), Maria Maddalena della Riviera (1611–1676), and Anna Zampieri (active 1678–at least 1679)—who collectively ran the manufacture from 1648 to 1679. The Crucifixion panel was begun under Rocci and finished by his widow, Caterina. As is seen in many works produced under the direction of widows, the panel bears the signature of the manufacture's founder "IAC DE RIV" (Giacomo della Riviera) and not the names of the female workshop head or her late husband, despite Giacomo having died four years before the *Life of Christ* series was begun. The image—somewhat simplified and modified for the woven medium—is based on a painting in the chapel of the Palazzo Barberini in Rome by the Baroque painter Pietro da Cortona.

In the Riviera workshop's series of five tapestries featuring the *Stories of Apollo* from Ovid's *Metamorphosis,* woven over a period of at least six years starting in 1659, conventions from painting were again borrowed and adapted by designer Clemente Maioli, this time from fresco traditions. In the panel showing *Apollo and Attendants Flaying Marsyas* (cat. no. 222), produced under the direction of Maria Maddalena, a fantastically lush frame populated by putti, shell-like cartouches, Barberini bees, and sculptural herms bearing floral bouquets invites viewers into a verdant woodland landscape. The bucolic setting plays host to the gruesome scene where the satyr Marsyas loses a musical contest to Apollo and is skinned alive as punishment. Series based on Ovid were popular throughout Europe and were a particularly fitting subject for tapestries made by women. The 1405 *Book of the City of Ladies* by Christine de Pizan (1364–1430) includes a section from the *Metamorphosis* about the maiden weaver Arachne, who "was the first person to invent the arts of dy[e]ing wool in different colours and of producing what we would call fine tapestries from weaving pictures on cloth that make them look like paintings."[1]

Despite the traditional assumption that tapestry production was isolated to male practitioners, surviving objects and documentary evidence indicate that women supported tapestry production at all levels. This ranged from commissions, as in the case of Madame de Montespan, to materials sourcing, preparation, and finishing, as seen with Poinsète, as well as the documentation of tapestry series by women like Küsel. Further, the locations for this work occurred in both private settings, such as the embroidery and weaving occurring in the Parisian convent, and professional ones, like the direction of major workshops for prominent families, as in the case of the Barberini workshop.

No matter whether it is tapestry, embroidery, or produced fabrics, the creation of textiles begins with design. In most European tapestry-making, the design is called a "cartoon" and the image is woven in such a way that the warp threads are not visible in the finished works, which were single-faced and largely made to be hung on walls. While also made on a loom, textiles such as woven silks were made in commercial workshops using a very different weaving process. While we know very little about the specific circumstances, sparse evidence indicates the employ of both female silk weavers and winders in eighteenth-century London.[2] Weaving was a lengthy and physically intense process. A weaver used their hands to pass the weft threads between the warp threads and beat them down to create a uniform cloth, while their feet pressed on treadles. From this dance of hands and feet, a drawn or

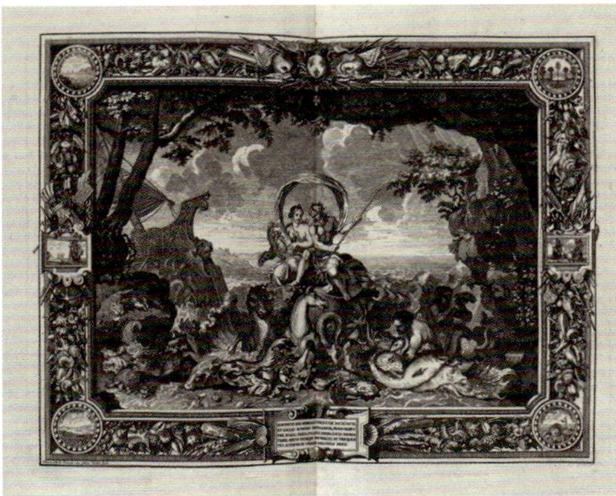

CAT. NO. 220
Engraver: Johanna Sibylla Küsel and Johann Ulrich Kraus after Sébastien Le Clerc the elder
Tapisseries du Roy : ou sont representez les quatre elemens et les quatre saisons : avec les devises qui les accompagnent et leur explication [*Tapestries of the four elements and four seasons*]
1687
Bound volume of engravings
Book (closed): 38.5 × 28.5 × 2.6 cm; book (open, spread): 37.5 × 47 cm; image: 24.9 × 32.8 cm
Art Gallery of Ontario, E.P. Taylor Library & Archives, Purchase funds generously donated by Janet E. Dewan in honour of Randall Speller and by the Janet E. Hutchison Foundation (2018)
R.B.F. 746.3944 L49 K86
Photo: Craig Boyko, AGO
Exhibited at AGO only

Opening illustrated: *The Element of Water*

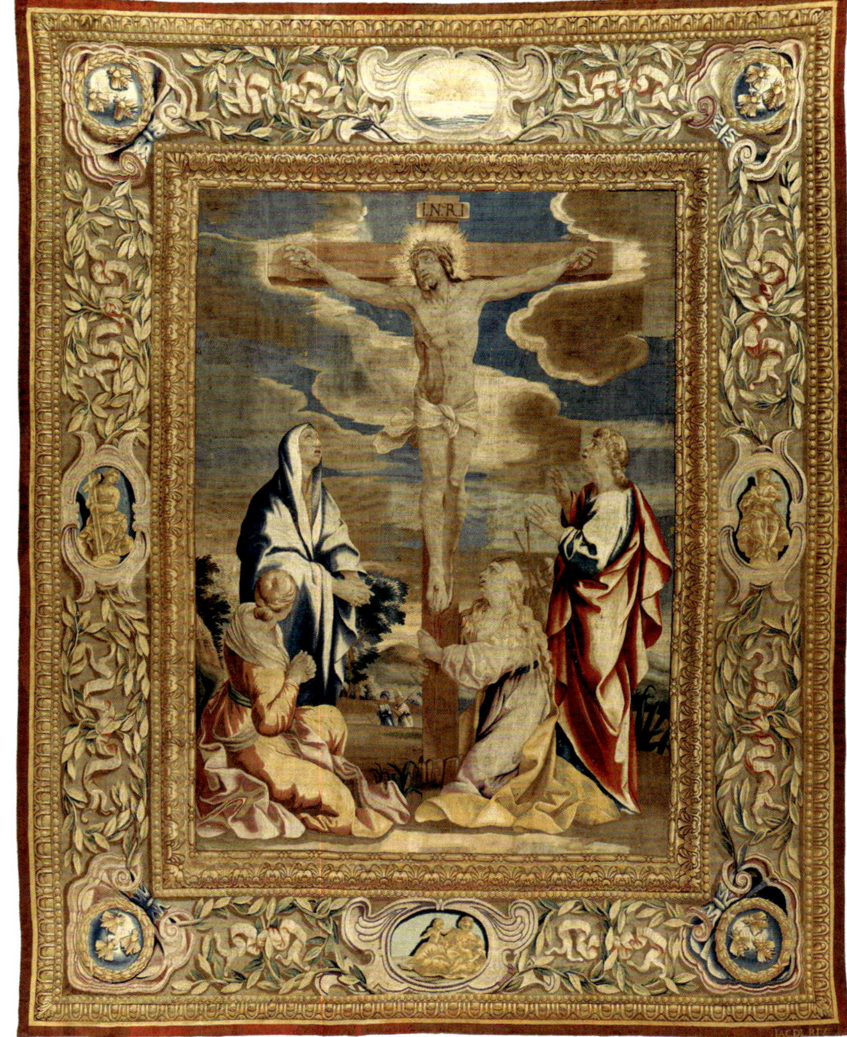

painted design on paper grew into an infinitely repeatable length of fabric.

Although not a weaver herself, the eighteenth-century Spitalfields silk designer Anna Maria Garthwaite (1688–1763) was one of Britain's most prominent and prolific textile designers. Despite not beginning her work at Spitalfields until she was nearly forty years old, Garthwaite worked for three decades and produced more than one thousand designs. Flowering vines, worked in watercolours, undulate and migrate down each of Garthwaite's pages. Elegantly curving lines characterize Garthwaite's style and the prevailing Rococo style more generally. In her design for a woven silk (cat. no. 233), she drew her thin brush horizontally in short lines to indicate where weft threads should create shading. It was probably the manufacturer Daniel Vautier, one of Garthwaite's best-known customers, who transformed this design of polychrome floral sprigs from paper to fabric (cat. no. 234), supported by hundreds of workers in his Spitalfields workshop whose names are now unknown.

Garthwaite's popular silk designs combined florals from Europe, the Americas, Africa, and Asia. Her designs mixed such European flowers as auriculas and sweet peas with exotic plants from far-flung corners of the world, including magnolias, palm trees, aloe, orchids, and hibiscus.[3] It was likely through her family connections that Garthwaite engaged with a circle of naturalists in London with access to specimens from around the world. In these lustrous silks, flora from thousands of miles apart were intermingled and literally interwoven. Like the natural specimens that inspired them, these woven silks also traversed the globe. From their East London workshops, they were shipped to ports close to home, such as Dublin, and to those across oceans, like New York and Philadelphia, for dispersal in the American colonies.[4] Although Garthwaite designed a silk lampas with flower-filled cornucopias in Spitalfields between 1726 and 1728, the silk was passed down from mother to daughter to granddaughter, reused in various gowns over multiple generations in the Americas. The current gown at Colonial Williamsburg (cat. no. 223) was assembled from this fabric sometime between 1775 and 1785, likely as a wedding dress for Sarah Greene's nuptials in 1784.[5]

A spectacular example of the reuse and recycling of fine fabrics in the period can be seen in the production of adorned or "dressed" prints, in which

CAT. NO. 221 (facing)
Workshop director: Caterina della Riviera
Manufacturer: Barberini Tapestry Workshop
Designer: Gaspare Rocci, after Pietro da Cortona
The Crucifixion, from the series *Life of Christ*
1647–1648
Wool warps, silk, and wool wefts
467.4 × 388.6 cm
Collection of the Cathedral of St. John the Divine, New York, NY, Gift of Elizabeth Underhill Coles, 1891
Photo: John Bigelow Taylor and Dianne Dubler
Exhibited at AGO only

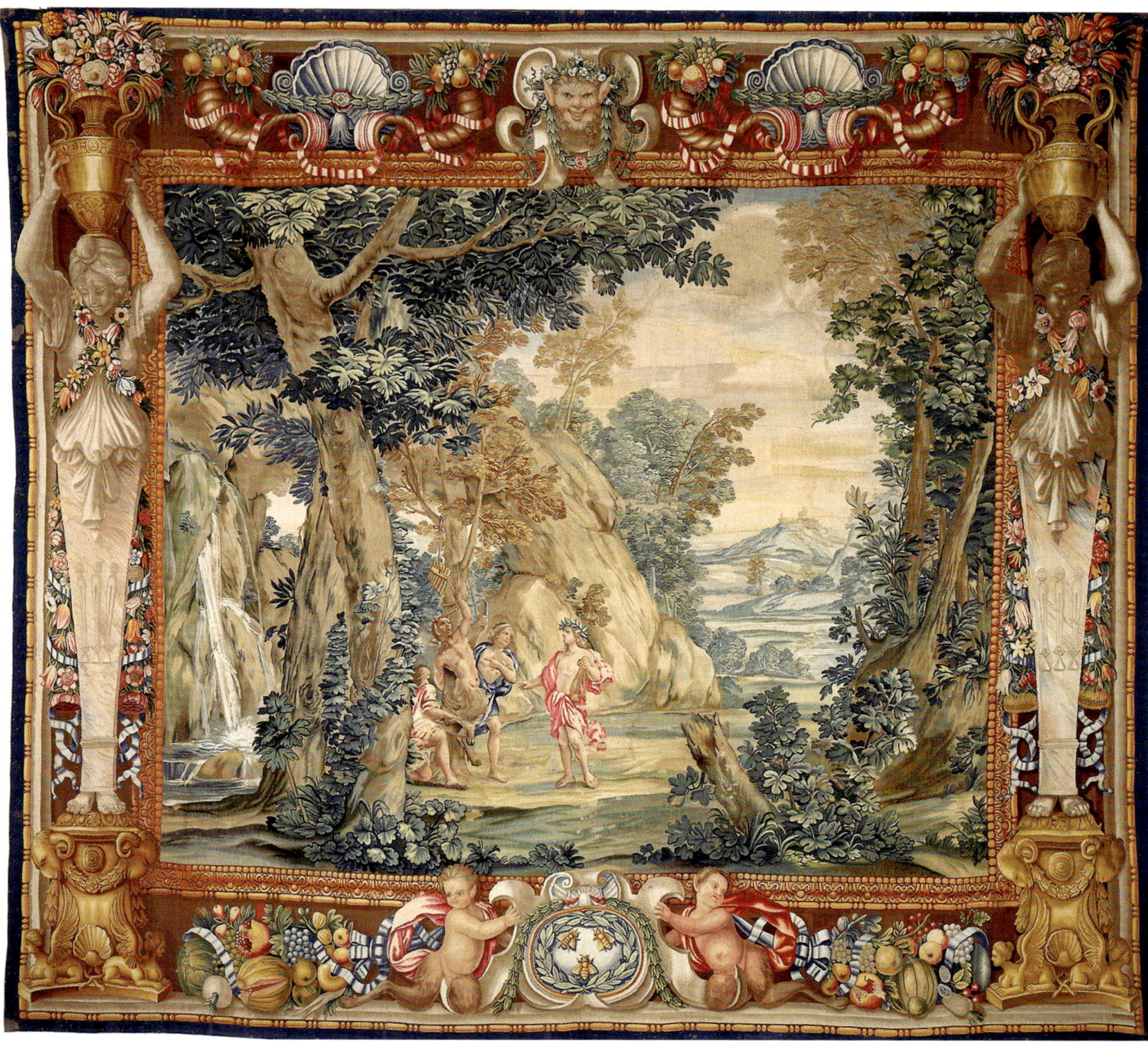

CAT. NO. 222 (right)
Workshop director: Maria Maddalena della Riviera
Manufacturer: Barberini Tapestry Workshop
Designer: Clemente Maioli
Apollo and Attendants Flaying Marsyas
c. 1662
Wool and silk; tapestry weave
419.1 × 476.9 cm
Lent by the Minneapolis Institute of Art, The Miscellaneous Works of Art Purchase Fund 57.19
Exhibited at BMA only

meticulously cut-out engravings are backed by pieces of fabric. This popular domestic craft, known as *découpe* (cut-out), was a pastime for women and men, and also occasionally professionally produced for a collector's market. An example printed between 1690 and 1710 by Robert Bonnart was "dressed" approximately fifty years later, around 1750, by a now unknown maker (cat. no. 219). This intervention updated the fashion of the central figure's dress, carefully cutting around the coloured printed folds to give dimension to the woven silk layered underneath. In another example, the introduction of layered fabrics provides a sumptuous update to the wardrobes of the holy family in a series of thirteen prints on the *Salus generis humani* (cat. no. 226). Worked for both secular and religious subjects, the adorned print offers a satisfying moment of cyclicality: a textile pattern originated on drawing paper; in these dressed works, they return to the page.

The publication and circulation of textile designs in books produced in centres like Germany and Italy created an interconnected network of makers in needlework as well as lace and paper work. Not just passive consumers, women like Elisabetta (or Isabella) Catanea Parasole (c. 1570–c. 1620) and Margaretha Helm (1659–1742) were involved in the production of widely copied and disseminated textile design texts.[6] In 1631, an Englishman named John Taylor published his book *The Needles Excellency*, featuring designs for embroidery and lacemaking that he had plucked from European pattern books, preceded by five sonnets and a long poem celebrating the needle and those who use it. It is in this poem that Taylor summarizes the importance of needlework to the early modern Englishwoman:

> Thus is a Needle prov'd an Instrument
> Of profit, pleasure, and of ornament:
> Which mighty Queenes have grac'd in hand
> to take,
> And high-borne Ladies such esteeme did make,
> That is their Daughters Daughters up did grow,
> The Needles Art, they to their children show.[7]

Embroidery, one of the primary forms of the "needles art" practised by centuries of women from every corner of Europe, was, just as Taylor described it, often passed down from mothers to daughters, and was indeed a means of profit and pleasure throughout the early modern world.

Although girls had always been taught to embroider by their mothers, this stitching education became more formalized beginning in the seventeenth century, when female academies emerged in ever-increasing numbers. In Catholic countries, much embroidery education was centred in convents, often as a means to support their community by selling their works. A work bag and box stitched by the English Bridgettine nuns living in Portugal is one such example (cat. no. 26). In the home, classroom, and convent, practical and decorative needlework were essential parts of a girl's education, not only providing her with the skills to sew, mend, and adorn clothing and household furnishings but also allowing her to demonstrate the diligence, femininity, and virtue associated with skilful stitching.

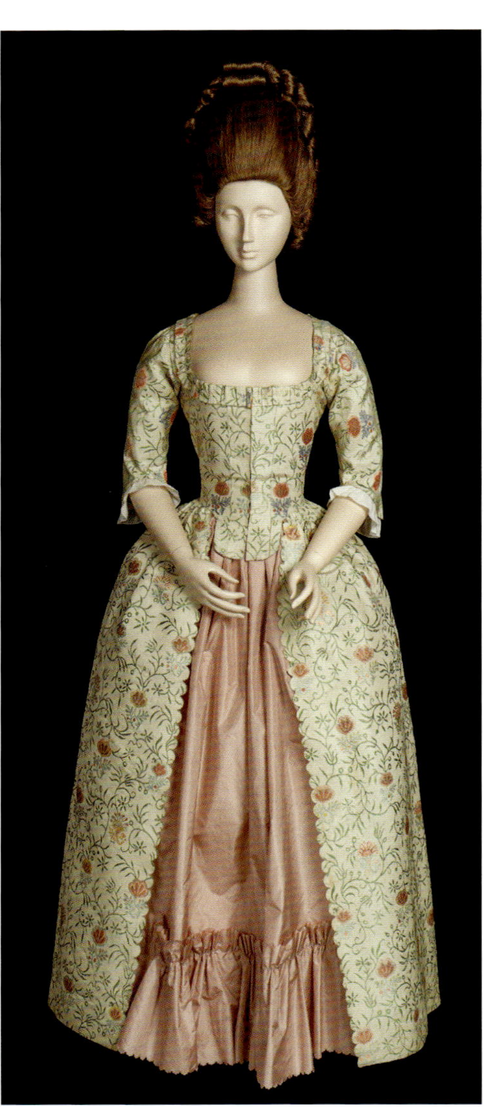

CAT. NO. 223 (below, left)
Anna Maria Garthwaite
Gown
1726–1728 (textile); 1775–1785 (gown)
Silk "lampas" brocaded with silk; linen bodice and sleeve lining
Length: 137.2 cm, waist: 55.9 cm, textile width: 53.3 cm, vertical repeat: 45.7 cm
Courtesy of The Colonial Williamsburg Foundation, Museum Purchase Accession #1951-150,1

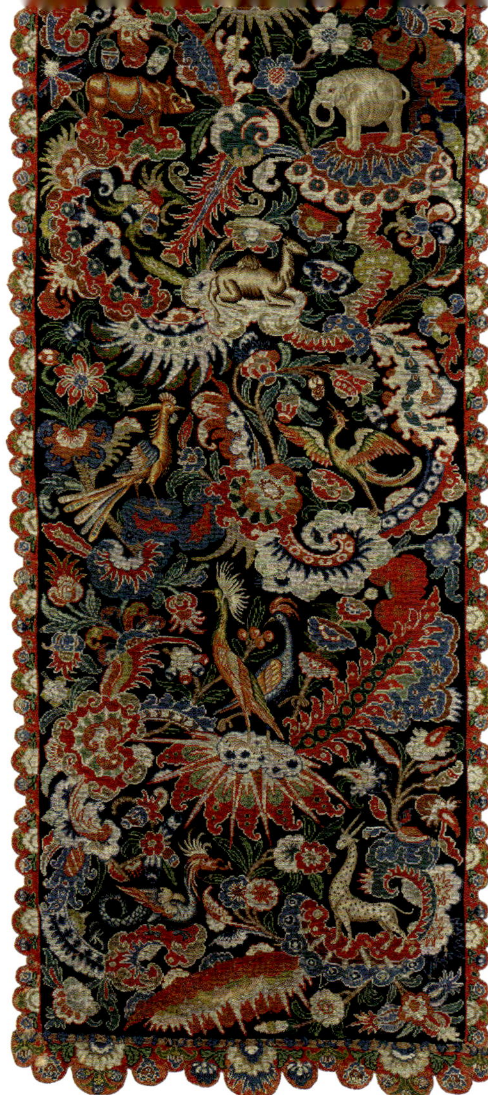

CAT. NO. 224 (above, right)
Unknown French embroiderer(s)
Bed hanging
18th century
Linen ground, wool, and silk embroidery threads
275.6 × 82.6 cm
Baltimore Museum of Art: Gift of Judge Irwin Untermyer, 1952.148b
Photo: Mitro Hood

At the centre of a girl's education was a sampler, a piece of embroidery created to practise or demonstrate stitching knowledge. Samplers range from the solely practical to the highly decorative; they are both educational exercises and biographical documents, providing unique glimpses into the lives of the girls who stitched them, with their inclusion of names, dates, and ages. In her sampler (cat. no. 228), Anna Bockett (active seventeenth century) inscribed an exact date—July 12, 1656—when she either began or ended her stitching.[8] Her sampler's upper band, illustrating a courting man and woman, shows the happy marriage for which Bockett aimed. The bands of her sampler come from sixteenth-century pattern books, the same ones Taylor used in *The Needles Excellency*. A Dutch sampler initialled "S.F." and dated 1798 (cat. no. 242) also utilizes motifs from early modern pattern books. By employing imagery from the same printed books, such as Helm's pattern book of embroidery designs (cat. no. 227), which contains guides for making everything from fans and stomachers to gloves and pockets, girls and their needlework teachers participated in a Europe-wide needlework network.

The S.F. sampler illustrates both whom and where in the world a stitcher was. S.F. stitched a building that was likely her home, school, or a hometown landmark, a common feature on samplers. Its inclusion speaks to a stitcher's community, whether it be classmates or family. The connection between stitch and place is also present in a map sampler depicting Europe (cat. no. 241) by Elizabeth Hawkins (active c. 1797) and the sampler by Spanish or Latin American Maria de la Luz Letona (active c. 1737) (cat. no. 235), which includes red-roofed, whitewashed houses, farms, and churches in a hilly landscape. It is difficult to ascertain if Letona's landscapes are accurate depictions of her surroundings or idealized pastoral scenes. Her sampler illustrates the spread of stitching knowledge beyond pattern books; the stitches and composition are shared by needlework made by girls in both Spain and its colonies, brought to Spanish America by not only books but also embroiderers themselves. In other cases, childhood stitching allows us to ascertain an embroiderer's locale via regional needlework styles. This is the case for a 1792 sampler (cat. no. 240) stitched in Norfolk, England, by Elizabeth Larter (born 1778). Larter's embroidery is typical of needlework from Norfolk, which usually features lozenge-shaped cartouches, detailed floral borders, and bands of linked octagons.

Regional influences are also found on other forms of childhood stitchery. The 1669 workbag by a ten-year-old with the initials "I. [or J.] S.," (cat. no. 230) features symmetrical, stylized floral motifs more typical of the Low Countries than the British Isles. Perhaps I.S. stitched her bag in eastern England, with its proximity to continental Europe.[9] I.S.'s work bag likely held sewing tools or its stitcher's precious possessions, as did the small tabletop boxes, called caskets and cabinets, that girls like Susanna Perwich (1636–1661) (cat. no. 218) and the stitcher of the anonymous example (cat. no. 247) worked toward the end of their needlework education. These boxes, with their beautiful exteriors and secret compartments, combined public consumption with private treasure-keeping. As girls became women, they continued to embroider, making objects for themselves and for others. Embroidered pockets (cat. no. 225), which were worn under skirts and tied at their owner's waists, offered spaces of privacy, just as cabinets and caskets did. In embroidering a pocket, a woman adorned a deeply personal object, a treasured container for her precious few possessions. Even more personal is a portrait (cat. no. 239) by Mary Anne Harvey Bonnell (1763–1853), worked in the hair of her close friends, each of whom are listed on the back of the framed embroidery. That Bonnell depicts herself at her embroidery hoop illustrates her passion for stitching and her self-fashioning as an artist. Bonnell also included a strand of hair collected in 1789 from the tomb of Edward IV of England. Located in pride of place as the thread of Bonnell's needle, this strand displays Bonnell's study of history and interest in scientific excavations.

Women embroidered not only their adornments but also their surroundings. An anonymous mid-seventeenth-century embroiderer worked tent stitches to create a cushion cover (cat. no. 246), likely used to decorate her bedchamber, depicting Abraham banishing Hagar and Ishmael. We can deduce that M.K. Herbert (active seventeenth century) also stitched her crewelwork bed curtain (cat. no. 245), finished in 1692, to adorn her sleeping quarters. Although Herbert's curtain was for personal use, the influences she drew from for her designs were from far afield. Like the bizarre-style French bed hanging (cat. no. 224), with its

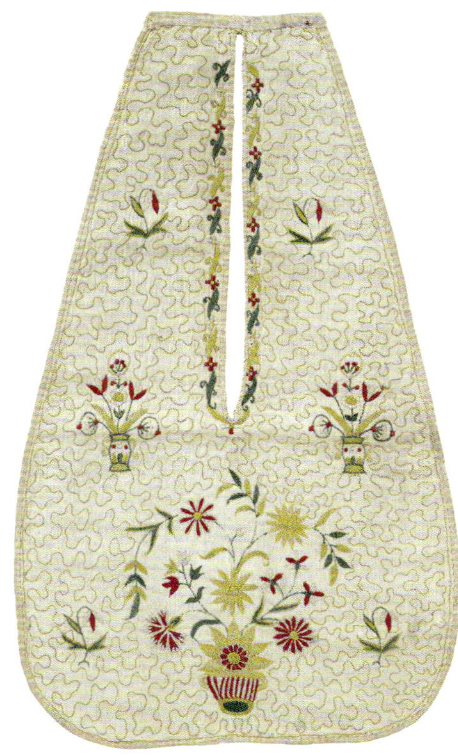

CAT. NO. 225
Unknown British embroiderer
Embroidered pocket
18th century
Linen plain weave and silk embroidery
41.1 × 25.4 cm
Lent by the Minneapolis Institute of Art, Gift of funds from Diane and Mary Lilly in memory of Irene Palmer
2017.42

variegated plants and menagerie of exotic animals ranging from a rhinoceros to a camel, Herbert's hanging features chinoiserie designs that draw inspiration from Asian textiles brought to Europe as global trade blossomed.

Just as women stitched for themselves, they stitched for loved ones. Jewish women in Italy often dedicated the Torah binders they stitched to their male family members, as Simcha (active 1696/97) did for her husband, Levi of Buttrio (cat. no. 231), and Beila Yehuditah (active 1764–1765) for her father, Emanuel Finzi di Rivarol (cat. no. 232).[10] The Roman Jewish liturgy encouraged this sort of familial production by devout women, entreating God to "bless every daughter of Israel who makes a mantle or cover in honour of the Torah." It is possible that a girl or woman also made the Elizabethan nightcap (cat. no. 229) for her husband, father, brother, or son. Crafting a nightcap, which was worn only in the home, suggests intimacy between maker and wearer. Growing out of these intimate embroidery traditions in seventeenth-century England was the incorporation of small glass beads into delicately crafted baskets, which were likely made or purchased to celebrate family milestones such as christenings or weddings. In the example by Anne Roundell (active mid-seventeenth century) at the Royal Ontario Museum (cat. no. 248), the inclusion of a verse that reads "Where vertue [sic] is the cause of love nothing but death can it remove" supports a reading of the work as a celebration of a marriage.

While some women plied their needles as a hobby, others did it for their livelihood. Contrary to popular belief, women sat alongside men in professional embroidery workshops as designers and stitchers. Mademoiselles Baulieu and Montalent (both active c. 1785) presumably worked alongside male and female makers, whose names are now unknown, to design embroidery at the Fabrique de Saint Ruf for embellished men's waistcoats that were popular in late-eighteenth-century Europe (cat. nos. 236–238). Although men and women coexisted in embroidery workshops, there was a gendered hierarchy of skill. It was often women who were tasked with embroidery rather than higher-status jobs like transferring designs and cutting out pieces.[11] The anonymity of the professional female embroiderer means it is sometimes difficult to know where exactly women's handiwork is present in embroidered objects.

But not all women who made their livelihood embroidering were anonymous. Mary Linwood (1755–1845) was a teacher and artist who displayed her needle paintings—embroidered renditions of famous paintings—in her London gallery and on tour across Scotland and Ireland. Linwood was the most renowned stitcher of needle paintings; the technique was also employed by Mary Morris Knowles (1703–1807) and Mary Delany (1700–1788). Linwood's picture *Tygress* (cat. no. 243), likely copied from John Dixon's mezzotint of George Stubbs's painting *A Tigress*, again returns to the close relationship of textiles to their origins as a design.[12] Before an embroidery design was transferred to linen or silk, it began on paper as printed designs and hand-drawn images. As also explored in the examination of woven silks designed by Garthwaite, drawing, painting, and stitching were inextricably intertwined for centuries by professional and amateur embroiderers, and women were involved in all steps of the design process. The appearance together of fine ivory embroidery tools and a tray with a stone mixing palette for watercolours in a work box from the late eighteenth century (cat. no. 244) neatly summarizes the unity of these media.

Textile production was universal, uniting European women across social classes, centuries, and borders. Although commonly held beliefs about women's needlework being relegated to the home and limited to pleasure rather than profit persist, the study of extant objects reveal that women were active participants in every type and stage of production, from elite tapestry commissions to educational samplers. Women designed, project managed, and embroidered both for themselves and the world around them.

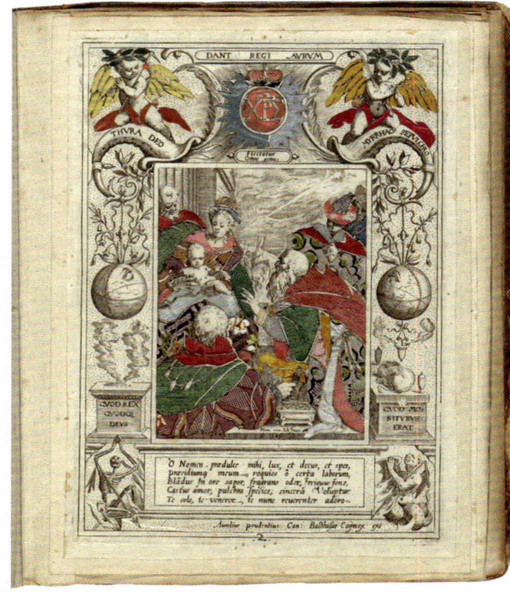

CAT. NO. 226 (above)
Unknown Northern European maker
Engraver: Balthasar Caimox
Adoration of the Magi
from *Salus generis humani* [*Salvation of Mankind*]
Originally printed c. 1600, altered 18th century
Bound volume of prints embellished with silk fabric lining
24 × 22 cm
Harvard University, Houghton Library, Philip Hofer Fund for Printing and Graphic Arts
TYP 630.00.454
Exhibited at AGO only

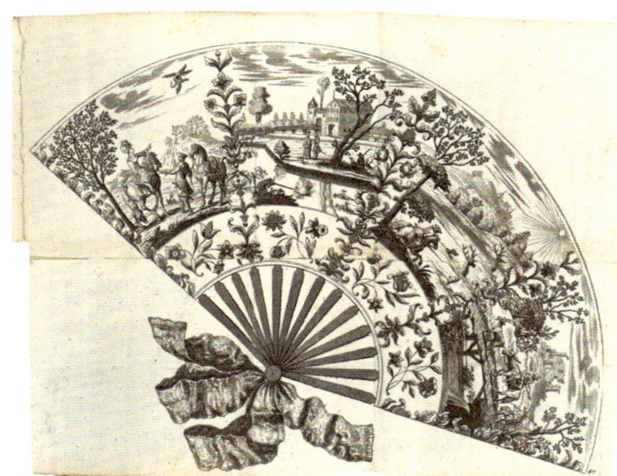
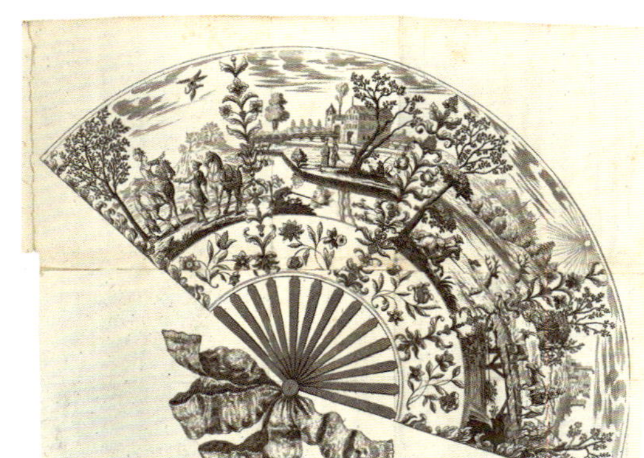

CAT. NO. 227 (below)
Margaretha Helm
Kunst- und Fleiss-übende Nadel-Ergötzungen... [*The Art and Diligence of Practicing Needle Delights*]
c. 1720–1746
Bound volume of engravings
Book: 21.2 × 34 × 3 cm; foldout page: 38.3 × 51 cm
Royal Ontario Museum, Toronto, Canada
RB TT 771 H45 1700z
Photo: courtesy of the Royal Ontario Museum, © ROM

Opening illustrated: *Design for a fan* (band 2, plate 47)

Resources Consulted

Adelson, Candace. *European Tapestry in the Minneapolis Institute of Arts.* New York: Harry N. Abrams, 1994.

Colby, Averil. *Samplers: Yesterday and Today.* London: Batsford, 1964.

Dyer, Serena. *Material Lives: Women Makers and Consumer Culture in the 18th Century.* London: Bloomsbury Visual Arts, 2021.

Eidelheit, Marlene, and James Gordon Harper. *The Barberini Tapestries: Woven Monuments of Baroque Rome.* Rome: Officina Libraria, 2017.

Goggin, Maureen Daly, and Beth Fowkes Tobin. *Women and the Material Culture of Needlework and Textiles, 1750–1950.* Farnham, UK: Ashgate, 2009.

Grossman, Cissy, "Womanly Arts: A Study of Italian Torah Binders in the New York Jewish Museum Collection." *Journal of Jewish Art* 7 (1980): 35–43.

Kane, Tina, trans. *The Troyes Mémoire: The Making of a Medieval Tapestry.* Suffolk: Boydell Press, 2010.

Kraak, Deborah. "Eighteenth-Century English Floral Silks." *Magazine Antiques* 153 (June 1998): 842–49.

Metropolitan Museum of Art. *Tapestry in the Renaissance: Art and Magnificence.* New Haven, CT: Yale University Press, 2002.

Parker, Rozsika. *The Subversive Stitch: Embroidery and the Making of the Feminine.* London: Women's Press, 1984.

Peck, Amelia, ed. *Interwoven Globe: The Worldwide Textile Trade, 1500–1800.* New York: Metropolitan Museum of Art, 2013.

Rosner, Isabella. "'A Cunning Skill Did Lurk': Susanna Perwich and the Mysteries of a Seventeenth-Century Needlework Cabinet." *Textile History* 49, no. 2 (November 2018): 140–63.

Rothstein, Natalie. *Silk Designs of the Eighteenth Century: In the Collection of the Victoria and Albert Museum, London.* London: Thames and Hudson, 1990.

Notes

1 This section also includes entries such as "About Pamphile, who discovered the art of gathering silk from worms, dyeing the thread, and making it into cloth," and "About Thamaris, who was a supremely gifted painter...." See Christine de Pizan, *The Book of the City of Ladies,* trans. Rosalind Brown-Grant (London: Penguin Classics, 1999), 73–77.

2 Viveka Hansen, "18th Century Weavers in London: A Case Study of Trade Cards and Bill-Heads," no. 113 (January 2, 2020), ikfoundation.org/itextilis/18th-century-weavers-in-london.html.

3 Zara Anishanslin, *Portrait of a Woman in Silk: Hidden Histories of the British Atlantic World* (New Haven, CT: Yale University Press, 2016), 82.

4 Anishanslin, *Portrait of a Woman in Silk*, 25–41.

5 "Gown," Works, The Colonial Williamsburg Foundation, accessed January 23, 2023, emuseum.history.org/objects/65868/gown?ctx=828ad05710ab239bec543896f915d8348269d150&idx=1.

6 For further discussion of the production and dissemination of textile design texts, see Alexa Greist's essay "Prints and Needles: Women Makers and European Textile Pattern Books, 1500–1800" on pages 30–41 of this volume.

7 John Taylor, *The Needles Excellency: A New Booke wherein are divers Admirable Workes wrought with the Needle, Newly invented and cut in Copper for the pleasure and profit of the industrious* (London: printed for James Baler, 1631), unnumbered page.

8 Elsewhere this name has been interpreted as "Buckett."

9 Andrew Morrall and Melinda Watt, eds., *English Embroidery from the Metropolitan Museum of Art, 1580–1700: 'Twixt Art and Nature* (New Haven, CT: Yale University Press, 2009), 158.

10 Maurice Berger and Joan Rosenbaum, *Masterworks of the Jewish Museum* (New Haven, CT: Yale University Press, 2004), 103.

11 Tabitha Baker, "The Embroidery Trade in Eighteenth-Century Paris and Lyon," PhD thesis diss., University of Warwick, 2019), 282.

12 "Tygress," Collections, Yale Center for British Art, collections. collections.britishart.yale.edu/catalog/orbis:11688941, accessed January 9, 2023.

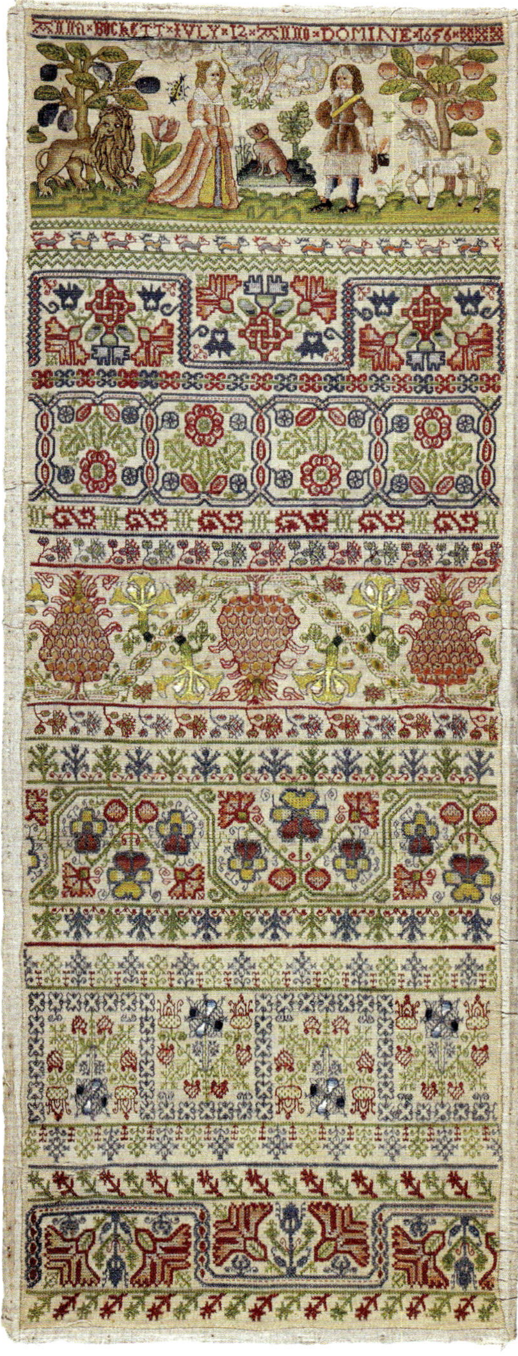

CAT. NO. 228
Anna Bockett
Sampler
1656
Linen worked with silk thread; long-and-short, split, stem, back, tent, cross, and satin stitches
70.8 × 26.4 cm
Lent by The Metropolitan Museum of Art, New York, Gift of Irwin Untermyer, 1964
64.101.1327

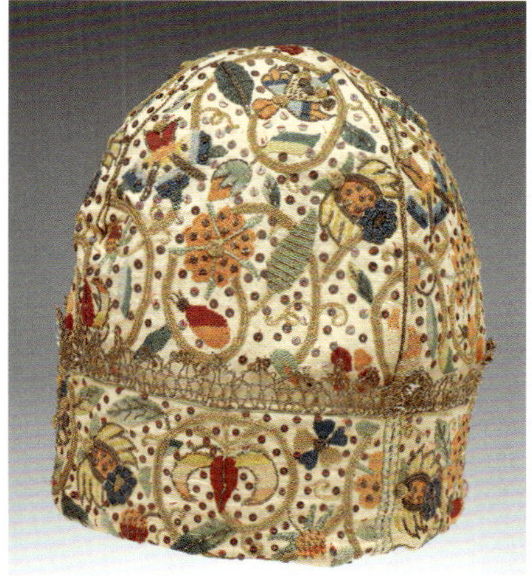

CAT. NO. 229
Unknown British embroiderer
Man's nightcap
c. 1580
Linen plain weave embroidered with silk, metallic thread, and metal sequins, and trimmed with metallic-thread lace
Height: 25.4 cm
Lent by Museum of Art, Rhode Island School of Design, Providence, Helen M. Danforth Acquisition Fund
1987.042
Image courtesy of the RISD Museum, Providence, RI

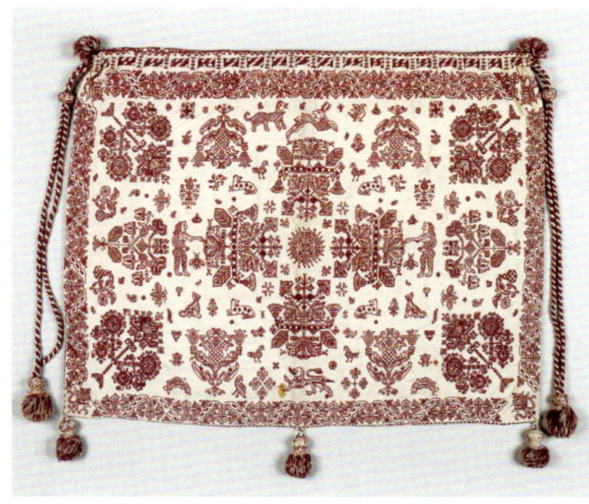

CAT. NO. 230
I.S.
Work bag
1669
Linen worked with wool thread; double running and herringbone stitches
Overall, excluding tasselled cords: 47 × 61 cm
Lent by The Metropolitan Museum of Art, New York, Purchase, Friends of European Sculpture and Decorative Arts Gifts and Rogers Fund, 2006
2006.263

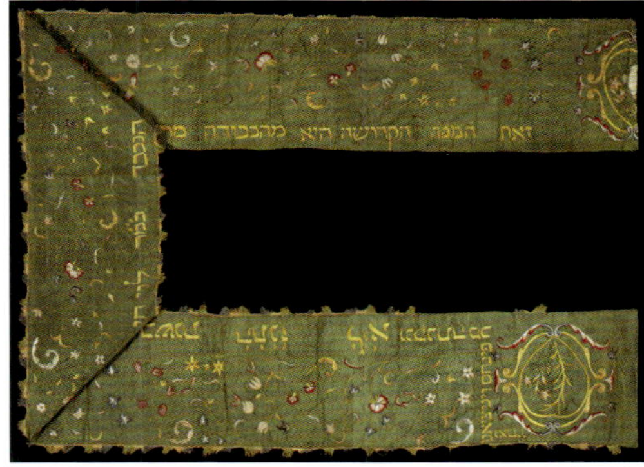

CAT. NO. 231
Simcha, wife of Levi of Buttrio
Torah binder
1696/1697
Silk embroidered with silk thread
21.6 × 248.9 cm
The Jewish Museum, New York, The H. Ephraim and Mordecai Benguiat Family Collection
S 16
Image courtesy the Jewish Museum, New York
Exhibited at AGO only

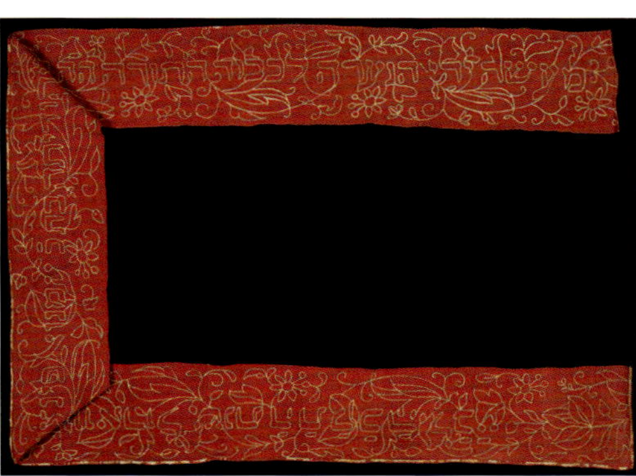

CAT. NO. 232
Beila Yehuditah, daughter of Emanuel Finzi di Rivarol
Torah binder
1764–1765
Linen embroidered with linen thread
17.8 × 289.6 cm
The Jewish Museum, New York, Gift of Dr. Harry G. Friedman
F 2405
Image courtesy the Jewish Museum, New York
Exhibited at BMA only

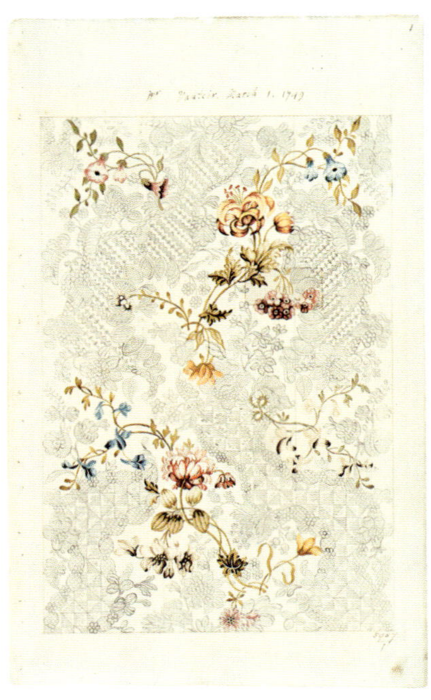

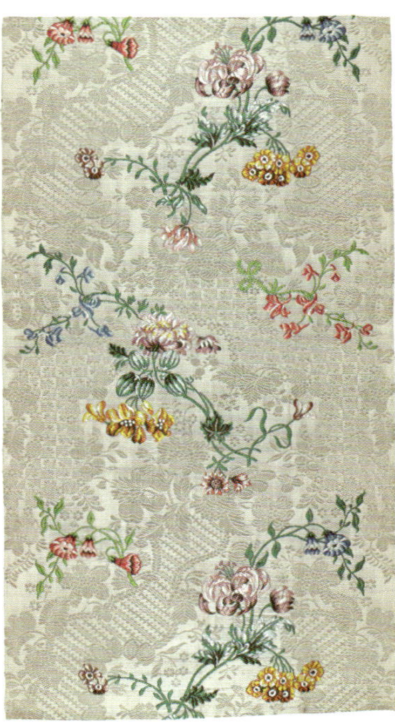

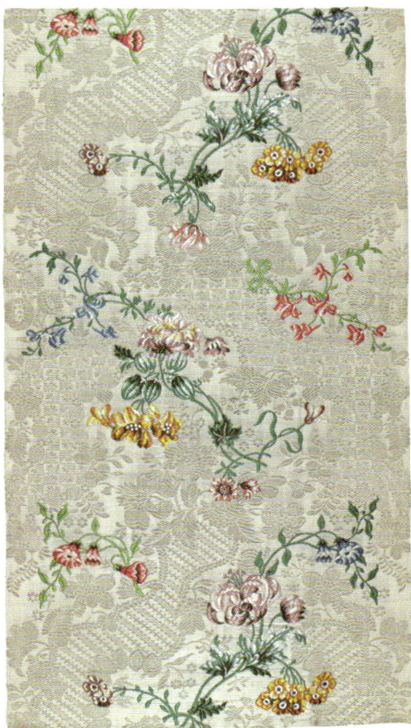

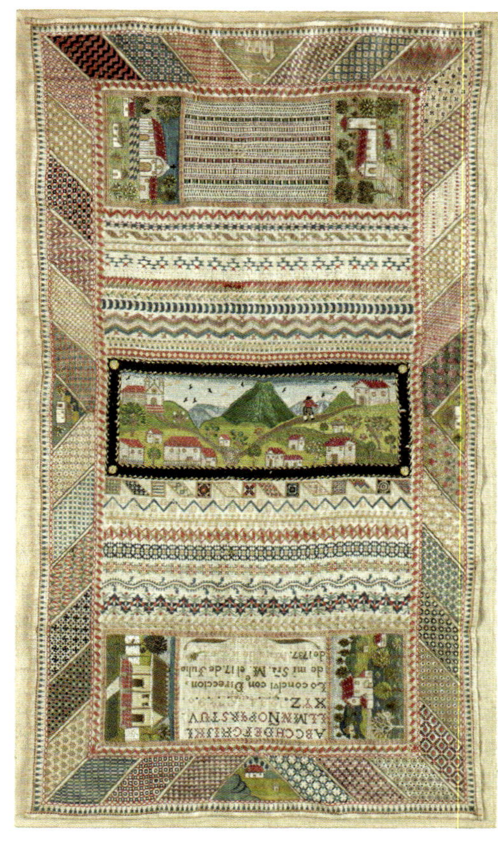

CAT. NO. 235 (right)
Maria de la Luz Letona
Sampler of country scene and border designs
1737
Silk and cotton embroidery floss on linen ground with cotton mount
64.8 × 38 cm
Frances Lehman Loeb Art Center, Vassar College, Transfer from Vassar College Libraries, Special Collections, Martha Clawson Reed Collection
1997.7.137
Photo: Frances Lehman Loeb Art Center, Vassar College, Poughkeepsie, NY / Art Resource, NY

CAT. NO. 233
Anna Maria Garthwaite
Design for a woven silk
1749
Watercolour on paper
39.4 × 25.4 cm
Victoria and Albert Museum, London
5987:1
Image © Victoria and Albert Museum, London

CAT. NO. 234
Anna Maria Garthwaite
Length of brocaded silk tobine
1749
Silk
88.3 × 49.5 cm
Baltimore Museum of Art: Angelica Yonge Pearre Fund, 1999.156
Photo: Mitro Hood

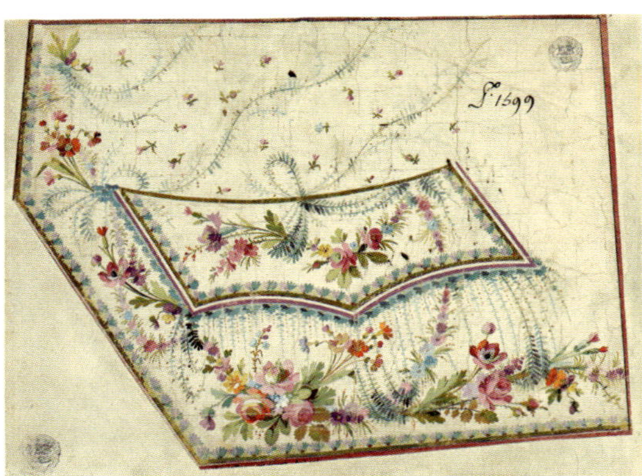

CAT. NO. 236
Mademoiselle Baulieu
Design for a gentleman's embroidered waistcoat
c. 1785
Pen and brown ink, brush, and opaque watercolour on off-white paper
22.8 × 37.5 cm
Cooper Hewitt, Smithsonian Design Museum, Smithsonian Institution, Gift of Eleanor and Sarah Hewitt
1921-22-241

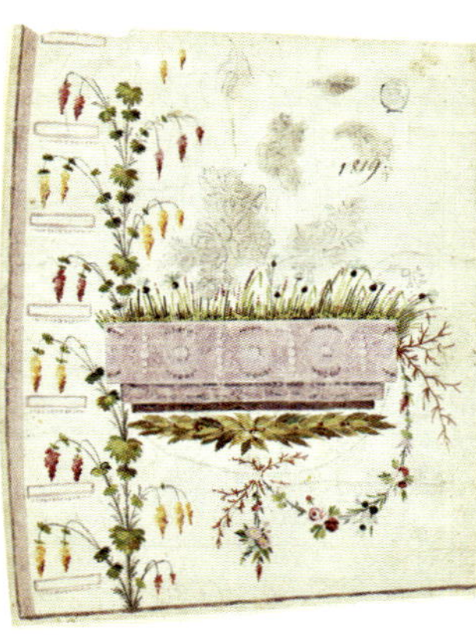

CAT. NO. 237
Mademoiselle Montalent
Design for embroidered waistcoat
c. 1785
Graphite, pen and ink, brush, and opaque watercolour on white paper
33.4 × 27.1 cm
Cooper Hewitt, Smithsonian Design Museum, Smithsonian Institution, Gift of Eleanor and Sarah Hewitt
1920-36-76

CAT. NO. 238
Unknown designer at the Fabrique de Saint Ruf, Lyon, France
Design for embroidery, gentleman's waistcoat pocket
c. 1785
Brush and watercolour, opaque watercolour, pen and purple ink, and graphite on cream paper
17.3 × 30.4 cm
Cooper Hewitt, Smithsonian Design Museum, Smithsonian Institution, Gift of Eleanor and Sarah Hewitt
1920-36-60

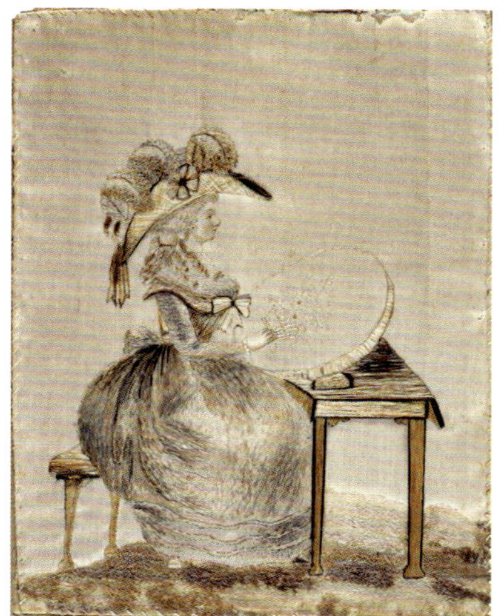

CAT. NO. 239
Mary Anne Harvey Bonnell
Self-Portrait
1789
Hair and silk
21.6 × 16.5 cm
Baltimore Museum of Art: Gift of Carlton Hobbs, 2022.94
Photo: Mitro Hood
Exhibited at BMA only

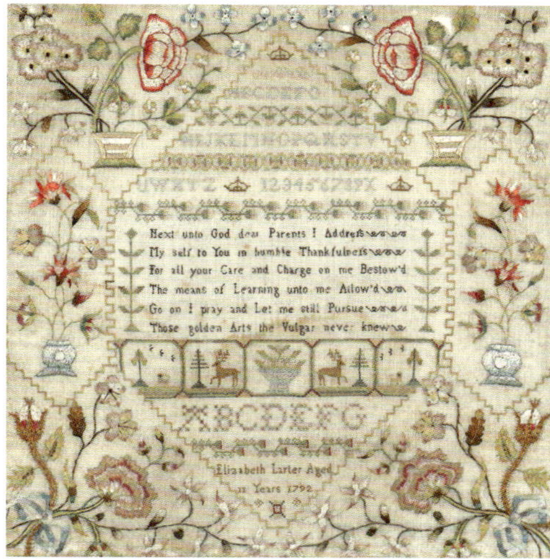

CAT. NO. 240
Elizabeth Larter
Sampler (Next Unto God…)
1792
Silk embroidery threads on wool ground
31.7 x 33 cm
Frances Lehman Loeb Art Center, Vassar College, Transfer from Vassar College Libraries, Special Collections, Martha Clawson Reed Collection 1997.7.74
Photo: Frances Lehman Loeb Art Center, Vassar College, Poughkeepsie, NY / Art Resource, NY

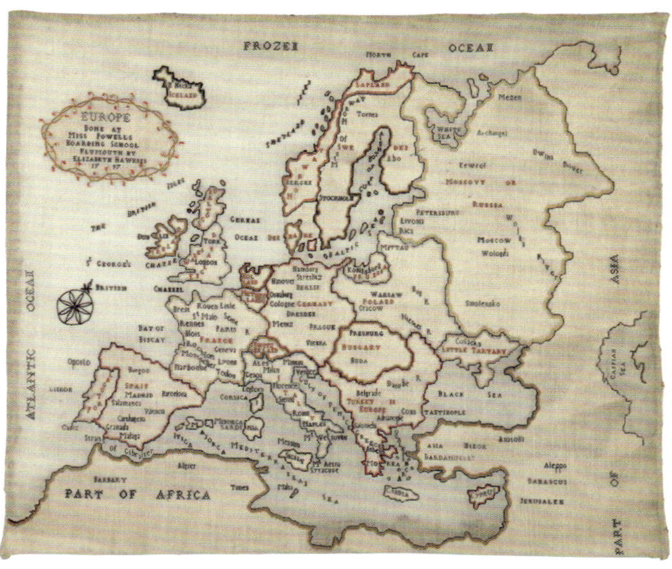

CAT. NO. 241
Elizabeth Hawkins
Map sampler
1797
Woollen sampler embroidered in silks
48.5 × 58.5 cm
Victoria and Albert Museum, London, Given by Miss A.P. Rean T.165-1959
Image © Victoria and Albert Museum, London

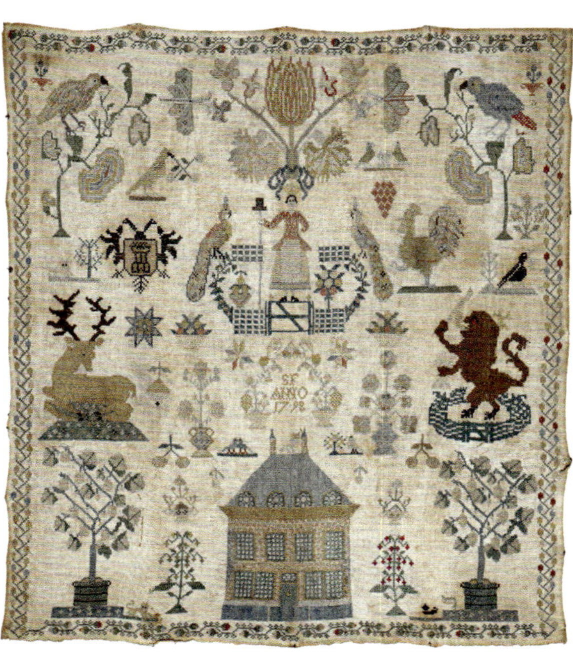

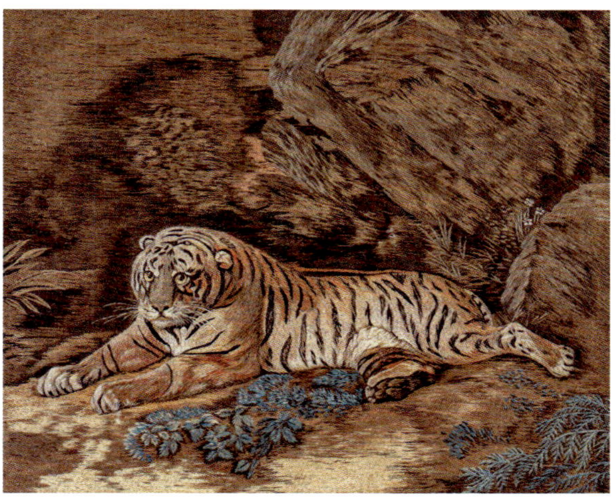

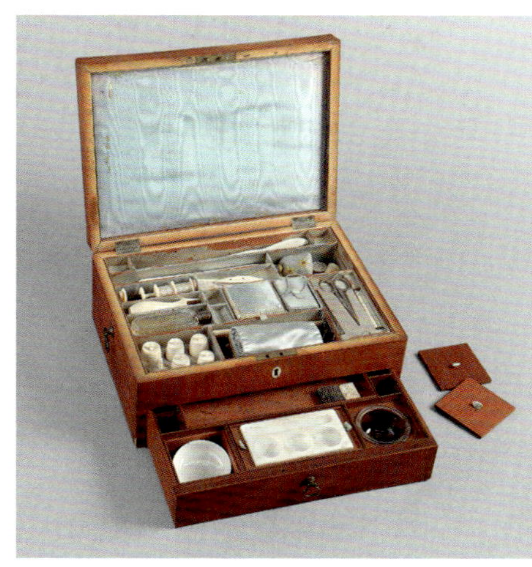

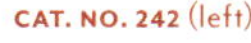

CAT. NO. 242 (left)
S.F.
Sampler
1798
Fabric
43.2 × 40.6 cm
Frances Lehman Loeb Art Center, Vassar College, Gift of Mrs. James W. Packard (Elizabeth Gillmer, Class of 1894)
1960.9.9
Photo: Frances Lehman Loeb Art Center, Vassar College, Poughkeepsie, NY / Art Resource, NY

CAT. NO. 243 (middle)
Mary Linwood, after George Stubbs
Tygress
c. 1798
Worsted wool needlework
46 × 59 cm
Yale Center for British Art, Paul Mellon Fund
QR.MC 3
Image Courtesy YCBA

CAT. NO. 244 (right)
Probably Reeves & Company
Combination sewing and painting box
c. 1800
Satinwood box lined with satin fabric, ivory sewing kit, watercolour pigment blocks, ceramic, alabaster, and glass tools
Closed: 24 × 36 × 13.3 cm
Katrin Bellinger Collection
2017-005
Photo: Matthew Hollow

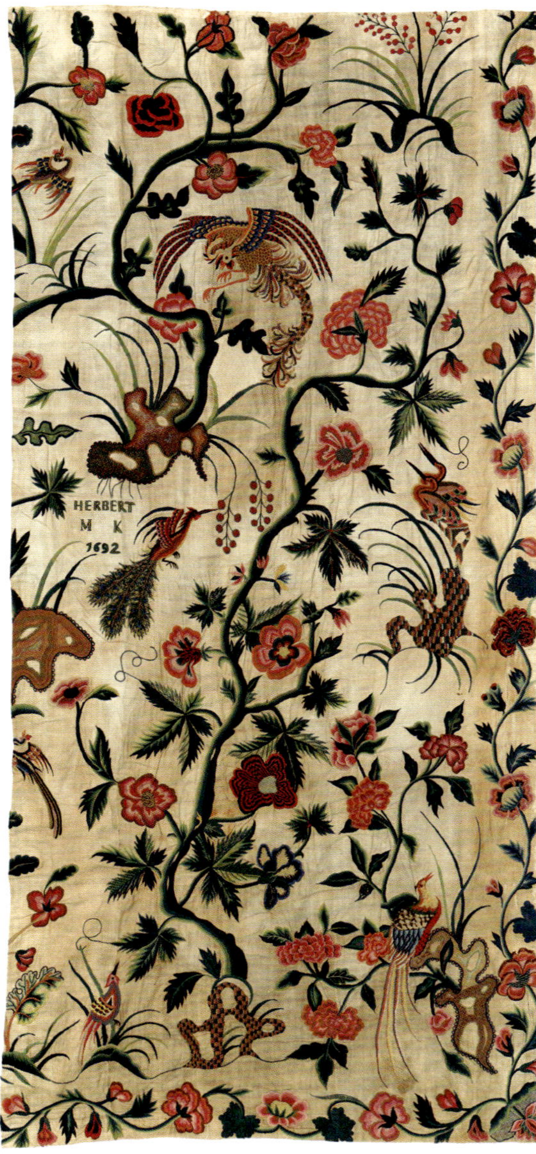

CAT. NO. 245
M.K. Herbert
Crewelwork bed curtain
1692
Linen (warp) and cotton (weft) ground; wool, silk, and cotton embroidery threads
246.4 × 111.8 cm
Baltimore Museum of Art: Gift of Judge Irwin Untermyer, New York, 1956.151a
Photo: Mitro Hood

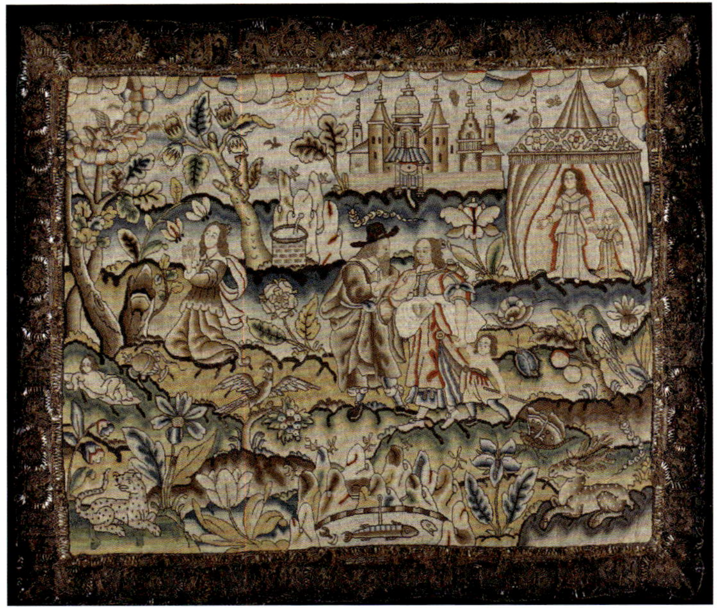

CAT. NO. 246
Unknown British embroiderer
Abraham Banishing Hagar and Ishmael
c. 1650
Linen canvas ground, silk embroidery threads, silk backing, and metallic bobbin lace
43.8 × 51.4 cm
Baltimore Museum of Art: Purchase with exchange funds from Gift of Mrs. A. Taylor Bragonier; Gift of Mrs. H.P. Bray; Gift of Mrs. Charles Collier; Gift of Mrs. Symington Dorsey; Gift of Mrs. J. Edward Duker; Gift of Maria Lovell Eaton and Mrs. Charles R. Weld, from the Estate of Mary M. Eaton; Gift of Mr. and Mrs. Manuel L. Hendler; Gift of Mrs. Gerald W. Johnson; Gift of Mrs. F.A. Korff; Gift of Ruth Young Lachman; Gift of Eleanor B. Leitch; Gift of Sara B. Lipscomb; Gift of Cornelius Ruxton Love, Jr.; Gift of Henry A. Ludwig; Gift of Fanny Lyon; Gift of Mrs. Florence Milliken; Gift of Mrs. Frank Primrose; Gift of Mrs. Jesse Rider; Gift of Mrs. Ralph K. Robertson; Gift of Mrs. C. Rogulih; Gift of Mrs. Dudley Shoemaker; and Gift of Louisa Gilmore Riach Wade, 1998.528
Photo: Mitro Hood

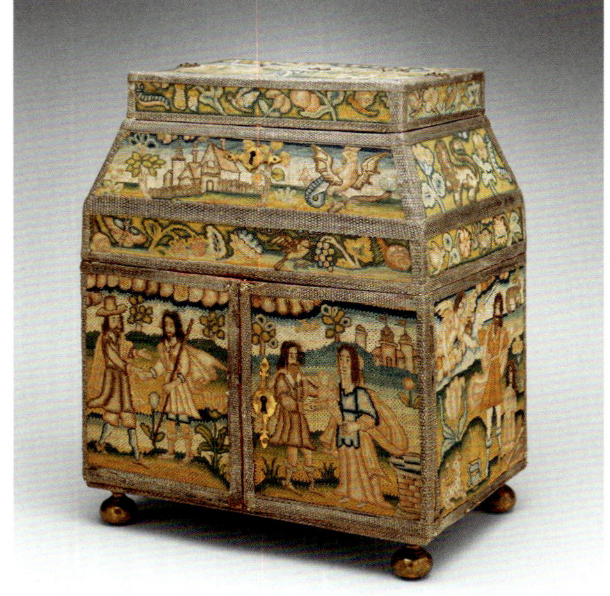

CAT. NO. 247
Unknown British embroiderer
Embroidered cabinet
c. 1665
Silk satin and linen plain weave with silk and metallic-thread embroidery, metal purl, metallic braid, silk plain weave, metallic-embossed paper, metal, and glass
31.8 × 26.7 × 19.1 cm
Los Angeles County Museum of Art, Gift of the Horowitz Family
M.84.46.9a-k

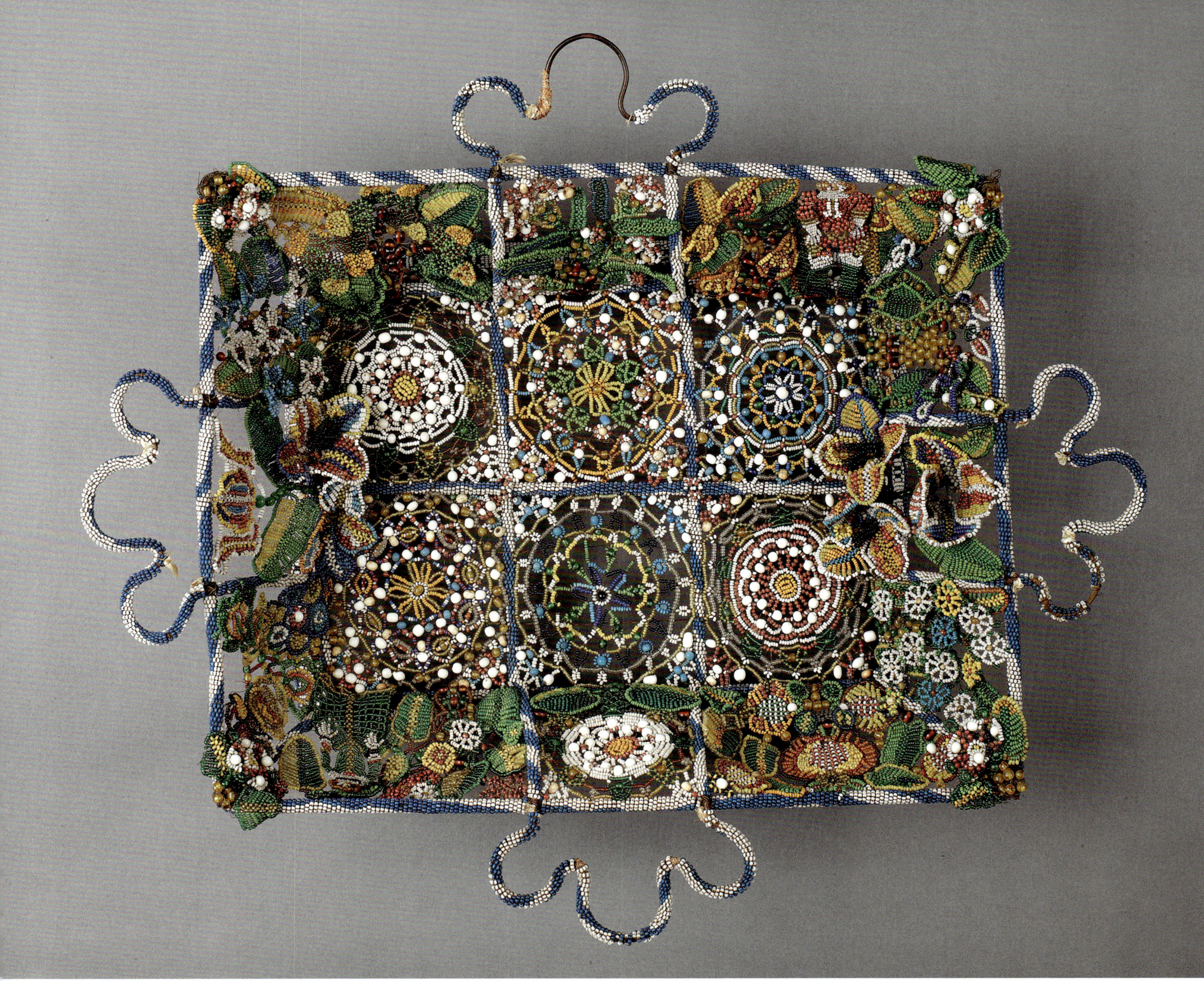

CAT. NO. 248
Anne Roundell
Commemorative beaded basket
1656
Iron frame and polychrome glass beads
12.5 × 44.5 × 53.3 cm

Royal Ontario Museum,
Toronto, Canada
960.126.3.A
Photo: courtesy of the Royal Ontario Museum, © ROM
Exhibited at AGO only

Index of Women Makers Illustrated

For the majority of women in this index, there is still much we do not know about their individual biographies and artistic careers. This is in part due to the difficulty of locating women in the types of documents used to chronicle the careers of men. Women's adoption of one or more married names often complicates their identification in archives, while many widows continued to operate workshops under their deceased husband's names or marks. The editors of this volume have attempted to standardize the names of the women represented throughout the volume for ease of identification and consistency, while recognizing shifts in their legal names during their careers and a wide variety of accepted spellings.

Italic indicates makers whose work is illustrated in the catalogue but not exhibited at either venue.

Regular type indicates makers and their work exhibited at both venues.

Alabaster, Mary Ann (British, 1805–1880)
Page 217 (cat. no. 128)

Allen, Anne (British, active in France, c. 1749/50–after 1808)
Page 153 (fig. 37); page 224 (cat. no. 152)

Alströmer, Anna Helena (Swedish, 1764–1792)
Page 183 (cat. nos. 52 & 53)

Andras, Catherine (British, 1775–1860)
Page 126 (fig. 10); page 238 (cat. no. 201)

Anguissola, Sofonisba (Italian, c. 1535–1625)
Page 44 (fig. 2); page 45 (figs. 3 & 4); page 141 (fig. 2); page 207 (cat. no. 101); page 208 (cat. nos. 102 & 103)

d'Arconville, Marie-Geneviève-Charlotte Darlus Thiroux (French, 1720–1805), attributed to
Page 117 (fig. 23); page 231 (cat. no. 177)

Ashfield, Mary (British, active second half of 17th century)
Page 187 (cat. no. 60)

Auffenwerth Hosennestel, Sabina (German, 1706–1782)
Page 98 (figs. 6, 7, 8); page 153 (fig. 39); page 166 (cat. no. 10); page 167 (cat. nos. 11 & 12)

Auffenwerth Wald, Anna Elizabeth (German, born 1696)
Page 98 (figs. 6, 7, 8); page 153 (fig. 39); page 166 (cat. no. 10); page 167 (cat. nos. 11 & 12)

Ayala, Josefa (Portuguese, c. 1630–1684)
Page 152 (fig. 34); page 197 (cat. no. 80); page 201 (cat. no. 89); page 214 (cat. nos. 118 & 119)

Backer, Catharina (Netherlandish, 1689–1766)
Page 116 (fig. 20)

Basseporte, Madeleine Françoise (French, 1701–1780), circle of
Page 115 (figs. 18 & 19); page 231 (cat. nos. 174 & 175)

Bateman, Hester (British, 1708–1794)
Page 98 (fig. 10); page 239 (cat. no. 202 & detail); page 243 (cat. nos. 213, 214, 215)

Baulieu, Mademoiselle (French, active c. 1785)
Page 12 (detail); page 252 (cat. no. 236)

Beale, Mary (British, 1633–1699)
Page 204 (cat. no. 95); page 208 (cat. no. 105)

Beauclerk, Diana (British, 1734–1808)
Page 101 (figs. 16 & 17); page 169 (cat. nos. 19 & 20); page 178 (cat. no. 39)

Beilby, Mary (Beilby Workshop) (British, 1749–1797)
Page 242 (cat. nos. 210 & 211)

Bembo, Illuminata (Italian, c. 1410–1496)
Page 194 (cat. no. 75)

Benoist, Marie-Guillemine (French, 1768–1826)
Page 134 (fig. 27); page 209 (cat. no. 111)

Benvenuti, Metilde (Italian, died 1772)
Page 175 (cat. no. 33)

Benwell, Mary (British, 1739–1811)
Page 124 (fig. 2)

Bertin, Marie-Jean, "Rose" (French, 1747–1813), attributed to
Page 88 (fig. 23)

Biffin, Sarah (British, 1784–1850)
Page 202 (detail); page 204 (cat. no. 96)

Blackwell, Elizabeth (British, 1699–c. 1758)
Page 230 (cat. nos. 169, 170, 171, 172, 173)

Bockett, Anna (British, active 17th century)
Front endpaper; page 82 (fig. 8); page 251 (cat. no. 228)

Bocquet Filleul, Anne-Rosalie (French, 1752–1794)
Page 131 (fig. 19); page 206 (cat. no. 99)

Boissier, Maria (French, active 1790s)
Page 233 (cat. no. 190)

Bonhomme, Yolande (French, c. 1490–1557)
Page 66 (fig. 11); page 161 (cat. no. 2)

Bonnell, Mary Anne Harvey (British, 1763–1853)
Page 186 (detail); page 189 (cat. no. 66); page 253 (cat. no. 239)

Bonnell, Sophia Jane Maria (British, c. 1748–1841)
Page 186 (detail); page 189 (cat. no. 66)

Bouchard, Magdalena (French, active c. 1772–1793)
Page 233 (cat. nos. 185, 186, 187, 188)

Bouillat, Geneviève-Louise (French, active 1776–1798)
Page 169 (cat. no. 22)

Bouzonnet Stella, Claudine (French, 1636–1697)
Page 65 (fig. 10)

Bowles Austin, Lydia (American, 1792–1824)
Page 148 (fig. 21)

Brandinn, Catherine (Austrian?, active 18th century)
Page 222 (cat. nos. 145 & 146)

Briot, Marie (French, active 17th century)
Page 228 (cat. no. 157)

Burlamacchi, Eufrasia (Italian, 1482–1548)
Page 194 (detail); page 196 (cat. nos. 77 & 78)

Campbell, Frances Mecia (American, active early 19th century)
Page 148 (fig. 20)

Candelot, Pierette, known as the Veuve Perrin (French, 1709–1794)
Page 153 (fig. 38); page 165 (cat. no. 9)

Capet, Marie Gabrielle (French, 1761–1818)
Page 180 (cat. no. 42)

Carew, Anna Maria (British, active 1660s)
Page 202 (cat. no. 92)

Carriera, Rosalba (Italian, 1673–1757)
Page 55 (fig. 24); page 177 (cat. no. 36); page 183 (cat. no. 50); page 204 (cat. no. 97); page 264 (detail)

Cosway, Maria Louisa Catherine Cecilia (British, 1759–1838)
Page 125 (fig. 4); page 185 (cat. no. 57)

Court, Suzanne de (French, active 1575–1625)
Page 95 (figs. 2 & 3); page 240 (cat. no. 203)

Courtauld, Louisa (British, 1729–1807)
Page 242 (cat. no. 212)

Coxed, Grace (British, active 1700–1735)
Page 189 (cat. no. 63)

Croswell, Mary Ann (British, died 1830), attributed to
Page 241 (cat. no. 204)

Damer, Anne Seymour (British, 1748–1828)
Page 234 (detail); page 125 (fig. 5); page 238 (cat. no. 200)

Dent, Catherine (British, active 18th century)
Page 167 (cat. no. 14)

Dietzsch, Barbara Regina (German, 1706–1783)
Page 225 (detail); page 231 (cat. nos. 178 & 179)

Dolci, Agnese (Italian, 1659–1686)
Page 46 (fig. 6); page 181 (cat. no. 44)

Drölling, Louise Adéone (French, 1797–1831)
Page 215 (detail); page 217 (cat. no. 127)

Duplessis, Mademoiselle (French, active c. 1753–1760)
Page 242 (cat. no. 209)

Edlin, Martha (British, 1660–1725)
Page 81 (fig. 7)

Eimmart, Maria Clara (German, 1676–1707)
Page 229 (cat. nos. 159, 160, 161, 162)

Emes, Rebecca (British, active 1808–1829)
Page 243 (cat. no. 217)

Faydherbe, Maria (Netherlandish, 1587–1643)
Page 234 (cat. no. 191)

Fessard, Barbe Michel Adam (French, active c. 1750–1775)
Page 231 (cat. no. 176)

Fontana, Lavinia (Italian, 1552–1614)
Page 49 (figs. 8 & 9); page 54 (fig. 23); page 200 (cat. no. 84); page 206 (cat. no. 100); page 208 (cat. no. 104)

Fontana, Veronica (Italian, 1651–1688)
Page 52 (fig. 18)

Fürst, Rosina Helena (German, 1642–1709)
Page 39 (fig. 12)

Galizia, Fede (Italian, 1578–c. 1630)
Page 197 (detail); page 201 (cat. no. 88); page 211 (cat. no. 113)

Garthwaite, Anna Maria (British, 1688–1763)
Front cover; page 84 (figs. 14 & 15); page 85 (figs. 16, 17, 18); page 148 (fig. 22); page 180 (cat. no. 41); page 248 (cat. no. 223); page 252 (cat. nos. 233 & 234)

Garzoni, Giovanna (Italian, 1600–1670)
Page 47 (fig. 7); page 109 (figs. 3 & 4); page 142 (fig. 5); page 143 (fig. 6); page 227 (cat. no. 155); page 228 (cat. no. 156)

Gentileschi, Artemisia (Italian, 1593–after 1654)
Page 200 (cat. no. 87); page 201 (cat. no. 90)

Gérard, Marguerite (French, 1761–1837)
Page 131 (fig. 20); page 217 (cat. nos. 125 & 126); page 223 (cat. no. 147)

Glisson, Bernice (British, active 18th century)
Page 167 (cat. no. 14)

Godfrey, Elizabeth (British, active c. 1720–1758)
Page 99 (figs. 11 & 12); page 153 (fig. 40); page 242 (cat. nos. 207 & 208)

Gravant, Marie-Henriette (French, active mid-1700s)
Page 101 (fig. 14); page 168 (cat. nos. 16 & 17)

Guéret, Anne (French, 1760–1805)
Front cover; page 185 (cat. no. 55)

Guillaume de Bassoncourt, Baronne de Molaret, Fanny (French, 1820–1888)
Page 176 (detail); page 185 (cat. nos. 58 & 59)

Hamerani, Beatrice (Italian, 1677–1704)
Page 238 (cat. no. 198)

Hamilton, Dame Ann (British, active 1762–1766)
Page 232 (cat. nos. 180, 181, 182, 183)

Hampton, Charlotte (British, active after 1789)
Page 164 (detail); page 168 (cat. no. 15)

Hawkins, Elizabeth (British, active c. 1797)
Page 154 (fig. 41); page 253 (cat. no. 241)

Helm, Margaretha (German, 1659–1742)
Page 40 (fig. 14); page 250 (cat. no. 227)

Hepplewhite, Alice (British, active 18th century)
Page 149 (figs. 23 & 24); page 188 (cat. nos. 61 & 62)

Herbert, M.K. (British, active 17th century)
Page 34 (fig. 5); page 153 (fig. 36); page 254 (cat. no. 245)

Herolt-Graff, Johanna Helena (German, 1668–c. 1723), attributed to
Page 230 (cat. no. 166)

d'Hervart, Sabine Louise, known as Lady Winn (Swiss, 1734–1798)
Page 83 (figs. 12 & 13)

Heul, Johanna van der (active early 18th century)
Page 97 (fig. 5)

Hill, Diana Dietz (British, c. 1760–1844)
Page 145 (figs. 10 & 11)

I.S. (British, born c. 1659)
Page 13 (detail); page 251 (cat. no. 230)

Inglis, Esther (British, c. 1569–1624)
Page 195 (cat. no. 76); page 196 (cat. no. 79)

Jaquotot, Marie-Victoire (French, 1772–1855)
Page 135 (fig. 29); page 170 (cat. no. 24)

Kauffmann, Angelica (Swiss, 1741–1807)
Page 117 (fig. 22); page 125 (fig. 7); page 126 (figs. 8 & 9); page 152 (figs. 32 & 33); page 198 (cat. no. 82); page 201 (cat. no. 91); page 223 (cat. no. 148); back endpaper

Königsmarck, Amalia von (Swedish, 1663–1740)
Page 216 (cat. no. 122)

Küsel, Johanna Sibylla (German, c. 1650–1717)
Page 63 (fig. 5); page 246 (cat. no. 220)

Labille-Guiard, Adélaïde (French, 1749–1803)
Page 133 (fig. 25); page 205 (cat. no. 98)

Lama, Giulia (Italian, 1681–1747)
Page 54 (fig. 22); page 116 (fig. 21); page 179 (cat. no. 40); page 182 (cat. nos. 45, 46, 47, 48, 49)

Landucci, Lucia Barbarossa (Italian, c. 1728–died after 1782), attributed to
Page 100 (fig. 13)

Larter, Elizabeth (British, born 1778)
Page 253 (cat. no. 240)

Lemoine, Marie Victoire (French, 1754–1820)
Page 87 (fig. 21); page 208 (cat. no. 106)

Letona, Maria de la Luz (Spanish or Guatemalan, active c. 1737)
Page 252 (cat. no. 235)

Leyster, Judith (Dutch, 1609–1660)
Pages 2–3 (detail); page 217 (cat. no. 123)

Linwood, Mary (British, 1755–1845)
Page 123 (fig. 1); page 128 (fig. 14); page 129 (fig. 16); page 253 (cat. no. 243)

Lister Knowler, Susanna (British, c. 1670–1738)
Page 114 (figs. 14, 15, 16); page 151 (fig. 29); page 232 (cat. no. 184)

Lister, Anna (British, 1671–1700)
Page 114 (figs. 14, 15, 16); page 151 (fig. 29); page 232 (cat. no. 184)

Longhi, Barbara (Italian, 1552–c. 1638)
Page 199 (cat. no. 83)

Lusurier, Catherine (French, c. 1753–1781), attributed to
Page 217 (cat. no. 124)

Mantuana, Diana, also known as Diana Scultori (Italian, c. 1547–1612)
Page 67 (fig. 14); page 71 (fig. 18); page 146 (fig. 13); page 221 (cat. nos. 133, 134, 135)

Mena y Bitoria, Andrea de (Spanish, 1654–1734)
Page 235 (cat. nos. 192 & 193)

Merian, Maria Sibylla (German, 1647–1717)
Page 110 (fig. 7); page 111 (figs. 8, 9, 10); page 113 (fig. 13); page 144 (fig. 9); page 225 (cat. no. 153); page 229 (cat. no. 164); page 230 (cat. nos. 167 & 168)

Mills, Ann (British, active 18th century)
Page 167 (cat. no. 14)

Moillon, Louise (French, c. 1610–c. 1696)
Page 8 (detail); page 213 (cat. no. 115)

Moninckx, Maria (Dutch, c. 1673–1757)
Page 110 (fig. 6); page 229 (cat. no. 165)

Montalent, Mademoiselle (French, active c. 1785)
Page 87 (fig. 20); page 252 (cat. no. 237)

Morandi Manzolini, Anna (Italian, 1714–1774)
Page 118 (fig. 24); page 119 (fig. 25)

Morris Knowles, Mary (British, 1703–1807)
Page 127 (fig. 11)

Moser, Mary (British, 1744–1819)
Page 178 (cat. no. 38); page 183 (cat. no. 51)

Muratori, Teresa (Italian, 1661–1708)
Page 52 (fig. 19)

Nelli, Plautilla (Italian, 1523–1588)
Page 45 (fig. 5)

Neuberger, Anna Felicitas (German, born 1630)
Page 236 (cat. no. 194)

Nuns (Bridgettine) of Syon House, Lisbon, Portugal (active c. 1787)
Page 34 (fig. 3); page 172 (cat. no. 26)

Nuns (Bridgettine) of Vadstena Abbey, Sweden (active c. 1350–1799)
Page 37 (fig. 10)

Nuns of the Convent of Saint Rose of Viterbo, Viterbo, Italy (active early 19th century)
Page 175 (cat. no. 34)

Nuns of the Convent of San Jacopo di Ripoli, Florence, Italy (15th century)
Page 64 (fig. 8); page 160 (cat. no. 1)

Nuns of the Convent of Santa Maria Maddalena, Venice, Italy (16th century)
Page 160 (detail); page 162 (cat. no. 3)

Nuns of the Discalced Mercedarians, Écija, Spain (17th–19th centuries)
Page 174 (cat. no. 27)

Nun (Ursuline) (probably French, 17th century)
Page 174 (cat. nos. 29 & 30)

Nun (Ursuline) (probably French, 18th century)
Page 174 (cat. no. 30)

Nun (Visitandine) (French, late 17th century)
Page 174 (cat. no. 28)

Oosterwijck, Maria van (Dutch, 1630–1693)
Page 210 (detail); page 213 (cat. no. 117)

Parasole, Elisabetta (or Isabella) Catanea (Italian, c. 1570–c. 1620)
Page 36 (fig. 8); page 38 (fig. 11); page 41 (detail); page 192 (cat. no. 70)

Parasole, Geronima Cagnaccia (Italian, c. 1569–1622)
Page 163 (cat. no. 4); page 220 (cat. no. 131)

Pars, Anne (British, born c. 1740)
Page 167 (cat. no. 14)

Passe, Magdalena van de (Dutch, 1600–1638)
Page 61 (figs. 2 & 3); page 147 (figs. 16 & 18); page 221 (cat. nos. 136, 137, 138, 139); back endpaper

Peeters, Clara (Flemish, c. 1587– after 1636)
Page 108 (fig. 1); page 109 (fig. 2); page 212 (cat. no. 114); back endpaper

Perwich, Susanna (British, 1636–1661)
Page 82 (fig. 9); page 244 (cat. no. 218); pages 259–62 (details)

Piccini, Elisabetta (Isabella) (Italian, 1644–1734)
Page 64 (figs. 6 & 7); page 150 (fig. 25); page 163 (cat. no. 5)

Piranesi, Laura (Italian, 1754–1785)
Page 223 (cat. nos. 150 & 151)

Poisson, Jeanne Antoinette, known as Madame de Pompadour (French, 1721–1764)
Page 69 (fig. 16)

Ponsonby, Sarah (Irish, 1755–1831)
Page 184 (cat. no. 54)

Prestel, Maria Catharina (German, 1747–1794)
Page 22 (fig. 5); page 65 (fig. 9); page 75 (detail); page 223 (cat. no. 149)

Read, Katharine (Scottish, 1723–1778), attributed to
Page 144 (fig. 8); page 208 (cat. no. 107)

Rifer de Courcelles, Pauline, known as Madame Knip (French, 1781–1851)
Page 134 (fig. 28); page 150 (figs. 27 & 28); page 165 (cat. no. 8); page 171 (cat. no. 25)

Riviera, Caterina della (Italian, active 1648–1653)
Page 246 (cat. no. 221)

Riviera, Maria Maddalena della (Italian, 1611–1676)
Page 244 (detail); page 247 (cat. no. 222)

Robusti, Marietta, known as Tintoretta (Italian, c. 1554/60–c. 1590)
Page 53 (figs. 20 & 21)

Roghman, Geertruydt (Dutch, 1625–1657)
Front endpaper; page 72 (fig. 20); page 222 (cat. nos. 141, 142, 143)

Roker, Elizabeth (British, active from 1776)
Page 243 (cat. no. 216)

Roldán, Luisa (Spanish, 1652–1706)
Page 142 (figs. 3 & 4); page 237 (cat. nos. 195, 196, 197); back cover

Rosse, Susannah-Penelope (British, c. 1655–1700)
Page 203 (cat. no. 93)

de' Rossi, Properzia (Italian, c. 1490/91–c. 1530), attributed to
Page 44 (fig. 1)

Roundell, Anne (British, active mid-17th century)
Page 255 (cat. no. 248)

Ruysch, Rachel (Dutch, 1664–1750)
Page 112 (figs. 11 & 12); page 121 (detail); page 210 (cat. no. 112); page 214 (cat. no. 120)

S.F. (Dutch, active late 18th century)
Page 253 (cat. no. 242)

Sánchez, María Josefa (Spanish, active mid-17th century)
Page 198 (cat. no. 81)

Sandrart, Susanne Maria von (German, 1658–1716)
Page 62 (fig. 4); page 218 (cat. no. 129)

Schmitz, Elizabeth Pieth (German, active c. 1650–1700)
Page 226 (cat. no. 154)

Schurman, Anna Maria van (Dutch, 1607–1678)
Page 68 (fig. 15); page 218 (detail); page 219 (cat. no. 130); page 222 (cat. no. 140)

Sharples, Ellen (British, 1769–1849), attributed to
Page 145 (fig. 12); page 185 (cat. no. 56)

Sheene, Alice (British, active 1700–c. 1714)
Page 241 (cat. nos. 205 & 206)

Simcha, wife of Levi of Buttrio (Italian, active 1696/97)
Page 251 (cat. no. 231)

Sirani, Elisabetta (Italian, 1638–1665)
Page 50 (figs. 10, 11, 12, 13); page 51 (figs. 14, 15, 16, 17); page 57 (detail); page 67 (figs. 12 & 13); page 176 (cat. no. 35); page 181 (cat. no. 43); page 200 (cat. nos. 85 & 86)

Sophia Fredericka Caroline Louise, Princess of Saxe-Coburg-Saalfeld (German, 1778–1835)
Page 70 (fig. 17)

Sperling-Heckel, Catharina (German, 1699–1741)
Page 163 (cat. nos. 6 & 7)

Stone, Sarah (British, c. 1760–1844)
Page 151 (figs. 30 & 31); page 159 (detail); page 233 (cat. no. 189)

Stonier Plaisted, Rebecca (British, active, c. 1668)
Page 82 (fig. 10)

Taillandier, Geneviève (French, active 1774–1798)
Page 169 (cat. no. 23)

Teerlinc, Levina (Netherlandish, c. 1510–1576), attributed to
Page 204 (cat. no. 94)

Templetown, Elizabeth Upton, known as Lady Templetown (British, 1746–1823)
Page 101 (fig. 15); page 169 (cat. nos. 18 & 21)

Thielen, Maria-Theresia van (Flemish, 1640–1706)
Page 213 (cat. no. 116)

Unknown porcelain flower makers, Chelsea-Derby Porcelain Factory (British, 1770–1784)
Page 158 (detail); page 167 (cat. no. 13)

Unknown cloistered maker (likely German, 18th century)
Page 172 (detail); page 175 (cat. no. 32)

Unknown designer, Fabrique de Saint Ruf, Lyon (French, active c. 1785)
Page 252 (cat. no. 238)

Unknown embroiderer (British, 16th century)
Page 34 (fig. 6); page 81 (fig. 6); page 251 (cat. no. 229); page 263 (detail)

Unknown embroiderer (British, 17th century)
Page 34 (fig. 4); page 254 (cat. nos. 246 & 247)

Unknown embroiderer (British, 18th century)
Page 249 (cat. no. 225)

Unknown embroiderer(s) (French, 18th century)
Page 153 (fig. 35); page 248 (cat. no. 224)

Unknown embroiderer (German, 17th century)
Page 39 (fig. 13)

Unknown lacemaker (Flemish, 18th century)
Page 190 (cat. no. 67)

Unknown lacemaker (Flemish, mid–late 17th century)
Page 193 (cat. no. 72)

Unknown lacemaker (French, 17th century)
Page 190 (detail); page 193 (cat. no. 73)

Unknown lacemaker (French or Italian, 17th century)
Page 193 (cat. no. 71)

Unknown lacemaker (Italian, 17th century)
Page 192 (cat. no. 69)

Unknown lacemaker (Italian, late 17th–early 18th century)
Page 193 (cat. no. 74)

Unknown lacemaker (Russian, 18th–19th century)
Page 1 (detail); page 191 (cat. no. 68)

Unknown maker (Europe, 18th century)
Front endpaper; page 5 (detail); page 83 (fig. 11); page 175 (cat. no. 31); page 189 (cat. no. 65); page 245 (cat. no. 219)

Unknown maker (Northern Europe, 18th century)
Page 250 (cat. no. 226)

Unknown textile makers at the Oberkampf manufactory (French, active 1760–1843)
Page 104 (fig. 21)

Vaiani, Anna Maria (Italian, active 1627–died c. 1655)
Page 220 (cat. no. 132); page 228 (cat. no. 158)

Vallayer-Coster, Anne (French, 1744–1818)
Page 115 (fig. 17); page 130 (fig. 18); page 214 (cat. no. 121)

Vandercruse, Françoise-Marguerite (French, 1731–1775)
Page 189 (cat. no. 64)

Vanni, Violante (Italian, 1732–1775/76)
Page 150 (fig. 26)

Verbruggen, Susanna (Flemish, c. 1684/50–1752)
Page 222 (cat. no. 144)

Vestier Dumont, Marie-Nicole (French, 1767–1846)
Page 133 (fig. 26)

Vigée-LeBrun, Elisabeth Louise (French, 1755–1842)
Page 125 (fig. 6); page 130 (fig. 17); page 133 (figs. 22, 23, 24); page 143 (fig. 7); page 177 (cat. no. 37); page 205 (detail); page 209 (cat. nos. 108, 109, 110)

Visscher, Maria Tesselschade Roemers (Dutch, 1594–1649), attributed to
Page 96 (fig. 4)

Wilcox, Sarah (British, born 1736)
Page 167 (cat. no. 14)

Withoos, Alida (Dutch, c. 1662–1730)
Page 110 (fig. 5); page 229 (cat. no. 163)

Wright, Patience Lovell (American, 1725–1786), attributed to
Page 131 (fig. 21); page 238 (cat. no. 199)

Yehuditah, Beila, daughter of Emanuel Finzi di Rivarol (Italian, active 1764–1765)
Page 251 (cat. no. 232)

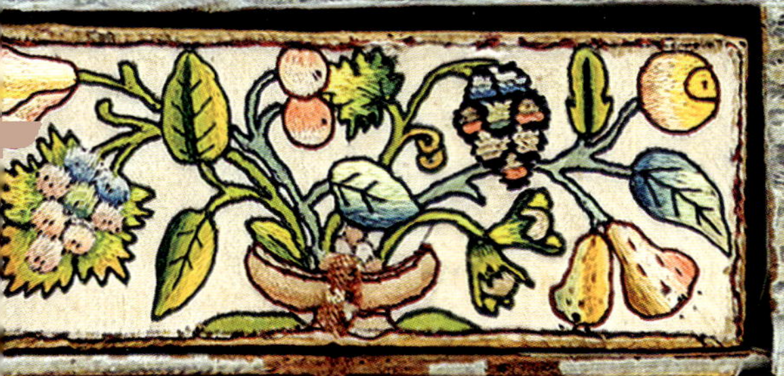
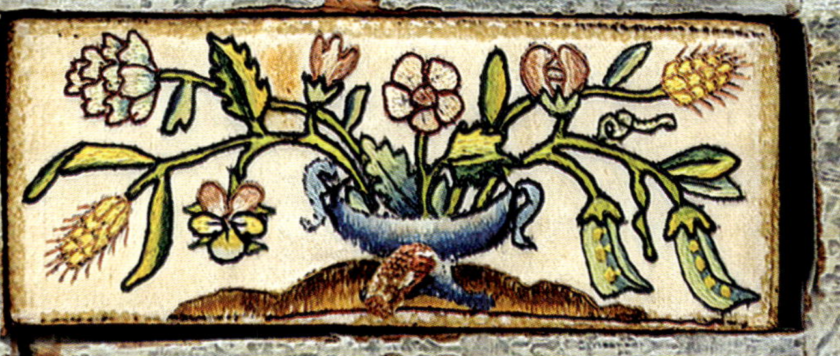
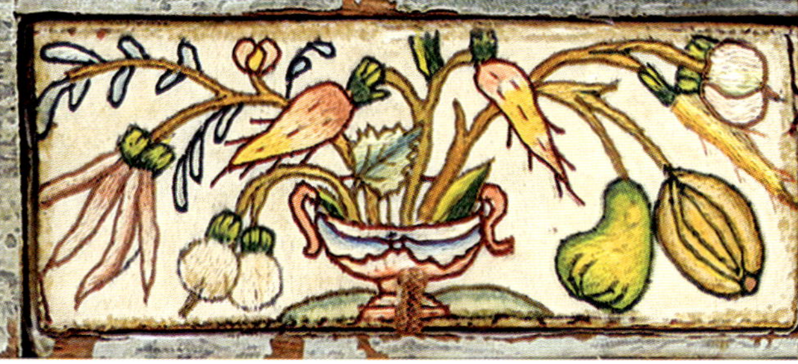

FRONT COVER:

Detail (cat. no. 55):
Anne Guéret (French, 1760–1805)
Portrait of an Artist with a Portfolio (Self-Portrait?)
c. 1793
Black chalk, pen and grey ink, and wash, heightened with white gouache on paper
32 × 40.4 cm
Katrin Bellinger Collection
2008-012
Photo: Matthew Hollow

Detail (cat. no. 234):
Anna Maria Garthwaite (British, 1688–1763)
Length of brocaded silk tobine
1749
Silk
88.3 × 49.5 cm
Baltimore Museum of Art:
Angelica Yonge Pearre Fund, 1999.156
Photo: Mitro Hood

BACK COVER:

Detail (cat. no. 195):
Luisa Roldán (Spanish, 1652–1706)
The Education of the Virgin
1680s
Polychrome paint and wood
76 × 63 × 43 cm
Los Angeles County Museum of Art, Gift of the 2019 Collectors Committee with additional funds from Linda Borick and Bill Davidson on behalf of the Louis L. Borick Foundation
M.2019.235

FRONT ENDPAPERS:

Detail (cat. no. 141):
Geertruydt Roghman
The Dressmakers
from the series *Domestic Occupations*
1640–1647

Detail (cat. no. 228):
Anna Bockett
Sampler
1656

Detail (cat. no. 65):
Unknown European maker
Tea caddy
late 18th century

PAGE 1:

Detail (cat. no. 68):
Unknown Russian lacemaker
Embroidered drawn net bed valance with bobbin lace border
1766–1833

PAGES 2–3:

Detail (cat. no. 123):
Judith Leyster
Self-Portrait
c. 1630

PAGE 8:

Detail (cat. no. 115):
Louise Moillon
Still Life with a Basket of Fruit and a Bunch of Asparagus
1630

PAGE 12:

Detail (cat. no. 236):
Mademoiselle Baulieu
Design for a gentleman's embroidered waistcoat
c. 1785

PAGE 13:

Detail (cat. no. 230):
I.S.
Work bag
1669

PAGE 158:

Detail (cat. no. 13):
Unknown porcelain flower makers, Chelsea-Derby Porcelain Factory
Pair of candlesticks
c. 1770–1775

PAGE 159:

Detail (cat. no. 189):
Sarah Stone
A Blue and Yellow Macaw
c. 1789

PAGES 259–262:

Detail (cat. no. 218):
Susanna Perwich
Embroidered cabinet
1645–1655

PAGE 263:

Detail (cat. no. 229):
Unknown British embroiderer
Man's nightcap
c. 1580

PAGE 264:

Detail (cat. no. 50):
Rosalba Carriera
Allegory of Painting
1730s

BACK ENDPAPERS:

Detail (cat. no. 114):
Clara Peeters
A Still Life of Lilies, Roses, Iris, Pansies, Columbine, Love-in-a-Mist, Larkspur and Other Flowers in a Glass Vase on a Table Top, Flanked by a Rose and a Carnation
c. 1610

Detail (cat. no. 82):
Angelica Kauffmann
Sappho Inspired by Love
1775

Detail (cat. no. 139):
Magdalena van de Passe
Winter
from the series *The Four Seasons*
c. 1614–1634

Contributors

ANDALEEB BADIEE BANTA, Senior Curator and Department Head, Prints, Drawings & Photographs, Baltimore Museum of Art

BABETTE BOHN, Professor Emerita of Art History, Texas Christian University

YASSANA CROIZAT-GLAZER, Independent Scholar, Founder of YCG Fine Art

ALEXA GREIST, Curator and R. Fraser Elliott Chair, Prints & Drawings, Art Gallery of Ontario

ELENA NAOMI KANAGY-LOUX, Collections Specialist, The Metropolitan Museum of Art

JOANNA KARLGAARD, Assistant Curator Prints, Drawings, and Photographs, Baltimore Museum of Art

THERESA KUTASZ CHRISTENSEN, Exhibition Research Assistant, Prints, Drawings & Photographs, Baltimore Museum of Art

BRITTANY LUBERDA, Anne Stone Associate Curator of Decorative Arts, Baltimore Museum of Art

CATHERINE POWELL-WARREN, Postdoctoral Research Fellow in Art History, Ghent University

ISABELLA ROSNER, King's College London

PARIS A. SPIES-GANS, Historian of Women and Gender

VIRGINIA TREANOR, Senior Curator, National Museum of Women in the Arts

ANNELIES VERELLEN, Doctoral Candidate, Art History, McGill University

MADELEINE C. VILJOEN, Curator of Prints and the Spencer Collection, The New York Public Library

LARA YEAGER-CRASSELT, Curator and Department Head, European Painting and Sculpture, Baltimore Museum of Art

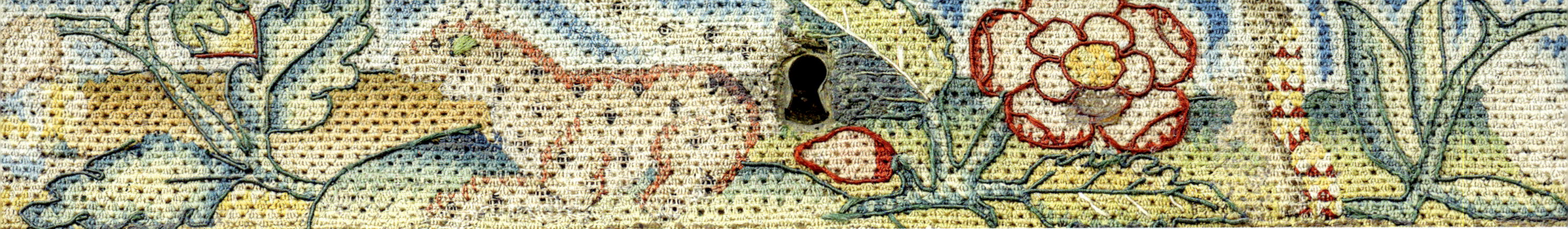

Land Acknowledgement

The Art Gallery of Ontario operates on land that is the territory of the Anishinaabe (Mississauga) nation and is also the territory of the Wendat and Haudenosaunee. The Dish with One Spoon Wampum Belt Covenant is an agreement between the Haudenosaunee Confederacy and the Anishinaabe Three Fires Confederacy to peaceably share and care for the resources around the Great Lakes. Toronto is also governed by a treaty between the federal government of Canada and the Mississaugas of the New Credit (Anishinaabe nation). Toronto has always been a trading centre for First Nations.

Goose Lane Editions is located on the unceded territory of the Wəlastəkwiyik whose ancestors along with the Mi'kmaq and Peskotomuhkati Nations signed Peace and Friendship Treaties with the British Crown in the 1700s.

Thank You

THE ART GALLERY OF ONTARIO GRATEFULLY ACKNOWLEDGES:

Lead Support
Volunteers of the AGO

Generous Support
Robert & Cecily Bradshaw
Philip R.L. Somerville
Women's Art Initiative

Supported by the Government of Canada / Avec l'appui du gouvernement du Canada

Canada

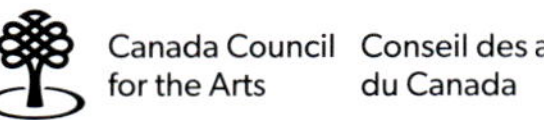

The Art Gallery of Ontario is partially funded by the Ontario Ministry of Culture. Additional operating support is received from the City of Toronto, the Department of Canadian Heritage, and the Canada Council for the Arts.

Goose Lane Editions acknowledges the generous support of the Government of Canada, the Canada Council for the Arts, and the Government of New Brunswick.

THE BALTIMORE MUSEUM OF ART GRATEFULLY ACKNOWLEDGES GENEROUS SUPPORT FOR THIS PROJECT BY:

National Endowment for the Humanities
Laura Freedlander
PNC Foundation
The Gladys Krieble Delmas Foundation
Samuel H. Kress Foundation
Sheela Murthy/MurthyNAYAK Foundation

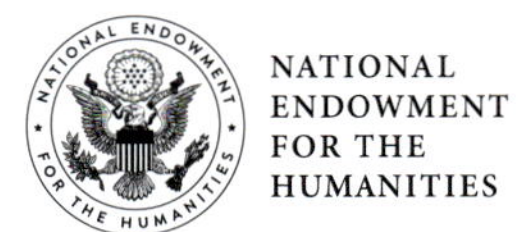

Any views, findings, conclusions, or recommendations expressed in this project do not necessarily represent those of the National Endowment for the Humanities.

This exhibition is supported by an indemnity from the Federal Council on the Arts and the Humanities.

This publication is supported as part of the Dutch Culture USA program by the Consulate General of the Netherlands in New York.

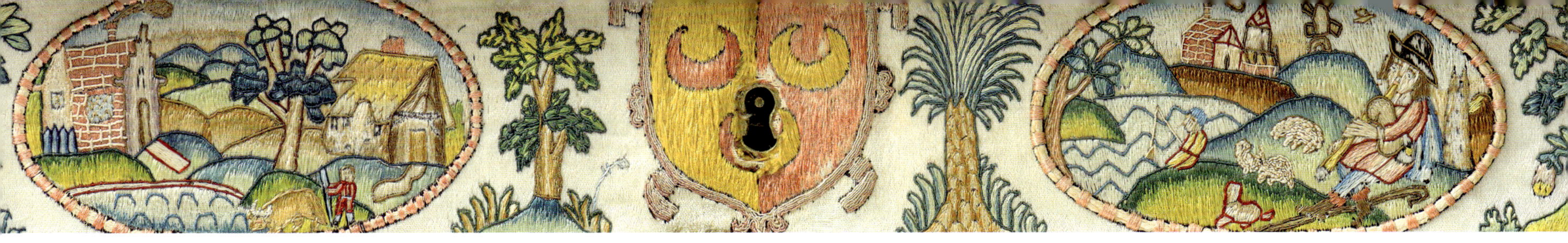

PUBLICATION

Editors: Andaleeb Badiee Banta, Alexa Greist, Theresa Kutasz Christensen
Publishing Director: Jim Shedden
Publishing Coordinator: Kathryn Yuen
Production and Content Editor: Nives Hajdin-Rorabeck
Proofreaders: David Marsh, Judy Phillips
Designer: Lara Minja of Lime Design
Photographers: Craig Boyko, Mitro Hood
Pre-Press: Paul Jerinkitsch
Printing: Friesens

AGO EXHIBITION

Deputy Director & Chief Curator: Julian Cox
Curator: Alexa Greist
Project Manager: Melissa Ramage
Curatorial Coordinator: Wendy Hebditch
Interpretive Planner: Nadia Abraham
Editor: Nives Hajdin-Rorabeck
Exhibition Designer: Theodora Doulamis
Graphic Designer: Evelina Petrauskas
Production: Malene Hjørngaard, Evelyn Quinn

EXHIBITIONS, COLLECTIONS, AND CONSERVATION

Chief, Exhibitions, Collections & Conservation: Jessica Bright
Director, Exhibitions: Laura Comerford
Registration: Donna Austria, Alison Beckett, Jerry Drozdowsky, Joel Herman, Alison Lindsay, Dale Mahar, Kristyn Rolanty, Sabine Schaefer
Collection Information: Alexander Arslanyan, Alexandra Cousins, Tracy Mallon-Jensen, Liana Radvak, Joe Venturella, Olga Zotova
Conservation: Julia Campbell-Such, Lisa Ellis, Christina McLean, Meaghan Monaghan, Valerie Moscato, Brent Roe, Rachel Stark, Maria Sullivan, Tessa Thomas, Joan Weir, Katharine Whitman, John Williams

LOGISTICS AND ART SERVICES

Director, Logistics and Art Services: Iain Hoadley
Manager, Art Services: Craig Whiteside

Curtis Amisich, Gregory Baszun, Michael Beynon, Andrew Bugden, Scott Cameron, Colin Campbell, Corinne Carlson, Iris Cheung, Meagan Christou, Brian Davis, Alex DiGiacomo, Christian Echeverri, Andre Ethier, Randal Fedje, Tina Giovinazzo, Eric Glavin, Ruth Jones, David Kinsman, Jason Laudadio, Paul Mathiesen, Ben Oakley, Angelo Pedari, David Ronchka, Brian Sasaki, Phil Scott, Damian Seguin, Jelena Sisko, Sasi Sivapalan, David Stasyna, Manny Trinh, Stephanie Vittas, Matthew Waples, Matthew Wells, Philip Woollam, Darin Yorston, Tanya Zhilinsky

EDUCATION AND PROGRAMMING

Richard & Elizabeth Currie Chief, Education & Programming: Audrey Hudson
Director, Engagement & Learning: Paola Poletto
Director, Strategic Projects & Operations: Deborah Nolan

Danah Abusido, Charlotte Big Canoe, Erica Chan, Maureen DaSilva, Sarah Febbraro, Nathan Huisman, Natalie Lam, Idalette Martins, Kathleen McLean, Zavette Quadros-Evangelista, Tiana Roebuck, Annie Roper, Melissa Smith, Bojana Stancic, Joey Suriano

MEDIA PRODUCTION

Manager, Digital Projects: Catherine Thomson
Media: Abbas Saifee, Matthew Scott, Fraser Wrighte
Photographers: Paul Ayers, Craig Boyko, Steve Jacobs, Ian Lefebvre, Leah Maghanoy, Tracey Owusu, Dean Tomlinson, Sean Weaver

DEVELOPMENT

Chief Development Officer: Kate Halpenny
Senior Director, Major Gifts and Campaign: Andrea Orr
Philanthropy: Marielle Bryck, Amanda Dudnik, Rebecca Fera, Anastasia Hare, Tanika Johnny, Christie Parker, May Rouhani, Erin Thadani
Corporate Partnerships: Madeleine Dalkie, Jordan Fee, Allison Miller, Jodi Spitzer

BMA EXHIBITION

Interim Chief Curator: Kevin Tervala
Curator: Andaleeb Badiee Banta
Exhibition Research Assistant: Theresa Kutasz Christensen
Exhibition Designer: David Zimmerman
Graphic Designers: Kristine Ferg, Olivia Tucker
Advancement: Elizabeth Courtemanche, Doug Levering, Saroyah Mevorach

EXHIBITIONS AND COLLECTIONS

Exhibitions: Kirsten MacKenzie, Steven Mann
Registration: Caitlin Perry-Vogelhut, Caitlyn Reid
Collections Research: Sarah Dansberger, Robin Joyce, Joanna Karlgaard, Brittany Luberda, Alexis Slater, Lara Yeager-Crasselt
Conservation: Mary Anne Arntzen, Christine Downie, Linda Owen, Adam Rush, Anne Shaffer, Louise Wheatley
Installation: John Bohl, Jeremy Hyman, Mike Klunk, Jeff McGrath, Asa Osborne, Maggie Robbins, Greg St. Pierre, David Verchomin

EDUCATION AND PROGRAMMING

Interpretive Planner: Verónica Betancourt
Education & Programming: Tracey Beale, Sabina Diaz-Rimal, Kaitlyn Garabino

MEDIA PRODUCTION

Marketing and Press: Meghan Gross, Colleen Hollister, Anne Mannix-Brown, Melanie Martin, Jessica Novak, Sarah Pedroni
Photographer: Mitro Hood

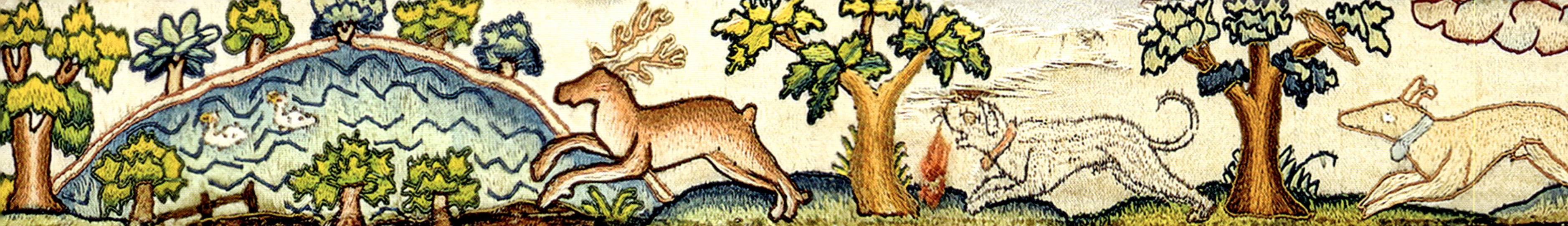

Published in 2023 by the Art Gallery of Ontario, Baltimore Museum of Art, and Goose Lane Editions.

LIBRARY AND ARCHIVES CANADA CATALOGUING IN PUBLICATION

Title: Making her mark : a history of women artists in Europe, 1400–1800 / edited by Andaleeb Badiee Banta and Alexa Greist, with Theresa Kutasz Christensen.
Names: Banta, Andaleeb, editor. | Greist, Alexa, editor. | Kutasz Christensen, Theresa, editor. | Baltimore Museum of Art, host institution. | Art Gallery of Ontario, host institution.
Description: This volume accompanies the exhibition of the same name and runs from October 1, 2023 to January 7, 2024 at the Baltimore Museum of Art, and then opens at the Art Gallery of Ontario from March 30, 2024 to July 1, 2024. | Includes bibliographical references.
Identifiers: Canadiana 20230218865 | ISBN 9781773103181 (hardcover)
Subjects: LCSH: Women artists—Europe—History—Exhibitions. | LCSH: Artists—Europe—History—Exhibitions. | LCSH: Art, European—Exhibitions. | LCGFT: Exhibition catalogs.
Classification: LCC N8354 .M34 2023 | DDC 704/.042094—dc23

This book was published on the occasion of *Making Her Mark: A History of Women Artists in Europe, 1400–1800*, co-organized by the Baltimore Museum of Art and Art Gallery of Ontario.

Baltimore Museum of Art
Baltimore, Maryland, United States
October 1, 2023 – January 7, 2024

Art Gallery of Ontario
Toronto, Ontario, Canada
March 30, 2024 – July 1, 2024

Art Gallery of Ontario
317 Dundas Street West
Toronto, Ontario M5T 1G4
Canada
ago.ca

Baltimore Museum of Art
10 Art Museum Drive
Baltimore, MD 21218
United States
artbma.org

Goose Lane Editions
500 Beaverbrook Court,
Suite 330
Fredericton,
New Brunswick E3B 5X4
Canada
gooselane.com

ISBN: 9781773103181

Printed and bound in Canada.
10 9 8 7 6 5 4 3 2 1

Printed on GardaMatt Art FSC White 100 lb.
Set in Minion Pro with Mrs Eaves, Mr Eaves, and Blue Goblet Ornaments.

Mrs Eaves is a typeface designed in 1996 by Zuzana Licko of the foundry Émigré. Licko based the typeface on Baskerville, a well-known typeface designed in 1757 by John Baskerville in Birmingham, England. The selection of the name "Mrs Eaves" honours one of the forgotten women in the history of typography. Sarah Eaves lived with and worked for Baskerville, later marrying him after the death of her first husband.

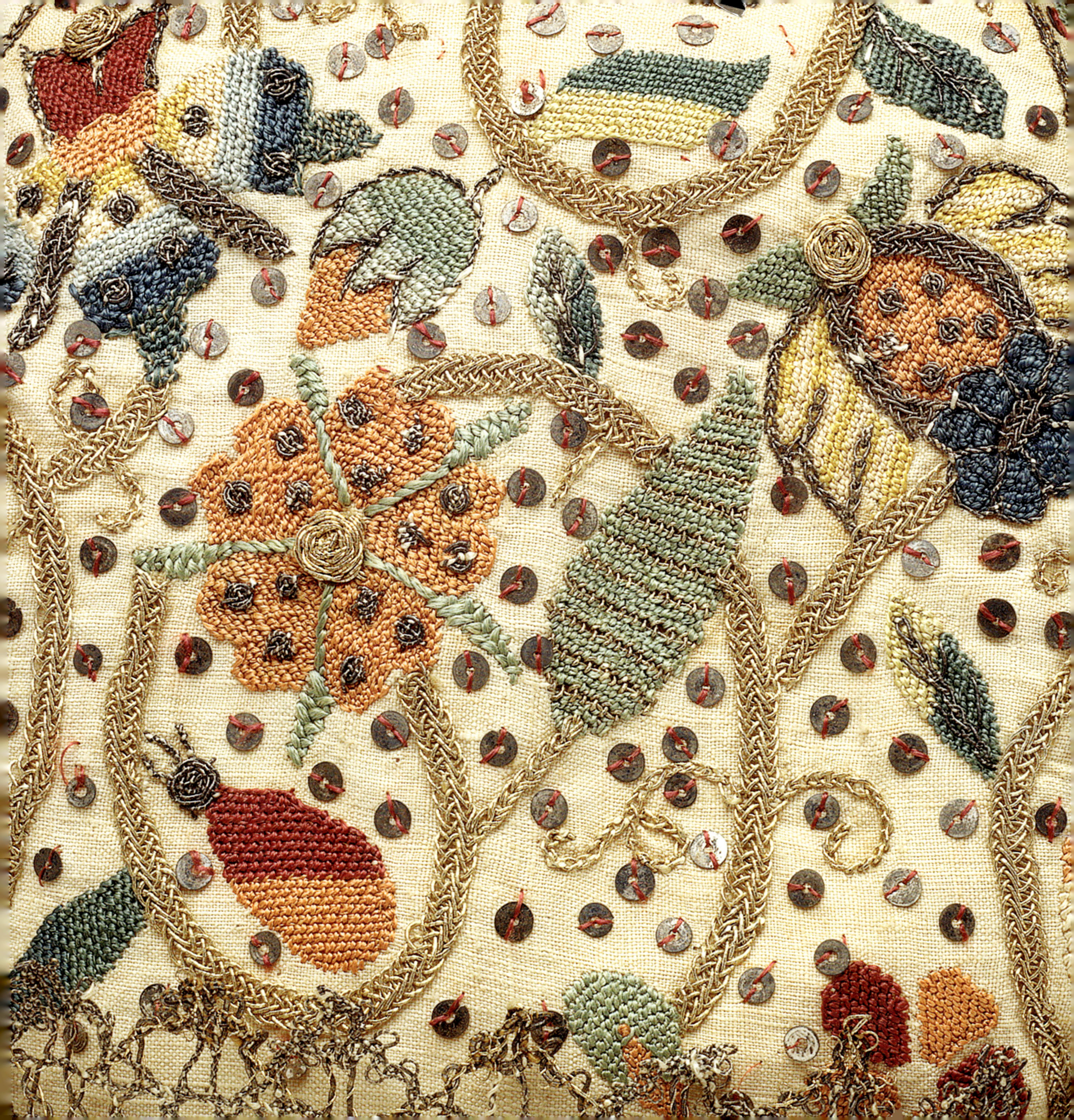

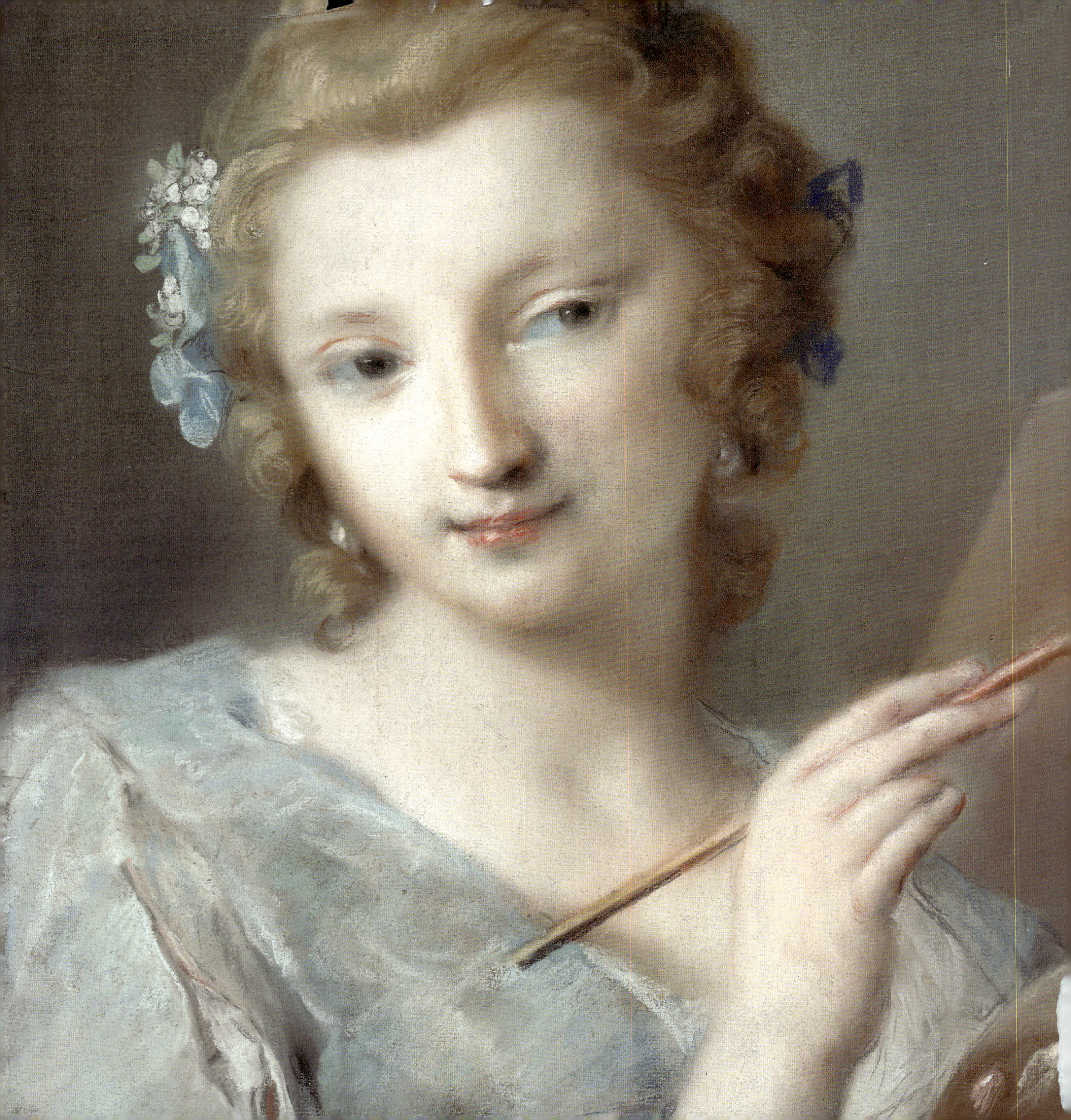